Readings in Western Civilization

ⲅⲋ Vere dignum

University of Chicago Readings in Western Civilization
John W. Boyer and Julius Kirshner, General Editors

University of Chicago
Readings in Western Civilization

John W. Boyer and Julius Kirshner, General Editors

6
Early Modern Europe: Crisis of Authority

Edited by Eric Cochrane, Charles M. Gray, and Mark A. Kishlansky

The University of Chicago Press

Chicago and London

Eric Cochrane, 1928–1985

ἀθάνατος μνήμη
Immortal memory

Eric Cochrane was born in Berkeley, California, in 1928. At the time of his death in 1985 he was professor of history at the University of Chicago. He authored *Florence in the Forgotten Centuries, 1527–1800: A History of Florence and the Florentines in the Age of the Grand Dukes* and *Historians and Historiography in the Italian Renaissance*, both published by the University of Chicago Press.

Charles M. Gray is professor in the Department of History and the College, lecturer in the Law School, and Master of the New Collegiate Division, University of Chicago.

Mark A. Kishlansky is professor in the Department of History and the College and a member of the Committee on General Studies in the Humanities at the University of Chicago, and an editor of *Journal of British Studies*.

The University of Chicago Press, Chicago 60637
The University of Chicago Press, Ltd., London
© 1987 by The University of Chicago
All rights reserved. Published 1987
Printed in the United States of America
96 95 94 93 92 91 90 89 88 87   5 4 3 2 1

Library of Congress Cataloging in Publication Data
(Revised for vol. 6)

University of Chicago readings in Western civilization.

    Includes bibliographies and indexes.
    Contents: 1. The Greek polis / edited by Arthur W. H. Adkins and Peter White—2. Rome : late republic and principate / edited by Walter Emil Kaegi, Jr., and Peter White—[etc.]— 6. Early modern Europe : crisis of authority / edited by Eric Cochrane, Charles M. Gray, and Mark A. Kishlansky.
    1. Civilization, Occidental—History—Sources.
2. Europe—Civilization—Sources. I. Boyer, John W. II. Kirshner, Julius.
III. Title. IV. Title: Readings in Western civilization.
CB245.U64   1986   909'.09821   85-16328
ISBN 0-226-06934-6 (v. 1)
ISBN 0-226-06935-4 (pbk. : v. 1)
ISBN 0-226-06947-8 (v. 6)
ISBN 0-226-06948-6 (pbk. : v. 6)

Contents

Series Editors' Foreword

This series is the result of almost four decades of teaching the History of Western Civilization course at the College of the University of Chicago. The course was founded in its present form in the late 1940s by a group of young historians at Chicago, including William H. McNeill, Christian Mackauer, and Sylvia Thrupp, and has been sustained during the past twenty-five years by the distinguished teaching of Eric Cochrane, Hanna H. Gray, Charles M. Gray, and Karl J. Weintraub. In the beginning it served as a counterpoint to the antihistorical and positivistic thrust of the general education curriculum in the social sciences in the Hutchins College. Western Civilization has since been incorporated as a year-long course into different parts of the College program, from the first to the last year. It now forms part of the general intercivilizational requirement for sophomores and juniors. It is still taught, as it has been almost constantly since its inception, in discussion groups ranging from twenty to thirty students.

Although both the readings and the instructors of the course have changed over the years, its purpose has remained the same. It seeks not to provide students with morsels of Western culture, nor to nourish their moral and aesthetic sensitivities, and much less to attract recruits for the history profession. Its purpose instead is to raise a whole set of complex conceptual questions regarding the nature of time and change and the intended and unintended consequences of human action and consciousness. Students in this course learn to analyze past events and ideas by rigorously examining a variety of texts. This is in contrast to parallel courses in the social sciences, which teach students to deploy synchronic and quantitative techniques in analyzing society, usually without reference to historical context or process.

Ours is a history course that aims not at imparting relevant facts or exotic ideas but at providing students with the critical tools by which to analyze texts produced in the distant or near past. It also serves a related purpose: to familiarize students with major epochs of that Western historical tradition to which most of them, albeit at times unknowingly, are heirs. The major curricular vehicle of the course is the *Readings in Western Civilization*, a nine-volume series of primary sources in translation, beginning with Periclean Athens and concluding with Europe in the twentieth century. The series is not meant to be a comprehensive survey of Western history. Rather, in each volume, we provide a large number of documents on specific themes in the belief that depth, not breadth, is the surest antidote to superficiality. The very extensiveness of the documentation in each volume allows for a variety of approaches to the same theme. At the same time the concentrated focus of individual volumes makes it possible for them to serve as source readings in more advanced and specialized courses.

Many people contributed to the publication of these volumes. The enthusiastic collaboration and labors of the members of the Western Civilization staff made it possible for these *Readings* to be published. We thank Barbara Boyer for providing superb editorial direction to the project and Mary Van Steenbergh for her dedication in creating beautifully text-edited manuscripts. Steven Wheatley's advice in procuring funding for this project was invaluable. Members of the University of Chicago Press have given their unstinting support and guidance. We also appreciate the confidence and support accorded by Donald N. Levine, the Dean of the College at the University of Chicago. Above all, we are deeply grateful for the extraordinary dedication, energy, and erudition which our late colleague and former chairperson of the course, Eric Cochrane, contributed to the *Readings in Western Civilization*.

We are grateful to the National Endowment for the Humanities for providing generous funding for the preparation and publication of the volumes.

John W. Boyer and Julius Kirshner

Note

Editorial work on this volume was interrupted by the tragic death of our colleague Eric Cochrane in November 1985. For their expertise and unselfish labor in bringing it to a successful conclusion, we wish to thank Lydia G. Cochrane, Brendan Dooley, Constantin Fasolt, and Kent Wright.

John Boyer and Julius Kirshner

General Introduction

All borders in history are indistinct, but landmarks should not be effaced in deference to that general truth. This volume in the *History of Western Civilization* series stands on a boundary more fundamental than any since the heavy line that divided Graeco-Roman antiquity from Christian civilization. It is designed to present the gateway to modernity in *one* intelligible perspective. Though its focus is on the seventeenth century, it also stretches back over the previous hundred and fifty years to tie together the strands of Renaissance and Reformation. By calling this volume *The Crisis of Authority* we mean to suggest that a wider range of authority was called more profoundly in question than ever before. Efforts to formulate resolutions to that crisis dominated Western thinking in the early modern era.

The pillars of pre-modern Western civilization were the Greek and Latin classics and the Christian faith. Their express authority had at length greatly diminished. The Renaissance and Reformation were celebrations of the fountains from which European culture had sprung. They were efforts to call the erring, self-conceited, overcomplicated "moderns" of the late middle ages back to those pure waters—in the one case to the eloquence and practical wisdom of the classical ancients, in the other to the core meaning of the Gospel. In the post-Renaissance, post-Reformation era to which we now turn, the mood of celebration and revival were not suddenly quenched, but gradually overcast. European classicism enjoyed its highest moment in that early modern period which this volume introduces and its sequel continues. Many of that period's struggles were over Christian causes; tensions between the classical and Christian inheritances came out more sharply in the early modern period than they had before even if the protagonists were still the ancient ones.

1

The old pillars remained the chief pillars, but their foundations were eroding. In the seventeenth century a seismic shift occurs and the tremors trouble authority itself.

The first part of this volume presents a picture of political thought in the wake of the Reformation. It begins with descriptive histories of the two great Protestant societies of the early modern period, England and Holland. They are juxtaposed to provide, as it were, a contrast of similars. England and Holland were the truest children of the Reformation, nations in which the reformed religion was crucial to their identities. If, however, they had remained inertly Protestant—merely the leaders of a coalition unified by religion in a period of religious conflict—their ultimate significance in history would be much less. In neither country did the Protestant culture stand still, in neither, as these readings demonstrate, was religion a sufficient or an unchallenged social bond. Gradually both societies assumed the shape of Europe's coming liberalism, and their religious toleration, free government, and commercial prosperity made them models for dissent and, ultimately, sources for the French Revolution.

Another set of documents more directly illustrates the pressures of overtly religious conflict or of political conflict with religious overtones. On the Protestant side one sees movement away from the highly conservative attitudes of Luther and Calvin, but one also sees how painful that break was and how a tradition of "passive obedience" to government, which Protestant religious ideas had originally reinforced, maintained their hold. Both Catholic and Protestant attitudes varied with the situations of the parties in the numerous countries afflicted by religious conflict and war; both sides contributed, as did medieval political thinkers before them, to the building of a fund of "liberal" ideas destined to become a central influence in the modern West—a complex body of ideas that turned on the notion that governments were constituted by the community for the fulfillment of its purposes, and are subject to legal limitations and guarantees of individual rights and subject to be judged by the communities from which they spring.

If one tendency was for political thinking grounded in religion to drift from its authoritarian roots and bequeath elements to the liberal creed of the future, and another was to revive the belief that governmental authority is the image of the Creator's, a third was sharply different from both. One consequence of the Reformation and its religious wars was a search for the secular principles of politics. There is no better illustration of the continuing influence of quintessentially Renaissance ideas, grounded in a deep fascination with classical antiquity, than the liveliness through the eighteenth century of a strain of political thought derived from Machiavelli. This strain, grounded in the experience of ideological schism, was in its first phase primarily solicitous for order. It found the source of civil peace in human need and reason's capacity to relieve it rather than in God's direct ordination or the charisma of the great prince. Order, peace, and a state capable of making its authority felt were its objectives. Later this strain of thought would discover more liberal potentialities in itself, ways of reconciling an effective state with individual rights. One of the pioneers in this reorientation of politics, the Frenchman Jean Bodin, is represented in this volume; the greatest figure (whose works are easily available elsewhere) was the Englishman Thomas Hobbes, whose thought was shaped by the origins and unfolding of the English Revolution.

II

As the first of the great European revolutions, the English Revolution continues to command our attention. It has been an attractive model for theorists of revolutionary events and Marx himself dubbed it the first bourgeois revolution. In the Soviet Union, modern history begins with the execution of Charles I. While Western historians are less confident of the universal, transforming power of the English Revolution, they have, nevertheless, devoted much energy to uncovering its causes and consequences. Its peculiar mixture of religious fervor, constitutional reform, and democratic participation have proven an enduring source of historiographical controversy. Changing emphases can be seen in the many labels that are attached to its events: the Great Rebellion; the Great Civil War; the Interregnum; the Puritan Revolution; the English Civil Wars; the English Revolution; and most recently the Wars of Religion.

However historians interpret the struggles of the period 1640–60, they all agree that they were times of excitement, achievement, enthusiasm, and creativity. The effects of the revolution were by no means wholly positive. The nation endured eight years of disrupting civil war. Probably one in ten male inhabitants was forced to take up arms, and the severe economic depression of the later 1640s can be attributed—at least in part—to the depredations of war. The divisions between royalists and parliamentarians tore local communities, and even families, apart, and they were not healed by the soothing rhetoric of the Declaration of Breda. Nevertheless, the Revolution sparked off a reexamination of the foundations of English society and encouraged efforts to achieve social and political justice as it was understood in the seventeenth century. If some of these were not successful it was not for lack of dedication or good will. The English Revolution was a time for aspirations and this is stamped upon its most visionary platforms of reform like the Grand Remonstrance, or the Army's Declaration of June 14, as well as upon its most mundane ordinances of regulation, like the Adultery Act.

One particular appeal of the English Revolution is the wealth of material that has survived from which to study actors and actions. Among the earliest changes of the revolutionary period was the effective ending of the church's control over the licensing of publications. This resulted in a flood of literature that continued unabated for twenty years. Over 80,000 tracts, pamphlets, and newsbooks were collected by a London bookseller, George Thomason, and preserved by his heirs. They range from scurrilous ephemera to works of enduring significance like Milton's *Aereopagetica* and Hobbes's *Leviathan*. Comprising mountains of public documents, an abundant collection of memoirs, and several contemporaneous histories, the sources for the study of the English Revolution are among the richest in Western History.

This array of material centers upon an event which was recognizably and self-consciously political: the primary motivation behind the English Revolution was the desire to locate the center of governmental authority in the nation and to enunciate the principles upon which that authority rested and the limits within which it could act. At first this took the form of a defense and attack upon the government of Charles I, and then upon the institution of monarchy itself. Subsequently it gave rise to theoretical and practical propositions for alternate forms of government ranging from a commonwealth supported by republican principles, to the rule of the saints supported by biblical prescription, to a centralized civil authority supported by a written constitution. In this quest to redefine authority, proposals of utopian vision like the Agreement of the People rubbed shoulders with programs of limited practical reform like the Instrument of Government. Ideal and practical comingled in a dynamic tension which was at once the strength of the revolutionary movement and its ultimate undoing.

The materials selected here are intended to bring out the variety of experiences which constituted the revolution. In the early sections it attempts to balance royalist and parliamentarian points of view and to demonstrate that the outcome of the civil war was not predetermined. In later sections the constitutional achievements of the revolutionaries can be contrasted with the alternative programs of the radicals. The largest concentration of documents is upon the trial and execution of Charles I. Here the central issues of the revolution are most starkly revealed both emotionally and intellectually. The crux of the issues which divided King and Parliament come to the fore as do the aspirations of those who believed that the execution of the king would inaugurate a new society. This section, composed of the Army's Agreement, the account of the king's trial and execution, his scaffold speech, and the famous tracts defending and defaming him, can be read alone to illustrate the seventeenth-century crisis, and can be usefully compared with the Investiture Controversy of the Middle Ages and the analogous episodes of the French Revolution. If the English Revolution serves as a case study for the continent-wide debate over the limits of loyalty and resistance, it also serves as an expression of the social consequences of the breaking apart of the shared Aristotelian world view.

III

One of the areas in which the crisis of authority proved to be the most acute was in philosophy—that discipline, or superdiscipline, that was expected to give order to all other aspects of human experience. Of the several philosophical systems transmitted from Antiquity, the one that won out in the high Middle Ages, and continued to dominate in the Renaissance, was the Aristotelian. Aristotle's writings had the advantage of covering many different fields: physics, metaphysics, logic, politics, ethics, poetics, biology. Other fields were added to this series by several of Aristotle's followers in the three centuries after his death: medicine by Galen, astronomy and geography by Ptolemy. Still another was added after the recovery of most of Aristotle's writings in the thirteenth century: Christian theology.

Every single compartment of the Aristotelian system was connected with all the others by a series of dialectical deductions from undisputable (or undisputed) first principles, and apparent defects in one compartment could be compensated for by the strengths of all the others. The system thus survived even the humanists' historicization of Aristotle—that is, their insistence that he was a fallible man like themselves and limited by the circumstances of the time and place in which he had lived. For, most humanists also admitted that Aristotle had discovered the correct method for discovering the truth; and they trusted the professional Aristotelians— in the literary academies as well as in the philosophy chairs of the universities—to fill in the gaps and correct the errors.

Just at the moment of its apparent triumph, however, this seemingly all-embracing system began to show signs of stress. For one thing, it never managed to embrace several fields that had become of considerable importance in the Renaissance (notably, painting, music, and history). For another, the humanist text hunters uncovered, or drew attention to, several alternate philosophic systems with equally valid credentials of antiquity. One was the Platonist, or Neoplatonist, strengthened after the late fifteenth century by the translation of all the relevant texts into Latin. Another was the atomic explanation of matter set forth in physics by Democritus and in ethics by Epicurus, and armed by Lucretius's poetic rendition of it, *De Rerum Natura* (On the Nature of Things). Still another was the heliocentric theory of the universe. That was one which attracted considerable attention, at least for its simplification of astronomical calculations, when it was revived by the mathematician Nicholas Copernicus in a highly technical treatise (*De Revolutionibus*) dedicated to Pope Paul III in 1543, the year of the author's death.

At the same time, internal developments in several of the Aristotelian disciplines made it increasingly difficult to keep them within an Aristotelian framework. Several of these disciplines were swamped with new information: geography with descriptions of extra-European lands that Ptolemy had never heard about, botany with thousands of new plants for which the Aristotelian scheme of categorization had no room, anatomy with a number of new muscles and bones that Galen had failed to fit into the human body. Machiavelli discovered that Aristotle's ideal state was totally inapplicable to the political realities of sixteenth century Italy. His contemporary, Pietro Pomponazzi, drew attention to the incurable antithesis between Christian revelation and the fundamental Aristotelian theses of the mortality of the soul and the eternity of the material universe. Artillery commanders could not make cannon balls follow one or another of the courses that the Aristotelian physicists prescribed for them. Literary critics disagreed violently about just what Aristotle might have said about such post-Aristotelian literary genres as the romance and the madrigal.

Such were the difficulties of maintaining the Aristotelian system that some philosophers gave up trying to patch it up and adopted a completely new one to take its place. Pierre de la Ramée (Ramus) proposed a totally different logic to replace what for Aristotle was the foundation of all the sciences. Giordano Bruno described a universe that was infinite, not finite, and that was commensurate with an infinite, but imminent, divine force. René Descartes substituted for Aristotle's fundamental axioms one that seemed to him much less irrefutable: "I think, therefore I am" (*Cogito, ergo sum*); and the universe of mind and extension that he deduced from that axiom turned out to be totally dissimilar from the Aristotelians' universe of four elements, four causes, and four humors.

Where the contrast between philosophical systems was most vivid, however, was in the field of astronomy. The Aristotelians had for centuries admitted the coexistence of two mutually exclusive explanations of planetary motions. Both Aristotle and Ptolemy put the earth in the center of the universe, with the planets and the "fixed stars" revolving around it. But in order to account for the motion of the planets, Aristotle had riveted them into contiguous and impermeable concentric spheres, all propelled, in varying degrees, by the precisely diurnal circular motion of the sphere of the fixed stars. Since circular motion could not be observed on earth, he divided the universe into two parts: the superlunary, where nothing ever changed, and the sublunary—everything below the closest of the heavenly spheres—which was the locus of linear motion, generation, and corruption.

Ptolemy, on the other hand, sought to systematize planetary motions in such a way that they could be predicted. To explain the observable phenomenon of "regression," when the planets at the same hour of the night move eastward rather than westward, he invented a series of "epicycles" that made the planets rotate not along a circular orbit, but along an axis revolving about a point on the orbit. In order to explain still further anomalies, he moved the center of the planetary orbits to the circumference of another "wheel" revolving about a point not coincident with the center of the earth.

The only way to avoid a confrontation between the two explanations was to suppose that Aristotle's system was "real," even if it was of no help in predicting the position of the planets, and that Ptolemy's was a purely artificial method of predicting them, which did not "really" exist even if the predictions proved to be fairly correct. Neither system could admit the existence of comets, which apparently traversed both spheres and orbits. And neither could admit the possibility of the "new stars" which, in the last decades of the sixteenth century, appeared, shone brightly, and then disappeared, to the consternation of all the Aristotelian astronomers and cosmographers. There was only one way out; and that was the one that seemed to be confirmed by the immense quantity of new empirical data suddenly made available by Galileo's telescope in January, 1610, and broadcast to the world in his eloquent and immediately best-selling pamphlet, *Sidereus Nuntius,* "The Starry Messenger."

How Galileo made these discoveries, and how he transferred the basis of cosmology from Aristotelian logic to Archimedian mathematics, is explained by Galileo himself in the selections here presented from his polemical pamphlet, *Il Saggiatore,* "The Assayer." How these substantive and methodological innovations led him into a violent confrontation with the adherents of the Aristotelian cosmos is explained in the letters of his disciples; they kept him informed of the gathering opposition that eventually won the support of at least one powerful organ of the Tridentine Church.

Agostino Scilla provides ample testimony to the manner in which Galileo's cosmological revolution defied the opposition, penetrated to the most distant corners of Europe, and entered into domains of scientific inquiry into which Galileo himself had never ventured. The selections from Pascal's *Pensées* reveal the consequences of the revolution in the realm of theology and religion, which was still one of great importance among the immediate heirs of the religious reformation of the sixteenth century. And those from Newton and from his editor Roger Cotes illustrate the divergences among alternative post-Aristotelian scientific systems and the way in which each of them attempted to come to terms with the same religious heritage.

The final section of this volume provides some explanation for the eventual victory of the new cosmos over the old. What a few brilliant individuals could not accomplish by themselves was accomplished by institutions that coordinated their efforts. That these institutions in the long run realized their aims was to some extent the result of their having won the support of those powers who were able to pay for and impose the philosophical revolution: the mixed monarchies of Naples and England, the paternalistic monarchies of Prussia and Tuscany, and, in these selections, the absolute monarchy of Louis XIV in France.

1
Cohesion and Division: Political Thought and the Making of States

Two Northern European States

1. Sir Thomas Smith, *De Republica Anglorum*

Sir Thomas Smith (1513–77) had a distinguished career in Elizabethan politics and diplomacy. He held several university degrees, and was an ordained clergyman, and a professor at Cambridge; but his primary profession was that of a civil (Roman) lawyer. Civil law was the only kind taught in the English universities; like many aspirants to the profession, however, Smith took his law degree on the Continent.

The practice of law, for most of the purposes we would associate with the trade today, required training in schools provided by professional societies, where common law—mainline English law—was taught. Civil lawyers, aside from practice in Church courts and some other specialized tribunals, could sometimes find a place in public service, especially in connection with foreign affairs, because the law they were versed in was the basis for that of the rest of Western Europe and such international law as then existed.

Over a long career in the service of the state, Smith was not so much a major league courtier-politician as the kind of man who today would be a top-rank professional civil servant. No formal distinction between the two classes existed in the world of monarchy; to have a political career was to be a courtier, and all careers were precarious. *De facto,* however, there was a difference between those who enjoyed great influence with the monarch and competed for it, and the reliable, competent, experienced men who kept the machinery running, and who tended to survive vicissi-

From Sir Thomas Smith, *De Republica Anglorum,* edited by L. Alston (Cambridge: Cambridge University Press, 1906), pp. 29–63.

tudes of personal favor and of policy. Smith is a good example of the latter type.

De Republica Anglorum is a consciously descriptive work. Although it opens with some theorizing, it is mostly devoted to describing English government and social structure with a particular interest in making England intelligible to foreigners. It is visibly the work of a practical man with long experience and a clear eye for reality, and also of a man who, as a civil lawyer and diplomat (he was ambassador to France at a critical time), could talk about England in an international vocabulary. It is rare and valuable to have a source which instead of reflecting ideals, partisan positions, or legalisms tries to "tell it like it was," in the terms a contemporary observer thought most relevant, and with the consciousness Smith had that reality does not always correspond to ideology.

Chapter 16: The division of the parts and persons of the common wealth

To make all thinges yet cleare before, as we shal go, there ariseth another division of the partes of the common wealth. For it is not enough to say that it consisteth of a multitude of houses and families which make stretes and villages, and the multitude of the stretes and villages make townes, and the multitude of townes the realme, and that freemen be considered only in this behalf, as subjects and citizens of the commonwealth, and not bondmen who can beare no rule nor jurisdiction over freemen, as they who be taken but as instruments and the goods and possessions of others. In which consideration also we do reject women, as those whom nature hath made to keepe home and to nourish their familie and children, and not to medle with matters abroad, nor to beare office in a citie or common wealth no more than children and infantes: except it be in such cases as the authoritie is annexed to the bloud and progenie, as the crowne, a dutchie, or an erledome for there the blood is respected, not the age nor the sexe. Whereby an absolute Queene, an absolute Dutches or Countesse, those I call absolute, which have the name, not by being maried to a king, duke, or erle, but by being the true, right and next successors in the dignitie, and upon whom by right of the blood that title is descended: These I say have the same authoritie although they be women or children in that kingdome, dutchie or earledome, as they shoulde have had if they had bin men of full age. For the right and honour of the blood, and the quietnes and suertie of the realme, is more to be considered, than either the tender age as yet impotent to rule, or the sexe not accustomed (otherwise) to intermeddle with publicke affaires, being by common intendment understood, that such personages never do lacke the counsell of such grave and discreete men as be able to supplie all other defectes. This (as I sayde) is not enough: But the division of these which be participant of the common wealth is one way of them that beare office, the other of them that beare none: the first are called magistrates, the second private men. Another the like was among the Romanes of *Patritij* and *plebei*, thone striving with thother a long time, the *patricij* many yeares excluding the *plebei* from bearing rule, untill at last all magistrates were made common between them: yet was there another division of the Romanes into *senatores, equites* and *plebs:* the Greekes had also ἐνγενεῖς καὶ Δημαυτιχοὺς. The French have also at this day, *les nobles* and *la populare,* or *gentils homes* and *villaines:* we in England divide our men commonly into foure sortes, gentlemen, citizens, yeomen artificers, and laborers. Of gentlemen the first and chiefe are the king, the prince, dukes, marquises, earles, vicountes, barrons, and these are called κατ᾽ ἐξοχὴν the nobility, and all these are called Lords and noblemen: next to these be knightes, esquiers and simple gentlemen.

Chapter 17: Of the first part of gentlemen of englande called *Nobilitas maior*

Dukes, marquises, erles, vicountes, and barrons, either be created by the prince or come to that honor by being the eldest sonnes, as highest and next in succession to their parentes. For the eldest of dukes sonnes during his fathers lyfe is called an earle, an earles sonne is called by the name of a vicount, or baron, or else according as the creation is. The creation I cal the first donation and condition of the honour (given by the prince, for good service done by him and advauncement that the prince will bestowe uppon him) which with the title of that honour is commonly (but not alwayes) given to him and to his heires, males onely: the rest of the sonnes of the nobilitie by the rigor of the lawe be but esquiers, yet in common speeche, all dukes and marquises sonnes, and the eldest sonne of an earle be called Lordes. The which name commonly doth agree to none of lower degree than barrons, excepting such onely, as be thereunto by some speciall office called. The barrony or degree of Lordes doeth answere to the dignitie of the Senators of Rome, and the title of our nobilitie to their *patricij:* when *patricij* did betoken *Senatores aut senatorum filios. Census Senatorius* was in Rome, at diverse times diverse, and in Englande no man is created barron, excepte he may dispend of yearly revenue, one thousand poundes or one thousand markes at the least. Vicountes, earles, marquises and dukes more according to the proportion of the degree and honour, but though by chaunce he or his sonne have lesse, he keepeth his degree: but if they decay by excesse, and be not able to maintaine the honour (as *senatores Romani* were *amoti senatu*) so sometimes they are not admitted to the upper house in the parliament, although they keepe the name of Lorde still.

Chapter 18: Of the second sort of gentlemen which may be called *Nobilitas minor,* and first of knightes

No man is a Knight by succession, not the king or prince. And the name of prince in england κατ' ἐξοχὴν betokeneth the kinges eldest sonne or prince of wales: although the king himselfe, his eldest sonne, and all dukes be called by generall name princes. But as in Fraunce the kinges eldest sonne hath the title of the daulphine, and he or the next heire apparant to the crowne is monsire, so in Englande the kinges eldest sonne is called κατ' ἐξοχὴν the prince. Knightes therefore be not borne but made, either before the battle to encourage them the more to adventure their lives, or after the conflict, as advauncement for their hardinesse and manhood alreadie shewed: or out of the warre for some great service done, or some good hope through the vertues which do appeare in them. And they are made either by the king himselfe, or by his commission and royall authoritie, given for the same purpose, or by his liuetenaunt in the warres, who hath his royall and absolute power committed to him for that time. And that order seemeth to aunswere in part to that which the Romanes called *Equites Romanos,* differing in some pointes, and agreeing in other, as their common wealth and ours do differ and agree: for never in all pointes one common wealth doth agree with an other, no nor long time any one common wealth with it selfe. For al chaungeth continually to more or lesse, and still to diverse and diverse orders, as the diversity of times do present occasion, and the mutabilitie of mens wittes doth invent and assay newe wayes, to reforme and amende that werein they do finde fault. *Equites Romani* were chosen *ex censu,* that is according to their substance and riches. So be knightes in England most commonly, according to the yearely revenew of their landes being able to maintaine that estate: yet all they that had *Equestrem censum, non legebantur equites.* No more are all made knightes in Englande that may dispende a knightes land or fee, but they onely whom the king wil so honour. The number of *Equites* was uncertaine, and so it is of knightes, at the pleasure of the prince. *Equites Romani* had *equum publicum.* The knightes of England have not so, but finde their own horse themselves in peace time, and most usually in warres.

Census equester was among the Romanes at diverse times of diverse valew: but in England whosoever may dispende of his free landes 40. l. sterling of yearely revenew by an olde law of Englande either at the coronation of the king, or mariage of his daughter, or at the dubbing of the prince, knight, or some such great occasion, may be by the king compelled to take that order and honour, or to pay a fine, which many not so desirous of honour as of riches, had rather disburse. Some who for causes ar not thought worthy of that honor and yet have abilitie, neither be made knightes though they would, and yet pay the fine. Xl. l. sterling, at that time when this order began, maketh now Cxx. l. of currant mony of Englande: as I have more at large declared in my booke of the diversitie of standardes or the valor of monies.

When the Romanes did write *senatus populusque Romanus,* they seemed to make but two orders, that is of the Senate and of the people of Rome, and so in the name of the people they contained *equites* and *plebem:* so when we in England do say the Lordes and the commons, the knights, esquires, and other gentlemen, with citizens, burgeses and yeomen be accompted to make the commons. In ordaining of lawes the senate of Lordes of England is one house, where the Archbishoppes and Bishops also be, and the king or Queene for the time being as chiefe: the Knights and all the rest of the gentlemen, citizens and burgeses which be admitted to consult upon the greatest affaires of the Realme be in an other house by themselves, and that is called the house of the commons, as we shal more clearely describe when we speake of the parliament. Whereupon this worde knight is derived, and whether it do betoken no more but that which *miles* doth in latine, which is a souldier, might be moved as a question. The word souldier now seemeth rather to come of sould and payment, and more to betoken a waged or hyred man to fight than otherwise, yet *Caesar* in his Commentaries called *soldures* in the tongue gallois, men who devoted and swore themselves in a certaine band or othe [oath] one to another and to the captaine, which order if the Almains did follow, it may be that they who were not hyred but being of the nation, uppon their owne charges and for their advauncement, and by such common oth or band that did follow the warres, were (possibly) κατ᾽ ἐξοχὴν called knightes or *milites,* and nowe among the Almaines some are called lanceknights as souldiers of their band not hyred, although at this day they be for the most part hirelings. Or peradventure it may be that they which were next about the prince as his garde or servauntes picked or chosen men out of the rest being called in the Almaine language, *knighten,* which is asmuch to say as servantes: these men being found of good service, the word afterward was taken for an honor, and for him who maketh profession of armes. Our language is so chaunged that I dare make no judgement therof. Now we call him knight in english that the french calleth *chevalier,* and the latine *equitem* or *equestris ordinis.*

And when any man is made a knight, he kneeling downe is stroken of the prince, with his sworde naked uppon the backe or shoulder, the prince saying: *sus* or *sois chivalier au nom de Dieu* and (in times past) they added S. *George,* and at his arising the prince saith, *avauncer.* This is the manner of dubbing of knights at this present: and that terme dubbing was the olde terme in this point, and not creation. At the coronation of a king or queene, there be knightes of the bath made with long and more curious ceremonies:

But howsoever one be dubbed or made a knight, his wife is by and by called a Ladie as well as a barons wife: he himselfe is not called Lorde, but hath to his name in common appellation added this syllable, Sir, as if he before were named, *Thomas, William, John,* or *Richard,* afterward he is alwayes called Sir *Thomas,* Sir *William,* Sir *John,* Sir *Richard,* and that is the title which men give to knightes in England. This may suffice at this time, to declare the order of knighthood, yet there is an other order of knightes in England which be called the knightes of the garter. King *Edward* the third, after he had obtained many notable victories, King *John* of Fraunce, King *James* of Scotland, being both prisoners in the tower of London at one time, and king *Henrie* of Castell the bastard expulsed out of his realme, and Don *Petro* restored unto it by the prince of Wales and Duke of Aquitaine called the blacke prince, invented a societie of honour, and made a choise out of his owne realme and dominions, and all Christendom: and the best and most excellent renouned persons in vertues and honour, he did adorne with that title to be knightes of his order, gave them a garter decked with golde, pearle and precious stones, with the buckle of gold, to weare daily on the left legge onely, a kirtle, gowne, cloke, chaperon, collar, and other august and magnificall apparell both of stuffe and fashion exquisite and heroicall, to weare at high feastes, as to so high and princely an order was meete: of which order he and his successors Kinges and Queenes of England to be the soveraigne, and the rest by certaine statues and lawes among themselves, be taken as brethren and fellowes in that order, to the number of xxvi. But because this is rather an ornament of the realme than any policie or government therof, I leave to speake any further of it.

Chapter 19: Of Esquiers

Escuier or esquier (which we call commonly squire) is a French worde, and betokeneth *Scutigerum* or *Armigerum,* and be all those which beare armes (as we call them) or armories (as they terme them in French) which to beare is a testimonie of the nobilitie or race from whence they do come. These be taken for no distinct order of the common wealth, but do goe with the residue of the gentlemen: save that (as I take it) they be those who beare armes, testimonies (as I have saide) of their race, and therefore have neither creation nor dubbing: or else they were at the first costerels or the bearers of the armes of Lordes or knightes, and by that had their name for a dignitie and honour given to distinguish them from a common souldier called in latine *Gregarius miles.*

Chapter 20: Of Gentlemen

Gentlemen be those whom their blood and race doth make noble and knowne, Ευγενεîς in Greeke, the Latines call them all *Nobiles,* as the

French *Nobles*, Ευγενεία or *Nobilitas* in Latine is defined, honour or title given, for that the auncestor hath bin notable in riches or vertues, or (in fewer wordes) old riches or prowes remaining in one stock. Which if the successors do keepe and followe, they be *verè nobiles* and Ευγενεῖς: if they doe not, yet the fame and wealth of their auncestors serve to cover them so long as it can, as a thing once gilted though it be copper within, till the gilt be worne away. This hath his reason, for the Etimologie of the name serveth thefficacie of the worde. *Gens* in Latine betokeneth the race and sirname, so the Romaines had *Cornelios, Sergios, Appios, Fabios, Aemilios, Pisones, Julios, Brutos, Valerios,* of which who were *Agnati,* and therefore kept the name, were also *Gentiles:* and remaining the memorie of the glorie of their progenitors fame, were gentlemen of that or that race. This matter made a great strife among the Romanes, when those which were *Novi homines* were more allowed, for their vertues new and newly showen, than the olde smell of auntient race newly defaced by the cowardise and evill life of their nephewes and discendauntes could make the other to be. . . .

But as other common wealthes were faine to doe, so must all princes necessarilie followe, that is, where vertue is to honour it: and although vertue of auncient race be easier to be obtained, as well by the example of the progenitors, which encourageth, as also through habilitie of education and bringing up, which enableth, and the lastly enraced love of tenants and neybors to such noblemen and gentlemen, of whom they holde and by whom they doe dwell, which pricketh forward to ensue in their fathers steps. So if all this doe faile (as it were great pitie it should) yet such is the nature of all humaine thinges, and so the world is subject to mutability, that it doth many times faile: but when it doth, the prince and common wealth have the same power that their predecessors had, and as the husbandman hath to plant a new tree where the olde fayleth, so hath the prince to honour vertue where he doth find it, to make gentlemen, esquiers, knights, barons, earles, marquises, and dukes, where he seeth vertue able to beare that honour or merits, and deserves it, and so it hath alwayes bin used among us. But ordinarily the king doth only make knights and create barons or higher degrees: for as for gentlemen, they be made good cheape in England. For whosoever studieth the lawes of the realme, who studieth in the universities, who professeth liberall sciences, and to be shorte, who can live idly and without manuall labour, and will beare the port, charge and countenaunce of a gentleman, he shall be called master, for that is the title which men give to esquires and other gentlemen, and shall be taken for a gentleman: for true it is with us as is saide, *Tanti eris alijs quanti tibi feceris:* (and if neede be) a king of Heraulds shal also give him for mony, armes newly made and invented, the title whereof shall pretende to have beene found by the sayd Herauld in perusing and viewing of olde registers, where his auncestors in times past had bin recorded to beare the same: Or if he wil do it more truely and of better faith, he will write that for the merittes of that man, and certaine qualities which he doth see in him, and for sundrie noble actes which he hath perfourmed, he by the authoritie which he hath as king of Heraldes and armes, giveth to him and his heires these and these armes, which being done I thinke he may be called a squire, for he beareth ever after those armes. Such men are called sometime in scorne gentlemen of the first head.

Chapter 21: Whether the maner of England in making gentlemen so easily is to be allowed

A man may make doubt and question whether this maner of making gentlemen is to be allowed or no, and for my part I am of that opinion that it is not amisse. For first the prince loseth nothing by it, as he shoulde doe if it were as in Fraunce: for the yeomen or husbandman is no more subject to taile or taxe in Englande than the gentleman: no, in every payment to the king the gentleman is more charged, which he beareth the gladlier and dareth not gainesaie for to save and keepe his honour and reputation. In any shew or muster or other particular charge of the towne where he is, he must open his purse wider and augment his portion above others, or else he doth diminish his reputation. As for their outward shew, a gentleman (if he wil be so accompted) must go like a gentleman, a yeoman like a yeoman, and a rascall like a rascall: and if he be called to the warres, he must and will (whatsoever it cost him) array himselfe and arme him according to the vocation which he pretendeth: he must shew also a more manly corage and tokens of better education, higher stomacke and bountifuller liberalitie than others, and keepe about him idle servauntes, who shall doe nothing but waite upon him. So that no man hath hurt by it but he himselfe, who hereby per chance will beare a bigger saile than he is able to maintaine. For as touching the policie and goverment of the common wealth, it is not those that have to do with it, which will magnifie them selves, and goe in higher buskins than their estate will beare: but they which are to be appointed, are persons tryed and well knowen, as shall be declared hereafter.

Chapter 22: Of Citizens and Burgesses

Next to gentlemen, be appointed citizens and burgesses, such as not onely be free and received as officers within the cities, but also be of some substance to beare the charges. But these citizens and burgesses, be to serve the common wealth, in their cities and burrowes, or in corporate townes where they dwell. Generally in the shyres they be of none accompt, save onely in the common assembly of the realme to make lawes, which is called the Parliament. The aunciet cities appoint iiij. and ech burrough ij.

to have voices in it, and to give their consent or dissent in the name of the citie or burrough for which they be appointed.

Chapter 23: Of Yeomen

Those whom we call yeomen next unto the nobilitie, knights and squires, have the greatest charge and doings in the common wealth, or rather are more travailed to serve in it than all the rest: as shall appear hereafter. I call him a yeoman whom our lawes doe call *Legalem hominem,* a worde familiar in writtes and enquestes, which is a freeman borne English, and may dispend of his own free lande in yerely revenue to the summe of xl. s. sterling: This maketh (if the just value were taken now to the proportion of monies) vi. l. of our currant mony at this present. This sort of people confesse themselves to be no gentlemen, but give the honour to al which be or take upon them to be gentlemen, and yet they have a certaine preheminence and more estimation than laborers and artificers, and commonly live welthilie, keepe goode houses, and do their businesse, and travaile to acquire riches: these be (for the most part) fermors unto gentlemen, which with grasing, frequenting of markettes, and keeping servauntes not idle as the gentleman doth, but such as get both their owne living and parte of their maisters: by these meanes doe come to such wealth, that they are able and daily doe buy the landes of unthriftie gentlemen, and after setting their sonnes to the schoole at the Universities, to the lawe of the Realme, or otherwise leaving them sufficient lands whereon they may live without labour, doe make their saide sonnes by those meanes gentlemen. These be not called masters, for that (as I saide) pertaineth to gentlemen onely: But to their surnames, men adde goodman: as if the surname be *Luter, Finch, White, Browne,* they are called, goodman *Luter,* goodman *White,* goodman *Finch,* goodman *Browne,* amongst their neighbours, I meane not in matters of importance or in lawe. But in matters of lawe and for distinction, if one were a knight they would write him (for example sake) sir *John Finch* knight, so if he be an esquier, *John Finch* esquier or gentleman, if he be no gentleman, *John Finch* yeoman. For amongst the gentlemen they which claime no higher degree, and yet be to be exempted out of the number of the lowest sort thereof, be written esquiers. So amongst the husbandmen labourers, lowest and rascall sort of the people such as be exempted out of the number of the rascabilitie of the popular be called and written yeomen, as in the degree next unto gentlemen. These are they which olde Cato calleth *Aratores* and *optimos cives in Republica:* and such as of whom the writers of common wealthes praise to have manie in it. *Aristoteles* namely reciteth πόμα μεσήτια ἄριστα: these tende their owne businesse, come not to meddle in publike matters and judgements but when they are called, and gladde when they are delivered thereof, are obe-

dient to the gentlemen and rulers, and in warre can abide travaile and labour as men used to it, yet wishing it soone at an ende that they might come
home and live of their owne. When they are foorth they fight for their
Lordes of whom they hold their landes, for their wives and children, for
their countrey and nation, for praise and honour, against they come home,
and to have the love of their Lorde and his children to be continued to-
wardes them and their children, which have adventured their lives to and
with him and his. These are they which in the old world gat that honour to
Englande, not that either for witte, conduction, or for power they are or
were ever to be compared to the gentlemen, but because they be so manie
in number, so obedient at the Lordes call, so strong of bodie, so heard to
endure paine, so couragious to adventure with their Lorde or Captaine
going with, or before them, for else they be not hastie nor never were, as
making no profession of knowledge of warre. These were the good archers
in times past, and the stable troupe of footemen that affaide all France, that
that would rather die all, than once abandon the knight or gentleman their
Captaine, who at those daies commonly was their Lorde, and whose ten-
auntes they were, readie (besides perpetuall shame) to be in danger of undoing of them selves, and all theirs if they should showe any signe of cowardise or abandon the Lorde, Knight or Gentlemen of whom they helde
their living. And this they have amongest them from their forefathers tolde
one to an other. The gentlemen of France and the yeomen of Englande are
renowned, because in battle of horsemen Fraunce was many times too
good for us, as we againe alway for them on foote. And Gentlemen for the
most part be men at armes and horsemen, and yeomen commonlie on
foote: howesoever it was, yet the gentlemen had alwaies the conduction of
the yeomen, and as their captaines were either a foote or upon a litle nagge
with them, and the Kinges of Englande in foughten battles remaining alwaies among the footemen, as the French Kinges amongst their horsemen.
Each Prince therby, as a man may gesse, did shew where he thought his
strength did consist. What a yeomen is I have declared, but from whence
the word is derived it is hard to say: it cannot be thought that yeomen
should be said a young man, for commonly wee doe not call any a yeoman
till he be married, and have children, and as it were have some authoritie
among his neighbours. Yonker in lowe dutch betokeneth a meane gentleman or a gay fellowe. Possible our yeomen not being so bolde as to name
themselves gentlemen, when they came home, were content when they had
heard by frequentation with lowe dutchmen of some small gentleman (but
yet that would be counted so) to be called amongst them, yonker man, the
calling so in warres in mockage or in sport thone an other, when they come
home, yonker man, and so yeoman: which worde now signifieth among us,
a man well at ease and having honestlie to live, and yet not a gentleman:

whatsoever that worde yonker man, yonke man, or yeoman doth more or less signifie to the dutch men.

Chapter 24: Of the fourth sort of men which doe not rule

The fourth sort or classe amongest us, is of those which the olde Romans called *capite censij proletarij* or *operae*, day labourers, poore husband-men, yea marchantes or retailers which have no free lande, copiholders, and all artificers, as Taylers, Shoomakers, Carpenters, Brickemakers, Bricklayers, Masons, &c. These have no voice nor authoritie in our common wealth, and no account is made of them but onelie to be ruled, not to rule other, and yet they be not altogether neglected. For in cities and corporate townes for default of yeomen, enquests and Juries are impaneled of such manner of people. And in villages they be commonly made Church-wardens, alecunners [inspectors of ale], and manie times Constables, which office toucheth more the common wealth, and at the first was not imployed uppon such lowe and base persons. Wherefore generally to speake of the common wealth, or policie of Englande, it is governed, ad-ministred, and manured by three sortes of persons, the Prince, Monarch, and head governer, which is called the king, or if the crowne fall to a woman, the Queene absolute, as I have heeretofore saide: In whose name and by whose authoritie all things are administred. The gentlemen, which be divided into two partes, the Baronie or estate of Lordes conteyning barons and all that bee above the degree of a baron, (as I have declared before): and those which be no Lords, as Knightes, Esquires, and simplely gentlemen. The thirde and last sort of persons is named the yeomanrie: each of these hath his part and administration in judgementes, corrections of defaultes, in election of offices, in appointing and collection of tributes and subsidies, or in making lawes, as shall appear heereafter.

The Second Booke

Chapter 1: Of the Parliament and the authoritie thereof

The most high and absolute power of the realme of Englande, consisteth in the Parliament. For as in warre where the king himselfe in person, the no-bilitie, the rest of the gentilitie, and the yeomanrie are, is the force and power of Englande: so in peace and consultation where the Prince is to give life, and the last and highest commaundement, the Baronie for the nobilitie and higher, the knightes, esquiers, gentlemen and commons for the lower part of the common wealth, the bishoppes for the clergie bee present to advertise, consult and shew what is good and necessarie for the common wealth, and to consult together, and upon mature deliberation everie bill or lawe being thrise reade and disputed upon in either house, the other two partes first each a part, and after the Prince himselfe in presence of both the parties doeth consent unto and alloweth. That is the Princes and whole realmes deede: whereupon justlie no man can complaine, but must accommodate himselfe to finde it good and obey it.

That which is doone by this consent is called firme, stable, and *sanctum,* and is taken for lawe. The Parliament abrogateth olde lawes, maketh newe, giveth orders for thinges past, and for thinges hereafter to be followed, changeth rightes, and possessions of private men, legittimateth bastards, establisheth formes of religion, altereth weightes and measures, giveth formes of succession to the crowne, defineth of doubtfull rightes, whereof is no lawe alreadie made, appointeth subsidies, tailes, taxes, and impositions, giveth most free pardons and absolutions, restoreth in bloud and name as the highest court, condemneth or absolveth them whom the Prince will put to that triall: And to be short, all that ever the people of Rome might do either in *Centuriatis comitijs* or *tributis,* the same may be doone by the parliament of Englande, which representeth and hath the power of the whole realme both the head and the bodie. For everie Englishman is entended to bee there present, either in person or by procuration and attornies, of what preheminence, state, dignitie, or qualitie soever he be, from the Prince (be he King or Queene) to the lowest person of Englande. And the consent of the Parliament is taken to be everie mans consent.

Chapter 2: The forme of holding the Parliament

The Prince sendeth foorth his rescripts or writtes to every duke, marques, baron, and every other Lorde temporall or spirituall who hath voice in the parliament, to be at his great counsell of Parliament such a day, (the space from the date of the writ is commonly at least fortie dayes): he sendeth also writtes to the Sherifes of every shyre to admonish the whole shire to choose two knightes of the parliament in the name of the shyre, to hearē and reason, and to give their advise and consent in the name of the shire, and to be present at that day: likewise to every citie and towne which of ancientie hath bin wont to finde burgesses of the parliament, so to make election that they might be present there at the first day of the parliament. The knightes of the shyre be chosen by all the gentlemen and yeomen of the shyre, present at the day assigned for the election: the voice of any absent can be counted for none. Yeomen I call here (as before) that may dispende at the least xl. s. of yearely rent of free lande of his owne. These meeting at one day, the two who have the more of their voices be chosen knightes of the shire for that parliament: likewise by the pluralitie of the voyces of the citizens and burgesses be the burgesses elected. The first day of the parliament the Prince and all the Lordes in their robes of parliament do meete in the higher house, where after prayers made, they that be present are written, and they that be absent upon sicknes or some other reasonable cause (which the prince will allowe) do constitute under their hande and seale some one of those who be present as their procurer or attorney to give voice for them, so that by presence or atturney and proxey they be all there, all the princes and barrons and all archbishops and bishops, and (when abbots were) so many abbots as had voice in parliament. The place where the assembly is, is richly tapessed and hanged, a princely and royal throne as appertaineth to a king, set in the middest of the higher place thereof. Next under the prince sitteth the Chancellor, who is the voyce and orator of the prince. On the one side of that house or chamber sitteth the archbishops and bishops, ech in his ranke, on the other side the dukes and barons. In the middest thereof uppon woolsackes sitteth the Judges of the realme, the master of the roules, and the secretaries of estate. But these that sit on the woolsacks have no voice in the house, but onely sit there to aunswere their knowledge in the law, when they be asked if any doubt arise among the Lordes. The secretaries to aunswere of such letters or thinges passed in counsell whereof they have the custodie and knowledge: and this is called the upper house, whose consent and dissent is given by ech man severally and by himselfe, first for himselfe, and then severally for so many as he hath letters and proxies, when it commeth to the question, saying onely content or not content, without further reasoning or replying. In this meane time the knights of the shires and burgesses of the parliament (for so they are called that have voice in parliament, and are chosen as I have said before, to the number betwixt iij. C. and iiij. C.) are called by such as it pleaseth the prince to appoint, into an other great house or chamber by name, to which they aunswere and declaring for what shyre or towne they aunswere: then they are willed to choose an able and discreete man to be as it were the mouth of them all, and to speake for and in the name of them, and to present him so chosen by them to the prince: which done they comming al with him to a barre, which is at the nether ende of the upper house, there he first praiseth the prince, then maketh his excuse of unabilitie, and prayeth the prince that he would command the commons to choose another. The chancellor in the princes name doth so much declare him able, as he did declare himselfe unable, and thanketh the commons for choosing so wise, discreete and eloquent a man, and willeth them to go and consult of lawes for the common wealth. Then the speaker maketh certaine requests to the prince in the name of the commons, first that his majestie would be content that they may use and enjoy all their liberties and priviledges that the common house was wont to enjoy. Secondly that they might franckely and freely saye their mindes in disputing of such matters as may come in question, and that without offence to his Majestie. Thirdly that if any should chaunce of that lower house to offend or not to do or say as should become him, or if any should offend any of them being called to that his highnes court: That they themselves might (according to the ancient custome) have the punishment of them. And fourthly, that if there came any doubt, whereupon they shal desire to have thadvise or conference with his Majestie or with any of the Lordes, that they might doe it: All which he promiseth in the commons names that they shall not abuse, but have such regarde as most faithfull, true and loving subjectes ought to have to their prince.

The Chauncelor answereth in the princes name, as apperteyneth. And this is all that is doone for one day, and sometime two. Besides the Chauncelor, there is one in the upper house who is called Clarke of the Parliament, who readeth the bils. For all that commeth in consultation either in the upper house or in the neather house, is put in writing first in paper, which being once read, he that will, riseth up and speaketh with it or against it: and so one after another so long as they shall thinke good. That doone they goe to another, and so an other bill. After it hath bin once or twise read, and doth appeare that it is somewhat liked as reasonable, with such amendment in wordes and peradventure some sentences as by disputation seemeth to be amended: In the upper house the Chauncelor asketh if they will have it engrossed, that is to say put into parchment: which doone, and read the third time, and that eftsoones if any be disposed to object disputed againe among them, the Chauncelor asketh if they will goe to the question: and if they agree to goe to the question, then he sayth, here is such a lawe or act concerning such a matter, which hath beene thrise read here in this house, are ye content that it be enacted or no? If the not contentes be moe, then the bill is dashed, that is to say the lawe is annihilated and goeth no further. If the contentes be the more, then the Clarke writeth underneath: *Soit baille aux commons*. And so when they see time they send such bils as they have approoved by two or three of those which doe sit on the woolsacks to the commons: who asking licence, and comming into the house, with due reverence, sayth to the speaker: Master speaker, my Lordes of the upper house have passed among them and thinke good, that there should be enacted by Parliament such an act, and such an act, and so readeth the titles of that act or actes. They pray you to consider of them, and shew them your advise, which doone they goe their way. They being gone and the doore againe shut, the speaker rehearseth to the house what they sayde. And if they be not busie disputing at that time in an other bill, he asketh them streightwaie if they will have that bill or (if there be mo) one of them.

In like maner in the lower house the speaker sitting in a seate or chaire for that purpose somewhat higher, that he may see and be seene of them all, hath before him in a lower seate his Clarke, who readeth such bils as be first propounded in the lower house, or be sent down from the Lords. For in that point ech house hath equal authoritie, to propounde what they thinke meete, either for thabrogating of some law made before, or for making of a newe. All bils be thrise in three diverse dayes read and disputed upon, before they come to the question. In the disputing is a mervelous good order used in the lower house. He that standeth uppe bareheadded is understanded that he will speake to the bill. If moe stande uppe, who that first is judged to arise, is first harde, though the one doe prayse the law, the other diswade it, yet there is no altercation. For everie man speaketh as to the speaker, not as one to an other, for that is against the order of the house. It is also taken against the order, to name him whom ye doe confute, but by circumlocution, as he that speaketh with the bill, or he that spake against the bill, and gave this and this reason. And so with perpetuall Oration not with altercation, he goeth through till he do make an end. He that once hath spoken in a bill though he be confuted straight, that day may not replie, no though he would chaunge his opinion. So that to one bill in one day one may not in that house speak twise, for else one or two with altercation woulde spende all the time. The next day he may, but then also but once.

No reviling or nipping wordes must be used. For then all the house will crie, it is against the order: and if any speake unreverently or seditiouslie against the Prince or the privie counsell, I have seene them not onely interrupted, but it hath beene moved after to the house, and they have sent them to the tower. So that in such a multitude, and in such diversitie of mindes, and opinions, there is the greatest modestie and temperance of speech that can be used. Neverthelesse with much doulce and gentle termes, they make their reasons as violent and as vehement the one against the other as they may ordinarily, except it bee for urgent causes and hasting of time. At the afternoone they keepe no parliament. The speaker hath no voice in the house, nor they will not suffer him to speake in any bill to moove or diswade it. But when any bill is read, the speakers office is as brieflie and as plainely as he may to declare the effect thereof to the house. If the commons doe assent to such billes as be sent to them first agreed upon from the Lords thus subscribed, *Les commons ont assentus,* so if the Lordes doe agree to such billes as be first agreed uppon by the Commons, they sende them downe to the speaker thus subscribed, *Les Seigneurs ont assentus.* If they cannot agree, the two houses (for everie bill from whence soever it doth come is thrise reade in each of the houses) if it be understoode that there is any sticking, sometimes the Lordes to the Commons, somtime the Commons to the Lordes doe require that a certaine of each house may meete together, and so ech part to be enformed of others meaning, and this is alwaies graunted. After which meeting for the most part not alwaies either parte agrees to others billes.

In the upper house they give their assent and dissent ech man severallie and by himselfe first for himselfe, and then for so manie as he hath proxie. When the Chaunceler hath demanded of them whether they will goe to the question after the bill hath beene thrise reade, they saying only content or not content, without further reasoning or replying: and as the more number doeth agree, so is it agreed on, or dashed.

In the neather house none of them that is elected either Knight or Burges can give his voice to an other nor his consent nor dissent by proxie. The more parte of them that be present onely maketh the consent or dissent. After the bill hath beene twise reade, and then engrossed and eftsoones reade and disputed on ynough as is thought: the speaker asketh if they will goe to the question. And if they agree he holdeth the bill up in his hande and sayeth, as many as will have this bill goe forwarde, which is concerning such a matter, say yea. Then they which allowe the bill crie yea, and as many as will not, say no: as the crie of yea or no is bigger, so the bill is allowed or dashed. If it be a doubt which crie is the bigger, they divide the house, the speaker saying, as many as doe alowe the bill goe downe with the bill, and as many as do not sitte still. So they divide themselves, and being so divided they are numbred who make the more part, and so the bill doeth speede. It chaunceth sometime that some part of the bil is allowed, some other part hath much contrariety and doubt made of it: and it is thought if it were amended it would goe forwarde. Then they chuse certaine *committees* of them who have spoken with the bil and against it to amende it, and bring it in againe so amended, as they amongest them shall thinke meete: and this is before it is engrossed, yea and some time after. But the agreement of these *committees* is no prejudice to the house. For at the last question they will either accept it or dash it as it shall seeme good, notwithstanding that whatsoever the *committees* have doone.

Thus no bill is an act of Parliament, ordinaunce, or edict of law, untill both the houses severallie have agreed unto it, after the order aforesaide, no nor then neither. But the last day of that Parliament or session the Prince commeth in person in his Parliament robes, and sitteth in his state: all the upper house sitteth about the Prince in their states and order in their robes. The speaker with all the common house commeth to the barre, and there after thankes given first in the Lordes name by the Chaunceller &c. and in the commons name by the speaker to the Prince, for that hee hath so great care of the good governement of his people, and for calling them together to advise of such thinges as should be for the reformation, establishing and ornament of the common wealth: the Chaunceller in the Princes name giveth thankes to the Lords and commons for their paines and travailes taken, which he saith the Prince will remember and recompence when time and occasion shall serve, and that he for his part is ready to declare his pleasure concerning their proceedings, whereby the same may have perfect life and accomplishment by his princelie authoritie, and so have the whole consent of the Realme. Then one reades the title of everie act which hath passed at that session, but only in this fashion: An act concerning such a thing &c. It is marked there what the Prince doth allowe, and to such he sayth: *Le roy* or *la royne le veult*. And those be taken nowe as perfect lawes and ordinances of the Realme of Englande and none other, and as shortlie as may be put in print, except it be some private cause or lawe made for the benefit or prejudice of some private man, which the Romans were wont to call *privilegia*. These be onelie exemplified under the seale of the Parliament, and for the most part not printed. To those which the Prince liketh not, he answereth, *Le roy* or *la royne saduisera*, and those be accounted utterly dashed and of no effect.

This is the order and forme of the highest and most authenticall court of Englande, by vertue whereof all those things be established whereof I spake before, and no other meanes accounted vailable to make any new forfaiture of life, member, or landes of any English man, where there was no lawe ordayned for it before. Nowe let us speake of the saide partes when they be severall.

Chapter 3: Of the Monarch King or Queene of Englande

The Prince whom I nowe call (as I have often before) the Monarch of Englande, King or Queene, hath absolutelie in his power the authoritie of warre and peace, to defie what Prince it shall please him, and to bid him warre, and againe to reconcile himselfe and enter into league or truce with him at his pleasure or the advice onely of his privie counsell. His privie counsell be chosen also at the Princes pleasure out of the nobilitie or baronie, and of the Knightes, and Esquiers, such and so many as he shal thinke good, who doth consult daily, or when neede is of the weightie matters of the Realme, to give therein to their Prince the best advice they can. The Prince doth participate to them all, or so many of them, as he shall thinke good, such legations and messages as come from forren Princes, such letters or occurrentes as be sent to himselfe or to his secretaries, and keepeth so many ambassades and letters sent unto him secret as he will, although these have a particular oth of a counceller touching faith and secrets administred unto them when they be first admitted into that companie. So that heerein the kingdome of Englande is farre more absolute than either the dukedome of Venice is, or the kingdome of the Lacedemonians was. In warre time, and in the field the Prince hath also absolute power, so that his worde is a law, he may put to death, or to other bodilie punishment, whom he shall thinke so to deserve, without processe of lawe or forme of judgement. This hath beene sometime used within the Realme before any open warre in sodden insurrections and rebellions, but that not allowed of wise and grave men, who in that their judgement had consideration of the consequence and example, asmuch as of the present necessitie, especiallie, when by anie meanes the punishment might have beene doone by order of lawe. This absolute power is called marciall lawe, and ever was and necessarilie must be used in all campes and hostes of men, where the time nor place do suffer the tariance of pleading and processe, be it never so short, and the important necessitie requireth speedie execution, that with more awe the souldier might be kept in more straight obedience, without which never captaine can doe anie thing vaileable in the warres.

The prince useth also absolute power in crying and decreeing the mony of the realme by his proclamation onely. The mony is always stamped with the princes image and title. The forme, fashion, maner, weight, finenesse, and basenesse therof, is at the discretion of the prince. For whom should the people trust more in that matter than their prince, seeing the coine is only to certifie the goodnes of the mettall and the weight, which is affirmed by the princes image and marke? But if the prince will deceave them and give them copper for silver or golde, or enhaunce his coyne more than it is worth, he is deceaved himselfe, aswell as he doth goe about to deceave his subjectes. For in the same sort they pay the prince his rentes and customes. And in time they will make him pay rateably or more for meate, drinke and victualles for him and his, and for their labour: which experience doth teach us nowe in our dayes to be doone in all regions. For there ever hath beene, and ever wil be a certaine proportion betweene the scarcity and plentie of other thinges, with gold and silver, as I have declared more at large in my booke of monie. For all other measures and weightes, aswell of drie thinges as of wet, they have accustomed to be established or altered by the Parliament, and not by the princes proclamation only.

The prince useth also to dispence with lawes made, whereas equitie requireth a moderation to be had, and with paynes for transgression of lawes, where the payne of the lawe is applyed onely to the prince. But where the forfaite (as in popular actions it chaunceth many times) is part to the prince, the other part to the declarator, detector or informer, there the prince doth dispence for his owne part onely. Where the criminall action is intended by inquisition (that maner is called with us at the princes suite) the prince giveth absolution or pardon: yet with a clause, *modo stet rectus in curia,* that is to say, that no man object against the offendor. Whereby notwithstanding that he hath the princes pardon if the person offended will take uppon him the accusation (which in our language is called the appeale) in cases where it lieth, the princes pardon doth not serve the offendor.

The prince giveth all the chiefe and highest offices or magistracies of the realme, be it of judgement or dignitie, temporall or spirituall, and hath the tenthes and first fruites of all Ecclesiasticall promotions, except in the Universities and certaine Colledges which be exempt.

All writtes, executions and commaundementes be done in the princes name. We doe say in England the life and member of the kinges subjectes are the kinges onely, that is to say no man hath *hault* nor *moyenne* justice but the king, nor can hold plea thereof. And therefore all those pleas, which touche the life or the mutilation of man, be called pleas of the crowne, nor can be doone in the name of any inferior person than he or shee that holdeth the crowne of Englande. And likewise no man can give pardon thereof but the prince onely: Although in times past there were certaine countie Palatines, as Chester, Durham, Elie, which were *hault* justicers, and writtes went in their name, and also some Lorde marchers of Wales, which claymed like priviledge. All these are nowe worne away. The supreme justice is done in the kinges name, and by his authoritie onely.

The Prince hath the wardshippe and first mariage of all those that hold landes of him in chiefe. And also the governement of all fooles naturall, or such as be made by adventure of sicknes, and so continue, if they be landed. This being once graunted by act of Parliament (although some inconvenience hath been thought to grow thereof, and sith that time it hath beene thought verie unreasonable) yet once annexed to the crowne who ought to go about to take the clubbe out of *Hercules* hand. And being governed justly and rightly, I see not so much inconvenience in it, as some men would make of it: diverse other rights and preeminences the prince hath which be called prerogatives royalles, or the prerogative of the king, which be declared particularly in the bookes of the common lawes of England.

To be short the prince is the life, the head, and the authoritie of all thinges that be doone in the realme of England. And to no prince is doone more honor and reverence than to the King and Queene of Englande, no man speaketh to the prince nor serveth at the table but in adoration and kneeling, all persons of the realme be bareheaded before him: insomuch that in the chamber of presence where the cloath of estate is set, no man dare walke, yea though the prince be not there, no man dare tarrie there but bareheaded. This is understood of the subjectes of the realme: For all strangers be suffered there and in all places to use the maner of their countrie, such is the civilitie of our nation.

2. Gregory King, *Naturall and Political Observations upon the State and Condition of England*

The landmark characteristic of *Naturall and Political Observations upon the State and Condition of England* (1696) is its use of numbers in drawing the profile of a country. An interest in what we would call statistics was a major aspect of the seventeenth-century "scientific revolution." The chief honors of that fundamental turn in Western intellectual history belong to high science, with its culminating achievement of Sir Isaac Newton's synthesis of classical physics. But in no place so much as in England were new enthusiasms and researches of a humbler sort so prominent in the total intellectual scene. The activities of collectors of facts and curiosities, experimenters, and practical improvers constituted a reaction against the divisive religious and political concerns of the Civil War period.

An interest in knowing more about the society and economy around one, and the perception that quantities matter for an appreciation of those everyday realities was one concern of the era. "Political arithmetic," as the early counters and number-estimators in England called their new field, was innocent of the mathematical sophistication of modern statistics and of anything we would recognize as economic theory, but counting it was—with conscious attention to the problems of getting the numbers right. The intention to be accurate does not guarantee the results, but for the first time in history we have figures from contemporaries to assist in the study of history.

Gregory King (1648–1712) was not the principal pioneer of political arithmetic (that title would go to his older contemporary Sir William Petty), but his comprehensive survey of England has proved its most durable product. King was a multitalented man—an engraver, map maker, and city planner, as well as an arithmetician—but if he is to be assigned to a primary profession, it would be that of a herald (an authenticator of genealogies and the right to use coats of arms). The step from keeping track of aristocratic family trees to keeping tabs on a wider range of social facts is not an illogical one, ironic though it may be to think of the feudal passion for heraldry among the ancestors of social science.

From George Chalmers, *An Estimate of the Comparative Strength of Great Britain*. To which is now annexed Gregory King's *Natural and Political Observations upon the State and Condition of England* (London: J. Stockdale, 1802), pp. 16–32, 49–56.

Whereas the ensuing Treatise depends cheifly upon the Knowledge of the true Number of People in England, and such other circumstances relating thereunto, as have been collected from the assessments on Marriages, Births, and Burials, Parish Registers, & other publick accounts; We shall first exhibit the calculation of the Number of People, as they appear by the said Assessments

1. As to the Number of People of England.

In this Calculation, We shall consider, (1) The Number of Inhabited Houses; (2) The Number of People to each House; (3) The Number of Transitory People, & vagrants.
The Number of Houses in the Kingdome, as charg'd in the Books of the Hearth Office at Lady Day 1690. Were . . . . 1,319,215.

The Kingdome increasing at this time about 9000 People per ann. as will appear in the ensuing Discourse.

The Increase of Houses should be about 2000 per ann. But by reason of the Present Warr with France not much above 1000 per ann So that by the year 1695 The Increase cannot have been above 6 or 7000. Which makes the present Number of Houses, that is to say such as were so charged in the Books of the Hearth office to be about . . . . 1,326,000.

But whereas the chimney Mony being charg'd on the Tennant or Inhabitant, The Divided Houses stand as so many distinct Dwellings in the Accounts of the said Hearth office; And whereas the Empty Houses, Smiths shops &c. are Included in the said account, All which may very well amount to 1 in 36 or 37 (or near 3 per Cent) which in the whole may be about 36,000 Houses, It Follows

That the true Number of Inhabited Houses in England,
is not Above 1,290,000
Which however in a Round Number, We shall call 1,300,000

And shall thus apportion,
	Houses
London & the Bills of Mortality	105,000
The other Cities, & Markett Towns	195,000
The Villages & Hamletts	1,000,000
	In all, 1,300,000

Haveing thus adjusted the Number of Inhabited Houses, We come to proportion the number of Souls to each House according to what we have observed from the said assessments on Marriages, Births, & Burials, in Several parts of the Kingdome viz.[1]

That London within the Walls produc'd at a medium
    almost .... $5\frac{1}{2}$ Souls per House.
    The 16 Parishes Without the Walls .... Full $4\frac{1}{2}$ Souls per House.
    And the Rest of the said Bills .... almost $4\frac{1}{2}$ Souls per House.
That the other Cities and Markett Towns produc'd at a
    medium .... $4\frac{1}{3}$ Souls per House.
    And the villages & Hamletts at a Medium   about 4 Souls per House.
    Accordingly the Number of People computed from
    the said assessments amounts to .... 5,318,100 Souls.

As by the following Scheme.

	Inhabited Houses.	Souls per House.	Number of Souls.
The 97 Parishes within the Walls	13,500	at 5'4	72,900 Souls.
The 16 Parishes without the Walls	32,500	at 4'6	149,500
The 15 Out Parishes in Midd.[x] & Surrey	35,000	at 4'4	154,000
The 7 Parishes in the City & Liberties of Westm.[r]	24,000	at 4'3	103,200
So London & the Bills of Mortality contain	105,000	at 4'57	479,600
The other Cities & Markett Towns	195,000	at 4'3	838,500
The Villages & Hamletts	1,000,000	at 4	4,000,000
In all	1,300,000	at 4'9	5,318,100

But considering that the omissions in the s.[d] assessm.[ts] may well be,

In London & the Bills of Mortality ..... 10 per Cent or 47,960 Souls.
In the Cities & Towns .... 2 per Cent or 16,500 Souls.
In the Villages & Hamletts .... 1 per Cent or 40,000 Souls.

In all 104,460 Souls.

It follows that the True number of People dwelling in the 1,300,000 Inhabited Houses should be 5,422,560 Souls, according to the following Scheme:

	People by the Assessm.[ts]	Omissions in the Assessm.[ts]	Number of People in all.		
The 97 Parishes ...	72,900	7,290	80,190	at almost 6	Heads per House.
The 16 Parishes ...	149,500	14,950	164,450	at above 5	Heads per House.

The 15 Parishes ...	154,000	15,400	169,400 at above 4'8	Heads per House.
The 7 Parishes ...	103,200	10,320	113,520 at almost 4	Heads per House.
The Bills of Mortal	479,600	47,960	527,560 at above 5	Heads per House.
The Cities & Towns	838,500	16,500	855,000 at almost 4'4	Heads per House.
The Villages	4,000,000	40,000	4,040,000 at 4'4	Heads per House.
Total	5,318,100	104,460	5,422,560 at above 4'17	Heads per House.

Lastly Whereas the Number of Transitory People as Seamen, & Souldiers, may be accounted 140,000 Whereof near onehalf or 60,000 have no place in the said assessm.ᵗˢ And that the number of vagrants viz.ᵗ Hawkers, Ped- lars, Crate Carriers, Gipsies, Theves & Beggars may be Reckond 30,000. Whereof above one half or 20,000 may not be taken notice of in the s.ᵈ assessm.ᵗˢ making in all 80,000 Persons.

It followes that the whole number of the People of England is much about . . . . 5,500,000 Souls.

viz.ᵗ London & the Bills of Mortality . . . .   530,000 Souls.
     The other Cities & Markett Towns . . . .   870,000 Souls.
     The Villages, & Hamletts . . . . 4,100,000 Souls.

                           In all 5,500,000 Souls.

2. The Proportion of England in Acres & People, To France and Holland, To Europe, & to the World in General, with a Calculation of the Number of People Now in the World

That England is in Proportion

	In Acres.	In Souls.
To the Globe of the Earth & Seas as	1 To 3,300	1 To 130
To the Known habitable World as	1 To 600	1 To 110
To Europe (Includ.ᵍ Muscovy) as	1 To 43	1 To 18
To France as	1 To $3\frac{1}{4}$	11 To 30
To Holland as	9 To 2	5 To 2
To France & Holl.ᵈ Together as	1 To $3\frac{1}{2}$	10 To 32

That England haveing but 7 Acres of Land to Each head:

It is between 5 & 6 Times better peopled than the Known world in General.
Above twice, but not 3 times better Peopled than Europe in General.
About $1\frac{1}{2}$ Times better peopled than Germany.
Above 3 Times better Peopled than Ireland Now is.
Almost 3 Times better Peopled than Scotland, or Spain.
Somewhat better Peopled than France, That Kingdome haveing at Least 9 Acres per head, as Italy likewise hath.

About as well Peopled as the Spanish Netherlands now are, or as the Countries about the Rhine, viz.[1] Alsatia, The Palatinate, Lorrain &c.

And Exceeded only in populousnesse by Holland & China, of all the Nations in the World.

That England hath 5 Times the number of People now in Scotland, and 6 times the number of People now in Ireland.

That Scotland & Ireland Together are near equall to England in number of Acres, but not $\frac{2}{5}$ths of Engl.[d] in Number of People.

That England Scotland & Ireland Together contain

About 75 Millions of Acres.

Somewhat more than 7 Millions of People.

Somewhat above 10 acres to Each Head.

About the 23.[d] part of Europe in Acres. And the 13.th or 14.th part of Europe in People.

Somewhat more than Half France in Acres & People.

Nine Times the bigness of the 7 Provinces of Holland in Acres.

And more than 3 Times, but not near 4 times the People of those Provinces

And in Proportion To France and Holland Together, as 10 To Nineteen in Acres, and as 10 To 22 in People.

As to the Number of People now in the World, We are to consider (1) The Number of Acres in the Habitable World; (2) The Proportion of People to the Number of Acres.

As to the Number of Acres:

The superficiall content of the Globe of Earth & Water at $69\frac{1}{2}$ miles to a Degree of Latitude, is 200 Millions of Square Miles, or 128,000 Mill.[s] of Acres, at 640 Acres to a square Mile.

The Land Discover'd & Undiscover'd is now Generally presum'd to be one Moity of the Globe, or 64,000 Mill.[s] of Acres.

The known part of the world contains about . . . . 23,000 Mill.[s] of acres.

And the Unknown Part . . . . 41,000 Mill.[s] of acres.

That of the known part of the world . . . . 20,000 Mill.[s] of acres is habitable.

And . . . . 3,000 Millions Uninhabitable.

That of the unknown part . . . . 25,000 Mill.[s] of acres may be Habitable.

And . . . . 16,000 Mill.[s] of acres Uninhabitable.

As to the Proportion of People to the Number of Acres.

That where there is more than 100 Acres to each Head, Such Country is Little better than Desert.

That there is no country besides Holland & China so Populous, as to have but 4 Acres per head.

That England haveing about 7 acres per head, France about 9 And Scottland & Ireland Together about 18 or 20 Acres per head we cannot suppose Europe in General has above 15 or 20 acres per Head.

That Asia being generally very rich & Populous, Especially India, Persia, & China, (w.ᶜʰ last is said to have 10 Millions of Large Families Containing 59 Millions of Men, besides Women & children, whereby the Number of Souls in China should be at Least 230 Millions for 1000 Millions of Acres) We cannot suppose but Asia must be near as well, if not better Peopled pro Rato than Europe.

That allowing Europe & Asia to be about 3 Times better Peopled pro rato than Affrica, and 6 Times better peopled pro Rato than America, It follows that the number of People in the Known part of the World should be about 600 Millions of Souls; And in the Unknown Part, above 100 Millions, In all . . . . 700 Millions of Souls.

	Acres.		Souls.
Europe	1,700 Millions at	17 Acres per Head.	100 Millions.
Asia	6,800 Millions at	20 Acres per Head.	340 Millions.
Affrica	6,100 Millions at	64 Acres per Head.	95 Millions.
America	8,400 Millions at	129 Acres per Head.	65 Millions.
	In all 23,000 Millions at 38 Acres per Head.		600 Millions.

3. The several Distinctions of the People, as to Males, & Females, Married, and unmarried, Children, Servants, & Sojourners

That the 5 Millions and a half of Souls in England Including the Transitory People, & vagrants, appear by the assessm.ᵗˢ on Marriages Births and Burials, to bear the following proportions in Relation to Males & Females viz.ᵗ

	Males. Females.	Males.	Females.	Both.
In London & the Bills of Mortal	10 To 13	230,000	300,000	530,000
In the other Cities & Market Towns	8 To 9	410,000	460,000	870,000
In the Villages & Hamletts	100 To 99	2,060,000	2,040,000	4,100,000
	27 To 28	2,700,000	2,800,000	5,500,000

That as to other Distinctions, they appear by the said Assessm.ᵗˢ to bear these Proportions.

		People.	Males.	Females.
Husbands & Wives at above	$34\frac{1}{2}$ per Cent.	1,900,000	950,000	950,000
Widdowers at above . .	$1\frac{1}{2}$ per Cent.	90,000	90,000	. . . .

Widdows at almost ...	$4\frac{1}{2}$ per Cent.	240,000	....	240,000
Children at above	45 per Cent.	2,500,000	1,300,000	1,200,000
Servants at almost	$10\frac{1}{2}$ per Cent.	560,000	260,000	300,000
Sojourners & Single Persons	4 per Cent.	210,000	100,000	110,000
	100	5,500,000	2,700,000	2,800,000

And that the Different Proportions in each of the said Articles Between London, The great Towns, & the villages may the better appear, We have exhibited the Following Scheme.

	London & Bills of Mortality.		The other Cities & great Towns.		The Villages & Hamletts.	
		Souls.		Souls.		Souls.
Husbands & Wives	37 per Cent	196,000	36 per Cent	313,200	34 per Cent	1,394,000
Widdowers	2 per Cent	10,600	2 per Cent	17,400	$1\frac{1}{2}$ per Cent	61,500
Widdows	7 per Cent	37,100	6 per Cent	52,200	$4\frac{1}{2}$ per Cent	184,500
Children	33 per Cent	174,900	40 per Cent	348,000	47 per Cent	1,927,000
Servants	13 per Cent	68,900	11 per Cent	95,700	10 per Cent	410,000
Sojourners &c.[a] ..	8 per Cent	42,400	5 per Cent	43,500	3 per Cent	123,000
	100	930,000	100	870,000	100	4,100,000

4. The Several Ages of the People.

That the Yearly Births of the Kingdome Being 190,000 Souls

	In all.	Males.	Females.
Those under 1 year old are	170,000	90,000	80,000
Those under 5 years old are	820,000	415,000	405,000
Those under 10 years old are	1,520,000	764,000	756,000
Those under 16 years old are	2,240,000	1,122,000	1,118,000.
Those above 16 years old are	3,260,000	1,578,000	1,682,000
Those above 21 years old are	2,700,000	1,300,000	1,400,000
Those above 25 years old are	2,400,000	1,150,000	1,250,000
Those above 60 years old are	600,000	270,000	330,000

So that the Number of Communicants is in all .... 3,260,000 Souls
And the Number of Fighting men between 16 & 60 is ...... 1,310,000.
That the Bachelors are about 28 per Cent of the Whole.
    Whereof those under 25 years are $25\frac{1}{2}$ per Cent.
    And those above 25 years are .... $2\frac{1}{2}$ per Cent.
That the Maidens are about $28\frac{1}{2}$ per Cent of the whole.
    Whereof those under 25 years are .... $26\frac{1}{2}$ per Cent.
    And those above 25 years are .... 2 per Cent.

That the Males & Females in the Kingdome in General are Aged one with
  another $27\frac{1}{2}$ years.

That in the Kingdome in General there is near as many People liveing
  under 20 years of age, as there is above 20. Whereof, one Half of the
  Males is under 19 Years, and one half of the Females, is under 21
  Years.

		At a Medium			Years.
That the Husbands are aged	43	Years apeice wch at	$17\frac{1}{4}$	per Cent Makes	742
The Wives	40	Years apeice	$17\frac{1}{4}$	. . . .	690
The Widdowers	56	Years apeice	$1\frac{1}{2}$	. . . .	84
The Widdows	60	Years apeice	$4\frac{1}{2}$	. . . .	270
The Children	12	Years apeice	45	. . . .	540
The Servants	27	Years apeice	$10\frac{1}{2}$	. . . .	284
The Sojourners	35	Years apeice	4	. . . .	140
At a Medium	$27\frac{1}{2}$		100	Persons	2750 Years.

5. The Origination & Increase of the People of England.

That if the World was Repeopled from 8 Persons after the Floud and that
  England was peopled originally by Two Persons, or by a number not
  exceeding 20 Persons; such first peopling was about the year of the
  World 2200 or 2300 vizt 600 years after the Floud; & 16 or 1700 Years
  before the Birth of our Saviour at which time the World had between
  one and two millions of People only.

But if the first Peopling of England was by a colony or colonies consisting
  of a number between 100 & 1000 People (wch is most Probable) Such
  colony or colonies were brought over between the year of the World
  2400 & 2600 vizt about 8 or 900 years after the Floud, and 14 or 1500
  years before the Birth of our Saviour at which time the World had
  about a Million of Families, and 4 or 5 Mill.^{s} of People.

From Which Hypothesis it will follow by an orderly series of Increase.

That when the Romans Invaded England 53 years before our Saviors Time,
  The Kingdome had about 360,000 People & at our Saviors Birth
  about 400,000 People;

That at the Norman conquest a.^{o} Christi 1066 The Kingdome had somewhere above Two Mill.^{s} of People;

That a.^{o} 1260 or about 200 Years after the Norman conquest the Kingdome
  had 2,750,000 People, or half the present Number so that the People
  of England have doubled in about 435 Years last past;

That in Probability the next doubling of the People of England will be in
  about 600 years to come, or by the year of our Lord 2300. At which

time it will have 11 Mill.ˢ of People; But that the next doubling after that, will not be (in all probability) in lesse than 12 or 1300 Years more, or by the Year of our Lord 3500 or 3600. At which time the Kingdome will have 22 Mill.ˢ of Souls, or 4 times it's present number in case the World should last so long.

Now the Kingdome containing but 39 Mill.ˢ of acres, it will then have Lesse than 2 Acres to each head, & consequently will not then be capable of any further Increase.

That the Increase of the Kingdome for every 100 Years of the Last preceeding Term of Doubling, and the Subsequent Term of Doubling, has been, and in probability will be according to the following scheme.

An.° Christi.	Number of People	Increase every 100 Years.
1300	2,860,000	440,000
1400	3,300,000	540,000
1500	3,840,000	780,000
1600	4,620,000	880,000
1700	5,500,000	920,000
1800	6,420,000	930,000
1900	7,350,000	930,000
2000	8,280,000	925,000
2100	9,205,000	910,000
2200	10,115,000	885,000
2300	11,000,000	

Whereby it appears, That the Increase of the Kingdome being 880,000 People in the last 100 Years, & 920,000 In the next succeeding 100 Years. The annual Increase at this time is about 9000 Souls per ann.

But whereas the Yearly Burials of the Kingdome are about, 1 in 32 or 170,000 Souls; And the yearly Births 1 in 28 or 190,000 Souls Whereby the yearly Increase Should be . . . . 20,000 Souls. It is to be noted.

1. That the Allowance for Plagues, & great Mortalities
   comes to at a Medium . . . .   4,000 per ann.
2. Forreign or Civil Warrs at a Medium . . . .   3,500 per ann.
3. The Sea constantly imploying about 40,000 Precipi-
   tates the Death of about . . . .   2,500 per ann.
4. The Plantations (over & above the accession of For-
   reigners) carry away . . . .   1,000 per ann.

                          In all . . . .   11,000 per ann.
Whereby the Neat annual Increase is but   9,000

                          In all   20,000

That of these 20,000 Souls which would be the annual Increase of the Kingdome by Procreation, were it not for the Foremention'd abatements.

The Country increases annually by Procreation . . . . 20,000 Souls
The Cities & Towns (Exclusive of London) . . . .   2,000 Souls
But Lond.° & the Bills of Mortality decrease annually . . . .   2,000 Souls

So that London requires a Supply of 2000 per ann. to keep it from Decreasing, besides a further Supply of about 3000 per ann. for its increase at this time. In all 5000 or a Moity of the Kingdoms Neat Increase.

That allowing London and the Bills of Mortality to have contain'd in Iulius Cæsars time between 4 & 5000 Souls; and at the Norman Conquest about 24,000 Souls, and at this time about 530,000 Souls. The Increase thereof hath been, and in probability will be according to the following Scheme of the Duplication of its Inhabitants.

Number of Souls.	Anno Christi.	Number of years in w.ʰ the People of Lond.° have doubled.
8,280	330	
16,560	830	500
33,120	1230	400
66,240	1500	270
132,480	1585	85
264,960	1621	36
529,920	1695	74
1,059,840	1900	205
2,119,680	3000	1100

Whereby it appears that London has doubled 3 Times since the year 1500. So that it is now 8 times as bigg as it was then. And the Present yearly Increase of London, and the Bills of Mortality would have been (had it not been for the Present Warr 3000 Souls per ann.

But in Relation to the Present Warr we are to consider,

That if the Nation do at this time Contain . . . .   5,500,000 Souls
It did contain An.° 1688 about 50,000 more or . . . . . .   5,550,000 Souls
For that Instead of a decrease of 11,000 per ann out of the yearly Increase by Procreation of 20,000. The said Decrease has been at a Medium 19,000 per ann. In all for 7 years   133,000
And that Instead of an Increase of 20,000 per ann by Procreation, the s.ᵈ Increase has been at a Medium but 12,000 per ann In all for 7 years   84,000

So that the Kingdome has decreased in 7 years   49,000

Observations about Procreation, Accounting the People to be
5,500,000 souls

By the foremention'd Assessments on Marriages Births and Burials, & the Collectors Returns thereupon, and by the Parish Registers, It appears that the Proportions of Marriages Births and Burials, is according to the following Scheme.

People		Annual Marriages.			
530,000	London & Bills of Mortal.	1 in 106	In all	5,000	Producing 4 children each.
870,000	The Cities & Market Towns	1 in 128	In all	6,800	Producing 4'5 children each.
4,100,000	The Villages & Hamletts	1 in 141	In all	29,200	Producing 4'8 children each.
5,500,000		1 in 134		41,000	4'64

	Annuall Births.			Annual Burials.		
London & Bills of Mortal.	1 in 26½	In all	20,000	1 in 14'1	In all	22,000
The Cities & Market Towns	1 in 28½	In all	30,000	1 in 30'4	In all	28,600
The Villages & Hamletts	1 in 29'4	In all	139,400	1 in 34'4	In all	119,400
	1 in 28'85		190,000	1 in 32'35		170,000

Whence We may observe That in 1000 coexisting Persons.

There are 71 or 72	. . . . . marriages in the Country	. . . . . Producing	. . . . . 34'3 children.
78	. . . . marriages in Towns	. . . . Producing	. . . . . 35'2 children.
94	. . . . marriages in London	. . . . Producing	. . . . . 37'6 children.

Whereby It followes.

1. That tho' each marriage in London produceth fewer people than in the Country, Yet London in General haveing a greater proportion of Breeders is more Prolifick than the other great Towns, and the great Towns are more Prolifick than the country.
2. That if the People of London of all Ages were as long liv'd as those in the Country, London would Increase in People much faster Pro rato than the Country.
3. That the Reason why each marriage in London produces fewer children, than the Country Marriages, seems to Be,

1. From the more frequent Fornications and Adulteries.
2. From a Greater Luxury & Intemperance.
3. From a Greater Intensnesse of Businesse.
4. From the Unhealthfullnesse of the Coal Smoak.
5. From a greater Inequality of age Between the Husbands & Wives.

And that it may appear what the effect is of the Inequality of ages in Married Couples, I have collected the following observations from a certain great Town (Litchfield), in the Middle of the Kingdome, consisting of Near 3000 Souls.

1. That there is no child of any Parents now Liveing in the said Town where the Wife is 17 years older than the Husband, or the Husband 19 years older than the Wife.
2. That the whole Number of children being 1060 the number of those where the Mother was older than the Father is 228 and where the Husband was older than the Wife 832.
3. That one Moity of the whole number of children in the said Town are the Product of such Parents, where the Husband is 4 or more years older than the Wife.
4. That the greatest Number of children with respect to any one number of years of Difference in age between the Husband and Wife, is where the Husband is Two years older than the Wife, the Product whereof is 147 or a $7.^{th}$ Part of the whole.
5. That an Equality in age in the Husband, & Wife, is not so Prolifick, as an Inequality, Provided that Inequality exceed not a Superiority of 4 Years in the Wife, or 10 Years in the Husband; For the equality of years produced but 23 children, whereas one years Inequality in the age of the Parents either way produc'd above 60.
6. That of the said 1060 Children in the whole Town near 3 Quarters of them are the Product of Coalitions from 2 years superiority of age in the Wife inclusive to 6 years superiority of age in the Husband Inclusive.
7. That the highest Powers in men & Women for Procreation is in that Town at 31 years of age in the Husband and 28 in the Wife, the Produce of the former being 86 children, & of the Latter 83.
8. That one moity of the said 1060 children are the Product of Fathers from 28 to 35 years of age Inclus. and of mothers from 25 to 32.
   Whence it followes that a just equality or too great an inequality of age in marriages, are prejudicial to the Increase of Mankind.
   And that the early or Late marriages in Men and Women, do tend little to the Propagation of Humane Race.

Lastly, From a consideration of the Male & Female children in the said Town, and the ages of their Parents, at the time when such children were respectively conceiv'd; A Scheme may be establish'd of the Powers of Generation, and the Inclination of the Several coalitions towards the Producing the one or the other Sex, according to the Superiority of Power in either Sex, at the time of Such respective coalitions.*

*Text continues on page 42.

Number of Families.	Ranks Degrees Titles and Qualifications.	Heads per Family.	Number of Persons.
160	Temporall Lords	40	6,400
26	Spirituall Lords	20	520
800	Baronets	16	12,800
600	Knights	13	7,800
3,000	Esquires	10	30,000
12,000	Gentlemen	8	96,000
5,000	Persons in offices	8	40,000
5,000	Persons in offices	6	30,000
2,000	M.'ch.ᵗˢ & Traders by Sea	8	16,000
8,000	M.'ch.ᵗˢ & Traders by Sea	6	48,000
10,000	Persons in the Law	7	70,000
2,000	Clergy Men	6	12,000
8,000	Clergy Men	5	40,000
40,000	Freeholders	7	280,000
140,000	Freeholders	5	700,000
150,000	Farmers	5	750,000
16,000	Persons in Sciences & Lib. arts	5	80,000
40,000	Shopkeep.ⁿˢ & Tradesmen	$4\frac{1}{2}$	180,000
60,000	Artizans & handycrafts	4	240,000
5,000	Naval officers	4	20,000
4,000	Military officers	4	16,000
511,586 Fam.			
		$5\frac{1}{4}$	2,675,520
50,000	Common Seamen	3	150,000
364,000	Labour.ˢ People & outserv.ᵗˢ	$3\frac{1}{2}$	1,275,000
400,000	Cottagers & Paupers	$3\frac{1}{4}$	1,300,000
35,000	Common Souldiers	2	70,000
849,000 Fam.ˢ		$3\frac{1}{4}$	2,795,000
. . . .	Vagrants	. . .	30,000
849,000		$3\frac{1}{4}$	2,825,000

So the General Account is.

511,586 Fam.	Increasing the wealth of the Kingd.	$5\frac{1}{4}$	2,675,520
849,000 Fam.	Decreas.ᵍ the wealth of the Kingdom	$3\frac{1}{4}$	2,825,000
1,360,586 Fam.	Neat Totalls	$4\frac{1}{20}$	5,500,520

Yearly Income per Family.	Totall of the Estates or Income.	Yearly Income per Head.	Expence per Head		Increase per Head.			Totall Increase per annum.
£	£	£	£		£	s	d	
2800	448,000	70	60		10	. .	. .	64,000£
1300	33,800	65	55		10	. .	. .	5,200
880	704,000	55	51		4	. .	. .	51,200
650	390,000	50	46		4	. .	. .	31,200
450	1,200,000	45	42		3	. .	. .	90,000
280	2,880,000	35	32	10	2	10	. .	240,000
240	1,200,000	30	27		3	. .	. .	120,000
120	600,000	20	18		2	. .	. .	60,000
400	800,000	50	40		10	. .	. .	160,000
200	1,600,000	33	28		5	. .	. .	240,000
140	1,400,000	20	17		3	. .	. .	210,000
60	120,000	10	9		1	. .	. .	12,000
45	360,000	9	8		1	. .	. .	40,000
84	3,360,000	12	11		1	. .	. .	280,000
50	7,000,000	10	9	10	. .	10	. .	350,000
44	6,600,000	8 15	8	10	. .	5	. .	187,000
60	960,000	12	11	10	1	10	. .	40,000
45	1,800,000	10	9	10	. .	10	. .	90,000
40	2,400,000	10	9	10	. .	10	. .	120,000
80	400,000	20	18	. .	2	. .	. .	40,000
60	240,000	15	14	. .	1	. .	. .	16,000

£		£ s	£			£ s d		
67	34,495,800	12 18	12	. .		. . 18 . .		2,447,100£
£	£	£	£ s			£ s d		Decrease
20	1,000,000	7 . .	7	10		. . 10 . .		75,000£
15	5,460,000	4 10	4	12		. . 2 . .		127,500
6 10	2,000,000	2 . .	2	5		. . 5 . .		325,000
14	490,000	7	7	10		. . 10 . .		35,000

| 10 10 | 8,950,000 | 3 5 | 3 | 9 | | . . 4 . . | | 562,000£ |
| . . . . . . | 60,000 | 2 . . | 3 | . . | | 1 . . . . | | 60,000 |

£ s								
10 10	9,010,000	3 3	3	7 6		. . 4 6		622,000£

£		£ s	£ s d			£ s d		
67	34,495,800	12 18	12			. . 18 . .		2,447,100£
10 10	9,010,000	3 3	3 7 6			. . 4 6		622,000
32	43,505,800	7 18	7 11 3			. . 6 9		1,825,100£

6. The Annual Income, & Expence of the Nation as it stood An.° 1688.

That the Yearly Income of the Nation a.° 1688 Was   43,500,000 Sterlg.
  That the Yearly Expence of the Nation Was   41,700,000
  That then the Yearly Increase of wealth was   1,800,000
That the Yearly Rent of the Lands were about   10,000,000
  of the Burgage or Houseing about   2,000,000
  of all other Heriditaments about   1,000,000

In all   13,000,000

That the yearly Produce of Trade arts & Labour was
  ab.'   30,500,000

In all   43,500,000

That the Number of Inhabited Houses being about .   1,300,000
  The Number of Families about   1,360,000
  And the Number of People about   5,500,000
  The People answer to 4¼ per House, & 4 per Family
That the Yearly Estates or Income of the several Families answer

	£	s.	d.	
In common To about	32	..	..	per Family
And about	7	18	..	per head
That the yearly expense of the Nation is about . . .	7	11	4	per head
And the yearly Increase about	..	6	8	per head

That the whole Value of the Kingdom in Gen." is
  about . . . .   650,000,000 Stlg.

Viz.'
  The 13 Millions of yearly Rents, at about 18 years
    Purchace . . . .   234,000,000 Sterlg.
  The 30 Millions and a Half per annum by Trade,
    arts, Labour &c. at near 11 years Purchase
    (which being the Value of the 5 Mill.ˢ & a half
    of people at 60ᶢ per head) comes To   330,000,000
  The Stock of the Kingdome in mony Plate Jewells
    and Household Goods about   28,000,000
  The Stock of the Kingdome in Shipping, Forts,
    Ammunition, Stores, Forreign or home Goods,
    Wares, and Provisions for Trade abroad, or con-
    sumption at home, and all Instruments, & Ma-
    terialls relating thereunto   33,000,000
  The Live Stock of the Kingdome in Cattle, Beasts,
    Fowle, &c.   25,000,000

In all . . . .   650,000,000 Sterlg.

[The table on pp. 40–41 comes here in the MS.]

3. Sir William Temple, *Observations upon the United Provinces of the Netherlands*

Sir William Temple (1628–99) was well qualified to write about Holland, for he saw extensive diplomatic service there and was throughout his life an advocate of friendship between England and Holland. Temple, though not a front-rank politician, was of some importance in public affairs; and after retirement—in the last two decades of his life—he made a second career of distinction as a prose writer on a variety of subjects. His *Observations upon the United Provinces of the Netherlands,* however, was written in 1672, when Temple was actively engaged in politics and diplomacy.

The histories of England and Holland were closely linked throughout the long Dutch struggle for independence from Spain, which began in the 1560s and had substantially succeeded by the end of the sixteenth century, even though success was not finally and formally secured until well into the seventeenth. English assistance was important to the Dutch cause, and England paid for her intervention by a dangerous war with Spain. The defeat of a massive Spanish expedition to invade England and settle Spain's interminable troubles in the Netherlands—the famous Armada of 1588—was as much a milestone in the Dutch revolt's success as it was in England's deliverance.

In the seventeenth century, independent Holland flourished as a commercial and maritime power with overseas possessions. Rivalry with England in the same departments led these cousinlike nations into three brief, immediately inconclusive, naval wars, the first when the Cromwellian regime was in power in England, the latter two under the restored Stuart king, Charles II, whose political flirtation with Louis XIV's France fueled English economic differences with Holland. These conflicts were the context of Sir William Temple's advocacy of a more traditional pro-Dutch policy of Protestant solidarity.

Although the seventeenth-century wars were not in themselves determinative, the commercial-maritime-imperial long run favored England. Holland suffered relative decline as, beginning in the eighteenth century, England advanced to predominance as a world power. But before this occurred, the symbiosis of England and Holland reasserted itself in the political arena when, in 1688, at the nearly unanimous invitation of the English ruling elite, the head of the Dutch state, William of Orange, invaded England and without bloodshed assured the deposition of the Catholic Stuart king, James II. William was made joint monarch with his wife Mary, a daughter of James II. Since this pair was childless, England

From Sir William Temple, *Works* (London: J. Round, 1740), pp. 30–43.

was not to have a part-Dutch ruling house for the future; but when it became apparent that nature would not guarantee a Protestant monarchy forever, it was guaranteed by law. Catholics were made ineligible by statute, and the crown passed to a German family descended from James I, where it still remains.

Holland's economic heyday in the seventeenth century was also a time of cultural flowering. Surely Protestant Europe's most distinguished early modern contributions to the heritage that outlasts politics and partisan religion were English literature and Dutch art. Holland preceded England in transcending narrow Protestantism and conservative anxiety lest intellectual variety threaten political order—that is, in becoming a country of refuge, where the air was free and dissent tolerated. As the seventeenth century passed into the eighteenth, both countries were beacons for those who aspired to a new freedom—twin pillars of liberal Europe in its first phase.

Chapter 2: Of Their Government

It is evident by what has been discoursed in the former Chapter concerning the Rise of this State (which is to be dated from the Union of *Utrecht*) that it cannot properly be styled a Commonwealth, but is rather a Confederacy of Seven Sovereign Provinces united together for their common and mutual Defence, without any Dependance one upon the other. But to discover the Nature of their Government from the first Springs and Motions, it must be taken yet into smaller Pieces, by which it will appear, that each of these Provinces is likewise composed of many little States or Cities, which have several Marks of Sovereign Power within themselves, and are not subject to the Sovereignty of their Provinces; not being concluded in many Things by the Majority, but only by the universal Concurrence of Voices in the Provincial States. For as the States-General cannot make War or Peace, or any new Alliance, or Levies of Money, without the Consent of every Province; so cannot the States-Provincial conclude of any of those Points, without the Consent of each of the Cities, that, by their Constitution, has a Voice in that Assembly. And tho' in many Civil Causes there lies an Appeal from the common Judicature of the Cities, to the Provincial Courts of Justice; yet in Criminal, there lies none at all; nor can the Sovereignty of a Province exercise any Judicature, seize upon any Offender, or pardon any Offence within the Jurisdiction of a City, or execute any common Resolution or Law, but by the Justice and Officers of the City itself. By this a certain Sovereignty in each City is discerned, the chief Marks whereof are, the Power of exercising Judicature, levying of Money, and making War and

Peace: For the other, of coining Money, is neither in particular Cities or Provinces, but in the Generality of the Union, by common Agreement.

The main Ingredients therefore into the Composition of this State are the Freedom of the Cities, the Sovereignty of the Provinces, the Agreements or Constitutions of the Union, and the Authority of the Princes of *Orange:* Which makes the Order I shall follow in the Account intended of this Government. But whereas, the several Provinces in the Union, and the several Cities in each Province, as they have, in their Orders and Constitutions, some particular Differences, as well as a general Resemblance; and the Account of each distinctly would swell this Discourse out of Measure, and to little Purpose: I shall confine myself to the Account of *Holland,* as the richest, strongest, and of most Authority among the Provinces; and of *Amsterdam* as that which has the same Preheminencies among the Cities.

Government of the City of Amsterdam

The Sovereign Authority of the City of *Amsterdam* consists in the Decrees or Results of their Senate, which is composed of six and thirty Men, by whom the Justice is administer'd, according to ancient Forms; in the Names of Officers, and Places of Judicature. But Monies are levied by Arbitrary Resolutions, and Proportions, according to what appears convenient or necessary upon the Change or Emergency of Occasions. These Senators are for their Lives, and the Senate was anciently chosen by the Voices of the richer Burghers, or Freemen of the City, who upon the Death of a Senator met together, either in a Church, a Market, or some other Place spacious enough to receive their Numbers; and there made an Election of the Person to succeed, by the Majority of Voices. But about a hundred and thirty, or forty Years ago, when the Towns of *Holland* began to increase in Circuit, and in People, so as those frequent Assemblies grew into Danger of Tumult and Disorder upon every Occasion, by reason of their Numbers and Contentions; this Election of Senators came, by the Resolution of the Burghers in one of their General Assemblies, to be devolved for ever upon the standing Senate at that Time; so, as ever since, when any one of their Number dies, a new one is chosen by the rest of the Senate, without any Intervention of the other Burghers; which makes the Government a sort of *Oligarchy,* and very different from a popular Government, as it is generally esteem'd by those, who, passing or living in these Countries, content themselves with common Observations, or Inquiries. And this Resolution of the Burghers either was agreed upon, or follow'd by general Consent or Example, about the same Time, in all the Towns of the Province, tho' with some Difference in Number of their Senators.

By this Senate are chosen the chief Magistrates of the Town, which are the Burgomasters, and the Eschevins: The Burgomasters of *Amsterdam* are Four, whereof Three are chosen every Year; so as one of them stays in Office two Years; but the Three last chosen are call'd the *Reigning-Burgomasters* for that Year, and preside by Turns, after the first three Months; for so long after a new Elect, the Burgomaster of the Year before presides; in which Time it is suppos'd the new ones will grow instructed in the Forms and Duties of their Office, and acquainted with the State of the City's Affairs.

The Burgomasters are chosen by most Voices of all those Persons in the Senate, who have been either Burgomasters or Eschevins; and their Authority resembles that of the Lord-Mayor and Aldermen in our Cities. They represent the Dignity of the Government, and do the Honour of the City upon all Occasions. They dispose of all Under-Offices that fall in their Time; and issue out all Monies out of the common Stock or Treasure, judging alone what is necessary for the Safety, Convenience, or Dignity of the City. They keep the Key of the Bank of *Amsterdam* (the common Treasure of so many Nations) which is never open'd without the Presence of one of them: And they inspect and pursue all the great Publick Works of the City, as the *Ramparts* and *Stadt-house,* now almost finished, with so great Magnificence, and so vast Expence.

This Office is a Charge of the greatest Trust, Authority, and Dignity; and so much the greater, by not being of Profit or Advantage, but only as a Way to other constant Employments in the City, that are so. The Salary of a Burgomaster of *Amsterdam* is but five hundred Gilders a Year, though there are Offices worth five thousand in their Disposal; but yet none of them known to have taken Money upon such Occasions, which would lose all their Credit in the Town, and thereby their Fortunes by any Publick Employments. They are oblig'd to no Sort of Expence more than ordinary modest Citizens, in their Habits, their Attendance, their Tables, or any Part of their own Domestick. They are upon all publick Occasions waited on by Men in Salary from the Town: and whatever Feasts they make upon solemn Days, or for the Entertainment of any Princes or Foreign Ministers, the Charge is defrayed out of the common Treasure; but proportion'd by their own Discretion. At other Times, they appear in all Places with the Simplicity and Modesty of other private Citizens. When the Burgomaster's Office expires, they are of course dispos'd into the other Charges or Employments of the Towns, which are very many and beneficial; unless they lose their Credit with the Senate, by any Want of Diligence or Fidelity in the Discharge of their Office, which seldom arrives.

The *Eschevins* are the Court of Justice in every Town. They are at *Amsterdam* Nine in Number; of which Seven are chosen annually; but Two of the preceding Year continue in Office. A double Number is named by the

Senate, out of which the Burgomasters now chuse, as the Prince of *Orange* did in the former Constitution. They are Sovereign Judges in all Criminal Causes. In Civil, after a certain Value, there lies Appeal to the Court of Justice of the Province. But they pass Sentence of Death upon no Man, without first advising with the Burgomasters; tho', after that Form is past, they proceed themselves, and are not bound to follow the Burgomasters Opinion, but are left to their own: This being only a Care or Favour of Supererogation to the Life of a Man, which is so soon cut off, and never to be retrieved or made amends for.

Under these Sovereign Magistrates, the chief subordinate Officers of the Town are the Treasurers, who receive and issue out all Monies that are properly the Revenues or Stock of the City: The *Scout,* who takes care of the Peace, seizes all Criminals, and sees the Sentences of Justice executed, and whose Authority is like that of a Sheriff in a County with us, or a Constable in a Parish: The *Pensioner,* who is a Civil-Lawyer, vers'd in the Customs, and Records, and Privileges of the Town, concerning which he informs the Magistracy upon Occasion, and vindicates them upon Disputes with other Towns; he is a Servant of the Senate and the Burgomasters, delivers their Messages, makes their Harangues upon all publick Occasions, and is not unlike the Recorder in one of our Towns.

In this City of *Amsterdam* is the famous Bank, which is the greatest Treasure, either real or imaginary, that is known any where in the World. The Place of it is a great Vault under the Stadthouse, made strong with all the Circumstances of Doors and Locks, and other appearing Cautions of Safety, that can be: And 'tis certain, that whoever is carried to see the Bank, shall never fail to find the Appearance of a mighty real Treasure, in Bars of Gold and Silver, Plate and infinite Bags of Metals, which are supposed to be all Gold and Silver, and may be so for aught I know. But the Burgomasters only having the Inspection of this Bank, and no Man ever taking any particular Account of what issues in and out, from Age to Age, 'tis impossible to make any Calculation, or guess what Proportion the real Treasure may hold to the Credit of it. Therefore the Security of the Bank lies not only in the Effects that are in it, but in the Credit of the whole Town or State of *Amsterdam,* whose Stock and Revenue is equal to that of some Kingdoms; and who are bound to make good all Monies that are brought into their Bank: The Tickets or Bills hereof make all the usual great Payments, that are made between Man and Man in the Town; and not only in most other Places of the *United Provinces,* but in many other Trading-parts of the World. So as this Bank is properly a general Cash, where every Man lodges his Money, because he esteems it safer, and easier paid in and out, than if it were in his Coffers at home: And the Bank is so far from paying any Interest for what is there brought in, that Money in the Bank is worth something more in common Payments, than what runs current in Coin from Hand to Hand; no other Money passing in the Bank, but in the Species of Coin the best known, the most ascertain'd, and the most generally current in all Parts of the Higher as well as the Lower *Germany*.

The Revenues of *Amsterdam* arise out of the constant Excise upon all Sorts of Commodities bought and sold within the Precinct: Or, out of the Rents of those Houses or Lands that belong in common to the City: Or, out of certain Duties and Impositions upon every House, towards the Uses of Charity, and the Repairs, or Adornments, or Fortifications, of the Place: Or else, out of extraordinary Levies consented to by the Senate, for furnishing their Part of the Publick Charge that is agreed to by their Deputies in the Provincial-States, for the Use of the Province: Or by the Deputies of the States of *Holland* in the States-General, for Support of the Union. And all these Payments are made into one Common Stock of the Town, not, as many of ours are, into that of the Parish, so as Attempts may be easier made at the Calculations of their whole Revenue: And I have heard it affirmed, that what is paid of all Kinds to Publick Uses of the States-General, the Province, and the City in *Amsterdam*, amounts to above sixteen hundred thousand Pounds *Sterling* a Year. But I enter into no Computations, nor give these for any thing more, than what I have heard from Men who pretended to make such Enquiries, which, I confess, I did not. 'Tis certain, that, in no Town, Strength, Beauty, and Convenience are better provided for, nor with more unlimited Expence, than in this, by the Magnificence of their Publick Buildings, as Stadthouse and Arsenals; the Number and Spaciousness, as well as Order and Revenues of their many Hospitals; the Commodiousness of their Canals, running through the chief Streets of Passage; the mighty Strength of their Bastions and Ramparts; and the Neatness, as well as Convenience, of their Streets, so far as can be compass'd in so great a Confluence of industrious People: All which could never be atchieved without a Charge much exceeding what seems proportioned to the Revenue of one single Town.

Government of the Province of Holland

The Senate chuses the Deputies, which are sent from this City to the States of *Holland;* the Sovereignty whereof is represented by Deputies of the Nobles and Towns, composing Nineteen Voices: Of which the Nobles have only the first, and the Cities Eighteen, according to the Number of those which are called *Stemms;* the other Cities and Towns of the Province having no Voice in the States. These Cities were originally but Six, *Dort, Haerlem, Delf, Leyden, Amsterdam,* and *Tergou.* But were encreased, by Prince

William of *Nassau,* to the Number of Eighteen, by the Addition of *Rotter-dam, Gorcum, Schedam, Schonoven, Briel, Alcmaer, Horne, Enchusen, Edam, Moninckdam, Medenblick,* and *Permeren.* This makes as great an Inequality in the Government of the Province, by such a small City as *Permeren* having an equal Voice in the Provincial-States with *Amsterdam* (which pays perhaps half of all Charges of the Province) as seems to be in the States-General, by so small a Province as *Overyssel* having an equal Voice in the States-General with that of *Holland,* which contributes more than half to the general Charge of the Union. But this was by some Writers of that Age interpreted to be done by the Prince's Authority, to lessen that of the Nobles, and balance that of the greater Cities, by the Voices of the smaller, whose Dependences were easier to be gained and secured.

The Nobles, though they are few in this Province, yet are not represented by all their Number, but by Eight or Nine, who as Deputies from their Body have Session in the States-Provincial; and who, when one among them dies, chuse another to succeed him. Though they have all together but One Voice equal to the smallest Town; yet they are very considerable in the Government, by possessing many of the best Charges both Civil and Military, by having the Direction of all the Ecclesiastical Revenue that was seiz'd by the State upon the Change of Religion; and by sending their Deputies to all the Councils both of the Generalty and the Province, and by the Nomination of One Counsellor in the two great Courts of Justice. They give their Voice first in the Assembly of the States, and thereby a great Weight to the Business in Consultation. The Pensioner of *Holland* is seated with them, delivers their Voice for them, and assists at all their Deliberations, before they come to the Assembly. He is, properly, but Minister or Servant of the Province, and so his Place or Rank is behind all their Deputies; but has always great Credit, because he is perpetual, or seldom discharged; though of Right he ought to be chosen or renewed every fifth Year. He has Place in all the several Assemblies of the Province, and in the States proposes all Affairs, gathers the Opinions, and forms or digests the Resolutions; pretending likewise a Power, not to conclude any very important Affair by Plurality of Voices, when he judges in his Conscience he ought not to do it, and that it will be of ill Consequence or Prejudice to the Province. He is likewise one of their Constant Deputies in the States-General.

The Deputies of the Cities are drawn out of the Magistrates and Senate of each Town: Their Number is uncertain and arbitrary, according to the Customs or Pleasure of the Cities that send them, because they have all together but one Voice, and are all maintained at their Cities Charge: But commonly one of the Burgomasters and the Pensioner are of the Number.

The States of *Holland* have their Session in the Court at the *Hague,* and assemble ordinarily four Times a Year, in *February, June, September,* and *November.* In the former Sessions, they provide for the filling up of all vacant Charges, and for renewing the Farms of all the several Taxes, and for consulting about any Matters that concern either the general Good of the Province, or any particular Differences arising between the Towns. But in *November,* they meet purposely to resolve upon the Continuance of the Charge which falls to the Share of their Province the following Year, according to what may have been agreed upon by the Deputies of the States-General, as necessary for the Support of the State of Union.

For extraordinary Occasions, they are convoked by a Council called the *Gecommitteerde Raeden,* or the Commissioned Counsellors, who are properly a Council of State, of the Province, composed of several Deputies; one from the Nobles; one from each of the chief Towns; and but one from three of the smaller Towns, each of the three chusing him by Turns. And this Council sits constantly at the *Hague,* and both proposes to the Provincial-States, at their extraordinary Assemblies, the Matters of Deliberation, and executes their Resolutions.

In these Assemblies, though all are equal in Voices and any one hinders a Result; yet it seldom happens, but that united by one common Bond of Interest, and having all one common End of publick Good, they come after full Debates to easy Resolutions; yielding to the Power of Reason, where it is clear and strong, and suppressing all private Passions or Interests, so as the smaller Part seldom contests, hard or long, what the greater agrees of. When the Deputies of the States agree in Opinion, they send some of their Number to their respective Towns, proposing the Affair and the Reasons alledged, and desiring Orders from them to conclude; which seldom fails, if the Necessity or Utility be evident: If it be more intricate, or suffers Delay, the States adjourn for such a Time, as admits the Return of all the Deputies to their Towns; where their Influence and Interest, and the Impressions of the Debates in their Provincial Assemblies, make the Consent of the Cities easier gain'd.

Besides the States and Council mention'd, the Province has likewise a Chamber of Accounts, who manage the general Revenues of the Province: And, besides this Trust, they have the absolute Disposition of the ancient Demesn of *Holland,* without giving any Account to the States of the Province. Only at Times, either upon usual Intervals, or upon a Necessity of Money, the States call upon them for a Subsidy of two or three hundred Crowns, or more, as they are press'd, or conceive the Chamber to be grown rich, beyond what is proportioned to the general Design of encreasing the Ease and Fortunes of those Persons who compose it. The States of *Holland* dispose of these Charges to Men grown aged in their Service, and who have pass'd through most of the Employments of State, with the Esteem of Prudence and Integrity; and such Persons find here an honourable and profitable Retreat.

The Provinces of *Holland* and *Zealand,* as they used formerly to have one Governor in the Time of the Houses of *Burgundy* and *Austria;* so they have long had one common Judicature, which is exercised by two Courts of Justice, each of them common to both the Provinces. The first is composed of twelve Counsellors, nine of *Holland,* and three of *Zealand,* of whom the Governor of the Provinces is the Head; by the old Constitution used to preside whenever he pleased, and to name all the Counsellors except one, who was chosen by the Nobles. This Court judges without Appeal in all Criminal Causes; but in Civil there lies Appeal to the other Court, which is called the High Council, from which there is no Appeal, but only by Petition to the States of the Province for a Revision: When these judge there is Reason for it, they grant Letters-patents to that Purpose, naming some *Syndiques* out of the Towns, who being added to the Counsellors of the two former Courts revise and judge the Cause in the last Resort. And this Course seems to have been instituted by Way of Supply or Imitation of the Chamber of *Mechlyn,* to which, before the Revolt of the Provinces, there lay an Appeal, by Way of Revision, from all or most of the Provincial Courts of Justice, as there still doth in the *Spanish* Provinces of the *Netherlands.*

Government of the United Provinces

The Union is made up of the Seven Sovereign Princes before named, who chuse their respective Deputies, and send them to the *Hague,* for the composing of three several Colleges, call'd The States-General, The Council of State, and the Chamber of Accounts. The Sovereign Power of this United State lies effectively in the Assembly of the States-General, which used at first to be convoked upon extraordinary Occasions, by the Council of State; but that seldom, in regard they usually consisted of above Eight Hundred Persons, whose meeting together in one Place, from so many several Parts, gave too great a Shake to the whole Body of the Union; made the Debates long, and sometimes confused; the Resolutions slow, and upon sudden Occasions, out of Time. In the Absence of the States-General, the Council of State represented their Authority, and executed their Resolutions, and judged of the Necessity of a new Convocation; 'till after the Earl of *Leicester*'s Departure from the Government, the Provincial-States desired of the General, that they might, by their constant respective Deputies, continue their Assemblies under the Name of *States-General,* which were never after assembled but at *Bergen ap Zoom,* for ratifying with more solemn Form and Authority the Truce concluded with Duke *Albert* and *Spain.*

This Desire of the Provinces was grounded upon the Pretences that the

Council of State convoked them but seldom, and at Will; and that being to execute all in their Absence, they thereby arrogated to themselves too great an Authority in the State. But a more secret Reason had greater Weight in this Affair, which was, That the *English* Ambassador had, by Agreement with Queen *Elizabeth,* a constant Place in their Council of State; and upon the Distastes arising between the Provinces and the Earl of *Leicester,* with some Jealousies of the Queen's Disposition to make a Peace with *Spain,* they had no Mind that her Ambassador should be present any longer in the first Digestion of their Affairs, which was then usually made in the Council of State. And hereupon they first framed the ordinary Council, called the *States-General,* which has ever since passed by that Name, and sits constantly in the Court at the *Hague,* represents the Sovereignty of the Union, gives Audience and Dispatches to all Foreign Ministers; but yet is indeed only a Representative of the States-General, the Assemblies whereof are wholly disused.

The Council of State, the Admiralty, and the Treasury, are all subordinate to this Council: All of which are continued in as near a Resemblance, as could be, to the several Councils used in the Time when the Provinces were subject to their several Principalities; or united under One in the Houses of *Burgundy* and *Austria:* Only the several Deputies (composing one Voice) now succeeding the single Persons employed under the former Governments: And the *Hague,* which was the ancient Seat of the Counts of *Holland,* still continues to be so of all these Councils; where, the Palace of the former Sovereigns, lodges the Prince of *Orange* as Governor, and receives these several Councils as attending still upon the Sovereignty, represented by the States-General.

The Members of all these Councils are placed and changed by the several Provinces according to their different or agreeing Customs. To the States-General every one sends their Deputies, in what Number they please; some Two, some Ten, or Twelve; which makes no Difference, because all Matters are carried, not by the Votes of Persons, but of Provinces; and all the Deputies from one Province, how few or many soever, have one single Vote. The Provinces differ likewise in the Time fixed for their Deputation; some sending for a Year, some for more, and others for Life. The Provinces of *Holland* send to the States-General One of their Nobles, who is perpetual; Two Deputies chosen out of their Eight chief Towns, and One out of *North-Holland;* and with these, Two of their Provincial Council of State, and their *Pensioner.*

Neither Stadtholder or Governor, or any Person in Military Charge, has Session in the States-General. Every Province presides their Week in Turns, and by the most qualified Person of the Deputies of that Province: He sits in a Chair with Arms, at the Middle of a long Table capable of holding about

Thirty Persons; for about that Number this Council is usually composed of. The *Gressier,* who is in Nature of a Secretary, sits at the lower End of the Table. When a Foreign Minister has Audience, he is seated at the Middle of this Table, over-against the President, who proposes all Matters in this Assembly; makes the *Gressier* read all Papers; puts the Question; calls the Voices of the Provinces; and forms the Conclusion. Or, if he refuses to conclude according to the Plurality, he is obliged to resign his Place to the President of the ensuing Week, who concludes for him.

This is the Course in all Affairs before them, except in Cases of Peace and War, of Foreign Alliances, of Raising or Coining of Monies, or the Privileges of each Province or Member of the Union. In all which, all the Provinces must concur, Plurality being not all weighed or observed. This Council is not Sovereign, but only represents the Sovereignty; and therefore, though Ambassadors are both received and sent in their Name; yet neither are their own chosen, nor Foreign Ministers answered, nor any of those mentioned Affairs resolved, without consulting first the States of each Province by their respective Deputies, and receiving Orders from them; and in other important Matters, though decided by Plurality, they frequently consult with the Council of State.

Nor has this Method or Constitution ever been broken since their State began, excepting only in one Affair, which was in *January* 1668, when His Majesty sent me over to propose a League of Mutual Defence with this State, and another for the Preservation of *Flanders,* from the Invasion of *France,* which had already conquered a great Part of the *Spanish* Provinces, and left the rest at the Mercy of the next Campaign. Upon this Occasion I had the Fortune to prevail with the States-General to conclude three Treaties, and upon them draw up and sign the several Instruments, in the Space of five Days, without passing the essential Forms of their Government by any Recourse to the Provinces, which must likewise have had it to the several Cities: There, I knew those Foreign Ministers, whose Duty and Interest it was to oppose this Affair, expected to meet, and to elude it; which could not have failed, in Case it had run that Circle, since engaging the Voice of one City must have broken it: 'Tis true, that in concluding these Alliances without Commission from their Principals, the Deputies of the States-General ventured their Heads, if they had been disowned by their Provinces; but being all unanimous, and led by the clear Evidence of so direct and so important an Interest (which must have been lost by the usual Delays) they all agreed to run the Hazard; and were so far from being disowned, that they were applauded by all the Members of every Province: Having thereby changed the whole Face of Affairs in Christendom, and laid the Foundation of the Triple-Alliance, and the Peace of *Aix* (which were concluded about four Months after.) So great has the Force of Reason and Interest ever proved in this State, not only to the uniting of all Voices in their Assemblies, but to the absolving of the greatest Breach of their Original Constitutions; even in a State whose Safety and Greatness has been chiefly founded upon the severe and exact Observance of Order and Method, in all their Counsels and Executions. Nor have they ever used, at any other Time, any greater Means to agree and unite the several Members of their Union, in the Resolutions necessary, upon the most pressing Occasions, than for the agreeing Provinces to name some of their ablest Persons to go and confer with the dissenting, and represent those Reasons and Interests by which they have been induced to their Opinions.

The Council of State is composed of Deputies from the several Provinces, but after another Manner than the States-General, the Number being fixed. *Gelderland* sends Two, *Holland* Three, *Zealand* and *Utrecht* Two apiece, *Friezland, Overyssel,* and *Groninghen,* each of them One, making in all Twelve. They vote not by Provinces, but by Personal Voices; and every Deputy presides by Turns. In this Council the Governor of the Provinces has Session, and a decisive Voice; and the Treasurer-General, Session, but a Voice only deliberative; yet he has much Credit here, being for Life; and so is the Person deputed to this Council from the Nobles of *Holland,* and the Deputies of the Province of *Zealand.* The rest are but for two, three, or four Years.

The Council of State executes the Resolution of the States-General; consults and proposes to them the most expedient Ways of raising Troops, and levying Monies, as well as the Proportions of both, which they conceive necessary in all Conjunctures and Revolutions of the State; superintends the Milice, the Fortifications, the Contributions out of the Enemies Country, the Forms and Disposal of all Passports, and the Affairs, Revenues, and Government of all Places conquer'd since the Union; which, being gain'd by the common Arms of this State, depend upon the States-General, and not upon any particular Province.

Towards the End of every Year, this Council forms a State of the Expence they conceive will be necessary for the Year ensuing; presents it to the States-General, desiring them to demand so much of the States-Provincial, to be raised according to the usual Proportions, which are, of 100,000 Guilders.

	GRS.	ST.	D.
Gelderland	3,612	05	00
Holland	58,309	01	10
Zealand	9,183	14	02
Utrecht	5,830	17	11
Friezland	11,661	15	10
Overyssel	3,571	08	04
Groningue	5,930	17	11

This Petition, as 'tis call'd, is made to the States-General, in the Name of the Governor and Council of State, which is but a Continuance of the Forms used in the Time of their Sovereigns, and still by the Governors and Council of State in the *Spanish Netherlands:* Petition signifying barely asking or demanding, tho' implying the Thing demanded to be wholly in the Right and Power of them that give. It was used by the first Counts, only upon extraordinary Occasions, and Necessities; but in the Time of the Houses of *Burgundy* and *Austria* grew to be a Thing of Course, and annual, as it is still in the *Spanish* Provinces.

The Council of State disposes of all Sums of Money destin'd for all extraordinary Affairs, and expedites the Orders for the whole Expence of the State, upon the Resolutions first taken, in the Main, by the States-General. The Orders must be signed by three Deputies of several Provinces, as well as by the Treasurer-General, and then register'd in the Chamber of Accounts, before the Receiver-General pays them, which is then done without any Difficulty, Charge, or Delay.

Every Province raises what Monies it pleases, and by what Ways or Means; sends its *Quota,* or Share, of the general Charge, to the Receiver-General, and converts the rest to the present Use, or reserves it for the future Occasions, of the Province.

The Chamber of Accounts was erected about sixty Years ago, for the Ease of the Council of State, to examine and state all Accounts of all the several Receivers, to control and register the Orders of the Council of State, which disposes of the Finances: And this Chamber is compos'd of two Deputies from each Province, who are changed every three Years.

Besides these Colleges, is the Council of the Admiralty; who, when the States-General, by Advice of the Council of State, have destin'd a Fleet of such a Number and Force to be set out, have the absolute Disposition of the Marine Affairs, as well in the Choice of Equipage of all the several Ships, as in issuing the Monies allotted for that Service.

This College is subdivided into Five, of which Three are in *Holland,* viz. One in *Amsterdam,* another at *Rotterdam,* and the third at *Horn:* the Fourth is at *Middlebourgh* in *Zealand,* and the Fifth at *Harlinguen* in *Friezland.* Each of these is composed of Seven Deputies, Four of that Province where the College resides; and Three named by the other Provinces. The Admiral, or, in his Absence, the Vice-Admiral, has Session in all these Colleges, and presides when he is present. They take Cognizance of all Crimes committed at Sea; judge all Pirates that are taken, and all Frauds or Negligences in the Payment or Collections of the Customs; which are particularly affected to the Admiralty, and applicable to no other Use. This *Fund,* being not sufficient in Times of War, is supplied by the States with whatever more is necessary from other *Funds;* but in Time of Peace, being little exhausted by other constant Charge, besides that of Convoys to their several Fleets of Merchants in all Parts, the Remainder of this Revenue is applied to the Building of great Ships of War, and Furnishing the several Arsenals and Stores with all Sorts of Provision necessary for the Building and Rigging of more Ships than can be needed by the Course of a long War.

So soon as the Number and Force of the Fleets design'd for any Expedition is agreed by the States-General, and given out by the Council of State to the Admiralty; each particular College furnishes their own Proportion, which is known as well as that of the several Provinces in all Monies that are to be raised. In all which, the Admiral has no other Share or Advantage, besides his bare Salary, and his Proportion in Prizes that are taken. The Captains and superior Officers of each Squadron are chosen by the several Colleges; the Number of Men appointed for every Ship: After which, each Captain uses his best Diligence and Credit to fill his Number with the best Men he can get, and takes the whole Care and Charge of Victualling his own Ship for the Time intended for that Expedition, and signify'd to him by the Admiralty; and this at a certain Rate of so much a Man. And by the good or ill Discharge of his Trust, as well as that of providing Chirurgeons, Medicines, and all Things necessary for the Health of the Men, each Captain grows into good or ill Credit with the Seamen, and by their Report, with the Admiralties; upon whose Opinion and Esteem the Fortune of all Sea-Officers depends: So as, in all their Expeditions, there appears rather an Emulation among the particular Captains who shall treat his Seamen best in these Points, and employ the Monies allotted for their Victualling to the best Advantage, than any little Knavish Practices, of filling their own Purses by keeping their Men's Bellies empty, or forcing them to corrupted unwholesome Diet: Upon which, and upon Cleanliness in their Ships, the Health of many People crowded up into so little Room seems chiefly to depend.

The Salaries of all the Great Officers of this State are very small: I have already mention'd that of a Burgomaster's of *Amsterdam* to be about Fifty Pounds *sterling* a Year: That of their Vice-Admiral (for since the last Prince of *Orange*'s Death, to the Year 1670, there had been no Admiral) is Five Hundred, and that of the *Pensioner* of *Holland* Two Hundred.

The Greatness of this State seems much to consist in these Orders, how confused soever, and of different Pieces, they may seem: But more in two main Effects of them, which are, The good Choice of the Officers of chief Trust in the Cities, Provinces, and State: And the great Simplicity and Modesty in the common Port or Living of their chiefest Ministers; without which, the Absoluteness of the Senates in each Town, and the Immensity of Taxes throughout the whole State, would never be endured by the People with any Patience; being both of them greater than in many of those Governments, which are esteem'd most Arbitrary among their Neighbours.

But in the Assemblies and Debates of their Senates, every Man's Abilities are discovered, as their Dispositions are in the Conduct of their Lives and Domestick among their Fellow-Citizens. The Observation of these either raises, or suppresses, the Credit of particular Men, both among the People, and the Senates of their Towns; who, to maintain their Authority with less popular Envy or Discontent, give much to the general Opinion of the People in the Choice of their Magistrates: By this Means it comes to pass, that, though perhaps the Nation generally be not wise, yet the Government is, because it is composed of the wisest of the Nation; which may give it an Advantage over many others, where Ability is of more common Growth, but of less Use to the Publick; if it happens that neither Wisdom nor Honesty are the Qualities, which bring Men to the Management of State-Affairs, as they usually do in this Commonwealth.

Besides, though these People, who are naturally cold and heavy, may not be ingenious enough to furnish a pleasant or agreeable Conversation, yet they want not plain down-right Sense to understand and do their Business both publick and private, which is a Talent very different from the other; and I know not whether they often meet: For the first proceeds from Heat of the Brain, which makes the Spirits more airy and volatile, and thereby the Motions of Thought lighter and quicker, and the Range of Imagination much greater than in cold Heads, where the Spirits are more earthy and dull: Thought moves slower and heavier, but thereby the Impressions of it are deeper, and last longer; one Imagination being not so frequently, nor so easily effaced by another, as where new ones are continually arising. This makes duller Men more constant and steady, and quicker Men more inconstant and uncertain; whereas the greatest Ability in Business seems to be the steady Pursuit of some one Thing, 'till there is an End of it, with perpetual Application and Endeavour not to be diverted by every Representation of new Hopes or Fears of Difficulty or Danger, or of some better Design. The first of these Talents cuts like a Razor, the other like a Hatchet: One has Thinness of Edge, and Fineness of Metal and Temper, but is easily turned by any Substance that is hard, and resists: T'other has Toughness and Weight, which makes it cut through, or go deep, whereever it falls; and therefore one is for Adornment, t'other for Use.

It may be said further, that the Heat of the Heart commonly goes along with that of the Brain; so that Passions are warmer, where Imaginations are quicker: And there are few Men (unless in Case of some evident natural Defect) but have Sense enough to distinguish in Gross between Right and Wrong, between Good and Bad, when represented to them; and consequently have Judgment enough to do their Business, if it be left to itself, and not swayed nor corrupted by some Humour or Passion, by Anger or Pride, by Love or by Scorn, Ambition or Avarice, Delight or Revenge; so that the Coldness of Passion seems to be the natural Ground of Ability and Honesty among Men, as the Government or Moderation of them the great End of Philosophical and Moral Instructions. These Speculations may perhaps a little lessen the common Wonder, how we should meet with in one Nation so little Shew of Parts and of Wit, and so great Evidence of Wisdom and Prudence, as has appeared in the Conduct and Successes of this State, for near an Hundred Years; which needs no other Testimony, than the mighty Growth and Power it arrived to, from so weak and contemptible Seeds and Beginnings.

The other Circumstance I mentioned, as an Occasion of their Greatness, was the Simplicity and Modesty of their Magistrates in their Way of Living; which is so general, that I never knew One among them exceed the common frugal popular Air; and so great, that of the two chief Officers in my Time, Vice-Admiral *De Ruiter,* and the Pensioner *De Wit;* (one generally esteemed by Foreign Nations as great a Seaman, and the other as great a Statesman, as any of their Age) I never saw the first in Cloaths better than the commonest Sea-Captain, nor with above one Man following him, nor in a Coach: And in his own House, neither was the Size, Building, Furniture, or Entertainment, at all exceeding the Use of every common Merchant and Tradesman in his Town. For the Pensioner *De Wit,* who had the great Influence in the Government, the whole Train and Expence of his Domestic went very equal with other common Deputies or Ministers of the State; his Habit grave, and plain, and popular; his Table, what only served Turn for his Family, or a Friend; his Train (besides Commissaries and Clerks kept for him in an Office adjoining to his House, at the publick Charge) was only one Man, who performed all the Menial Services of his House at Home; and upon his Visits of Ceremony, putting on a plain Livery-Cloak, attended his Coach abroad: For, upon other Occasions, he was seen usually in the Streets on Foot and alone, like the commonest Burgher of the Town. Nor was this Manner of Life affected, or used only by these particular Men, but was the general Fashion and Mode among all the Magistrates of the State: For I speak not of the Military Officers, who are reckoned their Servants, and live in a different Garb, though generally modester than in other Countries.

Thus this stomachful People, who could not endure the least Exercise of Arbitrary Power or Impositions, or the Sight of any Foreign Troops under the *Spanish* Government, have since been inured to all of them, in the highest Degree, under their own popular Magistrates; bridled with hard Laws, terrified with severe Executions, environed with Foreign Forces; and oppress'd with the most cruel Hardship and Variety of Taxes, that was ever known under any Government. But all this, whilst the Way to Office and Authority lies through those Qualities, which acquire the general Esteem of the People; whilst no Man is exempted from the Danger and Current of Laws; whilst Soldiers are confined to Frontier Garrisons (the Guard of Inland, or Trading Towns being left to the Burghers themselves;) and whilst no great Riches are seen to enter by publick Payments into private Purses, either to raise Families, or to feed the prodigal Expences of vain, extravagant, and luxurious Men; but all publick Monies are applied to the Safety, Greatness, or Honour of the State, and the Magistrates themselves bear an equal Share in all the Burthens they impose.

The Authority of the Princes of Orange

The Authority of the Princes of *Orange*, though intermitted upon the untimely Death of the last, and Infancy of this present Prince; yet, as it must be ever acknowledged to have had a most essential Part in the first Frame of this Government, and in all the Fortunes thereof, during the whole Growth and Progress of the State: So, has it ever preserved a very strong Root, not only in six of the Provinces, but even in the general and popular Affections of the Province of *Holland* itself, whose States have, for these last twenty Years, so much endeavoured to suppress, or exclude it.

This began in the Person of Prince *William* of *Nassau*, at the very Birth of the State; and not so much by the Quality of being Governor of *Holland* and *Zealand* in *Charles* the Fifth's and *Philip* the Second's Time; as by the Esteem of so great Wisdom, Goodness, and Courage, as excelled in that Prince, and seems to have been from him derived to his whole Race; being, indeed, the Qualities that naturally acquire Esteem and Authority among the People, in all Governments. Nor has this Nation in particular, since the Time perhaps of *Civilis*, ever been without some Head, under some Title or other; but always an Head subordinate to their Laws and Customs, and to the Sovereign Power of the State.

In the first Constitution of this Government, after the Revolt from *Spain*, all the Power and Rights of Prince *William* of *Orange*, as Governor of the Provinces, seem to have been carefully reserved. But those, which remained inherent in the Sovereign, were devolved upon the Assembly of the States-General, so as in them remained the Power of making Peace and War, and all Foreign Alliances, and of Raising and Coining of Monies. In the Prince, the Command of all Land and Sea-Forces, as Captain-General and Admiral, and thereby the Disposition of all Military Commands; the Power of pardoning the Penalty of Crimes; the chusing of Magistrates upon the Nomination of the Towns; for they presented three to the Prince, who elected one out of that Number. Originally the States-General were convoked by the Council of State, where the Prince had the greatest Influence: Nor, since that Change, have the States used to resolve any important Matter without his Advice. Besides all this, as the States-General represented the Sovereignty, so did the Prince of *Orange* the Dignity of this State, by publick Guards, and the Attendance of all Military Officers; by the Application of all Foreign Ministers, and all Pretenders at Home; by the Splendor of his Court, and Magnificence of his Expence, supported not only by the Pensions and Rights of his several Charges and Commands, but by a mighty Patrimonial Revenue in Lands and Sovereign Principalities, and Lordships, as well in *France, Germany,* and *Burgundy,* as in the several Parts of the Seventeen Provinces; so as Prince *Henry* was used to answer some, that would have flattered him into the Designs of a more Arbitrary Power, that he had as much as any wise Prince would desire in that State; since he wanted none indeed, besides that of punishing Men, and raising Money; whereas he had rather the Envy of the first should lie upon the Forms of the Government, and he knew the other could never be supported without the Consent of the People, to that Degree which was necessary for the Defence of so small a State, against so mighty Princes as their Neighbours.

Upon these Foundations was this State first established, and by these Orders maintained, 'till the Death of the last Prince of *Orange:* When, by the great Influence of the Province of *Holland* amongst the rest, the Authority of the Princes came to be shared among the several Magistracies of the State; those of the Cities assumed the last Nomination of their several Magistrates; the States Provincial, the Disposal of all Military Commands in those Troops, which their Share was to pay; and the States-General, the Command of the Armies, by Officers of their own Appointment, substituted and changed at their Will. No Power remained to pardon what was once condemned by Rigor of Law; nor any Person to represent the Port and Dignity of a Sovereign State: Both which could not fail of being sensibly missed by the People; since no Man in particular can be sure of offending, or would therefore absolutely despair of Impunity himself, though he would have others do so; and Men are generally pleased with the Pomp and Splendor of a Government, not only as it is an Amusement for idle People, but as it is a Mark of the Greatness, Honour, and Riches of their Country.

However, these Defects were for near Twenty Years supplied in some Measure, and this Frame supported by the great Authority and Riches of the Province of *Holland,* which drew a Sort of Dependance from the other Six; and by the great Sufficiency, Integrity, and Constancy of their chief Minister, and by the Effect of both in the prosperous Successes of their Affairs: Yet having been a Constitution strained against the current Vein and Humour of the People; it was always evident, that upon the Growth of this young Prince, the great Virtues and Qualities, he derived from the Mixture of such Royal and such Princely Blood, could not fail, in Time, of raising his Authority to equal, at least, if not to surpass that of his Glorious Ancestors.

Because the Curious may desire to know something of the other Provinces, as well as *Holland,* at least in general, and where they differ: It may be observed, That the Constitutions of *Gelderland, Zealand,* and *Utrecht* agree much with those of *Holland;* the States in each Province being composed of Deputies from the Nobles and the Cities: But with these small Differences; In *Gelderland,* all the Nobles, that have certain Fees or Lordships, in the Province, have Session, they compose one Half of the States, and the Deputies of the Towns the other; and though some certain Persons among them are deputed to the States-General, yet any of the Nobles of *Gelder* may have Place there, if he will attend at his own Charge.

In *Zealand,* the Nobility having been extinguished in the *Spanish* Wars, and the Prince of *Orange* possessing the Marquisates of *Flushing* and *Terveer,* his Highness alone makes that Part of the States in the Province, by the Quality and Title of First, or Solo Noble of *Zealand;* and thereby has, by his Deputy, the first Place and Voice in the States of the Province, the Council of State, and Chamber of Accounts: As Sovereign of *Flushing* and *Terveer,* he likewise creates the Magistrates, and consequently disposes the Voices, not only of the Nobles, but also of two Towns, whereas there are in all but Six that send their Deputies to the States, and make up the Sovereignty of the Province.

In *Utrecht,* besides the Deputies of the Nobles and Towns, Eight Delegates of the Clergy have Session, and make a third Member in the States of the Province. These are elected out of the four great Chapters of the Town, the Preferments and Revenues whereof (though anciently Ecclesiastical) yet are now possessed by Lay-persons, who are most of them Gentlemen of the Province.

The Government of the Province of *Friezland* is wholly different from that of the Four Provinces already mentioned; and is composed of Four Members, which are called, The Quarter of *Ostergo,* consisting of Eleven Baillages; Of *Westergo,* consisting of Nine; and of *Seveawolden,* consisting of Ten. Each Baillage comprehends a certain Number of Villages, Ten, Twelve, Fifteen, or Twenty, according to their several Extents. The Fourth Member consists of the Towns of the Province, which are Eleven in Number. These Four Members have each of them Right of sending their Deputies to the States, that is, Two chosen out of every Baillage, and Two out of every Town. And these represent the Sovereignty of the Province, and deliberate and conclude of all Affairs, of what Importance soever, without any Recourse to those who deputed them, or Obligation to know their Intentions, which the Deputies of all the former Provinces are strictly bound to, and either must follow the Instructions they bring with them to the Assembly, or know the Resolution of their Principals before they conclude of any new Affair that arises.

In the other Provinces, the Nobles of the Towns chuse the Deputies which compose the States, but in *Friezland* the Constitution is of quite another Sort. For every Baillage, which is composed of a certain Extent of Country and Number of Villages (as has been said) is governed by a Baily, whom in their Language they call *Greetman*, and this Officer governs his Circuit, with the Assistance of a certain Number of Persons who are called his Assessors, who, together, judge of all Civil Causes in the first Instance, but with Appeal to the Court of Justice of the Province. When the States are convoked, every Baily assembles together all the Persons of what Quality soever, who possess a certain Quantity of Land within his District, and these Men, by most Voices, name the Two Deputies which each Baillage sends to the Assembly of the States.

This Assembly, as it represents the Sovereignty of the Province, so it disposes of all vacant Charges, chuses the nine Deputies who compose that permanent College which is the Council of State of the Province, and likewise twelve Counsellors (that is, three for every Quarter) who compose the Court of Justice of the Province, and judge of all Civil Causes in the last Resort, but of all Criminal from the first Instance. There being no other Criminal Jurisdiction, but this only, through the Province: Whereas, in the other Provinces, there is no Town which has it not within itself: And several, both Lords, and Villages, have the High and Low Justice belonging to them.

In the Province of *Groningue,* which is upon the same Tract of Land, the Elections of the Deputies out of the Country are made as in *Friezland,* by Persons possess'd of set Proportions of Land; but, in *Overyssel,* all Nobles who are qualify'd by having Seigneurial Lands make a Part of the States.

These Three Provinces, with *Westphalia,* and all those Countries between the *Wezer,* the *Yssel,* and the *Rhine,* were the Seat of the ancient *Frizons,* who, under the Name of *Saxons* (given them from the Weapon they wore, made like a Sithe, with the Edge outwards, and called in their Language *Seaxes*) were the fierce Conquerors of our *British Island,* being called in upon the Desertion of the *Roman* Forces, and the cruel Incursions of the *Picts* against a People whose long Wars, at first with the *Romans,* and afterwards Servitude under them, had exhausted all the bravest Blood of their Nation, either in their own, or their Masters, succeeding Quarrels, and depressed the Hearts and Courages of the rest.

The Bishop of *Munster,* whose Territories lie in this Tract of Land, gave me the first certain Evidences of those being the Seats of our ancient *Saxons,* which have since been confirmed to me by many Things I have observed in reading the Stories of those Times, and by what has been affirmed to me upon Enquiry of the *Frizons* old Language having still so great Affinity with our old *English,* as to appear easily to have been the same;

most of their Words still retaining the same Signification and Sound; very different from the Language of the *Hollanders*. This is the most remarkable in a little Town called *Malcuera* upon the *Zudder* Sea, in *Friezland*, which is still built after the Fashion of the old *German* Villages, described by *Tacitus;* without any Use or Observation of Lines or Angles; but as if every Man had built in a common Field, just where he had a Mind, so as a Stranger, when he goes in, must have a Guide to find the Way out again.

Upon these Informations and Remarks, and the particular Account afterwards given me of the Constitutions of the Province of *Friezland,* so different from the others; I began to make Reflections upon them, as the likeliest Originals of many ancient Constitutions among us, of which no others can be found, and which may seem to have been introduc'd by the *Saxons* here, and by their long and absolute Possession of that Part of the Isle, called *England,* to have been so planted and rooted among us, as to have waded safe, in a great Measure, through the succeeding Inundations and Conquests of the *Danish* and *Norman* Nations. And, perhaps, there may be much Matter found for the curious Remarks of some diligent and studious Antiquaries, in the Comparisons of the *Bailli* or *Greetman* among the *Frizons,* with our *Sheriff:* Of their *Assessors,* with our *Justices* of Peace: Of their Judging Civil Causes in their District, upon the first Resort, but not without Appeal, with the Course of our Quarter-Sessions: Of their chief Judicature, being composed of Counsellors of four several Quarters, with our four Circuits. Of these being the common Criminal Judicature of the Country: Of the Composition of their States, with our Parliament, at least, our House of Commons: In the Particulars of two Deputies being chosen from each Town, as with us, and two from each Baillage, as from each County here: And these last by Voices of all Persons, possess'd of a certain Quantity of Land; and at a Meeting assembled by the *Greetman* to that Purpose: And these Deputies having Power to resolve of all Matters without Resort to those that chose them, or Knowledge of their Intentions; which are all Circumstances agreeing with our Constitutions, but absolutely differing from those of the other Provinces in the United States, and from the Composition, I think, of the States, either now, or formerly, used in the other Nations of *Europe*.

To this Original, I suppose, we likewise owe what I have often wonder'd at, that in *England* we neither see, nor find upon Record, any Lord, or Lordship, that pretends to have the Exercise of Judicature belong to it, either that which is called High or Low Justice, which seems to be a Badge of some ancient Sovereignty: Though we see them very frequent among our Neighbours, both under more arbitrary Monarchies, and under the most free and popular States.

The Justification of Resistance

4. John Knox, *The Appellation to the Nobility* (1558)

John Knox (1514−72) was the principal architect of the Protestant Reformation in Scotland, and a major influence on the Protestantization of England as well. We know very little about his original conversion. Like other reformers, he began as a priest of the old faith, but turned decisively away from it sometime in the 1540s. By then, England had broken from Rome on highly political and conservatively religious terms. King Henry VIII had set out in the late 1520s to obtain the annulment (by proceeding in the Church courts) of his marriage to the Spanish princess Catherine of Aragon. When, for complex reasons, this project failed, Henry and his advisers led England into a repudiation of Rome's authority—in effect, a nationalization of the ecclesiastical structure with the king declared supreme head of the church in England. Although this momentous break with the past encouraged Protestants abroad and those Englishmen touched by the new ideas, Henry VIII, from a mixture of personal preference and political caution, set himself against much religious change.

In Scotland, meanwhile, the Catholic government, strongly allied to France, remained very much in control. As a result of his early efforts on behalf of the incipient but weak Protestant movement in Scotland, Knox was taken prisoner in 1547 and spent about a year and a half as a French galley slave.

In 1547, Henry VIII was succeeded by his underaged son, Edward VI, and the Protestant interest assumed control of the English government. After his release from the galleys, Knox came to England where, as a preacher, he contributed to a government-sponsored effort to spread Protestant ideas and had a significant voice in the official recasting of the English state Church as a Protestant one. Edward VI died as an adolescent in 1553, to be succeeded by his elder half-sister Mary (daughter of Catherine of Aragon) who, without much forceful opposition, brought England back into allegiance to Rome. Many of the Englishmen most committed to Protestantism—a kind of intellectual elite—took refuge on the Continent; Knox, for whose version of Protestantism Calvin's influence was central, was among them. He was the minister of two congregations of English refugees, first in Germany and then at Geneva. During

From *The Works of John Knox*, collected and edited by David Laing (Edinburgh: Printed for the Bannatyne Club, 1846−64), pp. 104−46. Footnotes are author's notes.

this period of exile, he made a foray into Scotland, and his treatment on that occasion was the immediate provocation of his *Appellation*.

In 1558, Henry VIII's younger daughter, Elizabeth I, succeeded to the English throne and decided to return the English Church to the national independence her father had achieved and to the Protestantism established in her brother's reign. The exiles came home, both to lead the English Church and to be a thorn in its side, since some of them were zealots for a purer form of Protestantism than they thought they saw in the state church. That church, though Protestant enough in basic ways, was shaped by political compromise and by a policy of keeping the external forms of the church as inoffensive as possible to sentiment less zealously committed. Knox at this juncture returned to Scotland; his presence continued to be felt, however, in the councils of the ultra-Protestant party in England that came to be called the Puritan movement. He was far from Queen Elizabeth's favorite person.

Protestantism had meanwhile made great strides in Scotland. Back in his native country, Knox became the intellectual and—with his aristocratic allies—the practical leader of the cause during the most sensitive years of its struggle. In the upshot, with English assistance motivated by a realistic fear of what victory by the Catholic government of a virtual French protectorate would mean for England, the Protestants triumphed. Knox, victorious, went on to design a Protestant Church for Scotland on lines very different from those of the English Church. On its organizational—as opposed to doctrinal and liturgical—side, this design was the Presbyterian system, Scotland's contribution to the variety of mansions in the Protestant house, and for a long time to come an inspiration to Englishmen who hankered for a more strictly Protestant alternative, as they saw it, to the English system. Early Protestantism at its most militant, with its way of addressing political questions from a purely religious starting point, has no better illustration than Knox's writings, especially the *Appellation*.

The Appellation of John Knox from the cruel and most injust sentence pronounced against him by the false bishops of Scotland with his supplication and exhortation to the nobility, estates, and commonalty of the same realm

To the nobility and estates of Scotland John Knox wisheth grace, mercy, and peace from God, the father of our lord Jesus Christ, with the spirit of righteous judgment.

It is not only the love of life temporal, right honorable, neither yet the fear of corporal death that moveth me at this present to expone unto you the injuries done against me and to crave of you, as of lawful powers by God appointed, redress of the same; but partly it proceedeth from that reverence which every man oweth to God's eternal truth and partly from a love which I bear to your salvation and to the salvation of my brethren abused in that realm by such as have no fear of God before their eyes.

It hath pleased God of his infinite mercy not only so to illuminate the eyes of my mind and so to touch my dull heart that clearly I see and by his grace unfeignedly believe that, "there is no other name given to men under the heaven, in which salvation consisteth, save the name of Jesus alone," [1] "Who by that sacrifice which he did once offer upon the cross hath sanctified forever those that shall inherit the kingdom promised." [2] But also it hath pleased him of his super-abundant grace to make and appoint me, most wretched of many thousands, a witness, minister, and preacher of the same doctrine. The sum whereof I did not spare to communicate with my brethren, being with them in the realm of Scotland in the year 1556, because I know myself to be a steward, and that accompts of the talent committed to my charge shall be required to him who will admit no vain excuse which fearful men pretend. [3] I did therefore, as God did minister, during the time I was conversant with them (God is record and witness), truly and sincerely, according to the gift granted unto me, divide the word of salvation, teaching all men to hate sin—which before God was and is so odious that none other sacrifice could satisfy his justice except the death of his only son; and to magnify the great mercies of our heavenly Father—who did not spare the substance of his glory but did give him to the world to suffer the ignominious and cruel death of the cross, by that means to reconcile his chosen children to himself; teaching further what is the duty of such as to believe themselves purged by such a price from their former filthiness, to wit, that they are bound to walk in the newness of life, fight ing against the lusts of the flesh, and studying at all times to glorify God by such good works as he hath prepared his children to walk in. [4] In doctrine I did further affirm, so taught by my master Christ Jesus, that, "whosoever denieth him, yea, or is ashamed of him before this wicked generation, him shall Christ Jesus deny, and of him shall he be ashamed when he shall appear in majesty." [5] And therefore I fear not to affirm that of necessity it is that such as hope for life everlasting avoid all superstition, vain religion,

1. Acts 4:12.   2. Heb. 10:10.
3. 1 Cor. 4; Matt. 25.
4. John 3; Rom. 5; Rom. 8; 2 Cor. 5; Rom. 6; Eph. 2, 4, 5.
5. Matt. 10:33.

and idolatry. Vain religion and idolatry I call whatsoever is done in God's service or honor without the express commandment of his own word.

This doctrine did I believe to be so conformable to God's Holy Scriptures that I thought no creature could have been so impudent as to have damned any point or article of the same. Yet nevertheless, me, as an heretic, and this doctrine as heretical have your false bishops and ungodly clergy damned, pronouncing against me a sentence of death, in testification whereof they have burned a picture. From which false and cruel sentence and from all judgment of that wicked generation, I make it known to your honors that I appeal to a lawful and general council, to such, I mean, as the most ancient laws and canons do approve to be holden, but such as whose manifest impiety is not to be reformed in the same. Most humbly requiring of your honors that, as God hath appointed you princes in that people and by reason thereof requireth of your hands the defense of innocents troubled in your dominion, in the meantime, and till the controversies that this day be in religion be lawfully decided, ye receive me and such others, as most unjustly by those cruel beasts are persecuted, in your defense and protection.

Your honors are not ignorant that it is not I alone who doth sustain this cause against the pestilent generation of papists, but that the most part of Germany, the country of Helvetia, the King of Denmark, the nobility of Polonia, together with many other cities and churches reformed, appeal from the tyranny of that Antichrist and most earnestly do call for a lawful and general council wherein may all controversies in religion be decided by the authority of God's most sacred word. And unto this same, as said is, do I appeal yet once again, requiring of your honors to hold my simple and plain appellation of no less value nor effect than if it had been made with greater circumstance, solemnity, and ceremony, and that ye receive me, calling unto you as to the powers of God ordained, in your protection and defense against the rage of tyrants, not to maintain me in any iniquity, error, or false opinion but to let me have such equity as God by his word, ancient laws, and determinations of most godly councils grant to men accused or infamed.

The word of God will that no man shall die except he be found criminal and worthy of death for offence committed, of the which he must be manifestly convicted by two or three witnesses.[6] Ancient laws do permit just defenses to such as be accused (be their crimes never so horrible), and godly councils will that neither bishop nor person ecclesiastical whatsoever, accused of any crime, shall sit in judgment, consultation, or council

6. Deut. 17.

where the cause of such men as do accuse them is to be tried. These things require I of your honors to be granted unto me, to wit, that the doctrine which our adversaries condemn for heresy may be tried by the simple and plain word of God, that just defenses be admitted to us that sustain the battle against this pestilent generation of Antichrist, and that they be removed from judgment in our cause, seeing that our accusation is not intended against any one particular person but against that whole kingdom which we doubt not to prove to be a power usurped against God, against his commandment, and against the ordinance of Christ Jesus established in his Church by his chief Apostles. Yea, we doubt not to prove the kingdom of the pope to be the kingdom and power of Antichrist. And therefore, my lords, I cannot cease in the name of Christ Jesus to require of you that the matter may come in examination, and that ye, the estates of the realm, by your authority compel such as will be called bishops not only to desist from their cruel murdering of such as do study to promote God's glory in detecting and disclosing the damnable impiety of that man of sin, the Roman Antichrist, but also that ye compel them to answer to such crimes as shall be laid to their charge for not righteously instructing the flock committed to their cares.

But here I know two things shall be doubted. The former, whether that my appellation is lawful and to be admitted, seeing that I am damned as an heretic; and secondarily, whether your honors be bound to defend such as call for your support in that case, seeing that your bishops, who in matters of religion claim all authority to appertain to them, have by their sentence already condemned me. The one and the other I nothing doubt most clearly to prove: first, that my appellation is most lawful and just; and secondarily, that your honors cannot refuse to defend me, thus calling for your aid, but that in so doing ye declare yourselves rebellious to God, maintainers of murderers, and shedders of innocent blood.

How just cause I have by the civil law (as for their canon, it is accursed of God) to appeal from their unjust sentence, my purpose is not to make long discourse. Only I will touch the points which all men confess to be just causes of appellation. First, lawfully could I not be summoned by them, being for that time absent from their jurisdiction, charged with the preaching of Christ's Evangel in a free city not subject to their tyranny. Secondarily, to me was no intimation made of their summons, but so secret was their surmised malice that, the copy of the summons being required, was denied. Thirdly, to the realm of Scotland could I have had no free nor sure access, being before exiled from the same by their unjust tyranny. And last, to me they neither could nor can be competent and indifferent judges; for that before any summons were raised against me, I had accused them by my letters published to the Queen Dowager and had intended against them all crimes, offering myself with hazard of life to prove the same, for the which they are not only unworthy of ecclesiastical authority but also of any sufferance within a commonwealth professing Christ.

This, my accusation, preceding their summons, neither by the law of God neither yet by the law of man can they be to me competent judges till place be granted unto me openly to prove my accusation intended against them and they be compelled to make answer as criminals. For I will plainly prove that not only bishops but also popes have been removed from all authority and pronouncing of judgment till they have purged themselves of accusations laid against them. Yea, further I will prove that bishops and popes most justly have been deprived from all honors and administration for smaller crimes than I have to charge the whole rabble of your bishops. But because this is not my chief ground, I will stand content for this present to shew that lawful it is to God's prophets and to preachers of Christ Jesus to appeal from the sentence and judgment of the visible church to the knowledge of the temporal magistrate, who by God's law is bound to hear their causes and to defend them from tyranny.

The Prophet Jeremiah was commanded by God to stand in the court of the house of the Lord and to preach this sermon in effect: that Jerusalem should be destroyed and be exponed in opprobry, to all nations of the earth, and that also that famous temple of God should be made desolate, like unto Shiloh, because the priests, the prophets, and the people did not walk in the law which God had proposed unto them, neither would they obey the voices of the prophets whom God sent to call them to repentance.[7] For this sermon was Jeremiah apprehended, and a sentence of death was pronounced against him and that by the priests, by the prophets, and by the people; which things being bruited in the ears of the princes of Judah, they passed up from the king's house to the temple of the Lord and sat down in judgment for further knowledge of the cause. But the priests and prophets continued in their cruel sentence, which before they had pronounced, saying, "This man is worthy of the death, for he hath prophesied against this city as your ears have heard." But Jeremiah, so moved by the Holy Ghost, began his defense against that their tyrannous sentence in these words: "The Lord," saith he, "hath sent me to prophesy against this house and against this city all the words which you have heard. Now therefore make good your ways and hear the voice of the Lord your God, and then shall he repent of the evil which he hath spoken against you. As for me, behold I am in your hands" (so doth he speak to the princes), "do to me as you think good and righteous. Nevertheless know you this most assuredly, that if ye murder or slay me, ye shall make yourselves, this city, and the inhabitants

7. Jer. 26.

of the same criminal and guilty of innocent blood. For of a truth the Lord hath sent me to speak in your ears all those words." Then the princes and the people, saith the text, said, "this man is not worthy of death, for he hath spoken to us in the name of the Lord our God." And so after some contention was the Prophet delivered from that danger.

This fact and history manifestly proveth whatsoever before I have affirmed, to wit, that it is lawful for the servants of God to call for the help of the civil magistrate against the sentence of death if it be unjust, by whomsoever it be pronounced, and also that the civil sword hath power to repress the fury of the priests and to absolve whom they have condemned. For the Prophet of God was damned by those who then only in earth were known to be the visible church, to wit, priests and prophets who then were in Jerusalem, the successors of Aaron to whom was given a charge to speak to the people in the name of God, and a precept given to the people to hear the law from their mouths—to the which if any should be rebellious or inobedient, he should die the death without mercy.[8] These men, I say, thus authorized by God first did excommunicate Jeremiah for that he did preach otherwise than did the common sort of prophets in Jerusalem, and last apprehended him, as you have heard, pronouncing against him this sentence aforewritten, from the which, nevertheless, the Prophet appealed—that is, sought help and defense against the same, and that most earnestly did he crave of the princes. For albeit he saith, "I am in your hands, do with me as ye think righteous," he doth not contemn nor neglect his life as though he regarded not what should become of him, but in those his words most vehemently did he admonish the princes and rulers of the people, giving them to understand what God should require of them.[9]

As he should say: "You princes of Judah and rulers of the people, to whom appertaineth indifferently to judge betwixt party and party, to justify the just man, and to condemn the malefactor, you have heard a sentence of death pronounced against me by those whose lips ought to speak no decept because they are sanctified and appointed by God himself to speak his law and pronounce judgment with equity; but as they have left the living God and have taught the people to follow vanity, so are they becomed mortal enemies to all God's true servants, of whom I am one, rebuking their iniquity, apostasy, and defection from God which is the only cause they seek my life. But a thing most contrary to all equity, law, and justice it is that I, a man sent of God to call them, this people, and you again to the true service of God, from the which you are all declined, shall suffer the death because that my enemies do so pronounce sentence. I stand in your presence, whom God hath made princes; your power is above their tyranny; before you do I

8. Deut. 17.   9. Jer. 1; Deut. 1, 10, 17.

expone my cause. I am in your hands and cannot resist to suffer what ye think just. But lest that my lenity and patience should either make you negligent in the defense of me in my just cause appealing to your judgment, either yet encourage my enemies in seeking my blood, this one thing I dare not conceal: that if you murder me (which thing ye do if ye defend me not), ye make not only my enemies guilty of my blood but also yourselves and this whole city."

By these words, I say, it is evident that the Prophet of God, being damned to death by the priests and the prophets of the visible church, did seek aid, support, and defense at the princes and temporal magistrates, threatening his blood to be required of their hands if they by their authority did not defend him from the fury of his enemies, alleging also just cause of his appellation and why he ought to have been defended, to wit, that he was sent of God to rebuke their vices and defection from God, that he taught no doctrine which God before had not pronounced in his law, that he desired their conversion to God, continually calling upon them to walk in ways which God had approved, and therefore doth he boldly crave of the princes, as of God's lieutenants, to be defended from the blind rage and tyranny of the priests, notwithstanding that they claimed to themselves authority to judge in all matters of religion.

And the same did he what time he was cast in prison and thereafter was brought to the presence of King Zedekiah. After, I say, that he had defended his innocence, affirming that he neither had offended against the King, against his servants, nor against the people, at last he made intercession to the King for his life, saying, "But now my Lord the King take heed, I beseech thee, let my prayer fall into thy presence, command me not to be carried again into the house of Jonathan the scribe that I die not there." And the text witnesseth that the King commanded the place of his imprisonment to be changed.[10] Whereof it is evident that the Prophet did ofter than once seek help at the civil power, and that first the princes and thereafter the King did acknowledge that it appertained to their office to deliver him from the injust sentence which was pronounced against him.

If any think that Jeremiah did not appeal because he only declared the wrong done unto him and did but crave defense according to his innocence, let the same man understand that none otherwise do I appeal from that false and cruel sentence which your bishops have pronounced against me. Neither yet can there be any other just cause of appellation but innocence hurt or suspected to be hurt, whether it be by ignorance of a judge or by malice and corruption of those who under the title of justice do exercise tyranny. If I were a thief, murderer, blasphemer, open adulterer, or any offender

10. Jer. 38.

whom God's word commandeth to suffer for a crime committed, my appellation were vain and to be rejected; but I being innocent (yea, the doctrine which your bishops have condemned in me being God's eternal verity), have no less liberty to crave your defense against that cruelty than had the Prophet Jeremiah to seek the aid of the princes and King of Judah.

But this shall more plainly appear in the fact of St. Paul, who, after that he was apprehended in Jerusalem, did first claim to the liberty of Roman citizens for avoiding torment what time that the captain would have examined him by questions. Thereafter in the council, where no righteous judgment was to be hoped for, he affirmed that he was a Pharisee and that he was accused of the resurrection of the dead. And last in the presence of Festus he appealed from all knowledge and judgment in the priests of Jerusalem to the Emperor (of which last point, because it doth chiefly appertain to this my cause, I will somewhat speak.)[11]

After that Paul had divers times been accused, as in the Acts of the Apostles it is manifest, at the last the chief priests and their faction came to Caesarea with Festus the president, who presented to them Paul in judgment, whom they accused of horrible crimes, which nevertheless they could not prove, the Apostle defending that he had not offended neither against the law, neither against the temple, neither yet against the Emperor. But Festus, willing to gratify the Jews, said to Paul, "Wilt thou go up to Jerusalem, and there be judged of these things in my presence?" But Paul said, "I stand at the justice seat of the Emperor where it behooveth me to be judged. I have done no injury to the Jews, as thou better knowest. If I have done anything injustly, or yet committed crime worthy of death, I refuse not to die; but if there be nothing of these things true whereof they accuse me, no man may give me to them. I appeal to Caesar."[12]

It may appear at the first sight that Paul did great injury to Festus, the judge, and to the whole order of the priesthood, who did hope greater equity in a cruel tyrant than in all that session and learned company. Which thing no doubt Festus did understand, pronouncing these words: "Hast thou appealed to Caesar? Thou shalt go to Caesar." As he would say: "I, as a man willing to understand the truth before I pronounce sentence, have required of thee to go to Jerusalem where the learned of thine own nation may hear thy cause and discern in the same. The controversy standeth in matters of religion. Thou art accused as an apostate from the law, as a violator of the temple, and transgressor of the traditions of their fathers, in which matters I am ignorant and therefore desire information by those that be learned in the same religion whereof the question is. And yet dost thou refuse so many godly fathers to hear thy cause and dost appeal to the Em-

11. Acts 22, 23, 24, 25.   12. Acts 25:9, 10, 11.

peror, preferring him to all our judgments, of no purpose belike but to delay time."

Thus, I say, it might have appeared that Paul did not only injury to the judge and to the priests, but also that his cause was greatly to be suspected—partly for that he did refuse the judgment of those that had most knowledge, as all men supposed, of God's will and religion, and partly because he appealed to the Emperor, who then was at Rome far absent from Jerusalem, a man also ignorant of God and enemy to all virtue. But the Apostle, considering the nature of his enemies and what things they had intended against him even from the first day that he began freely to speak in the name of Christ, did not fear to appeal from them and from the judge that would have gratified them. They had professed themselves plain enemies of Christ Jesus and to his blessed Evangel, and had sought the death of Paul, yea, even by factions and treasonable conspiracy, and therefore by no means would he admit them either judges in his cause, either auditors of the same as Festus required. But grounding himself upon strong reasons, to wit, that he had not offended the Jews, neither yet the law, but that he was innocent, and therefore that no judge ought to give him in the hands of his enemies; grounding, I say, his appellation upon these reasons, he neither regarded the displeasure of Festus, neither yet the bruit of the ignorant multitude, but boldly did appeal from all cognition of them to the judgment of the Emperor, as said is.

By these two examples I doubt not but your honors do understand that lawful it is to the servants of God, oppressed by tyranny, to seek remedy against the same, be it by appellation from their sentence or by imploring the help of civil magistrates. For what God hath approved in Jeremiah and Paul, he can condemn in none that likewise be entreated. I might allege some histories of the primitive church serving to the same purpose: as of Ambrose and Athanasius, of whom the one would not be judged but at Milan where that his doctrine was heard of all his church and received and approved by many; and the other would in nowise give place to those councils where he knew that men, conspired against the truth of God, should sit in judgment and consultation. But because the Scriptures of God are my only foundation and assurance in all matters of weight and importance, I have thought the two former testimonies sufficient as well to prove my appellation reasonable and just, as to declare to your honors that with safe conscience ye cannot refuse to admit the same.

If any think it arrogance or foolishness in me to compare myself with Jeremiah and Paul, let the same man understand that, as God is immutable, so is the verity of his glorious Evangel of equal dignity whensoever it is impugned, be the members suffering never so weak. What I think touching mine own person God shall reveal when the secrets of all hearts shall be disclosed, and such as with whom I have been conversant can partly witness what arrogance or pride they espy in me. But touching the doctrine and cause which that adulterous and pestilent generation of Antichrist's servants—who will be called bishops amongst you—have condemned in me, I neither fear nor shame to confess and avow before man and angel to be the eternal truth of the eternal God. And in that case I doubt not to compare myself with any member in whom the truth hath been impugned since the beginning, for as it was the truth which Jeremiah did preach in these words: "The priests have not known me, saith the Lord, but the pastors have traitorously declined and fallen back from me. The prophets have prophesied in Baal and have gone after those things which cannot help. My people have left the fountain of living waters and have digged to themselves pits which can contain no water." [13]

As it was a truth that the pastors and watchmen in the days of Isaiah were becomed dumb dogs, blind, ignorant, proud, and avaricious, and finally as it was a truth that the princes and the priests were murderers of Christ Jesus and cruel persecutors of his Apostles, so likewise it is a truth—and that most infallible—that those that have condemned me (the whole rabble of the papistical clergy) have declined from the true faith, have given ear to deceivable spirits and to doctrine of devils, are the stars fallen from the heaven to the earth, are fountains without water, and finally are enemies to Christ Jesus, deniers of his virtue, and horrible blasphemers of his death and passion. [14] And further, as that visible church had no crime whereof justly they could accuse either the Prophets either the Apostles, except their doctrine, so have not such as seek my blood other crime to lay to my charge except that I affirm, as always I offer to prove, that the religion which now is maintained by fire and sword is no less contrarious to the true religion taught and established by the Apostles than is darkness to light, or the devil to God, and also that such as now do claim the title and name of the church are no more the elect spouse of Christ Jesus than was the synagogue of the Jews the true church of God what time it crucified Christ Jesus, damned his doctrine, and persecuted his Apostles. And therefore, seeing that my battle is against the proud and cruel hypocrites of this age as that battle of those most excellent instruments was against the false prophets and malignant church of their ages, neither ought any man think it strange that I compare myself with them with whom I sustain a common cause, neither ought you, my lords, judge yourselves less addebted and bound to me, calling for your support, than did the princes of Judah think themselves bound to Jeremiah, whom for that time they delivered notwith-

13. Jer. 2:8, 13.
14. Isa. 56; Acts 3, 4; 2 Tim. 4; Jude 1; 2 Pet. 2.

standing the sentence of death pronounced against him by the visible church. And thus much for the right of my appellation which in the bowels of Christ Jesus I require your honors not to esteem as a thing superfluous and vain but that ye admit and also accept me in your protection and defense that, by you assured, I may have access to my native country, which I never offended, to the end that freely and openly in the presence of the whole realm I may give my confession of all such points as this day be in controversy, and also that you, by your authority which ye have of God, compel such as of long time have blinded and deceived both yourselves and the people to answer to such things as shall be laid to their charge.

But, lest some doubt remain that I require more of you than you of conscience are bound to grant, in few words I hope to prove my petition to be such, as without God's heavy displeasure, ye cannot deny. My petition is that ye, whom God hath appointed heads in your commonwealth, with single eye do study to promote the glory of God, to provide that your subjects be rightly instructed in his true religion, that they be defended from all oppression and tyranny, that true teachers may be maintained, and such as blind and deceive the people together also with all idle bellies which do rob and oppress the flock may be removed and punished as God's law prescribeth. And to the performance of every one of these do your offices and names, the honors and benefits which ye receive, the law of God universally given to all men, and the examples of most [godly] princes, bind and oblige you.

My purpose is not greatly to labor to prove that your whole study ought to be to promote the glory of God; neither yet will I study to allege all reasons that justly may be brought to prove that ye are not exalted to reign above your brethren as men without care and solicitude. For these be principles so grafted in nature that very ethnics have confessed the same. For seeing that God only hath placed you in his chair, hath appointed you to be his lieutenants, and by his own seal hath marked you to be magistrates and to rule above your brethren, to whom nature nevertheless hath made you like in all points (for in conception, birth, life, and death ye differ nothing from the common sort of men, but God only, as said is, hath promoted you and of his especial favor hath given unto you this prerogative to be called gods), how horrible ingratitude were it then that you should be found unfaithful to him that thus hath honored you. And further what a monster were it that you should be proved unmerciful to them above whom ye are appointed to reign as fathers above their children. Because I say that very ethnics have granted that the chief and first care of princes and of such as be appointed to rule above others ought to be to promote the glory and honor of their gods and to maintain that religion which they supposed to have been true, and that their second care was to maintain and defend the subjects committed to their charge in all equity and justice, I will not labor to shew unto you what ought to be your study in maintaining God's true honor, lest that in so doing I should seem to make you less careful over God's true religion than were the ethnics over their idolatry.

But because other petitions may appear more hard and difficile to be granted, I purpose briefly but yet freely to speak what God by his word doth assure me to be true: to wit, first, that in conscience you are bound to punish malefactors and to defend innocents imploring your help; secondarily, that God requireth of you to provide that your subjects be rightly instructed in his true religion and that the same by you be reformed whensoever abuses do creep in by malice of Satan and negligence of men; and last, that ye are bound to remove from honor and to punish with death—if the crime so require—such as deceive the people or defraud them of that food of their souls—I mean God's lively word.

The first and second are most plain by the words of St. Paul, thus speaking of lawful powers: "Let every soul," saith he, "submit himself unto the higher powers. For there is no power but of God. The powers that be are ordained of God, and they that resist shall receive to themselves damnation. For rulers are not to be feared of those that do well, but of those that do evil. Wilt thou then be without fear of the power? Do that which is good, and so shalt thou be praised of the same. For he is the minister of God for thy wealth. But if thou do that which is evil, fear. For he beareth not the sword for nought, for he is the minister of God to take vengeance on them that do evil." [15]

As the Apostle in these words most straitly commandeth obedience to be given to lawful powers, pronouncing God's wrath and vengeance against such as shall resist the ordinance of God, so doth he assign to the powers their offices which be to take vengeance upon evil-doers, to maintain the well-doers, and so to minister and rule in their office that the subjects by them may have a benefit and be praised in well doing. Now if you be powers ordained by God—and that I hope all men will grant, then by the plain words of the Apostle is the sword given unto you by God for maintenance of the innocent and for punishment of malefactors. But I and my brethren with me accused do offer not only to prove ourselves innocents in all things laid to our charge but also we offer most evidently to prove your bishops to be the very pestilence who have infected all Christianity. And therefore by the plain doctrine of the Apostle you are bound to maintain us and to punish the other, being convict and proved criminal.

Moreover the former words of the Apostle do teach how far high powers be bound to their subjects, to wit, that because they are God's ministers by

15. Rom. 13: 1, 2, 3, 4.

him ordained for the profit and utility of others, most diligently ought they to intend upon the same. For that cause assigneth the Holy Ghost, commanding subjects to obey and to pay tribute, saying, "for this do you pay tribute and toll," that is, because they are God's ministers, bearing the sword for your utility.[16] Whereof it is plain that there is no honor without a charge annexed. And this one point I wish your wisdoms deeply to consider: that God hath not placed you above your brethren to reign as tyrants without respect of their profit and commodity. You hear the Holy Ghost witness the contrary, affirming that all lawful powers be God's ministers ordained for the wealth, profit, and salvation of their subjects and not for their destruction. Could it be said, I beseech you, that magistrates, enclosing their subjects in a city without all victuals or giving unto them no other victuals but such as were poisoned, did rule for the profit of their subjects? I trust that none would be so foolish as so to affirm, but that rather every discreet person would boldly affirm that such as so did were tyrants unworthy of all regiment. If we will not deny that which Christ Jesus affirmeth to be a truth infallible, to wit, that the soul is greater and more precious than is the body, then shall we easily espy how unworthy of authority be those that this day debar their subjects from the hearing of God's word and by fire and sword compel them to feed upon the very poison of their souls—the damnable doctrine of Antichrist. And therefore in this point I say I cannot cease to admonish your honors diligently to take heed over your charge, which is greater than the most part of men suppose.

It is not enough that you abstain from violent wrong and oppression, which ungodly men exercise against their subjects; but ye are further bound, to wit, that ye rule above them for their wealth, which ye cannot do if that ye either by negligence, not providing true pastors, or yet by your maintenance of such as be ravening wolves suffer their souls to starve and perish for lack of the true food which is Christ's Evangel sincerely preached. It will not excuse you in his presence, who will require accompt of every talent committed to your charge, to say that ye supposed that the charge of the souls had been committed to your bishops. No, no, my lords, for ye cannot escape God's judgment. For if your bishops be proved to be no bishops but deceivable thieves and ravening wolves (which I offer myself to prove by God's word, by law and councils, yea, by the judgment of all the godly learned from the primitive church to this day), then shall your permission and defense of them be reputed before God a participation with their theft and murder. For thus accused the Prophet Isaiah the princes of Jerusalem: "Thy princes," saith he, "are apostates," that is, obstinate refusers of God, "and they are companions of thieves."[17] This grievous ac-

16. Rom. 13:6.   17. Isa. 1:23.

cusation was laid against them (albeit that they ruled in that city which sometime was called holy, where then were the temple, rites, and ordinances of God), because that not only they were wicked themselves but chiefly because they maintained wicked men, their priests and false prophets, in honors and authority. If they did not escape this accusation of the Holy Ghost in that age, look ye neither to escape the accusation nor judgment which is pronounced against the maintainers of wicked men, to wit, that the one and the other shall drink the cup of God's wrath and vengeance together.[18]

And, lest ye should deceive yourselves, esteeming your bishops to be virtuous and godly, this do I affirm and offer myself to prove the same: that more wicked men than be the whole rabble of your clergy were never from the beginning universally known in any age; yea, Sodom and Gomorrah may be justified in their respect. For they permitted just Lot to dwell amongst them without any violence done to his body, which that pestilent generation of your shaven sort doth not but most cruelly persecute by fire and sword the true members of Christ's body for no other cause but for the true service and honoring of God.

And therefore I fear not to affirm that which God shall one day justify: that by your offices ye be bound not only to repress their tyranny but also to punish them as thieves and murderers, as idolaters and blasphemers of God; and in their rooms ye are bound to place true preachers of Christ's Evangel for the instruction, comfort, and salvation of your subjects, above whom else shall never the Holy Ghost acknowledge that you rule in justice for their profit. If ye pretend to possess the kingdom with Christ Jesus, ye may not take example neither by the ignorant multitude of princes, neither by the ungodly and cruel rulers of the earth, of whom some pass their time in sloth, insolence, and riot without respect had to God's honor or to the salvation of their brethren, and other most cruelly oppress with Nimrod such as be subject to them. But your pattern and example must be the practice of those whom God hath approved by the testimony of his word, as after shall be declared.

Of the premises it is evident that to lawful powers is given the sword for punishment of malefactors, for maintenance of innocents, and for the profit and utility of their subjects. Now let us consider whether the reformation of religion fallen in decay and punishment of false teachers do appertain to the civil magistrate and nobility of any realm. I am not ignorant that Satan of old time for maintenance of his darkness hath obtained of the blind world two chief points: former, he hath persuaded to princes, rulers, and magistrates that the feeding of Christ's flock appertaineth nothing to their

18. Jer. 23, 27; Ezek. 13; Hos. 4.

charge, but that it is rejected upon the bishops and estate ecclesiastical; and secondarily, that the reformation of religion, be it never so corrupt, and the punishment of such as be sworn soldiers in their kingdom are exempted from all civil power and are reserved to themselves and to their own cognition. But that no offender can justly be exempted from punishment and that the ordering and reformation of religion with the instruction of subjects doth especially appertain to the civil magistrate, shall God's perfect ordinance, his plain word, and the facts and examples of those that of God are highly praised, most evidently declare.

When God did establish his law, statutes, and ceremonies in the midst of Israel, he did not exempt the matters of religion from the power of Moses; but as he gave him charge over the civil polity, so he put in his mouth and in his hand, that is, he first revealed to him and thereafter commanded to put in practice whatsoever was to be taught or done in matters [of] religion. Nothing did God reveal particularly to Aaron, but altogether was he commanded to depend from the mouth of Moses.[19] Yea, nothing was he permitted to do himself or to his children either in his or their inauguration and sanctification to the priesthood, but all was committed to the care of Moses, and therefore were these words so frequently repeated to Moses: "Thou shalt separate Aaron and his sons from the midst of the people of Israel that they may execute the office of priesthood. Thou shalt make unto them garments, thou shalt annoint them, thou shalt wash them, thou shalt fill their hands with the sacrifice."[20] And so forth of every rite and ceremony that was to be done unto them, especial commandment was given unto Moses that he should do it. Now if Aaron and his sons were subject to Moses that they did nothing but at his commandment, who dare be so bold as to affirm that the civil magistrate hath nothing to do in matters of religion? For seeing that then God did so straitly require that even those who did bear the figure of Christ should receive from the civil power, as it were, their sanctification and entrance to their office, and seeing also that Moses was so far preferred to Aaron that the one commanded and the other did obey, who dare esteem that the civil power is now becomed so profane in God's eyes that it is sequestered from all intromission with the matters of religion.

The Holy Ghost in divers places declareth the contrary. For one of the chief precepts commanded to the king, when that he should be placed in his throne, was to write the example of the book of the Lord's law that it should be with him, that he might read in it all the days of his life, that he might learn to fear the Lord his God, and to keep all the words of his law, and his statutes to do them. This precept requireth not only that the king should

19. Exod. 21, 24, 25.   20. Exod. 28, 29.

himself fear God, keep his law and statutes, but that also he as the chief ruler should provide that God's true religion should be kept inviolated of the people and flock which by God was committed to his charge. And this did not only David and Solomon perfectly understand, but also some godly kings in Judah, after the apostasy and idolatry that infected Israel by the means of Jeroboam, did practice their understanding and execute their power in some notable reformations. For Asa and Jehoshaphat, Kings in Judah, finding the religion altogether corrupt, did apply their hearts, saith the Holy Ghost, to serve the Lord and to walk in his ways. And thereafter doth witness that Asa removed from honors his mother—some say grand-mother—because she had committed and labored to maintain horrible idol-atry. And Jehoshaphat did not only refuse strange gods himself, but also, destroying the chief monuments of idolatry, did send forth the Levites to instruct the people. Whereof it is plain that the one and the other did under-stand such reformations to appertain to their duties.[21]

But the facts of Hezekiah and of Josiah do more clearly prove the power and duty of the civil magistrate in the reformation of religion. Before the reign of Hezekiah so corrupt was the religion that the doors of the house of the Lord were shut up, the lamps were extinguished, no sacrifice was orderly made; but in the first year of his reign, the first month of the same, did the King open the doors of the temple, bring in the priests and Levites and, assembling them together, did speak unto them as followeth: "Hear me, O ye Levites, and be sanctified now, and sanctify also the house of the Lord God of your fathers, and carry forth from the sanctuary all filthiness" (he meaneth all monuments and vessels of idolatry), "for our fathers have transgressed and have committed wickedness in the eyes of the eternal our God; they have left him and have turned their faces from the tabernacle of the Lord, and therefore is the wrath of the Lord comed upon Judah and Jerusalem. Behold our fathers have fallen by the sword, our sons, daugh-ters, and wives are led in captivity, but now have I purposed in my heart to make a covenant with the Lord God of Israel that he may turn the wrath of his fury from us. And therefore, my sons," he sweetly exhorteth, "be not faint, for the Lord hath chosen you to stand in his presence to serve him." [22]

Such as be not more than blind, clearly may perceive that the King doth acknowledge that it appertained to his charge to reform the religion, to ap-point the Levites to their charge, and to admonish them of their duty and office; which thing he more evidently declareth, writing his letters to all Israel, to Ephraim, and Manasseh and sent the same by the hands of mes-sengers, having this tenor: "You sons of Israel, return to the Lord God of Abraham, Isaac, and Israel, and he shall return to the residue that resteth

21. 2 Chron. 14, 17.   22. 2 Chron. 29:5-11.

from the hands of Assyria. Be not as yours and as your brethren were, who have transgressed against the Lord God of their fathers, who hath made them desolate as you see. Hold not your heart therefore, but give your hand unto the Lord. Return unto his sanctuary, serve him, and he shall shew mercy unto you, to your sons and daughters that be in bondage, for he is pitiful and easy to be entreated." [23]

Thus far did Hezekiah by letters and messengers provoke the people, declined from God, to repentence, not only in Judah where he reigned lawful King but also in Israel, subject then to another King. And albeit that by some wicked men his messengers were mocked; yet as they lacked not their just punishment (for within six years after, Samaria was destroyed and Israel led captive by Shalmaneser), so did not the zealous King Hezekiah desist to prosecute his duty in restoring the religion of God's perfect ordinance, removing all abominations.

The same is to be read of Josiah, who did not only restore the religion but did further destroy all monuments of idolatry which of long time had remained. [24] For it is written of him that, after that the book of the Law was found and that he had asked counsel at the Prophetess Huldah, he sent and gathered all the elders of Judah and Jerusalem; and standing in the temple of the Lord, he made a covenant that all the people from the great to the small should walk after the Lord, should observe his law, statutes, and testimonies with all their heart and all their soul, and that they should ratify and confirm whatsoever was written in the book of God. He further commanded Helkiah the high priest and the priests of the inferior order that they should carry forth of the temple of the Lord all vessels that were made to Baal, which he burnt and did carry their powder to Bethel. He did further destroy all monuments of idolatry, yea, even those that had remained from the days of Solomon. He did burn them, stamp them to powder, whereof one part he scattered in the brook Kidron and the other upon the sepulchers and graves of the idolaters, whose bones he did burn upon the altars, where before they made sacrifice not only in Judah but also in Bethel, where Jeroboam had erected his idolatry. Yea, he further proceeded and did kill the priests of the high places, who were idolaters and had deceived the people; he did kill them, I say, and did burn their bones upon their own altars, and so returned to Jerusalem. This reformation made Josiah, and for the same obtained this testimony of the Holy Ghost that neither before him neither after him was there any such king who returned to God with his whole soul and with all his strength according to the law of Moses. [25]

23. 2 Chron. 30:6, 7, 8.   24. 2 Chron. 34.
25. 2 Kings 23.

Of which histories it is evident that the reformation of religion in all points, together with the punishment of false teachers doth appertain to the power of the civil magistrate. For what God required of them, his justice must require of others having the like charge and authority; what he did approve in them, he cannot but approve in all others who with like zeal and sincerity do enterprise to purge the Lord's temple and sanctuary. What God required of them it is before declared, to wit, that most diligently they should observe his law, statutes, and ceremonies, and how acceptable were their facts to God doth he himself witness. For to some he gave most notable victories without the hand of man, and in their most desperate dangers did declare his especial favors towards them by signs supernatural; to other he so established the kingdom that their enemies were compelled to stoop under their feet.[26] And the names of all he hath registered not only in the book of life but also in the blessed remembrance of all posterity since their days, which also shall continue till the coming of the Lord Jesus, who shall reward with the crown of immortality not only them but also such as unfeignedly study to do the will and to promote the glory of his heavenly father in the midst of this corrupted generation. In consideration whereof ought you, my lords, all delay set apart to provide for the reformation of religion in your dominions and bounds, which now is so corrupt that no part of Christ's institution remaineth in the original purity; and therefore of necessity it is that speedily ye provide for reformation [or] else ye declare yourselves not only void of love towards your subjects but also to live without care of your own salvation, yea, without all fear and true reverence of God.

Two things perchance may move you to esteem these histories, before briefly touched, to appertain nothing to you. First, because you are no Jews but gentiles, and secondarily, because you are no kings but nobles in your realm. But be not deceived. For neither of both can excuse you in God's presence from doing your duty, for it is a thing more than certain that, whatsoever God required of the civil magistrate in Israel or Judah, concerning the observation of true religion during the time of the Law, the same doth he require of lawful magistrates, professing Christ Jesus in the time of the Gospel, as the Holy Ghost hath taught us by the mouth of David, saying, Psalm 2, "Be learned you that judge the earth, kiss the son, lest that the Lord wax angry and that ye perish from the way." This admonition did not extend to the judges under the Law only but doth also include all such as be promoted to honors in the time of the Gospel, when Christ Jesus doth reign and fight in his spiritual kingdom, whose enemies in that Psalm be first most sharply taxed, their fury expressed, and vanity mocked.

26. 2 Chron. 32.

And then are kings and judges, who think themselves free from all law and obedience, commanded to repent their former blind rage, and judges are charged to be learned; and last are all commanded to serve the eternal in fear, to rejoice before him in trembling, to kiss the son, that is, to give unto him most humble obedience, whereof it is evident that the rulers, magistrates, and judges now in Christ's kingdom are no less bound to obedience unto God than were those under the Law.

And how is it possible that any shall be obedient who despise his religion, in which standeth the chief glory that man can give to God and is a service which God especially requireth of kings and rulers? Which thing St. Augustine plainly did note, writing to one Bonifacius, a man of war, according to the same argument and purpose which I labor to persuade your honors. For after that he hath in that his epistle declared the difference betwixt the heresy of the Donatists and Arians and hath somewhat spoken of their cruelty, he sheweth the way how their fury should and ought to be repressed and that it is lawful for the injustly afflicted to seek support and defense at godly magistrates. For thus he writeth: "Either must the verity be kept close, or else must their cruelty be sustained. But if the verity should be concealed, not only should none be saved nor delivered by such silence, but also should many be lost through their decept. But if by preaching of the verity their fury should be provoked more to rage, and by that means yet some were delivered, yet should fear hinder many weaklings to follow the verity, if their rage be not stayed."

In these first words Augustine sheweth three reasons why the afflicted church in those days called for the help of the emperor and of godly magistrates against the fury of the persecutors. The first, the verity must be spoken, or else mankind shall perish in error. The second, the verity, being plainly spoken, provoketh the adversaries to rage. And because that some did allege that rather we ought to suffer all injury than to seek support by man, he addeth the third reason, to wit, that many weak ones be not able to suffer persecution and death for the truth's sake, to whom not the less respect ought to be had that they may be won from error and so be brought to greater strength.

O that rulers of this age should ponder and weigh the reasons of this godly writer and provide the remedy which he requireth in these words following: "Now when the church was thus afflicted if any think that rather they should have sustained all calamity than that the help of God should have been asked by Christian Emperors, he doth not well advert that of such negligence no good compts or reason could be given. For where such as would that no just laws should be made against their impiety allege that the Apostles sought no such things of the kings of the earth, they do not consider that then the time was other than it is now, and that all things are done in their own time. What emperor then believed in Christ that should serve him in making laws for godliness against impiety? While yet that saying of the prophet was complete, "Why hath nations raged, and people have imagined vanity? The kings of the earth have stand up, and princes have convented together against the Lord and against his annointed," that which is after said in the same Psalm was not yet come to pass: "And now understand, O you kings, be learned you that judge the earth serve the Lord in fear and rejoice to him with trembling." How do kings serve the Lord in fear but in punishing and by a godly severity forbidding those things which are done against the commandment of the Lord. For otherwise doth he serve insofar as he is man, otherwise insofar as he is king. Insofar as he is man, he serveth him by living faithfully; but because he is also king, he serveth, establishing laws that command the things that be just and that with a convenient rigor forbid things contrary. As Hezekiah served, destroying the groves, the temples of idols, and the places which were builded against God's commandment; so served also Josiah, doing the same; so served the King of Ninevites, compelling the whole city to mitigate the Lord; so served Darius, giving in the power of Daniel the idol to be broken and his enemies to be cast to the lions; so served Nebuchadnezzar by a terrible law, forbidding all that were in his realm to blaspheme God. Herein therefore do kings serve the Lord insofar as they are kings when they do those things to serve him which none except kings be able to do." [27] He further proceedeth and concludeth that, as when wicked kings do reign, impiety cannot be bridled by laws but rather is tyranny exercised under the title of the same, so it is a thing without all reason that kings, professing the knowledge and honor of God, should not regard nor care who did defend nor who did oppugn the church of God in their dominions.

By these words of this ancient and godly writer, your honors may perceive what I require of you, to wit, to repress the tyranny of your bishops and to defend the innocents professing the truth. He did require of the emperor and kings of his days, professing Christ, and manifestly concludeth that they cannot serve Christ except that so they do. Let not your bishops think that Augustine speaketh for them because he nameth the church. Let them read and understand that Augustine writeth for that church which professeth the truth and doth suffer persecution for the defense of the same, which your bishops do not, but rather with the Donatists and Arians do cruelly persecute all such as boldly speak Christ's eternal verity to manifest their impiety and abomination. But thus much we have of Augustine that it appertaineth to the obedience and service which kings owe to God, as well

27. Augustine *Letters* 185.

now in the time of the Gospel as before under the Law, to defend the afflicted for matters of religion and repress the fury of the persecutors by the rigor and severity of godly laws. For which cause, no doubt, doth Isaiah the Prophet say that, "kings should be nourishers to the church of God, that they should abase their heads, and lovingly embrace the children of God." [28] And thus, I say, your honors may evidently see that the same obedience doth God require of rulers and princes in the time of the Gospel that he required in the time of the Law.

If you do think that the reformation of religion and defense of the afflicted doth not appertain to you because you are no kings but nobles and estates of a realm, in two things you are deceived. Former, in that you do not advert that David requireth as well that the princes and judges of the earth be learned and that they serve and fear God, as that he requireth that the kings repent. If you therefore be judges and princes, as no man can deny you to be, then by the plain words of David you are charged to be learned, to serve and fear God, which ye cannot do if you despise the reformation of his religion. And this is your first error.

The second is that ye neither know your duty which ye owe to God, neither yet your authority which of him ye have received, if ye for pleasure or fear of any earthly man despise God's true religion and contemn your brethren that in his name call for your support. Your duty is to hear the voice of the eternal, your God, and unfeignedly to study to follow his precepts, who, as is before said, of especial mercy hath promoted you to honors and dignity. His chief and principal precept is that with reverence ye receive and embrace his only beloved son Jesus, that ye promote to the uttermost of your powers his true religion, and that ye defend your brethren and subjects whom he hath put under your charge and care.

Now, if your king be a man ignorant of God, enemy to his true religion, blinded by superstition, and a persecutor of Christ's members, shall ye be excused if with silence ye pass over his iniquity? Be not deceived, my lords, ye are placed in authority for another purpose than to flatter your king in his folly and blind rage, to wit, that as with your bodies, strength, riches, and wisdom ye are bound to assist and defend him in all things which by your advice he shall take in hand for God's glory and for the preservation of his commonwealth and subjects, so by your gravities, counsel, and admonition ye are bound to correct and repress whatsoever ye know him to attempt expressedly repugning to God's word, honor, and glory, or what ye shall espy him to do, be it by ignorance or be it by malice, against his subjects great or small. Of which last part of your obedience if ye de-

28. Isa. 49:23.

fraud your king, ye commit against him no less treason than if ye did extract from him your due and promised support what time by his enemies injustly he were pursued.

But this part of their duty, I fear, do a small number of the nobility of this age rightly consider; neither yet will they understand that for that purpose hath God promoted them. For now the common song of all men is, we must obey our kings, be they good or be they bad, for God hath so commanded. But horrible shall the vengeance be that shall be poured forth upon such blasphemers of God, his holy name, and ordinance. For it is no less blasphemy to say that God hath commanded kings to be obeyed when they command impiety than to say that God by his precept is author and maintainer of all iniquity. True it is God hath commanded kings to be obeyed, but like true it is that in things which they commit against his glory, or when cruelly without cause they rage against their brethren the members of Christ's body, he hath commanded no obedience, but rather he hath approved, yea, and greatly rewarded such as have opponed themselves to their ungodly commandments and blind rage, as in the examples of the three children, of Daniel, and Ebedmelech it is evident.

The three children would neither bow nor stoop before the golden image at the commandment of the great King Nebuchadnezzar. Daniel did openly pray, his windows being open, against the established law of Darius and of his council. And Ebedmelech feared not to enter in before the presence of Zedekiah and boldly to defend the cause and innocency of Jeremiah the Prophet, whom the King and his council had condemned to death.[29] Every one of these facts should this day be judged foolish by such as will not understand what confession God doth require of his children when his verity is oppugned or his glory called in doubt; such men, I say, as prefer man to God and things present to the heavenly inheritance, should have judged every one of these facts stubborn inobedience, foolish presumption and singularity, or else bold controlling of the king and his wise council. But how acceptable in God's presence was this resistance to the ungodly commandments and determinations of their king, the end did witness. For the three children were delivered from the furnace of fire and Daniel from the den of lions to the confusion of their enemies, to better instruction of the ignorant king, and to the perpetual comfort of God's afflicted children.

And Ebedmelech, in the day of the Lord's visitation when the King and his council did drink the bitter cup of God's vengeance, did find his life for a prey and did not fall in the edge of the sword when many thousands did perish. And this was signified unto him by the Prophet himself at the com-

29. Jer. 38.

mandment of God before that Jerusalem was destroyed. The promise and cause were recited unto him in these words: "I will bring my words upon this city unto evil and not unto good, but most assuredly I shall deliver thee because thou hast trusted in me, saith the Lord." The trust and hope which Ebedmelech had in God made him bold to oppone himself, being but one, to the King and to his whole council who had condemned to death the Prophet, whom his conscience did acknowledge to be innocent. For this did he speak in the presence of the King, sitting in the port of Benjamin: "My Lord, the King," saith Ebedmelech, "these men do wickedly in all things that they have done to Jeremiah the Prophet." [30]

Advert and take heed, my lords, that the men who had condemned the Prophet were the King, his princes, and council, and yet did one man accuse them all of iniquity and did boldly speak in the defense of him whose innocence he was persuaded. And the same, I say, is the duty of every man in his vocation, but chiefly of the nobility which is joined with their kings to bridle and repress their folly and blind rage. Which thing, if the nobility do not neither yet labor to do, as they are traitors to their kings, so do they provoke the wrath of God against themselves and against the realm in which they abuse the authority which they have received of God to maintain virtue and to repress vice. For hereof I would your honors were most certainly persuaded that God will neither excuse nobility nor people, but the nobility least of all, that obey and follow their kings in manifest iniquity; but with the same vengeance will God punish the prince, people, and nobility, conspiring together against him and his holy ordinances, as in the punishment taken upon Pharaoh, Israel, Judah, and Babylon is evidently to be seen. For Pharaoh was not drowned alone, but his captains, chariots, and great army drank the same cup with him. The kings of Israel and Judah were not punished without company, but with them were murdered the councillors, their princes imprisoned, and their people led captive. And why? Because none was found so faithful to God that he durst enterprise to resist nor againststand the manifest impiety of their princes. And therefore was God's wrath poured forth upon the one and the other. But the more ample discourse of this argument I defer to better opportunity; only at this time I thought expedient to admonish you that before God it shall not excuse you to allege, we are no kings and therefore neither can we reform religion nor yet defend such as be persecuted. Consider, my lords, that ye are powers ordained by God, as is before declared; and therefore doth the reformation of religion and the defense of such as injustly are oppressed appertain to your charge and care, which thing shall the law of God, uni-

30. Jer. 39:16; Jer. 38:9.

versally given to be kept of all men, most evidently declare, which is my last and most assured reason why I say ye ought to remove from honors and to punish with death such as God hath condemned by his own mouth.

After that Moses had declared what was true religion, to wit, to honor God as he commanded, adding nothing to his word, neither yet diminishing anything from it, after also that vehemently he had exhorted the same law to be observed, he denounceth the punishment against the transgressors in these words:[31] "If thy brother, son, daughter, wife, or neighbor, whom thou lovest as thine own life, solicitate thee secretly, saying, let us go serve other gods whom neither thou nor thy fathers have known, consent not to hear him, hear him not, let not thine eye spare him, shew him no indulgency or favor, hide him not, but utterly kill him; let thy hand be the first upon him that he may be slain, and after the hand of the whole people."[32] Of these words of Moses are two things appertaining to our purpose to be noted. Former, that such as solicitate only to idolatry ought to be punished to death without favor or respect of person. For he that will not suffer man to spare his son, his daughter, nor his wife, but straitly commandeth punishment to be taken upon the idolaters—have they never so nigh conjunction with us—will not wink at the idolatry of others of what estate or condition soever they be.

It is not unknown that the Prophets had revelations of God which were not common to the people, as Samuel had the revelation that Eli and his posterity should be destroyed, that Saul should first be king and thereafter that he should be rejected, that David should reign for him.[33] Micaiah understood by vision that Ahab should be killed in battle against the Syrians.[34] Elijah saw that dogs should eat Jezebel in the fortress of Jezreel.[35] Elisha did see hunger come upon Israel by the space of seven years.[36] Jeremiah did foresee the destruction of Jerusalem and the time of their captivity, and so divers other Prophets had divers revelations of God which the people did not otherwise understand but by their affirmation; and therefore in those days were the Prophets named seers, because that God did open unto them that which was hid from the multitude. Now if any man might have claimed any privilege from the rigor of the law or might have justified his fact, it should have been the Prophet. For he might have alleged for himself his singular prerogative that he had above other men to have God's will revealed unto him by vision or by dream, or that God had declared particularly unto him that his pleasure was to be honored in that manner, in such a place, and by such means. But all such excuses doth God remove, commanding that the Prophet that shall solicitate the people to serve

31. Deut. 12.
32. Deut. 13; 6, 7, 8, 9.
33. 1 Sam. 3, 9, 15, 16.
34. 1 Kings 22.
35. 1 Kings 21.
36. 2 Kings 8.

strange gods shall die the death, notwithstanding that he allege for himself dream, vision, or revelation. Yea, although he promise miracles and also that such things as he promiseth come to pass, yet, I say, commandeth God that no credit be given to him, but that he die the death, because he teacheth apostasy and defection from God.

Hereof your honors may easily espy that none provoking the people to idolatry ought to be exempted from the punishment of death. For if neither that inseparable conjunction which God himself hath sanctified betwixt man and wife, neither that unspeakable love grafted in nature which is betwixt the father and the son, neither yet that reverence which God's people ought to bear to the Prophets, can excuse any man to spare the offender or to conceal his offense, what excuse can man pretend which God will accept? Evident it is that no estate, condition, nor honor can exempt the idolater from the hands of God when he shall call him to accompts or shall inflict punishment upon him for his offense; how shall it then excuse the people that they, according to God's commandment, punish not to death such as shall solicitate or violently draw the people to idolatry? And this is the first which I would your honors should note of the former words, to wit, that no person is exempted from punishment if he can be manifestly convicted to have provoked or led the people to idolatry. And this is most evidently declared in that solemn oath and covenant which Asa made with the people to serve God and to maintain his religion, adding this penalty to the transgressors of it, to wit, that "whosoever should not seek the Lord God of Israel should be killed, were he great or were he small, were it man or were it woman." [37] And of this oath was the Lord compleased; he was fond of them and gave them rest on every part, because they sought him with their whole heart and did swear to punish the offenders according to the precept of his law, without respect of persons. And this is it which, I say, I would your honors should note for the first: that no idolater can be exempted from punishment by God's law.

The second is that the punishment of such crimes as are idolatry, blasphemy, and others that touch the majesty of God doth not appertain to kings and chief rulers only but also to the whole body of that people and to every member of the same, according to the vocation of every man and according to that possibility and occasion which God doth minister to revenge the injury done against his glory what time that impiety is manifestly known. And that doth Moses more plainly speak in these words: "If in any of thy cities," saith he, "which the Lord thy God giveth unto thee to dwell in them, thou shalt hear this bruit: there are some men, the sons of Belial, passed forth from thee and have solicited the citizens of their cities

37. 2 Chron. 15:13.

by these words: let us go and serve strange gods which you have not known, search and inquire diligently; and if it be true that such abomination is done in the midst of thee, thou shalt utterly strike the inhabitants of that city with the sword, thou shalt destroy it and whatsoever is within it, thou shalt gather the spoil of it in the midst of the marketplace, thou shalt burn that city with fire and the spoil of it to the Lord thy God that it may be a heap of stones forever, neither shall it be any more builded. Let nothing of that execration cleave to thy hand that the Lord may turn from the fury of his wrath and be moved towards thee with inward affection." [38] Plain it is that Moses speaketh nor giveth not charge to kings, rulers, and judges only, but he commandeth the whole body of the people, yea, and every member of the same according to their possibility.

And who dare to be so impudent as to deny this to be most reasonable and just? For, seeing that God had delivered the whole body from bondage, and to the whole multitude had given his law, and to the twelve tribes had he so distributed the inheritance of the land of Canaan that no family could complain that it was neglected, was not the whole and every member addebted to confess and acknowledge the benefits of God, yea, had it not been the part of every man to have studied to keep the possession which he had received? Which thing God did plainly pronounce they should not do, except that in their hearts they did sanctify the Lord God, that they embraced and inviolably kept his religion established, and finally except they did cut out iniquity from amongst them, declaring themselves earnest enemies to those abominations which God declared himself so vehemently to hate that first he commanded the whole inhabitants of that country to be destroyed and all monuments of their idolatry to be broken down, and thereafter he also straitly commandeth that a city declining to idolatry should fall in the edge of the sword, and that the whole spoil of the same should be burned, no portion of it reserved. [39]

To the carnal man this may appear a rigorous and severe judgment, yea, it may rather seem to be pronounced in a rage than in wisdom. For what city was ever yet in which, to man's judgment, were not to be found many innocent persons, as infants, children, and some simple and ignorant souls who neither did nor could consent to such impiety? And yet we find no exception, but all are appointed to the cruel death. And as concerning the city and the spoil of the same, man's reason cannot think but that it might have been better bestowed than to be consumed with fire and so profit no man. But in such cases will God that all creatures stoop, cover their faces, and desist from reasoning when commandment is given to execute his judgment.

Albeit I could adduce divers causes of such severity, yet will I search

38. Deut. 13:12-17.   39. Deut. 7, 13, 28, 30.

none other than the Holy Ghost hath assigned. First, that all Israel, hearing the judgment, should fear to commit the like abomination; and secondarily, that the Lord might turn from the fury of his anger, might be moved towards the people with inward affection, be merciful unto them, and multiply them according to his oath made unto their fathers. Which reasons, as they are sufficient in God's children to correct the murmuring of the grudging flesh, so ought they to provoke every man, as before I have said, to declare himself enemy to that which so highly provoketh the wrath of God against the whole people. For where Moses saith, "let the city be burned, and let no part of the spoil cleave to thy hand that the Lord may return from the fury of his wrath," etc., he plainly doth signify that by the defection and idolatry of a few God's wrath is kindled against the whole, which is never quenched till such punishment be taken upon the offenders: that whatsoever served them in their idolatry be brought to destruction, because that it is execrable and accursed before God. And therefore he will not that it be reserved for any use of his people.

I am not ignorant that this law was not put in execution as God commanded; but what did thereof ensue and follow histories declare, to wit, plague after plague till Israel and Judah were led in captivity, as the Books of Kings do witness. The consideration whereof maketh me more bold to affirm that it is the duty of every man that list to escape the plague and punishments of God to declare himself enemy to idolatry not only in heart, hating the same, but also in external gesture, declaring that he lamenteth, if he can do no more, for such abominations. Which thing was shewed to the Prophet Ezekiel what time he gave him to understand why he would destroy Judah with Israel, and that he would remove his glory from the temple and place that he had chosen, and so pour forth his wrath and indignation upon the city that was full of blood and apostasy—which became so impudent that it durst be bold to say, "the Lord hath left the earth and seeth not." At this time, I say, the Lord revealed in vision to his Prophet who they were that should find favor in that miserable destruction, to wit, "those that did mourn and lament for all the abominations done in the city, in whose foreheads did God command to print and seal Tau" to the end that the destroyer, who was commanded to strike the rest without mercy, should not hurt them in whom the sign was found.[40]

Of these premises I suppose it be evident that the punishment of idolatry doth not appertain to kings only but also to the whole people, yea, to every member of the same according to his possibility. For that is a thing most assured that no man can mourn, lament, and bewail for those things which he will not remove to the uttermost of his power. If this be required of the

40. Ezek. 8:12; 9:4.

whole people and of every man in his vocation, what shall be required of you, my lords, whom God hath raised up to be princes and rulers above your brethren, whose hands he hath armed with the sword of his justice, yea, whom he hath appointed to be as bridles to repress the rage and insolency of your kings whensoever they pretend manifestly to transgress God's blessed ordinance?

If any think that this my affirmation, touching the punishment of idolaters, be contrary to the practice of the Apostles who, finding the gentiles in idolatry, did call them to repentance, requiring no such punishment, let the same man understand that the gentiles, before the preaching of Christ, lived, as the Apostle speaketh, without God in the world, drowned in idolatry, according to the blindness and ignorance in which then they were holden, as a profane nation, whom God had never openly avowed to be his people, had never received in his household, neither given unto them laws to be kept in religion nor polity; and therefore did not his Holy Ghost, calling them to repentance, require of them any corporal punishment according to the rigor of the law unto the which they were never subjects, as they that were strangers from the commonwealth of Israel.[41] But if any think that, after that the gentiles were called from their vain conversation, and, by embracing Christ, were received in the number of Abraham's children, and so made one people with the Jews believing, if any think, I say, that then they were not bound to the same obedience which God required of his people Israel what time he confirmed his league and covenant with them, the same man appeareth to make Christ inferior to Moses and contrarious to the law of his heavenly father. For if the contempt or transgression of Moses' law was worthy of death, what should we judge the contempt of Christ's ordinance to be (I mean after they be once received)? And if Christ be not comed to dissolve but to fulfill the world of his heavenly father, shall the liberty of his Gospel be an occasion that the especial glory of his father be trodden underfoot and regarded of no man? God forbid.

The especial glory of God is that such as profess them to be his people should hearken to his voice; and amongst all the voices of God revealed to the world, touching punishment of vices, is none more evident neither more severe than is that which is pronounced against idolatry, the teachers and maintainers of the same.[42] And therefore I fear not to affirm that the gentiles (I mean every city, realm, province, or nation amongst the gentiles, embracing Christ Jesus and his true religion) be bound to the same league and covenant that God made with his people Israel what time he promised to root out nations before them in these words: "Beware that thou make any covenant with the inhabitants of the land to the which thou

41. Eph. 2.   42. 1 Sam. 15.

comest, lest perchance, that this come in ruin, that is, be destruction to thee; but thou shalt destroy their altars, break their idols, and cut down their groves. Fear no strange gods, worship them not, neither yet make you sacrifice to them. But the Lord, who in his greater power and outstretched arm hath brought you out of the land of Egypt, shall you fear, him shall you honor, him shall you worship, to him shall you make sacrifice; his statutes, judgments, laws, and commandments you shall keep and observe. This is the covenant which I have made with you, saith the Eternal, forget it not, neither yet fear ye other gods; but fear you the Lord your God, and he shall deliver you from the hands of all your enemies." [43]

To this same law, I say, and covenant are the gentiles no less bound than sometimes were the Jews. Whensoever God doth illuminate the eyes of any multitude, province, people or city and putteth the sword in their own hand to remove such enormities from amongst them as, before God, they know to be abominable, then, I say, are they no less bound to purge their dominions, cities, and countries from idolatry than were the Israelites what time they received the possession of the land of Canaan. And moreover, I say, if any go about to erect and set up idolatry or to teach defection from God after that the verity hath been received and approved, that then, not only the magistrates to whom the sword is committed, but also the people are bound by that oath which they have made to God to revenge to the uttermost of their power the injury done against his majesty.

In universal defections and in a general revolt, such as was in Israel after Jeroboam, there is a diverse consideration. For then because the whole people were together conspired against God, there could none be found that would execute the punishment which God had commanded till God raised up Jehu, whom he had appointed for that purpose. And the same is to be considered in all other general defections, such as this day be in the papistry where all are blinded and all are declined from God, and that of long continuance, so that no ordinary justice can be executed, but the punishment must be reserved to God and unto such means as he shall appoint.

But I do speak of such a number as, after they have received God's perfect religion, do boldly profess the same, notwithstanding that some or the most part fall back, as of late days was in England; unto such a number, I say, it is lawful to punish the idolaters with death, if by any means God give them the power. For so did Joshua and Israel determine to have done against the children of Reuben, Gad, and Manasseh for their suspect apostasy and defection from God. And the whole tribes did in very deed execute the sharp judgment against the tribe of Benjamin for a less offense than for idolatry. And the same ought to be done wheresoever Christ Jesus and his

43. Exod. 34:12-16.

Evangel is so received in any realm, province, or city that the magistrates and people have solemnly avowed and promised to defend the same, as under King Edward of late days was done in England. In such places, I say, it is not only lawful to punish to the death such as labor to subvert the true religion, but the magistrates and people are bound so to do unless they will provoke the wrath of God against themselves. And therefore I fear not to affirm that it had been the duty of the nobility, judges, rulers, and people of England not only to have resisted and againststanded Mary, that Jezebel whom they call their Queen, but also to have punished her to the death with all the sort of her idolatrous priests together with all such as should have assisted her what time that she and they openly began to suppress Christ's Evangel, to shed the blood of the saints of God, and to erect that most devilish idolatry—the papistical abominations and his usurped tyranny, which once most justly by common oath was banished from that realm.

But because I cannot at this present discuss this argument as it appertaineth, I am compelled to omit it to better opportunity; and so, returning to your honors, I say that if ye confess yourselves baptised in the Lord Jesus, of necessity ye must confess that the care of his religion doth appertain to your charge. And if ye know that in your hands God hath put the sword for the causes above expressed, then can ye not deny but that the punishment of obstinate and malapert idolaters, such as all your bishops be, doth appertain to your office, if after admonition they continue obstinate.

I am not ignorant what be the vain defenses of your proud prelates. They claim first a prerogative and privilege that they are exempted, and that by consent of councils and emperors, from all jurisdiction of the temporality. And secondarily, when they are convicted of manifest impieties, abuses, and enormities—as well in their manners as in religion, neither fear nor shame they to affirm that things so long established cannot suddenly be reformed, although they be corrupted; but with process of time they promise to take order. But in a few words I answer that no privilege granted against the ordinance and statutes of God is to be observed, although all councils and men in the earth have appointed the same. But against God's ordinance it is that idolaters, murderers, false teachers, and blasphemers shall be exempted from punishment, as before is declared; and therefore in vain it is that they claim for privilege when that God saith, "the murderer shalt thou rive from my altar that he may die the death." And as to the order and reformation which they promise, that is to be looked or hoped for when Satan, whose children and slaves they are, can change his nature. This answer, I doubt not, shall suffice the sober and godly reader.

But yet to the end that they may further see their own confusion and that your honors may better understand what ye ought to do in so manifest a corruption and defection from God, I ask of themselves what assurance they have for this their immunity, exemption, or privilege? Who is the author of it, and what fruit it hath produced?

And first I say that of God they have no assurance neither yet can he be proved to be author of any such privilege. But the contrary is easy to be seen. For God, in establishing his orders in Israel, did so subject Aaron (in his priesthood being the figure of Christ) to Moses that he feared not to call him in judgment and to constrain him to give accompt of his wicked deed in consenting to idolatry, as the history doth plainly witness. For thus it is written: "Then Moses took the calf which they had made, and burned it with fire, and did grind it to powder, and scattering it in the water, gave it to drink to the children of Israel" (declaring hereby the vanity of their idol and the abomination of the same); and thereafter, "Moses said to Aaron, 'what hath this people done to thee that thou shouldst bring upon it so great a sin?'"[44] Thus, I say, doth Moses call and accuse Aaron of the destruction of the whole people, and yet he perfectly understood that God had appointed him to be the high priest that he should bear upon his shoulders and upon his breast the names of the twelve tribes of Israel, for whom he was appointed to make sacrifice, prayers, and supplications. He knew his dignity was so great that only he might enter within the most holy place, but neither could his office nor dignity exempt him from judgment when he had offended.

If any object Aaron at that time was not anointed and therefore was he subject to Moses, I have answered that Moses, being taught by the mouth of God, did perfectly understand to what dignity Aaron was appointed, and yet he feared not to call him in judgment and to compel him to make answer for his wicked fact. But if this answer doth not suffice, yet shall the Holy Ghost witness further in the matter.

Solomon removed from honor Abiathar, being the high priest, and commanded him to cease from all function and to live as a private man. Now if the unction did exempt the priest from jurisdiction of the civil magistrate, Solomon did offend, and injured Abiathar. For he was anointed and had carried the ark before David. But God doth not reprove the fact of Solomon, neither yet doth Abiathar claim any prerogative by the reason of his office; but rather doth the Holy Ghost approve the fact of Solomon, saying, "Solomon ejected forth Abiathar that he should not be the priest of the Lord, that the word of the Lord might be performed which he spake unto the house of Eli." And Abiathar did think that he obtained great favor in that he did escape the present death which by his conspiracy he had deserved.[45] If any yet reason that Abiathar was no otherwise subject to the

44. Exod. 32:20, 21.   45. 1 Kings 2:27.

judgment of the King, but as he was appointed to be the executor of that sentence which God before had pronounced, as I will not greatly deny that reason, so require I that every man consider that the same God who pronounced sentence against Eli and his house hath pronounced also that idolaters, whoremongers, murderers, and blasphemers shall neither have portion in the kingdom of God neither ought to be permitted to bear any rule in his church and congregation.[46]

Now if the unction and office saved not Abiathar, because that God's sentence must needs be performed, can any privilege granted by man be a buckler to malefactors that they shall not be subject to the punishments pronounced by God? I think no man will be so foolish as so to affirm. For a thing more than evident it is that the whole priesthood in the time of the Law was bound to give obedience to the civil powers. And if any member of the same was found criminal, the same was subject to the punishment of the sword which God had put in the hand of the magistrate.

And this ordinance of his father did not Christ disannul but rather did confirm the same, commanding tribute to be paid for himself and for Peter, who, perfectly knowing the mind of his master, thus writeth in this Epistle: "Submit yourselves to all manner ordinance of man" (he excepteth such as be expressly repugning to God's commandment) "for the Lord's sake, whether it be to king as to the chief head, or unto rulers as unto them that are sent by him for punishment of evil doers and for the praise of them that do well." [47] The same doth the Apostle St. Paul most plainly command in these words: "Let every soul be subject to the superior powers." [48] Which places make evident that neither Christ neither his Apostles hath given any assurance of this immunity and privilege which men of church, as they will be termed, do this day claim.

Yea, it was a thing unknown to the primitive church many years after the days of the Apostles. For Chrysostom, who served in the church at Constantinople four hundred years after Christ's ascension and after that corruption was greatly increased, doth yet thus write upon the foresaid words of the Apostle: "This precept," saith he, "doth not appertain to such as be called seculars only but even to those that be priests and religious men." And after he addeth: "Whether thou be Apostle, Evangelist, Prophet, or whosoever thou be thou canst not be exempted from this subjection." [49] Hereof it is plain that Chrysostom did not understand that God had exempted any person from obedience and subjection of the civil power, neither yet that he was author of such exemption and privilege, as papists do

46. 1 Tim. 3.   47. Matt. 17; Acts 4, 5; 1 Pet. 2:13, 14.
48. Rom. 13:1.
49. Chrysostom *The Epistle to the Romans* 23.

this day claim. And the same was the judgment and uniform doctrine of the primitive church many years after Christ.

Your honors do wonder, I doubt not, from what fountain then did this their immunity, as they term it, and singular privilege spring. I shall shortly touch that which is evident in their own laws and histories. When the Bishops of Rome, the very Antichrists, had, partly by fraud and partly by violence, usurped the superiority of some places in Italy, and most injustly had spoiled the emperors of their rents and possessions, and had also murdered some of their officers—as histories do witness, then began pope after pope to practice and devise how they should be exempted from judgment of princes and from equity of laws. And in this point they were most vigilant, till at length iniquity did so prevail in their hands, according as Daniel had before prophesied of them, that this sentence was pronounced: "Neither by the emperor, neither by the clergy, neither yet by the people shall the judge be judged." "God will," saith Symmachus, "that the causes of others be determined by men, but without all question he hath reserved the bishop of this seat" (understanding Rome) "to his own judgment." [50] And hereof divers popes and expositors of their laws would seem to give reasons, for, saith Agatho, "all the precepts of the apostolic seat are assured as by the voice of God himself." [51] The author of the gloss upon their canon affirmeth that if all the world should pronounce sentence against the pope, yet should his sentence prevail, for, saith he: "The pope hath a heavenly will, and therefore he may change the nature of things; he may apply the substance of one thing to another, and of nothing he may make somewhat; and that sentence which was nothing, that is, by his mind false and injust, he may make somewhat that is true and just." "For," saith he, "in all things that please him his will is for reason. Neither is there any man that may ask of him, why dost thou so. For he may dispense above the law, and of injustice he may make justice. For he hath the fullness of all power." [52] And many other most blasphemous sentences did they pronounce every one after other, which for shortness sake I omit, till at the end they obtained this most horrible decree: that albeit in life and conversation they were so wicked and detestable that not only they condemned themselves but that also they drew to hell and perdition many thousands with them, yet that none should presume to reprehend or rebuke them. [53]

This being established for the head (albeit not without some contradiction, for some emperors did require due obedience of them, as God's word

50. *Decretum Gratiani*, quaest. iii, dist. 9.
51. *Decretum Gratiani*, dist. 19.
52. *Decretum Gratiani*, Liber 2, 7, (*de translatione episcopi*) 2.
53. *Decretum Gratiani*, dist. 40.

commanded and ancient bishops had given before to emperors and to their laws; but Satan so prevailed in his suit before the blind world that the former sentences were confirmed, which power being granted to the head), then began provision to be made for the rest of the members in all realms and countries where they made residence. The fruit whereof we see to be this: that none of that pestilent generation—I mean the vermin of the papistical order—will be subject to any civil magistrate how enormous that ever his crime be, but will be reserved to their own ordinary, as they term it.

And what fruits have hereof ensued, be the world never so blind, it cannot but witness. For how their head, that Roman Antichrist, hath been occupied ever since the granting of such privileges histories do witness, and of late the most part of Europa, subject to the plague of God, to fire and sword by his procurement, hath felt and this day doth feel. The pride, ambition, envy, excess, fraud, spoil, oppression, murder, filthy life, and incest that is used and maintained among that rabble of priests, friars, monks, canons, bishops, and cardinals cannot be expressed. I fear not to affirm, neither doubt I to prove, that the papistical church is further degenerate from the purity of Christ's doctrine, from the footsteps of the Apostles, and from the manners of the primitive church than was the church of the Jews from God's holy statutes what time it did crucify Christ Jesus, the only Messiah, and most cruelly persecute his Apostles.

And yet will our papists claim their privileges and ancient liberties, which, if you grant unto them, my lords, ye shall assuredly drink the cup of God's vengeance with them and shall be reputed before his presence companions of thieves and maintainers of murderers, as is before declared. For their immunity and privilege, whereof so greatly they boast, is nothing else but as if thieves, murderers, or brigands should conspire amongst themselves that they would never answer in judgment before any lawful magistrate to the end that their theft and murder should not be punished; even such, I say, is their wicked privilege which neither they have of God the father, neither of Christ Jesus who hath revealed his father's will to the world, neither yet of the Apostles, nor primitive church, as before is declared. But it is a thing conspired amongst themselves to the end that their iniquity, detestable life, and tyranny shall neither be repressed nor reformed.

And if they object that godly emperors did grant and confirm the same, I answer that the godliness of no man is or can be of sufficient authority to justify a foolish and ungodly fact—such, I mean, as God hath not allowed by his word. For Abraham was a godly man, but the denial of his wife was such a fact as no godly man ought to imitate. The same I might shew of David, Hezekiah, and Josiah, unto whom I think no man of judgment will prefer any emperor since Christ in holiness and wisdom; and yet are not all their facts, not even such as they appeared to have done for good causes, to be approved nor followed. And therefore, I say, as error and ignorance remain always with the most perfect man in his life, so must their works be examined by another rule than by their own holiness, if they shall be approved.

But if this answer doth not suffice, then will I answer more shortly that no godly emperor since Christ's ascension hath granted any such privilege to any such church or person as they—the whole generation of papists—be at this day. I am not ignorant that some emperors of a certain zeal and for some considerations granted liberties to the true church afflicted, for their maintenance against tyrants. But what serveth this for the defense of their tyranny? If the law must be understanded according to the mind of the lawgiver, then must they first prove themselves Christ's true and afflicted church before they can claim any privilege to appertain to them. For only to that church were the privileges granted. It will not be their glorious titles, neither yet the long possession of the name that can prevail in this so weighty a cause. For all those had the church of Jerusalem which did crucify Christ and did condemn his doctrine.

We offer to prove by their fruits and tyranny, by the Prophets, and plain Scriptures of God what trees and generation they be, to wit, unfruitful and rotten, apt for nothing but to be cut and cast in hell fire, yea, that they are the very kingdom of Antichrist, of whom we are commanded to be beware. And therefore, my lords, to return to you, seeing that God hath armed your hands with the sword of justice, seeing that his law most straitly commandeth idolaters and false prophets to be punished with death, and that you be placed above your subjects to reign as fathers over their children, and further seeing that not only I but with me many thousand famous, godly, and learned persons accuse your bishops and the whole rabble of the papistical clergy of idolatry, of murder, and of blasphemy against God committed, it appertaineth to your honors to be vigilant and careful in so weighty a matter. The question is not of earthly substance but of the glory of God and of the salvation of yourselves and of your brethren subject to your charge, in which, if you after this plain admonition be negligent, there resteth no excuse by reason of ignorance. For in the name of God I require of you that the cause of religion may be tried in your presence by the plain and simple word of God, that your bishops be compelled to desist from their tyranny, that they be compelled to make answer for the neglecting of their office, for the substance of the poor—which unjustly they usurp and prodigally they do spend, but principally for the false and deceivable doctrine which is taught and defended by their false prophets, flattering friars, and other such venomous locusts. Which thing, if with single eyes ye do—preferring God's glory and the salvation of your brethren to all worldly commodity, then shall the same God, who solemnly doth pronounce to honor those that do honor him, pour his benediction plentifully upon you; he shall be your buckler, protection, and captain, and shall repress by his strength and wisdom whatsoever Satan by his supposts shall imagine against you.

I am not ignorant that great troubles shall ensue your enterprise. For Satan will not be expelled from the possession of his usurped kingdom without resistance. But if you, as is said, preferring God's glory to your own lives, unfeignedly seek and study to obey his blessed will, then shall your deliverance be such, as evidently it shall be known, that the angels of the eternal do watch, make war, and fight for those that unfeignedly fear the Lord. But if you refuse this, my most reasonable and just petition, what defense that ever you appear to have before men, then shall God, whom in me you contemn, refuse you. He shall pour forth contempt upon you and upon your posterity after you.[54] The spirit of boldness and wisdom shall be taken from you; your enemies shall reign, and you shall die in bondage; yea, God shall cut down the unfruitful trees when they do appear most beautifully to flourish and shall so burn the root that after of you shall neither twig nor branch again spring to glory.[55]

Hereof I need not to adduce unto you examples from the former ages and ancient histories. For your brethren, the nobility of England, are a mirror and glass in the which ye may behold God's just punishment. For as they have refused him and his Evangel, which once in mouth they did profess, so hath he refused them and hath taken from them the spirit of wisdom, boldness, and of counsel. They see and feel their own misery, and yet they have no grace to avoid it. They hate the bondage of strangers, the pride of priests, and the monstriferous empire of a wicked woman, and yet are they compelled to bow their necks to the yoke of the devil, to obey whatsoever the proud Spaniards and wicked Jezebel list to command, and finally to stand with cap in hand till the servants of Satan, the shaven sort, call them to council. This fruit do they reap and gather of their former rebellion and unfaithfulness towards God. They are left confused in their own counsels. He, whom in his members for the pleasure of a wicked woman they have exiled, persecuted, and blasphemed, doth now laugh them to scorn, suffereth them to be penned in bondage of most wicked men, and finally shall adjudge them to the fire everlasting, except that speedily and openly they repent their horrible treason which against God, against his son Christ Jesus, and against the liberty of their own native realm they have committed.

The same plague shall fall upon you, be you assured, if ye refuse the defense of his servants that call for your support. My words are sharp; but consider, my lords, that they are not mine, but that they are the threaten-

54. Deut. 28; Lev. 26.   55. Isa. 27, 30.

ings of the Omnipotent, who assuredly will perform the voices of his prophets how that ever carnal men despise his admonitions. The sword of God's wrath is already drawn which, of necessity, must needs strike when grace offered is obstinately refused.[56]

You have been long in bondage of the devil; blindness, error, and idolatry prevailing against the simple truth of God in that your realm in which God hath made you princes and rulers. But now doth God of his great mercy call you to repentance before he pour forth the uttermost of his vengeance; he crieth to your ears that your religion is nothing but idolatry; he accuseth you of the blood of his saints, which hath been shed by your permission, assistance, and powers. For the tyranny of those raging beasts should have no force, if by your strength they were not maintained. Of those horrible crimes doth now God accuse you, not of purpose to condemn you, but mercifully to absolve and pardon you, as sometime he did those whom Peter accused to have killed the son of God, so that ye be not of mind nor purpose to justify your former iniquity.[57]

Iniquity I call not only the crimes and offenses which have been and yet remain in your manners and lives; but that also which appeareth before men most holy, with hazard of my life, I offer to prove abomination before God, that is, your whole religion to be so corrupt and vain that no true servant of God can communicate with it, because that in so doing, he should manifestly deny Christ Jesus and his eternal verity. I know that your bishops, accompanied with the swarm of the papistical vermin, shall cry, "a damned heretic ought not to be heard." But remember, my lords, what in the beginning I have protested, upon which ground I continually stand, to wit, that I am no heretic nor deceivable teacher, but the servant of Christ Jesus, a preacher of his infallible verity, innocent in all that they can lay to my charge concerning my doctrine, and that therefore by them, being enemies to Christ, I am injustly damned.

From which cruel sentence I have appealed and do appeal, as before mention is made; in the meantime most humbly requiring your honors to take me in your protection, to be auditors of my just defenses, granting unto me the same liberty which Ahab, a wicked King, and Israel, at that a blinded people, granted to Elijah in the like case, that is, that your bishops and the whole rabble of your clergy may be called before you and before the people whom they have deceived, that I be not condemned by multitude, by custom, by authority or law devised by man, but that God himself may be judge betwixt me and my adversaries.[58] Let God, I say, speak by his law, by his Prophets, by Christ Jesus or by his Apostles, and so let him

56. Let England and Scotland both advert.
57. Acts 2.   58. 1 Kings 18.

pronounce what religion he approveth; and then, be my enemies never so many and appear they never so strong and so learned, no more do I fear victory than did Elijah, being but one man against the multitude of Baal's priests.

And if they think to have advantage by their councils and doctors, this I further offer: to admit the one and the other as witnesses in all matters debatable, three things—which justly cannot be denied—being granted unto me. First, that the most ancient councils, nighest to the primitive church, in which the learned and godly fathers did examine all matters by God's word, may be holden of most authority. Secondarily, that no determination of council nor man be admitted against the plain verity of God's word nor against the determination of those four chief councils whose authority hath been and is holden by them equal with the authority of the four Evangelists. And last, that no doctor be given greater authority than Augustine requireth to be given to his writings, to wit, if he plainly prove not his affirmation by God's infallible word, that then his sentence be rejected and imputed to the error of man.[59] These things granted and admitted, I shall no more refuse the testimonies of councils and doctors than shall my adversaries. But and if they will justify those councils which maintain their pride and usurped authority and will reject those which plainly have condemned all such tyranny, negligence, and wicked life, as bishops now do use, and if further they will snatch a doubtful sentence of a doctor and refuse his mind when he speaketh plainly, then will I say that all man is a liar, that credit ought not to be given to an unconstant witness, and that no council ought to prevail nor be admitted against the sentence which God hath pronounced.

And thus, my lords, in few words to conclude: I have offered unto you what God requireth of you, being placed above his people as rulers and princes; I have offered unto you and to the inhabitants of the realms the verity of Christ Jesus; and with the hazard of my life I presently offer to prove the religion which amongst you is maintained by fire and sword to be false, damnable, and diabolical. Which things if ye refuse, defending tyrants in their tyranny, then dare I not flatter; but as it was commanded to Ezekiel boldly to proclaim, so must I cry to you that "you shall perish in your iniquity," that the Lord Jesus shall refuse so many of you as maliciously withstand his eternal verity, and in the days of his apparition, when all flesh shall appear before him, that he shall repel you from his company and shall command you to the fire which never shall be quenched; and then neither shall the multitude be able to resist neither yet the counsels of man be able to prevail against that sentence which he shall pronounce.[60]

God, the father of our Lord Jesus Christ, by the power of his Holy

59. Augustine *Retractions*, Prologue.   60. Ezek. 33; Dan. 12; Matt. 24, 25, 26.

Spirit, so rule and dispose your hearts that with simplicity ye may consider the things that be offered, and that ye may take such order in the same as God in you may be glorified and Christ's flock by you may be edified and comforted to the praise and glory of our Lord Jesus Christ, whose omnipotent spirit rule your hearts in his true fear to the end. Amen.

5. Philippe Duplessis-Mornay, *Vindiciae contra Tyrannos*

The *Vindiciae contra Tyrannos* is the most important statement of political doctrine to come out of the series of disturbances in France usually called the Wars of Religion, which extended from the 1560s to the 1590s. "Vindiciae" was originally a Roman law term meaning the statement of a claim, but its use spread to some other legal contexts. The title adopted in the late seventeenth century by the first English translator—*A Defense of Liberty against Tyrants*—is close enough.

The *Vindiciae* was written in 1579, in the heat of a struggle that pitted Protestant against Catholic, while conflict among aristocratic factions and localistic interests intensified religious differences. The almost-certain author was Philippe Duplessis-Mornay (1549–1623), a Protestant nobleman who was both a major activist and a prolific writer on politics and religion. His career was essentially in the service of fellow-Protestant Henry of Navarre, dynastically connected with the French royal house and, in 1589, successor to the throne as Henry IV—the first of the Bourbon kings. This apparent success for the Protestants was undercut by Henry's politically-motivated acceptance of Catholicism. Although the extension of toleration to Protestants followed the king's conversion, Duplessis-Mornay lost his influence in high affairs: he was a committed stalwart not only of the French Protestant party, but of Protestantism as an international cause—which it was in a very self-conscious way. In his youth he wrote in support of the Dutch rebellion against Spanish domination, a struggle both Protestant and nationalistic; and he had connections with the Protestant elites of Germany and England. The *Vindiciae,* however, is not a narrow expression of a partisan religious interest and a religious mentality; it rises to general principles of political obligation. The French Protestant (or Huguenot—a name of obscure origin) tradition descended primarily from John Calvin, and the *Vindiciae* belongs in a

From Philippe Mornay du Plessis, *Vindiciae Contra Tyrannos* (n.p., 1589), pp. A2, 15–16, 18–20, 23–26, 29–32, 35–36, 39–40, 43–44, 46–48, 50–51, 55–60, 62–64, 72–77, 79–81, 83, 87–90, 93–96, 99–108, 110–13, 116–17, 121, 124, 134, 136–40, 143–44, 148–49, 153, 156–62, 166–67, 177–79, 181, 184–85, 187, 189–96, 198–99, 201–2, 206–11, 219–21, 225–26. Translated for this volume by Constantin Fasolt.

line of reflection and polemic on political duty that started with Calvin himself.

An accepted and thriving minority through much of the seventeenth century, the Huguenots were nearly reduced to extinction in France when Louis XIV reversed the policy of toleration and drove large numbers of them into exile, mostly in Holland and England. A remnant survived to see the return of toleration at the time of the Revolution, and the Reformed Church and Frenchmen of Protestant heritage remain a significant element in the pluralistic culture of modern France.

Edict of Emperor Theodosius and Caesar Valentinianus to the Pretorian Prefect Volusianus: It is a maxim worthy of the ruler's majesty for the prince to declare that he is bound by the laws, for our authority depends upon the authority of the law. Indeed, to subject the principate to the laws is a greater thing than empire itself. By the present edict, therefore, we shall indicate to others what we do not suffer to be permitted to ourselves. Given in Ravenna on the third day before the Ides of June during the consulship of Florentius and Dionysius.

Iustinus in book two of *Lycurgus the Legislator:* Since the Spartans had no laws, he instituted laws for them, distinguished not so much by his ability to invent laws as by his exemplary conduct. For he imposed no law upon others to which he had not first subjected himself. Thus he confirmed the people's obedience to the princes and tied the princes' empire to justice.

First Question: Must Subjects Obey Princes Who Issue Orders Counter to the Law of God?

At first sight this question might appear to waste our time to no purpose because it seems to call the most evident axiom of Christianity into doubt as if it were still controversial, although it has been corroborated by so many testimonies of sacred Scripture, so many examples accumulated over the centuries, and the pyres of so many pious martyrs. What other reason, it might be asked, could explain the willingness of the pious to undergo such extraordinary suffering if not their conviction that God is to be obeyed simply and absolutely, kings, however, only so long as they do not issue orders counter to the law of God? How else are we to understand the apostolic precept to obey God rather than men? And since God's will alone is always just, whereas the will of anybody else can be unjust at any time, who could doubt that only the former is to be obeyed without exception, but the latter always with reservations?

There are, however, many princes nowadays who boast the name of Christ, yet dare to arrogate an immense power that most assuredly does not depend from God. There are also many adulators who worship them as gods on earth, and many others seized by fear, or else coerced by force, who either really believe that obedience is never to be denied to princes or at least wish to seem to believe it. The vice of our times indeed appears to be that nothing is so firm as that it could not be uprooted, nothing so certain that it could not be disputed, and nothing so sacred that it could not be violated. Therefore I am afraid that anyone carefully weighing the matter will consider this question to be not only far from useless, but even absolutely necessary, especially in our century. . . .

The question then is whether subjects are obliged to obey kings whose orders are in conflict with the law of God. Who of the two, in other words, is rather to be obeyed, God or the king? If an answer can be given for the king, whose power is deemed the greatest of all, the same answer will apply to other magistrates.

First of all, sacred letters teach us that God rules by his own authority, kings, however, by a borrowed power, as it were; that God rules through himself, but kings through God; that God applies his own jurisdiction, but kings merely delegated jurisdiction. Hence it follows in the books of *Wisdom* 6, *Proverbs* 8, *Job* 12 and elsewhere that God's jurisdiction is unmeasured, that of kings measured; God's power infinite, that of kings finite; God's realm surrounded by no limits, that of kings, on the other hand, limited to fixed regions and terminated by borders. Furthermore God created heaven and earth out of nothing. Therefore he is the rightful lord of heaven and earth and their true owner. Whoever inhabits the earth, on the other hand, is only like a tenant or lessee, and whoever has the right to say the law on earth, or is set above others for some other reason, is only God's beneficiary and client, obliged to let himself be invested by God and to acknowledge him as his lord. God is sole owner and lord, whereas human beings of whatever rank are merely tenants, stewards, ministers, and vassals. The richer their income, the more dues they owe, the greater their authority, the more strictly are they obliged to render account, and the brighter their honors, the heavier the burdens placed upon their shoulders. . . .

Kings, therefore, are vassals of the king of kings, invested with the sword denoting royal power in order that they use that sword for the defense of divine law, the protection of the good, and the destruction of the bad, in no other way than vassals invested with a fief by a higher lord obtain sword, shield and flag under the obligation to use their arms for the defense of the fief whenever necessary. In order for us to define kings as vassals, whatever applies to vassals must also apply to kings, and especially so. The vassal receives his fief from a superior lord together with the right to say justice and the duty to serve with arms. The king receives his kingdom from God in order to judge his people and defend them against enemies. The vassal receives his law and condition from a superior lord, the king from God, who commands him to observe his law always and keep it before his eyes. If he does so, he and his offspring will possess their realm for a long time, but if not, they will experience the opposite. The vassal pledges himself to a superior lord by an oath and promises faith and obedience. The king similarly swears to govern according to the prescriptions of divine law. Finally, unless the vassal keeps his oath, he forfeits his fief and deprives himself of any right to his prerogatives. And if the king neglects God, goes over to his enemies, or commits a felony against God, he forfeits all rights to his kingdom, and usually he loses it in fact as well.

These matters clearly follow from the covenant that is regularly concluded between God and king (since God condescends to treat those who are actually his slaves as his partners in a covenant). We read of two covenants concluded at the inauguration of kings, however, the first between God, king and people, requiring the people to be God's people, and the second between king and people, requiring the people to obey a good ruler. We shall consider the second one later on. Now we need to deal with the first.

The Covenant between God and Kings

We read that at the inauguration of Joash a covenant was concluded between God, the king, and the people or, as is said elsewhere, between the high priest Jehoiada, the entire people, and the king, so that they would be a people of God. Likewise we read that Josiah and the entire people entered into a covenant with God. We learn that in making this covenant the high priest asked the king and the people in the name of God whether they would take care to worship God in the Jewish kingdom in purity and according to the proper rites; whether the king would rule in such a way as to let the people serve God and keep them within the law of God; and finally whether the people would obey the king in such a way as nonetheless to obey God above all. The king and the people acknowledged their liability for that promise by swearing to keep the law of God and by binding themselves with a solemn oath to worship God above all. Hence, as soon as that covenant was established, Josiah and Joash destroyed the idolatry of Baal and restored the worship of God. The main chapters of this covenant were that the king and the people would individually worship God according to the prescriptions of his law and that they would protect his worship collectively. If they were to do so, God would be in their midst and preside over their commonwealth. But if not, he would abandon and ruin them. . . .

If a king, therefore, assaults the law of God and goes over from God to his enemies, to the gods of the heathens, I say, this is frequently and fittingly a reason why he is deprived of the fief he accepted from God. Since equal punishments fit equal crimes, we read in Holy Scripture that all the kings of Israel and Judah who committed such acts suffered a similarly extreme end. Now although the form of both the Jewish church and the Jewish kingdom limited to Judah through the entire world, the same can nevertheless be said about Christian kings. The Gospel succeeded to the law and Christian kings have taken the place of Jewish ones, but the pact and the conditions are the same, as are the penalties when the conditions are not fulfilled, and omnipotent God remains the judge of perfidy. Just as Jewish kings are held to observe the law, so are Christian kings held to observe the Gospel, which each of them promises at his inauguration to propagate above all other things. . . .

But what shall we say about heathen kings? Although their exterior is not anointed by God, they doubtless are his vassals and have received their power from him alone, whether they are chosen by lot or in some other manner. If by vote, because God rules the hearts of men and directs them where he wills. If by lot, because a lot is thrown in the midst, as Solomon says, and its decision stems from God. It is always he who raises, establishes, confirms and overturns kings according to his discretion. For this reason Isaiah calls Cyrus the anointed of the lord, and Daniel says that Nebuchadnezzar and the rest received their power from God, as Paul also says of all magistrates in general. For although God did not commend his law as explicitly to heathen kings as to others, they nevertheless acknowledge that they owe their rule to God as the supreme king. Hence, if they do not take care to pay tribute to God on that account, or at least do not try to collect and render to God what is owed to him by their subjects, or if they arrogate divine jurisdiction in any other way, they are usurping the kingdom, a crime for which God has wreaked severe vengeance upon heathen kings. . . .

In short, we see that kings are invested with their kingdoms by God in almost the same manner in which vassals are invested with their fiefs by their superior lords, and that they are deprived of their benefices for the same reasons. Therefore we must on all counts conclude that the former are in an almost identical place as the latter and that all kings are vassals of God. Having said this, our question is easily finished. For if God occupies the place of a superior lord, and the king that of a vassal, who will not declare that one should rather obey the lord than the vassal? If God commands this, and the king the other, who will consider someone refusing to obey the king as a rebel? Who will not on the contrary condemn it as rebellion if he fails to obey God promptly or if he obeys the king instead?

And finally, if the king calls us to this choice and God to that, who will not declare that we must desert the king in order to fight for God? Thus we are not only not obliged to obey a king who orders something against the law of God, but we even commit rebellion if we do obey him, in no other way than a landholder does who fights for a senior vassal against the king, or who prefers to obey the edict of the inferior rather than the superior, of the vicar rather than the prince, and of the minister rather than the king. . . .

We do not even lack an explicitly formulated law for this. Whenever the apostles admonish Christians to obey kings and magistrates, they always, as though on purpose, admonish them first to obey God above of everything else. You will never find more than superficial grounds for that preposterous kind of obedience which the adulators of princes urge upon the simpleminded. "Let every soul," says Paul, "be subject to the higher powers, for there is no power but of God." He says "every soul" in order to shut out all exceptions. These words alone are enough to conclude that one ought to obey God rather than the king. If one ought to obey the king because of God, then one should certainly not obey him against God. But because Paul wishes to remove all ambiguity, he adds that the prince is a minister of God, set up for our good in order to establish justice. The conclusion is still the same: one should obey the lord rather than the minister. Paul, however, thinks this is still not enough. Render, he says in the end, tribute to whom tribute is due, honor to whom honor is due, and fear to whom fear is due, as if he were repeating Christ's saying: render unto Caesar what is Caesar's, unto God what is God's. . . .

Second Question: Is it Permitted to Resist a Prince Who Violates the Law of God and Devastates His Church? Who May Resist, in What Manner, and to What Extent?

At first sight this question appears to be so much the more arduous as it is superfluous under pious princes and dangerous under impious ones. One can hardly touch it without impudence. Nevertheless there really is a question whether it is permissible to resist a prince who invalidates the law of God, destroys the church, or impedes its establishment. Holy Scripture, provided we accept its judgment, will give us the answer. For if, as can easily be proved with its help, resistance is not only permitted, but even enjoined upon the Jewish people as a whole, no one, I think, will deny that the same must plainly apply to the Christian people of any kingdom as a whole. . . .

The Covenant between God and the People

We have said that two covenants were entered into at the inauguration of the king, of which the first was between God, the king, and the people or alternatively between the high priest, the people, and the king (in 2 Chronicles the people are mentioned before the king). Its purpose was that the people should be God's people, that is, that they should be God's church. We have already shown the meaning of the covenant between God and the king. We still need to examine the meaning of the covenant between God and the people.

If anything is certain, then it is that God did not conclude this covenant in vain. But obviously it would have been superfluous unless the people retained some authority both to make and to fulfill their promise. God thus seems to have done what creditors are used to do with borrowers of doubtful reputation, which is to obligate several of them at the same time, so that two or more debtors assume liability for a single loan and each of them can be held responsible for the entire sum as though he were the principal debtor. To entrust the entire church to the weakness of a single human being would have been risky. This is the reason why God entrusted it to the entire people. The king, raised to a slippery height, could easily have lapsed into impiety. Lest the entire church should collapse, God wished the people to intervene.

In the engagement under consideration, God, or in his stead the high priest, thus stipulate the condition. The king and the entire people, that is, Israel, on the other hand, promise to keep it, both of them of their own free will, both of them obligated for one and the same thing. The priest requires the people to promise that they will be God's people and make every effort for God to have his temple and his church forever in their midst where he can be worshiped according to the proper rite. The king gives his promise, Israel gives its promise, with the entire people acting as a single person, and they do so together, not separately, simultaneously, not one after the other, as appears from the wording of the covenant itself. Both of them, the king and Israel, thus assume liability and they are equally obligated for the whole promise. And just as Caius and Titius are each legally bound to pay the entire sum if they conjointly contracted for the same amount of money with Seius, and just as the entire sum can be collected from either one of them, so the king and Israel are each bound to protect the church from any harm. If either one of them is negligent, God may collect the whole from either. Indeed he may collect it from the people so much the more than from the king as many people are less likely to fall and more able to pay than one. . . .

Now how can consent possibly be requested from the entire people, how can Israel and Judah be held responsible for observing divine law, and how can they swear to be God's people always, unless an appropriate authority or faculty is also granted them with which to save themselves from perjury and the church from devastation? What could be the purpose of a covenant with the people to be God's people if they permit, are even obliged to per-

mit their kings to lead them to the worship of strange gods? Why a covenant to worship God in purity if the people are in the condition of a slave,
with whom no contract is possible? If, finally, the people are not allowed
an effort to fulfill what they promised, would God have entered into a covenant with them although they have the right neither to give nor to fulfill
their promise? Or is it not rather the case that when he confirmed his covenant with the people and placed that condition upon them, he evidently
wished to show that they had the right to give the promise, fulfill it, and
take the measures necessary in order to do so? If we ridicule a man who
makes a contract with a slave or a household member because he cannot
enforce his claims against them in court, would we not be impudent to attribute something like that to God? . . .

If the king overturns the law of God or the church, therefore, Israel is
permitted to resist him. Not only that, but it will even be guilty of the same
crime as the king and pay the same penalty unless it does resist him. If it is
attacked with words, it shall resist with words; if with force, with force;
and if with fraud, I say, with craft, war, and even counter-fraud, for if the
war is just, it makes no difference whether you fight in the open or with
deception, provided that wiliness is always carefully distinguished from
perfidy, which is never permissible.

I can already see the objection that will here be raised. What, it will be
asked: Is it really necessary that that entire multitude, that enormous monster with innumerable heads must be raised in tumult and run together as if
to form an army? What kind of order can there be in such a crowd? What
sort of counsel or well-planned action? When we speak of the people as a
whole, however, we only mean those who have received authority from the
people, that is, the magistrates inferior to the king but elected by the
people or constituted in some other way as partners in government and
overseers of the king. They represent the assembly of the entire people. We
also mean the assemblies of the estates, which are nothing other than the
kingdom in abbreviation, so to speak, to which all public business is
referred.

Of that kind were the seventy elders in the kingdom of Israel who judged
all the most important issues under the presidency of the high priest, as it
were. Originally they were elected six at a time from the seventy families
that had gone down to Egypt. Then there were the dukes or princes of the
tribes, one of each. There were also the judges and prefects of the several
towns, that is, the captains of the thousands, the captains of the hundreds
and as many other officials as there were families to be represented. And
finally there were the nobles, the men with purple robes, and all the rest
who made up the public council. This council, we read, was frequently
opened with words like "the elders were assembled at Raman," as at the

election of Saul, "all of Israel was assembled," and "all of Judah" or "all of Benjamin," and so on, when it is hardly likely that the entire multitude assembled.

In every well established kingdom there are similar officers of the kingdom, princes, peers, patricians, nobles and others delegated by the estates. They meet in ordinary or extraordinary assemblies, parlements, diets and all those other meetings whose names differ from region to region, where provision is made that the commonwealth and the church suffer no harm. Now although they are below the king individually, collectively they are superior. The councils of Basel and Constance rightly declared an ecumenical synod to be superior to the pope, and a cathedral chapter is superior to a bishop, a corporate body above its representative, and a court above its president. Conversely someone who has received his authority from an assembly is below that assembly, although above its individual members. There can be no doubt at all, therefore, that Israel, which requested and constituted the king as a public representative, is superior to Saul, who had been requested by Israel and who was constituted for its sake, as we shall show later on.

Order is necessary if matters are to be well-governed, but no order can be maintained by too great a multitude. On the contrary there often are issues that cannot be divulged to the multitude without the risk of endangering the common good. Whatever we said to have been conceded and entrusted to the entire people, we therefore mean to be conceded and entrusted to the officers of the kingdom, not to Israel, but to the princes and elders of Israel, a usage that is confirmed by custom.

In sum, as it is permitted to the entire people to fight back, so also is it permitted to the princes of the kingdom, who represent the people, in no other way than municipal officers are entitled to make contracts for the common good. And just as actions publicly taken by a majority are considered to have been taken by the collectivity, so actions taken by a majority of princes or nobles are considered to have been taken by all of them together, and what all of them have done is in turn considered to have been done by the entire people.

May a Part of the Kingdom Resist?

Here we are confronted with another question. Let us assume that a king abolishes the law of God and the church, that the people as a whole or at least their majority are giving their consent to this, and that all or most of the princes are going along, while only a small part of the people or just one of the princes and magistrates wish to retain the law of God and worship God according to the rite. What, do you think, may be done when the king wishes to force that small part to perform impious rites or prevents them from performing pious ones? Here we are not speaking of individual or private persons, who are no more considered to be parts of the community strictly speaking than planks, nails, and pegs are the parts of a ship, or stones, beams, and mortar the parts of a house. We are rather speaking of a province or a town and the magistrate representing that province or town. They do constitute parts of the kingdom in the same way as prow, stern, and keel are said to constitute the parts of a ship, or roof, walls, and foundations of a house. . . .

We have already said that the king swore an oath to keep the law of God and promised to conserve the church as far as possible. Likewise that all of Israel, as though a single person, promised to keep God's conditions. Now we say that individual cities, too, in their function as parts of the kingdom, as well as their magistrates individually and expressly promised the same as far as it directly concerned themselves. It follows that all Christian cities and communities have tacitly done the same. . . . Hence not only the king, but the kingdom, not only the kingdom, but all of the kingdom's parts promised faith and obedience to God. Not only the king, I say, but Israel, not only Israel, but each of Israel's cities and their prefects subjected themselves to God by a sacred oath and, as if by liege homage, forever tied themselves to him against anyone else.

An example taken from contemporary customs will clarify the matter. When an emperor is to be inaugurated in the German empire, the electors and the princes ecclesiastical and temporal are present, either in person or by representative, as are the prelates, counts, barons and deputies of all imperial cities, equipped with a special mandate to submit themselves as well as those they represent to the emperor under certain conditions. Now if someone tries to depose the emperor in violation of his oath and grasps the empire for himself, while the princes and barons deny to Caesar the aid that is his due as well as the tributes he usually gets, not only failing to go along with him but even breaking their faith and collaborating with his adversary, do you not think that the people of Strasbourg or Nuremberg, for example, who have promised their faith to the emperor, have every right to keep that robber at a distance and to shut him out of their towns? If they fail to do so and do not aid the emperor in his distress, would you say that they kept the faith they pledged? Especially since he who does not protect a superior although he is able to do so must be considered just as guilty as the one who took the initiative? . . .

We must therefore state that the entire people, under the leadership of those who are equipped with the people's authority, may and must use force against a prince who orders impiety or prohibits piety. All of the inhabitants of the regions and cities, or at least the leading citizens, under the leadership of the most important magistrates, constituted first by God, as it were, then by the king, thus have the right to keep impious rites outside their walls and protect the pious ones within them. For there is only one church, and they may extend its confines. If they do not do so, although they could, they are guilty of violating the majesty of God.

May Private Individuals Resist with Arms?

It only remains to deal with private persons. First of all, individuals as such are not bound by the covenant that is established between God and the people as a whole, that they should be God's people. For just as what is owed to a community is not owed to individuals, so individuals do not owe what the community owes. Furthermore they have none of the duties of office. The obligation to serve God depends upon the position to which one has been called. Private individuals, however, have no power, perform no magistracy, have no dominion and no power of punishment. God did not give the sword to private persons and therefore does not require them to use it. To private persons it is said: "Put thy sword into its scabbard"; to magistrates, however: "You do not bear the sword in vain." The former are guilty if they draw the sword, the latter are guilty of grave negligence unless they draw it when necessary.

But, you may ask, is there no covenant between God and individuals at all, as there is between God and the community? No covenant with private persons as with magistrates? What could then be the purpose of circumcision and baptism? Why else is this sacred covenant mentioned over and over again in Scripture? Of course there is a covenant, but of a wholly different sort. For just as all the subjects of a just prince in general, of whatever rank they may be, are obliged to obey him, but only some of them have a special obligation, for example in the form of a magistracy, to take care that the others will be obedient, too, so all human beings in general are indeed obliged to serve God, but only some of them have taken on a greater burden along with their higher position so that, if they neglect their duty, they are responsible up to a point for the guilt of the rest. Kings, the community, and magistrates who have received the sword from the community must take care that the body of the church is governed according to the rite. Individuals, however, have no other function than to be members of that church. The former must pay heed that the temple of the lord is not polluted and does not collapse, but is safe from all internal corruption and external injury; the latter only that their body, which is the temple of God, is not impure, so that God's spirit can live in it. "Whosoever shall destroy God's temple, which you are," says Paul, "him shall God destroy." This is the reason why the former have been given a sword that can be fastened to their belts, whereas only the sword of the spirit has been entrusted to the latter, that is, the word of the lord with which Paul girds all Christians against the devil's attack.

What then shall private individuals do when the king urges impious rites upon them? If the nobles with authority from the entire people, or at least their own magistrates, oppose themselves to the king, they shall obey, follow, and assist the pious striving of the pious with all of their might as soldiers of God. As one example among many they may take the swift obedience of the officers and soldiers to the princes of Judah who acted at Jehoiada's urging to save the church from idolatry and the kingdom from queen Athaliah's tyranny. If the nobles and magistrates applaud a raging king, however, or if at least they fail to resist him, the advice of Christ should be taken to heart: they should withdraw to another city. For this they have the example of the faithful members of the ten tribes of Israel who withdrew to the king of Judah, where the worship of God had remained intact, while all the others consented to Jeroboam's abolition of the true worship of God. But if there is nowhere to escape to, they should rather forsake their lives than God, rather let themselves be crucified than, as the apostle says, crucify Christ once again. Do not, says our lord, fear those who can only kill the body, a lesson that has been taught to us by his own example as well as that of the apostles and innumerable pious martyrs.

Is no private person at all then permitted to resist with arms? But what about Moses, who led Israel out of Egypt against the will of Pharaoh? What about Ehud, who killed king Eglon of Moab and liberated Israel from the yoke of the Moabites after their rule had already lasted for eighteen years, when they might have seemed to acquire a right to the kingdom? And what about Jehu, who killed king Jehoram, for whom he himself had used to fight, who destroyed the line of Ahab and killed all the worshipers of Baal? Were they not private persons? As such you may of course consider them as private persons because they were not equipped with power in the normal way. But since we know them to have been called by extraordinary means, God himself, so to speak, evidently girding them with their swords, we may regard them not only as more than mere private persons, but also as placed above anyone equipped with power by ordinary means. The vocation of Moses is confirmed by an express word of God and by the most obvious signs. Ehud is explicitly said to have been incited by God to kill the tyrant and save Israel. And Jehu, anointed at the command of the prophet Elijah, was ordered to destroy the line of Ahab, although the leading people had greeted him as the king earlier on. The same can be shown for all others like them who can be adduced from Scripture.

But when God has spoken neither himself nor through prophets out of the ordinary, we must be especially sober and circumspect. If someone arrogates authority by reason of divine inspiration, he must find out whether he is not rather swelled up with arrogance, does not confuse God with himself, and creates his great spirits out of himself, lest he should conceive vanity and beget a lie. And the people, although they may be desiring to fight under the sign of Christ, must find out whether they are not perhaps fighting to their own great damage for some Theudas from Galilee or a Bar-Kochba, as happened not so long ago in Germany to the people of Münster. I do not say that the same God who is sending us Pharaohs and Ahabs in this century does not occasionally also inspire liberators in an extraordinary way. His justice and his mercy have certainly never waned. But when external signs are lacking, we must at least recognize the inner ones by their effects, a mind devoid of all ambition, true and fervid zeal, good conscience, and knowledge, too, lest someone misled by error should serve false gods or being driven mad by ambition should serve himself rather than the true God.

May Arms be Justly Taken up for the Sake of Religion?

In order to remove all remaining scruples, we should now give a general answer to those who believe that the church may not be defended by arms or, as is more likely, wish at least to seem to believe it. . . . But why would John then have prophesied that the ten kings under the spell of the whore of Babylon would take up arms to exterminate her in the end? What about the war of Constantine against Maxentius and Licinius that has been celebrated in so many songs and approved by the reasoning of so many learned men? And finally, what should we say about the campaigns of Christian princes against Turks and Saracens? All of these had, or ought to have had, but a single purpose, namely to prevent the finished temple of the lord from being destroyed and to protect its construction from strife. Although the church, therefore, is not really expanded by arms, it can nevertheless be justly defended with arms. The men who die in a sacred war are martyrs no less than those who suffer the cross for the sake of religion. Indeed, the former seem to be so much the more praiseworthy as they undergo death with knowledge and of their own accord, whereas the latter merely do not object to a death that is urged upon them by somebody else. . . .

The people as a whole and the officers of the kingdom who were constituted by the people, or a majority of these, or any one of them should therefore recognize that they are gravely sinning against their covenant with God unless they properly restrain someone who corrupts the law of God or prohibits its restoration; that the same penalty is inflicted upon residents of towns and provinces that constitute parts of the kingdom, however small they may be, unless they keep impieties that the king wishes to introduce away from their borders and retain pious doctrine by any means within their power, even if they have to secede for a while; and that private persons, finally, cannot at all be excused for obedience to impious orders, yet have no right to take up arms on their own authority either, unless they have clearly been called to such a function in an extraordinary way. And all of this is proved from Holy Scripture.

Third Question: Is it Permitted to Resist a Prince who Oppresses or Destroys the Commonwealth? To What Extent, by Whom, in What Fashion, and by What Right?

Kings are Created by the People

We have previously shown that it is God who sets up kings, gives them their kingdoms, and chooses them. Now we add that it is the people who constitute kings, deliver them their kingdoms, and approve their election by vote. God wanted it to be like that so that, next to himself, the kings would receive all of their authority and power from the people. That is why they should devote all of their care, thought, and energy to the good of the people, but should not deem themselves to have been raised above the rest by some natural preeminence, as men are raised above sheep and cattle. They should rather remember that they have been born to exactly the same lot as all other human beings and that they have been raised from the earth to their rank by the votes of the people, as if by shoulders on which the burdens of the commonwealth may later for the greater part fall back again. . . .

To be sure, God promised eternal light to his people from David's seed, and the hereditary succession of the kings of Israel was confirmed by God's word itself. But we also see that the kings did not begin to reign before they were solemnly established by the people. We may therefore conclude that the kingdom of Israel was hereditary only as far as the actual line of descent was concerned, but that it was elective as far as the people's choice of individual kings was concerned. . . .

In general, since no one is born as a king, can turn himself into a king, or is able to rule without a people, whereas the people can very well exist on their own before there are kings, all kings were obviously first created by the people. Although the sons and nephews of kings may seem to have turned their kingdoms into hereditary possessions by imitating their fathers' virtues, and although the power of free election seems to have vanished in certain regions, it thus remains the custom in all well-established kingdoms that children do not succeed to their fathers until they are constituted by the people, as if they had had no claims upon the throne at all. They are not born to their fathers as heirs of a family property, but are only considered kings as soon as those who represent the people's majesty have invested them with the kingdom through scepter and crown. Even in Christian kingdoms that are nowadays said to descend by hereditary succession there are obvious traces of this fact. In France, Spain, England, and other countries it thus is the custom that kings are inaugurated and put in possession of the kingdom, so to speak, by the estates of the realm, the peers, the patricians, and the magnates who represent the community of the people, just as the emperors of Germany are created by electors and the kings of Poland by the Wojewodowie, or members of the court, where the right of election has remained completely intact. . . .

In sum, all kings were elected in the beginning. Those who nowadays appear to obtain their kingdom by hereditary succession must first be established by the people. And although in certain regions the people are accustomed to choose their kings from a particular line with outstanding merits, they choose from the line as a whole and are not restricted to any of its branches, nor is their choice so restricted that, should the line degenerate, they could not choose another one. Even those most closely related to that line are not born as kings, but are made such. They are therefore not considered kings, but only candidates for kingship.

The People as a Whole is Ordinarily Represented by the Officers of the Kingdom and Extraordinarily or Annually by Assemblies of Estates

To continue, what we have said about the people as a whole should also apply to those who legitimately represent the people of the entire kingdom or one of its cities, as in the second question. They are commonly considered to be officers of the kingdom, not of the king. Officers of the king are created and removed at his discretion, and when he dies they lose their office. They are even considered to have suffered a kind of death themselves. Officers of the kingdom, on the other hand, receive, or at least used to receive, their authority from the people in a public assembly and they cannot be removed without the people's participation. The former therefore depend upon the king, the latter on the kingdom; the former on the highest officer of the kingdom, namely, the king himself, the latter on the supreme dominion of the people upon which the king himself along with his officers ought to depend. The duty of the former is to care for the king; of the latter, to protect the commonwealth from harm; of the former, to assist and serve the king as domestics serve their master; of the latter, to guard the rights and privileges of the people and to pay attention that the prince does nothing to ruin the people by commission or omission. The former are the king's ministers, slaves, and domestics, appointed only to obey. The latter, on the other hand, are like assessors participating in the king's jurisdiction or partners in the king's dominion. All of them are just as responsible for the administration of the kingdom as the king himself, although he is a kind of president who takes first place among them. As the people as a whole is superior to the king, so the officers of the kingdom must be considered superior to him, too, although they are inferior to him as individuals.

How limited the power of the earliest kings used to be can easily be inferred from the fact that Ephron, king of the Hittites, did not dare to grant Abraham the right of burial without consulting the people, and Hemor, the Hevite king of Sichem, to conclude a pact with Jacob, since important business used to be referred to the people. At the time this was an easy thing to do, for those empires were limited to little more than a single city. But when kings began to extend the borders of their kingdoms and the whole people could no longer meet in a single place without confusion, officers of the kingdom were appointed as ordinary guardians of the rights of the people, but on condition that an extraordinary assembly of the people as a whole, or at least a meeting of the people in abbreviation, so to speak, should be called whenever necessary.

The Officers of the Kingdom in Israel

This form of organization existed in the kingdom of Israel, the best established kingdom of all according to the judgment of virtually all political thinkers. The king had his cupbearers, butlers, chamberlains, stewards, and managers who took care of his family, and the kingdom had its own officers, the seventy-one elders, the dukes elected by the individual tribes, who cared for the commonwealth in times of peace as well as war, and the magistrates of each of the cities, each of whom guarded his city as the former guarded the entire kingdom. When it was necessary to deliberate on a really important matter, they met. Unless they had been consulted, nothing pertaining to the fate of the commonwealth could be decided. Thus David convoked them when he desired to invest Solomon with the kingdom, when his reform of the constitution was to be examined and approved, when the Ark was to be returned, and so on. And since they represented the people as a whole, the entire people were said to have been assembled. . . .

But what shall we say about kingdoms that are said to devolve by hereditary succession? Their condition is in no way different. The kingdom of France, which not so long ago used to be preferred to all the others because of the excellence of its laws and estates, was once constituted in this way. And even though the men in these positions may not in fact be exercising their office as they ought, they are nevertheless still obliged to do so. The king has his own grand steward, his chamberlains, masters of the hunt, shieldbearers, cupbearers, and the rest, whose offices once used to depend so exclusively upon him, that they lost them as soon as he died. This is why even now, when mourning for the king is over, the custom is for the grand steward to dismiss the royal household ceremoniously and ask them to look after themselves. In the same fashion the French kingdom has officers of its own, the mayor of the palace, who was later called the constable, marshals, admirals, the chancellor or grand referee, secretaries, examiners and the rest, who used to be appointed only by the public assembly of the three estates, that is, the clergy, the nobility, and the people. Ever since parlement has settled down in Paris, however, they are considered to have entered their offices when they have been accepted and approved by the Senate of Paris, and they cannot be deposed without its consent and authorization. Now all of these first promise to be faithful to the kingdom, that is, the people as a whole, then to the king as its guardian, as is obvious from the wording of their oath. And the constable above all promises to guard and defend the commonwealth, as is apparent from the words pronounced by the king when he girds the chancellor with the sword of fleur-de-lis.

The French kingdom also has its peers, meaning partners of the king, or patricians, meaning fathers of the commonwealth, who are individually nominated by the several provinces of the kingdom and to whom, as representatives of the entire kingdom, the king customarily promises his faith at his inauguration. Hence they are clearly superior to the king. They in turn swear an oath to protect, not the king, but the crown, and to participate in the holy princely council in times of peace and war in order to assist the commonwealth with advice, as is manifest from the oath of the patricians. Just like the peers of the court in Lombard law not only used to assist a feudal lord in sentencing others, but often decided suits between himself and his vassals as well, these patricians of France have often decided suits between the king and his subjects. This is why they opposed Charles VI when he wanted to sentence the Duke of Brittany, and stated that such a judgment was not the king's business, but the peers', whose authority he could not evade. To a certain extent the Senate of Paris, which is called the court of peers or patricians, functions as a judge between the king and the people, indeed, between the king and any private individual. Hence even nowadays it is obliged to represent individuals against the royal procurator whenever the king invades their rights. Furthermore, when the king issues a statute or edict at home, when he makes peace with neighboring princes, and when matters of war or peace are to be decided upon, as happened recently with Charles V, the Senate's authorization is required. Whatever pertains to the commonwealth must therefore be entered into its records. No such acts become valid before they have been approved by the Senate. And so that the Senators would have no fear of the king, no one used to become Senator unless he had been nominated by the Senate, and no one could be deposed except for a legitimate reason and with the Senate's authorization. Royal letters, finally, have no validity unless they are subscribed by a secretary of the kingdom, and royal rescripts, unless they are countersigned by the chancellor, who has the power to annul them. Finally there are also dukes, marquises, counts, viscounts, barons, and chatelains, and in the cities there are mayors, vicars, consuls, syndics, aldermen, and the rest, each of whom has been entrusted with some region or city in order to protect the people within his jurisdiction. Some of these dignities, however, are now regarded as hereditary.

So much for ordinary means of representation. In addition there is the assembly of the three estates to which every region and city of any importance used to send delegates separately representing the commoners, nobility, and clergy. This is where affairs concerning the commonwealth were decided in public. In the beginning it used to meet annually, thereafter at least as often as necessary. The authority of that assembly was always such, not only that its statutes were held to be sacred, regardless whether they had to do with making peace, conducting war, appointing procurators of the kingdom, or imposing a tax, but also that it could send kings off to monasteries for dissipation, sloth, or tyranny, and deprive an entire family from the right to succeed to the kingdom, since the people had called it to kingship in the first place. Whom consent had raised up high, dissent thus overturned, and who had almost become hereditary kings by imitating their fathers' virtues were incapacitated, dishonored, and disinherited by their degenerate and thankless hearts—which proves that hereditary succession was merely tolerated in order to avoid graft, secession, interregna, and other disadvantages of election. But if even graver dangers threatened, where tyranny was about to seize the kingdom or a tyrant about to occupy the throne of the king, the legitimate assembly of the people always retained full authority to expel a tyrant or a negligent king, to transfer the kingdom to his relatives, and to approve a good king in his place. According to Caesar, *The Gallic War* book 5, the Franks may very well have adopted this practice from the Gauls. For Ambiorix, King of the Eburones, says there that the power of the kings of Gaul was such that the people properly assembled had no less authority over the king than the king over the people. This is also hinted by the case of Vercingetorix, who pleaded his case before the assembly of the people.

In the kingdoms of Spain, especially in Aragonian Valencia and Catalonia, things are the same. The highest authority of the Aragonian kingdom rests with the assembly that they call their *iustitia*. The magnates in this assembly who represent the people are not afraid to dictate the following words to the king in public, at the time of his inauguration as well as in the third year of his rule: "We have as much authority as you, but above us both there is someone whose dominion is greater than yours (meaning the *iustitia*)." The *iustitia* often repeals the king's laws and prohibits his edicts, and the king does not dare to impose any tribute without its authorization. In England and Scotland the highest authority rests with the Parliament, which meets about every year. What they call Parliament is the assembly of the estates of the kingdom, where bishops, counts, barons and delegates from towns and regions in common decide the affairs of the commonwealth by vote. Its authority is so sacred that it is a crime for the king to abrogate whatever it has ratified. And all ordinary officers of the kingdom who participate in the king's or queen's council are accustomed to receive their insignia from this assembly. To sum up, the other Christian kingdoms, Hungary, Bohemia, Denmark, Sweden, and the rest, all have their officers of the kingdom or partners in royal government, whom history teaches and recent memory plainly shows to have used their authority at times and even to have deposed their kings.

It is not the case, however, that we should therefore consider royal power to have been diminished in any way, as if kings had suffered a loss of rights. We certainly do not consider God to be any less powerful because he is incapable of sinning, nor his empire as somewhat restricted because it is incapable of being ruined. Because the king is capable of sinning, the same is true for him if he is sustained by someone else's help or if he retains an empire for a long time through someone else's foresight that he himself might have lost through negligence or guilt. . . .

Can Prescription be Used as an Objection?

Now perhaps you will say: You are talking to me about patricians, nobles, and officers of the kingdom. I, however, see nothing but masks and ancient coats of the kind that are used in theater. I hardly perceive traces of ancient liberty or authority. Wherever one looks one finds that most of these men are taking care of their own affairs, complying with the king, and deceiving the people. You can hardly find anyone who takes pity on an emaciated people, in need of pity though they are. But if someone does take heart and feels pity, or if he should only be thought to do so, he is judged a rebel and a traitor and driven into exile, if he is not even reduced to searching for his daily bread.

This is indeed the case. The audacity of the kings and the improbity, or sheer incompetence, of the nobles has been so great for such a long time and in so many places, that kings seem to have acquired a right of prescription to that licence to which most of them are nowadays accustomed. The people, on the other hand, seem to have ceded their authority tacitly, or to have lost it through disuse, because most of the time it turns out that no one cares for something that everyone should care for, and no one considers himself responsible for something that has been entrusted to everyone. Against the people, however, neither prescription nor improbity have any effect. It is public knowledge that no prescription runs against the fisc. So much the less does it run against the people as a whole. They are above the king and his privilege exists only for their sake. How could it be otherwise, since the prince is merely the administrator of the fisc, but the people, as shall be proved below, its true owner? Is it, furthermore, not known that liberty cannot be prescribed by any violence at all, not even by the longest servitude? And if you should object that the kings were established by a people that lived perhaps 500 years ago, and not by the people in existence today, I shall say that though kings may die, the people, like any other corporate body, never dies. . . .

The Purpose of Having Kings

Since kings were constituted by the people, and certain men who are superior to the king as a collectivity, although inferior as individuals, were joined to kings as partners in dominion, so to speak, in order to restrict them in the exercise of their office, we ought to inspect the purpose for which kings were established to begin with and what their primary duty is. For something is deemed to be just and good if it attains the end for which it has been set up. First of all, since men are free by nature and impatient of servitude, born to rule rather than to obey, they would obviously not have gone so far as to elect someone else to rule and renounced the law of their nature in order to subject themselves to another law, unless this was an extremely useful thing to do. As Aesop says, the horse, used to roaming about in freedom, would never have accepted rein and rider had it not hoped to conquer the bull.

We do therefore not believe that kings were elected in order to use goods for their own purposes that the many had acquired by their labor, for everybody loves his own affairs, nor do we believe that they were elected in order to abuse public power as they please, for almost everybody hates or envies those more powerful than himself. . . . Rather, when Mine and Thine entered the world, when fights over property arose between citizens, and wars over the borders with their neighbors were added as well, the people began to seek safety from some single person who should ensure with justice and with strength that neither the poorer among them should have to suffer the force of the richer, nor all of them together that of their neighbors. And when strife and wars continued further to increase, they elected someone as king of whose strength and energy all of them were firmly convinced. Kings, therefore, were once created in order to say the law at home and lead the army abroad, not only in order to ward off inimical campaigns, devastation of the fields, and other harm to the body, but even more so in order to keep sacrilege, crime and vice away from the commonwealth, if necessary by force. . . .

Now since the people were looking for an equitable law, they were certainly satisfied if they obtained it from a just and good man. But that could hardly happen because such a man occurs only rarely. So long as free decision took the place of laws, however, it often happened that kings gave contradictory judgments. That is why laws, which speak with the same voice to everybody, were next invented by the more prudent men and other magistrates. The principal duty entrusted to the kings thus became to act as custodians, ministers, and conservers of the laws. At times, because the law could not foresee all eventualities, they were to supply its deficiencies from natural equity. But in order to prevent them from doing violence to the law, nobles, who were discussed above, were joined to the kings by the people. Kings should consequently obey the law and recognize it as their queen. The attitude expressed by the satirist Juvenal as "this is what I will, this is what I order, my will is reason enough," however, is womanly weakness rather than true strength, and they should be aware that it must have nothing to do with themselves. The law is like an instrument given by God with which human societies are best governed and directed to their end, namely, happiness. Kings who consider it shameful to obey the law therefore make themselves as ridiculous as a geometer who considers it absurd and indecorous to use the ruler, the pointer, and the other instruments with which experts are accustomed to survey the land, or as a sailor who recklessly prefers to cruise and drift off course with fancy as his guide, rather than to direct the course of his ship with his compass. . . .

Can a Prince Make New Laws?

Shall it then not be permitted to the prince to make new laws and repeal old ones? Not at all, because the function of the king is not only to pay attention that the laws are neither violated nor cheated, but also that nothing is missing from them or superfluous in them, lest they should grow decrepit with age and be buried with oblivion. If he thinks that a law should be abrogated, amplified, or shortened, he should advise the people or convoke their ordinary or extraordinary officers and request a new law. But he shall not put it into force until they have considered and approved it according to the regular procedure. Once he has put it into force, however, he may no longer change his mind, but is obliged to keep it on all counts. Examples have more effect than words. Therefore he must obey a law he has enacted, for it is futile and even, in a sense, iniquitous for a prince to require obedience to the laws from his subjects if he himself, who is obliged to guard them, neglects them. Kings ought to differ from their subjects, not by greater impunity, but by greater equity and justice. . . .

Does the King Own Everything?

Since we have shown that the king cannot be considered the owner of his subjects' lives, we should now inquire whether he can at least be considered the owner of their belongings. First of all we should inspect the case of private property. Nowadays no one among the followers of princes is heard perhaps more frequently than those who say that everything belongs to the king. According to them one cannot say that the king takes something away if he seizes his subjects' belongings, but must say, on the contrary, that he allows them to enjoy the use of whatever he does not take away. This opinion has come to be so firmly settled in the minds of some princes that they dare to claim for themselves whatever their wretched subjects may have plowed and ground, as though they were oxen. And this is how it is in fact, except that it plainly contradicts the law.

Here we should always remember that kings were created for the good of the people and that only those who labor for the people's advantage are to be considered kings, but those who labor for their own as tyrants, as Aristotle says. Since each man loves his own belongings and most strive for those of others as well, is it likely that human beings would have looked for someone to whom they could give all the goods they had acquired by their labor, or that they would rather have looked for someone who would make an effort that rich and poor alike would rest secure in their possessions? . . . Hence the king of Germany, France, or England can rightfully assert a claim to his kingdom. But if he excludes an upright individual from his private property as though he who owns the goods of the community should or could legally possess the goods of individuals as well, he manifestly violates the law.

Does the King Own the Kingdom?

Is the king then the proprietor of the royal patrimony, or public domain? This question must be treated in a little more detail. First it is to be noted that there is a difference between the patrimony of the fisc and that of the prince, between, in other words, the possessions of emperor, king, and prince on the one hand, and those of Antoninus, Henry, and Philip on the other. Possessions of the king are those which he possesses as king, possessions of Antoninus which he possesses as Antoninus. He receives the former from the people and the latter from his parents. . . . Concerning the private belongings of the prince, if there are such, he doubtless owns them in the same way as individual citizens own their belongings, and civil law entitles him to sell or spend them as he sees fit. But there is no reason at all to consider him the owner of fisc, kingdom, and royal patrimony, what is commonly called the domain.

How could it be otherwise? If someone has made you the shepherd of his flock, has he delivered the flock to you to be skinned, sold, or driven away at your pleasure? Or if the people have appointed you to be the duke or judge of a city or region, have they given you the power to alienate, sell, or destroy this city or region? And since the people are alienated along with the region, did they authorize you to sell, prostitute, and enslave them to whomever you like? Is the royal dignity a possession, or not rather a function? If it is a function, what does it have in common with property? And if it is a possession, is it not at least of a kind in which the people who handed it over always retain their rights of ownership? And finally, if it is correct to say that the patrimony of the fisc, or domain, is a kind of dowry of the commonwealth, by whose sale or waste the commonwealth, the kingdom, and in the end even the king are destroyed, which is the law that would permit the alienation of such a dowry? . . .

To be sure, when kings were established it was necessary to supply them with the means required to protect the royal dignity and, more importantly, to sustain the burdens of kingship. Honesty and utility demanded it. After all it pertained to the kings's duties to establish judges everywhere who would not take gifts and prostitute the law for money. He also had to be prepared to assist the law with force whenever necessary, to protect the roads, commerce, and so on. When war was threatening, he had to garrison towns against the enemies, surround them with walls, furnish an army, and build arsenals. Now everybody knows that there can be no peace without war, no war without soldiers, no soldiers without pay, and no pay without tribute. The domain was therefore established in order to sustain the burdens of peace, and tribute (what the jurists call *canon*) to sustain those of war, in such a way, however, that extraordinary levies could be raised in order to make up for unusually heavy expenses. . . .

It has then been established that whatever ordinary or extraordinary revenues are assigned to the king in the form of tribute, taxes, and the entire domain, including harbor dues, fees of entry and exit, regalities, escheated, forfeited, or confiscated lands, and so on, have all been assigned for the good and defense of the people and for the sustenance of the kingdom. When these nerves are cut, the people weakens, and when these foundations are undermined, the kingdom collapses of necessity. It follows that someone who burdens the people to their detriment, who gains from its losses and cuts its throat with his sword, is not a king; that a true king on the contrary, in his function as caretaker of public business, is an administrator of public resources, but not their proprietor. . . .

Is the King the Usufructuary of the Kingdom?

Now granted that the king is not the owner of the kingdom, can he at least be called the usufructuary of the kingdom and the domain? Not even that. A usufructuary can mortgage his possessions. But kings, we have said, cannot mortgage the patrimony of the fisc. A usufructuary can give his income away as he pleases. Unmeasured gifts by a king, on the other hand, are considered invalid, unnecessary expenditures are rescinded, super-fluous ones are cut, and whatever he has turned to any other purposes than public ones he is considered to have stolen. He is no less bound by the *lex Cincia* than any private Roman citizen. According to this law, especially in Gaul, he can make no gifts without the consent of the so-called Chamber of Accounts. Hence the usual note by this chamber about wasteful kings: "trop donné, soit répété," that is, this gift was excessive and should be recovered. This chamber also swears a sacred oath never to accept any re-script from the king that might damage the kingdom or the commonwealth, even though its observance of this oath has been rather less than sacred. And finally the law does not care how a usufructuary uses or enjoys his income. To the king, however, it prescribes the purposes for which he must use it. . . . We must conclude that kings are neither owners nor usufructu-aries of the royal patrimony, but only administrators. So much the less can they claim the ownership or usufruct of anyone's private property or of the public property belonging to individual townships. . . .

The Covenant or Pact between the King and the People

We have said that there was a twofold covenant when the king was estab-lished, the first between god, king, and people, which has been treated above, the second between the king and the people, which we must now consider. When Saul was established as king, he was given a law of king-ship according to which he had to rule. David in Hebron in the presence of God, that is, with God as witness, entered into a covenant with all the elders of Israel who represented the entire people. Only thereafter was he anointed as king. Joash also covenanted in the house of the Lord with the entire people of the land, with the high priest Jehoiada presiding. And along with the crown a "testimony" is said to have been imposed upon him, which most interpreters take to mean the law of God, as the law of God is often referred to by that term. Josiah similarly promised to observe the precepts, testimonies and statutes contained in the book of the cove-nant, meaning the laws pertaining to both piety and justice.

In all of these cases a covenant is said to have been entered into with the entire people, the entire multitude, all the elders, or all men of Judah. Thus we understand, as is also specifically stated, that not only the princes of the tribes, but also all the leaders of the thousands and the hundreds, and all lower magistrates were present in their cities' names, each of them covenanting with the king on their own.

That pact dealt with the creation of the king. The people made the king, not the king the people. Hence there is no doubt that the people is the stipulating, the king the promising party. The law, however, considers the stipulator to be in a stronger position. The king was asked to promise that he would rule justly and according to the laws, and he did promise to do so. Then the people promised faithfully to obey him, provided his orders would be just. Hence the king gave an unrestricted promise, the people a conditional one. Consequently the law would absolve people from any obligation should the condition not be fulfilled. In the first covenant or pact, piety became an obligation, in the second, justice; in the former the king promised to obey God faithfully, in the latter, to rule over the people justly; in the former, to care for the glory of God, in the latter, for the good of the people; in the former the condition is "if you will observe my law," in the latter "if you give to each his own." If the former is not fulfilled, God is the proper avenger, if the latter, the entire people or the nobles of the kingdom who have undertaken to guard the entire people will have the right to do so.

This is how it has always been observed in all legitimate governments. . . . And if we inspect the kingdoms of today, we find that there is none considered worthy of its name where no such pact intervenes between the prince and his subjects. In the German empire, not so long ago, the king of the Germans used to swear fealty and homage to the empire when he was about to be crowned emperor, just like a vassal being invested with a fief by his lord. And even though the words of his oath were slightly altered by the pontiffs, the content always remained the same. Thus we know Charles V of Austria as well as his successors to have been promoted to the empire under certain laws and conditions, whose essence was that he would guard existing laws, not enact new ones without consulting the electors, follow public counsel in public affairs, not alienate or mortgage any of the empire's belongings, and other conditions which the historians tell in detail. And when the emperor is crowned at Aachen, the archbishop of Cologne first asks him whether he will defend the church, administer justice, preserve the empire and protect widows, orphans, and all others deserving of pity. When he has solemnly sworn before the altar that he will do so, the princes and the representatives of the empire are asked if they will promise him the same. He is neither anointed nor does he receive the sword standing for the defense of the commonwealth and the other imperial insignia until he has sworn that oath. That manifestly proves that the emperor is obliged without restriction, the princes of the empire however only conditionally. No one familiar with the rite recently observed at the election and

coronation of Henry of Anjou will doubt, moreover, that the same observance is followed in the Polish kingdom, especially since a condition requiring the king to preserve both the evangelical and the Roman religion
was added, which was thrice explicitly put by the nobles and thrice accepted by the king. The same thing plainly happens in Hungary, Bohemia,
and other kingdoms, which it would lead too far to list in detail.

These same conditions, furthermore, are not only set up in kingdoms
where the law of election has so far remained intact, but also where purely
hereditary succession is thought to have taken its place. When the king of
France is inaugurated, the bishops of Laon and Beauvais, as peers of the
church, first ask the entire people present whether they wish and order this
man to be the king. This is why in the inauguration formula he is even said
to have been elected by the people. When the people has consented, he
swears to guard all laws, privileges, and rights of France in their entirety,
not to alienate the domain, and so on, and although there may be interpola-
tions in his oath, which differs widely from the ancient formula that can be
found in the library of the cathedral chapter of Beauvais and to which
Philip I is known to have sworn, the words are nevertheless perfectly clear.
He is not girded with the sword, anointed, and crowned by the peers, who
are adorned with wreaths themselves, he does not receive the scepter and
rod of justice, and he is not proclaimed king until the people has so
ordered. Nor do the peers swear fealty to him until he has given them his
promise that he will strictly observe the laws, that is, that he will not di-
lapidate the public patrimony, impose or collect taxes, duties, and tributes,
decree war or make peace at his own discretion, and take any measures
concerning the public without public counsel. He likewise promises that
the Senate, the assemblies, and the officers of the kingdom shall remain
firm in their authority, like everything else that has always been observed in
the kingdom of France. And when he enters a province or city, he is obliged
to confirm its privileges and subjects himself by oath to its laws and customs. This explicitly applies to Toulouse, Dauphiné, Brittany, Provence,
and La Rochelle, whose agreements with the kings are the most detailed
and would have to be considered futile were they not functioning like
clauses in a contract. . . .

Now even if these rites, these sacred ceremonies, and these oaths had
never taken place, does nature itself not teach us sufficiently clearly that
kings are established by the people on condition that they govern well,
judges, that they say justice, and generals, that they lead the army against
the enemy? If they grow violent, inflict harm, and themselves become the
enemy, they are therefore no longer kings and should not be acknowledged
by the people. But what, you may say, if the prince forces a people suppressed by violence to swear an oath at his dictate? What then, I shall reply,

if a robber, a pirate, or a tyrant, with whom no one considers it possible to enter into a lawful agreement, uses his sword to extort a promise? Is it not commonly known that a promise obtained by force is not binding? Especially if it violates good morals and the law of nature? And what could be more repugnant to nature than a people tying itself with chains and fetters and, which is evidently the same thing, promising to the prince to offer its throat to his dagger and use violence against itself? There is thus a mutual obligation between the king and the people, whether it is by civil or natural law, tacit or explicit, that cannot be superseded by any pact, violated by any law, or rescinded by any force. Its strength is so great that a prince who violates it contumaciously can truly be said to be a tyrant, and a people that breaks it, seditious.

The Nature of Tyranny

So far we have described a king. Now we shall describe tyrants a little more accurately. We have said that a king is someone legitimately ruling over a kingdom conveyed to him by inheritance or election and properly committed to his care. It follows that a tyrant, as the direct opposite of a king, is someone who has either usurped power by force or fraud or who governs a kingdom that has been freely conveyed to him against human and divine law and persists in administering it in violation of the laws and pacts to which he has bound himself by oath. A single individual may of course fall into both kinds of tyranny at the same time. The former is commonly called a tyrant without title, the latter a tyrant by conduct. It can, however, also happen that someone governs justly over a kingdom that he has occupied by force, or governs unjustly over a kingdom legally conveyed to him. In that case, since kingship is a matter of right rather than of heredity, a function rather than a possession, someone administering his office badly is worthier of being called a tyrant than someone who has not entered his office in the proper way. . . .

How to Resist a Tyrant without Title

First we should deal with so-called tyrants without title. Some Ninus uses force to invade a people that owes him nothing and has done him no harm; a Caesar oppresses his country and the Roman commonwealth; a Popelus tries by fraud or parricide to make the kingdom of Poland hereditary rather than elective; a Bruenhilde and her Protadius transfer the entire administration of France to themselves; an Ebroinus, placing his hope on Theodoric's cowardice, seizes the reins of government and oppresses the people with servitude: what shall we say is the law?

Natural law, first of all, teaches us to preserve and protect our lives and liberty, without which life can hardly be lived, against all violence and injury. This is what nature has instilled in dogs against wolves, bulls against lions, doves against hawks, and chickens against kites. So much the more in man against man, if man becomes a wolf to man. Hence no doubt is permitted whether one should fight back, for nature herself is fighting here.

In addition there is the law of nations, which distinguishes between countries, fixes limits and sets up borders that everybody is obliged to defend against foreign enemies. Hence it is just as permissible to resist Alexander if he mounts an enormous fleet in order to invade a people over which he has no rights and from which he has suffered no harm as it is to resist the pirate Diomedes if he raids the sea with but a single ship. Under such circumstances Alexander outdoes Diomedes, not by his greater right, but merely by his greater impunity. One may also resist Alexander's devastation of a region as though he were a vagabond stealing a cloak, and resist an enemy putting a city under siege as though he were a burglar breaking into a house.

Above all there is civil law, by which all human societies are constituted according to particular laws, so that each of them is governed by its own laws. Some societies are ruled by one man, others by several, and still others by all; some reject government by women, others accept it; some elect kings from a specific line, others do not; and so on. If anyone should try to break this law by force or fraud, all are obliged to resist him, because he violates society, to which everything is owed, and undermines the foundations of the fatherland, to which we are bound by nature, laws, and sacred oaths. If we neglect to resist him, we are truly traitors of our fatherland, deserters of human society, and contemners of law. Since the laws of nature, of nations, and civil law all command us to take up arms against tyrants of that kind, no reason at all can be offered to dissuade us from our obligation. No oath, no pact, no obligation of any kind, whether private or public, can intervene. Even a private individual is therefore permitted to resist usurpations by a tyrant of this sort. . . .

These considerations apply while the tyranny is still in the happening, as they say, that is, while the tyrant is still getting in motion, plotting, and tunneling. As soon, however, as he has gotten so much control over things that the people are conquered and swear an oath to him, that the commonwealth has been suppressed and transferred its power to him, and that the kingdom has regularly consented to a change in its laws, he has acquired the title that he was formerly lacking. He is then not only in factual but also in legal possession. Even though the people has only superficially agreed to accept his yoke, but has acted against the will of its heart, it is nevertheless right for it to obey and calmly to acquiesce in the will of God, who transfers kingdoms from one hand to another as he pleases. Otherwise there would be no kingdom at all whose jurisdiction could not be called into doubt. But this shall only apply if he who used to be a tyrant without title governs legitimately after he has acquired his title and does not continue to act as a tyrant by conduct. . . .

What the Law Permits to be Done against Tyrants by Conduct

We must be rather careful in examining the case of those who are tyrants by conduct, regardless of whether they acquired power by law or by force. First of all we must take into consideration that all princes are mere human beings. Their reason cannot be protected from passion any more than their souls can be separated from their bodies. It is therefore not the case that we should wish for none but perfect princes. We should rather regard ourselves lucky if we have been furnished middling ones. If a prince occasionally exceeds the proper measure, if he does not always follow reason, if he is a little lazy about the public good, a little negligent about providing justice, or not so keen on military defense, he is not really a tyrant at all times. Since a man does not govern other men as a god, as men do with oxen, but rather as a human being born to the same lot as they, it is not only presumptuous of a prince to mistreat human beings as though they were brutes, but also iniquitous of the people to look for a god in their prince, and a divinity in his fallible nature. If the prince, however, overturns the commonwealth on purpose, if he unabashedly demolishes the laws, if he cares not a bit about promises, conventions, justice, and piety, if he becomes an enemy to his people, and finally if he exercises all or the most important tyrannical skills that we have mentioned, then he can really be judged a tyrant, that is (although there was a time when that word had more pleasant connotations) an enemy of God and man. . . .

We have already proved that all kings accept the royal dignity from the people, that the people as a whole are superior to the king, that the king is only the supreme minister and representative of the kingdom, and the emperor the supreme representative of the empire, whereas the people are its true lord. It follows that a tyrant by conduct commits a felony against the people in their capacity as lord of his fief, that he is guilty of *lèse majesté* against the kingdom and the empire, and that he is a rebel. The laws against rebellion thus apply to him, although he deserves far greater punishment. Bartolus says that someone like that can be deposed by his superior or be justly punished under the *lex Julia* for public acts of violence. His superior, however, is the people as a whole or those who represent it, the electors, members of the court, patricians, assemblies of estates, and so on. But should he have established himself so firmly that he cannot be expelled without armed force, they shall be permitted to call the people to arms, enlist an army, and mount force, deceit, and all possible machinery against him as against a declared enemy of the fatherland and the commonwealth. . . .

That is why it is permitted to the officers of the kingdom in their entirety, or at least their majority, to use force against a tyrant by conduct. Not only is it permitted, but it is even their official duty, from which they can on no account be excused. Electors, members of the court, patricians, and the other nobles should not believe that they have been created and established for no other purpose than once to exhibit themselves at the king's inauguration, dressed up for all to see in military coats of bygone times in order to enact some costume comedy and on that day to wear the masks of Roland, Oliver, Renaud, and all the others, as though they were on stage, representing a sort of King Arthur's round table, as it is called. And when the crowd has been dismissed and the poet has bid his farewell, they may not believe that they played their parts in the best possible way. . . . The nobles should rather be aware that the king may play the first part in administering the commonwealth, but they play the second, the third, and so on, each in his place. If he plays his part badly, they should therefore not follow him, and if he destroys the commonwealth they should not collaborate with him, for the commonwealth is entrusted to them no less than to him. They are not only obliged to administer their own offices well, but also to keep the prince within the limits of his office. Finally, as the king has promised to take care of the public interest, so they have, too. If he breaks his promise, they may therefore not consider themselves to be released from their oaths any more than bishops may if the pope falls into heresy or ruins the church. On the contrary, they should consider themselves to be the more obliged to fulfill their oaths the more flagrantly he has broken the covenant. If they collaborate with him, they violate their duty; if they connive, they are deserters and traitors; and if they do not save the commonwealth from tyranny, they must themselves be counted among tyrants, just as on the other hand they are true patrons, guardians and kinglets, as it were, if they guard and defend by all means what they undertook to guard. . . .

Is this not even true for the Pope himself? They say that the cardinals, who elected him, or, if the cardinals fail to exercise their duty, the patriarchs, who are primates next in ranks to the cardinals, can for certain reasons convoke a council against the will of the pope in order to judge him if he scandalizes the universal church by notorious crimes, if he is incorrigible, if reform in head and members is required, if he refuses to assemble a council in violation of his oath, and so on. We read that many popes have in fact been deposed by the authority of councils. And if, says Baldus, they persist in abusing their power even then, words are to be used at first, then herbs, that is, remedies, and finally stones, and where the talents of virtue are not enough, arms must afford protection. Now if it is proved by the reasoning of almost all learned men, by the decrees of councils, and by the course of events itself that a council has the right to depose a pope, as they say, even though he boasts of being the king of kings, claims to be as much superior to the emperor as the sun is to the moon, and even arrogates the authority to depose kings and emperors at will, who can have any doubt that the public council of any kingdom can depose not only a tyrant but also a king who is dangerously mad? . . .

It is not the case after all, as we have said before, that the people entrust the entire administration of the kingdom to the king, just as the pope, they say, is not entrusted with the church's entire episcopacy. They rather entrust a part of the administration to each of the nobles according to his capacity. Of course the king holds the highest position in the administration of the commonwealth and was set up in order to provide for concord in the community and prevent rivalries among the peers. So he swears to take care of the kingdom's welfare. But so also does each of the nobles. Now if the king or a majority of the nobles neglect their promise and destroy the commonwealth, or desert it when it is in jeopardy, should all the rest therefore desert it as well? Will they be any less obliged to defend it, as though they were released from their oaths? Should they not keep their promise more than ever if the others neglect to do so, especially since this is precisely the purpose for which, as overseers, they were set up, and since only that is considered just which serves its purpose? If several promised the same thing, does the perjury of one end the obligation of another? If several debtors are liable for the same sum of money, does the fraud of one redeem the others? If several guardians protect their ward badly, does their guilt diminish the burdens of guardianship on the single good man among them? Or is it not rather the case that the former cannot avoid the charge of perfidy unless they try to fulfill their promise as best they can, and that the latter cannot avoid the risk of being convicted for neglect of guardianship unless they bring a suit against their co-guardians, especially since not only someone appointed as guardian can bring suit against the others in order to have them removed, but even someone who is no guardian at all.

Those who have promised their strength and their efforts to the kingdom or empire as a whole, such as the constables, marshals, peers and the rest, and those who have done so for a specified region or city constituting a part of the kingdom, such as dukes, marquises, counts, mayors and the rest are therefore bound, next to the king, to aid the commonwealth when it is oppressed by tyranny. The former, if they can, must save the kingdom as a whole from tyranny, the latter, in the capacity of guardians given to the regions, must save that part of the kingdom for which they have undertaken guardianship. The former, I say, must attack the tyrant with force and the latter keep him away from their borders. . . .

Does this mean that such resistance shall even be permitted to servants? Shall people like Herdonius the Sabine, Eunus of Syria, or maybe Spartacus the gladiator—shall any private individual be permitted to incite slaves to rebellion, call subjects to arms, and enter into combat with the prince when there is danger of tyranny? By no means. The commonwealth is not entrusted to individuals or private persons, but private individuals are, on the contrary, entrusted to the care of nobles and magistrates like wards. Since they cannot even guard themselves, they are not obliged to guard the commonwealth. Neither God nor the people have conceded the sword to individuals. If they draw the sword without being ordered to do so, they are seditious, however just their cause may be. Not individuals, finally, establish the prince, but only the people as a whole. Hence they must wait for an order from the people as a whole, meaning those who represent the people in the kingdom, the regions, and the cities constituting parts of the kingdom, or at least for an order by one of them, before they may undertake anything against the prince. A ward cannot bring an action except under the authority of his guardian, even though the ward is the true principal and the guardian only takes the principal's place inasmuch as he provides for his ward. Neither can the people take action, except under the authority of those upon whom they have conferred their authority and power, whether they are ordinary magistrates or constituted by an extraordinary public assembly. They are the ones whom for that purpose the people have girded with their sword, to whose government and care they have surrendered themselves, and who, like that Roman praetor who provided for justice between slaves and their lords, have truly been put in their position so that they can offer themselves as judges and defenders in any quarrels that may arise between the king and his subjects, lest the subjects should pass sentence in their own cause. . . .

In sum, and in order to conclude with this question, princes are elected by God and constituted by the people. As individuals are inferior to the prince, so are the collectivity and the officers representing the kingdom superior to the prince. When the prince is constituted there is a covenant between himself and the people, which may be tacit or explicit, founded on natural or civil law. Its content is that they will follow him well if he orders well, serve him if he serves the commonwealth, obey him if he obeys the laws, and so on. Of this covenant or pact the officers of the kingdom are guardians and defenders. Someone who violates this pact perfidiously and persistently is a tyrant by conduct. Therefore the officers of the kingdom may judge him according to the laws, and if he resists they have the duty to use force against him, if they fail to succeed by other means. These officers are of two kinds. Those who guard the kingdom as a whole, such as constables, marshals, patricians, members of the court, and the rest, must use force against the tyrant on their own if the others connive or conspire with him. Those who represent a part of the kingdom, or a region, such as dukes, marquises, counts, consuls, and mayors have the right to keep tyranny and the tyrant away from their region or city. Individuals or private persons, finally, may not draw the sword against tyrants by conduct because they were not constituted by individuals but by the people as a whole. But everybody is allowed to fight against tyrants usurping power without title, because in that case no pact has taken place. Those, moreover, who take advantage of the negligence or sloth of a legitimate prince in order to exercise tyranny over his subjects may be considered to be tyrants of the same kind. So much for this question. If anything should have been left out, it can be supplied from the second question.

Fourth Question: Does the Law Permit or Oblige Neighboring Princes to Aid the Subjects of Other Princes Who are Afflicted for the Sake of Religion or Manifestly Oppressed by Tyranny?

The question that now follows must be answered by conscience rather than knowledge. If charity were given the place it deserves in this century, it would be an idle question. But since our present habits are such that there is nothing dearer or rarer than charity among human beings, it appears that we must briefly treat it. Tyrants over souls as well as tyrants over bodies, over the church as well as over the commonwealth or kingdom, may be coerced, expelled, and punished by the people. For both we have already established the reasons. But the deceptiveness of tyrants and the simple-mindedness of subjects is often such that the former are barely recognized before they have already seized power, and the latter do not think about their salvation until they have almost perished. The people therefore are reduced to straits from which they cannot emerge by their own strength, but are forced to implore the help of others. The question then is whether Christian princes can help a people which is trying to protect religion, the commonwealth and kingdom of Christ, and their own kingdom. . . .

First of all it is firmly established that there is only one church, whose head is Christ and whose members are so closely united to each other that not even the least of them can suffer force or injury without the rest being wounded as well and feeling the pain, as all Scripture teaches. . . . As the church is one, it is in its entirety entrusted to each Christian prince. Since it would have been risky to entrust the entire church to a single prince, and plainly foreign to its unitary nature to entrust it in parts to individual princes, God entrusted the whole of it to each of them and each of its parts to all of them, not only for them to defend it, but also to expand it whenever possible. If a prince in charge of one of the church's parts, say Germany or England, takes care of that area, but neglects to fight against the oppression of another one and abandons it, although he could bring help, he must be deemed to have abandoned the church itself because there is only one bride of Christ, whom he must protect and guard with all his strength from being violated or corrupted anywhere. . . .

But is it permitted to say the same about princes who do not send their help to a people that is oppressed by tyranny or tries to defend its commonwealth against tyranny? In this case neither necessity nor covenant provide equally clear grounds for action since it has nothing to do with the church, which is one and the same for all and entrusted to each prince in its entirety, but rather with commonwealths, which differ from case to case and are entrusted to different people. But Christ says that a Jew has not only Jews as his neighbors, but also Samaritans and all other human beings. Now we should love our neighbors like ourselves. Hence, if he wants to do his duty, a Jew is not only obliged to rescue another Jew from a robber, if possible, but also any traveler on the road whether he knows him or not. . . .

Since all human beings have the same nature, as Cicero says, nature itself prescribes that man ought to wish another man well, whoever he may be, for the simple reason that he is a human being. Otherwise every human association would of necessity dissolve. There are two foundations of justice, then, the first requiring us to do no harm to any one and the second, to serve the good of everyone wherever possible. Accordingly there are two kinds of injustice as well, one that itself commits injustice, and another that fails to protect those upon whom injustice is inflicted, although it could protect them. Someone doing an injustice to another, whether out of anger or passion, lays violent hands upon his fellow. But someone who does not fend off injury or does not put himself in the way, although he could, is just as guilty of the same vice as if he were abandoning his parents, friends, or country. . . .

In brief, if a prince violently transgresses the limits fixed for piety and justice, his neighbor can in piety and justice transgress the limits fixed for himself, not in order to invade the rights of another, but in order to command him to be content with his own. If he neglects to do so, he is impious and unjust. If, on the other hand, a prince exercises tyranny over the people, his neighbor should help them just as much and just as quickly as he should help the prince when the people become seditious. Indeed, he should act so much the more promptly as the suffering of many deserves greater pity than that of one. . . . Since tyrants have existed always and everywhere, all of the historians afford plentiful examples of princes who saved their neighbors from tyranny and defended the people. The princes of today ought to imitate these examples in using force against tyrants over bodies and souls, over the commonwealth, and over the church of Christ, lest they themselves should be justly branded as tyrants.

At last, in order to conclude this treatise, let us say in a word that piety commands us both to observe the law of God and to guard the church, justice commands us to use force against both tyrants and subverters of the law and the commonwealth, and charity commands us both to assist the oppressed and to lend them a helping hand. Whoever denies this wants to abolish and extinguish piety, justice and charity.

6. Juan de Mariana, *The King and the Education of the King*

Juan de Mariana (1536–1624) was a Spanish Jesuit scholar and a man of independent mind. He was a second-generation member of the Society of Jesus, which was given official recognition as a religious order only in 1540, and whose founder, Ignatius Loyola, lived until 1556. The order grew rapidly and was at the heart of the Church's activity in Europe and throughout the world. Mariana's life testifies to the diversity of the Jesuits and their intellectuality, rather than to the practical influence and venturesome spirit for which they were also renowned. He spent the greater part of his life quietly at Toledo in his native Spain, writing books for some of which he got into trouble with the Church. His *magnum opus* was a history of Spain, written in Latin and translated into Spanish by himself. His *De rege et regis institutione* (1598), some of which is reproduced here, is too much its author's own book to reduce to the expression of a tradition, but it nevertheless draws on one. The limits of state power and the right of resistance to tyrants were discussed by medieval political thinkers and discussed again with distinction by sixteenth-century Catholic scholars, rediscovering the strength of their forebears—especially Thomas Aquinas—in an age too ready to dismiss medieval philosophy. Mariana's style is not "neoscholastic," but along with some of his contemporaries in the Roman Church to whom that term is appropriate, he was a transmitter and reinterpreter of an old vein in liberal thought; when the fires of politicized religious conflict eventually abated, even Protestant political thinkers acknowledged a debt to it.

From Juan de Mariana, *The King and the Education of the King,* translated by Albert Moore (Washington, D.C.: Country Dollars Press, 1948), pp. 135–79.

Chapter 5: Difference between a King and a Tyrant

There are six kinds of governments and forms of ruling commonwealths. The main points should be sketched at this stage before we explain the difference between the benevolence of a king and the insanities of a tyrant.

Regal power results from handing over the supreme direction to one man, and it is thus based upon the judgment and decision of this one individual.

The rule of the best men, which the Greeks call aristocracy, is sanctioned when the power is divided among the few who are preeminent because of outstanding quality.

On the other hand, what is spoken of as republic in the proper sense exists when the whole people participate in the government, with the limitation that the more important honors and offices are entrusted to the better men, the lesser, to the others, as befits the worth and merit of each.

Then, that which is called democracy exists when in a government of the people office is given promiscuously, and without selection, to the greater, the lesser and the middle group; it is a great perversion to place on the same footing those whom nature or a higher power has made unequal.

So democracy is contrasted to a republic in the same manner as the rule of the few, which among the Greeks is called oligarchy, is differentiated from the direction by the Optimates; for although in each case the power is given to a certain few, in the latter case character is the deciding factor, while in the rule by oligarchy wealth is weighed; the higher each is in the assessor's list, the more preference he gets over the others.

Tyranny which is the most evil and disadvantageous type of government, as compared with the kingly, exercises an oppressive power over its subjects, and is built up generally by force. Or at least, starting from a sane beginning of a reign, the tyrant declines into vices, and especially avarice, license and cruelty. And although the duties of a real king are to protect innocence, punish wickedness, provide safety, to enlarge the commonwealth with every blessing and success, on the contrary the tyrant establishes his maximum power on himself—abandonment to boundless licentiousness and the advantages therefrom, thinks no crime to be a disgrace to him, no villainy so great that he may not attempt it; through force he brings blemish to the chaste, he ruins the resources of the powerful, violently snatches life away from the good, and there is no kind of infamous deed that he does not undertake during the course of his life.

The King shows himself to be tractable and free from harshness, he is easy of access, he lives under the law on a level with the others. The tyrant, in his distrust and fear of the citizens, has the habit of terrifying them with the trappings of State and with the weight of his high position, by the severity of his caprices and by the barbarity of his judgments.

Now a few more differences between a king and a tyrant must be stressed, and the beginnings, development and progress of both types of government ought to be considered.

The King exercises the power received from his subjects with distinguished modesty, oppressive to none, molesting nothing except wickedness and madness; he uses severity upon those that storm recklessly against the property and lives of others. Toward the remainder he displays a fatherly solicitude. And he lays aside with pleasure the character of the strict judge which wicked men force him to assume, as soon as the criminals have been punished for their misdeeds.

He makes himself available to all in every duty of life; no one in his helplessness, no one in his loneliness is kept away, not only from his office, but not even from his dwelling and court. His ears are open to the complaints of all. Finally, nothing about his rule is harsh, nothing cruel; on the contrary, there are abundant examples of clemency, gentleness and humaneness.

Thus it comes about that he rules his subjects not like slaves, as the tyrants do, but he is over them as if they were his children; and he who got his power from the people makes it his first care that throughout his whole life he rules with their consent. Also his popularity for his good qualities gains the good will of his subjects, especially of the virtuous.

So, protected by this affection of his people, he has no great need of an escort for his personal protection, nor for hired and mercenary soldiers against external enemies. Indeed his subjects are prepared to fight in defence of his honor and safety, to sacrifice blood and life the same as for their children, wives and native land, to rush onto the sword and into the flame, if circumstances require, quickly, with high spirits, spreading terror in their wake.

Accordingly, he does not take away from the citizens their arms and horses, and he does not permit them to become enfeebled by ease and idleness, as the tyrants do, who enervate their people with sedentary occupations and the nobles with an abundance of sensual pleasures, pandering and wine. On the contrary, he will see that the cavalry and infantry are drilled in wrestling, boxing and leaping, both unarmed and equipped with weapons; and he will attach to their manliness greater importance as a defense than to low cunning and deceit. Is it right that in time of danger the arms of our sons be taken away and given to slaves?

On the other hand, we observe that under a just and temperate king the citizens consider themselves happy and abounding in all good things; which is a great inducement for good will and love toward a prince. Thus he will have no need to incur great expenses either for the trappings of royalty or for war, for he is secured by the many virtues of the company of good citizens and comes off most handsomely. He has close at hand, with all the orders spontaneously assisting, their public and private resources for warding off war, or even undertaking it, if there should be need.

In this way we observe that in Spain our kings, with a slender tax list, have carried on many considerable wars, especially against the Moors, with unconquered valor; and on this the very wide foundations of our power were placed, which, as we see today, are hardly limited by the very ends of the earth. Therefore he will not have need to impose heavy and unusual taxes on the provinces, and, if at any time adverse circumstances or a war not of his own choosing forces him, he will assess them with their own consent, as need demands. He will not extort this consent either with terrorism or threats, and not even by deceiving his people (what sort, indeed, of a consent would that be?) but by a full explanation of the peril of imminent war and of the weak exchequer.

Now the king will not view himself as the owner of the commonwealth and the individuals—although the flatterers are constantly whispering that into his ear—but as a director with an allowance set by the citizens, which he will consider wrong to increase without their consent. However, he will build up the magazines, he will enrich the public treasury without groaning on the part of the subjects—but later also, with the spoils from the enemies, as Lucius Aemilius Paulus did. He was the one who, having possessed himself of all the treasure of the Macedonians, which was enormous, delivered to the treasury so much money that the booty of one commander-in-chief put an end to taxes; at that time the duty of looking after the public revenues consisted in seeing that they did not become the booty of the courtiers and other attendants. And how much of the public property does peculation get away with? How much does fraud pluck off?

Moreover, a great restraint in the court is an important commendation for the Prince, replacing extensive taxes and sufficing for war and peace. The real resources are those which are made available harmlessly and without exciting complaint.

Henry III, King of Castile, cured by this method the lack of funds in a treasury depleted by the misfortunes of the times, and at his death he left to his son great resources gathered together without deceit, and without complaint or rancour on the part of his subjects. His philosophy was that he feared the curses of his people more than the arms of his enemies.

Now, this is the main point, that the King shows the citizens their duties more by the example of the temperateness of his life than by precepts. Indeed, as someone has said, it is a long process by way of words, but example is short and efficacious; and I certainly wish that there were as many good doers as good talkers. The King will exhibit every whit as much probity, modesty, fairness and virtue as he requires from others. Nor will he exercise his authority more harshly toward others than toward his own family and self. He will attain this more easily, if first he will remove far away from his thoughts any hope of concealment of any of his actions and deliberations; also he will be convinced that nothing greedy, unjust or intemperate should be done, even if it could be hidden and concealed from God and man. Nor if he should have the ring of Gyges, as the stories have it, should he give himself more licence than if he were acting right out in the open. Indeed, pretense cannot last long, for the acts of the Prince cannot stay hidden. Majesty is like the light; it puts its good and bad deeds out in public and it does not permit its activities to be hidden.

Then, if he will only drive away the flatterers—a most pestilent type of men—from the court; for they carefully examine the character of the Prince, praise those things that should be condemned, attack the opposite, veering in the direction that most pleases the Prince. This very base conduct springs from the lucky successes of too many people.

After he has driven the flatterers far away, he will summon the best men from every province. These he will use as his eyes and ears, but they will be upright and uncorrupted by defects. Let him give them access to himself for reporting not only the truth, but everything that is said about him, even the vain and empty gossip of the crowd. His objective of public service and the safety of the province as a whole will balance the grief that he feels because of these rumors and this frankness. Truth's roots are bitter; its fruits, most sweet.

Further, in my opinion at least, it seems that the Prince ought to consider everything with a view to promoting good will in the minds of his subjects, and so that under his rule they should be both in estimation and actuality as happy as possible. It is the duty of him who presides not only over the citizens but also over their dumb herds, to look out for the welfare and interests over which he rules.

These are the kingly virtues; by this path does one try to attain immortality.

Now that those matters above have been set forth and summed up, one is prompted to say something about the tyrant; for befouled by every taint of baseness he moves to overturn the commonwealth by a different and wholly opposite path.

In the first place, indeed, he seizes on his own initiative and by force the supreme power in the nation, which has not been given to him on account of merit, but because of his wealth, bribery and armed power. Or else he exercises his power violently, though he got it from a willing people, and he values it, not in accordance with his service to the people, but for his own convenience, indulgence and sinful lack of restraint.

In fact, at the beginning, in his mildness and pleasantness with everybody, or living along with the others under the same laws, he deceives them by an appearance of gentleness and kindness, while he consolidates his power and buttresses his position with the aid of armed forces. So even Domitius Nero, according to Trajan, acted for five years. After getting firmly in the saddle he changes into the exact opposite, not being able to conceal for long his inborn monstrousness; like an untamed and frightful beast he rages against every level of society. He seizes and wastes the possessions of private individuals, impregnated as he is with the destructive vices of licentiousness, avarice, cruelty and deceit. Such monsters as these were found only between the covers of the stories of ancient times, the three-headed Geryons in Spain, Antaeus in Lybia, the Hydra in Boeotia, the Chimaera in Lycia. In banishing these and freeing the peoples from their wretched slavery the great heroes industriously and manfully put forth their great efforts.

The tyrants try to do hurt indeed to all, violently to lay all low, but especially do they make their effort against the rich, honorable men, with all their authority; they hold the good more suspect than the bad, and the virtue of another always makes them more apprehensive. Just as physicians separate harmful things from the body by healing draughts, they are resolved to drive the better men from the State.

This is the doctrine of the tyrant. Whatever is lofty in the realm, let it be cast down. This they accomplish either by open force, or by working on it through secret calumnies. They exhaust all the other people, lest they be able to bother them, by ordering new taxes daily, by planting discord among the citizens, by weaving wars out of wars. Moreover, great works pile up huge burdens at the expense of, and with the sighs of, their citizens. Thus grew the pyramids in Egypt, the foundations of Olympus in Thessaly, as Aristotle tells us. And in Holy Writ we read how Nimrod, who was the first to impose tyranny on the world, and is said in the Bible to have been a mighty hunter, began to build in Babylon a high tower of great mass out of hewn rock to weaken his subjects and protect himself. Thence the fable of the Greeks was born, it is believed. Once upon a time the Giants, in order to cast Jove headlong from the skies, piled mountains on mountains on the plain of Macedonia, which is called Phlegra. Philaster is the authority for this. I pass over the Jewish tribes, how they were tricked by Pharaoh lest they should aspire to freedom, and were conquered by misfortune, compelled to build cities in Egypt by the sweat of their brows.

It is unavoidable that the tyrant be afraid of those whom he puts in a state of dread; and he must diligently take care, by removing all their means of protection and by taking their weapons away, not leaving them even their personal arms, that those whom he holds as slaves get no opportunity to engage in any of the liberal arts, worthy of a freeman, or strengthen their bodily robustness and their spiritual confidence by military activities.

Of course, the tyrant fears, and the King fears. But the King is concerned for his subjects; the tyrant fears for himself, and he is afraid of his subjects, for those whom he considers as enemies may snatch away his wealth and kingdom.

Consequently he forbids the citizens to congregate, to come together in political meetings and societies, and to talk at all about public business; this he accomplishes by secret inquisitions, and by taking away the means of speaking and hearing freely, which is the height of servitude. He does not even allow them the freedom of complaint in such bad conditions.

Thus since he distrusts the citizens, he seeks his support in intrigue; he diligently cultivates friendship with foreign princes, so that he may be prepared for every eventuality; he calls in foreigners, who are just about barbarians, but he puts his trust in them. He supports a mercenary army, in his mistrust of his citizens, which is great calamity.

When Domitius Nero was emperor, the footsoldiers and cavalrymen, with a mixture of Germans, swarmed through the forums, homes, country places and the environs of the towns; the ruler was depending on these virtual foreigners. (I am reporting the very words of Tacitus.)

Tarquinius Superbus, the first of the Kings of Rome, as it is told, stopped the custom of consulting the senate about everything; he managed the state by family councils. He himself alone, without the consent of the people and senate, made war and declared peace, made and broke off pacts and agreements with whomever he wished. He conciliated the tribe of the Latins to himself as fully as possible, so that by means of these foreign resources also he might be safer among his own citizens. So Livy says in his first book.

Yes, he even says that Tarquin killed the leaders of the community and named no one in their places, so that the order might be more despicable on account of its smallness; he himself conducted trials of capital crimes alone without advice. All these things are the proper marks of a tyrant.

Finally, he ruins the whole state; he considers it as his spoil in his wretched methods with no respect for the laws, from which he thinks himself exempt; and though he professes to be planning for the public safety, he carries on in such a way that the citizens are crushed by every kind of evil and lead a most unhappy existence. Individually and en masse he drives them wrongfully from their paternal possessions, so that he is the sole ruler in all the estates. The common people are deprived of all their benefits, and no evil can possibly be imagined which is not a part of the misfortunes of the citizens.

Chapter 6: Whether It Is Right to Destroy a Tyrant

Such are the character and habits of a tyrant, hated equally by Heaven and men. Though he may seem very fortunate, his shameful acts become his punishment. Like bodies cut with the whip, his distorted mind and conscience are tortured by his savagery, caprice and fear. Those whom the vengeance of Heaven pursues and presses on to destruction it deprives of mind and counsel.

Many examples, both ancient and modern, are available to demonstrate how great is the strength of a multitude angered with hatred for a ruler, and that the ill will of the people results in the destruction of the prince.

Lately in France a well-known example occurred, from which it may be seen how important it is that the spirits of the people be pacified, which are ruled not exactly as their bodies—a remarkable calamity to be kept in mind. Henry III, King of France, lies dead, stabbed by a monk in the intestines with a poisoned knife, a detestable spectacle and one especially to be remembered; but also by this princes are taught that impious attempts by no means go unpunished, and that the power of princes is weak once reverence has departed from the minds of the subjects.

Henry III was planning, since he had no heir, to leave the kingdom to Henry of Vendôme, husband of his sister, although the brother-in-law from an early age had been infected with wrong ideas of religion, being at that time under an excommunication from the Roman Pontiffs and cut off from the succession by law; though now he is King of France, after a change of heart.

When the plan became known a great part of the nobles, after the matter had been talked over with the other princes, both in France and abroad, took up arms for the safety of the fatherland and for their religion; from everywhere came aid. The leader was Guise, in whose manliness and family the hopes and fortunes of France in this storm were resting.

The designs and plans of kings remain constant. Henry, preparing to punish the attempts of the nobles, resolved on killing Guise, and called him to Paris. Since the plan did not go well, as the people were enraged and incited to take up arms, he quickly departed from the city, and after a short interval he pretended that he was won over to better counsels and wanted a public consultation on the common safety.

After all classes had come together at his summons, he killed at Blois on the Loire, in his palace, Guise and his brother the cardinal, who felt safe in the good faith of the meeting. Nevertheless after the killing the crimes of treason were imputed to them, in order that it might seem to have been done justifiably. They were accused with no one defending them, and it was decreed that they were punished under the law of treason. He seized others, among them the Bourbon cardinal, upon whom, although in an advanced age, the next hope of ruling rested by the law of blood.

This matter stirred up the minds of a large part of France; and many cities, after having renounced Henry, publicly renewed the fight for the common safety. At the head was Paris, to which no city in Europe is comparable in resources, extent and pursuit of wisdom. But the insurrection of a people is like a torrent; it is swollen for but a short time.

As the people were quieting down, while Henry had his camp about four miles out, still looking forward to punishing the city, and though matters were almost despaired of, the audacity of one young man in a short time definitely restored them.

Jacques Clement, born among the Aedui in the obscure district of Sorbon, was studying theology in the Dominican college of his order. He was told by the theologians, whom he had consulted, that a tyrant may be killed legally. He then obtained letters from people in the city whom he had ascertained by investigation to be loyal to Henry privately or openly; and keeping his own counsel, he resolved to kill the king. He then went out into his camp on July 31, in the year of our Lord 1589.

There was no delay. On the ground that he wished to tell secrets of the citizens to the king, he was admitted at once. After he had delivered the letters that he was carrying, he was directed to wait till the next day.

So, on the very first day of August, which is sacred to the feast of Peter the Apostle in Chains, after Clement performed the service, he was summoned by the king. He went in as the king was arising and was not yet fully dressed. They had some conversation. As he approached under color of handing over some letter into his hands, he inflicted a deep wound above the bladder with a knife treated with poison which he was concealing in his hand—a deed of remarkable resolution and an exploit to be remembered. Grievously wounded, the king struck back at the murderer, wounding him in the eye and breast with the same knife, crying out against the traitor and king-killer.

The courtiers break in, aroused by this unusual occurrence. Though Clement is prostrate and senseless, they inflict many wounds on him in their wildness and savagery. He says nothing, rather is glad, as appears from his countenance, because with the deed accomplished he missed the other tortures which he feared would be due him. At the same time he rejoiced that by his own blood the liberty of the common fatherland and nation had been redeemed, though, alas, at the great cost of his blows and wounds.

By the death of the king he made a great name for himself. A killing was expiated by a killing, and at his hands the betrayal and death of the Duke of Guise were avenged with the royal blood.

Thus Clement died, an eternal honor to France, as it has seemed to very many, twenty-four years of age, a young man of simple temperament and not strong of body; but a greater power strengthened his normal powers and spirit.

The king breathed his last the next night, in the second hour after midnight—though he had great hope of recovery and therefore had been administered no sacraments—pronouncing these words of David: "Behold, I was shapen in iniquity; and in sin did my mother conceive me." He would have been lucky, if he had made his latter acts correspond with his earlier life, and if he had proved himself to be such a prince as in the reign of his brother Charles he was believed to have been, when leading troops in war against traitors. This rank was his in the kingdom of Poland by the choice of the chiefs of this nation. But his character deteriorated as he grew older, and his later life blotted out the good deeds of his youth by shameful crime. After the death of his brother he was recalled to his native land and proclaimed king of France. He turned everything into a mockery; with the result that he seemed to have been raised to the pinnacle of things for no other reason than that he might crash down in greater disaster.

Thus fortune, or a mightier force, makes sport of human affairs.

There was no unanimity of opinion about the deed of the monk. While many praised him and deemed him worthy of immortality, others, eminent in their reputations for wisdom and learning, condemned him, denying that it is right for anyone on his own private authority to kill a king who has been proclaimed by the agreement of the people and anointed and sanctified according to the custom with the holy oil, even though he be profligate in his morals and also has degenerated into tyranny. This they assert positively with many arguments and examples.

Think how great, they say, was the wickedness of Saul, the King of the Jews, in the olden times, and how dissolute was his life and morals! His mind was agitated with his evil plans, and as the punishments of his crimes drove him on he swayed along blindly in his course. After he had been disclaimed by the authority of God, the right of ruling was transferred to David, along with the mystical anointing. Nevertheless, though Saul was ruling unjustly and had slipped down into folly and crimes, his rival, David, did not dare to injure him and he was put back into power time and again. Yet David seemed to be in a position to do it legally either by making rightful claim to the dominion, or on the grounds of looking out for his own safety; while Saul, unprovoked by any wrongs, was plotting in every way to take even his life, and dogging the footsteps of the innocent man wherever he presented himself. Now, not only did David himself spare his enemy; but he slew with the sword, as impious and imprudent, the young Amalechite, who told him that he had killed Saul, at the latter's request, when he was conquered in battle and leaning on his sword, because the Amalechite had dared to injure the Prince sacred to God (for that is what the ceremony of anointing signifies).

Who ever judged that the monstrousness of the Roman emperors, at the time of the birth of the Church, ought to be avenged and punished with the sword, although in hunting down the pious folk they indulged in savage tortures throughout the provinces and employed every bodily torment; but did they not rather urge that they must fight cruelty with patience and challenge evil-doing with submission, especially since Paul teaches that whoever resists a magistrate resists the will of God? And if it is unlawful to raise hands against a praetor although he is in the act of assaulting someone unjustly and inconsiderately, how much less may one assault Kings, though they have profligate morals? These God and the Commonwealth have placed at the head of things, to be viewed by the subjects as divinities, as more than mortals.

Further, they who try to change princes often bring great misfortune to the state; nor is government overturned without serious disturbance, during which the instigators themselves generally are crushed. The histories are full of examples; ordinary life is replete with them.

For what did it profit the Shechemites to form a conspiracy against Abimelech with the object of avenging, as they wished it to appear, the seventy brothers, whom Abimelech impiously and monstrously killed, though he was born of an inferior mother? He was led on by the evil ambition of ruling—than which there is no purer evil. The result was that all perished at one blow, the city was completely destroyed, and the site was sowed over with salt.

And to pass over the most ancient cases, after Domitius Nero was overthrown, what did the citizens of Rome do except to bring on Otho and Vitellius, not lesser plagues to the commonwealth? So, to make the butcheries fewer their reigns were made shorter.

Therefore, people conclude that the unjust prince must be accepted like the just, and that the rule of the former must be alleviated by passive obedience. The mildness of kings and leaders depends not only on their own characters but also on that of their subjects. Quite a number think that was the case when Peter was king of Castile, and that the name Cruel was commonly given him not so much through his own fault as that the intemperate nobles, greedy in every way, imposed on him the necessity of punishing wrongs and restraining their impudence. But this is the way with human affairs. Unfortunately virtue is now considered as a fault; and we judge plans by their results.

Moreover, how will respect for princes (and what is government without this?) remain constant, if the people are persuaded that it is right for the subjects to punish the sins of the rulers? The tranquillity of the commonwealth will often be disturbed with pretended as well as real reasons. And when a revolt takes place every sort of calamity strikes, with one section of the populace armed against another part. If anyone does not think these evils must be avoided by every means, he would be heartless, wanting in the universal commonsense of mankind. Thus they argue who protect the interests of the tyrant.

The protectors of the people have no fewer and lesser arguments. Assuredly the republic, whence the regal power has its source, can call a king into court, when circumstances require and, if he persists in senseless conduct, it can strip him of his principate.

For the commonwealth did not transfer the rights to rule into the hands of a prince to such a degree that it has not reserved a greater power to itself; for we see that in the matters of laying taxes and making permanent laws the state has made the reservation that except with its consent no change can be made. We do not here discuss how this agreement ought to be effected. But nevertheless, only with the desire of the people are new imposts ordered and new laws made; and, what is more, the rights to rule, though hereditary, are settled by the agreement of the people on a successor.

Besides, we reflect, in all history, that whoever took the lead in killing tyrants was held in great honor. What indeed carried the name of Thrasybulus in glory to the heavens unless it was the fact that he freed his country from the oppressive domination of the Thirty Tyrants? Why should I mention Harmodius and Aristogiton. Why the two Brutuses, whose praise is most gratefully enshrined in the memory of posterity and is borne witness to with the peoples' approval? Many conspired against Domitius Nero with luckless result, and yet without censure, but rather with the praise of all ages. Thus Caius, a grievous and sinful monster, was killed by the conspiracy of Charea; Domitian fell by the sword of Stephen, Caracalla, by Martial's. The praetorians slew Elagabalus, a monstrosity and disgrace of the empire—his sin atoned for by his own blood.

Whoever criticized the boldness of these men, and not rather considered it worthy of the highest commendations? Also, common sense, like the voice of nature, has been put into our minds, a law sounding in our ears, by which we distinguish the honest from the base.

You may add, that a tyrant is like a beast, wild and monstrous, that throws himself in every possible direction, lays everything waste, seizes, burns, and spreads carnage and grief with tooth, nail and horn.

Would you be of the opinion that anyone who delivered the State safely at the peril of his own life ought to be ignored, or rather would you not honor him? Would you determine that all must make an armed fight against something resembling a cruel monster that is burdening the earth? And that an end to butchery would not be reached so long as he lived? If you should see your most dear mother or your wife misused in your presence, and not aid if you were able, you would be cruel and you incur the opprobrium of worthlessness and impiety. Would you leave to the tyrant your native land, to which you owe more than to your parents, to be harassed and disturbed at his pleasure? Out with such iniquity and depravity! Even if life, safety, fortune are imperilled, we will save our country free from danger, we will save our country from destruction.

These are the arguments of both sides; and after we have considered them carefully it will not be difficult to set forth what must be decided about the main point under discussion. Indeed in this I see that both the philosophers and theologians agree, that the Prince who seizes the State with force and arms, and with no legal right, no public, civic approval, may be killed by anyone and deprived of his life and position. Since he is a public enemy and afflicts his fatherland with every evil, since truly and in a proper sense he is clothed with the title and character of tyrant, he may be removed by any means and gotten rid of by as much violence as he used in seizing his power.

Thus meritoriously did Ehud, having worked himself by gifts into the favor of Eglon, King of the Moabites, stab him in the belly with a poniard and slay him; he snatched his own people from a hard slavery, by which they had been oppressed for then eighteen years.

It is true that if the prince holds the power with the consent of the people or by hereditary right, his vices and licentiousness must be tolerated up to the point when he goes beyond those laws of honor and decency by which he is bound. Rulers, really, should not be lightly changed, lest we run into greater evils, and serious disturbances arise, as was set forth at the beginning of this discussion.

But if he is destroying the state, considers public and private fortunes as his prey, is holding the laws of the land and our holy religion in contempt, if he makes a virtue out of haughtiness, audacity, and irreverence against Heaven, one must not ignore it.

Nevertheless, careful consideration must be given to what measures should be adopted to get rid of the ruler, lest evil pile on evil, and crime is avenged with crime.

Now, if the opportunity for public meeting exists, a very quick and safe way is to deliberate about the issue in an atmosphere of public harmony, and to confirm and ratify what has developed as the common sentiment.

In this the procedure should be by the following steps: First the prince must be warned and invited to come to his senses. If he complies, if he satisfies the commonwealth, and corrects the error of his way, I think that it must stop there, and sharper remedies must not be attempted. If he refuses to mend his ways, and if no hope of a safe course remains, after the resolution has been announced, it will be permissible for the commonwealth to rescind his first grant of power. And since war will necessarily be stirred up, it will be in order to arrange the plans for driving him out, for providing arms, for imposing levies on the people for the expenses of the war. Also, if circumstances require, and the commonwealth is not able otherwise to protect itself, it is right, by the same law of defense and even by an authority more potent and explicit, to declare the prince a public enemy and put him to the sword.

Let the same means be available to any individual, who, having given up the hope of escaping punishment and with disregard for his personal safety, wishes to make the attempt to aid the commonwealth.

You would ask what must be done, if the practicability of public assembly is taken away, as can often happen. There will be, truly, in my opinion at least, no change in the decision, since, when the state is crushed by the tyranny of the ruler and facility for assembly is taken away from the citizens, there would be no lack of desire to destroy the tyrant, to avenge the crimes of the ruler, now plainly seen and intolerable, and to crush his destructive attempts. And so, if the sacred fatherland is falling in ruins and its fall is attracting the public enemies into the province, I think that he who bows to the public's prayers and tries to kill the tyrant will have acted in no wise unjustly. And this is strengthened enough by those arguments against the tyrant which are put at a later place in this discussion.

So the question of fact remains, who justly may be held to be a tyrant, for the question of law is plain that it is right to kill one.

Now there is no danger that many, because of this theory, will make mad attempts against the lives of the princes on the pretext that they are tyrants. For we do not leave this to the decision of any individual, or even to the judgment of many, unless the voice of the people publicly takes part, and learned and serious men are associated in the deliberation.

Human affairs would be very admirably carried on, if many men of brave heart were found in defense of the liberty of the fatherland, contemptuous of life and safety; but the desire for self-preservation, often not disposed to attempt big things, will hold back very many people.

Therefore out of so great a number of tyrants, such as existed in the ancient times, one may count only a few that have perished by the swords of their own people; in Spain, hardly more than one or two; though this may be due to the loyalty of the subjects and the mildness of the princes, who got their power with the best right and exercised it modestly and kindly.

Nevertheless, it is a salutary reflection that the princes have been persuaded that if they oppress the state, if they are unbearable on account of their vices and foulness, their position is such that they can be killed not only justly but with praise and glory. Perhaps this fear will give some pause lest they deliver themselves up to be deeply corrupted by vice and flattery; it will put reins on madness.

This is the main point, that the prince should be persuaded that the authority of the commonwealth as a whole is greater than that of one man alone; and he should not put faith in the very worst men when they affirm the contrary in their desire to please him; which is a great disaster.

There was not sufficient reason for David to kill Saul (a cause which was cited against my position), since he was able to ensure his safety by flight; and for this reason, if, for the sake of protecting himself, he should kill a king especially appointed by God, it would be impiety, not love of country. And Saul was not of such base morals that he was oppressing his subjects with tyranny, was overturning God's and man's laws, and was looking upon the citizens as his prey. The rights of government were transferred to David so that he might succeed a man when he had passed on, but not in such a way that he might snatch life and power from one still living.

And further, Augustine says in the seventeenth chapter in his book *Against Adimantus,* that David did not want to kill Saul, although it was permissible.

We find no difficulty about the Roman emperors. The foundations of the Church, marked out by the very borders of the earth, were laid with the blood and suffering of the pious; and the miracle was the greater that in oppression the Church kept growing, and though lessened in membership temporarily, it continued daily to gain and increase anew. In truth, in accordance with its philosophy, it was not expedient at that time, and is not even at this time, to do everything that has been granted to it by right and statutes. Therefore the well-known historian, Sozomen, in chapter two of his sixth book says that if it was a fact that some soldier had killed Julian the emperor, as some at that time were claiming, he did it rightly and laudably.

Finally, we are of the opinion that upheavals in the commonwealth must be avoided. Precaution must be taken lest joy run wild briefly on account of the deposition of a tyrant and then turn out sterile. On the other hand, every remedy must be tried to bring the ruler to right views before that extreme and most serious course is reached. But if every hope is gone, if the public safety and the sanctity of religion are put in danger, who will be so unintelligent as not to admit that it is permissible to take arms and kill the tyrant, justly and according to the statutes? Would one, perhaps, be influenced unduly that the proposition was disapproved by the Fathers in the fifteenth session of the Council of Constance, that "a tyrant may and ought to be killed by any subject, not only openly with violence but also through conspiracy and plots"? But this decision I do not find approved by the Roman Pontiff, Martin V, nor by Eugenius or his successors, by whose consent the legality of the proceedings of ecclesiastical councils is confirmed; this council's decrees especially needed approval, since we know that it was held not without disturbance of the Church on account of the three-way disagreement of claimants struggling for the supreme pontificate.

Also it was proposed to the fathers that the license of the Hussites be restrained, that the opinions of those be disapproved that think that the princes fall from office whenever they commit crime, that they can be deprived with impunity by anyone of the power that they have seized unjustly.

And appropriately there was an inclination to disapprove the idle talk of Jean Petit, Parisian theologian, who was excusing the murder of Louis of Orleans at Paris at the instigation of John of Burgundy with this comment, that it was right to crush him, on individual authority, if he was on the verge of becoming a tyrant. But the way he did it was not lawful, especially since an oath had been violated, and the approval of his superior was not obtained—if, of course, the opportunity was given to get it. This, indeed, is what the Fathers say.

This is our opinion, advanced certainly from a sincere mind, but in this, since I am able to err as a human being, if anyone has a better set of ideas, I should acknowledge my obligation to him.

This discussion I should like to conclude with the words of the tribune Flavius, who when convicted of conspiracy against Domitius Nero, and asked why he had gone ahead forgetful of his allegiance, said, "I hated you, but none of your soldiers was more faithful, while you deserved to be loved. I began to hate you after you became the murderer of your mother and wife, a charioteer and actor and an incendiary."

The spirit of a soldier and robust man! Tacitus tells us about it in his fifteenth book.

Chapter 7: Whether It Is Lawful to Kill a Tyrant with Poison

A polluted mind has tortures that cannot be described. Or the very conscience itself of the tyrant is his torturer. Even if no outside adversary happens along, the very baseness of his life and morals gives a bitter taste to all life's pleasantness and freedom.

What a condition of life and how wretched, indeed, to singe the beard and shorten the hair of the head by red-hot charcoal for fear of the barber, as Dionysius, the tyrant, used to do! What pleasure had a man who was hiding himself like a snake in a citadel at the time of quiet sleep, as did Clearchus of Pontus, the tyrant! What joy in ruling had Aristodemus of Greece who hid himself away in a garret and used a hanging entrance made by putting up and taking down ladders? Or could there be any greater unhappiness than trusting no one, not even friends and family? To quake at every noise and shadow, as if there was an uprising and the people were enraged? Plainly he leads a wretched life whose murderer is to be not only in great favor but even lauded.

It is glorious to exterminate wholly from human association this type of deathly pest. Rotten limbs indeed are cut off lest they infect the remainder of the body. And likewise that monstrosity of a beast in the human species must be cut out with the sword and so removed from the commonwealth.

Truly must he fear who spreads terror; but the terror that he inspires is no greater than the fear that he suffers. There is not as much protection in resources, arms and troops as there is in danger in the people's hate; and from this ruin threatens.

All orders bend their best efforts to do away with a monster who is infamous for foul base worthlessness and wantonness. After the hatreds have mounted from day to day, arms are publicly taken up and an open insurrection forcefully breaks out—an admirable spirit that we ought naturally to restore to the fatherland, by which means quite a number of tyrants have perished openly by violence! Or else they succumb by deceit and from plots, if one or more conspire secretly against the tyrant's life and at their own peril labor to redeem the safety of the commonwealth. Now if the conspirators come through all this, they are regarded in every walk of life as great heroes; if it turns out otherwise, and they fall as a sacrifice that is sweet to the heavenly choir and pleasing to man, all posterity holds them in honored memory for their noble attempt.

So, it is generally known that it is legal to kill a tyrant openly by force of arms, either by breaking into his palace or by starting a civil disturbance.

But it has been undertaken also by guile and treachery. This Ehud did; by bringing gifts and feigning a message from above he got close enough, and when the witnesses had left he killed Eglon, King of the Moabites.

It is, indeed, more manly and spirited to show your hate openly, to rush upon the enemy of the state in public; but it is not less prudent to seize the opportunity for guileful stratagems, which may be carried out without commotion and surely with less public and individual danger.

So, I praise the custom of the Lacedaemonians in their sacrificing to Mars, the protector in battle (as deluded antiquity thought), with a white cock, that is, when the victory had been gained in battle. When, however, the enemy were overcome by ambushes and cunning, they sacrificed a fat bull; as if it is more outstanding to conquer the enemy and keep the army intact by prudence and reasoning power, which distinguish us as men, than by main strength and robustness, in which we are surpassed by the beasts. Besides, there is the point of great loss on one's side.

Yet there is a question whether there is equal virtue in killing a public enemy and tyrant (indeed, they are considered the same) by poison and lethal herbs. A certain prince asked me this years ago in Sicily, when I was teaching theology in that island. We know that it has often been done. We do not think that there will be anyone, bent on killing, who, because of the opinion of the theologians, will neglect and pass up the offered opportunity of inflicting this kind of death and prefer to make the assault with the sword; especially in view of the lesser danger and the greater hope of escape. By this method the public joy is not less, when the enemy is destroyed, but the author and architect of the public safety and liberty is saved.

However, we regard not what men are likely to do but what is permitted by natural law; and from a rational standpoint, what difference does it make whether you kill by steel or poison, especially since the means of acting by fraud and deceit are conceded? Now, there are many examples in ancient and modern history of enemies killed in this manner. It is, of course, hard to poison a prince, surrounded as he is by his ministers of the court; besides, he is in the habit of having his food tried by a taster. It is difficult to break through the massive citadel of the regal mode of life.

But if an opportune occasion would be offered, who will have such an acute intellect, be so keen in discrimination as to strive to distinguish between the two kinds of death? At least, I will not deny that great force inheres in these arguments; that there will be those that are led on by these reasons and will approve this type of death, as in consonance with justice and equity and in agreement with what has been said—namely, that a tyrant or public enemy is killed justly by using not only an assassin but also a poisoner.

Nevertheless we see that it is not in accordance with our customs to do what was done at Athens and Rome frequently in the olden time, in that those convicted of capital crimes were gotten rid of by poison. Truly we think it cruel, and also foreign to Christian principles to drive a man, though covered with infamy, to the point that he commit suicide by plunging a dagger into his abdomen, or by taking deadly poison which has been put into his food or drink. It is equally contrary to the laws of humanity and the natural law; since it is forbidden that anyone take his own life.

We deny therefore that the enemy, whom we admit it is lawful to kill by treachery, may be made away with by poison.

What difference is there, indeed, whether drink is given to one that knows what he is getting or to one that is uninformed? Since the murderer cannot possibly be ignorant of the fact that the kind of death he is using is really against the laws of nature, the blame for a crime committed in ignorance falls on the author. What did it profit Laban to have substituted Leah for Rachel, whom Jacob married, that Jacob did not at all realize it? Does it help to make people innocent when, deceived by their fraud, others have gone wrong unknowingly? The very voice of nature's common sense reproaches when anyone uses poison against others though they be enemies. On this ground Charles, King of Navarre, surnamed the Cruel, was generally accused of having sought the lives of many princes by poison, even to procuring the poisoners for the King of France, the Dukes of Burgundy and Berry and the Count of Foix. These reports, whether fact or counterfeit, though there is reason rather to believe the latter, were spread into the senseless crowd, and what great hatred did they kindle against him among both French and Spanish peoples!

Therefore, to my way of thinking, neither may a deadly draught be given to an enemy nor deadly poison be put into his food and drink for his destruction.

Yet we may in this discussion have this qualification in the use of poison—that the man who is being done away with is not compelled to drink it, by taking which into his very marrow he perishes; but it may be employed externally by another, provided that he who is to die does not cooperate in any way. For the strength of poison is so great that it has the power to kill if even a chair or robe is smeared with it.

By this practice I find that other princes were done away with by the Moorish kings who sent them gifts of valuable clothing, linens, arms and saddles. It was spread abroad by numerous reports that some fine greaves, sent as a gift by a certain Moorish leader, were ill-omened for Henry the Sufferer, King of Castile. For after he put them on, his feet were actually affected with the poison, and to the end of his days he was afflicted with poor health. Likewise a purple robe, stiff with gold work, sent by the King of Fez to Yusuf, King of Granada, brought him to death in thirty days. The belief was confirmed that this robe was steeped in poison, because his limbs in consequence of the drug melted away as the flesh disappeared.

The report had it that this happened to Mahommed of Guadix, King of Granada, in the time of Henry III, King of Castile, that he died from a drugged undergarment.

Our Ferdinand Garcia, after he had forsworn the Moorish superstition, wrote all these things in a letter to Prince Ferdinand, the one who afterwards was King of Aragon, advising him, in the matter of the Moorish gifts sent him by Yusuf, King of Granada, that he should beware of treachery and that he should fear the Moors who were very deceitful under the guise of friendship.

They certainly act improperly, who deceive under color of well-doing and plot ruin, though provoked by no evil deed, or though they have made a sincere pact of amity in reconciliation after a period of hostility.

But a tyrant ought not to hope that his citizens have been reconciled except he be a changed man and ought to fear even those bearing gifts; it has been granted to proceed violently against his life in any manner. Only he should not, knowingly or unawares, be forced to be an accomplice in his own death; because we judge it to be wrong to mix poison or any like thing in the food or drink to be consumed by the man who must die. And this was the point that we had begun to discuss.

Chapter 8: Whether the Authority of the Commonwealth or the King Is Greater

A serious discussion now follows, a discussion which is complicated and difficult, and it is all the harder and more troublesome because we take a route unworn by footsteps.

The question is, whether the authority of the King is greater than that of the whole commonwealth over which he is placed.

The subject is slippery, and there is danger lest we seem to have wished to flatter the Princes, or to have been careless of offending those in whose hands lies the power of life and death. In delivering a suitable opinion I injure one of the two to the degree that I favor the other; there is a slender hope for successful achievement. You may indeed, more quickly break the things that have been confirmed by time than mend them. We love our moles and scars, and we like others also to love them. The one course would be fickle and characteristic of one eager to win favor; the other would have a mark of rashness and madness. Still it must be tried, since in no way can one err more deeply against the best interests of the commonwealth than by increasing or decreasing the power of the Prince.

Of a truth, fate claims for itself, as if of its own right, a very great part in setting up a state and promulgating its laws; the people are often led not by any discriminating choice and wisdom, but by impetuosity and unfounded opinion; and for this reason wise men in those circumstances have decided that what the people had done must be tolerated, though in many cases it ought not be praised.

However, my view is this: the regal power, if it is lawful, ever has its source from the citizens; by their grant the first kings were placed in each state on the seat of supreme authority. That authority they hedged about with laws and obligations, lest it puff itself up too much, run riot, result in the ruin of the subjects, and degenerate into tyranny.

The Lacedaemonians in Greece at one time had things this way, for they gave to the King only the management of war and the administration of religious matters; so says Aristotle.

The Aragonians in Spain in recent memory, keenly incited by a desire of protecting their liberty, made like provision, for they were not ignorant that the rights of liberty are much weakened by small initial encroachments. Therefore they set up an intermediate magistracy, like a tribune's authority (commonly at this time it is called the Lord Chief-Justiceship of Aragon), which, backed with the laws, authority and zealous affection of the people, has thus far held the regal power bound by sure limits. Especially it had been granted to the nobles that it would not be treachery if they took counsel among themselves and held meetings for the purpose of preserving the laws and defending their liberty, even without the knowledge of the King.

No one will doubt that in these nations and those like them the authority of the commonwealth is greater than that of the kings. Otherwise, how would it be possible, unless it were greater, to restrain the power of the kings and to resist their will? In other provinces where the authority of the people is less and that of the kings is greater, it must be considered whether the arrangement should be the same and whether it would be for the common interests.

Almost all grant that the king is the governor and head of the state, that he has the supreme and very greatest authority in management of affairs, whether war should be declared against an enemy, or laws must be made for his subjects in time of peace. And they do not doubt that the authority of the one to rule is greater than that of individuals, be they citizens or peoples. These same people, however, deny that the king has an equal authority to command whenever the commonwealth as a whole, or men of the first rank who have been selected out of all the orders and who are carrying on the public functions, gather into one place and come to a common decision. It was proved in Spain that the king was unable to lay taxes if the people disagree. The king will indeed use cunning measures, will hold out promises to the citizens, sometimes in drawing others to his way of thinking he will threaten; he will persuade by words, hope and promises (whether he does this properly we are not now discussing), but if the orders resist, their decision will prevail rather than the wish of the king.

Our view will be the same with regard to making laws. According to St. Augustine, these enter into force when they are promulgated; they are confirmed, when they are approved by the acceptance of those for whom they are passed.

And perhaps nothing different ought to be observed when a successor is to be designated by the solemn affirmation of the Estates. Especially, if the new king must be taken from a different family because the old king has no progeny and there are no cognates, these functions will pertain to the citizens and not only to the Prince.

Besides, how could this same state subdue, and if necessary deprive of office and life, a king who is vexing it with his low morals and is degenerating into open tyranny, unless it retained within itself the greater power when it delegated some of its authority to the king? And it is not likely that the citizens as a whole would have wanted entirely to deprive themselves of their own authority, to transfer it to another without exceptions, without limitations and restrictions; it was not necessary for them to have arranged things in such a way that a prince, who is subject to corruption and depravity, have a greater power than all the citizens; the offspring would be more distinguished than the parent, the river than its source. And anyone would think that the authority of the commonwealth, whose strength is greater and which has the larger resources, would be even greater than that of the prince, if he should disagree, no matter on how great authority he relies.

I see, however, that there are men, outstanding in their reputation for erudition, who think otherwise. They think that the king is greater not only than the individual citizens but also than the whole body, and for the following reasons. Otherwise, the government would be popular rather than regal, if the chief power remains in the hands of many and even reposes in all the people. If this opinion is adopted, appeal would be permitted from the decision of the king to the commonwealth. If this liberty of action is adopted, there would be great general confusion and great disturbance of judgments.

For it must not be thought that the king has less authority in the province than the head of the family in the house; for the king is equivalent to a ruler of the whole people, as Aristotle says. The same reasoning must be applied to the minor rulers if they are considered in connection with their own subject peoples. The bishops take precedence not only over the individuals in their dioceses, but over the whole body, in authority, powers and majesty. This matter can be illustrated by many other examples as fully as one wishes; but its characteristics are clear. Moreover, since no one can deny that the commonwealth could confer upon the prince the supreme and maximum authority, without exception, what hinders granting that this has been done so that the power to rule be greater, the necessity of the people to obey be greater, and the facility of rebelling be less, and thus the safety of all and the tranquillity of the state are maintained? What is the majesty of power if it is not the safeguard of the best interests of the whole body? Thus they argue who wish to amplify the regal authority and do not permit it to be circumscribed by any limits.

Now it is clear that this arrangement flourishes in some nations where the custom of general concurrence does not obtain, and the people or the nobles never come together to deliberate about public affairs; the necessity for compliance only is pressing, no matter whether the rule of the king is equitable or not—too much power, without doubt, and verging very nearly on tyranny. Aristotle has asserted that this was in vogue among barbarian tribes. Nor is it to be wondered at, since some men have been born to slavery, with only their bodily strength, without ability to do their own thinking, without sagacity. However onerous the rule of the prince, such men bear it whether they want to or not.

We are not discussing barbarians at this point, but the principate that flourishes—and rightly—in our nation and the best and most healthful type of government.

Now at the beginning I shall grant freely that the regal authority is supreme in the kingdom for all those matters which in accordance with the custom of the nation, its statute and undoubted law have been committed to the judgment of the Prince, whether it is a question of carrying on war, or dispensing justice to his subjects, or appointing leaders or magistrates. In these matters he will have greater authority not only than the individuals but also than the whole body, so that he stops for nothing and does not give an account of his actions to anyone. This we see as fixed in the customs of almost all peoples, lest anyone be permitted to reopen what has been determined by the king, or to debate about those matters.

Nevertheless I would believe, in certain other functions, that the authority of the Commonwealth is greater than that of the Prince, provided that the people are wholly united in one resolution. Assuredly, in levying taxes, or abrogating laws, and especially in the matters that concern the succession, if the multitude opposes, the authority of the Prince is not a match for it. And if any other things, according to the customs of the nation, have been reserved to the whole body politic, they are by no means placed within the discretion of the Prince.

Finally, and this is the main point, I prefer that the power of restraining the Prince abide in the Commonwealth, if he is infected with vices and wickedness, and, ignoring the true path of glory, prefers to be feared by the citizens rather than to be loved, and if, become a tyrant, he continues to rule his subjects, who are shaken and quaking with terror, and is set to do them hurt.

Appeal to the Commonwealth has been taken away for a double reason (though this right has been retained by the Aragonians): because, I suppose, the power of the King is supreme in deciding private suits; and because a practice had to be devised for punishing crimes and ending suits, lest the latter go on without end. Who indeed would say that the state has been given preference and that the government is in the hands of the people, when no power is left to the people and none to the nobles in the administration of the individual functions of the state?

About the status of the head of the household, the minor kings and the bishops we have no difficulty. About the first, the paterfamilias is over his subjects as over slaves in despotic rule. The lesser king is over the citizens in a civil and free principate. Nothing stands in the way of giving preference to the latter two over their subordinates as a whole, since there is in the commonwealth a greater authority, namely that of the king and the Roman Pontiff; and by this is corrected with a better and rather severe censorship any wrong that the others may have done.

Who is able to set the King aright, if the Commonwealth's power is completely subordinated?

And since mention is made of the Roman Pontiff, not even his authority, though next to divine (which some use as an argument), can cause maximum authority without limitation to be given to kings as against the Commonwealth as a whole.

Indeed, many wise and serious men of the greatest erudition make the Roman Pontiffs subject to the Church Universal when, in fact, it is deliberating in general council about religion and morals—whether rightly or wrongly I am not saying. But they nevertheless make them subordinate, after the fashion of regal power.

Those who think and act otherwise, in their preference for the pontifical authority over the universal, when their opinion is attacked on the grounds that the regal power is subject to the State, get around it with the following distinction. The regal authority has sprung from the State and is rightly subject to it; while the pontifical is answerable to God, whom the Pope considers his sole source of authority through Christ, because He, while on earth, delegated sacred jurisdiction to Peter and his successors over the whole world, whether the conduct of the people is to be regulated, or a decision is to be taken on matters of faith or divine worship.

From this answer it may be plainly concluded that while they disagree on the Pope's authority they agree on the regal, that it is less than the State's.

Now, if you persist in asking inquisitively whether it is within the prerogative of the commonwealth to abdicate and give full authority, without limitation, to the Prince—concerning which there is controversy—indeed I would not argue the matter much, nor would it make much difference to me how it is decided; provided that it is granted that the Commonwealth would act unwisely if it surrendered, that the Prince would be rash to accept that power which will make the subjects slaves instead of free men, and that the principate, constituted for the public good, would degenerate into tyranny.

Indeed, government is kingly which restrains itself within the bounds of modesty and moderation, while by an excess of power, which the unwise are busy at increasing daily, it is reduced and weakened through and through. We foolishly are deceived with an appearance of greater power and slip off into the opposite error, not giving the matter sufficient consideration, and not realizing that power is finally safe only when it places a limit on its own strength.

In the regal principate it does not apply as it does in possessions, that the more the latter are increased, the richer we become; the opposite, indeed, is the fact. Though the prince ought to be ruling over willing subjects, to be eliciting the good will of his citizens, and to be serving their interests, if his rule becomes irritating, as King he will lose their good will and exchange power for weakness.

Theopompus, King of the Lacedaemonians, made a correct and wise rejoinder to his wife, after he had set up the ephors like tribunes in that city to restrain the license of the kings. As he was being led back home amid the plaudits of the people, his wife protested to him and reproachfully said: "You will leave to your sons a rule diminished by your deed." His reply was, "Less, but more stable."

The princes, by placing reins on their own fortune, rule themselves, that fortune, and their subjects more easily. But when they are unmindful of human feeling and moderation, the higher they go up, the harder they fall. Our ancestors, seeing this danger ahead, like prudent men, adopted many outstandingly wise measures to keep their kings within bounds of moderation and temperance, lest they should pride themselves on too much power, whence ruin comes to the public.

How prudently did they act in these matters, in that they wanted nothing transacted of rather great moment without the consent of the nobles and the people; and in accordance with this plan it was the custom to summon bishops of the whole jurisdiction, the nobles and the deputies of the commonwealths, selected out of all the Estates, to the convocation of the realm. This at the present time has been retained in Aragon and in other provinces, and I would wish that our princes would restore it. Why, in fact, has it been put aside, in greater part, by excluding the bishops and nobles, unless that, by obviating the custom of general agreement, through which the public safety is maintained, the public and private business may be left to the decision of the King and to the whim of a few? The people far and wide complain that private individuals, such as the procurators of the towns, who are the only ones left from that storm [destruction of the Spanish Armada], are corrupted by gifts and hopes; especially since they are not chosen deliberately but are designated by the chance of luck, a new means of corruption and a proof of a confused commonwealth. This the more wise bemoan; yet no one dares to mutter a complaint.

But in tranquil moments we must think of the storm, lest the gale catch us unawares and crush us; and it is no wonder that the provincials groan that so many safeguards of the State have been destroyed; that they must daily meet the attack of many heavy calamities; that events prove the spread of the kingly power in war and peace; and that they are enmeshed in many misfortunes.

Now, lest the authority of the Commonwealth be lifeless and without strength, it was provided quite wisely that the chief men of the State have great resources and great power, by giving full jurisdiction to many towns and fortified places, not only to the nobles of the realms, but also to the bishops and priests as custodians of the public safety, as love of country and the consecrated order require; because historical events have often proved these to be friends of justice and protectors of the paternal religion. It must be hoped that they will rightly be a deterrent to anyone who thinks of busying himself to the detriment of the public interests.

They err, and they err greatly, whoever determine that it is necessary to deprive churchmen of jurisdictions and towns, on the grounds that these are an unprofitable burden and a responsibility the least suitable to the church. They do not think that the safety of the State cannot persist if this most noble part of it is weakened; and they must remember that the bishops are not only the heads of the churches, but also they are prime personages of the State, and that they also are true princes.

Those who strive to change this arrangement tear up every foundation of liberty, public safety and the principate; and I should rather believe, if we want to be sound, that the authority of the prelates must be enlarged, their jurisdiction must be increased, and the key fortified places must be entrusted to them.

Why, indeed, should the public weal, the sanctity of religion, and the fortunes of all be risked in the hands of one man, who is so continuously beset with the flatteries of the court, the crowd of fawners, and their un-bridled desires as hardly to have control of himself, and who certainly is too exposed to the many perils not to be marred by vices and pravity? Or, by weakening the sacred order should we yield to profane men, such as live in the court of the Prince, the decisions in business, religion, and state? The mind shudders to think how great evils impend from such a source.

Aristotle wisely, as in many things, wanted the State to have not only greater authority but also the stronger forces. His words I want to include here as translated from the Greek to the Latin.

"The question then is whether the King ought to have forces about him-self so that he is strong enough to coerce the disobedient by punishment; or under what agreement shall he exercise the power. For if he have power restricted by laws, so that he does nothing in accordance merely with his own desire but rather as a consequence of the prescription of the laws, he must have the necessary resources by which he may be able to maintain the laws. Perhaps it would be fitting that the King have resources of this kind, but only so great that he be more powerful than individuals and even large groups, and still less powerful than the whole body politic. Thus the an-cients were in the habit of limiting the escorts of those whom they put over the state, whom they called judges or tyrants. And when Dionysius was seeking companions as a guard, someone suggested that the same number of guardians ought to be granted to the Syracusans." That is what Aristotle thought.

Just one example will suffice me to tell how great authority the Commonwealth had in the time of our ancestors and how much the nobility had. Alphonso VIII, King of Castile, was besieging Cuenca, a town situated in the roughest part of the Celtiberi, the strongest fortress in that part of the Moorish jurisdiction. There was no money for the campaign, and consequently there was a lack of supplies. The King hastened to Burgos. In the Cortes he asked that, since the people were wearied with taxes, each noble put into the public treasury five maravedis of gold to carry on the war in an honorable manner. He was arguing that the opportunity should not be passed up for destroying the Moorish cause. The originator of this plan was Diego de Haro, ruler of Cantabria. Peter, Count of Lara, who opposed these attempts, got a band of nobles together and left the assembly, prepared to protect by force the exemption won by the arms and courage of his ancestors; and he stated that he would not allow that a start be made by this entering wedge to oppress the nobility and vex them with new levies. To crush the Moors was not so important as for them to permit the commonwealth to be enmeshed in a more grievous slavery. The King was thoroughly moved by the threat and desisted from his idea.

The nobles, after the resolution had been made known, determined to honor Peter, himself, and his posterity annually with a banquet, as a reward for the assistance rendered and as a future memorial and proof of a deed well done, lest on any other occasion they should suffer the right of liberty to be lessened.

Therefore, it should be considered as established that those who keep the regal principate in order and described by limits and bounds certain are taking thought for the weal of the State and for the authority of the Princes; while the liars, flatterers and the deceitful, who want to expand it without limit, weaken both Prince and State. Of these evil men a great number are seen in the courts of Princes, mighty in resources, favor and influence. This pest will always be condemned and will always exist.

Chapter 9: The Prince Is Not Free from the Laws

It is a difficult matter to keep Princes of great and distinguished power within the bounds of moderation. It is hard to persuade them, if they are corrupted by an abundance of wealth and puffed up by the empty talk of their courtiers, not to be thinking that it is pertinent to their dignified status and to the increase of their grandeur to augment their resources and power, or that they are considered to be subject to the authority of anybody.

However, the fact really is otherwise. Nothing, indeed, strengthens regal power more than moderation, if it is fixed in the minds and impressed on the very innermost consciences of Princes, when they are about to adopt a manner of thought and life, that they should serve first God, whose will governs the countries of the world and at whose nod empires rise and fall; secondly, that they should be modest and honest, for by these good qualities we merit divine protection, and the well-wishing of men is thus won to them in whose hands rests the governance of affairs. Also, the judgment of the citizens should be heeded, and one should often reflect as to what history will indeed say in the far distant future. As a matter of fact, it is characteristic of a noble spirit to aspire, next to heaven, to an immortal name.

Despise fame and you despise virtue; the very best personalities have the very highest aims; mean-spirited men, because of their personal inadequacy, are despised by their contemporaries and do not bestir themselves about the future. Feeling this way, men in early times were accustomed to place in heaven those princes who have fulfilled their destiny, whose services to the state stood out very preeminently, and to honor them with temples. Stupidly, you say, and uselessly. Who would not agree to that? Especially since this custom, though it began in no unreasonable manner, degenerated into such a madness that they granted divinity even to princes sunk in debauchery and vices, both living and dead. However, even in spite of this perversity it is plain enough that, to excite posterity to seek virtue, the praise of ancestors is very valuable, and by the love of fame virtues and the zeal for justice are nurtured.

Lastly, the Prince must be convinced that the sacrosanct laws, by which the public weal is maintained, will at last be stable only if he makes them hallowed by his own example. He therefore so orders his life that he permits neither himself nor anyone else to be mightier than the laws.

Since indeed divine and human law and right are expressed by the laws in every phase of life, it is unavoidable that he who violates the laws thereby departs from justice and uprightness.

What is conceded to no one is permitted still less to the king. His attention and power are employed in keeping justice sacred and in punishing depravity; and to this end are devoted the energies and best thought of the ruler. Kings will be permitted when circumstances require to ask for new laws, and to interpret and lessen the severity of old ones; to make adequate provision, if any eventuality is not covered by the law. However, the King should believe that it is the distinguishing mark of a tyrant to lack reverence for the customs and institutions of the fathers, to overturn the laws at his own whim, to refer to his own license and convenience everything that he does. Nor is it consistent that lawful princes so conduct themselves that they seem to possess and use a power untrammeled by law.

Now, how dangerous it is that the Prince wants to have his subjects well disciplined and outstanding in probity, though he himself by his lewd living sanctions sensuality and wickedness, is seen by the fact that the people indeed give more credit to example than to laws, and to imitate the zealous activities of the princes is considered to be a kind of obedience, whether they are improper or wholesome.

That prince is unfit who honors his own edicts and the laws of the fathers only in word but tears them up by the roots and destroys them by his licentious vices.

Moreover, the prince has no greater power than the people as a whole would have, if the government were democratic, or than the leading men, if the supreme authority had devolved on them—a form of government which the Greeks call aristocracy. Therefore he should not think himself more free from his own laws than the degree to which the citizens or the nobles would have been exempted from those laws sanctioned by virtue of the power that they might have secured. Especially is this so since more laws are made by the will of the commonwealth as a whole than are decreed by the prince. The State has greater authority for ordering and prohibiting—a greater power, than the prince, if what we have put down in this discussion above is true.

And furthermore the prince ought not only to obey these laws, but he will not be permitted to alter them, unless with the consent and expressed vote of the whole community; among these are the laws of the succession among the princes, taxes, and the form of religion.

Zaleucus of Lorci and Charondas of Tyre did not consider themselves unbound by the laws. The former of these, indeed, when his son had committed adultery, although the citizens had remitted the penalty, [by] which the adulterers were deprived of their sight, first tore out his own and then his son's eye, satisfying by this compromise both mankind and the nobles. Thus he upheld the authority of the laws.

And Charondas, since he had made the law that one should not enter the assembly armed, and since, coming out of the field into a hastily called meeting, he had not laid aside his sword, when his attention was called to the law, drew his weapon and fell upon it.

Imbued with these precepts and examples the Prince demonstrates the ideal of probity and moderation. He exhibits the same obedience to the laws that he exacts from his subjects. He loves the customs and institutions of his fatherland. In no degree does he degenerate into foreign and unusual rites. He enjoys the paternal religion, costume and tongues. This is the most sure proof of regal dignity, constancy and love for fatherland. And he takes thought to allow himself nothing that will cause the destruction of the laws and ruin of his country, if his people were to follow in it.

He considers as most certainly prejudicial the kind of court talk that in its desire to please the king proclaims that he has greater power than the laws and the fatherland, that he is the master alone of whatever is possessed publicly or privately by his subjects, or that everything hangs on his decision, and that all law consists in serving the desire of the prince. This view Thrasymachus of Chalcedon supported, in defining justice and equity as what the princes wanted and found to their personal advantage.

The Prince should reject the shameful artificiality of the soothsayers. When Cambyses of Persia wanted to marry his sister, whom he loved to distraction, and inquired of them whether he could do it legally, they said at first that it was not in accordance with the Persian common law; nevertheless, they said that here was a law which decreed that kings were permitted to do anything that they pleased, and that by this law the license of this marriage was permissible, though it was forbidden to others under any circumstances. O men born to slavery!

The Prince should not heed even Anaxarchus who thus attempted to console Alexander after he had killed Clitus and was thereby prostrated with grief: "Are you really ignorant, Sire, that Themis and Justice were right at hand for Zeus, so that they could approve whatever might be at the moment dear to him?" Certainly, he explained, it was humanly and divinely right for kings to do what Alexander had done.

The Roman people and senate took the same view of it when they said by decree that Augustus would be freed from the restraint of the laws. For when the republic was oppressed by the armed power of Caesar and was unable to do anything else but quake, dissemble and agree, why wonder if the whole multitude, driven by unwonted apprehension, turned themselves to the adulation of the one! However, while they freed the Prince from the laws, they made him by the same decree a tyrant. That famous man was indeed merciful and benign; nevertheless a person would have to be bereft of reason to deny that he was a tyrant. For a tyrant is he who rules over unwilling subjects, who crushes the liberty of the commonwealth by arms, who does not serve above all the interests of the people, but rather considers his own advantage and the enlargement of the power that he has seized. All these specifications fit Caesar and Augustus. Who will be so blind as not to see that?

But you say it is ridiculous to want to subject the person to the laws who surpasses all the others in resources and power and to put him by law on a par with them; for the laws order fair treatment; what else indeed is justice? Therefore there is no place for him among those who in every respect are not his equals. For this reason at Athens it was the custom to sentence to exile men excelling all the others, a practice which they called ostracism. Indeed they thought it wrong to put those men by law on a level with the others, and that it was deleterious to the commonwealth for them to be living in it who were more powerful in private and public life than the laws.

Next, you say it seems inappropriate to impede with laws a person whom you are unable to coerce with fear of trial and judgment since he has arms at his beck and call and is surrounded with every protection. For the laws would be in vain unless they are supported by the fear of superior power. Lastly, there are many laws that though they limit the multitude are not applicable to the Prince; certainly those that limit expenses, prescribe the type of clothing, and take away arms from the people. That is true; and we are not so mad as to attempt to cast down from their position the kings who have been set on the pinnacle and to put them into the crowd. Our intention is not that the Prince be subjected to all the laws without any degree of exception, but only to those laws that may be obeyed without insult to majesty and without interfering with the duties of the Prince—those passed about the obligations of life in which the Prince is no different from the people, such as are promulgated concerning wicked deceit, violence, adulteries, and about moderation in style of life.

The Prince will be acting prudently if he supports even the sumptuary laws by the example of his own life, lest he induce the citizens to hold the other laws in contempt and lest the impression become common that it is beneath one's dignity to obey the laws. If however, he overlooks these sumptuary laws, by no means will I have anything to say, nor will I greatly censure him, provided he shows proper respect for the others, whether divine or human. In any event, he who is more distinguished than all the others ought to bear in mind that he is a man and a member of the commonwealth.

The Athenian law that drove the chief men from the state is sometimes condemned; it would have been better to accustom them from an early age to live under the law on a level with the others; and to remember that all— high, low and middle class—exist in one commonwealth and therefore are held bound by a certain social law.

The great philosophers say that the Prince is guided by precept and that he is not forced by legal penalty against his will. Although the double force of ordering and coercing the disobedient exists, they subject the Prince to the law only from the first of these, that is, by precept—making it a matter for his conscience, if he forsakes his obligation under the law. They claim that other people are subject to the law under both its aspects. This reasoning is agreeable to me.

I might even grant that the Prince, when there is question of those laws which the State has made, whose power we have said is greater than the Princes, may be, if necessary, coerced by penalties. For it has been conceded above that he is to be removed from office and even punished with death under exceptional circumstances. On the other hand, if he obeys of his own accord those laws which he himself has made, I am satisfied; I grant that no one should force him, against his will, or coerce him with sanctions. But above all the mind of the Prince should be trained from an early age to be convinced that he himself is more bound by the laws than the others who obey his rule; that he involves himself seriously in conscience if he resists; that he is the protector and guarantor of the laws; and that he will effect this better by example than by fear, which latter does not teach us lasting lessons of duty.

If he will acknowledge that he is bound by the laws, he will govern the state very easily, he will keep it happy, he will curb the insolence of the nobles, so that they will not think it more in consonance with their dignity to despise their fathers' customs and show that they are free from the laws.

But, you say the majesty of the Prince is lessened by this moderation. Not at all: folly will be increased if the privilege of violating the laws shall have been granted. But it is characteristic of a craven and slavish mind, you say, to respect the laws. Rather, I think, it is profligate and contumacious to despise them. One is happy, you say, in doing what one wishes. Yes, and one is wretched in wanting to do what is not allowed, and it is lamentable to be able to do what is dishonorable. Madness armed with a sword will pave the way to ruin for itself and others.

Therefore it should be clear that the moderation of the Prince, by which he manifests what is true and what is becoming, namely, that he is amenable to the laws, is honorable for him and salutary for his citizens; that it defends and protects his whole realm in a vigorous and robust manner; and that it makes his empire permanently prosperous and happy.

Chapter 10: The Prince Should Determine Nothing about Religion

If all this is true, that the Prince is subject neither to his own laws nor those of the Commonwealth, who would grant him the right to change the sacred rites and ceremonies, to alter ecclesiastical laws and to decide about divine matters?

If any Prince may reopen for discussion in accordance with his own opinion or that of his people what should be the thought on religion, how can there be concord and agreement between all the provinces, so that the German does not have one idea about God and immortality and the Spaniard another, and so that both the Frenchman and the Italian, the Englishman and the Sicilian may have the same opinion, the same understanding and expression about divine matters?

Rather do we believe that in a short time as many opinions on religion would be spread throughout the world, and the sacred rites and the character of ecclesiastical organization would be as varied as there are different human judgments.

For the above reason it is necessary to have a chief authority, who would have the responsibility for sacred matters and have charge of the sacred ceremonies and laws to which other Princes throughout the world would submit, to whose power all would look, and very especially the ministers of religion, who for this reason are free of the rule of other Princes through the decision of our ancestors, in consonance with the divine laws.

Indeed in the most ancient times it is very clear that sacred matters were attended to by the temporal princes; in the same hands reposed the care for the state and religious matters. This we see from the Holy Scriptures; Noah, Melchisedec, and Job sacrificed with their own hands; the same word indicated both priest and leader. In Xenophon we see that Cyrus the Persian offered sacrifices to the gods. In Athens and Rome the kings performed the functions of priest. When Codrus the king was killed at Athens, the office of chief priest was established. After the kings of Rome were driven out, the Romans designated for themselves a chief priest, or king for sacrificing, for the purpose of carrying on the traditional sacrifices which the kings had been performing, and also lest in any way a longing for a king should arise. However, they made him subject to the Pontificate, so that no honor would be added to the name and thus injury be done to liberty, concern for which was the prime consideration.

This institution was abolished at the time of the Roman emperors, and the Augusti were made Pontiffs. A fresh stole was customarily sent to the newly created emperors to show them that they were adopted as members of the college. Honorius Augustus was the first one, indeed, among the Christian emperors to consider this a sacred matter, and he refused it; so Zosimus tells us.

Many other facts can be adduced which we must omit. Nevertheless this custom resulted in the practice of religion being in the care of the state and the princes; the ministers of religion were very close to the magistrates, and there was one national head for these two main groups.

Moses was the first one to change this custom, and in accordance with the will of God he delegated jurisdiction over sacred matters to his own brother, Aaron, while he retained in his own hands the duty of ruling over the people; and with good reason. For he understood that with the extensive religious observance, and the assiduous care for the multitude of ceremonies, the strength of one man was not equal to both offices.

With greater reason after Christ had shown himself in the flesh He separated the two powers, gave Peter and his successors the responsibility for religious matters and left to the kings and princes the power that the latter had received from their fathers. He did not, however, arrange matters—as some nefarious men have always charged—in such a way that he denied to the bishops and other priests all access to wealth and principates on the ground that they were grossly unsuited, provided that any of them, under divine inspiration, wanted by this splendor to increase and amplify the majesty of religion. Who may rightly censure this arrangement which has been used in all the nations as far and wide as the name of Christian reaches.

If the authority of each is wholly separate, care must be taken that the two orders are bound together with good will and the fulfilment of mutual obligations toward each other. And this is best accomplished if each has access to the honors and duties of the other. Thus united in spirit, the churchmen will look after the safety of the state, and the princes and chief men will apply themselves with greater effort to the protection of the established religion; and from this each has a sure and evident hope of benefitting himself and his own by honors and wealth.

So let the prince first endeavor to conciliate both estates and to keep them at peace, lest they disagree to the public disadvantage; and in this zeal he should admit the churchmen to the responsibility of the government. This I see was habitual with our ancestors, when the bishops were invited to the realm's assembly. They did not want anything of major importance done unless it was approved by the bishops' agreement and assent; I do not know why in our times this practice has become outmoded. Is it right, especially when the prince is surrounded by so many corrupt persons, to risk on him alone the safety of the state and the preservation of the religion of our fathers? And should we commit to the judgment of the courtiers and secular magistrates the decision in matters of the ceremonies, sacred laws and customs?

Let us avoid such great danger! He who does not see it is blind; he who does not desire to apply a remedy holds public and private safety in contempt. In a condition of corrupt morals will the state expect a remedy more readily from the prelates or from private individuals and laymen, such as are the office-holders in the towns? Which will show the greater forethought in healing such great wounds?

Further, the Prince ought to see that the immunities and rights of the clergy remain intact. No cleric should be held subject to civil punishment, though deserving it. The Prince should not deprive them, as they flee to the shrines for asylum, of the privilege granted by our ancestors. It is better that misdeeds go unpunished than that laws hallowed by time be abrogated. And he should reflect on this, for he is not risking that the impious in any event go unpunished. We know that it turned out badly for Eutropius when he persuaded Emperor Arcadius that the law of the immunity of the temples should be abrogated. The author was among the first to find this advice deadly. For he was dragged out of the shrine to which he had fled from the wrath of the emperor for safety and paid the penalty with his life, though a little before he had been happy and important, chamberlain of the emperor and consul, a position that was considered the first among the eunuchs.

If any pestilential and wicked fellow should be found in Holy Orders, if the people shamefully abuse the sanctuary of the shrines, the prince should take the initiative in proposing to the prelates that they remedy the situation; by no means should he on his own authority and for his own aggrandizement violate the sacrosanct laws, which have been especially set up by our forbears for augmenting and amplifying the practice and majesty of religion.

The more he grants to religion, the greater shall be his reward from heaven in resources, honors and authority.

In addition the Prince should never permit the towns and strong points to be taken away from the bishops and churches to which they have been given; for, if the holy estate is weakened in resources and power, who will beat back the attempts of wicked men to overturn the state or to hold religion in derision, as often happens? They act very wisely who take thought about the tempest while the state is tranquil.

Imagine a prince left by his father at an early and weak age. Restless men are accustomed to make full use of this predicament for harassing the state. Imagine (for what prevents it since it is in the range of possibilities?) that he has low morals and is contaminated with new ideas about religion, with the result that he changes the established ancestral religious practices. Imagine that a conspiracy is formed and a civil war is stirred up by the nobles. Is it proper that the Church be without protection? Rather it should be reinforced by troops, supplies and authority, to resist wickedness and to protect our most holy religion. It has been my view all along that the present bad conditions are mere trifles in comparison with what I have in mind as possible, and I would rather desire not only that the grants by our ancestors be not taken away from the bishops, but that even the strongest citadels be handed over to their care; so that wickedness, impiety and the eagerness for change which shows itself everywhere may be so bound and fettered that it can not stir. It is possible that some churchmen are corrupt, but this happens rather rarely.

Now we know that if there is any safety at all left in France and Germany, due to the very frequent changes there and the extreme fierceness of the times, it is almost wholly attributable to the strength and power of the bishops. In Spain when Alphonso, King of Leon, died, his son Ferdinand, whose righteous life earned him the title of Saint, while the nobles were in discord and were excited to armed sedition, kept his position purely with the assistance of the bishops, to whom it seemed wrong that a son should be excluded from his paternal inheritance. Indeed, the duties of the bishops, as Roderigo, the archbishop, says, are not only to conduct the Church's affairs but also to support the state. For they nurture fairness with greater zeal because consideration for their office and person requires it; or because they are perturbed less in their advanced stage of life and settled state of mind; or because, separated from marriage and not at all solicitous about sons—a condition that often forced great men into a dilemma—they use every care and solicitude for the universal public interests.

For this reason I find that eunuchs were associated by the Persian kings and other princes with the court offices in ancient times, since they thought that these, having no children, would have greater affection and faithfulness toward their princes; and from this goodwill some think that the word itself, eunuch, has been derived.

Lastly, we are convinced that the possession of property by the churches, whether it consists of rich vessels of gold and silver, annual incomes, field titles or estates, is especially beneficial to the state. There is a certain limit in this matter, as also in others, and a certain moderation in all things; nevertheless these means of increasing the majesty of religion, by which the public safety is maintained and the churchmen are maintained in their allegiance, not only do not hinder, but even help to the greatest possible degree.

Therefore we see that in those nations in which the care of the shrines is neglected and churchmen are cramped by a lack of means of sustenance, religion is at a low ebb, and the morals of the holy orders are likely to be lowered all the more foully. For we men are influenced by our senses, we are very much taken with the attractiveness of outward appearance, and dignity means a great deal to a person, so that even if his morals are not blameless, at least he will sin with greater reluctance.

God had a purpose in wanting the tabernacle and temple in the Jewish nation to abound in purple and gold, and in granting the tithes of the fields to the priests. Not even Christ nor the apostles condemned this custom or abrogated it, as if it were abhorrent to our institutions. We would do an excellent work if by the purity of our habits we were to win respect for ourselves and our religion, and if there were no need for external appearance. But since our times do not attain such distinction, they who strive to despoil the churches of their resources, to take away their possessions from the ministers of the churches, do it that contempt may be the greater, moderation, less—and with small danger, with light expense and with no shame.

In the next place, a great crowd of poor is supported with the resources of the church, for which purpose chiefly our forbears gave these means. I would prefer, indeed, that they be used with more restraint and with greater advantage. And I am not able to deny that not a few misuse these means for low reasons; I contend, however, that, if these expenditures are compared with the use of resources by the laymen, they contribute much more to the public good.

On the other hand, look at the great annual incomes of the nobles. You will not deny that they are consumed in superfluous care and adornment of the body, hunting dogs, an idle crowd of servants, and with little profit. This does not apply to the means of the churches. Even where the worst expenditures are made, many poor are fed, from which considerable benefits accrue to the state in war and peace. I ask you to consider that the incomes of the monasteries are not great, that by these means a great number of men are kept, born of honest, and in many cases noble parents. These are content with little and have enough to sustain life with cheap clothing and food. We pass over the other poor in the neighborhood, who in great numbers often are succored by these means.

If this income were given to any layman, one is sorry to say how easily and with what slender profit it would disappear, serving the stomach and appetite. It would certainly be expended for the upkeep of only a few servants and sons. Therefore they who argue that resources and incomes of the churches are useless and contend that they ought to be turned to better use are really mistaken in their view and do the state great harm if they are believed. Also I prefer to seek safety not by taking these riches away, but by seeing that they are devoted to the original uses and to feeding the poor. No one who has the story of antiquity explained and clearly understands it can doubt that this was the proposal of our ancestors.

In addition, the ornaments, the annual incomes and the churches' gold and silver coins serve the state in supreme crises as a kind of sacred treasury. When an enemy, ferocious and fearsome in victory, harasses it with war, or there is strife over our most holy religion, I do not think it will be out of place if the commonwealth uses these resources for protecting the public safety. I read often that the gold and silver vessels of the shrines were melted down to redeem the captives by very holy men, Ambrose, Cyril of Jerusalem, and others. Also I find that the Estates agreed at Medina del Campo in 1477 to allow Ferdinand the Catholic of recent memory to borrow half of the church gold to further his opposition to the armed assaults of Alphonso of Portugal, with the understanding that he would repay it in full in good faith when times became tranquil. And indeed the majesty of religion is not obscured by removing the treasure but is rather increased by this salutary use. Men are encouraged to vie in offering more still, for they see this as the most certain protection in difficult times.

The influence of the priests and the revenues of the cathedral of Toledo grew for no other reason to the amplitude that we see today (none in the whole world can be compared to it) than by the salutary use of its wealth. And particularly I find that Rodrigo Semen, archbishop of Toledo, in the very extremity of a lean harvest, when the cultivation of the fields was neglected and the towns were deserted far and wide, contributed much from his own resources and encouraged others by sermons to relieve the emergency; and that Alphonso, King of Castile, because of this meritorious action endowed the Toledo church with a new jurisdiction over many towns, since he had the idea that reserves were being deposited to the best purpose in the equivalent of a public treasury. I find further that the archbishop of Toledo was designated by the King as the Chancellor of the realm by perpetual and permanent legal right. This magistracy was thereafter the supreme and greatest authority next to that of the King. Therefore, neither the majesty nor the resources are diminished, but both are rather increased by salutary use.

However, the Prince should make use of these resources only if the situation be very grave and if all other agencies have been tried and aid from other sources should not suffice, indeed if the people have been untouched and the immunity of the nobles has been preserved, he ought not to take possession of the sacred treasures. That is sacrilegious, since they are sacred to God when given by our ancestors, whose testaments no one ought to change. In view of the fact that they have always been considered especially immune, is it right to lay hands on them first? At all events, if the former owners were in possession of these resources, the Prince would not touch them. How great is the pravity to take these same things away once they have been given to the churches and are protected with that sanctity? Moreover, who would dare to touch the support of the widows and orphans if one remembered the punishments for that sort of thing which Heliodorus mentions? And will anyone be so very impudent as to resolve to take possession of the sacred treasures, which are doubly pledged to the use of those who are helpless, first the widows and orphans, and then, of necessity, the churches and the holy orders, who are in the nature of wards and especially have need of the protection of the Prince?

At the same time I think that this property must be held inviolate to avoid discussion, which is a great factor in carrying on the public business well or badly. Indeed the people shun a person as impious if he touches the things sacred to God, and they think him and also the commonwealth fettered by an inexpiable curse through such a deed. If any adversity comes, it is interpreted as punishment for the crime.

For this reason when Ferdinand, King of Castile, surnamed Saint, was besieging Seville, there was a great and even supreme lack of supplies, and although certain people were urging him to relieve this with church property, lest he be forced to give up his campaign with deep shame to the Christian name, he absolutely refused to do it, declaring that he put greater faith in the prayers of the priests than in all their physical possessions and money. The reward for this moderation and piety was that the city, a well filled one, on the next day was reduced to his conditions of surrender.

On the other hand, the common opinion was that John I of Castile was defeated at Aljubarrota by a much smaller number of enemy solely because the votive offerings of the church at Guadaloupe, which it was sacrilegious to remove, were melted down for his war uses. The people considered the Virgin an avenging protectress of her shrine and possessions.

The consent of the church authorities would respond to the needs of the prince and the wish of the Roman Pontiff; this was a frequent practice in ancient times, and I do not know why it is disregarded now. But the bishops ought not to make themselves too difficult; rather they should help the prince and the commonwealth to the utmost of their abilities with their own and the churches' resources. For this is one of the very best uses to which consecrated means are devoted. Is it proper to want to avert a great common peril only with the resources of somebody else and not contribute something of one's own? Further, it is clear that in the time of Ambrose the estates of the Church paid a tax to the Christian emperors. Also we must take care that if the churches refuse their obligation recourse may be had to the other extreme and their consent may not even be asked; and the property would be seized from their unwilling hands, which is much more serious.

It ought to be diligently avoided that help once granted become permanent. But when the actual need has been met and provision has been made for the emergency, the rights and liberty of the churches should be restored; the resources should be turned to the ordinary uses.

The churches should assist by equipping the army and navy at their own expense and by providing subsistence. This will be better than if they are forced to pay ready money, which after peace has been gained the prince may turn to other uses, and then order a new levy for new difficulties that have arisen. There would be no end to the exaction.

It seems to me that the Prince must consider these matters, that the clergy must consider them, and that they must be done. And if they are neglected, the sacred order may indeed be too late in groaning over their lost liberty and reduced means, while the Prince in vain would plead necessity and an empty treasury.

Many serious misfortunes, indeed, can be cited, and history is full of examples of those princes whom the defiling of the holy treasures has driven out headlong. I pass over those who did it on their own responsibility, who are not of our religion, M. Crassus, Gneus Pompey, Antiochus, Heliodorus, Nebuchadnezzar. Then in our nation, Queen Urraca, daughter of Alphonso VI, died rent asunder on the portal of the church that she had robbed. And there were Charles Martel, prefect of the palace of the Franks, Aistulf, King of the Lombards, Emperor Frederick, and countless others whose unhappy deaths resulted from taking the treasures of the churches.

The story is that the Virgin of Thecla gave King Peter IV of Aragon a slap that proved fatal, for he died on the sixth day thereafter, and the rights of the Church of Tarragona which he had violated were vindicated by this punishment.

Sancho, King of Aragon, had seized on his own responsibility the good of the churches and priests; the poor condition of the treasury and the great expenses of the wars seemed to excuse him; besides, permission had been given him by Pope Gregory VII to change, transfer and give to whom he pleased, in accordance with his own decision, the tithes and revenues of the churches which had been built up or recently seized from the Moors. The king himself, by a remarkable example of Christian respect and piety, allayed the unpopularity and curse engendered by his acts, by publicly asking forgiveness in most humble attire, groaning and in tears, in the church of St. Victor in Rota, near the shrine of Saint Vincent. Ramon Dalmago, bishop of that city, was present, to whom he ordered everything that had been taken away to be returned with inviolate faith. And I marvel that in our time certain princes, whose conduct is similar, when they seize the goods of the churches, are neither moved by this King's lamentations nor shudder at his fate. In fact, at the siege of Osca, as he came near the wall, he perished by an arrow in the armpit—a man otherwise of great endowments of mind and body, but because of this one defect of avarice of less fame. Indeed, the people interpreted the seizure of the churches' goods as the cause of his unlucky death.

Yet Pope Urban II granted his son, King Peter, and his descendants the tithes and revenues of the churches which recently had been collected or taken from the Moors, excepting only those churches where the seats of the bishops were. So great was the desire to root out these impious people that they did not give consideration to the inconvenience that would be caused to posterity by this grant. Relying on the pontifical indulgence, Alphonso, brother of Peter, husband of Urraca, encouraged moreover by the King of Portugal, took the treasures of the churches for war purposes, which it was sacrilegious to take away. Isidore and the other saints avenged this wrong by despoiling Alphonso of his dowry kingdom of Castile, his wife, and finally his life at Fraga. The popular hate and the critics of this impious deed who were saying that heavy penalties were in store for the violators also were parties to this revenge.

Pope Gregory X gave the tithes of the churches to King Alphonso the Wise. This was compensation for the lost Roman power, but it was, indeed, not lasting and of no permanent benefit, as events showed. Bereft of his kingdom by the revolt of his son, he died in need and deserted, a prince who a little while before could be compared with great kings.

This certainly has as much effect as the treasurers and administrators of the royal estate admit and the facts themselves teach us: that by no means have alleged needs been relieved by the church revenues, but rather a greater crisis oppresses us, as if the touching of the property of the church consumed also the revenues of the king. Pliny therefore has some basis for his story that the wings of eagles feed on the wings of other birds mingled with them; and people say when lyre strings from the wolf are stretched on a tortoise shell with those from a sheep the former naturally gnaw on the latter with a certain secret force. Let us believe that the same applies in the present matter.

In any event, we wonder and deplore, although the royal revenues have been immeasurably augmented, a great treasure has been brought in from the Indian trade and from the annual voyages, the tithes of the churches, besides, for a great part have been seized, and all the estates are groaning under the impositions of a heavy burden, that still the money is not at all equal to the demand in peace and war. We wonder and deplore that the state is pressed by a very serious exigency and much smaller victories are gained than formerly on land and sea.

Now the people and also the leaders of the nation put an interpretation on the violation of the sacred possessions; they say, this violation weakens might and causes other resources and revenues to decline.

The vessels of the temple of Jerusalem, in fact, were seized by Titus Vespasian; they were carried from Rome by Genseric, the Vandal, with other spoils into Africa, and they wandered through many Roman Vandal families. After all their possessors had been punished and overthrown, they did not come to rest until, after the empire of the Vandals had been destroyed by the generalship of Belisarius, and after Gelimer, the last king of that nation, had been captured, they were returned by the order of Justinian Augustus to Jerusalem, thus gaining a most conspicuous triumph after so many ages over the enemies of religion and their own violators.

But enough about the royal power. We ought, therefore, to restrain the Prince by precepts and education, holding a rein on the perilous time of his life, to keep him from going wild in pleasures and degenerating through wealth into tyranny. He should, on his part, exhibit that benevolence toward his citizens, that moderation in every phase of his life, that reverence of law and religion which is pleasing to God, fair to himself, and conducive to the safety of the Commonwealth as a whole.

And let all love him, admire and cherish him, not as if he were of mortal mould, but as the most brilliant star, a gift from Heaven, of divine descent.

7. John Lilburne, *A Work of the Beast*

John Lilburne (1614–57) fits no pigeonhole that existed in his day; if "radical" can be considered a human type in modern history without reference to the aims of a particular cause, there is no early modern prototype to match Lilburne. The story of his personal struggles against the authorities and "the system" is inseparable from the evolution of his ideas. Lilburne's social position was middling: he was a cloth merchant turned brewer, and subsequently a successful officer on Parliament's side in the English Civil War. The first of his major clashes with authority occurred in 1638, and it is his manner of dealing with this episode—typically, by writing a pamphlet—that *A Work of the Beast* documents. His first cause was the Puritan one; his first oppressor a regime in Protestant England that was rather more intent than earlier ones to define a distance between the state church and the party of Protestant zeal: heavy-handed measures were taken against a few agitators. The regime was the government of Charles I (son of James I), its ecclesiastical branch headed by Archbishop William Laud. This was the regime that drove some Englishmen of Puritan persuasion to Massachusetts, and provoked many whose Protestantism was too commonplace to call puritan, and whose respect for law and authority would have shrunk from Lilburne-like attitudes, into aggrievement.

   The face of established authority changed drastically during the course of the Civil War, but there were many more occasions when Lilburne squared off against it—many more pamphlets. The prophetic voice of Protestant zeal, first heard in a specifically religious cause, though adapted to the more secular issues of his later conflicts with authority, continued to be Lilburne's. For such men, the religious and the secular are ultimately indivisible. While there is no such thing as *the* cause of liberty, much that Lilburne agitated for came in time to count among the truisms of the liberal creed.

A Work of the Beast, or, A Relation of a Most Unchristian Censure, executed upon John Lilburne (now prisoner in the fleet) the 18th of April 1638 with the heavenly speech uttered by him at the time of his suffering

Upon Wednesday the said 18 of April, having no certain notice of the execution of my censure, till this present morning, I prepared myself by prayer

From John Lilburne, *A Work of the Beast* (London, 1638).

unto God, that He would make good His promise, to be with me and enable me to undergo my affliction with joyfulness and courage: and that He would be a mouth and utterance unto me to enable me to speak that which might make for His greatest honour. And in any meditations my soul did principally pitch upon these three places of Scripture.

First, that in Isaiah 41.10.11.12.13. Fear thou not for I am with thee, be not dismayed for I am thy God, I will strengthen thee, yea I will help thee, yea I will uphold thee with the right hand of my righteousness. Behold all they that were incensed against thee shall be ashamed and confounded, they shall be as nothing, and they that strive with thee shall perish. Thou shalt seek them and shall not find them, even them that contended with thee, they that war against thee shall be as nothing and as a thing of nought. For I the Lord thy God will hold thee by the right hand, saying unto thee, fear not, I will help thee, fear not thou worm Jacob, and yee men of Israel, I will help, thus sayth the Lord and thy Redeemer the Holy one of Israel. Etc.

Secondly, that place in Isaiah 43.1.2. Where God speaks thus to his elect. Fear not for I have redeemed thee, I have called thee by thy name thou art mine. When thou passest through the waters I will be with thee, and through the rivers they shall not overflow thee, when thou walkest through the fire thou shalt not be burnt, neither shall the flame kindle upon thee.

Thirdly, that in Hebrews 13.5.6. In these words for he hath said I will never leave thee nor forsake thee, so that we may boldly say the Lord is my helper, I will not fear what man can do to me.

With the consideration of these and other gracious promises, made to His people, I being one of His chosen ones, did claim my share and interest in them, and the Lord of His infinite goodness enabled me to cast myself upon and rest in them, knowing and steadfastly believing that He is a God of faithfulness and power, who is able and willing to make good these His promises to the utmost, and (to His praise be it spoken I desire to speak it) my soul was that morning exceedingly lifted up with spiritual consolation and I felt within me such a divine supportation, that the baseness of my punishment I was to undergo did seem as a matter of nothing to me. And I went to my suffering with as willing and joyful heart as if I had been going to solemnize the day of my marriage with one of the choicest creatures this world could afford. The Warden of the Fleet having sent his men for my old fellow soldier Mr. John Wharton, and myself being both in one chamber, we made ourselves ready to go to the place of execution. I took the old man by the hand and led him down three pair of stairs, and so along the yard till we came to the gate. And when we came there George Harrington the Porter told me I must stay a little, and after our parting (commending one another to the protection of our all sufficient God) I was bid go to the Porter's

Lodge, no sooner was I gone in, but came John Hawes, the other Porter to me saying these words.

Mr. Lilburne, I am very sorry for your punishment, you are now to undergo, you must strip you, and be whipt from hence to Westminster.

I replied, the will of my God be done, for I know He will carry me through it with an undaunted spirit; but I must confess it seemed at the first a little strange to me, in regard I had no more notice given me for my preparation for so sore a punishment. For I thought I should not have been whipt through the street but only at the pillory: and so passing along the lane being attended with many staves and halberds, as Christ was when He was apprehended by His enemies and led to the High Priest's Hall. Matthew 26, we came to Fleet-bridge where was a cart standing ready for me. And I being commanded to strip me, I did it with all willingness and cheerfulness, where upon the executioner took out a cord and tied my hands to the cart's ass, which caused me to utter these words, Welcome be the Cross of Christ.

With that there drew near a young man of my acquaintance, and bid me put on a courageous resolution to suffer cheerfully and not to dishonor my cause for you suffer (said he) for a good cause, I gave him thanks, for his Christian encouragement, I replying I know the cause is good, for it is God's cause, and for my own part I am cheerful and merry in the Lord, and am as well contented with this my present portion as if I were to receive my present liberty. For I know my God that hath gone along with me hither to, will carry me through to the end. And for the affliction itself, though it be the punishment inflicted upon rogues, yet I esteem it not the least disgrace, but the greatest honour that can be done unto me, that the Lord counts me worthy to suffer anything for His great name.

And you my Brethren that do now here behold my present condition this day, be not discouraged, be not discouraged at the ways of Godliness by reason of the Cross which accompanies it, for it is the lot and portion of all which will live Godly in Christ Jesus to suffer persecution.

The cart being ready to go forward, I spoke to the executioner (when I saw him pull out his corded whip out of his pocket) after this manner, Well my friend do thy office. To which he replied I have whipt many a rogue but now I shall whip an honest man. But be not discouraged (said he) it will be soon over.

To which I replied, I know my God hath not only enabled me to believe in His name, but also to suffer for His sake. So the cartman drove forward his cart, and I laboured with my God for strength to submit my back with cheerfulness unto the smiter. And He heard my desire and granted my request, for when the first stripe was given I felt not the least pain but said, Blessed be Thy name O Lord my God that hast counted me worthy to suffer for Thy glorious name's sake; And at the giving of the second, I cried out with a loud voice, Hallelujah, Hallelujah, Glory, Honour, and Praise, be given to thee O Lord forever, and to the Lamb that sits upon the Throne. So we went up Fleet Street, the Lord enabling me to endure the stripes with such patience and cheerfulness, that I did not in the least manner show the least discontent at them, for my God hardened my back, and steeled my veins and took away the smart and pain of the stripes from me.

But I must confess, if I had had no more but my own natural strength, I had sunk under the burden of my punishment, for to the flesh the pain was very grevious and heavy: But my God in whom I did trust was higher and stronger than myself, who strengthened and enabled me not only to undergo the punishment with cheerfulness: but made me triumph and with a holy disdain to insult over my torments.

And as we went along the Strand, many friends spoke to me and asked how I did, and bid me be cheerful, to whom I replied, I was merry and cheerful: and was upheld with a divine and heavenly supportation, comforted with the sweet consolations of God's spirit. And about the middle of the Strand, there came a friend and bid me speak with boldness. To whom I replied, when the time comes so I will. For then if I should have spoken and spent my strength, it would have been but as water spilt on the ground, in regard of the noise and press of people. And also at that time I was not in a fit temper to speak: because the dust much troubled me, and the sun shined very hot upon me. And the Tipstaff man at the first would not let me have my hat to keep the vehement heat of the sun from my head. Also he many times spoke to the cartman to drive softly, so that the heat of the sun exceedingly pierced my head: and made me undergo it with a joyful heart. And when I came to Chearing Cross some Christian friends spoke to me and bid me to be of good cheer.

So I am (said I) for I rest not in my own strength, but I fight under the Banner of my great and mighty Captain the Lord Jesus Christ who hath conquered all his enemies, and I doubt not but through His strength I shall conquer and overcome all my sufferings, for His power upholds me, His strength enables me, His presence cheers me, and His Spirit comforts me, and I look for an immortal Crown which never shall fade nor decay, the assured hope and expectation whereof makes me to contemn my sufferings, and count them as nothing, for my momentary affliction will work for me a far more exceeding Crown and weight of glory. And as I went by the King's palace a great multitude of people came to look upon me. And passing through the gate into Westminster, many demanded what was the matter.

To whom I replied, my Brethren, against the Law of God, against the law of the land, against the King or State have I not committed the least offence that deserves this punishment, but only I suffer as an object of the Prelate's cruelty and malice; and hereupon, one of the Wardens of the Fleets-officers, began to interrupt me, and tells me my suffering was just and therefore I should hold my tongue; Whom I bid meddle with his own business, for I would speak come what would, for my cause was good for which I suffered, and here I was ready to shed my dearest blood for it.

And as we went through Kings Street, many encouraged me, and bid me be cheerful; Others whose faces (to my knowledge) I never saw before, and who I verily think knew not the cause of my suffering, but feeling my cheerfulness under it, beseeched the Lord to bless me and strengthen me.

At the last we came to the pillory, where I was unloosed from the cart, and having put on some of my clothes we went to the tavern, where I staid a pretty while waiting for my surgeon, who was not yet come to dress me. Where were many of my friends, who exceedingly rejoiced to see my courage, that the Lord had enabled me to undergo my punishment so willingly.

Who asked me how I did, I told them, as well as ever I was in my life I blessed my God for it, for I felt such inward joy and comfort, cheering up my soul, that I lightly esteemed my sufferings. And this I counted my wedding day in which I was married to the Lord Jesus Christ; for now I know He loves me in that He hath bestowed so rich apparel this day upon me, and counted me worthy to suffer for His sake. I having a desire to retire into a private room from the multitude of people that were about me, which made me like to faint: I had not been there long but Mr. Lightburne the Tipstaff of the Star Chamber, came to me saying the Lords sent him to me, to know if I would acknowledge myself to be in a fault and then he knew what to say unto me. To whom I replied, Have their Honours caused me to be whipt from the Fleet to Westminster, and do they now send to know if I will acknowledge a fault. They should have done this before I had been whipt; for now seeing I have undergone the greatest part of my punishment, I hope the Lord will assist me to go through it all. And besides, if I would have done this at the first I needed not to have come to this, but as I told the Lords when I was before them at the Bar, so I desire you to tell them again, that I am not conscious to myself of doing.anything that deserves a submission, but yet I do willingly submit to their Lordships' pleasures in my censure. He told me if I would confess a fault it would save me astanding on the pillory, otherwise I must undergo the burden of it.

Well, (said I) regard not a little outward disgrace for the cause of my God, I have found already that sweetness in Him in whom I have believed, that through His strength I am able to undergo anything that shall be inflicted on me; But me thinks that I had very hard measure that I should be condemned and thus punished upon two oaths, in which the party hath most falsely foresworn himself: and because I would not take an oath to betray mine own innocence; Why Paul found more favor and mercy from the Heathen Roman Governors, for they would not put him to an oath to accuse himself, but suffered him to make the best defence he could for himself, neither would they condemn him before his accusers and he were brought face to face, to justify and fully to prove their accusation: But the Lords have not dealt so with me, for my accusers and I were never brought face to face to justify their accusation against me: it is true two false oaths were sworn against me: and I was thereupon condemned, and because I would not accuse myself. It is true (said he) it was so with Paul but the Laws of this Land are otherwise than their Laws were in those days. Then said I, they are worse and more cruel, than the Laws of the Pagans and Heathen Romans were, who would condemn no man without witnesses, and they should be brought face to face, to justify their accusations. And so he went away, and I prepared myself for the Pillory, to which I went with a joyful courage. And when I was upon it, I made obeisance to the Lords, some of them (I suppose) looking out at the Star-Chamber window, towards me. And so I put my neck into the hole, which being a great deal too low for me, it was very painful to me in regard of the continuance of time that I stood on the Pillory: which was about two hours, my back also being very sore, and the Sun shining exceeding hot. And the Tipstaff man, not suffering me to keep on my hat, to defend my head from the heat of the Sun. So that I stood there in great pain. Yet through the strength of my God I underwent it with courage: to the very last minute. And lifting up my heart and spirit unto my God,

While I was thus standing on the Pillory, I craved his Powerful assistance: with the spirit of wisdom and courage, that I might open my mouth with boldness: and speak those things that might make for His greatest glory, and the good of his people, and so casting my eyes on the multitude, I began to speak after this manner.

My Christian Brethren, to all you that love the Lord Jesus Christ, and desire that He should reign and rule in your hearts and lives, to you especially: and to as many as hear me this day: I direct my speech.

I stand here in the place of ignominy and shame. Yet to me it is not so, but I own and embrace it, as the Welcome Cross of Christ. And as a badge of my Christian Profession. I have been already whipt from the Fleet to this place, by virtue of a Censure: from the Honourable Lords of the Star Chamber hereunto, the cause of my Censure I shall declare unto you as briefly as I can.

The Lord by his special hand of providence so ordered it, that not long ago I was in Holland. Where I was like to have settled myself in a course of trading, that might have brought me in a pretty large portion of earthly things; (after which my heart did too much run) but the Lord having a better portion in store for me, and more durable riches to bestow upon my soul. By the same hand of providence: brought me back again. And cast me into easy affliction, that thereby I might be weaned from the world, and see the vanity and emptiness of all things therein. And He hath now pitched my soul upon such an object of beauty, amiableness, and excellence, as is as permanent and endurable as eternity itself, namely the personal excellence of the Lord Jesus Christ, the sweetness of whose presence, no affliction can ever be able to wrest out of my soul.

Now while I was in Holland, it seems there were diverse books of that noble and renowned Dr. John Bastwick's sent into England which came to the hands of one Edmond Chillington, for the sending over which I was taken, and apprehended, the plot being before laid, by one John Chilliburne (whom I supposed and took to be my friend) servant to my old fellow soldier Mr. John Wharton living in Bow Lane (after this manner).

I walking in the street with the said John Chilliburne, was taken by the Pursuant and his men, the said John as I verily believe, having given direction to them: where to stand, and he himself was the third man that laid hands on me to hold me.

Now at my Censure before the Lords: I there declared upon the word of a Christian that I sent not over those books, neither did I know the ship that brought them, nor any of the men that belonged to the ship, nor to my knowledge did I ever see, either ship, or any appertaining to it, in all my days.

Besides this, I was accused at my examination, before the King's Attorney at his Chamber, by the said Edmond Chillington, button seller living in Canon Street near Abchurch Lane, and late prisoner in Bridewell and Newgate, for printing ten or twelve thousand books in Holland, and that I would have printed *The Unmasking the Mystery of Iniquity* if I could have got a true copy of it, and that I had a chamber in Mr. John Foot's house at Delft where he thinks the books were kept. Now here I declare before you all, upon the word of a suffering Christian: that he might have as well accused me of printing a hundred thousand books, and that been as true as the other; and for the printing *The Unmasking the Mystery of Iniquity,* upon the word of an honest man I never saw, nor to my knowledge heard of the book till I came back again into England: And for my having a chamber in Mr. John Foot's house at Delft, where he thinks the books were kept, I was so far from having a chamber there, as I never lay in his house, but twice or thrice at the most. And upon the last Friday of the last term I was brought to the Star Chamber Bar, where before me was read the said Edmond Chillington's affidavit, upon oath, against Mr. John Wharton and myself. The sum of which oath was that he and I had printed (at Rotterdam in Holland,) Dr. Bastwick's *Answer* and his *Litany* with divers other scandalous books.

Now here again I speak it in the presence of God and all you that hear me, that Mr. Wharton and I never joined together in printing, either these or any other books whatsoever. Neither did I receive any money from him toward the printing any.

Withall, in his first oath he peremptorily swore that we had printed them at Rotterdam, unto which I likewise say that he hath in this particular forsworn himself. For my own part, I never in all my days either printed, or caused to be printed, either for myself or Mr. Wharton any books at Rotterdam. Neither did I come into any printing house there all the time I was in the city.

And then upon the twelfth day after he swore against both of us again. The sum of which oath was that I had confessed to him (which is most false) that I had printed Dr. Bastwick's *Answer to Sir John Banks,* his *Information,* and his *Litany;* and another book called *Certain Answers to Certain Objections;* and another book called *The Vanity and Impiety of the Old Litany;* and that I had diverse other books of the said Dr. Bastwick's in printing; and that Mr. Wharton had been at the charges of printing a book called *A Breviat* of the Bishop's late proceeding; and another book called *Sixteen New Queries,* and in this oath hath sworn they were printed at Rotterdam or somewhere else in Holland; and that one James Oldam, a turner keeping shop at Westminster Hall Gate, dispersed divers of these books. Now in his oath he hath again forsworn himself in a high degree, for whereas he took his oath that I had printed the book called *The Vanity and Impiety of the Old Litany,* I here speak it before you all, that I never in all my days did see one of them in print, but I must confess, I have seen and read it, in written hand, before the Dr. was censured, and as for the other books, of which he saith I have diverse in printing, to that I answer that for mine own particular I never read nor saw any of the Drs. books: but the forenamed four in English and one little thing more of about two sheets of paper which is annexed to the *Vanity of the Old Litany.* And as for the Latin books, I never saw but two: Namely his *Flagellum,* for which he was first censured in the High Commission Court; and his *Apologeticus,* which were both in print long before I knew the Doctor. But it is true, there is a second edition of his *Flagellum,* but that was at the press about two years ago: namely Anno 1634. And some of this impression was in England before I came out of Holland.

And these are the main things for which I was Censured and Condemned, being two oaths in which the said Chillington hath palpably forsworn himself. Yet by the law (as I am given to understand) I might have excepted against him, being a guilty person himself and a prisoner, and did that which he did against me for purchasing his own liberty which he hath by such Judasly means got and obtained, who is also known to be a lying fellow, as I told the Lords I was able to prove and make good.

But besides all this, there was an inquisition oath tendered unto me (which I refused to take) on four several days; the sum of which oath is thus much. You shall swear that you shall make true answer to all things that shall be asked of you: So help you God. Now this oath I refused as a sinful and unlawful oath: it being the High Commission Oath, with which the Prelates ever have and still do so butcherly torment, afflict and undo the dear Saints and Servants of God. It is also an oath against the Law of the Land, as Mr. Nicholas Fuller in his argument doth prove. And also it is expressly against the Petition of Right, an act of Parliament enacted in the second year of our King. Again, it is absolutely against the Law of God, for that law requires no man to accuse himself, but if anything be laid to his charge: there must come two or three witnesses at the least to prove it. It is also against the practice of Christ himself, who in all His examinations before the High Priest would not accuse Himself: but upon their demands, returned this answer: Why ask ye me, go to them that heard me.

With all this oath is against the very law of nature, for nature is always a preserver of itself and not a destroyer. But if a man takes this wicked oath he destroys and undoes himself, as daily experience doth witness. Nay it is worse than the Law of the Heathen Romans, as we may read Acts 25.16. For when Paul stood before the Pagan Governors, and the Jews required judgement against him, the Governor replied, it is not the manner of the Romans to condemn any man before his accusers and he were brought face to face to justify their accusation. But for my own part, if I had been proceeded against by a Bill, I would have answered and justified all that they could have proved against me, and by the strength of my God would have sealed whatsoever I have done with my blood, for I am privy to mine own actions, and my conscience bears me witness that I have labored ever since the Lord in mercy made the riches of his grace known to my soul, to keep a good conscience and to walk inoffensably both towards God and man. But as for the oath that was put unto me, I did refuse to take it, as a sinful and unlawful oath, and by the strength of my God enabling me I will never take it though I be pulled in pieces with wild horses as the ancient Christians were by the bloody tyrants in the Primitive Church, neither shall I think that man a faithful subject of Christ's Kingdom that shall at any time hereafter take it, seeing the wickedness of it hath been so apparently laid open by so many, for the refusal whereof many do suffer cruel persecution to this day. Thus have I as briefly as I could declared unto you the whole cause of my standing here this day, I being, upon these grounds censured by the Lords at the Star Chamber on the last Court day of the last term to pay 500 po. to the King and to receive punishment which with rejoicing I have undergone, unto whose censure I do with willingness and cheerfulness submit myself.

But seeing I now stand here at this present, I intend, the Lord assisting me with His power, and guiding me by His spirit, to declare my mind unto you.

I have nothing to say to any man's person, and therefore will not meddle with that. Only the things that I have to say in the first place, are concerning the Bishops and their calling. They challenge their callings to be *Jure Divino,* and for the opposing of which, those three renowned living martyrs of the Lord, Dr. Bastwick, M. Burton, and M. Prinne: did suffer in this place, and they have sufficiently proved that their (the Bishops') Calling is not from God, which men I love and honour, and do persuade myself their souls are dear and precious in the sight of God, though they were so butcherly dealt with by the Prelates, and as for Mr. Burton and Mr. Prinne they are worthy and learned men, but yet did not in main things write so fully as the Doctor did, who hath sufficiently and plentifully set forth the wickedness, both of the Prelates themselves and of their Callings (as you may read in his books), that they are not *Jure Divino.* Which noble and reverend Doctor I love with my soul, and as he is a man that stands for the truth and glory of God, my very life and heart's blood I will lay down for his honour, and the maintaining of his cause, for which he suffered, it being God's cause. As for the Bishops, they used in former times to challenge their jurisdiction, callings, and power from the King. But they have now openly in the High Commission Court renounced that as was heard by many, at the Censure of that noble Doctor. And as you may fully read in his *Apollogeticus,* and in his *Answer to Sir John Bankes,* and his *Information,* now I will maintain it before them all, that their Calling is so far from being *Jure Divino* (as they say they are) that they are rather *Jure Diabollico.* Which if I be not able to prove, let me be hanged up at the Hall Gate. But my Brethren, for your better satisfaction, read the 9th and 13th Chapters of the Revelation, and there you shall see, that there came locusts out of the Bottomless Pit, part of whom they are, and they are there lively described. Also you shall there find that the Beast (which is the Pope, or Roman State and Government) hath given him by the Dragon (the Devil) his power and seat, and great authority, so that the Pope's authority comes from the Devil, and the Prelates, and their Creatures in their printed books, do challenge their authority, jurisdiction, and power (that they exercise over all sorts of people) is from Rome.

And for proving of the Church of England to be a true Church, their best and strongest argument is: that the Bishops are lineally descended from his Holiness (or impiousness) of Rome: as you may read in Pocklington's book called *Sunday no Sabbath.* So by their own confession they stand by the same power and authority that they have received from the Pope. So that their calling is not from God but from the Devil. For the Pope cannot give a better authority or calling to them than he himself hath. But his authority and calling is from the Devil: Therefore the Prelates calling and authority is from the Devil also. Revelations 9.3. And there came out of the smoke, Locusts upon the earth: and unto them was given power as the Scorpions of the earth have power to hurt and undo men, as the Prelates daily do. And also Revelations 9.3. And the Beast which I saw (saith St. John) was like unto a Leopard, and his feet were as the feet of a Bear, and his mouth as the mouth of a Lion, and the Dragon (that is to say the Devil) gave him his power, his seat, and great authority. And verse 15.16.17. And whether the Prelates as well as the Pope do not daily the same things, let every man that hath but common reason judge.

For do not their daily practices and cruel burdens imposed on all sorts of people, high and low, rich and poor witness that their descent is from the Beast, part of his state and kingdom. So also Revelations 16.13.14. All which places do declare that their power and authority being from the Pope (as they themselves confess) therefore it must needs originally come from the Devil. For their power and callings must of necessity proceed either from God or else from the Devil. But it proceeds not from God, as the Scriptures sufficiently declare. Therefore their calling and power proceeds from the Devil, as both Scripture and their own daily practices do demonstrate and prove. And as for that last place cited Revelations 16.13.14. if you please read the second and third parts of Dr. Bastwick's *Litany,* you shall find he there proves that the Prelates' practices do every way suit with and make good that portion of Scripture to the utmost. For in their sermons that they preach before his Majesty, how do they incense the King and Nobles against the people of God, labouring to make them odious in his sight and stirring him up to execute vengeance upon them, though they be the most harmless generation of all others.

And as for all these officers that are under them and made by them, for mine own particular I cannot see but that their callings are as unlawful as the Bishops themselves, and in particular for the callings of the ministers, I do not, nor will not speak against their persons for I know some of them to be very able men, and men of excellent gifts and qualifications, and I persuade myself their souls are very dear and precious in the sight of God.

Yet not withstanding, this proves not their callings to be ever the better. As it is in civil government, if the King (whom God hath made a lawful Magistrate) make a wicked man an officer, he is as true an officer and as well to be obeyed, comming in the King's name, as the best man in the world comming with the same authority. For in such a case, he that is a wicked man hath his calling from as good authority as the godliest man hath. And therefore his calling is as good as the others.

But on the other side, if he that hath no authority make officers, though the men themselves be ever so good and holy, yet their holiness makes their calling never a whit the truer, but still is a false calling: in regard his authority was not good nor lawful that made them; and so the ministers, be they ever so good and holy, yet they have one and the same calling with the wickedest that is amongst them. Their holiness proves not their callings to be ever the truer: seeing their authority that made them ministers is false, and therefore they have more to answer for than any of the rest: by how much the more God hath bestowed greater gifts upon them than upon others, and yet they detain the truth in unrighteousness from God's people: and do not make known to them as they ought the whole will and counsel of God.

And again, the greater is their sin if their callings be unlawful (as I verily believe they are), in that they still hold them and do not willingly lay them down and renounce them, for they do but deceive the people and highly dishonour God, and sin against their own souls, while they preach unto the people by virtue of an Antichristian and unlawful Calling, and the more godly and able the minister is that still preaches by virtue of this calling, the more hurt he doth, for the people that have such a minister will not be persuaded of the truth of things, though one speak and inform them in the name of the Lord; but will be ready to reply, Our Minister that preaches still by virtue of this Calling, is so holy a man, that were not his calling right and good, I do assure myself he would no longer preach by virtue thereof. And thus the holiness of the minister is a cloak to cover the unlawfulness of his calling, and make the people continue rebels against Christ's his Scepter and Kingdom, which is an aggravation of his sin. For by this means the people are kept off from receiving the whole truth into their souls, and rest in being but almost Christians, or but Christians in part. But Oh my Brethren, it behooves all you that fear God and tender the salvation of your own souls to look about you and to shake off that long security and formality in religion that you have lain in, for the God of all things cannot endure "Lukewarmness" Revelations 3.16. And search out diligently the truth of things, and try them in the Balance of the Sanctuary. I beseech you take things no more upon truth, as hitherto you have done, but take pains to search and find out those spiritual and hidden truths that God hath enwrapped in his sacred Book, and find out a bottom for your own souls. For if you will have the comforts of them, you must bestow some labour for the getting of them, and you must search diligently before you find them. Proverbs 2. Labour also to withdraw your necks from under that spiritual and Antichristian bondage (unto which you have for a long time subjected yourselves) lest the Lord cause his plagues and the fierceness of his wrath to seize both upon your bodies and souls: seeing you are now warned of the danger of these things.

For he Himself hath said Revelations 14.9.10.11. "That if any man worship the Beast and his Image, and receive his marks in his forehead or in his hand, the same shall drink of the wine of His wrath: which is poured out without mixture into the cup of His indignation, and he shall be tormented with fire and brimstone in the presence of the holy angels and in the presence of the Lamb, and the smoke of their torment ascended up for ever and ever, and they have no rest day nor night who worship the Beast and his Image and whosoever receiveth the mark of his name." Therefore as you love your own souls and look for that immortal Crown of happiness in the world to come, look that you withdraw yourselves from that Antichristian power and slavery that you are now under, even as God himself hath commanded and enjoined you in Revelations 18.4. saying "Come out of her my people that you be not partaker of her sins and that ye receive not of her plagues, for her sins have reached unto heaven, and God hath remembered her iniquities." Here is the voice of God himself commanding all his chosen ones, though they have lived under this Antichristian slavish power and estate a long time, yet at last to withdraw their obedience and subjection from it. My Brethren, we are all at this present in a very dangerous and fearful condition, under the idolatrous and spiritual bondage of the Prelates, in regard we have turned traitors unto our God, in seeing his Almighty name and his Heavenly truth troden under foot, and so highly dishonoured by them, and yet we not only let them alone in holding our peace, but most slavishly and wickedly subject ourselves unto them, fearing the face of a piece of dirt more than the Almighty great God of heaven and earth, who is able to cast both body and soul into everlasting damnation.

Oh repent, I beseech you therefore repent, for the great dishonour you have suffered to be done unto God by your fearfulness and cowardliness, and for the time to come, put on courageous resolutions like valiant soldiers of Jesus Christ, and fight manfully in this His spiritual battle, in which battle some of His soldiers have already lost part of their blood, and withall study the Book of Revelation, and there you shall find the mystery of iniquity fully unfolded and explained; and also you shall see what great spiritual battles have been fought betwixt the Lamb and his Servants and the Dragon (the Devil) and his vassals, and some are yet to fight.

Therefore gird on your spiritual armour spoken of in Ephesians 6. that you may quit yourselves like good and faithful soldiers, and fear no colours the victory and conquest is ours already, for we are sure to have it (I do not speak of any bodily and temporal battle, but only of a spiritual one), and be not discouraged and knocked off from the study of it because of the obscurity and darkness of it, for the Lord hath promised his enlightening spirit unto all his people that are labourious and studious to know him aright, and also he hath promised a blessing and pronounced a blessedness unto all that read and labour to keep the things contained in this Book. Revelations 1.3. My Christian Brethren, in the bowels of Jesus Christ I beseech you do not condemn the things that are delivered to you, in regard of the meanness and weakness of me the instrument, being but one of the meanest and unworthiest of the servants of Jesus Christ, for the Lord many times doth great things by weak means, that His power may be more seen, for we are too ready to cast our eye upon the means and instrument: not looking up unto that Almighty power that is in God, who is able to do the greatest things by the weakest means, and therefore out of the mouths of "Babes and Sucklings" He hath ordained strength. Psalms 8.2. And He hath chosen the foolish things of the world to confound the wise, and God hath chosen the weak things of the world to confound the things which are mighty, and base things of the world, and things which are dispised hath God chosen, yea things which are not, to bring to nought things that are. I Corinthians 1.27.28. And He gives the reason wherefore He is pleased so to do: "That no flesh should glory in His presence." So you see God is not tied to any instrument and means to effect His own glory, but He by the least instrument is able to bring to pass the greatest things.

It is true, I am a young man and no scholar, according to that which the world counts scholarship, yet I have obtained mercy of the Lord to be faithful, and He by a divine providence hath brought me hither this day, and I speak to you in the name of the Lord, being assisted with the spirit and power of the God of heaven and earth, and I speak not the words of rashness or inconsiderateness, but the words of soberness and mature de-liberation, for I did consult with my God before I came hither and desired Him that He would direct and enable me to speak that which might be for His glory and the good of His people. And as I am a soldier fighting under the banner of the great and mighty Captain and Lord Jesus Christ, and as I look for that Crown of immortality which one day I know shall be set upon my temples, being in the condition that I am in, I dare not hold my peace, but speak unto you with boldness in the might and strength of my God, the things which the Lord in mercy hath made known unto my soul, come life come death.

When I was here about, there came a fat Lawyer, I do not know his name, and commanded me to hold my peace and leave my preaching. To whom I replied and said, "Sir, I will not hold my peace but speak my mind freely though I be hanged at Tiburne for my pains." It seems he himself was galled and touched as the Lawyers were in Christ's time when He spoke against the Scribes and Pharisees, which made them say, "Master in saying thus thou revilest us also." So he went away and (I think) com-plained to the Lords, but I went on with my speech and said,

My Brethren, be not discouraged at the ways of God for the affliction and Cross that doth accompany them, for it is sweet and comfortable drawing in the Yoke of Christ for all that, and I have found it so by experience, for my soul is filled so full of spiritual and heavenly joy, that with my tongue I am not able to express it, neither are any capable (I think) to partake of so great a degree of consolation but only those upon whom the Lord's gracious afflicting hand is.

And for mine own part I stand this day in the place of an evil doer, but my conscience witnesseth that I am not so. And here about I put my hand in my pocket and pulled out three of worthy Dr. Bastwick's books and threw them among the people and said, "There is part of the books for which I suffer, take them among you, and read them, and see if you find anything in them against the Law of God, the Law of the Land, the glory of God, the honour of the King or state."

I am the son of a Gentleman, and my Friends are of rank and quality in the Country where I live, which is 200 miles from this place, and I am in my present condition deserted of them all, for I know not one of them dare meddle with me in my present estate, being I am stung by the Scorpions (the Prelates) and for anything I know, it may be I shall never have a favourable countenance from any of them again; and with all, I am a young man and likely to have lived well and in plenty, according to the fashion of the world. Yet not withstanding, for the cause of Christ, and to do Him service, I have and do bid adieu to Father, Friends, Riches, pleasures, ease, contented life and blood, and lay down all at the Footstoole of Jesus Christ, being willing to part with all rather than I will dishonour Him or in the least measure part with the peace of a good conscience, and that sweetness and joy which I have found in him, for in naked Christ is the quintessence of sweetness and I am so far from thinking my affliction and punishment which this day I have endured and still do endure and groan under (a disgrace) that I receive it as the welcome Cross of Christ, and do think myself this day more honoured by my sufferings than if a Crown of gold had been set upon my head, for I have in some part been made conformable to my Lord and Master, and have in some measure drunk of the same Cup which He Himself drank of, while He was in this sinful world, for He shed His most precious blood for the salvation of my poor soul, that so I might be reconciled to his Father, therefore I am willing to undergo anything for His sake, and that inward joy and consolation within me that carries me high above all my pains and torments, and you (My Brethren) if you be willing to have Christ, you must own Him and take Him upon His own terms, and know that Christ and the Cross are inseparable, for he that will live godly in Christ Jesus must suffer persecution and affliction, it is the lot and portion of all his chosen ones, through many afflictions and trials we must enter into glory and the Apostle saith "that if we be without afflictions whereof all are partakers, then are ye Bastards and not Sons." And therefore if you will have Christ sit down and reckon before ever you make profession of Him what He will cost you, lest when you come to trial you dishonour Him, and if you be not willing and contented to part withall and let all go for His sake, you are not worthy of Him.

If parents, husband, wife, or children, lands or livings, riches or honours, pleasure or ease, life or blood stand in the way, you must be willing to part with all these and to entertain Christ naked and alone, though you have nothing but the Cross, or else you are not worthy of Him. Matthew 10.37.38.

Oh my Brethren there is such sweetness and contentedness in enjoying the Lord Jesus alone, that it is able where it is felt, to make a man go through all difficulties and endure all hardships that may possibly come upon him. Therefore if He call you to it, do not deny Him nor His truth in the least manner for He hath said, "He that denies Him before men, him will He deny before His Father which is in Heaven." And now is the time that we must show ourselves good Soldiers of Jesus Christ, for His truth, His cause and glory lies at stake in a high degree, therefore put on courageous resolutions, and withdraw your necks and souls from all false power and worship, and fight with courage and boldness in this spiritual Battle, in which Battle the Lord before your eyes hath raised up some valiant Champions that fought up to the ears in blood, therefore be courageous Soldiers and fight it out bravely, that your God may be glorified in you, and let Him only have the service, both of your inward and outward man, and stand to his cause, and love your own souls, and fear not the face of any mortal man, for God hath promised to be with you and uphold you that they shall not prevail against you. Isaiah 45.10.11. But, alas, how few are there that dare throw their courage for God and His cause, though His glory lies at stake, but think themselves happy and well, and count themselves wise men if they can sleep in a whole skin when Christ hath said, "He that will save his life shall lose it, and he that will lose his life for His sake shall find it. What shall it profit a man if he gain the whole world and lose his own soul?"

Therefore is it better for a man to be willing and contented to let all go for the enjoying of Christ and doing him service, than to sit down and sleep in a whole skin though in so doing he gain all the world and see Him dishonoured, His glory and truth troden under foot, and the blood of His servants shed and spilt? Yes without a doubt it is. But many are in these times so far from suffering valiantly for Christ, that they rather dissuade men from it, and count it a point of singularity and pride and selfish ends for a man to put himself forward to do God service; asking, what calling and warrant any private man hath thereunto, seeing it belongs to the ministers to speak of these things. Yes so it doth, but alas they are so cowardly and fearful that they dare not speak.

And therefore it belongs also to thee, or me, or any other man, if thou beest a Soldier of Jesus Christ, whatsoever by place or Calling thy rank or degree be, be it higher or lower, yet if He call for thy service, thou art bound though others stand still, to maintain His power and glory to the utmost of thy power and strength, yea to the shedding the last drop of thy blood, for He hath not loved His life unto the death for thy sake, but shed His precious blood for the redemption of thy soul, hath He done this for thee, and darest thou see Him dishonoured and His glory lie at the stake, and not speak on His behalf, or do Him the best service thou canst?

If out of a base and cowardly Spirit thus thou dost, let me tell thee here and that truly to thy face, thou hast a Dalila in thy heart which thou lovest more than God, and that thou shalt one day certainly find by woefull experience. Alas if men should hold their peace in such times as these, the Lord would cause the very stones to speak to convince man of his cowardly baseness.

Having proceeded in a manner thus far by strength of my God, with boldness and courage in my speech, the Warden of the Fleete came with the fat Lawyer, and commanded me to hold my peace. To whom I replied, I would speak and declare my cause and mind, though I were to be hanged at the gate for my speaking. And he caused proclamation to be made upon the Pillory: for bringing to him the books. So then he commanded me to be gagged, and if I spoke any more that then I should be whipt again upon the Pillory.

So I remained about an hour and a half gagged, being intercepted of much matter which by God's assistance I intended to have spoken. But yet with their cruelty I was nothing at all daunted, for I was full of comfort and courage, being mightily strengthened with the power of the Almighty which made me with cheerfulness triumph over all my sufferings, not showing one sad countenance or a discontented heart.

And when I was to come down having taken out my head out of the Pillory, I looked about me upon the people and said I am more than a conqueror through Him that loved me. Vivat Rex. Let the King live forever, and so I came down, and was had back again to the Tavern, where I together with Mr Wharton, stayed a while till one went to the Warden to know what should be done with me, who gave order we should be carried back again to the Fleete, and as I went by land through the streets, great store of people stood all along to behold me, and many of them blessed God for enabling me to undergo my sufferings with such cheerfulness and courage as I did, for I was mightily filled with the sweet presence of God's

Spirit, which caused me notwithstanding the pains of my sufferings to go along the streets with a joyful countenance not showing the least discontentedness, as if I had been going to take possession of some great treasures.

After I came back to the prison, none were suffered to come at me but the Surgeon to dress me, and I feeling myself somewhat feverish I went to bed, and my Surgeon doubting the same also, gave me a Glister, and appointed to come the next morning and let me blood, but when he came, he could not be permitted to come at me nor anyone else, for the Porter kept the key, and locked me up very close: saying the Warden gave him straight command so to do. Where upon I desired the Surgeon to go to Westminster to the Warden and certify him how it was with me (being very ill), and that he might have liberty to come at me and to let me blood and dress me, which could not be obtained till the Warden himself came home. About one of the clock John Hawes, the Porter, came to me, to know what I had to say to the warden, to whom I said, Mr. Hawes, this is very cruel and harsh dealing, that after so sore whipping my Surgeon shall not be admitted to come and dress me, nor any other be suffered to administer to my necessities, not having eaten all this day nor the last evening but a little Caudle, I hope the Lords will be more merciful than after the undergoing the extremity of my Censure to take my life from me by letting me perish for want of looking to, therefore I pray speak to Mr. Warden that he would be pleased to give leave to my Surgeon to come dress me and let me blood; otherwise I was in danger of a fever which might take away my life. So he wished me to have written to the Warden; I told him, if he would help me to pen, ink, and paper, so I would. No (said he) I dare not do that. Then I desired him to deliver my mind to the Warden by word of mouth; who then went away, and after I was in my bed, he came to me again, and said thus unto me: Mr. Lilburne I have one suit to you. What is that, said I? It is this, said he, that you would help me to one of those books that you threw abroad at the Pillory, that I might read it, for I never read any of them. I speak not for it to do you any hurt, only I have a great desire to read one of them. Sir, I think you do not (said I) but I cannot satisfy your desire, for if I had had more of them, they should yesterday have all gone. I verily believe you, said he, and so we parted.

And in a very little while after, came the Warden himself with the Porter, and I being in my bed, he asked me how I did? Said I, I am well, I bless my God for it, and am very merry and cheerful. Well (said he) you have undone yourself with speaking what you did yesterday. Sir (said I) I am not sorry for what I said, but am heartily glad that the Lord gave me strength and courage to speak what I did, and were I to speak again, I would speak twice as much as I did, if I could have liberty, though I were immediately to lose my life after it. Wouldst thou so, said he? Aye indeed Sir would I, with the Lord's assistance, said I, for I fear not the face of man; And concerning what I yesterday spoke, I did not in the least manner speak against any of the Lords, but did openly declare that I did willingly with all contentedness submit myself to their Censure, and as for the Bishops, I said nothing against any of their persons, but only against their callings. Aye, said the Warden, and thou saidest their calling was from the Devil. Yes Sir so I did, said I, and I will prove it, and make it good, or else I will be willing to lose my dearest blood. For if you please to read the 9th and 13th chapters of Revelations you shall there find that the Beast which ascended out of the bottomless Pit (which is the Pope and Roman State) hath his power and authority given him by the Dragon (the Devil) so that all the power which the Pope hath and doth exercise, originally comes from the Devil. If you read also from books lately set forth by the Prelates themselves and their Creatures, you shall there find that they claim their jurisdiction, standing, and power from the Pope. Now, if their power and calling be from the Pope (as they themselves say it is) then it must needs be from the Devil also. For the Pope's power and calling is from the Devil, and he cannot give a better power and calling to them than he himself hath; and I pray Sir, if the Bishop of Canterbury be offended at that which I spoke yesterday, tell him I will seal it with my blood; And if he please to send for me, I will justify it to his face, and if I be not able to make it good before any noble man in the Kingdom, let me lose my life. Aye, but it had been a great deal better, said he, for thine own particular good to have been more sparing of thy speech at that time. No Sir, said I, nothing at all, for my life and blood is not dear and precious to me, so I may glorify God, and do him any service therewith. I assure thee, said he, I was exceedingly chided about thee; and also there were old businesses rubbed up against me concerning Dr. Laiton and Mr. Burton, for that Liberty that they had. Wherefore were you chided for me, said I? About the books, said he, that you threw abroad, in regard you were close prisoner, and yet had those books about you; I would ask you one question: Did you bring those books to the Fleete with you or were they since brought to you by any other? I beseech you Sir pardon me for revealing that, said I. Then he would have known who they were that most resorted to me. I desired I might be excused in that also. Aye, but you must give me an answer, said he, for I must certify the Lords thereof. Then, said I, I pray you tell their Honours, I am unwilling to tell you. What were those books, said he, that you threw abroad, were they all of one sort? Those that have them, said I, can certify you of that. I myself have one of them, said he, and have read it, and I can find no wit in it, there is nothing but railing in it. Sir, said I, I conceive you are mistaken, for the Book is all full of wit. It is true, this book which you lighted on, is not so full of solidity as other of his books are; but you must understand, that at that time when the Doctor made that book, he was full of heaviness and in danger of a great punishment, for the Prelates had breathed out more cruelty against him for writing his *Apology;* And at that time also he was compassed about on every side with the Pestilence; Therefore he made that book to make himself merry. But, said he, he doth not write anything in it to the purpose against the Bishops' callings. Sir, said I, I must confess, you lighted on the worst of the three. And it is true, there is not much solidity and force of argument in it but only mirth; But the other two are as full of solidity as this is of mirth. What, were they of three sorts, said he? Yes, Sir, that they were, said I. What were the other two called, said he? The one (said I) was his *Answer to Sr. John Banks* his *Information;* The other is an *Answer to Some Objections* that are made against that book which you have. But if ever you read his Latin books, you shall there find solidity enough, and the wickedness and unlawfulness of the Bishops' callings and practices set forth to the full. What Latin books be they, said he? His *Flagellum,* for which he was first Censured, said I. What hath he been twice Censured, said he? Yes, said I, he was Censured in the High Commission Court for writing his *Flagellum;* And after that he wrote his *Apology* and that little book which you have, which were the cause of his Censure in the Star Chamber. But hast thou any more of those books, said he? Sir, said I, if I had had twenty of them more, they should all have gone yesterday. But, hast thou any more of them now, said he? Sir, said I, I verily think, that if I should tell you, I had not, you would not believe me, and therefore if you please, you may search my Chamber. So I must (said he) for the Lords have commanded me so to do, therefore open your trunk. Sir, said I, it is open already. Search it John Hawes, said he. So he searched it, and found nothing there. Open the Cupboard, said he. So I gave the Porter the key of my Cupboard, to search it, and he found nothing there but my victuals. Search his pocket, said the Warden. Indeed Sir, said I, there is none in them. Yet he searched them, and found as I said. Then he searched all my Chamber over, but found nothing at all. Well Sir, said I, now you can certify the Lords how you find things with me. But I pray Sir, must I still be kept close prisoner? I hope, now the Lords have inflicted their Censure on me, they will not still keep me close. No, said he, within a little time you will be eased of it. So we took our leaves each of other, and he went away.

And the next day, being Friday and a Star Chamber day, I hoped I should have had the Liberty of the prison; but instead thereof, news was brought me at evening that I must be removed to the Common Jail, or a worse place, and that I must be put in Irons. Well, for all this my God enabled me to keep my hold still, and not to let my confidence go; For (blessed be His name for it) this news did not in the least manner trouble me.

And upon Saturday morning John Hawes the Porter came with the woman that looked to me to my Chamber, to stand by her that none might speak with me till she had made my bed and done other things for me. What is it, said I? I hear, said he, that the Lords have ordered that you must be put into the Wards and kept close prisoner there, and lie in irons, and none must be suffered to come at you to bring you anything; but you must live upon the Poor Man's Box. Sir, that's very hard, said I, but the will of my God be done; For mine own part, it nothing at all troubles me, for I know in whom I have believed, and I know not one hair of my head shall fall to the ground without His providence; And I have cast up my account already what it will cost me. Therefore I weigh not anything that can be inflicted on me, for I know that God, that made Paul and Silas to sing in the Stocks at midnight, will also make me rejoice in my Chains. But it is very much that they will let none come to me to bring me anything. It seems they will be more cruel to me than the very Heathens and Pagan Romans were to Paul, who when he was in prison did never refuse to let any come to him to administer to his necessities. But I weigh it not, for I know my God is and will be with me, to make me go through all my afflictions with cheerfulness, for I feel His power within me so mightly supporting and upholding me, that no condition in this World can make me miserable. And for mine own part, I do no more set by my life and blood in this cause than I do a piece of bread when I have newly dined.

Afterwards the woman telling me she hoped I should not have so sore a punishment laid on me, but that I might have things brought me from my friends, I told her I did not much care how it went with me, for Jeremy's Dungeon, or Daniel's Den, or the Three Children's Furnace, is as pleasant and welcome to me as a Palace; for wheresoever I am I shall find God there, and if I have Him, that is enough to me. And for victuals, I told her I did not doubt but that God that fed the Prophet Elijah by a Raven would preserve me, and fill me to the full by the way of His providence; and if no meat should be brought me, I knew, if they take away my meat, God would take away my stomach. Therefore I weighed not their cruelty; And thereupon uttered to her these four verses:

I do not fear nor dread the face of any mortal man,
Let him against me bend his power and do the worst he can,
For my whole trust, strength, confidence,
My hope, and all my aide
Is in the Lord JEHOVAH's fence
Which Heaven and Earth hath made.

The rest that I intended by the strength of my God to have spoken (if I had not been prevented by the Gag) I now forbear to set down, in regard I

hear I am to come into the Field again to fight a second battle, unto which
time I reserve it, if the Lord so order it that I may have Liberty to speak, I
doubt not but by the might and power of my God, in whom I rest and trust,
valiantly to display the weapons of a good Soldier of Jesus Christ; Come
life, come death; And in the meantime to what I have here said and written,
I set to my name, by me JOHN LILBURNE, being written with part of my
own blood, the rest of which by the Lord's assistance I will willingly shed if
He call for it, in the maintaining of his Truth and Glory, and that which I
have here said and written by me

JOHN LILBURNE

My verses are to follow here.

I do not fear the face nor power of any mortal man,
Though he against me rise to do the worst he can,
Because my trust, my hope, my strength, my confidence and aide
Is in the Lord Jehovah's power, both now and ever staid.
Therefore my soul shall never cease triumphantly to sing,
Thou art my Fort, my sure defence, my Saviour and my King,
For in my straits and trials all, Thou well with me hath delt.
Thou hath in my distresses great, my stripes and bitter smart
So held my soul as from Thy truth, I never once did start.
But to Thy truth with cheerfulness and courage have I stood
Though tortured for it were my flesh, and lost my dearest blood,
When from Fleete-bridge to Westminster, at Cart's Arsse I was whipt,
Then Thou with joy my soul upheldst, so that I never wept.
Likewise when I on Pillory, in Palace-yard did stand,
Then by Thy help against my foes, I had the upper-hand,
For openly I to their face, did there truely declare,
That from the Pope our Prelates all descended still they are,
And that I might for what I said, make confirmation;
I named Chapters 9 and 13 of Revelation.
Likewise I then did fearlessly, unto the people show
That what Pocklington hath writ is found now very true,
Namely, that they come lineally, from Antichrist his Chair,
Even to him that now doth reign, the great Arch-Bishop here.
All which I did on Pillory, there offer to make good,
Or else I would lose willingly, my best and dearest blood.
Moreover there to God's people, I did most plainly show
That we have been, and so are still, ruled by a Popish crew;
Therefore against them valiantly, we must fight in the field,
And to their Laws at any hand, not ever once to yield.
But from their Yoke without delay, we must our necks outdraw,

If that we will true Subjects be, unto our Saviour's Law.
Therefore my Friends, if that you will, Christ Jesus here enjoy,
Withdraw yourselves from these vile men, and every Popish toy
And naked Christ be willing still, and ready to embrace;
Though for the same you suffer shame, and wicked men's disgrace,
Because in Him is more content, more full and sweeter bless
Than can be found in anything that in the world now is.
And this I have by trial found, what here I do declare
That to the comforts of our God, the Earthly nothing are.
And he that will not quite deny, all things for Jesus' sake,
The joys of Christ he neither here, nor after shall partake;
Therefore my friends if you, your souls, will really preserve,
Reject their Antichristian Laws, and from Christ never swerve,
Because the Lord hath said on those, His wrath shall surely come,
His foremost ire, his greatest strokes, his deepest plagues and doom
That do on hand or head receive, the Hell-mark of the Hour,
Or do the Beast and his image, not cease for to adore
Thus and much more on Pillory, there openly I said,
Till at the last my mouth was gaged, and by them basely staid,
And threatened there once again, that my back should be whipt
If that my tongue but one word more, against Rome's Priests let slipt.
Thus with a straight gag in my mouth, about an hour stood I,
Having my God to comfort me, in all my misery;
And having stood a long time there, I was at length down brought;
Most sweetly cheered with His blood that had my poor soul bought;
And when I was come down, I cheerfully did say,
I am more than a Conqueror, through Christ that is my stay.
Hallelujah, all blessing, glory, honour, laud and praise,
Be rendered to Thee my God, of me and Thine always,
For though that I was in myself a Creature poor and weak,
Yet was I made through Thy great strength with boldness for to speak.
It was Thou Lord that didst uphold with mercy and Thy grace,
My feeble flesh so that I did rejoice in my disgrace,
Thou filledst my soul so full of joy and inward felling peace
As that my tongue Thy praise to tell no time shall ever cease,
And now, O Lord, keep Thou my soul most humbly I Thee pray
That from Thy just Commandments, I never run astray,
But unto Thee, and to Thy Truth, my heart may still be fast,
And not offend in anything, so long as life doth last,
And as Thou hast in me begun, the saving work of grace,
So grant, that I Thy poor servant, may still therein increase

And when I shall lay down the House of frail mortality,
Then let thy Angels bring my soul, sweet Jesus unto Thee.

These Verses were my Meditation the next day, after the Execution of my Censure; after the Warden of the Fleete had been with me, from the Lords of the Council and had searched my Chamber, it being afternoon, and I being not well, wrote them in my bed.

By me JOHN LILBURNE

Allegiance and Sovereignty

8. James VI and I, *The Trew Law of Free Monarchies*

James VI of Scotland, later James I of England, was a *rara avis* for combining the role of monarch with that of an author of at least minor note: His best-known authorial excursions outside polities were into witchcraft, which he thought there was reason to be alarmed about, and tobacco, a new vice of which he disapproved.

Born in 1566, the son of Mary Queen of Scots, James succeeded to the Scottish throne as a baby in the wake of his mother's deposition, and in 1603 (on the basis of the most plausible and widely accepted reading of a somewhat tangled dynastic situation of the Tudor house) assumed the throne of England, on the death of the unmarried Queen Elizabeth I. England and Scotland were not united into a single political entity until 1707, so down to his death in 1625 he was simultaneously king of two realms—a position which his successors of the Stuart house also occupied.

James's premature accession in Scotland was the result of the triumph of the Protestant party there, just as his mother's eclipse was centrally due to her championship of the Catholic cause. In order to retain the crown, it was necessary that James be raised as a Protestant. In his childhood and youth, he was a captive of rival Protestant factions in Scotland, and though he remained throughout his life a convinced Calvinist in religious principle, this experience made him wary of Protestant churches and of church-

From *The Political Works of James I*, reprinted from the edition of 1616 with an introduction by Charles Howard McIlwain (Cambridge, Mass.: Harvard University Press, 1918), pp. 53–70. Footnotes are author's notes.

men too independent of secular control. When, as king of England, he became head of a state-managed Protestant church with a tradition of moderation, he found himself in a new and welcome situation, and one he meant to preserve. In more general terms as well, when James acceded to England he came from a rough life, and struggles to assert his kingly authority, into an inheritance of wealth and relative political stability. His reign in England was troubled by the religious and factional conflicts that had plagued his predecessors: it was none the easier for his being a foreigner (in a way Englishmen and Scots, after centuries of union, have ceased to be seriously foreign to each other), as well as an eccentric and extravagant individual who was possibly too much an intellectual for a politician. But, despite his failings, he appears to have been a fairly shrewd and commonsensical ruler, basically in tune with the ideas and policies of Queen Elizabeth, whose luck and theatrical flair cast a shadow over King James in his lifetime and beyond.

The Trew Law of Free Monarchies, written just before he added England to his realms, is the most general of James's several writings on political subjects. The ideas of kingship and allegiance it expounds can be seen as natural aspirations of a king whose lot was not an entirely happy one; they are also very much in line with the political orthodoxy of Tudor England, to which King James was an apt intellectual heir. They draw on one vein of Protestant political thought as they dispute another. For all his disapproval of over-eager Protestants, James considered that the real threat to intellectual soundness and practical order came from Roman Catholicism, and, with different degrees of explicitness, his political writings primarily reply to a vein of contemporary Catholic theory.

An Advertisement to the Reader

Accept, I pray you (my deare countreymen) as thankefully this Pamphlet that I offer unto you, as lovingly it is written for your weale. I would be loath both to be faschious, and fectlesse: And therefore, if it be not sententious, at least it is short. It may be yee misse many things that yee looke for in it: But for excuse thereof, consider rightly that I onely lay downe herein the trew grounds, to teach you the rightway, without wasting time upon refuting the adversaries. And yet I trust, if ye will take narrow tent, ye shall finde most of their great gunnes payed home againe, either with contrary conclusions, or tacite objections, suppose in a dairned forme, and indirectly: For my intention is to instruct, and not irritat, if I may eschew it. The profite I would wish you to make of it, is, as well so to frame all your actions according to these grounds, as may confirme you in the course of honest and obedient Subjects to your King in all times comming, as also, when ye shall fall in purpose with any that shall praise or excuse the by-past rebellions that brake foorth either in this countrey, or in any other, ye shall herewith bee armed against their Sirene songs, laying their particular examples to the square of these grounds. Whereby yee shall soundly keepe the course of righteous Judgement, decerning wisely of every action onely according to the qualitie thereof, and not according to your pre-judged conceits of the committers: So shall ye, by reaping profit to your selves, turne my paine into pleasure. But least the whole Pamphlet runne out at the gaping mouth of this Preface, if it were any more enlarged; I end, with committing you to God, and me to your charitable censures.

The Trew Law of Free Monarchies: or the Reciprock and Mutuall Duetie betwixt a Free King and His Naturall Subjects

As there is not a thing so necessarie to be knowne by the people of any land, next the knowledge of their God, as the right knowledge of their alleageance, according to the forme of governement established among them, especially in a *Monarchie* (which forme of government, as resembling the Divinitie, approacheth nearest to perfection, as all the learned and wise men from the beginning have agreed upon; Unitie being the perfection of all things,) So hath the ignorance, and (which is worse) the seduced opinion of the multitude blinded by them, who thinke themselves able to teach and instruct the ignorants, procured the wracke and overthrow of sundry flourishing Common-wealths; and heaped heavy calamities, threatning utter destruction upon others. And the smiling successe, that unlawfull rebellions have oftentimes had against Princes in aages past (such hath bene the misery, and iniquitie of the time) hath by way of practise strengthned many in their errour: albeit there cannot be a more deceiveable argument; then to judge ay the justnesse of the cause by the event thereof; as hereafter shall be proved more at length. And among others, no Commonwealth, that ever hath bene since the beginning, hath had greater need of the trew knowledge of this ground, then this our so long disordered, and distracted Common-wealth hath: the misknowledge hereof being the onely spring, from whence have flowed so many endlesse calamities, miseries, and confusions, as is better felt by many, then the cause thereof well knowne, and deepely considered. The naturall zeale therefore, that I beare to this my native countrie, with the great pittie I have to see the so-long disturbance thereof for lacke of the trew knowledge of this ground (as I have said before) hath compelled me at last to breake silence, to discharge my conscience to you my deare country men herein, that knowing the ground from whence these your many endlesse troubles have proceeded, as well as ye have already too-long tasted the bitter fruites thereof, ye may by knowledge, and eschewing of the cause escape, and divert the lamentable effects that ever necessarily follow thereupon. I have chosen then onely to set downe in this short Treatise, the trew grounds of the mutuall duetie, and alleageance betwixt a free and absolute *Monarche,* and his people; not to trouble your patience with answering the contrary propositions, which some have not bene ashamed to set downe in writ, to the poysoning of infinite number of simple soules, and their owne perpetuall, and well deserved infamie: For by answering them, I could not have eschewed whiles to pick, and byte wel saltly their persons; which would rather have bred contentiousnesse among the readers (as they had liked or misliked) then sound instruction of the trewth: Which I protest to him that is the searcher of all hearts, is the onely marke that I shoot at herein.

First then, I will set downe the trew grounds, whereupon I am to build, out of the Scriptures, since *Monarchie* is the trew paterne of Divinitie, as I have already said: next, from the fundamental Lawes of our owne Kingdome, which nearest must concerne us: thirdly, from the law of Nature, by divers similitudes drawne out of the same: and will conclude syne by answering the most waighty and appearing incommodities that can be objected.

The Princes duetie to his Subjects is so clearly set downe in many places of the Scriptures, and so openly confessed by all the good Princes, according to their oath in their Coronation, as not needing to be long therein, I shall as shortly as I can runne through it.

Kings are called Gods [1] by the propheticall King *David,* because they sit upon GOD his Throne in the earth, and have the count of their administration to give unto him. Their office is, *To minister Justice and Judgement to the people,* [2] as the same *David* saith: *To advance the good, and punish the evill,* [3] as he likewise saith: *To establish good Lawes to his people, and procure obedience to the same,* [4] as divers good Kings of *Judah* [5] did: *To procure the peace of the people,* as the same *David* saith:* [6] To decide all controversies that can arise among them* [7] as *Salomon* did: *To be the Minister of God for the weale of them that doe well, and as the minister of God, to take vengeance upon them that doe evill,* [8] as S. *Paul* saith. And finally, *As a good Pastour, to goe out and in before his people* [9] as is said in the first of *Samuel: That through the Princes prosperitie, the peoples peace may be procured,* [10] as *Jeremie* saith.

1. Psal. 82. 6.   2. Psal. 101.
3. Psal. 101.   4. 2 King. 18.
5. 2 Chron. 29; 2 King. 22; and 23. 2; chro. 34, & 35.
6. Psal. 72.   7. 1 King 3.
8. Rom. 13.   9. 1 Sam. 8.
10. Jerem. 29.

And therefore in the Coronation of our owne Kings, as well as of every Christian *Monarche* they give their Oath, first to maintaine the Religion presently professed within their countrie, according to their lawes, whereby it is established, and to punish all those that should presse to alter, or disturbe the profession thereof; And next to maintaine all the lowable and good Lawes made by their predecessours: to see them put in execution, and the breakers and violaters thereof, to be punished, according to the tenour of the same: And lastly, to maintaine the whole countrey, and every state therein, in all their ancient Priviledges and Liberties, as well against all forreine enemies, as among themselves: And shortly to procure the weale and flourishing of his people, not onely in maintaining and putting to execution the olde lowable lawes of the countrey, and by establishing of new (as necessitie and evill maners will require) but by all other meanes possible to fore-see and prevent all dangers, that are likely to fall upon them, and to maintaine concord, wealth, and civilitie among them, as a loving Father, and careful watchman, caring for them more then for himselfe, knowing himselfe to be ordained for them, and they not for him; and therefore countable to that great God, who placed him as his lieutenant over them, upon the perill of his soule to procure the weale of both soules and bodies, as farre as in him lieth, of all them that are committed to his charge. And this oath in the Coronation is the clearest, civill, and fundamentall Law, whereby the Kings office is properly defined.

By the Law of Nature the King becomes a naturall Father to all his Lieges at his Coronation: And as the Father of his fatherly duty is bound to care for the nourishing, education, and vertuous government of his children; even so is the king bound to care for all his subjects. As all the toile and paine that the father can take for his children, will be thought light and well bestowed by him, so that the effect thereof redound to their profite and weale; so ought the Prince to doe towards his people. As the kindly father ought to foresee all inconvenients and dangers that may arise towards his children, and though with the hazard of his owne person presse to prevent the same; so ought the King towards his people. As the fathers wrath and correction upon any of his children that offendeth, ought to be by a fatherly chastisement seasoned with pitie, as long as there is any hope of amendment in them; so ought the King towards any of his Lieges that offend in that measure. And shortly, as the Fathers chiefe joy ought to be in procuring his childrens welfare, rejoycing at their weale, sorrowing and pitying at their evill, to hazard for their safetie, travell for their rest, wake for their sleepe; and in a word, to thinke that his earthly felicitie and life standeth and liveth more in them, nor in himselfe; so ought a good Prince thinke of his people.

As to the other branch of this mutuall and reciprock band, is the duety and alleageance that the Lieges owe to their King: the ground whereof, I take out of the words of *Samuel,* dited by Gods Spirit, when God had given him commandement to heare the peoples voice in choosing and annointing them a King. And because that place of Scripture being well understood, is so pertinent for our purpose, I have insert herein the very words of the Text.

9   *Now therefore hearken to their voice: howbeit yet testifie unto them, and shew them the maner of the King, that shall raigne over them.*

10 *So* Samuel *tolde all the wordes of the Lord unto the people that asked a King of him.*

11 *And he said, This shall be the maner of the King that shall raigne over you: he will take your sonnes, and appoint them to his Charets, and to be his horsemen, and some shall runne before his Charet.*

12 *Also, hee will make them his captaines over thousands, and captaines ouer fifties, and to eare his ground, and to reape his harvest, and to make instruments of warre and the things that serve for his charets:*

13 *Hee will also take your daughters, and make them Apothicaries, and Cookes, and Bakers.*

14 *And hee will take your fields, and your vineyards, and your best Olive trees, and give them to his servants.*

15 *And he will take the tenth of your seed, and of your Vineyards, and give it to his Eunuches, and to his servants.*

16 *And he will take your men servants, and your maid-servants, and the chiefe of your young men, and your asses, and put them to his worke.*

17 *He will take the tenth of your sheepe: and ye shall be his servants.*

18 *And ye shall cry out at that day, because of your King, whom ye have chosen you: and the Lord God will not heare you at that day.*

19 *But the people would not heare the voice of* Samuel, *but did say: Nay, but there shalbe a King over us.*

20 *And we also will be all like other Nations, and our King shall judge us, and goe out before us, and fight our battels.*

That these words, and discourses of Samuel were dited by Gods Spirit, it needs no further probation, but that it is a place of Scripture; since the whole Scripture is dited by that inspiration, as *Paul* saith: which ground no good Christian will, or dare denie. Whereupon it must necessarily follow, that these speeches proceeded not from any ambition in *Samuel,* as one loath to quite the reines that he so long had ruled, and therefore desirous, by making odious the government of a King, to disswade the people from their farther importunate craving of one: For, as the text proveth it plainly, he then conveened them to give them a resolute grant of their demand, as God by his owne mouth commanded him, saying,

Hearken to the voice of the people.

And to presse to disswade them from that, which he then came to grant unto them, were a thing very impertinent in a wise man; much more in the Prophet of the most high God. And likewise, it well appeared in all the course of his life after, that so long refusing of their sute before came not of any ambition in him: which he well proved in praying, & as it were importuning God for the weale of *Saul*. Yea, after God had declared his reprobation unto him, yet he desisted not, while God himselfe was wrath at his praying, and discharged his fathers suit in that errand. And that these words of *Samuel* were not uttered as a prophecie of *Saul* their first Kings defection, it well appeareth, as well because we heare no mention made in the Scripture of any his tyrannie and oppression, (which, if it had beene, would not have been left unpainted out therein, as well as his other faults were, as in a trew mirrour of all the Kings behaviours, whom it describeth) as likewise in respect that *Saul* was chosen by God for his vertue, and meet qualities to governe his people: whereas his defection sprung after-hand from the corruption of his owne nature, & not through any default in God, whom they that thinke so, would make as a step-father to his people, in making wilfully a choise of the unmeetest for governing them, since the election of that King lay absolutely and immediatly in Gods hand. But by the contrary it is plaine, and evident, that this speech of *Samuel* to the people, was to prepare their hearts before the hand to the due obedience of that King, which God was to give unto them; and therefore opened up unto them, what might be the intollerable qualities that might fall in some of their kings, thereby preparing them to patience, not to resist to Gods ordinance: but as he would have said; Since God hath granted your importunate suit in giving you a king, as yee have else committed an errour in shaking off Gods yoke, and over-hastie seeking of a King; so beware yee fall not into the next, in casting off also rashly that yoke, which God at your earnest suite hath laid upon you, how hard that ever it seeme to be: For as ye could not have obtained one without the permission and ordinance of God, so may yee no more, fro hee be once set over you, shake him off without the same warrant. And therefore in time arme your selves with patience and humilitie, since he that hath the only power to make him, hath the onely power to unmake him; and ye onely to obey, bearing with these straits that I now foreshew you, as with the finger of God, which lieth not in you to take off.

And will ye consider the very wordes of the text in order, as they are set downe, it shall plainely declare the obedience that the people owe to their King in all respects.

First, God commandeth *Samuel* to doe two things: the one, to grant the people their suit in giving them a king; the other, to forewarne them, what

some kings will doe unto them, that they may not thereafter in their grudging and murmuring say, when they shal feele the snares here fore-spoken;
We would never have had a king of God, in case when we craved him, hee
had let us know how wee would have beene used by him, as now we finde
but over-late. And this is meant by these words:

> *Now therefore hearken unto their voice: howbeit yet testifie unto them,
> and shew them the maner of the King that shall rule over them.*

And next, *Samuel* in execution of this commandement of God, hee likewise doeth two things.

First, hee declares unto them, what points of justice and equitie their
king will breake in his behaviour unto them: And next he putteth them out
of hope, that wearie as they will, they shall not have leave to shake off that
yoke, which God through their importunitie hath laide upon them. The
points of equitie that the King shall breake unto them, are expressed in
these words:

11 *He will take your sonnes, and appoint them to his Charets, and to
be his horsemen, and some shall run before his Charet.*
12 *Also he will make them his captaines over thousands, and captaines over fifties, and to eare his ground, and to reape his harvest, and to make instruments of warre, and the things that serve
for his charets.*
13 *He will also take your daughters, and make them Apothecaries,
and Cookes, and Bakers.*

The points of Justice, that hee shall breake unto them, are expressed in
these wordes:

14 *Hee will take your fields, and your vineyards, and your best Olive
trees, and give them to his servants.*
15 *And he will take the tenth of your seede, and of your vineyards,
and give it to his Eunuches and to his servants: and also the tenth
of your sheepe.*

As if he would say; The best and noblest of your blood shall be compelled in slavish and servile offices to serve him: and not content of his
owne patrimonie, will make up a rent to his owne use out of your best
lands, vineyards, orchards, and store of cattell: So as inverting the Law of
nature, and office of a King, your persons and the persons of your posteri-
tie, together with your lands, and all that ye possesse shall serve his private
use, and inordinate appetite.

And as unto the next point (which is his fore-warning them, that, weary
as they will, they shall not have leave to shake off the yoke, which God
thorow their importunity hath laid upon them) it is expressed in these
words:

18 *And yee shall crie out at that day, because of your King whom yee*
    have chosen you: and the Lord will not heare you at that day.

As he would say; When ye shall finde these things in proofe that now I
fore-warne you of, although you shall grudge and murmure, yet it shal not
be lawful to you to cast it off, in respect it is not only the ordinance of God,
but also your selves have chosen him unto you, thereby renouncing for ever
all priviledges, by your willing consent out of your hands, whereby in any
time hereafter ye would claime, and call backe unto your selves againe that
power, which God shall not permit you to doe. And for further taking away
of all excuse, and retraction of this their contract, after their consent to
under-lie this yoke with all the burthens that hee hath declared unto them,
he craves their answere, and consent to his proposition: which appeareth by
their answere, as it is expressed in these words:

19 *Nay, but there shall be a King over us.*
20 *And we also will be like all other nations: and our king shall judge*
    us, and goe out before us and fight our battels.

As if they would have said; All your speeches and hard conditions shall
not skarre us, but we will take the good and evill of it upon us, and we will
be content to beare whatsoever burthen it shal please our King to lay upon
us, aswell as other nations doe. And for the good we will get of him in
fighting our battels, we will more patiently beare any burden that shall
please him to lay on us.

Now then, since the erection of this Kingdome and Monarchie among
the Jewes, and the law thereof may, and ought to bee a paterne to all Christian and well founded Monarchies, as beeing founded by God himselfe,
who by his Oracle, and out of his owne mouth gave the law thereof: what
liberty can broiling spirits, and rebellious minds claime justly to against
any Christian Monarchie; since they can claime to no greater libertie on
their part, nor the people of God might have done, and no greater tyranny
was ever executed by any Prince or tyrant, whom they can object, nor was
here fore-warned to the people of God, (and yet all rebellion counter-
manded unto them) if tyrannizing over mens persons, sonnes, daughters
and servants; redacting noble houses, and men, and women of noble blood,
to slavish and servile offices; and extortion, and spoile of their lands and
goods to the princes owne private use and commoditie, and of his cour-
teours, and servants, may be called a tyrannie?

And that this proposition grounded upon the Scripture, may the more
clearly appeare to be trew by the practise oft prooved in the same booke,
we never reade, that ever the Prophets perswaded the people to rebell
against the Prince, how wicked soever he was.

When *Samuel* by Gods command pronounced to the same king *Saul,* that his kingdome was rent from him, and given to another (which in effect was a degrading of him) yet his next action following that, was peaceably to turne home, and with floods of teares to pray to God to have some compassion upon him.[11]

And *David,* notwithstanding hee was inaugurate in that same degraded Kings roome, not onely (when he was cruelly persecuted, for no offence; but good service done unto him) would not presume, having him in his power, skantly, but with great reverence, to touch the garment of the annoynted of the Lord, and in his words blessed him:[12] but likewise, when one came to him vanting himselfe untrewly to have slaine *Saul,* hee, without forme of proces, or triall of his guilt, caused onely for guiltinesse of his tongue, put him to sodaine death.[13]

And although there was never a more monstrous persecutor, and tyrant nor *Achab* was: yet all the rebellion, that *Elias* ever raised against him, was to flie to the wildernes: where for fault of sustentation, he was fed with the Corbies. And I thinke no man will doubt but *Samuel, David,* and *Elias,* had as great power to perswade the people, if they had like to have employed their credite to uproares & rebellions against these wicked kings, as any of our seditious preachers in these daies of whatsoever religion, either in this countrey or in France, had, that busied themselves most to stir up rebellion under cloake of religion. This farre the only love of veritie, I protest, without hatred at their persons, have mooved me to be somewhat satyricke.

And if any will leane to the extraordinarie examples of degrading or killing of kings in the Scriptures, thereby to cloake the peoples rebellion, as by the deed of *Jehu,* and such like extraordinaries: I answere, besides that they want the like warrant that they had, if extraordinarie examples of the Scripture shall bee drawne in daily practise; murther under traist as in the persons of *Ahud,* and *Jael;* theft, as in the persons of the *Israelites* comming out of *Egypt;* lying to their parents to the hurt of their brother, as in the person of *Jacob,* shall all be counted as lawfull and allowable vertues, as rebellion against Princes. And to conclude, the practise through the whole Scripture prooveth the peoples obedience given to that sentence in the law of God:

> *Thou shalt not rayle upon the Judges, neither speake evill of the ruler of thy people.*

To end then the ground of my proposition taken out of the Scripture, let two speciall, and notable examples, one under the law, another under the

11. 1 Sam. 15.   12. 1 Sam. 24.
13. 2 Sam. 1.

Evangel, conclude this part of my alleageance. Under the lawe, *Jeremie* threatneth the people of God with utter destruction for rebellion to *Nabuchadnezar* the king of Babel:[14] who although he was an idolatrous persecuter, a forraine King, a Tyrant, and usurper of their liberties; yet in respect they had once received and acknowledged him for their king, he not only commandeth them to obey him, but even to pray for his prosperitie, adjoyning the reason to it; because in his prosperitie stood their peace.[15]

And under the Evangel, that king, whom *Paul* bids the *Romanes obey* and serve *for conscience sake,* was *Nero* that bloody tyrant, an infamie to his aage, and a monster to the world, being also an idolatrous persecuter, as the King of *Babel* was. If then Idolatrie and defection from God, tyranny over their people, and persecution of the Saints, for their profession sake, hindred not the Spirit of God to command his people under all highest paine to give them all due and heartie obedience for conscience sake, giving to *Caesar* that which was *Caesars,* and to God that which was Gods, as Christ saith; and that this practise throughout the booke of God agreeth with this lawe, which he made in the erection of that Monarchie (as is at length before deduced) what shamelesse presumption is it to any Christian people now adayes to claime to that unlawfull libertie, which God refused to his owne peculiar and chosen people?[16] Shortly then to take up in two or three sentences, grounded upon all these arguments, out of the lawe of God, the duetie, and alleageance of the people to their lawfull king, their obedience, I say, ought to be to him, as to Gods Lieutenant in earth, obeying his commands in all thing, except directly against God, as the commands of Gods Minister, acknowledging him a Judge set by GOD over them, having power to judge them, but to be judged onely by GOD, whom to onely hee must give count of his judgement; fearing him as their Judge, loving him as their father; praying for him as their protectour; for his continuance, if he be good; for his amendement, if he be wicked; following and obeying his lawfull commands, eschewing and flying his fury in his unlawfull, without resistance, but by sobbes and teares to God, according to that sentence used in the primitive Church in the time of the persecution.

Preces, & Lachrymae sunt arma Ecclesiae.

Now, as for the describing the allegeance, that the lieges owe to their native King, out of the fundamentall and civill Lawe, especially of this contrey, as I promised, the ground must first be set downe of the first maner of establishing the Lawes and forme of governement among us; that the ground being first right laide, we may thereafter build rightly thereupon.

14. Jer. 27.   15. Jere. 29.
16. Jere. 13.

Although it be trew (according to the affirmation of those that pryde them-selves to be the scourges of Tyrants) that in the first beginning of Kings rising among the Gentiles, in the time of the first aage, divers common-wealthes and societies of men choosed out one among themselves, who for his vertues and valour, being more eminent then the rest, was chosen out by them, and set up in that roome, to maintaine the weakest in their right, to throw downe oppressours, and to foster and continue the societie among men; which could not otherwise, but by vertue of that unitie be wel done: yet these examples are nothing pertinent to us; because our Kingdome and divers other Monarchies are not in that case, but had their beginning in a farre contrary fashion.

For as our Chronicles beare witnesse, this Ile, and especially our part of it, being scantly inhabited, but by very few, and they as barbarous and scant of civilitie, as number, there comes our first King *Fergus,* with a great number with him, out of *Ireland,* which was long inhabited before us, and making himself master of the countrey, by his owne friendship, and force, as well of the *Irelandmen* that came with him, as of the countrey-men that willingly fell to him, hee made himselfe King and Lord, as well of the whole landes, as of the whole inhabitants within the same. Thereafter he and his successours, a long while after their being Kinges, made and estab-lished their lawes from time to time, and as the occasion required. So the trewth is directly contrarie in our state to the false affirmation of such sedi-tious writers, as would perswade us, that the Lawes and state of our coun-trey were established before the admitting of a king: where by the coun-trarie ye see it plainely prooved, that a wise king comming in among barbares, first established the estate and forme of governement, and there-after made lawes by himselfe, and his successours according thereto.

The kings therefore in *Scotland* were before any estates or rankes of men within the same, before any Parliaments were holden, or lawes made: and by them was the land distributed (which at the first was whole theirs) states erected and decerned, and formes of governement devised and estab-lished: And so it followes of necessitie, that the kings were the authors and makers of the Lawes, and not the Lawes of the kings. And to proove this my assertion more clearly, it is evident by the rolles of our Chancellery (which containe our eldest and fundamentall Lawes) that the King is *Domi-nus omnium bonorum,* and *Dominus directus totius Dominij,* the whole subiects being but his vassals, and from him holding all their lands as their over-lord, who according to good services done unto him, chaungeth their holdings from tacke to few, from ward to blanch, erecteth new Baronies, and uniteth olde, without advice or authoritie of either Parliament or any other subalterin judiciall seate: So as if wrong might bee admitted in play (albeit I grant wrong should be wrong in all persons) the King might have a better colour for his pleasure, without further reason, to take the land from his lieges, as overlord of the whole, and doe with it as pleaseth him, since all that they hold is of him, then, as foolish writers say, the people might unmake the king, and put an other in his roome: But either of them as unlawful, and against the ordinance of God, ought to be alike odious to be thought, much lesse put in practise.

And according to these fundamentall Lawes already alledged, we daily see that in the Parliament (which is nothing else but the head Court of the king and his vassals) the lawes are but craved by his subjects, and onely made by him at their rogation, and with their advice: For albeit the king made daily statutes and ordinances, enjoyning such paines thereto as hee thinkes meet, without any advice of Parliament or estates; yet it lies in the power of no Parliament, to make any kinde of Lawe or Statute, without his Scepter be to it, for giving it the force of a Law: And although divers changes have beene in other countries of the blood Royall, and kingly house, the kingdome being reft by conquest from one to another, as in our neighbour countrey in *England,* (which was never in ours) yet the same ground of the kings right over all the land, and subjects thereof remaineth alike in all other free Monarchies, as well as in this: For when the Bastard of *Normandie* came into *England,* and made himselfe king, was it not by force, and with a mighty army? Where he gave the Law, and tooke none, changed the Lawes, inverted the order of governement, set downe the strangers his followers in many of the old possessours roomes, as at this day well appeareth a great part of the Gentlemen in *England,* beeing come of the *Norman* blood, and their old Lawes, which to this day they are ruled by, are written in his language, and not in theirs: And yet his successours have with great happinesse enjoyed the Crowne to this day; Whereof the like was also done by all them that conquested them before.

And for conclusion of this point, that the king is over-lord over the whole lands, it is likewise daily proved by the Law of our hoordes, of want of Heires, and of Bastardies: For if a hoord be found under the earth, because it is no more in the keeping or use of any person, it of the law pertains to the king. If a person, inheritour of any lands or goods, dye without any sort of heires, all his landes and goods returne to the king. And if a bastard die unrehabled without heires of his bodie (which rehabling onely lyes in the kings hands) all that hee hath likewise returnes to the king. And as ye see it manifest, that the King is over-Lord of the whole land: so is he Master over every person that inhabiteth the same, having power over the life and death of every one of them: For although a just Prince will not take the life of any of his subjects without a cleare law; yet the same lawes whereby he taketh them, are made by himselfe, or his predecessours; and so the power flowes alwaies from him selfe; as by daily experience we see, good and just Princes will from time to time make new lawes and statutes, adjoyning the penalties to the breakers thereof, which before the law was made, had beene no crime to the subject to have committed. Not that I deny the old definition of a King, and of a law; which makes the king to bee a speaking law, and the Law a dumbe king: for certainely a king that governes not by his lawe, can neither be countable to God for his administration, nor have a happy and established raigne: For albeit it be trew that I have at length prooved, that the King is above the law, as both the author and giver of strength thereto; yet a good king will not onely delight to rule his subjects by the lawe, but even will conforme himselfe in his owne actions thereuneto, alwaies keeping that ground, that the health of the common-wealth be his chiefe law: And where he sees the lawe doubtsome or rigorous, hee may interpret or mitigate the same, lest otherwise *Summum ius* bee *summa iniuria:* And therefore generall lawes, made publikely in Parliament, may upon knowen respects to the King by his authoritie bee mitigated, and suspended upon causes onely knowen to him.

As likewise, although I have said, a good king will frame all his actions to be according to the Law; yet is hee not bound thereto but of his good will, and for good example-giving to his subjects: For as in the law of abstaining from eating of flesh in *Lenton,* the king will, for examples sake, make his owne house to observe the Law; yet no man will thinke he needs to take a licence to eate flesh. And although by our Lawes, the bearing and wearing of hag-buts, and pistolets be forbidden, yet no man can find any fault in the King, for causing his traine use them in any raide upon the Borderers, or other malefactours or rebellious subjects. So as I have alreadie said, a good King, although hee be above the Law, will subject and frame his actions thereto, for examples sake to his subjects, and of his owne free-will, but not as subject or bound thereto.

Since I have so clearly prooved then out of the fundamentall lawes and practise of this country, what right & power a king hath over his land and subjects, it is easie to be understood, what allegeance & obedience his lieges owe unto him; I meane alwaies of such free Monarchies as our king is, and not of elective kings, and much lesse of such sort of governors, as the dukes of *Venice* are, whose Aristocratick and limited government, is nothing like to free Monarchies; although the malice of some writers hath not beene ashamed to mis-know any difference to be betwixt them. And if it be not lawfull to any particular Lordes tenants or vassals, upon whatsoever pretext, to controll and displace their Master, and over-lord (as is clearer nor the Sunne by all Lawes of the world) how much lesse may the subjects and vassals of the great over-lord the KING controll or displace him? And since in all inferiour judgements in the land, the people may not upon any respects displace their Magistrates, although but subaltern: for the people of a borough, cannot displace their Provost before the time of their election: nor in Ecclesiasticall policie the flocke can upon any pretence displace the Pastor, nor judge of him: yea even the poore Schoolemaster cannot be displaced by his schollers: If these, I say (whereof some are but inferiour, subaltern, and temporall Magistrates, and none of them equall in any sort to the dignitie of a King) cannot be displaced for any occasion or pretext by them that are ruled by them: how much lesse is it lawfull upon any pretext to controll or displace the great Provost, and great Schoole-master of the whole land: except by inverting the order of all Law and reason, the commanded may be made to command their commander, the judged to judge their Judge, and they that are governed, to governe their time about their Lord and governour.

And the agreement of the Law of nature in this our ground with the Lawes and constitutions of God, and man, already alledged, will by two similitudes easily appeare. The King towards his people is rightly compared to a father of children, and to a head of a body composed of divers members: For as fathers, the good Princes, and Magistrates of the people of God acknowledged themselves to their subjects. And for all other well ruled Common-wealths, the stile of *Pater patriae* was ever, and is commonly used to Kings. And the proper office of a King towards his Subjects, agrees very wel with the office of the head towards the body, and all members thereof: For from the head, being the seate of Judgement, proceedeth the care and foresight of guiding, and preventing all evill that may come to the body or any part thereof. The head cares for the body, so doeth the King for his people. As the discourse and direction flowes from the head, and the execution according thereunto belongs to the rest of the members, every one according to their office: so it is betwixt a wise Prince, and his people. As the judgement comming from the head may not onely imploy the members, every one in their owne office, as long as they are able for it; but likewise in case any of them be affected with any infirmitie must care and provide for their remedy, in-case it be curable, and if otherwise, gar cut them off for feare of infecting of the rest: even so is it betwixt the Prince, and his people. And as there is ever hope of curing any diseased member by the direction of the head, as long as it is whole; but by the contrary, if it be troubled, all the members are partakers of that paine, so is it betwixt the Prince and his people.

And now first for the fathers part (whose naturall love to his children I described in the first part of this my discourse, speaking of the dutie that Kings owe to their Subjects) consider, I pray you what duetie his children owe to him, & whether upon any pretext whatsoever, it wil not be thought monstrous and unnaturall to his sons, to rise up against him, to control him at their appetite, and when they thinke good to sley him, or to cut him off, and adopt to themselves any other they please in his roome: Or can any pretence of wickednes or rigor on his part be a just excuse for his children to put hand into him? And although wee see by the course of nature, that love useth to descend more than to ascend, in case it were trew, that the father hated and wronged the children never so much, will any man, endued with the least sponke of reason, thinke it lawfull for them to meet him with the line? Yea, suppose the father were furiously following his sonnes with a drawen sword, is it lawfull for them to turne and strike againe, or make any resistance but by flight? I thinke surely, if there were no more but the example of bruit beasts & unreasonable creatures, it may serve well enough to qualifie and prove this my argument. We reade often the pietie that the Storkes have to their olde and decayed parents: And generally wee know, that there are many sorts of beasts and fowles, that with violence and many bloody strokes will beat and banish their yong ones from them, how soone they perceive them to be able to fend themselves; but wee never read or heard of any resistance on their part, except among the vipers; which prooves such persons, as ought to be reasonable creatures, and yet unnaturally follow this example, to be endued with their viperous nature.

And for the similitude of the head and the body, it may very well fall out that the head will be forced to garre cut off some rotten members (as I haue already said) to keep the rest of the body in integritie: but what state the body can be in, if the head, for any infirmitie that can fall to it, be cut off, I leave it to the readers judgement.

So as (to conclude this part) if the children may upon any pretext that can be imagined, lawfully rise up against their Father, cut him off, & choose any other whom they please in his roome; and if the body for the weale of it, may for any infirmitie that can be in the head, strike it off, then I cannot deny that the people may rebell, controll, and displace, or cut off their king at their owne pleasure, and upon respects mooving them. And whether these similitudes represent better the office of a King, or the offices of Masters or Deacons of crafts, or Doctors in Physicke (which jolly comparisons are used by such writers as maintaine the contrary proposition) I leave it also to the readers discretion.

And in case any doubts might arise in any part of this treatise, I wil (according to my promise) with the solution of foure principall and most weightie doubts, that the adversaries may object, conclude this discourse. And first it is casten up by divers, that employ their pennes upon Apologies for rebellions and treasons, that every man is borne to carry such a naturall zeale and duety to his commonwealth, as to his mother; that seeing it so rent and deadly wounded, as whiles it will be by wicked and tyrannous Kings, good Citizens will be forced, for the naturall zeale and duety they owe to their owne native countrey, to put their hand to worke for freeing their common-wealth from such a pest.

Whereunto I give two answeres: First, it is a sure Axiome in *Theologie,* that evill should not be done, that good may come of it: The wickednesse therefore of the King can never make them that are ordained to be judged by him, to become his Judges. And if it be not lawfull to a private man to revenge his private injury upon his private adversary (since God hath onely given the sword to the Magistrate) how much lesse is it lawfull to the people, or any part of them (who all are but private men, the authoritie being alwayes with the Magistrate, as I have already proved) to take upon them the use of the sword, whom to it belongs not, against the publicke Magistrate, whom to onely it belongeth.

Next, in place of relieving the common-wealth out of distresse (which is their onely excuse and colour) they shall heape double distresse and deso-lation upon it; and so their rebellion shall procure the contrary effects that they pretend it for: For a king cannot be imagined to be so unruly and tyran-nous, but the common-wealth will be kept in better order, notwithstanding thereof, by him, then it can be by his way-taking. For first, all sudden muta-tions are perillous in common-wealths, hope being thereby given to all bare men to set up themselves, and flie with other mens feathers, the reines being loosed to all the insolencies that disordered people can commit by hope of impunitie, because of the loosenesse of all things.

And next, it is certaine that a king can never be so monstrously vicious, but hee will generally favour justice, and maintaine some order, except in the particulars, wherein his inordinate lustes and passions carry him away; where by the contrary, no King being, nothing is unlawfull to none: And so the olde opinion of the Philosophers prooves trew, That better it is to live in a Common-wealth, where nothing is lawfull, then where all things are law-full to all men; the Common-wealth at that time resembling an undanted young horse that hath casten his rider: For as the divine Poet Du Bartas sayth, *Better it were to suffer some disorder in the estate, and some spots in the Common-wealth, then in pretending to reforme, utterly to overthrow the Republicke.*

The second objection they ground upon the curse that hangs over the common-wealth, where a wicked king reigneth: and, say they, there cannot be a more acceptable deed in the sight of God, nor more dutifull to their common-weale, then to free the countrey of such a curse, and vindicate to them their libertie, which is naturall to all creatures to crave.

Whereunto for answere, I grant indeed, that a wicked king is sent by God for a curse to his people, and a plague for their sinnes: but that it is lawfull to them to shake off that curse at their owne hand, which God hath laid on them, that I deny, and may so do justly. Will any deny that the king of *Babel* was a curse to the people of God, as was plainly fore-spoken and threatned unto them in the prophecie of their captivtie? And what was *Nero* to the Christian Church in his time? And yet *Jeremy* and *Paul* (as yee have else heard) commanded them not onely to obey them, but heartily to pray for their welfare.

It is certaine then (as I have already by the Law of God sufficiently proved) that patience, earnest prayers to God, and amendment of their lives, are the onely lawful means to move God to relieve them of that heavie curse. As for vindicating to themselves their owne libertie, what lawfull power have they to revoke to themselves againe those priviledges, which by their owne consent before were so fully put out of their hands? for if a Prince cannot justly bring backe againe to himself the priviledges once bestowed by him or his predecessors upon any state or ranke of his subjects; how much lesse may the subjects reave out of the princes hand that superioritie, which he and his Predecessors have so long brooked over them?

But the unhappy iniquitie of the time, which hath oft times given over good successe to their treasonable attempts, furnisheth them the ground of their third objection: For, say they, the fortunate successe that God hath so oft given to such enterprises, prooveth plainely by the practise, that God favoured the justnesse of their quarrell.

To the which I answere, that it is trew indeed, that all the successe of battels, as well as other worldly things, lyeth onely in Gods hand: And therefore it is that in the Scripture he takes to himselfe the style of God of Hosts. But upon that generall to conclude, that hee ever gives victory to the just quarrell, would proove the *Philistims,* and divers other neighbour enemies of the people of God to have oft times had the just quarrel against the people of God, in respect of the many victories they obtained against them. And by that same argument they had also just quarrell against the Arke of God: For they wan it in the field, and kept it long prisoner in their countrey. As likewise by all good Writers, as well Theologues, as other, the Duels and singular combats are disallowed; which are onely made upon pretence, that GOD will kith thereby the justice of the quarrell: For wee must consider that the innocent partie is not innocent before God: And therefore God will make oft times them that have the wrong side revenge justly his quarrell; and when he hath done, cast his scourge in the fire; as he oft times did to his owne people, stirring up and strengthening their enemies, while they were humbled in his sight, and then delivered them in their hands. So God, as the great Judge may justly punish his Deputie, and for his rebellion against him stir up his rebels to meet him with the like: And when it is done, the part of the instrument is no better then the divels part is in tempting and torturing such as God committeth to him as his hangman to doe: Therefore, as I said in the beginning, it is oft times a very deceiveable argument, to judge of the cause by the event.

And the last objection is grounded upon the mutuall paction and adstipulation (as they call it) betwixt the King and his people, at the time of his coronation: For there, say they, there is a mutuall paction, and contract bound up, and sworne betwixt the king, and the people: Whereupon it followeth, that if the one part of the contract or the Indent bee broken upon the Kings side, the people are no longer bound to keep their part of it, but are thereby freed of their oath: For (say they) a contract betwixt two parties, of all Law frees the one partie, if the other breake unto him.

As to this contract alledged made at the coronation of a King, although I deny any such contract to bee made then, especially containing such a clause irritant as they alledge; yet I confesse, that a king at his coronation, or at the entry to his kingdome, willingly promiseth to his people, to discharge honorably and trewly the office given him by God over them: But presuming that thereafter he breaks his promise unto them never so inexcusable; the question is, who should bee judge of the breake, giving unto them, this contract were made unto them never so sicker, according to their alleageance. I thinke no man that hath but the smallest entrance into the civill Law, will doubt that of all Law, either civil or municipal of any nation, a contract cannot be thought broken by the one partie, and so the other likewise to be freed therefro, except that first a lawfull triall and cognition be had by the ordinary Judge of the breakers thereof: Or else every man may be both party and Judge in his owne cause; which is absurd once to be thought. Now in this contract (I say) betwixt the king and his people, God is doubtles the only Judge, both because to him onely the king must make count of his administration (as is oft said before) as likewise by the oath in the coronation, God is made judge and revenger of the breakers: For in his presence, as only judge of oaths, all oaths ought to be made. Then since God is the onely Judge betwixt the two parties contractors, the cognition and revenge must onely appertaine to him: It followes therefore of necessitie, that God must first give sentence upon the King that breaketh, before the people can thinke themselves freed of their oath. What justice then is it, that the partie shall be both judge and partie, usurping upon himselfe the office of God, may by this argument easily appeare: And shall it lie in the hands of headlesse multitude, when they please to weary off subjection, to cast off the yoake of governement that God hath laid upon them, to judge and punish him, whom-by they should be judged and punished, and in that case, wherein by their violence they kythe themselves to be most passionate parties, to use the office of an ungracious Judge or Arbiter? Nay, to speak trewly of that case, as it stands betwixt the king and his people, none of them ought to judge of the others break: For considering rightly the two parties at the time of their mutuall promise, the king is the one party, and the whole people in one body are the other party. And therfore since it is certaine, that a king, in case so it should fal out, that his people in one body had rebelled against him, hee should not in that case, as thinking him-selfe free of his promise and oath, become an utter enemy, and practise the wreake of his whole people and native country: although he ought justly to punish the principall authours and bellowes of that universall rebellion: how much lesse then ought the people (that are alwaies subject unto him, and naked of all authoritie on their part) presse to judge and over-throw him? otherwise the people, as the one partie contracters, shall no sooner challenge the king as breaker, but hee assoone shall judge them as breakers: so as the victors making the tyners the traitors (as our proverbe is) the par-tie shall aye become both judge and partie in his owne particular, as I have alreadie said.

And it is here likewise to be noted, that the duty and alleageance, which the people sweareth to their prince, is not only bound to themselves, but likewise to their lawfull heires and posterity, the lineall succession of crowns being begun among the people of God, and happily continued in divers christian common-wealths: So as no objection either of heresie, or whatsoever private statute or law may free the people from their oath-giving to their king, and his succession, established by the old fundamen-tall lawes of the kingdome: For, as hee is their heritable over-lord, and so by birth, not by any right in the coronation, commeth to his crowne; it is a like unlawful (the crowne ever standing full) to displace him that suc-ceedeth thereto, as to eject the former: For at the very moment of the expir-ing of the king reigning, the nearest and lawful heire entreth in his place: And so to refuse him, or intrude another, is not to holde out uncomming in, but to expell and put out their righteous King. And I trust at this time whole *France* acknowledgeth the superstitious rebellion of the liguers, who upon pretence of heresie, by force of armes held so long out, to the great desolation of their whole countrey, their native and righteous king from possessing of his owne crowne and naturall kingdome.

Not that by all this former discourse of mine, and Apologie for kings, I meane that whatsoever errors and intollerable abominations a sovereigne prince commit, hee ought to escape all punishment, as if thereby the world were only ordained for kings, & they without controlment to turne it upside down at their pleasure: but by the contrary, by remitting them to God (who is their onely ordinary Judge) I remit them to the sorest and sharpest schoolemaster that can be devised for them: for the further a king is pre-ferred by God above all other ranks & degrees of men, and the higher that his seat is above theirs, the greater is his obligation to his maker. And ther-fore in case he forget himselfe (his unthankfulnes being in the same mea-sure of height) the sadder and sharper will his correction be; and according to the greatnes of the height he is in, the weight of his fall wil recompense the same: for the further that any person is obliged to God, his offence becomes and growes so much the greater, then it would be in any other. *Joves* thunderclaps light oftner and sorer upon the high & stately oakes, then on the low and supple willow trees: and the highest bench is sliddriest to sit upon. Neither is it ever heard that any king forgets himselfe towards God, or in his vocation; but God with the greatnesse of the plague revengeth the greatnes of his ingratitude: Neither thinke I by the force and argument of this my discourse so to perswade the people, that none will hereafter be raised up, and rebell against wicked Princes. But remitting to the justice and providence of God to stirre up such scourges as pleaseth him, for punishment of wicked kings (who made the very vermine and filthy dust of the earth to bridle the insolencie of proud *Pharaoh*) my onely purpose and intention in this treatise is to perswade, as farre as lieth in me, by these sure and infallible grounds, all such good Christian readers, as beare not onely the naked name of a Christian, but kith the fruites thereof in their daily forme of life, to keep their hearts and hands free from such monstrous and unnaturall rebellions, whensoever the wickednesse of a Prince shall procure the same at Gods hands: that, when it shall please God to cast such scourges of princes, and instruments of his fury in the fire, ye may stand up with cleane handes, and unspotted consciences, having prooved your selves in all your actions trew Christians toward God, and dutifull subjects towards your King, having remitted the judgement and punishment of all his wrongs to him, whom to onely of right it appertaineth.

But craving at God, and hoping that God shall continue his blessing with us, in not sending such fearefull desolation, I heartily wish our kings behaviour so to be, and continue among us, as our God in earth, and loving Father, endued with such properties as I described a King in the first part of this Treatise. And that ye (my deare countreymen, and charitable readers) may presse by all means to procure the prosperitie and welfare of your King; that as hee must on the one part thinke all his earthly felicitie and happinesse grounded upon your weale, caring more for himselfe for your sake then for his owne, thinking himselfe onely ordained for your weale; such holy and happy emulation may arise betwixt him and you, as his care for your quietnes, and your care for his honour and preservation, may in all your actions daily strive together, that the Land may thinke themselves blessed with such a King, and the king may thinke himselfe most happy in ruling over so loving and obedient subjects.

9. Jean Bodin, *Six Books of a Commonweale*

Jean Bodin (1530–96) is a major name in the history of political theory. By profession he was a civil lawyer, in which pursuit he was at different stages of his life a professor, a practitioner, and a judge. "Civil" lawyer means one trained in Roman law (the "corpus of civil law" compiled by the Emperor Justinian in the sixth century) and the long medieval and post-medieval tradition of commentary and adaptation based on that material. The legal system of France in Bodin's time was complicated, but Roman law, as adapted, furnished most of its substance and procedure. For about a decade of his life, Bodin had a certain role in contemporary politics as an adviser to the brother of King Henry III. In that capacity, during the period of bitter Catholic-Protestant conflict in France, he was rather too much of an advocate of peace for his employers' taste. He was a loyal Catholic personally but, in contrast with many of his contemporaries, not someone whose thinking was primarily powered by religious conviction; in one of his literary works he wrote about comparative religion in a rather ecumenical vein.

Although experience of France in his time contributed to Bodin's thinking about the need and sources of political order, he was essentially a lawyer and independent scholar, whose ideas by no means reduce to projection of a partisan stance or of an agonized revulsion from all partisans. His political thought is collected in *Six Books of the Republic,* first published in 1576 and later reissued in a drastically revised form. The early English translation "Commonweale" (1600) renders the meaning of Bodin's "république" much better than our "republic." The word does not refer to a form of government, but to the classical definition (as in Cicero's *De Republica*)—a lasting political society in which people are united by shared law and community of purpose. The *Six Books* are a vast and vastly learned work, whence only small excerpts on especially important subjects are reproduced here. Bodin was one of the heirs and transmitters of the tradition of European humanism, with the legal accent of one of its branches. He is important as a theorist of history as well as of politics by virtue of his *Method for the Easy Comprehension of History.*

From Jean Bodin, *Six Books of the Commonwealth,* abridged and edited by M. J. Tooley (New York: Barnes and Noble, 1967), pp. 1–21, 25–36, 40–49, 51–56, 174–80. Published by permission of Barnes & Noble Books, Totowa, New Jersey. Footnotes deleted.

Book One

Chapter 1: The Final End of the Well-ordered Commonwealth

A commonwealth may be defined as the rightly ordered government of a number of families, and of those things which are their common concern, by a sovereign power. We must start in this way with a definition because the final end of any subject must first be understood before the means of attaining it can profitably be considered, and the definition indicates what that end is. If then the definition is not exact and true, all that is deduced from it is valueless. One can, of course, have an accurate perception of the end, and yet lack the means to attain it, as has the indifferent archer who sees the bull's-eye but cannot hit it. With care and attention however he may come very near it, and provided he uses his best endeavours, he will not be without honour, even if he cannot find the exact centre of the target. But the man who does not comprehend the end, and cannot rightly define his subject, has no hope of finding the means of attaining it, any more than the man who shoots at random into the air can hope to hit the mark.

Let us consider more particularly the terms of this definition. We say in the first place *right* ordering to distinguish a commonwealth from a band of thieves or pirates. With them one should have neither intercourse, commerce, nor alliance. Care has always been taken in well-ordered commonwealths not to include robber-chiefs and their followers in any agreements in which honour is pledged, peace treated, war declared, offensive or defensive alliances agreed upon, frontiers defined, or the disputes of princes and sovereign lords submitted to arbitration, except under the pressure of an absolute necessity. Such desperate occasions however do not come within the bounds of normal conventions. The law has always distinguished robbers and pirates from those who are recognized to be enemies legitimately at war, in that they are members of some commonwealth founded upon that principle of justice that brigands and pirates seek to subvert. For this reason brigands cannot claim that the conventions of war, recognized by all peoples, should be observed in their case, nor are they entitled to those guarantees that the victors normally accord to the vanquished. . . .

It is true that we see brigands living amicably and sociably together, sharing the spoil fairly among themselves. Nevertheless the terms *amity, society, share* cannot properly be used of such associations. They should rather be called *conspiracies, robberies,* and *spoliations.* Such associations lack that which is the true mark of a community, a rightly ordered government in accordance with the laws of nature. This is why the ancients define a commonwealth as a society of men gathered together for the good and happy life. This definition however falls short on the one hand, and goes beyond the mark on the other. It omits the three principal elements of a commonwealth, the family, sovereign power, and that which is of common concern, while the term "happy," as they understood it, is not essential. If it were, the good life would depend on the wind always blowing fair, a conclusion no right-thinking man would agree to. A commonwealth can be well-ordered and yet stricken with poverty, abandoned by its friends, beset by its enemies, and brought low by every sort of misfortune. Cicero saw this happen to the city of Marseilles in Provence, yet he thought it the best-ordered and most civilized city, without exception, of any in the world. On the same showing the commonwealth that is well-situated, wealthy, populous, respected by its allies, feared by its enemies, invincible in war, impregnable, furnished with splendid buildings, and of great reputation, must be considered well-ordered, even if given over to every wickedness and abandoned to vicious habits. But there is surely no more fatal enemy to virtue than worldly success of this sort, fortunate as it is accounted to be, for they are contraries not to be reconciled. Therefore we do not include the term "happy" as an essential term in our definition. We aim higher in our attempt to attain, or at least approximate, to the true image of a rightly ordered government. Not that we intend to describe a purely ideal and unrealizable commonwealth, such as that imagined by Plato, or Thomas More the Chancellor of England. We intend to confine ourselves as far as possible to those political forms that are practicable. We cannot therefore be blamed if we do not succeed in describing the state which is rightly ordered absolutely, any more than the pilot, blown out of his course by a storm, or the doctor defeated by a mortal disease, is to be blamed, provided he has managed his ship or his patient in the right way.

The conditions of true felicity are one and the same for the commonwealth and the individual. The sovereign good of the commonwealth in general, and of each of its citizens in particular lies in the intellective and contemplative virtues, for so wise men have determined. It is generally agreed that the ultimate purpose, and therefore sovereign good, of the individual, consists in the constant contemplation of things human, natural, and divine. If we admit that this is the principal purpose whose fulfilment means a happy life for the individual, we must also conclude that it is the goal and the condition of well-being in the commonwealth too. Men of the world and princes however have never accepted this, each measuring his own particular well-being by the number of his pleasures and satisfactions. Even those who have agreed that the sovereign good of the individual is contemplation, have not always agreed that the good of the individual and good of the commonwealth are identical, and that to be a good man is also to be a good citizen. For this reason there has always been a great variety of laws, customs, and policies attendant on the desires and passions of princes and governors. Since however the wise man is the measure of justice and of truth, and those reputed wise have always agreed that the end of the individual and the end of the commonwealth are one, without distinction of the good man and the good citizen, we also must conclude that contemplation is the end and form of the good to which the government of the commonwealth should be directed.

Aristotle was not always consistent in what he had to say on the subject. At times he compromised with the views of various people, coupling now riches, now power, now health, with virtue, in order to take into account commonly received opinions. But in moments of greatest insight he made contemplation the height of felicity. It may have been similar considerations which prompted Marcus Varro to say that human felicity springs from the union of action and contemplation. To my mind this is so, because whereas the well-being of a simple organism may be simple in character, that of a dual organism, composed of diverse elements, must itself be of a dual nature. The well-being of the body comes from health, strength, vigour, and the beauty of well-proportioned members. The well-being of the active principle of the soul, which is the link between body and soul, consists in the subordination of appetite to reason, in other words, the exercise of the moral virtues. The well-being of the intellective part of the soul lies in the intellectual virtues of prudence, knowledge, and faith. By the first we distinguish good and evil, by the second truth and falsehood, and by the third piety and impiety, and what is to be sought and what avoided. These are the sum of true wisdom, which is the highest felicity attainable in this world.

If one turns from the microcosm to the macrocosm, it follows by parity of argument that the commonwealth should have a territory which is large enough, and sufficiently fertile and well stocked, to feed and clothe its inhabitants. It should have a mild and equable climate, and an adequate supply of good water for health. If the geography of the country is not in itself its best defence, it should have sites capable of fortification against the danger of attack. These are the basic needs which are the first objects of concern in all commonwealths. These secured, one looks for such luxuries as minerals, medicinal plants, and dyes. Offensive weapons must also be provided if one would extend one's frontiers and subjugate the enemy, for the appetites of men being for the most part insatiable, they desire to secure great abundance not only of what is necessary and useful, but of what is pleasant merely, and redundant. But just as one does not think of educating a child until it is grown and capable of instruction, so commonwealths do not concern themselves with the moral and mental sciences, still less with philosophy, till they are amply furnished with all that they regard as necessities. They are contented to cultivate that modest degree of prudence which is sufficient for the defence of the state against its enemies, the prevention of disorders among its subjects, and the reparation of injuries.

A man of good disposition however who finds himself well provided with the necessities and comforts of life, secure and at peace, turns away from unworthy companions and seeks the society of wise and virtuous men. When he has purged his soul of troubling passions and desires, he is free to give his attention to observing his fellows, and interests himself in the difference that age and temperament makes between them, the causes of the greatness of some and the failure of others, and of the fluctuations of states. From men he turns to the contemplation of nature, and considers the great chain of being, minerals, plants, and animals in their hierarchical order, the forms, qualities, and virtues of all generated things, and their mutual attractions and repulsions. From the world of material things he moves forward to the contemplation of the immaterial world of the heavens, where the splendour, beauty, and power of the stars is manifested in their proud, remote, and majestic movements, comprehending the whole universe in a single harmony. The ecstasy of this vision inspires him with a perpetual longing to penetrate to the first cause and author of this perfect creation. But there he must pause, for the greatness, the power, the wisdom, and goodness of the Supreme Being, being infinite, must for ever remain inscrutable in its essence. By such a progression a wise and thoughtful man reaches the concept of the one infinite and eternal God, and thereby as it were attains the true felicity of mankind.

If such a man is adjudged both wise and happy, so also will be the commonwealth which has many such citizens, even though it be neither large nor rich, for in it the pomps and vanities of proud citizens, given over to pleasure, are contemned. But it must not be assumed from this account that felicity comes from a confusion of many elements. Man is made up of a mortal body and an immortal soul, but his final good pertains to the more noble part of himself . . . For though those activities such as eating and drinking by which life is supported are necessary, no thoughtful man finds in them his sovereign good. The habit of good deeds is of the first importance, for the soul that is not illumined and purified by the moral virtues cannot enjoy the fruits of contemplation. The moral virtues are therefore ordained to the intellectual. Felicity cannot be found in that imperfect state in which there is still some good yet to be realized; that which is less noble is ordained to that which is more noble as its final end, body to spirit, spirit to intellect, appetite to reason, living to right living. Therefore when Varro found felicity in both contemplation and action, he would have done better, in my opinion, to have said that a man has need of both action and contemplation in this life, but that his sovereign good lies in contemplation.

Nevertheless it is certain that a commonwealth is not rightly ordered which neglects altogether, or even for any length of time, mundane activities such as the administration of justice, the defence of the subject, the provision of the necessary means of subsistence, any more than a man whose soul is so absorbed in contemplation that he forgets to eat and drink can hope to live long. . . .

The same principles hold good for the well-ordered commonwealth. It is ordained to the contemplative virtues as its final end, and those things which are least in order of dignity come first in order of necessity. Those material things necessary to the sustenance and defence of the subject must first be secured. Nevertheless such activities are ordained to moral activities, and moral activities to intellectual, or the contemplation of the noblest subjects within the scope of men's imaginations. Thus we see that God allotted six days for all those labours to which the greater part of man's life is dedicated. But He ordained that these labours should cease on the seventh day, and He blessed it above all other days as the holy day of rest, so that men might then have leisure to contemplate His works, His law, and His glory. Such is the final end of well-ordered commonwealths, and they are the more happy the more nearly they come to realizing it. For just as there are degrees of felicity among men, so are there among commonwealths, some greater, some less, in accordance with the end which each sets out to attain. It was said of the Spartans that they were courageous and magnanimous, but for the rest unjust and perfidious, if they could thereby further the public interest. The sole purpose of their laws, their customs, their institutions was to make men brave and indifferent to hardship and pain, contemptuous of ease and pleasure, and totally devoted to the state. The Roman Republic on the other hand was distinguished for its justice, and surpassed that of the Spartans, for its citizens were not only magnanimous, but justice was the mainspring of all their actions.

In treating of the commonwealth we must therefore try and find means whereby it may come as near as possible to realizing the felicity we have described, and conforming to the definition we have postulated. Let us continue with the terms of the definition and pass on to the family.

Chapters 2–5: Concerning the Family

A family may be defined as the right ordering of a group of persons owing obedience to a head of a household, and of those interests which are his proper concern. The second term of our definition of the commonwealth refers to the family because it is not only the true source and origin of the commonwealth, but also its principal constituent. Xenophon and Aristotle divorced economy or household management from police or disciplinary power, without good reason to my mind . . . I understand by domestic government the right ordering of family matters, together with the authority which the head of the family has over his dependants, and the obedience due from them to him, things which Aristotle and Xenophon neglect. Thus the well-ordered family is a true image of the commonwealth, and domestic comparable with sovereign authority. It follows that the household is the model of right order in the commonwealth. And just as the whole body enjoys health when every particular member performs its proper function, so all will be well with the commonwealth when families are properly regulated.

We have said that a commonwealth is the rightly ordered government of a number of families and of those matters which are their common concern, by a sovereign power. The phrase *a number* cannot mean just two, for the law requires at least three persons to constitute a college, and the same number to constitute a family in addition to its head, whether they be his children, slaves, freedmen, or free dependants who have voluntarily submitted to his authority. He is the fourth member of the group. Furthermore, since households, colleges and corporate bodies of all sorts, commonwealths, and indeed the whole human race would perish unless perpetuated from generation to generation, no family is complete without the wife, who is therefore called the mother of the family. By this reckoning, a minimum of five persons is required to constitute a family. I think this is the reason why ancient writers, such as Apuleius, said that fifteen persons could become a political community, meaning by that three complete households. Otherwise, even if the head of the family had three hundred wives and six hundred children, like Hermotinus, King of Parthia, or five hundred slaves like Crassus, if all these persons were a single household under the authority of a single head, they would not constitute either a political community or a commonwealth, but only a family. . . .

The law says that the people never dies, but that after the lapse of a hundred or even a thousand years it is still the same people. The presumption is that although all individuals alive at any one moment will be dead a century later, the people is immortal by succession of persons, as was Theseus' ship which lasted as long as pains were taken to repair it. But a ship is no more than a load of timber unless there is a keel to hold together the ribs, the prow, the poop and the tiller. Similarly a commonwealth without sovereign power to unite all its several members, whether families, colleges, or corporate bodies, is not a true commonwealth. It is neither the town nor its inhabitants that makes a city state, but their union under a sovereign ruler, even if they are only three households. Just as the mouse is as much numbered among animals as is the elephant, so the rightly ordered government of only three households, provided they are subject to a sovereign authority, is just as much a commonwealth as a great empire. The principality of Ragusa, which is one of the smallest in Europe, is no less a commonwealth than the empires of the Turks and the Tartars, which are among the greatest in the world. . . .

But besides sovereign power there must also be something enjoyed in common such as the public domain, a public treasury, the buildings used by the whole community, the roads, walls, squares, churches, and markets, as well as the usages, laws, customs, courts, penalties, and rewards which are either shared in common or of public concern. There is no commonwealth where there is no common interest. . . . It is not desirable however that all things, including women and children, should be possessed in common as Plato advocated in his *Republic*. His intention was to banish from the city the words "mine" and "thine," since he thought them the cause of all the misfortunes and disasters that befall commonwealths. He forgot that even if this could be achieved, then the peculiar mark of a commonwealth would be lost. For nothing could properly be regarded as public if there were nothing at all to distinguish it from what was private. Nothing can be thought of as shared in common, except by contrast with what is privately owned. If all citizens were kings there would be no king. There can be no harmony if the subtle combination of various chords, which is the charm of harmony, is reduced to a monotone. Moreover such a commonwealth would be directly contrary to the law of God and of nature, for that law not only condemns the incests, adulteries, and parricides which would be the inevitable consequence of women being possessed in common, but forbids theft, or even the mere coveting of that which is the private possession of another. We see therefore that commonwealths were ordained of God to the end that men should render to the community that which is required in the public interest, and to each individual that which is proper to him. . . .

It is of course possible for all the subjects of a commonwealth to live in common, as did the Cretans and the Spartans in ancient times . . . or as the Anabaptists attempted to do when they founded their community in the city of Münster. They ruled that all things should be possessed in common save only women and personal belongings, thinking this would promote amity and mutual concord. They soon discovered their mistake however. So far from accomplishing what they expected, and banishing quarrels and animosities, they destroyed affection between husband and wife, and the love of parents for their children, the reverence of children for their parents, and the goodwill of parents towards one another. Such are the consequences of ignoring the tie of blood, the strongest bond there is. It is common knowledge that no one feels any very strong affection for that which is common to all. Common possession brings in its train all sorts of quarrels and antagonisms. They deceive themselves who think that persons and property possessed in common will be much cared for, for it may be observed every-

where, that those things which are public property are habitually neglected, unless someone calculates that he may extract some private advantage from looking after them. The proper organization of the household
requires the separation and distinction of the goods, the women, the children, and servants, of one family from another, and that which pertains to
each from that which is common to all, or in other words pertains to the
public good. . . .

So much for the difference and the resemblance that there is between the
family and the commonwealth in general. Let us now consider the members of the family. The government of all commonwealths, colleges, corporate bodies, or households whatsoever, rests on the right to command on
one side, and the obligation to obey on the other, which arises when the
natural liberty which each man has to live as he chooses, is exercised subject to the power of another. The right to command another is either of a
public or a private character; public when vested in a sovereign who declares the law, or in the magistrate who executes it, and issues orders binding on his subordinates and private citizens generally; private when vested
in heads of households, or in the collective authority which colleges and
corporate bodies exercise over their particular members, or the minority of
the whole body. Authority in the family rests on the fourfold relationship
between husband and wife, father and child, master and servant, owner
and slave. And since the rightful government of any society, public or private, depends on a proper understanding of how to command and how to
obey, we will consider the household in the order described.

We understand by natural liberty the right under God to be subject to no
man living and amenable only to those commands which are self-imposed,
that is to say the commands of right reason conformable to the will of God.
The first of all commandments was the commandment to subordinate animal appetite to reason, for before a man can govern others he must learn to
govern himself, surrendering to reason the power of direction, and school-
ing the appetites to obedience. In this way each man will achieve that
which truly pertains to his nature, which is the original and purest form of
justice. The Hebrews expressed this proverbially in their saying "Charity
begins at home," meaning that one should subordinate appetite to reason in
accordance with the first express commandment of God, laid upon him
who killed his brother. The commandment that He had given the husband
to rule over his wife has a double significance, first in the literal sense of
marital authority, and second in the moral sense of the soul over the body,
and the reason over concupiscence, which the Scriptures always identify
with the woman. . . .

From the moment a marriage is consummated the woman is subject to
her husband, unless he is still living as a dependant in his father's house.

Neither slaves nor other dependants have any authority over their wives, still less over their children. They are all subject to the head of the family until such time as he shall have given his married son his independence. No household can have more than one head, one master, one seigneur. If there were more than one head there would be a conflict of command and incessant family disturbances . . . wherefore a woman marrying a man still living in his father's house is subject to her father-in-law. . . .

By a law of Romulus the husband was not only given full authority over his wife but could without any formal process of law take her life on four occasions, when she was taken in adultery, for substituting a child not his own, for having duplicate keys, or for being habitually drunk. . . . In order to show how general among all people has been this subjection of women, I will add two or three examples. We read that by the laws of the Lombards wives were held in the same subjection as had been customary among the ancient Romans, and their husbands had a power of life and death over them that they were still exercising when Baldus was writing, only two hundred and sixty years ago. As for our ancestors, the Gauls, nowhere in the world have husbands enjoyed a more absolute power than among them. Caesar makes this clear in his *Memoirs* when he says that they had the same absolute power of life and death over their wives and children as over their slaves. . . .

With regard to divorce, the law of God permitted the husband to repudiate his wife, if she did not please him, on condition that he never took her back, but married another. This was at one time a custom common to all peoples, and is still practised in Africa and throughout the East. It was a means of humbling proud wives, while the knowledge that he had repudiated one wife without sufficient provocation made it difficult for an exacting husband to find another. If it is objected that it does not seem right that a man should be able to repudiate his wife without giving any reason, I appeal to the common usage in the matter. There is nothing more ill-advised than to compel two people to go on living together unless they are willing to publish the reason for the separation that they desire. The honour of both parties is at stake, whereas it is safeguarded if no reason has to be alleged. . . .

However great the variety, and subsequent changes in law, it has never been customary anywhere to exempt wives from the obedience, and even the reverence which they owe their husbands . . . Therefore in all systems of law the husband is regarded as the master of his wife's actions, and entitled to the usufruct of any property she may have, while the wife cannot come into the courts either as plaintiff or defendant save with the consent of her husband, or should he withhold it, the permission of the magistrate. The power, authority, and command that a husband has over his wife is allowed by both divine and positive law to be honourable and right. I know that in marriage alliances and settlements clauses are sometimes included exempting the wife from subjection to her husband. But such stipulations cannot detract from the authority of the husband, for they are contrary to both divine and positive law, as well as to the public interest. They are therefore invalid, and oaths to observe them cannot in consequence bind the husband.

The rightly ordered government of a father over his children lies first in the proper exercise of that power which God gives to a father over his natural children, and the law over his adopted ones, and second in the obedience, love, and reverence that children owe their father. Authority properly belongs to all those who have recognized power to command another. So, says Seneca, the prince commands his subjects, the magistrate the citizens, the master his pupils, the captain his soldiers, and the lord his slaves. But of all these there is none that has a natural right to command save only the father, who is the image of Almighty God, the Father of all things. Therefore Plato, having first defined the laws which touch the honour of God, speaks of them as an introduction to the reverence that a son owes his father, from whom, after God, he draws his life and all he may expect to enjoy in this world. And just as nature impels the father to foster his child so long as he is defenceless, and educate him in honourable and virtuous principles, so the child is prompted, and by an even stronger impulse, to love, honour, serve, and care for his father, to be obedient to his commands, support him, protect him, conceal all his infirmities and imperfections, and to spare neither goods nor life to preserve the life of him from whom he draws his own. This obligation is obvious, and founded in nature. But if one wishes further proof, one has only to remember that it was the first commandment in the second table of the law, and the only one of the ten commandments of the Decalogue that carried with it any promise of reward, for it is not usual to reward one who simply does that which he is under a strict obligation to do by both divine and positive law. Conversely we find the first curse recorded in Scripture was the curse laid on Ham for not concealing his father's shame. . . .

In any rightly ordered commonwealth, that power of life and death over their children which belongs to them under the law of God and of nature, should be restored to parents. This most primitive of customs was observed in ancient times by the Persians, and people of Asia generally, by the Romans and the Celts; it was also recognized throughout the New World till the time of the Spanish conquests. If this power is not restored, there is no hope of any restoration of good morals, honour, virtue, or the ancient splendour of commonwealths. Justinian and those who have repeated him are wrong in saying that the Romans alone recognized such power of parents over their children. We have the testimony of the law of God which ought to be regarded as holy and inviolate by all peoples. We also have the evidence of Greek and Roman historians such as Caesar, of the customs of the Persians, the Romans, and the Celts. He said of the Gauls that they had power of life and death as much over their wives and children as over their slaves. Moreover by the laws of Romulus, whereas the power of life and death which a husband had over his wife was restricted to four occasions only, that which he had over his children was unqualified, being a plenary power to dispense life or death to them as he thought fit, and to be seized of all property which they might acquire. Roman fathers had such authority not only over their natural children, but also over their children by adoption. . . .

A father is bound to educate and instruct his children, especially in the fear of God. But if he fails of his duty, the son is not excused his, though Solon in his laws acquitted children from the obligation of supporting their father if he had failed to apprentice them to some trade by which they could earn a living. There is no need to enter into any discussion of this particular point since we are only concerned here with the question of paternal authority. One of the greatest benefits which resulted from it in ancient times was the proper upbringing of children. Public courts do not take cognizance of the contempt, disobedience, and irreverence of children towards their parents, nor the vices to which their indiscipline disposes the young, such vices as extravagance, drunkenness, fornication, and gambling, not to mention those graver crimes punishable by law, which their unhappy parents neither dare to discover, nor have the power to punish. For children who stand in little awe of their parents, and have even less fear of the wrath of God, readily set at defiance the authority of magistrates, who in any case are chiefly occupied with the habitual criminal. It is therefore impossible that a commonwealth should prosper while the families which are its foundation are ill-regulated. . . .

Yet paternal power was gradually undermined in the time of the decline of the Roman Empire. The antique virtue thereupon vanished and with it the glory of the Republic, and a million vices and evil habits replaced the old loyalty and upright ways. For the paternal power of life and death was gradually restricted by the ambition of the magistrates, who wished to extend their own jurisdiction over all such matters. . . . Nowadays, fathers having been deprived of their paternal authority, and any claim to property acquired by their children, it is even suggested that the son can defend himself and resist by force any unjust attempt at coercion on the part of his father, and there are those that agree that he can. . . . But I hold that it is imperative that princes and legislators should revive the ancient laws touching the power of fathers over their children, and restore the usages prescribed by the law of God. . . .

It may be objected that an enraged father may abuse the power which he has over the life and property of his children. The law however puts those who are truly mad under ward, and takes from them any power over others when they do not possess it over themselves. But if a father is not out of his mind, he will never be tempted to kill his own child without cause, and if the son has merited such a fate, it is not for the magistrate to intervene. The affection of parents for their children is so strong, that the law has always rightly presumed that they will only do those things which are of benefit and honour to their children. The real danger lies in the temptation of parents to be too partial. Indeed there are innumerable cases of parents setting at defiance both divine and positive law in order to advance the interests of their children by fair means or foul. Therefore the father who kills his son is not liable to the same penalty as the parricide, for the law presumes he would only commit such an act upon good and just grounds. The law moreover gives him, to the exclusion of all others, the right to kill the adultress, or his daughter taken in sin. All these instances show that parents are not suspected of being liable to abuse their authority. Even if it be true that there have been cases where such powers have been misused, one cannot refuse to establish a good custom because certain ill consequences might occasionally ensue. No law, however just, natural, and necessary, but carries with it some risks. Anyone who wished to abolish all those laws which were liable to give rise to difficulties would abolish all laws whatsoever. But I hold that the natural affection of parents for their children is incompatible with cruelty and abuse of power. . . .

The third type of government in the household is that of the lord over his slaves and the master over his servants. . . . And seeing that there are slaves all over the world except in that quarter which is Europe, we must necessarily consider the power of masters over their slaves, and the advantages and disadvantages of the institution. It is a matter of moment both to families and to commonwealths everywhere.

Slaves are either naturally so, being born of slave women, or slaves by right of conquest, or in punishment for some crime, or because they have sold or gambled away their liberty to another. . . . Household servants are in no sense slaves but free men, and both before the law, and in fact, have an equal liberty of action. All the same they are not simply paid employees or day labourers over whom those who have hired their services have no such authority or right of punishment as the master has over his servants. For so long as they are members of their master's household they owe him service, respect, and obedience, and he can correct and punish them, though with discretion and moderation. Such briefly is the power of masters over their servants, for we do not want here to enter into any discussion of the rules which should govern the conduct proper on each side.

But the institution of slavery raises difficulties which have never been satisfactorily resolved. First of all, is slavery natural and useful, or contrary to nature? And second, what power should the master have over the slave? Aristotle was of opinion that servitude was natural, and alleged as proof that it is obvious that some are born fit only to serve and obey, others to govern and command. On the other hand jurists, who are less concerned with philosophical arguments than with commonly received opinions, hold that servitude is directly contrary to nature, and have always done what they could to defend personal liberty, despite the obscurity of laws, testaments, legal decisions, and contracts. . . .

Let us consider which of these two opinions is the better founded. There is a certain plausibility in the argument that slavery is natural and useful to the commonwealth. That which is contrary to nature cannot endure, and despite any force and violence that one can use, the natural order will always re-establish itself, as is clear from the behaviour of all natural agents. Slavery appeared suddenly in the world after the flood, and at the very same time that the first commonwealths began to take shape, and has persisted from that day to this. Although in the last three or four hundred years it has been abolished in many places, one continually sees it reappearing in some form. For instance in the West Indies, which are three times as extensive as the whole of Europe, people who have no knowledge of divine and positive laws to the contrary, have always had great numbers of slaves. There is not a commonwealth to be found anywhere that has never known the institution, and wise and good men in all ages have owned and employed slaves. What is more, in all commonwealths the master is always recognized as having absolute power to dispose of the lives and belongings of his slaves as he thinks fit, save in a few cases where princes and lawgivers have restricted this power. It cannot be that so many rulers and legislators have upheld an institution which was unnatural, or so many wise and virtuous men approved of them for doing so, or so many peoples for so many centuries maintained the practice of slavery, and even restricted the right of manumission, and still prospered in peace and war, if it had been against nature.

Again, who would deny that it is laudible and charitable to spare the life of a prisoner taken in legitimate warfare who cannot find a ransom, instead of killing him in cold blood, for this was generally the origin of enslavement. Moreover a man is required by divine and positive law to submit to corporal punishment if he cannot pay the forfeit for any act he has committed. No one doubts that those who make violent assaults upon the goods and lives of others are brigands and robbers, deserving of death. It cannot be against nature in such a case to exact services from the malefactor instead of killing him. If it were against nature to have power of life and death over another, all kingdoms and lordships in the world would be against nature, seeing that kings and princes have the like power over their subjects, noble and simple, if they are proved guilty of a capital crime.

All these arguments tend to prove that slavery is natural, useful, and right. I think however that strong objections can be urged against them all. I agree that servitude is natural where the strong, brutal, rich, and ignorant obey the wise, prudent, and humble, poor though they may be. But no one would deny that to subject wise men to fools, the well-informed to the ignorant, saints to sinners is against nature. . . . One sees in fact how often quiet and peaceable men are the prey of evildoers. When princes attempt to settle their differences by war, it is always claimed that the victor had right on his side, and the vanquished were in the wrong. If the vanquished did indeed make war without just cause, as do brigands, ought one not rather to make an example of them and put them to death, than to show them mercy? As for the argument that slavery could not have been so enduring if it had been contrary to nature, I would answer that the principle holds good for natural agents whose property it is to obey of necessity the unchanging laws of God. But man, being given the choice between good and evil, inclines for the most part to that which is forbidden, and chooses the evil, defying the laws of God and of nature. So much is such a one under the domination of his corrupt imagination, that he takes his own will for the law. There is no sort of impiety or wickedness which in this way has not come to be accounted virtuous and good. I will be content with one instance. It is sufficiently obvious that there can be no more cruel and detestable practice than human sacrifice. Yet there is hardly a people which has not practised it, and each and all have done so for centuries under the cover of piety. In our own times it was common throughout the Western Isles. . . . Such things show how little the laws of nature can be deduced from the practices of men, however inveterate, and one cannot on these grounds accept slavery as natural. Again, what charity is there in sparing captives in order to derive some profit or advantage from them as if they were cattle? For where is the man who would spare the lives of the vanquished if he saw more profit in killing than in sparing them? . . .

I will refrain from setting down in words the base humiliations that slaves have been made to suffer. But the cruelties one reads about are unbelievable, and yet only the thousandth part has been told. For writers only refer to the subject incidentally, and such accounts as we have, come from the most civilized races in the world. Slaves were made to work in the fields chained, as they still do in Barbary, and sleep in the open when work was done, as they still do everywhere in the East, for fear that they would abscond, or fire the house, or murder their masters. . . . So much have cities and commonwealths always feared their slaves that they have never dared to permit them the use of arms, or to be enrolled for service. It was forbidden on pain of death. . . . Yet they never succeeded so well but that some desperate man, by promising liberty to the slaves, threw the whole state into confusion, as did Viriat the pirate who made himself King of Portugal, Cinna, Spartacus, and others down to Simon Gerson the Jew. All these raised themselves from humble origins to be powerful rulers simply by enfranchising the slaves who joined them. . . .

Since the Christian religion was established however the number of slaves has diminished. The process was hastened by the publication of the law of Mahomet, which enfranchised all who professed that faith. By the year 1200 slavery had been abolished nearly everywhere save in the West Indies, where great numbers were found at the time of their discovery. . . . It may be objected that if the Mohammedans really enfranchised their co-religionists, who cover the whole of Asia, the greater part of Africa and even a considerable area of Europe, and the Christians have done the same, how come there to be still so many slaves in the world? For the Jews by the terms of their law may not make slaves of their own people either, nor yet of Christians if they live in a Christian country, still less of Mohammedans among whom they are chiefly settled. The answer is that those who profess all these three religions only partially observe the law of God with regard to slaves, for by the law of God it is forbidden to make any man a slave except with his own entire good will and consent. . . . Seeing that the experience of four thousand years has shown us the insurrections, the civil commotions, the disasters and revolutions that commonwealths have suffered at the hands of slaves, and the homicides, the cruelties and barbarities inflicted on slaves by their masters, it was an unmitigated catastrophe that the institution was ever introduced, and then, that once it had been declared abolished, it should ever have been allowed to persist.

Chapters 6 and 7: Concerning the Citizen

. . . When the head of the family leaves the household over which he presides and joins with other heads of families in order to treat of those things which are of common interest, he ceases to be a lord and master, and becomes an equal and associate with the rest. He sets aside his private concerns to attend to public affairs. In so doing he ceases to be a master and becomes a citizen, and a citizen may be defined as a free subject dependent on the authority of another.

Before such things as cities and citizens, or any form of commonwealth whatsoever, were known among men, each head of a family was sovereign in his household, having power of life and death over his wife and children. But force, violence, ambition, avarice, and the passion for vengeance, armed men against one another. The result of the ensuing conflicts was to give victory to some, and to reduce the rest to slavery. Moreover the man who had been chosen captain and leader by the victors, under whose command success had been won, retained authority over his followers, who became his loyal and faithful adherents, and imposed it on the others, who became his slaves. Thus was lost the full and entire liberty of each man to live according to his own free will, without subjection to anyone. It was completely lost to the vanquished and converted into unmitigated servitude; it was qualified in the case of the victors in that they now rendered obedience to a sovereign leader. Anyone who did not wish to abandon part of his liberty, and live under the laws and commands of another, lost it altogether. Thus the words, hitherto unknown, of master and servant, ruler and subject, came into use.

Reason and common sense alike point to the conclusion that the origin and foundation of commonwealths was in force and violence. If this is not enough, it can be shown on the testimony of such historians as Thucydides, Plutarch, Caesar, and even by the laws of Solon, that the first generations of men were unacquainted with the sentiments of honour, and their highest endeavour was to kill, torture, rob, and enslave their fellows. So says Plutarch. We also have the evidence of sacred history, where it is said that Nimrod, the youngest son of Ham, was the first to subject his followers by force and violence. Wherefore he has called the mighty hunter, which to the Hebrews suggests the robber and despoiler. Demosthenes, Aristotle, and Cicero laboured under a misapprehension in repeating the error of Herodotus, who held that the first kings were chosen for their justice and their virtue, in what were believed to be heroic times. I have rebutted this view elsewhere on the grounds that in the first commonwealths, and for a long time after Abraham, there were innumerable slaves, as indeed was also found to be the case in the West Indies. This could hardly be unless there had been some violent forcing of the laws of nature. . . .

Such being the origin of commonwealths, it is clear why a citizen is to be defined as a free subject who is dependent on the sovereignty of another. I use the term *free subject,* because although a slave is as much, or more, subject to the commonwealth as is his lord, it has always been a matter of common agreement that the slave is not a citizen, and in law has no personality. This is not the case with women and children, who are free of any servile dependence, though their rights and liberties, especially their power of disposing of property, is limited by the domestic authority of the head of the household. We can say then that every citizen is a subject since his liberty is limited by the sovereign power to which he owes obedience. We cannot say that every subject is a citizen. This is clear from the case of slaves. The same applies to aliens. Being subject to the authority of another, they have no part in the rights and privileges of the community. . . .

Just as slaves can be slaves either by birth or by convention, so citizens can be either natural or naturalized. The natural citizen is the free subject who is a native of the commonwealth, in that both, or one or other of his parents, was born there. . . . The naturalized citizen is one who makes a voluntary submission to the sovereign authority of another, and is accepted by him as his subject. An honorary citizen who has been granted certain privileges such as civic rights, either as the reward of merit, or an act of grace and favour, is not properly a citizen because he does not thereby become a subject. The whole body of the citizens, whether citizens by birth, by adoption or by enfranchisement (for these are the three ways in which citizen rights are acquired) when subjected to the single sovereign power of one or more rulers, constitutes a commonwealth, even if there is diversity of laws, language, customs, religion, and race. If all the citizens are subject to a single uniform system of laws and customs they form not only a commonwealth but a commune, even though they be dispersed in divers townships, villages, or the open countryside. The town is not the commune, as some have held, any more than the house is the household, for dependants and children can live in widely separated places, yet still form a household, if they are subject to a single head of the family. The same applies to the commune. It can consist of a number of townships and villages, provided they share the same customs, as is the case with the bailliwicks of this realm. Similarly the commonwealth can include a number of communes and provinces which all have different customs. But so long as they are subject to the authority of a single sovereign, and the laws and ordinances made by it, they constitute a commonwealth. . . .

It is a very grave error to suppose that no one is a citizen unless he is eligible for public office, and has a voice in the popular estates, either in a judicial or deliberative capacity. This is Aristotle's view. Later he corrects himself when he observes that it only applies to popular states. But he himself said in another place that a definition is valueless unless it is of universal application. . . . Plutarch improved on this description when he said that citizenship implied a right to a share in the rights and privileges of a city-state, implying that he meant such a share as accorded with the standing of each, nobles, commoners, women, and children too, according to the differences of age, sex, and condition. . . . It must however be emphasized that it is not the rights and privileges which he enjoys which makes a man a citizen, but the mutual obligation between subject and sovereign, by which, in return for the faith and obedience rendered to him, the sovereign must do justice and give counsel, assistance, encouragement, and protection to the subject. He does not owe this to aliens. . . . Moreover, although a man can be a slave of more than one master, or a vassal of more than one lord provided they all hold of the same overlord, a citizen cannot be the subject of more than one sovereign, unless they are both members of a federated state. For princes are not subject to any jurisdiction which delimits their claims over their subjects, as are lords and masters in respect of their vassals and slaves. Neglect of this principle is the reason why there are so frequently frontier wars between neighbouring princes. Each claims the population of the march country as his own. These latter recognize one or other disputant as it suits them, or escape dependence on either, and in consequence are invaded and pillaged by both sides equally. . . .

It is a generally accepted principle of public right that mere change of domicile from one country to another does not deprive the subject of his citizen rights, nor his prince of his sovereign authority over him. The case is parallel to that of the vassal who under feudal custom cannot escape the faith he owes his lord, any more than his lord can excuse himself from the obligation to protect his vassal, unless there has been agreement between them to this effect, seeing that the obligation is mutual and reciprocal. But if both parties have expressly or tacitly consented, and the prince has suffered his subject to renounce his subjection and submit to another, then the subject is no longer bound in obedience to his former sovereign. . . . In order then to acquire full rights of citizenship, it is not sufficient to have been domiciled for the statutory period. Letters of naturalization must also have been asked for and obtained. A settlement cannot be made on anyone unless the benefactor has offered, and the beneficiary duly accepted, the gift offered. Similarly an alien does not become a citizen, nor the subject of a foreign prince, until he has been received as such by that prince, but remains the subject of his natural prince. The same is the case if he has asked for admission to citizenship and been refused. . . .

It is therefore the submission and obedience of a free subject to his prince, and the tuition, protection, and jurisdiction exercised by the prince over his subject that makes the citizen. This is the essential distinction between the citizen and the foreigner. . . .

Chapter 8: Concerning Sovereignty

Sovereignty is that absolute and perpetual power vested in a commonwealth which in Latin is termed *majestas*. . . . The term needs careful definition, because although it is the distinguishing mark of a commonwealth, and an understanding of its nature fundamental to any treatment of politics, no jurist or political philosopher has in fact attempted to define it. . . .

I have described it as *perpetual* because one can give absolute power to a person or group of persons for a period of time, but that time expired they become subjects once more. Therefore even while they enjoy power, they cannot properly be regarded as sovereign rulers, but only as the lieutenants and agents of the sovereign ruler, till the moment comes when it pleases the prince or the people to revoke the gift. The true sovereign remains always seized of his power. Just as a feudal lord who grants lands to another retains his eminent domain over them, so the ruler who delegates authority to judge and command, whether it be for a short period, or during pleasure, remains seized of those rights of jurisdiction actually exercised by another in the form of a revocable grant, or precarious tenancy. For this reason the law requires the governor of a province, or the prince's lieutenant, to make a formal surrender of the authority committed to him, at the expiration of his term of office. In this respect there is no difference between the highest officer of state and his humblest subordinate. If it were otherwise, and the absolute authority delegated by the prince to a lieutenant was regarded as itself sovereign power, the latter could use it against his prince who would thereby forfeit his eminence, and the subject could command his lord, the servant his master. This is a manifest absurdity, considering that the sovereign is always excepted personally, as a matter of right, in all delegations of authority, however extensive. However much he gives there always remains a reserve of right in his own person, whereby he may command, or intervene by way of prevention, confirmation, evocation, or any other way he thinks fit, in all matters delegated to a subject, whether in virtue of an office or a commission. Any authority exercised in virtue of an office or a commission can be revoked, or made tenable for as long or short a period as the sovereign wills.

These principles accepted as the foundations of sovereignty, it follows that neither the Roman Dictator, the Harmost of Sparta, the Esymnete of Salonika, the Archus of Malta, nor the ancient Balia of Florence (who had the same sort of authority), nor regents of kingdoms, nor holders of any other sort of commission, nor magistrates whatsoever, who have absolute power to govern the commonwealth for a certain term only, are possessed of sovereign authority. . . .

But supposing the king grants absolute power to a lieutenant for the term of his life, is not that a perpetual sovereign power? For if one confines *perpetual* to that which has no termination whatever, then sovereignty cannot subsist save in aristocracies and popular states, which never die. If one is to include monarchy too, sovereignty must be vested not in the king alone, but in the king and the heirs of his body, which supposes a strictly hereditary monarchy. In that case there can be very few sovereign kings, since there are only a very few strictly hereditary monarchies. Those especially who come to the throne by election could not be included.

A perpetual authority therefore must be understood to mean one that lasts for the lifetime of him who exercises it. If a sovereign magistrate is given office for one year, or for any other predetermined period, and continues to exercise the authority bestowed on him after the conclusion of his term, he does so either by consent or by force and violence. If he does so by force, it is manifest tyranny. The tyrant is a true sovereign for all that. The robber's possession by violence is true and natural possession although contrary to the law, for those who were formerly in possession have been disseized. But if the magistrate continues in office by consent, he is not a sovereign prince, seeing that he only exercises power on sufferance. Still less is he a sovereign if the term of his office is not fixed, for in that case he has no more than a precarious commission. . . .

What bearing have these considerations on the case of the man to whom the people has given absolute power for the term of his natural life? One must distinguish. If such absolute power is given him simply and unconditionally, and not in virtue of some office or commission, nor in the form of a revocable grant, the recipient certainly is, and should be acknowledged to be, a sovereign. The people has renounced and alienated its sovereign power in order to invest him with it and put him in possession, and it thereby transfers to him all its powers, authority, and sovereign rights, just as does the man who gives to another possessory and proprietary rights over what he formerly owned. The civil law expresses this in the phrase "all power is conveyed to him and vested in him."

But if the people give such power for the term of his natural life to anyone as its official or lieutenant, or only gives the exercise of such power, in such a case he is not a sovereign, but simply an officer, lieutenant, regent, governor, or agent, and as such has the exercise only of a power inhering in another. When a magistrate institutes a perpetual lieutenant, even if he abandons all his rights of jurisdiction and leaves their exercise entirely to his lieutenant, the authority to command and to judge nevertheless does not reside in the lieutenant, nor the action and force of the law derive from him. If he exceeds his authority his acts have no validity, unless approved and confirmed by him from whom he draws his authority. For this reason King John, after his return from captivity in England, solemnly ratified all the acts of his son Charles, who had acted in his name as regent, in order, as was necessary, to regularize the position.

Whether then one exercises the power of another by commission, by institution, or by delegation, or whether such exercise is for a set term, or in perpetuity, such a power is not a sovereign power, even if there is no mention of such words as representative, lieutenant, governor, or regent, in the letters of appointment, or even if such powers are a consequence of the normal working of the laws of the country. In ancient times in Scotland, for instance, the law vested the entire governance of the realm in the next of kin, if the king should be a minor, on condition that everything that was done, was done in the king's name. But this law was later altered because of its inconvenient consequences.

Let us now turn to the other term of our definition and consider the force of the word *absolute*. The people or the magnates of a commonwealth can bestow simply and unconditionally upon someone of their choice a sovereign and perpetual power to dispose of their property and persons, to govern the state as he thinks fit, and to order the succession, in the same way that any proprietor, out of his liberality, can freely and unconditionally make a gift of his property to another. Such a form of gift, not being qualified in any way, is the only true gift, being at once unconditional and irrevocable. Gifts burdened with obligations and hedged with conditions are not true gifts. Similarly sovereign power given to a prince charged with conditions is neither properly sovereign, nor absolute, unless the conditions of appointment are only such as are inherent in the laws of God and of nature. . . .

If we insist however that absolute power means exemption from all law whatsoever, there is no prince in the world who can be regarded as sovereign, since all the princes of the earth are subject to the laws of God and of nature, and even to certain human laws common to all nations. On the other hand, it is possible for a subject who is neither a prince nor a ruler, to be exempted from all the laws, ordinances, and customs of the commonwealth. We have an example in Pompey the Great who was dispensed from the laws for five years, by express enactment of the Roman people, at the instance of the Tribune Gabinius. . . . But notwithstanding such exemptions from the operations of the law, the subject remains under the authority of him who exercises sovereign power, and owes him obedience.

On the other hand it is the distinguishing mark of the sovereign that he cannot in any way be subject to the commands of another, for it is he who makes law for the subject, abrogates law already made, and amends obsolete law. No one who is subject either to the law or to some other person can do this. That is why it is laid down in the civil law that the prince is above the law, for the word *law* in Latin implies the command of him who is invested with sovereign power. Therefore we find in all statutes the phrase "notwithstanding all edicts and ordinances to the contrary that we have infringed, or do infringe by these present." This clause applies both to former acts of the prince himself, and to those of his predecessors. For all laws, ordinances, letters patent, privileges, and grants whatsoever issued by the prince, have force only during his own lifetime, and must be expressly, or at least tacitly, confirmed by the reigning prince who has cognizance of them. . . . In proof of which, it is the custom of this realm for all corporations and corporate bodies to ask for the confirmation of their privileges, rights, and jurisdictions, on the accession of a new king. Even Parlements and high courts do this, as well as individual officers of the crown.

If the prince is not bound by the laws of his predecessors, still less can he be bound by his own laws. One may be subject to laws made by another, but it is impossible to bind oneself in any matter which is the subject of one's own free exercise of will. As the law says, "there can be no obligation in any matter which proceeds from the free will of the undertaker." It follows of necessity that the king cannot be subject to his own laws. Just as, according to the canonists, the Pope can never tie his own hands, so the sovereign prince cannot bind himself, even if he wishes. For this reason edicts and ordinances conclude with the formula "for such is our good pleasure," thus intimating that the laws of a sovereign prince, even when founded on truth and right reason, proceed simply from his own free will.

It is far otherwise with divine and natural laws. All the princes of the earth are subject to them, and cannot contravene them without treason and rebellion against God. His yoke is upon them, and they must bow their heads in fear and reverence before His divine majesty. The absolute power of princes and sovereign lords does not extend to the laws of God and of nature. He who best understood the meaning of absolute power, and made kings and emperors submit to his will, defined his sovereignty as a power to override positive law; he did not claim power to set aside divine and natural law.

But supposing the prince should swear to keep the laws and customs of his country, is he not bound by that oath? One must distinguish. If a prince promises in his own heart to obey his own laws, he is nevertheless not bound to do so, any more than anyone is bound by an oath taken to himself. Even private citizens are not bound by private oaths to keep agreements. The law permits them to cancel them, even if the agreements are in themselves reasonable and good. But if one sovereign prince promises another sovereign prince to keep the agreements entered into by his predecessors, he is bound to do so even if not under oath, if that other prince's interests are involved. If they are not, he is not bound either by a promise, or even by an oath.

The same holds good of promises made by the sovereign to the subject, even if the promises were made prior to his election (for this does not make the difference that many suppose). It is not that the prince is bound either by his own laws or those of his predecessors. But he is bound by the just covenants and promises he has made, whether under oath to do so or not, to exactly the same extent that a private individual is bound in like case. A private individual can be released from a promise that was unjust or unreasonable, or beyond his competence to fulfil, or extracted from him by misrepresentations or fraud, or made in error, or under restraint and by intimidation, because of the injury the keeping of it does him. In the same way a sovereign prince can make good any invasion of his sovereign rights, and for the same reasons. So the principle stands, that the prince is not subject to his own laws, or those of his predecessors, but is bound by the just and reasonable engagements which touch the interests of his subjects individually or collectively.

Many have been led astray by confusing the laws of the prince with covenants entered into by him. This confusion has led some to call these covenants contractual laws. This is the term used in Aragon when the king issues an ordinance upon the petition of the Estates, and in return receives some aid or subsidy. It is claimed that he is strictly bound by these laws, even though he is not by any of his other enactments. It is however admitted that he may override even these when the purpose of their enactment no longer holds. All this is true enough, and well-founded in reason and authority. But no bribe or oath is required to bind a sovereign prince to keep a law which is in the interests of his subjects. The bare word of a prince should be as sacred as a divine pronouncement. It loses its force if he is ill-thought of as one who cannot be trusted except under oath, nor relied on to keep a promise unless paid to do so. Nevertheless it remains true in principle that the sovereign prince can set aside the laws which he has promised or sworn to observe, if they no longer satisfy the requirements of justice, and he may do this without the consent of his subjects. It should however be added that the abrogation must be express and explicit in its reference, and not just in the form of a general repudiation. But if on the other hand there is no just cause for breaking a law which the prince has promised to keep, the prince ought not to do so, and indeed cannot contravene it, though he is not bound to the same extent by the promises and covenants of his predecessors unless he succeeds by strict hereditary right.

A law and a covenant must therefore not be confused. A law proceeds from him who has sovereign power, and by it he binds the subject to obedience, but cannot bind himself. A covenant is a mutual undertaking between a prince and his subjects, equally binding on both parties, and neither can contravene it to the prejudice of the other, without his consent. The prince has no greater privilege than the subject in this matter. But in the case of laws, a prince is no longer bound by his promise to keep them when they cease to satisfy the claims of justice. Subjects however must keep their engagements to one another in all circumstances, unless the prince releases them from such obligations. Sovereign princes are not bound by oath to keep the laws of their predecessors. If they are so bound, they are not properly speaking sovereign. . . .

The constitutional laws of the realm, especially those that concern the king's estate being, like the salic law, annexed and united to the Crown, cannot be infringed by the prince. Should he do so, his successor can always annul any act prejudicial to the traditional form of the monarchy, since on this is founded and sustained his very claim to sovereign majesty. . . .

As for laws relating to the subject, whether general or particular, which do not involve any question of the constitution, it has always been usual only to change them with the concurrence of the three estates, either assembled in the States-General of the whole of France, or in each bailliwick separately. Not that the king is bound to take their advice, or debarred from acting in a way quite contrary to what they wish, if his acts are based on justice and natural reason. At the same time the majesty of the prince is most fully manifested in the assembly of the three estates of the whole realm, humbly petitioning and supplicating him, without any power of commanding or determining, or any right to a deliberative voice. Only that which it pleases the prince to assent to or dissent from, to command or to forbid, has the force of law and is embodied in his edict or ordinance.

Those who have written books about the duties of magistrates and such like matters are in error in maintaining that the authority of the Estates is superior to that of the prince. Such doctrines serve only to encourage subjects to resist their sovereign rulers. Besides, such views bear no relation to the facts, except when the king is in captivity, lunatic or a minor. If he were normally subject to the Estates, he would be neither a prince nor a sovereign, and the commonwealth would not be a kingdom or a monarchy, but a pure aristocracy where authority is shared equally between the members of the ruling class. . . .

Although in the Parliaments of the kingdom of England, which meet every three years, all three orders use great freedom of speech, as is characteristic of northern peoples, they still must proceed by petitions and supplications. . . . Moreover Parliaments in England can only assemble, as in this kingdom and in Spain, under letters patent expressly summoning them in the king's name. This is sufficient proof that Parliaments have no independent power of considering, commanding or determining, seeing that they can neither assemble nor adjourn without express royal command. . . . It may be objected that no extraordinary taxes or subsidies can be imposed without the agreement and consent of Parliament. King Edward I agreed to this principle in the Great Charter, which is always appealed to by the people against the claims of the king. But I hold that in this matter no other king has any more right than has the King of England, since it is not within the competence of any prince in the world to levy taxes at will on his people, or seize the goods of another arbitrarily, as Philippe de Comines very wisely argued at the Estates at Tours, as we may read in his *Memoirs*.

We must agree then that the sovereignty of the king is in no wise qualified or diminished by the existence of Estates. On the contrary his majesty appears more illustrious when formally recognized by his assembled subjects, even though in such assemblies princes, not wishing to fall out with their people, agree to many things which they would not have consented to, unless urged by the petitions, prayers, and just complaints of a people burdened by grievances unknown to the prince. After all, he depends for his information on the eyes and ears and reports of others.

From all this it is clear that the principal mark of sovereign majesty and absolute power is the right to impose laws generally on all subjects regardless of their consent. . . . And if it is expedient that if he is to govern his state well, a sovereign prince must be above the law, it is even more expedient that the ruling class in an aristocracy should be so, and inevitable in a popular state. A monarch in a kingdom is set apart from his subjects, and the ruling class from the people in an aristocracy. There are therefore in each case two parties, those that rule on the one hand, and those that are ruled on the other. This is the cause of the disputes about sovereignty that arise in them, but cannot in a popular state. . . . There the people, rulers and ruled, form a single body and so cannot bind themselves by their own laws. . . .

When edicts are ratified by Estates or Parlements, it is for the purpose of securing obedience to them, and not because otherwise a sovereign prince could not validly make law. As Theodosius said with reference to the consent of the Senate, "it is not a matter of necessity but of expediency." He also remarked that it was most becoming in a sovereign prince to keep his own laws, for this is what makes him feared and respected by his subjects, whereas nothing so undermines his authority as contempt for them. As a Roman Senator observed "it is more foolish and ill-judged to break your own laws than those of another."

But may it not be objected that if the prince forbids a sin, such as homicide, on pain of death, he is in this case bound to keep his own law? The answer is that this is not properly the prince's own law, but a law of God and nature, to which he is more strictly bound than any of his subjects. Neither his council, nor the whole body of the people, can exempt him from his perpetual responsibility before the judgement-seat of God, as Solomon said in unequivocal terms. Marcus Aurelius also observed that the magistrate is the judge of persons, the prince of the magistrates, and God of the prince. Such was the opinion of the two wisest rulers the world has ever known. Those who say without qualification that the prince is bound neither by any law whatsoever, nor by his own express engagements, insult the majesty of God, unless they intend to except the laws of God and of nature, and all just covenants and solemn agreements. Even Dionysius, tyrant of Syracuse, said to his mother that he could exempt her from the laws and customs of Syracuse, but not from the laws of God and of nature. For just as contracts and deeds of gift of private individuals must not derogate from the ordinances of the magistrate, nor his ordinances from the law of the land, nor the law of the land from the enactments of a sovereign prince, so the laws of a sovereign prince cannot override or modify the laws of God and of nature. . . .

There is one other point. If the prince is bound by the laws of nature, and the civil law is reasonable and equitable, it would seem to follow that the prince is also bound by the civil law. As Pacatius said to the Emperor Theodosius "as much is permitted to you as is permitted by the laws." In answer to this I would point out that the laws of a sovereign prince concern either public or private interests or both together. All laws moreover can be either profitable at the expense of honour, or profitable without involving honour at all, or honourable without profit, or neither honourable nor profitable. When I say "honour" I mean that which conforms with what is natural and right, and it has already been shown that the prince is bound in such cases. Laws of this kind, though published by the prince's authority, are properly natural laws. Laws which are profitable as well as just are even more binding on him. One need hardly concern oneself about the sanctity of laws which involve neither profit nor honour. But if it is a question of weighing honour against profit, honour should always be preferred. Aristides the Just said of Themistocles that his advice was always very useful to the people, but shameful and dishonourable.

But if a law is simply useful and does not involve any principle of natural justice, the prince is not bound by it, but can amend it or annul it altogether as he chooses, provided that with the alteration of the law the profit to some does not do damage to others without just cause. The prince then can annul an ordinance which is merely useful in order to substitute one more or less advantageous, for profit, honour, and justice all have degrees of more and less. And just as the prince can choose the most useful among profitable laws, so he can choose the most just among equitable laws, even though while some profit by them others suffer, provided it is the public that profits, and only the private individual that suffers. It is however never proper for the subject to disobey the laws of the prince under the pretext that honour and justice require it. . . .

Edicts and ordinances therefore do not bind the ruler except in so far as they embody the principles of natural justice; that ceasing, the obligation ceases. But subjects are bound till the ruler has expressly abrogated the law, for it is a law both divine and natural that we should obey the edicts and ordinances of him whom God has set in authority over us, providing his edicts are not contrary to God's law. For just as the rear-vassal owes an oath of fealty in respect of and against all others, saving his sovereign prince, so the subject owes allegiance to his sovereign prince in respect of and against all others, saving the majesty of God, who is lord of all the princes of this world. From this principle we can deduce that other rule, that the sovereign prince is bound by the covenants he makes either with his subjects, or some other prince. Just because he enforces the covenants and mutual engagements entered into by his subjects among themselves, he must be the mirror of justice in all his own acts. . . . He has a double obligation in this case. He is bound in the first place by the principles of natural equity, which require that conventions and solemn promises should be kept, and in the second place in the interests of his own good faith, which he ought to preserve even to his own disadvantage, because he is the formal guarantor to all his subjects of the mutual faith they owe one another. . . .

A distinction must therefore be made between right and law, for one implies what is equitable and the other what is commanded. Law is nothing else than the command of the sovereign in the exercise of his sovereign power. A sovereign prince is not subject to the laws of the Greeks, or any other alien power, or even those of the Romans, much less to his own laws, except in so far as they embody the law of nature which, according to Pindar, is the law to which all kings and princes are subject. Neither Pope nor Emperor is exempt from this law, though certain flatterers say they can take the goods of their subjects at will. But both civilians and canonists have repudiated this opinion as contrary to the law of God. They err who assert that in virtue of their sovereign power princes can do this. It is rather the law of the jungle, an act of force and violence. For as we have shown above, absolute power only implies freedom in relation to positive laws, and not in relation to the law of God. God has declared explicitly in His Law that it is not just to take, or even to covet, the goods of another. Those who defend such opinions are even more dangerous than those who act on them. They show the lion his claws, and arm princes under a cover of just claims. The evil will of a tyrant, drunk with such flatteries, urges him to an abuse of absolute power and excites his violent passions to the pitch where avarice issues in confiscations, desire in adultery, and anger in murder. . . .

Since then the prince has no power to exceed the laws of nature which God Himself, whose image he is, has decreed, he cannot take his subjects' property without just and reasonable cause, that is to say by purchase, exchange, legitimate confiscation, or to secure peace with the enemy when it cannot be otherwise achieved. Natural reason instructs us that the public good must be preferred to the particular, and that subjects should give up not only their mutual antagonisms and animosities, but also their possessions, for the safety of the commonwealth. . . .

It remains to be determined whether the prince is bound by the covenants of his predecessors, and whether, if so, it is a derogation of his sovereign power. . . . A distinction must be made between the ruler who succeeds because he is the natural heir of his predecessor, and the ruler who succeeds in virtue of the laws and customs of the realm. In the first case the heir is bound by the oaths and promises of his predecessors just as is any ordinary heir. In the second case he is not so bound even if he is sworn, for the oath of the predecessor does not bind the successor. He is bound however in all that tends to the benefit of the kingdom.

There are those who will say that there is no need of such distinctions since the prince is bound in any case by the law of nations, under which covenants are guaranteed. But I consider that these distinctions are necessary nevertheless, since the prince is bound as much by the law of nations, but no more, than by any of his own enactments. If the law of nations is iniquitous in any respect, he can disallow it within his own kingdom, and forbid his subjects to observe it, as was done in France in regard to slavery. He can do the same in relation to any other of its provisions, so long as he does nothing against the law of God. If justice is the end of the law, the law the work of the prince, and the prince the image of God, it follows of necessity that the law of the prince should be modelled on the law of God. . . .

Chapter 10: The True Attributes of Sovereignty

Because there are none on earth, after God, greater than sovereign princes, whom God establishes as His lieutenants to command the rest of mankind, we must enquire carefully into their estate, that we may respect and revere their majesty in all due obedience, speak and think of them with all due honour. He who contemns his sovereign prince, contemns God whose image he is. . . .

Aristotle, Polybius, and Dionysius Halicarnassus alone among the Greeks discussed the attributes of sovereignty. But they treated the subject so briefly that one can see at a glance that they did not really understand the principles involved. I quote Aristotle. "There are," he says, "three parts of a commonwealth. There must be provision for the taking and giving of counsel, for appointing to office and assigning to each citizen his duties, for the administration of justice." If he did not mean by *parts* attributes of sovereignty, he never treated of the subject at all, since this is the only passage which has any bearing. Polybius does not define the rights and duties of sovereignty either, but he says of the Romans that their constitution was a mixture of monarchy, aristocracy, and popular government, since the people made law and appointed to office, the Senate administered the provinces and conducted great affairs of state, the consuls enjoyed the pre-eminence of honour accorded to kings, especially in the field, where they exercised supreme command. This passage appears to imply a treatment of sovereign rights, since he says that those who enjoyed those rights had sovereign power. Dionysius Halicarnassus however had a clearer and better understanding of the matter than the others. When he was explaining how the King Servius deprived the Senate of authority, he observed that he transferred to the people the power to make and unmake law, to determine war and peace, to institute and deprive magistrates, and the right of hearing appeals from all courts whatsoever. In another passage, when describing the third conflict between the nobles and the people, he reported how the Consul Marcus Valerius rebuked the people and said that they should be content with the powers of making law, appointing to office and hearing appeals. Other matters should be left to the Senate.

Since ancient times civilians, and especially those of more recent years, have elaborated these rights, especially in their treatises on what they call regalian rights. Under this heading they have collected an immense number of particular rights and privileges enjoyed by dukes, counts, bishops, and various officials, and even subjects of sovereign princes. As a result they describe dukes, such as those of Milan, Mantua, Ferrara, and Savoy, and even counts, as sovereign princes. However reasonable it may appear, this is an error. How can these rulers be regarded as anything but sovereign, they argue, when they make law for their subjects, levy war and conclude peace, appoint to all office in their dominions, levy taxes, make a free man of whom they please, pardon those who have forfeited their lives. What other powers has any sovereign prince?

But we have already shown above that the Dukes of Milan, Mantua, Ferrara, Florence, and Savoy hold of the Empire. Their most honourable title is that of Imperial Vicar and Prince of the Empire. . . . We have also pointed out the absurdities that ensue if one makes sovereigns of vassals, since the lord and his subject, the master and his servant, the man who makes the law and the man on whom it is imposed, the man who issues orders and the man who obeys them, are thereby placed on an equal footing. Since this cannot be, it follows that dukes, counts, and all those who hold of another, or are bound by his laws and subject to his commands, whether of right or by constraint, are not sovereign. The same holds good of the highest officers of state, lieutenant-generals of the king, governors, regents, dictators, whatever the extent of their powers. They are not sovereigns since they are subject to the laws and commands of another and may be appealed against.

The attributes of sovereignty are therefore peculiar to the sovereign prince, for if communicable to the subject, they cannot be called attributes of sovereignty. . . . Just as Almighty God cannot create another God equal with Himself, since He is infinite and two infinities cannot co-exist, so the sovereign prince, who is the image of God, cannot make a subject equal with himself without self-destruction.

If this is so, it follows that rights of jurisdiction are not attributes of sovereignty since they are exercised by subjects as well as the prince. The same is true of the appointment and dismissal of officials, for this power also the prince shares with the subject, not only in regard to the lesser offices of justice, of police, of the armed forces, or of the revenues, but also in regard to responsible commanders in peace and war. . . . The infliction of penalties and the bestowing of awards is not an attribute of sovereignty either, for the magistrate has this power, though it is true he derives it from the sovereign. Nor is taking counsel about affairs of state an attribute of sovereignty, for such is the proper function of the privy council or senate in the commonwealth, a body always distinct from that in which sovereignty is vested. Even in the popular state, where sovereignty lies in the assembly of the people, so far from it being the function of the assembly to take counsel, it ought never be permitted to do so, as I shall show later.

It is clear therefore that none of the three functions of the state that Aristotle distinguishes are properly attributes of sovereignty. As for what Halicarnassus says about Marcus Valerius' speech to the people of Rome, when trying to pacify them, that they should be content with the prerogatives of making law and appointing magistrates, he does not make the point sufficiently clear. As I have already said, appointing to office is not an attribute of sovereignty. Moreover some further explanation is necessary of the nature of the law-making power. A magistrate can make laws binding on those subject to his jurisdiction, provided such laws do not conflict with the edicts and ordinances of his sovereign prince.

Before going any further, one must consider what is meant by *law*. The word law signifies the right command of that person, or those persons, who have absolute authority over all the rest without exception, saving only the law-giver himself, whether the command touches all subjects in general or only some in particular. To put it another way, the law is the rightful command of the sovereign touching all his subjects in general, or matters of general application. . . . As to the commands of the magistrate, they are not properly speaking laws but only edicts. "An edict," says Varro, "is an order issued by a magistrate." Such orders are only binding on those subject to his jurisdiction, and are only in force for his term of office.

The first attribute of the sovereign prince therefore is the power to make law binding on all his subjects in general and on each in particular. But to avoid any ambiguity one must add that he does so without the consent of any superior, equal, or inferior being necessary. If the prince can only make law with the consent of a superior he is a subject; if of an equal he shares his sovereignty; if of an inferior, whether it be a council of magnates or the people, it is not he who is sovereign. The names of the magnates that one finds appended to a royal edict are not there to give force to the law, but as witnesses, and to make it more acceptable. . . . When I say that the first attribute of sovereignty is to give law to all in general and each in particular, I mean by this last phrase the grant of privileges. I mean by a privilege a concession to one or a small group of individuals which concerns the profit or loss of those persons only. . . .

It may be objected however that not only have magistrates the power of issuing edicts and ordinances, each according to his competence and within his own sphere of jurisdiction, but private citizens can make law in the form of general or local custom. It is agreed that customary law is as binding as statute law. But if the sovereign prince is author of the law, his subjects are the authors of custom. But there is a difference between law and custom. Custom establishes itself gradually over a long period of years, and by common consent, or at any rate the consent of the greater part. Law is made on the instant and draws its force from him who has the right to bind all the rest. Custom is established imperceptibly and without any exercise of compulsion. Law is promulgated and imposed by authority, and often against the wishes of the subject. For this reason Dion Chrysostom compared custom to the king and law to the tyrant. Moreover law can break custom, but custom cannot derogate from the law, nor can the magistrate, or any other responsible for the administration of law, use his discretion about the enforcement of law as he can about custom. Law, unless it is permissive and relaxes the severity of another law, always carries penalties for its breach. Custom only has binding force by the sufferance and during the good pleasure of the sovereign prince, and so far as he is willing to authorize it. Thus the force of both statutes and customary law derives from the authorization of the prince. . . . Included in the power of making and unmaking law is that of promulgating it and amending it when it is obscure, or when the magistrates find contradictions and absurdities. . . .

All the other attributes and rights of sovereignty are included in this power of making and unmaking law, so that strictly speaking this is the unique attribute of sovereign power. It includes all other rights of sovereignty, that is to say of making peace and war, of hearing appeals from the sentences of all courts whatsoever, of appointing and dismissing the great officers of state; of taxing, or granting privileges of exemption to all subjects, of appreciating or depreciating the value and weight of the coinage, of receiving oaths of fidelity from subjects and liege-vassals alike, without exception of any other to whom faith is due. . . .

But because *law* is an unprecise and general term, it is as well to specify the other attributes of sovereignty comprised in it, such as the making of war and peace. This is one of the most important rights of sovereignty, since it brings in its train either the ruin or the salvation of the state. This was a right of sovereignty not only among the ancient Romans, but has always been so among all other peoples. . . . Sovereign princes are therefore accustomed to keep themselves informed of the smallest accidents and undertakings connected with warfare. Whatever latitude they may give to their representatives to negotiate peace or an alliance, they never grant the authority to conclude without their own express consent. This was illustrated in the negotiations leading up to the recent treaty of Câteaux-Cambrésis, when the king's envoys kept him almost hourly informed of all proposals and counter-proposals. . . . In popular states and aristocracies the difficulty of assembling the people, and the danger of making public all the secrets of diplomacy has meant that the people have generally handed responsibility over to the council. Nevertheless it remains true that the commissions and the orders that it issues in discharge of this function proceed from the authority of the people, and are despatched by the council in the name of the people. . . .

The third attribute of sovereignty is the power to institute the great officers of state. It has never been questioned that the right is an attribute of sovereignty, at any rate as far as the great officers are concerned. I confine it however to high officials, for there is no commonwealth in which these officers, and many guilds and corporate bodies besides, have not some power of appointing their subordinate officials. They do this in virtue of their office, which carries with it the power to delegate. For instance, those who hold feudal rights of jurisdiction of their sovereign prince in faith and homage have the power to appoint the judges in their courts, and their assistants. But this power is devolved upon them by the prince. . . . It is therefore not the mere appointment of officials that implies sovereign right, but the authorization and confirmation of such appointments. It is true however that in so far as the exercise of this right is delegated, the sovereignty of the prince is to that extent qualified, unless his concurrence and express consent is required.

The fourth attribute of sovereignty, and one which has always been among its principal rights, is that the prince should be the final resort of appeal from all other courts. . . . Even though the prince may have published a law, as did Caligula, forbidding any appeal or petition against the sentences of his officers, nevertheless the subject cannot be deprived of the right to make an appeal, or present a petition, to the prince in person. For the prince cannot tie his own hands in this respect, nor take from his subjects the means of redress, supplication, and petition, notwithstanding the fact that all rules governing appeals and jurisdictions are matters of positive law, which we have shown does not bind the prince. This is why the Privy Council, including the Chancellor de l'Hôpital, considered the action of the commissioners deputed to hold an enquiry into the conduct of the President l'Alemant irregular and unprecedented. They had forbidden him to approach within twenty leagues of the court, with the intention of denying him any opportunity of appeal. The king himself could not deny this right to the subject, though he is free to make whatsoever reply to the appeal, favourable or unfavourable, that he pleases. . . . Were it otherwise, and the prince could acquit his subjects or his vassals from the obligation to submit their causes to him in the last instance, he would make of them sovereigns equal with himself. . . . But if he would preserve his authority, the surest way of doing so is to avoid ever devolving any of the attributes of sovereignty upon a subject. . . .

With this right is coupled the right of pardoning convicted persons, and so of overruling the sentences of his own courts, in mitigation of the severity of the law, whether touching life, property, honour, or domicile. It is not in the power of any magistrate, whatever his station, to do any of these things, or to make any revision of the judgement he has once given. . . . In a well-ordered commonwealth the right should never be delegated either to a special commission, or to any high officer of state, save in those circumstances where it is necessary to establish a regency, either because the king is abroad in some distant place, or in captivity, or incapable, or under age. For instance, during the minority of Louis IX, the authority of the Crown was vested in his mother Blanche of Castile as his guardian. . . . Princes however tend to abuse this right, thinking that to pardon is pleasing to God, whereas to exact the utmost punishment is displeasing to Him. But I hold, subject to correction, that the sovereign prince cannot remit any penalty imposed by the law of God, any more than he can dispense any one from the operation of the law of God, to which he himself is subject. If the magistrate who dispenses anyone from obedience to the ordinance of his king merits death, how much more unwarrantable is it for the prince to acquit a man of the punishment ordained by God's law? If a sovereign prince cannot deny a subject his civil rights, how can he acquit him of the penalties imposed by God, such as the death penalty exacted by divine law for treacherous murder?

It may be objected that the prince can never show the quality of mercy if he cannot remit punishments prescribed by divine law. But in my opinion there are other means of showing clemency, such as pardoning breaches of positive laws. For instance, if the prince forbids the carrying of arms, or the selling of foodstuffs to the enemy in time of war, on pain of death, he can very properly pardon the offence of carrying arms if it was done in self-defence, or the selling of provisions if done under the pressure of extreme poverty. Again, the penalty for larceny under the civil law is death. A merciful prince can reduce this to fourfold restitution, which is what is required by divine law. It has always been the custom among Christian kings to pardon unpardonable offences on Good Friday. But pardons of this kind bring in their train pestilences, famine, war, and the downfall of states. That is why it is said in the law of God that in punishing those who have merited death one averts the curse on the whole people. Of a hundred criminals only two are brought to justice, and of those brought to justice only one half are proved guilty. If the few proven cases of guilt are pardoned, how can punishment act as a deterrent to evil-doers? . . . The best way for a prince to exercise his prerogative of mercy is to pardon offences against his own person. Of all exercises of mercy none is more pleasing to God. But what can one hope of the prince who cruelly avenges all injuries to himself, but pardons those inflicted on others? . . .

Faith and homage are also among the most important attributes of sovereignty, as was made clear when the prince was described as the one to whom obedience was due without exception.

As for the right of coinage, it is contained within the law-making power, for only he who can make law can regulate currency. This is illustrated in the very terms used by Greeks, Romans, and French alike, for the word *nummus* comes from the Greek *nomos* signifying both law and alloy. There is nothing of more moment to a country, after the law, than the denomination, the value, and the weight of the coinage; as we have already shown in a separate treatise. Therefore in every well-ordered commonwealth the prince reserves this right exclusively to himself. . . . And although in this kingdom many private persons, such as the Vicomte de Touraine, the Bishops of Meaux, Cahors, Agde, Ambrun and the Counts of St. Pol, de la Marche, Nevers, Blois, and others enjoyed this right, Francis I in a general edict cancelled all such rights whatsoever, declaring the concessions null and void. This right and attribute of sovereignty ought not ever to be granted to a subject. . . .

The right of levying taxes and imposing dues, or of exempting persons from the payment of such, is also part of the power of making law and granting privileges. Not that the levying of taxation is inseparable from the essence of the commonwealth, for as President Le Maître has shown, there was none levied in France till the time of Louis IX. But if any necessity should arise of imposing or withdrawing a tax, it can only be done by him who has sovereign authority. . . . It is true that many seigneurs have prescriptive rights of levying tallages, dues, and imposts. Even in this kingdom many seigneurs can levy tallage on four occasions in virtue of privileges confirmed by judgements in the courts, and by custom. Even seigneurs who have no rights of jurisdiction enjoy this privilege. But in my opinion the privilege started as an abuse which in consequence of long years of enjoyment acquired the dignity of a prescriptive right. But there is no abuse, of however long standing, that the law cannot amend, for the law exists to amend all abuses. Therefore, by the Edict of Moulins it was ordained that all rights of tallage claimed by seigneurs over their dependants could no longer be levied, notwithstanding immemorial prescription. . . .

I have left out of this discussion those lesser prerogatives that individual sovereign princes claim in their own particular realms, as I have confined myself to those general attributes of sovereignty proper to all sovereign princes as such, but which, being inalienable and imprescriptible, cannot, of their very nature, be communicated to subordinate persons such as feudal lords, magistrates, or subjects of any degree whatsoever. Whatever grant a sovereign prince makes of lands or jurisdiction, the rights of the crown are always reserved. This was implied in a judgement of the High Court relating to appanages in France, that no passage of time could justify the usurpation of royal rights. If common lands cannot be acquired by prescription, how can the rights and attributes of sovereignty? It is certain, on the evidence of various edicts and ordinances, that the public domain is inalienable, and cannot be acquired by prescription. Over two thousand years ago Themistocles, in recovering common lands occupied by private persons, said in his speech to the people of Athens that men could acquire no prescriptive rights against God nor private citizens against the commonwealth. . . .

Such are the principal characteristics of sovereign majesty, treated as briefly as possible, since I have already written at greater length on the subject in my book *De Imperio*. It is most expedient for the preservation of the state that the rights of sovereignty should never be granted out to a subject, still less to a foreigner, for to do so is to provide a stepping-stone whereby the grantee himself becomes the sovereign.

Book Two

Chapter 1: Of the Different Kinds of Commonwealth

Now that we have determined what sovereignty is, and have described its rights and attributes, we must consider in whom it is vested in every kind of commonwealth, in order to determine what are the various possible types of state. If sovereignty is vested in a single prince we call the state a monarchy. If all the people share in it, it is a popular state. If only a minority, it is an aristocracy.

It is desirable to be exact in the use of these terms in order to avoid the confusion which has arisen as a result of the great variety of governments, good and bad. This has misled some into distinguishing more than three kinds of commonwealth. But if one adopts the principle of distinguishing between commonwealths according to the particular virtues and vices that are characteristic of each, one is soon faced with an infinity of variations. It is a principle of all sound definition that one should pay no regard to accidental properties, which are innumerable, but confine oneself to formal and essential distinctions. Otherwise one becomes entangled in a labyrinth which defies exact analysis. For there is no reason why one should stop short at the difference between good and bad. There are other inessential variations. A king can be chosen for his strength, his beauty, his fame, his noble birth, his wealth, all of them matters of indifference. Or he may be chosen because he is the most warlike or most peace-loving, the wisest, the most just, a lover of display, of great learning, the most prudent, the most modest, the simplest, the most chaste. One could add to the list indefinitely and arrive at an infinity of types of monarchy. It would be the same in the case of aristocracies. The ruling class might be drawn from the rich, the nobles, or those esteemed as wise, or just, or warlike. Moreover, one would have to make a similar reckoning of bad qualities. The result would be merely absurd, and for this reason such a method of classification must be rejected.

Since then the nature of things is not changed by their accidental properties, we conclude that there are only three types of state, or commonwealth, monarchy, aristocracy, and democracy. A state is called a monarchy when sovereignty is vested in one person, and the rest have only to obey. Democracy, or the popular state, is one in which all the people, or a majority among them, exercise sovereign power collectively. A state is an aristocracy when a minority collectively enjoy sovereign power and impose law on the rest, generally and severally.

All the ancients agree that there are at least three types of commonwealth. Some have added a fourth composed of a mixture of the other three. Plato added a fourth type, or rule of the wise. But this, properly speaking, is only the purest form that aristocracy can take. He did not accept a mixed state as a fourth type. Aristotle accepted both Plato's fourth type and the mixed state, making five in all. Polybius distinguished seven, three good, three bad, and one composed of a mixture of the three good. Dionysius Halicarnassus only admitted four, the three pure types, and a mixture of them. Cicero, and following his example, Sir Thomas More in his *Commonwealth,* Contarini, Machiavelli, and many others have held the same opinion. This view has the dignity of antiquity. It was not new when propounded by Polybius, who is generally credited with its invention, nor by Aristotle. It goes back four hundred years earlier to Herodotus. He said that many thought that the mixed was the best type, but for his part he thought there were only three types, and all others were imperfect forms. I should have been convinced by the authority of such great names, but that reason and common sense compels me to hold the opposing view. One must show then not only why these views are erroneous but why the arguments and examples they rely on do not really prove their point. . . .

If sovereignty is, of its very nature, indivisible, as we have shown, how can a prince, a ruling class, and the people, all have a part in it at the same time? The first attribute of sovereignty is the power to make law binding on the subject. But in such a case who will be the subjects that obey, if they also have a share in the law-making power? And who will be the law-giver if he is also himself forced to receive it from those upon whom he has imposed it? One is forced to the conclusion that if no one in particular has the power to make law, but it belongs to all indifferently, then the commonwealth is a popular state. If power is given to the people to make law, and appoint to office, but all other powers are denied them, it must nevertheless be recognized that these other powers, vested in officials, really belong to the people, and are only entrusted by them to the magistrates. The people, having instituted the latter, can also deprive them, and the state therefore remains a popular one. In order to confirm what I have just said, let us look more closely at the examples of mixed states cited by Polybius, Contarini and others. . . .

One of the examples given is Rome, whose constitution, it is alleged, was a mixture of monarchy, democracy, and aristocracy, in such a way that according to Polybius the Consuls embody the monarchical principle, the Senate the aristocratic, the Estates of the people the democratic. Halicarnassus, Cicero, Contarini, and others have accepted this analysis, inaccurate as it is. In the first place monarchical power cannot subsist in two persons simultaneously, since monarchy by definition is the rule of one. If it is divided, there is either no monarchy, or no kingdom. One could, with more reason, describe the Doge of Genoa or Venice as a monarch. But in any case what kingly power could be ascribed to the Consuls, seeing that they could not make law, declare war and peace, appoint any officials, pardon any offenders, spend a penny of public money, or even condemn a citizen to corporal punishment except in time of war? This last power belongs to any leader in the field. These would also have to be called kings, and with more reason. The Constable in this realm, and the great Pascha in Turkey have ten times the power of the two Consuls put together, yet they are no more than the subjects and slaves of the prince, as the Consuls were of the people. . . .

Again, conduct of affairs of state undertaken by the Senate, and the decisions reached by it, had no force unless confirmed by the people, or assented to by the tribunes, as will be explained more fully when we come to deal with the council in the state. There can be no real doubt that the Roman constitution, from the moment that the kings were expelled, was popular, except for the two years of the Decemvirate, erected to revise the laws and customs. This temporarily converted the constitution into an aristocracy, or rather, oligarchy. I have said above that the authority of magistrates, of whatever degree they may be, is never properly their own, but enjoyed by them as a trust. It is clear that the people originally elected the Senate, but in order to get rid of the burden of so doing, they committed this power to the censors, who were, of course, also elected by the people. Thus all the authority of the Senate derived from the people. The people were accustomed to confirm or annul, ratify or veto the decisions of the Senate according to their good pleasure.

Contarini has analysed the Republic of Venice in the same way, describing it as a mixture of three pure types, as was that of Rome. He identifies royal power with that of the Doge, aristocratic with the Senate, and popular with the Great Council. . . . But it is only a small minority of Venetians, drawn from noble families, that enjoys sovereign power. By no means all gentlemen who are natives of Venice are participants, for some of these citizens are eligible for the Great Council and others are not, although they may be of the same extraction, the same kin, and even bear the same names. I need not explain how this comes to be so, for it is all in Sabellico. The Great Council, says Contarini, has power to make and unmake laws, institute and deprive officials, hear appeals, determine peace and war, pardon the convicted. But in saying this Contarini is condemned out of his own mouth. If it is as he says, it follows that the constitution of the Republic is an aristocracy, even though the Great Council's only direct power is the institution to office, for whatever power these officials enjoy, they hold them in trust. It follows that neither the Ten, nor the Senate, nor the Ministers of State, nor even the Doge himself with the six ducal councillors have any authority save by commission, and depend on the good pleasure of the Great Council. . . .

There are those who say, and have published in writing, that the constitution of France is a mixture of the three pure types, the Parlement representing aristocracy, the Estates-General democracy, and the King monarchy. But this is an opinion not only absurd but treasonable. It is treasonable to exalt the subjects to be the equals and colleagues of their sovereign prince. And what resemblance is there to a popular form of government in the Estates, seeing that each particular member and all in general, kneel in the king's presence, and address him by humble prayers and supplications, which he accepts or rejects as he thinks fit. What counter-weight of popular sovereignty can be set against the monarchy in an assembly of the three estates, or even an assembly of the entire people, were that physically possible, seeing that they approach the king with supplication and entreaty, and address him in terms of reverence? So far from diminishing the power of a sovereign prince, such an assembly enhances and emphasizes it. The king can attain no higher degree of honour, power, and glory, than he enjoys at the moment when an infinite number of princes and seigneurs, an innumerable multitude of people of all sorts and conditions, cast themselves at his feet, and pay homage to his majesty. The honour, glory, and power of princes lies in the obedience, homage, and service of their subjects.

If then there is no vestige of popular sovereignty in the assembly of the three estates of this realm, no more, or even less, than there is in those of Spain and England, still less is there any trace of aristocratic authority either in the Court of Peers, or any assembly of the officers of the kingdom, seeing that in the king's presence the authority of all corporations and colleges, of all officers of the realm collectively or severally, is suspended, so that no magistrate whatsoever has power to issue commands in his presence, as we shall show in due course. . . .

But, someone may say, could you not have a commonwealth where the people appointed to office, controlled the expenditure of the revenue and had the right of pardon, which are three of the attributes of sovereignty; where the nobles made laws, determined peace and war, and levied taxes, which are also attributes of sovereignty; and where there was a supreme magistrate set over all the rest, to whom liege-homage was due by all the people severally and collectively, and who was the final and absolute resort of justice. Would not such arrangements involve a division of sovereign rights, and imply a composite commonwealth which was at once monarchical, aristocratic and popular? I would reply that none such has ever existed, and could never exist or even be clearly imagined, seeing that the attributes of sovereignty are indivisible. Whoever could make laws for all the rest, that is to say command or forbid whatever he wished, without there being any right to appeal against or resist his orders, could forbid the declaration of war, the levying of taxes, the swearing of oaths of fealty, without his consent. Or the man to whom liege-homage was due could forbid both nobles and people from obedience to any person but himself. Such situations could only be resolved by an appeal to arms, until by this means it was decided whether final authority remained in the prince, or a ruling class, or in the people. . . . Since the King of Denmark has been compelled to share sovereign power with the nobility, that kingdom has never enjoyed any secure peace. The same is true of Sweden, where the King is so mistrustful of the nobles that he employs a German as Chancellor, and a Norman gentleman called Varennes as Constable. . . .

There is just one other point to be considered. The Republic of Rome, under the Empire of Augustus, and for long after, was called a principality.

This appears to be a form of commonwealth not mentioned by Herodotus, Plato, Aristotle or even Polybius, who enumerated seven. . . . But I would reply that in many aristocratic or popular states one particular magistrate has precedence over all the rest in dignity and authority. Such are the Emperor in Germany, the Doge in Venice, and in ancient times the Archon in Athens. But this does not change the form of the state. . . . A principality is nothing but an aristocracy or a democracy which has a single person as president or premier of the republic, but who nevertheless holds of those in whom sovereign power resides.

Chapter 2: Concerning Despotic Monarchy

. . . All monarchies are either despotic, royal, or tyrannical. These however are not different species of commonwealth, but different modes of operation in their governments. It is important that a clear distinction be made between the form of the state, and the form of the government, which is merely the machinery of policing the state, though no one has yet considered it in that light. To illustrate, a state may be a monarchy, but it is governed democratically if the prince distributes lands, magistracies, offices, and honours indifferently to all, without regard to the claims of either birth or wealth or virtue. Or a monarchy can be governed aristocratically when the prince confines the distribution of lands and offices to the nobles, the most worthy, or the rich, as the case may be. Again, an aristocracy can conduct its government democratically if it bestows honours and rewards on all alike, or aristocratically if it reserves them for the rich and nobly born. This variety in forms of government has misled those who have written confusedly about politics, through failure to distinguish the form of the commonwealth from the form of the government. . . .

Book 5
Chapter 6: The Keeping of Treaties and Alliances between Princes

This discussion arises out of the foregoing, and must on no account be omitted, seeing that writers on law and politics have never treated of it, though there is no matter of state that more exercises the minds of princes and rulers than the securing of treaties, whether with friends, enemies, neutrals, or their own subjects. Some rely on mutual good faith simply. Others demand hostages. Many add the surrender of fortified places. Others cannot feel safe unless they totally disarm the conquered. It has always been considered that the best guarantee of a treaty is ratification by a marriage alliance. But just as there is a difference between friends and enemies, victors and vanquished, equals in power and the weak, princes and subjects, so also must the forms of treaties and their appropriate guarantees be diversified. But there is one general and indisputable principle to be observed, and that is that in all treaties there is no better guarantee of its observation than that the clauses and conditions included in it should be suitable to the parties concerned, and conformable to the matters in dispute. . . .

As we have shown, true protection is given where a prince freely undertakes to defend another without recompense of any kind. Nevertheless, for the better securing of these treaties of protection or commendation, it is customary to offer a pension to the protector or advocate, in the hope that the protector, being bound not only by his oath, but by the payments received, will be more ready to succour his adherent when need arises. It is true that the ancients never followed such a proceeding. But now that honour is weighed against profit, protection is sold for money. This is why a Salvian of Marseilles complains that when the weak seek the protection of the strong, they have to part with all they have to secure it. One knows what enormous sums the people of Lucca, Parma, and Siena, and many other towns, disbursed for their protection. Often enough the pension is paid not so much to secure oneself against one's enemies, as against the protector himself. This happened after the battle of Pavia. All the rulers of Italy turned their attention to the Spaniards, and in order to buy themselves off from the threat of invasion, put themselves under their protection. . . .

Treaties of protection expose the protected party to much greater risks than any other kind of alliance, and therefore it is important that the guarantees should be most carefully considered. For lack of such, how often has one not seen an obligation to protect transformed into sovereign rights. He feels safe indeed who commits the sheep to the care of the wolf. It is therefore in the first instance important that treaties of protection should be limited in time, even in the case of aristocracies and popular states where the ruler never dies. For this reason when Geneva put itself under the protection of Berne, the citizens did not wish to bind themselves for more than thirty years. The treaty expired in 1558, when Geneva proposed an alliance with Berne on equal terms. This was only concluded with great difficulty, and only after a crisis in which the city was nearly brought into subjection through the machinations of certain citizens who paid the penalty with their lives. . . . But the best guarantee for the protected party is to prevent, if possible, the seizure of the fortresses of their towns by the troops of the protector and the introduction of his garrisons into them. The words of the Tribune Brutus to the nobles and people of Rome should never be forgotten, that the only protection that the weak have against the strong whom they fear, is that the latter should not be able to harm them even if they wish to, for the desire to do harm is never lacking in ambitious men who have power to inflict it. On these grounds the Scots were wise when in the treaty which they made in 1559 with the Queen of England, to secure her protection, they stipulated that the hostages surrendered should be changed every six months, and that no fortress should be constructed in Scotland without the consent of the Scots themselves. . . .

Many think that it is safest for a prince to adopt a policy of neutrality, and so keep out of other people's wars. The principal argument in support of this view is that whereas loss and expense is shared in common, the fruits of victory all accrue to the ruler on whose behalf the quarrel is sustained, added to which one must declare oneself the enemy of princes who have in no way offended one's interests. But he who remains neutral often finds means to reconcile enemies, and so remains himself everyone's friend, and receives honours and rewards at the hands of both parties. If all princes were aligned against one another in hostile camps, who could compose their differences? And again, what better way is there of maintaining one's state in all its strength than to stand aside while one's neighbours ruin one another? In truth, the greatness of a prince largely depends on the decline and fall of his neighbours, and his strength is measured by other people's weakness. . . .

But the arguments on the other side appear stronger. First of all, in matters of state one ought always to be either the stronger, or of the stronger party. There are few exceptions to this rule, whether one is considering a single commonwealth, or a number of princes. Otherwise one falls a prey to the whim of the victor. . . . Without looking further afield, we have the example of the Florentines. Having abandoned their alliance with the French royal house, but at the same time refusing to join the league of the Pope, the Emperor, the Kings of England and of Spain, they almost immediately felt the evil effects of their neutrality. Someone may object that it was not open to them to join the League. That is true. But it was not open to them either to abandon their obligations to an ally at will, as they did. . . . One cannot take up a neutral position if one owes assistance to one of the parties under some treaty. The only way of remaining neutral without going in fear of the victor is to secure the consent of the other parties to such a course of action. In fact the duchies of Lorraine, Burgundy, and Savoy maintained their independence so long as they followed a policy of neutrality. But as soon as the Duke of Savoy took sides with the Spaniards, the French drove him from his principality. But there is a great difference in being neutral because the friend of neither party, and neutral because the ally of both. The latter situation is much the safer, since one is secure from attack by the victors, and if any treaties are agreed upon by the contending parties, one is included by both sides.

If neutrality is to be commended in such a case, it is even more laudable in a great prince who surpasses all others in power and dignity. To him falls the honour of being judge and arbiter, for it always happens that the quarrels between princes are composed by some common friend, especially by those who stand above all the others in greatness. In former times many popes, who rightly understood their office, made it their business to reconcile Christian princes and thereby win honour and respect, and favours and protection for their own person and for their office. But those who took sides with one or other party brought ruin on others. The Spaniards thought it very unfitting that Alexander VI, himself a Spaniard by birth, should ally with Louis XII against them. But when the Spaniards themselves had the mastery, he said to the French ambassador that he considered it his role to remain neutral. But it was a little late to try and extinguish the fire he had kindled by putting on a show of piety. . . .

Good faith is little regarded by many princes in the alliances which they make with one another. What is more, there are those so perfidious that they only enter into solemn engagements with the intention of deceiving, in this emulating the captain Lysander, who boasted that he cheated adults by his sworn assurances, and children by his conjuring. But God punished his perfidy according to his merits. Perjury is more to be detested than atheism. Since the atheist does not believe in God, he cannot sin so gravely against one in whose existence he does not believe, as the man who does believe, and mocks God in perjuring himself. Perjury therefore always implies impiety and a wicked heart, for he who swears in order to deceive evidently mocks God, fearing only his enemy. It would be better never to call God to witness, or that power one believes to be God, only to mock Him, but only call oneself to witness. That is what Richard, Count of Poitiers, son of the King of England did when he confirmed the privileges of La Rochelle, he simply added the words *teste meipso*.

Since faith is the sole foundation and prop of that justice on which all commonwealths, alliances, and associations of men whatsoever, is founded, it should be preserved sacred and inviolable in all cases where no injustice is contemplated. This applies most particularly to the relations between princes, for seeing that they are the guarantors of good faith and sworn engagements, what assurance will those subject to them have of their own mutual undertakings if the rulers themselves are the principal breakers and violators of good faith? I have added, "in all cases where no injustice is contemplated," for it is a double sin to engage one's faith to do an evil act. In such a case he who fails of his promise, so far from being perfidious, is to be commended. In like case, if the prince promises not to do something permitted by natural law, he is not perjured if he breaks his oath. Even the subject is not foresworn who breaks his oath regarding any action permitted by the law. But wise princes should never bind themselves by oath to other princes to do anything forbidden by natural law, or the law of nations, nor should they ever compel princes weaker than themselves to swear to an agreement quite unreasonable in its terms. . . . Not that princes who fail to carry out promises to their disadvantage, which have been exacted from them by their conquerors, escape the dishonour of perjury, as certain doctors argue. These doctors are as ill-informed about the character of the commonwealth as they are about past history, and the true foundations of justice. They treat engagements between sovereign princes as if they were of the same order as contracts and agreements between private citizens. The consequences have been most unfortunate. During the last two to three hundred years this opinion has gained ground, with the result that there has been no treaty, however beneficial, which has not been infringed. It is remarkable that the first legislators and jurists, and the Romans who were models of justice, never thought of such subtleties. For it is very obvious that most treaties of peace are made under constraint, from fear of the victor, or of him who is the stronger party. What fear is more excusable than fear for one's life? Yet the Consul Attilius Regulus, having sworn to the Carthaginians to return, knowing that he was going to his death, took refuge in no such subtle excuses. . . .

Jurists rightly hold that faith is not to be kept with him who breaks it. But they go further. They allege that by the decree of the Council of Constance it was laid down that one is not bound to keep faith with enemies of the faith. The Emperor Sigismund had pledged his word to Wenceslas, King of Bohemia, and given a safe-conduct to John Huss and Jerome of Prague, and therefore resisted proceedings against them. To satisfy his conscience a number of jurists, canonists, and theologians, especially Nicholas, Abbot of Palermo, and Luigi da Ponte surnamed Romanus elaborated this opinion, and it was given the backing of a decree published by the Council. John Huss and his companion were executed, though neither the Council nor the Emperor had any jurisdiction over them, and their natural lord, the King of Bohemia, did not give his consent. But no attention was paid to these things. This is no matter for surprise seeing that Bartolus, the first jurist of his age, maintained that one was not bound to keep faith with individuals in the enemy camp who were not responsible leaders. . . .

But if faith should not be kept with the enemy, it ought never to be pledged. On the contrary, if it is permissible to treat with the enemy, it follows that one is bound to honour one's engagements to him. This raises the question as to whether it is permissible to treat with pagans and infidels, as the Emperor Charles V treated with the King of Persia. . . . The Kings of Poland, the Venetians, Genoese, and Ragusans, all made similar alliances with them. The Emperor Charles V himself pledged his word to Martin Luther, though he had been denounced as an enemy to the faith in a Papal bull, that he might safely attend the Imperial Diet at Worms in 1519. There van Eyck, seeing that Luther would not renounce his opinions, cited the decree of Constance as grounds for proceeding against him regardless of the pledged word of the Emperor. But there was not a prince present that did not express horror at van Eyck's petition, and in fact the Emperor dismissed Luther with a safe-conduct, and under armed protection. I do not wish to discuss the merits of the decree, but the opinion of Bartolus, and those who maintain that one need not keep faith with the enemy is not worthy of formal refutation, so contrary is it to ordinary common sense. . . .

There have been no greater exponents of the principles of justice and good faith than the ancient Romans. Pompey the Great treated with sea-rovers and pirates, and allowed them to take refuge in certain towns and territories where they could settle under the authority of Rome. But he was well aware that the pirates had a fleet of nine hundred sail, and access to some five hundred coastal towns and villages. Governors could not reach their provinces, nor merchants carry on their business of trading. War could not be made on such a power without exposing the whole Roman state to danger, whereas its dignity was preserved intact by this treaty. If he had not honoured the agreement he made with them, or the Senate had refused to ratify the treaty, the honour of the Republic would have been smirched, and the glory of Pompey's achievement obscured. In normal circumstances however we do not hold that one should either give or receive pledges where pirates are concerned, for one should have no dealings with them, nor observe the rules of the law of nations where they are concerned. . . . But once one has pledged one's faith to an outlaw, one should keep the engagement. I can think of no better instance of this than that afforded by the Emperor Augustus. He caused it to be published, to the sound of trumpets, that he would give twenty-five thousand *scudi* to anyone who could deliver to him Crocotas, leader of the Spanish brigands. Crocotas, hearing of it, presented himself before Augustus and claimed the reward of twenty-five thousand *scudi*. Augustus ordered that he should be paid, and then granted him a free pardon, in order to give a good example of keeping faith, for in such matters the honour of God and of the Republic is involved. . . .

2
The English Revolution

The King and Parliament

10. The Calling of the Long Parliament (Selections from Clarendon)

The Long Parliament was so called because it sat in almost continuous session from 4 November 1640 to 23 April 1653. It was the body that legislated the enduring constitutional reforms of the revolutionary period and raised a war against the king of England. Among its members was Edward Hyde (1609–74) who sat for the Cornish borough of Saltash. A country gentleman by birth and a lawyer by training, Hyde was among a number of moderate reformers who broke ranks with the radicals over the passage and publication of the Grand Remonstrance in November 1641 (see document 13). He was with the king during the Civil War and was given charge of the Prince of Wales. After the Restoration, Hyde was raised to the peerage as earl of Clarendon and served as Lord Chancellor of England. He was driven out of politics and into his own exile in France in 1667. There he resumed writing his *History of the Rebellion and Civil Wars in England* which he had begun in 1646. He based his history upon his own participation in political affairs and on an extensive collection of contemporary documents that had been gathered by the exiled court in the 1650s. At the same time he composed the *Life of Edward Hyde, Earl of Clarendon* for the instruction and edification of his children. *The History of the Rebellion* was first published in 1702–4 and remains one of the great works of western historiography. Subsequent editions, including

From Edward, Lord Clarendon, *The History of the Great Rebellion*, edited by W. D. Macray (Oxford: The Clarendon Press, 1888), pp. 218–37. Footnotes deleted.

the following selections, have interspersed relevant sections of the *Life* into the *History*.

Book 3

1. The Parliament met upon the third of November, 1640, with a fuller appearance than could be reasonably expected from the short time for elections after the issuing out of the writs. Insomuch as at the first many members were absent, it had a sad and a melancholic aspect upon the first entrance, which presaged some unusual and unnatural events. The King himself did not ride with his accustomed equipage nor in his usual majesty to Westminster, but went privately in his barge to the Parliament-stairs, and so to the church, as if it had been to a return of a prorogued or adjourned Parliament. And there was likewise an untoward, and in truth an unheard of, accident, which brake many of the King's measures, and infinitely disordered his service beyond a capacity of reparation. From the time the calling a Parliament was resolved upon, the King designed sir Thomas Gardiner, who was Recorder of London, to be Speaker in the House of Commons; a man of gravity and quickness, that had somewhat of authority and gracefulness in his person and presence, and in all respects equal to the service. There was little doubt but that he would be chosen to serve in one of the four places for the city of London, which had very rarely rejected their Recorder upon that occasion; and lest that should fail, diligence was used in one or two other places that he might be elected. The opposition was so great, and the faction so strong, to hinder his being elected in the city, that four others were chosen for that service, without hardly mentioning his name, nor was there less industry used to prevent his being chosen in other places; clerks were corrupted not to make out the writ for one place, and ways were found to hinder the writ from being executed in another time enough for the return before the meeting: so great a fear there was that a man of entire affections to the King, and of prudence enough to manage those affections, and to regulate the contrary, should be put into that chair. So that the very morning the Parliament was to meet, and when the King intended to go thither, he was informed that sir Thomas Gardiner was not returned to serve as a member in the House of Commons, and so was not capable of being chosen to be Speaker; so that his majesty deferred his going to the House till the afternoon, by which time he was to think of another Speaker.

2. Upon the perusal of all the returns into the Crown Office, there were not found many lawyers of eminent name (though many of them proved

very eminent men afterwards) or who had served long in former Parliaments, the experience whereof was to be wished; and men of that profession had been always thought the most proper for that service, and the putting it out of that channel at that time was thought too hazardous; so that, after all the deliberation that time would admit, Mr. Lenthall (a bencher of Lincoln's Inn) a lawyer of competent practice, and no ill reputation for his affection to the government both of Church and State, was pitched upon by the King, and with very great difficulty rather prevailed with than persuaded to accept the charge. And no doubt a worse could not have been deputed of all that profession who were then returned; for he was a man of a very narrow timorous nature, and of no experience or conversation in the affairs of the kingdom, beyond what the very drudgery in his profession (in which all his design was to make himself rich) engaged him in. In a word, he was in all respects very unequal to the work; and not knowing how to preserve his own dignity, or to restrain the license and exorbitance of others, his weakness contributed as much to the growing mischiefs as the malice of the principal contrivers. However, after the King had that afternoon commended the distracted condition of the kingdom, with too little majesty, to the wisdom of the two Houses of Parliament, to have such reformation and remedies applied as they should think fit, proposing to them as the best rule for their counsels that all things should be reduced to the practice of the time of Queen Elizabeth, the House of Commons no sooner returned to their house than they chose Mr. Lenthall to be their Speaker; and two days after, with the usual ceremonies and circumstances, presented him to the King, who declared his acceptation; and so both Houses were ready for their work.

3. There was observed a marvellous elated countenance in most of the members of Parliament before they met together in the house; the same men who six months before were observed to be of very moderate tempers, and to wish that gentle remedies might be applied without opening the wound too wide and exposing it to the air, and rather to cure what was amiss than too strictly to make inquisition into the causes and original of the malady, talked now in another dialect both of things and persons. Mr. Hyde, who was returned to serve for a borough in Cornwall, met Mr. Pimm [Pym] in Westminster Hall some few days before the Parliament, and conferring together upon the state of affairs, the other told him, [Hyde,] and said, "that they must now be of another temper than they were the last Parliament; that they must not only sweep the house clean below, but must pull down all the cobwebs which hung in the top and corners, that they might not breed dust and so make a foul house hereafter; that they had now an opportunity to make their country happy, by removing all grievances and pulling up the causes of them by the roots, if all men would do their du-

ties"; and used much other sharp discourse to him to the same purpose: by which it was discerned that the warmest and boldest counsels and overtures would find a much better reception than those of a more temperate allay; which fell out accordingly. And the very first day they met together in which they could enter upon business, Mr. Pimm, in a long, formed discourse, lamented the miserable state and condition of the kingdom, aggravated all the particulars which had been done amiss in the government as done and contrived maliciously, and upon deliberation, to change the whole frame, and to deprive the nation of all the liberty and property which was their birthright by the laws of the land, which were now no more considered, but subjected to the arbitrary power of the Privy-Council, which governed the kingdom according to their will and pleasure; these calamities falling upon us in the reign of a pious and virtuous King, who loved his people and was a great lover of justice. And thereupon enlarging in some specious commendation of the nature and goodness of the King, that he might wound him with less suspicion, he said, "We must inquire from what fountain these waters of bitterness flowed; what persons they were who had so far insinuated themselves into his royal affections as to be able to pervert his excellent judgment, to abuse his name, and wickedly apply his authority to countenance and support their own corrupt designs. Though he doubted there would be many found of this *classis,* who had contributed their joint endeavours to bring this misery upon the nation, yet he believed there was one more signal in that administration than the rest, being a man of great parts and contrivance, and of great industry to bring what he designed to pass; a man who in the memory of many present had sat in that house an earnest vindicator of the laws, and a most zealous assertor and champion for the liberties of the people; but that it was long since he turned apostate from those good affections, and, according to the custom and nature of apostates, was become the greatest enemy to the liberties of his country, and the greatest promoter of tyranny, that any age had produced"; and then named "the earl of Strafford, Lord Lieutenant of Ireland, and Lord President of the Council established in York for the northern parts of the kingdom: who," he said, "had in both places, and in all other provinces wherein his service had been used by the King, raised ample monuments of his tyrannical nature: and that he believed, if they took a short survey of his actions and behaviour, they would find him the principal author and promoter of all those counsels which had exposed the kingdom to so much ruin"; and so instanced some high and imperious actions done by him in England and in Ireland, some proud and over-confident expressions in discourse, and some passionate advices he had given in the most secret councils and debates of the affairs of state; adding some lighter passages of his vanity and amours, that they who were not inflamed with anger and detestation against him for the former might have less esteem and reverence for his prudence and discretion: and so concluded, "that they would well consider how to provide a remedy proportionable to the disease, and to prevent the farther mischiefs which they were to expect from the continuance of this great man's power and credit with the King and his influence upon his councils."

4. From the time that the earl of Strafford was named most men believed that there would be some committee named to receive information of all his miscarriages, and that upon report thereof they would farther consider what course to take in the examination and prosecution thereof: but they had already prepared and digested their business to a riper period.

5. Mr. Pimm had no sooner finished his discourse, than sir John Clotworthy (a gentleman of Ireland, and utterly unknown in England, who was by the contrivance and recommendation of some powerful persons returned to serve for a borough in Devon, that so he might be enabled to act this part against the Lord Lieutenant) made a long and confused relation of his tyrannical carriage in that kingdom; of the army he had raised there to invade Scotland; how he had threatened the Parliament if they granted not such supplies as he required; of an oath he had framed to be administered to all the Scots' nation which inhabited that kingdom, and his severe proceeding against some persons of quality who refused to take that oath; and that he had with great pride and passion publicly declared at his leaving that kingdom, "If ever he should return to that sword he would not leave a Scotchman to inhabit in Ireland": with a multitude of very exalted expressions, and some very high actions, in his administration of that government, in which the lives as well as the fortunes of men had been disposed of out of the common road of justice: all which made him to be looked upon as a man very terrible, and under whose authority men would not choose to put themselves.

6. Several other persons appearing ready to continue the discourse, and the morning being spent, so that, according to the observation of parliament hours, the time of rising being come, an order was suddenly made that the door should be shut, and nobody suffered to go out of the house; which had been rarely practised: care having been first taken to give such advertisement to some of the Lords that that House might likewise be kept from rising; which would very much have broken their measures.

7. Then sir John Hotham, and some other Yorkshire men who had received some disobligation from the earl in the country, continued the invective, mentioning many particulars of his imperious carriage, and that he had, in the face of the country, upon the execution of some illegal commission, declared, "that they should find the little finger of the King's prerogative heavier upon them than the loins of the law"; which expression,

though upon after-examination it was found to have a quite contrary sense, marvellously increased the passion and prejudice towards him.

8. In conclusion, after many hours of bitter inveighing, and ripping up the course of his life before his coming to Court and his actions after, it was moved, according to the secret resolution taken before, "that he might be forthwith impeached of high treason"; which was no sooner mentioned than it found an universal approbation and consent from the whole: nor was there in the whole debate one person who offered to stop the torrent by any favourable testimony concerning the earl's carriage, save only that the lord Falkland, who was very well known to be far from having any kindness for him, when the proposition was made for the present accusing him of high treason, modestly desired the House to consider, "Whether it would not suit better with the gravity of their proceedings first to digest many of those particulars which had been mentioned, by a committee?" declaring himself to be abundantly satisfied that there was enough to charge him before they sent up to accuse him: which was very ingenuously and frankly answered by Mr. Pymm, "That such a delay might probably blast all their hopes, and put it out of their power to proceed farther than they had done already; that the earl's power and credit with the King, and with all those who had most credit with King or Queen, was so great, that when he should come to know that so much of his wickedness was discovered his own conscience would tell him what he was to expect, and therefore he would undoubtedly procure the Parliament to be dissolved rather than undergo the justice of it, or take some other desperate course to preserve himself, though with the hazard of the kingdom's ruin: whereas, if they presently sent up to impeach him of high treason before the House of Peers, in the name and on the behalf of all the Commons of England, who were represented by them, the Lords would be obliged in justice to commit him into safe custody, and so sequester him from resorting to Council or having access to his majesty: and then they should proceed against him in the usual form with all necessary expedition."

9. To those who were known to have no kindness for him, and seemed to doubt whether all the particulars alleged, being proved, would amount to high treason, it was alleged that the House of Commons were not judges but only accusers, and that the Lords were the proper judges whether such a complication of enormous crimes in one person did not amount to the highest offence the law took notice of, and therefore that it was fit to present it to them. These reasons of the haste they made, so clearly delivered, gave that universal satisfaction, that, without farther considering the injustice and unreasonableness of it, they voted unanimously (for aught appeared to the contrary by any avowed contradiction) "That they would forthwith send up to the Lords and accuse the earl of Strafford of high trea-

son and several other crimes and misdemeanours, and desire that he might be presently sequestered from Council, and committed to safe custody"; and Mr. Pimm was made choice of for the messenger to perform that office. And this being determined, the doors were opened, and most of the House accompanied him on the errand.

10. It was about three of the clock in the afternoon, when the earl of Strafford (being infirm and not well disposed in his health, and so not having stirred out of his house that morning) hearing that both Houses still sat, thought fit to go thither. It was believed by some (upon what ground was never clear enough) that he made that haste then to accuse the lord Say and some others of having induced the Scots to invade the kingdom: but he was scarce entered into the House of Peers when the message from the House of Commons was called in, and when Mr. Pymm at the bar, and in the name of all the Commons of England, impeached Thomas earl of Strafford (with the addition of all his other titles) of high treason and several other heinous crimes and misdemeanours, of which, he said, the Commons would in due time make proof in form; and in the mean time desired in their name, that he might be sequestered from all councils and be put into safe custody; and so withdrawing, the earl was, with more clamour than was suitable to the gravity of that supreme court, called upon to withdraw, hardly obtaining leave to be first heard in his place, which could not be denied him.

11. And he then lamented his great misfortune to lie under so heavy a charge; professed his innocence and integrity, which he made no doubt he should make appear to them; desired he might have his liberty until some guilt should be made appear: and desired them to consider what mischief they should bring upon themselves, if upon such a general charge, without the mention of any one crime, a peer of the realm should be committed to prison, and so deprived of his place in that House where he was summoned by the King's writ to assist in the council, and of what consequence such a precedent might be to their own privilege and birthright; and then withdrew. And with very little debate the Peers resolved that he should be committed to the custody of the gentleman usher of the Black Rod, there to remain until the House of Commons should bring in a particular charge against him: which determination of the House was pronounced to him at the bar upon his knees by the Lord Keeper of the Great Seal upon the woolsack: and so being taken away by Maxwell, gentleman usher, Mr. Pymm was called in and informed what the House had done; after which (it being then about four of the clock) both Houses adjourned till the next day.

12. When this work was so prosperously over they began to consider that, notwithstanding all the industry that had been used to procure such members to be chosen, or returned though not chosen, who had been most refractory to the government of the Church and State, yet that the House

was so constituted that when the first heat (which almost all men brought with them) should be a little allayed, violent counsels would not be long hearkened to: and therefore, as they took great care by their committee of elections to remove as many of those members as they suspected not to be inclinable to their passions upon pretence that they were not regularly chosen, that so they might bring in others more compliable in their places; (in which no rule of justice was so much as pretended to be observed by them, insomuch as it was often said by leading men amongst them, "That they ought in those cases of elections to be guided by the fitness and worthiness of the person, whatever the desire of those was in whom the right of election remained"; and therefore one man hath been admitted upon the same rule by which another hath been rejected): so they declared, that no person, how lawfully and regularly soever chosen and returned, should be and sit as a member with them who had been a party or a favourer of any project, or who had been employed in any illegal commission.

13. And by this means (contrary to the custom and rights of Parliament) many gentlemen of good quality were removed, in whose places commonly others were chosen of more agreeable dispositions: but in this likewise there was no rule observed; for no person was hereby removed of whom there was any hope that he might be applied to the violent courses which were intended. Upon which occasion the King charged them in one of his Declarations that when under that notion of projectors they expelled many, they yet never questioned sir H. Mildmay, or Mr. Laurence Whitaker, who had been most scandalously engaged in those pressures, though since more scandalously in all enterprises against his majesty; to which never any answer or reply was made.

14. The next art was to make the severity and rigour of the House as formidable as was possible, and to make as many men apprehend themselves obnoxious to the House as had been in any trust or employment in the kingdom. Thus they passed many general votes concerning ship-money, in which all who had been high sheriffs, and so collected it, were highly concerned; the like sharp conclusions upon all lords lieutenants and their deputies, which were the prime gentlemen of quality in all the counties of England. Then upon some disquisition of the proceedings in the Star-Chamber and at the Council-table, all who concurred in such a sentence, and consented to such an order, were declared criminous and to be proceeded against. So that, in a moment, all the lords of the Council, all who had been deputy lieutenants or high sheriffs during the late years, found themselves within the mercy of these grand inquisitors: and hearing new terms of art, that a complication of several misdemeanours might grow up to treason, and the like, it was no wonder if men desired by all means to get their favour and protection.

15. When they had sufficiently startled men by these proceedings, and

upon half an hour's debate sent up an accusation against the lord arch-bishop of Canterbury of high treason, and so removed him likewise from the King's Council, they rested satisfied with their general rules, votes, and orders, without making haste to proceed either against things or persons; being willing rather to keep men in suspense and to have the advantage of their fears, than, by letting them see the worst that could befall them, lose the benefit of their application. For this reason they used their utmost skill to keep off any debate of ship-money, that that whole business might hang like a meteor over the heads of those that were in any degree faulty in it; and it was observable, when, notwithstanding all their diversions, that business was brought into debate, and upon that (which could not be avoided) the lord Finch named as an avowed factor and procurer of that odious judgment (who, if their rule were true that an endeavour to alter the government by law and to introduce an arbitrary power were treason, was the most notoriously and unexcusably guilty of that crime of any man that could be named) before they would endure the mention of an accusation of high treason, they appointed a committee, with great deliberation and sol-emnity, to bring in a charge formally prepared, which had not been done in the case of the lord archbishop or the earl of Strafford and then gave him a day to be heard for himself at the House of Commons' bar, and so, against all order, to take notice of what was handled in the House concerning him; and then, finding that by their own rules he would be likewise accused of high treason, they continued the debate so long that the Lords' house was risen, so that the accusation was not carried up till the next morning. And before that time the Lord Keeper (being well informed of all that had passed) had withdrawn himself, and shortly after went into Holland; the lord Littleton, then Chief Justice of the court of Common Pleas, being made Keeper of the Great Seal of England in his place.

16. About the same time, sir Francis Wynnibanke, [Windebank,] one of the principal Secretaries of State, and then a member of the House of Com-mons, was accused of many transactions on the behalf of the Papists of several natures (whose extraordinary patron indeed he was) and, he being then present in the House, several warrants under his own hand were produced for the discharge of prosecutions against priests and for the re-lease of priests out of prison; whereupon, whilst the matter should be de-bated, according to custom he was ordered to withdraw, and so went into the usual place, the committee-chamber; immediately whereupon, the House of Commons went to a conference with the Lords upon some other occasion, and returning from that conference, no more resumed the debate of the Secretary, but, having considered some other business, rose at their usual hour. And so the Secretary had liberty to go to his own house, from whence, observing the disposition of the House, and well knowing what they were able to say against him, he had no more mind to trust himself in

that company, but the same night withdrew himself from any place where inquiry might be made for him, and was no more heard of till the news came of his being landed in France.

17. So that within less than six weeks, for no more time was yet elapsed, these terrible reformers had caused the two greatest counsellors of the kingdom, and whom they most feared and so hated, to be removed from the King and imprisoned under an accusation of high treason, and frighted away the Lord Keeper of the Great Seal of England and one of the principal Secretaries of State into foreign kingdoms, for fear of the like; besides the preparing all the lords of the Council, and very many of the principal gentlemen throughout England, who (as was said before) had been high shrieves and deputy lieutenants, to expect such measure of punishment from their general votes and resolutions as their future demeanour should draw upon them for their past offences; by which means, they were like to find no very vigorous resistance or opposition in their farther designs.

18. I could never yet learn the reason, why they suffered Secretary Winnibanke to escape their justice (for the lord Finch, it was visible he was in their favour, and they would gladly have preserved him in the place) against whom they had more pregnant testimony of offences within the verge of the law than against any person they have accused since this Parliament, and of some that, it may be, might have proved capital, and so their appetite of blood might have been satisfied. For, besides his frequent letters of intercession in his own name and signification of his majesty's pleasure on the behalf of Papists and priests to the judges and to other ministers of justice, and protections granted by himself to priests that nobody should molest them, he harboured some priests in his own house, knowing them to be such, which by the statute made in the twenty-ninth year of Queen Elizabeth is made felony; and there were some warrants under his own hand for the release of priests out of Newgate who were actually attainted of treason and condemned to be hanged, drawn, and quartered; which by the strict letter of the statute, the lawyers said, would have been very penal to him.

11. The Root and Branch Petition (11 December 1640)

One of the most contentious issues in the early days of the Long Parliament was that of religion. The innovations in doctrine, practice, and ceremony instituted by Archbishop William Laud during the 1630s had heightened fears that England was being reintroduced into the Church of Rome. Laud's persecution of religious dissidents, opprobriously named

From S. R. Gardiner, *Constitutional Documents of the Puritan Revolution* (Oxford: The Clarendon Press, 1906), pp. 171–75.

Puritans, led to forced emigrations to Holland and America and drove the movement for religious reform further to the left. By 1640 even the most moderate of the reform groups were ready to support sweeping changes in the established church. The most radical of these was the abolition of the office of bishop. "Root and branch" was the metaphorical expression of the idea of form and substance; a complete uprooting of the hierarchical church structure.

To the Right Honourable the Commons House of Parliament.

The humble petition of many of his Majesty's subjects in and about the City of London, and several counties of the kingdom, showeth,

That whereas the government of archbishops and lord bishops, deans and archdeacons, etc., with their courts and ministrations in them, have proved prejudicial and very dangerous both to the Church and Commonwealth, they themselves having formerly held, that they have their jurisdiction or authority of human authority, till of these later times, being further pressed about the unlawfulness, that they have claimed their calling immediately from the Lord Jesus Christ, which is against the Laws of this kingdom, and derogatory to his Majesty and his state royal. And whereas the said government is found by woeful experience to be a main cause and occasion of many foul evils, pressures and grievances of a very high nature unto his Majesty's subjects in their own consciences, liberties and estates, as in a schedule of particulars hereunto annexed may in part appear.

We therefore most humbly pray and beseech this honourable assembly, the premises considered, that the said government, with all its dependencies, roots and branches, may be abolished, and all laws in their behalf made void, and the government according to God's Word may be rightly placed amongst us. And we your humble suppliants, as in duty we are bound, will daily pray for his Majesty's long and happy reign over us, and for the prosperous success of this high and honourable Court of Parliament.

A Particular of the Manifold Evils, Pressures and Grievances Caused, Practised and Occasioned by the Prelates and Their Dependants

1. The subjecting and enthralling all ministers under them and their authority, and so by degrees exempting them from the temporal power; whence follows:

2. The faint-heartedness of ministers to preach the Truth of God, lest they should displease the prelates; as namely, the doctrine of Predestination, of Free-Grace, of Perseverance, of Original Sin remaining after baptism, of the Sabbath, the doctrine against Universal Grace, Election for

Faith foreseen, Free Will, against Anti-Christ, Non-Residents, human Inventions in God's Worship; all which are generally withheld from the people's knowledge, because not relishing to the bishops.

3. The encouragement of ministers to despise the temporal magistracy, the nobles and gentry of the land, to abuse the subjects and live contentiously with their neighbours, knowing that they, being the bishops' creatures, shall be supported.

4. The restraint of many godly and able men from the ministry, and thrusting out of many congregations their faithful, diligent and powerful ministers, who lived peaceably with them, and did them good, only because they cannot in conscience submit to and maintain the bishops' needless devices; nay, sometimes for no other cause but for their zeal in preaching or great auditories. . . .

6. The great increase of idle, lewd and dissolute, ignorant and erroneous men in the ministry, which swarm like the locusts of Egypt over the whole kingdom, and will they but wear a canonical cap, a surplice, a hood, bow at the name of Jesus, and be zealous of superstitious ceremonies, they may live as they list, confront whom they please, preach and vent what errors they will, and neglect preaching at their pleasures without control. . . .

9. The hindering of godly books to be printed, the blotting out or perverting those which they suffer, all or most of that which strikes either at Popery or Arminianism, the adding of what or where pleaseth them, and the restraint of reprinting books formerly licensed, without relicensing. . . .

11. The growth of Popery and increase of Papists, priests and Jesuits in sundry places, but especially about London since the Reformation; the frequent venting of crucifixes and Popish pictures both engraved and printed, and the placing of such in Bibles. . . .

13. Moreover, the offices and jurisdictions of archbishops, lordbishops, deans, archdeacons, being the same way of Church government which is in the Romish Church, and which was in England in the time of Popery, little change thereof being made (except only the head from whence it was derived), the same arguments supporting the Pope which do uphold the prelates, and overthrowing the prelates which do pull down the Pope; and other Reformed Churches having, upon their rejection of the Pope, cast the prelates out also, as members of the Beast; hence it is that the prelates here in England, by themselves or their disciples, plead and maintain that the Pope is not Anti-Christ, and that the Church of Rome is a true Church, hath not erred in fundamental points, and that salvation is attainable in that religion, and therefore have restrained to pray for the conversion of our Sovereign Lady the Queen. Hence also hath come:

14. The great conformity and likeness both continued and increased of

our Church to the Church of Rome, in vestures, postures, ceremonies and administrations, namely as bishops' rotchets and the lawn-sleeves, the four-cornered cap, the cope and surplice, the tippet, the hood and the canonical coat, the pulpits clothed, especially now of late, with the Jesuits' badge upon them every way.

15. The standing up at *Gloria Patri,* and at the reading of the Gospel, praying towards the east, bowing at the name of Jesus, the bowing to the altar towards the east, cross in baptism, the kneeling at the Communion.

16. The turning of the Communion Table altar-wise, setting images, crucifixes and conceits over them, and tapers and books upon them, and bowing or adoring to, or before them, . . . which is a plain device to usher in the Mass. . . .

19. The multitude of canons formerly made, wherein among other things excommunication, *ipso facto,* is denounced for speaking of a word against the devices above said, or subscription thereunto, though no law enjoined a restraint from the ministry without subscription, and appeal is denied to any that should refuse subscription or unlawful conformity, though he be never so much wronged by the inferior judges. Also the canons made in the late sacred synod, as they call it, wherein are many strange and dangerous devices to undermine the Gospel, and the subjects' liberties, to propagate Popery, to spoil God's People, ensnare ministers and other students, and so to draw all into an absolute subjection and thraldom to them and their government, spoiling both the King and the Parliament of their power.

20. The countenancing plurality of benefices, prohibiting of marriages without their licence, at certain times almost half the year, and licensing of marriages without banns asking.

21. Profanation of the Lord's Day, pleading for it, and enjoining ministers to read a declaration set forth (as 'tis thought) by their procurement for tolerating of sports upon that day, suspending and depriving many godly ministers for not reading the same, only out of conscience, because it was against the Law of God so to do, and no law of the land to enjoin it. . . .

25. . . . The pride and ambition of the prelates being boundless, unwilling to be subject either to man or laws, they claim their office and jurisdiction to be *jure divino,* exercise ecclesiastical authority in their own names and rights, and under their own seals, and take upon them temporal dignities, places and offices in the Commonwealth, that they may sway both Swords.

26. Whence follows the taking commissions in their own courts and consistories, and where else they sit, in matters determinable of right at Common Law, the putting of ministers upon parishes without the patron's and people's consent. . . .

28. The exercising of the oath *ex officio,* and other proceedings by way of Inquisition, reaching even to men's thoughts, the apprehending and detaining of men by pursuivants, the frequent suspending and depriving of ministers, fining and imprisoning of all sorts of people, breaking up of men's houses and studies, . . . and the doing of many other outrages, to the utter infringing of the laws of the realm and the subjects' liberties, and ruining of them and their families; and of later time the judges of the land are so awed with the power and greatness of the prelates, and other ways promoted, that neither prohibition, *habeas corpus,* nor any other lawful remedy can be had, or take place, for the distressed subjects in most cases; only Papists, Jesuits, priests and such others as propagate Popery or Arminianism, are countenanced, spared, and have much liberty; and from hence followed amongst others these dangerous consequences:

First, The general hope and expectation of the Romish party, that their superstitious religion will ere long be fully planted in this kingdom again, and so they are encouraged to persist therein, and to practice the same openly in divers places, to the high dishonour of God, and contrary to the laws of the realm.

2. The discouragement and destruction of all good subjects, of whom are multitudes, both clothiers, merchants and others, who being deprived of their ministers and overburdened with these pressures have departed the kingdom, to Holland and other parts, and have drawn with them a great manufacture of cloth, and trading, out of the land into other places where they reside, whereby wool, the great staple of the kingdom, is become of small value, and vends not, trading is decayed, many poor people want work, seamen lose employment and the whole land is much impoverished, to the great dishonour of this kingdom, and blemishment to the government thereof.

3. The present wars and commotions happened between his Majesty and his subjects of Scotland, wherein his Majesty and all his kingdoms are endangered, and suffer greatly, and are like to become a prey to the common enemy, in case the wars go on, which we exceedingly fear will not only go on, but also increase, to an utter ruin of all, unless the prelates with their dependencies be removed out of England, and also they and their practises, who, as we under your Honours' favours do verily believe and conceive, have occasioned the quarrel.

All which we humbly refer to the consideration of this Honourable Assembly, desiring the Lord of Heaven to direct you in the right way to redress all these evils.

12. The Triennial Act (15 February 1641)

Though Parliaments had been convened annually in the early thirteenth century, modern practice was less regular. Parliaments always met after the accession of a new monarch and were thereafter summoned at the discretion of the Crown. Its convocation, continuance, and dissolution were among the royal prerogatives. In the seventeenth century, James I (1603–25) had summoned a Parliament in 1604 which continued, through prorogations, until 1610; in 1614 (which was dissolved within two months); in 1621 and 1624. Charles I (1625–49) summoned Parliaments in 1625, 1626, and 1628. In April 1640 he convened the Short Parliament, which lasted less than a month. The Triennial Act received the royal assent and, with some modifications, was reconfirmed after the Restoration of Charles II.

An Act for the Preventing of Inconveniences Happening by the Long Intermission of Parliaments

1. Whereas by the laws and statutes of this realm the Parliament ought to be holden at least once every year for the redress of grievances, but the appointment of the time and place for the holding thereof hath always belonged, as it ought, to His Majesty and his royal progenitors: and whereas it is by experience found that the not holding of Parliaments accordingly hath produced sundry and great mischiefs and inconveniences to the King's Majesty, the Church and Commonwealth; for the prevention of the like mischiefs and inconveniences in time to come:

2. Be it enacted by the King's Most Excellent Majesty, with the consent of the Lord's spiritual and temporal, and the Commons in this present Parliament assembled, that the said laws and statutes be from henceforth duly kept and observed; and your Majesty's loyal and obedient subjects, in this present Parliament now assembled, do humbly pray that it be enacted: and be it enacted accordingly, by the authority of this present Parliament, that in case there be not a Parliament summoned by writ under the Great Seal of England, and assembled and held before the 10th of September, which shall be in the third year next after the last day of the last meeting and sitting in this present Parliament, the beginning of the first year to be accounted from the said last day of the last meeting and sitting in Parliament;

and so from time to time, and in all times hereafter, if there shall not be a Parliament assembled and held before the 10th day of September, which shall be in the third year next after the last day of the last meeting and sitting in Parliament before the time assembled and held; the beginning of the first year to be accounted from the said last day of the last meeting and sitting in Parliament; that then in every such case as aforesaid, the Parliament shall assemble and be held in the usual place at Westminster, in such manner, and by such means only, as is hereafter in this present Act declared and enacted, and not otherwise, on the second Monday, which shall be in the month of November, then next ensuing. And in case this present Parliament now assembled and held, or any other Parliament which shall at any time hereafter be assembled and held by writ under the Great Seal of England, or in case any Parliament shall be assembled and held by authority of this present Act; and such Parliaments, or any of them, shall be prorogued, or adjourned, or continued by prorogation or adjournment, until the 10th day of September, which shall be in the third year next after the last day of the last meeting and sitting in Parliament, to be accounted as aforesaid; that then in every such case, every such Parliament so prorogued or adjourned, or so continued by prorogation or adjournment, as aforesaid, shall from the said 10th day of September be thenceforth clearly and absolutely dissolved, and the Lord Chancellor of England, the Lord Keeper of the Great Seal of England, and every Commissioner and Commissioners, for the keeping of the Great Seal of England, for the time being, shall within six days after the said 10th day of September, in every such third year as aforesaid, in due form of law and without any further warrant or direction from His Majesty, his heirs or successors, seal, issue forth, and send abroad several and respective writs to the several and respective peers of this realm, commanding every such peer that he personally be at the Parliament to be held at Westminster on the second Monday which shall be in November next following the said 10th day of September, then and there to treat concerning the high and urgent affairs concerning His Majesty, the state and defence of the kingdom and Church of England; and shall also seal and issue forth, and send abroad several and respective writs to the several and respective sheriffs of the several and respective counties, cities and boroughs of England and Wales, and to the Constable of the Castle of Dover, Lord Warden of the Cinque Ports, or his lieutenant for the time being, and to the Mayor and Bailiffs of Berwick upon Tweed, and to all and every other officers and persons to whom writs have used to be directed, for the electing of the knights, citizens, barons and burgesses of and for the said Counties, Cities, Cinque Ports and Boroughs of England and Wales respectively, in the accustomed form, to appear and serve in the Parliament to be held at Westminster on the said second Monday, which shall be in

November aforesaid; which said peers, after the said writs received, and which said knights, citizens, barons and burgesses chosen by virtue of the said writs, shall then and there appear and serve in Parliament accordingly. And the said Lord Chancellor, Lord Keeper, Commissioner and Commissioners aforesaid, shall respectively take a solemn oath upon the Holy Evangelists for the due issuing of writs, according to the tenor of this Act, *in haec verba,*—

"You shall swear that you shall truly and faithfully issue forth, and send abroad all writs of summons to Parliament for both Houses, at such time, and in such manner, as is expressed and enjoined by an Act of Parliament, entitled, 'An Act for the preventing of inconveniences happening by the long intermission of Parliaments.'"

Which oath is forthwith to be taken by the present Lord Keeper, and to be administered by the Clerk of the Crown to every Lord Chancellor, Lord Keeper, Commissioner and Commissioners aforesaid; and that none of the said officers respectively shall henceforth execute any the said offices before they have taken the said oath. And if the said Lord Chancellor, Lord Keeper, or any of the said Commissioners shall fail, or forbear so to issue out the said writs, according to the true meaning of this Act, then he or they respectively shall, beside the incurring of the grievous sin of perjury, be disabled, and become, by virtue of this Act, incapable, *ipso facto,* to bear his and their said offices respectively; and be further liable to such punishments as shall be inflicted upon him or them by the next, or any other ensuing Parliament. And in case the said Lord Chancellor, Lord Keeper, Commissioner or Commissioners aforesaid, shall not issue forth the said writs as aforesaid: or in case that the Parliament do not assemble and be held at the time and place before appointed, then the Parliament shall assemble and be held in the usual place at Westminster, in such manner, and by such means only, as is hereafter in this present Act declared and enacted, and not otherwise, on the third Monday which shall be in the month of January then next ensuing. And the peers of this realm shall by virtue of this Act be enabled, and are enjoined to meet in the Old Palace of Westminster, in the usual place there, on the third Monday in the said month of November: and they or any twelve or more of them, then and there assembled, shall on or before the last Monday of November next following the tenth day of September aforesaid, by virtue of this Act, without other warrant, issue out writs in the usual form, in the name of the King's Majesty, his heirs or successors, attested under the hands and seals of twelve or more of the said peers, to the several and respective sheriffs of the several and respective counties, cities, and boroughs of England and Wales; and to the Constable of the Castle of Dover, Lord Warden of the Cinque Ports, or his lieutenant for the time being, and to the Mayor and Bailiffs of Berwick upon Tweed;

and to all and every other the said officers and persons to whom writs have been used to be directed, for the electing of the knights, citizens, barons and burgesses, of and for the said Counties, Cities, Cinque Ports and Boroughs, to be and appear at the Parliament at Westminster aforesaid, to be held on the third Monday in January then next following: all and every which writs the Clerks of the Petty Bag, and other clerks, to whom the writing of the writs for summons to the Parliament doth and shall belong, or whom the said Lords, or twelve or more of them shall appoint, shall at the command of the said Lords so assembled, or of any twelve or more of them, make and prepare ready for the signature of the said Lords, or any twelve or more of them, under pain of the loss of their places and offices, and of such other punishment as in the next, or any other ensuing Parliament, shall be inflicted on him or them: and it is enacted that the said writs so issued shall be of the same power and force to all intents and purposes, as the writs or summons to Parliament under the Great Seal of England have ever been or ought to be. And all the messengers of the Chamber or others who shall be appointed by the said Lords, or any twelve or more, are hereby required faithfully and speedily to deliver the said writs to every person and persons, sheriffs, officers, and others, to whom the same shall be directed: which if the said messengers or any of them shall fail to perform, they shall forfeit their respective places, and incur such other pains and punishments as by that or any other ensuing Parliament shall be imposed on them.

3. And it is also further enacted, that all and every the peers of this realm shall make their appearance, and shall assemble on the said third Monday in January, in such manner, and to such effect, and with such power, as if they had received every of them writs of summons to Parliament under the Great Seal of England, in the usual and accustomed manner. And in case the said Lords, or twelve or more of them, shall fail to issue forth such writs, or that the said writs do not come to the said several Counties, Cities, Cinque Ports and Boroughs, so that an election be not thereupon made; and in case there be not a Parliament assembled and held before the 23rd day of the said month of January, and so from time to time; and in all times hereafter, if there shall not be a Parliament assembled and held before the said 23rd day of January, then in every such case as aforesaid the Parliament shall assemble, and be held in the usual place at Westminster, in such manner, and by such means only, as is hereafter in this present Act declared and enacted, and not otherwise, on the second Tuesday which shall be in the month of March next after the said 23rd day of January; at which Parliament the peers of this realm shall make their appearance, and shall assemble at the time and place aforesaid, and shall each of them be liable unto such pains and censures for his and their not

appearing and serving then and there in Parliament, as if he or they had
been summoned by writ under the Great Seal of England, and had not appeared and served; and to such further pains and censures, as by the rest of
the peers in Parliament assembled they shall be adjudged unto.

4. And for the better assembling of the knights, citizens, barons, and
burgesses to the said Parliament, as aforesaid, it is further enacted, that the
several and respective sheriffs of the several and respective Counties,
Cities and Boroughs of England and Wales, and the Chancellors, Masters
and Scholars of both and every of the Universities, and the Mayor and Bailiffs of the borough of Berwick upon Tweed, shall at the several courts and
places to be held and appointed for their respective Counties, Universities,
Cities and Boroughs, next after the said 23rd day of January, cause such
knight and knights, citizen and citizens, burgess and burgesses of their said
Counties, Universities, Cities and Boroughs respectively, to be chosen by
such persons, and in such manner, as if several and respective writs of
summons to Parliament, under the Great Seal of England, had issued, and
been awarded. And in case any of the several Sheriffs, or the Chancellors,
Masters and Scholars of either of the Universities, or the Mayor and Bailiffs of Berwick respectively, do not before ten of the clock in the forenoon
of the same day wherein the several and respective courts and places shall
be held or appointed for their several and respective Counties, Universities, Cities and Boroughs as aforesaid, begin and proceed on according to
the meaning of this law, in causing elections to be made of such knight and
knights, citizen and citizens, burgess and burgesses, of their said Counties,
Universities, Cities and Boroughs as aforesaid, then the freeholders of each
County, and the Masters and Scholars of every the Universities, and the
citizens and others having voices in such election respectively, in each University, City and Borough, that shall be assembled at the said courts or
places to be held, or appointed, as aforesaid, shall forthwith, without further warrant or direction, proceed to the election of such knight or knights,
citizen or citizens, burgess or burgesses aforesaid, in such manner as is
usual in cases of writs of summons issued and awarded.

5. And it is further enacted that the several and respective sheriffs of
their several and respective counties, and the Constables of the Castle of
Dover, and Lord Warden of the Cinque Ports, or his lieutenant for the time
being respectively, shall after the said 23rd day of January, and before the
8th day of February then immediately next ensuing, award and send forth
their precepts to the several and respective cities and boroughs within their
several counties, and likewise unto the said Cinque Ports respectively,
commanding them respectively to make choice of such citizen and citizens, barons, burgess and burgesses, to serve in the said Parliament, at the
time and place aforesaid: which said Cities, Cinque Ports and Boroughs

respectively, shall before the last day of the said month of February make election of such citizen and citizens, barons, burgess and burgesses, as if writs for summoning of a Parliament, under the Great Seal of England, has issued and been awarded. And in case no such precept shall come unto the said Cities, Cinque Ports and Boroughs respectively, by the time herein limited: or in case any precept shall come, and no election be made thereupon, before the said last day of February, that then the several citizens, burgesses, and other persons that ought to elect and send citizens, barons, and burgesses to the Parliament, shall on the first Tuesday in March then next ensuing the said last day of February make choice of such citizen and citizens, barons, burgess and burgesses, as if a writ of summons under the Great Seal of England had issued and been awarded, and precepts thereupon issued, to such Cities, Cinque Ports and Boroughs: which knights, citizens, barons and burgesses so chosen shall appear and serve in Parliament at the time and place aforesaid, and shall each of them be liable unto such pains and censures for his and their not appearing and serving then and there in Parliament, as if he or they had been elected and chosen by virtue of a writ under the Great Seal of England, and shall be likewise subject unto such further pains and censures for his and their not appearing and serving then and there in Parliament, as if he or they had been elected and chosen by virtue of a writ under the Great Seal of England, and shall be likewise subject to such further pains and censures as by the rest of the knights, citizens and burgesses assembled in the Commons House of Parliament, he or they shall be adjudged unto. And the sheriffs and other officers and persons to whom it appertaineth shall make returns, and accept and receive the returns of such elections in like manner as if writs of summons had issued, and been executed, as hath been used and accustomed: and in default of the sheriffs and other officers respectively, in not accepting or making return of such elections, it shall and may be lawful to and for the several freeholders, and other persons that have elected, to make returns of the knights, citizens, barons and burgesses by them elected, which shall be as good and effectual to all intents and purposes as if the sheriff or other officers had received a writ of summons for a Parliament, and had made such returns: and that such elections, precepts and returns shall be had and made at such times, by such persons, and in such manner, as before in this Act is expressed and declared, according to the true intent and meaning of this law; any writ, proclamation, edict, act, restraint, inhibition, order or warrant to the contrary in any wise notwithstanding. And in case any person or persons shall be so hardy to advise, frame, contrive, serve or put in execution any such writs, proclamation, edict, act, restraint, inhibition, order or warrant thereupon, then he or they so offending shall incur and sustain the pains, penalties and forfeitures limited, ordained and provided in and by the Statute of Provision and Premunire made in the 16th year of King Richard the Second, and shall from thenceforth be disabled, during his life, to sue and implead any person in any action real or personal, or to make any gift, grant, conveyance, or other disposition of any his lands, tenements, hereditaments, goods or chattels which he hath to his own use, either by act executed in his lifetime, or by his last will, or otherwise, or to take any gift, conveyance, or legacy to his own use: and if any Sheriff, Constable of the Castle of Dover, or Lord Warden of the Cinque Ports, shall not perform his duty enjoined by this Act, then he shall lose and forfeit the sum of £1000, and every County, City, Cinque Port and Borough that shall not make election of their knights, citizens, barons and burgesses, respectively, shall incur the penalties following (that is to say) every County the sum of £1000, and every City, which is no County, £200, and every Cinque Port and Borough the sum of £100; all and every of which several forfeitures, and all other forfeitures in this Act mentioned, shall and may be recovered in any of the King's Courts of Record at Westminster, without naming the Christian name and surname of the said Mayor for the time being, by action of debt, bill, plaint or information, wherein no essoine, protection, wager of law, aid, prayer, privilege, injunction, or order of restraint, shall be in any wise prayed, granted or allowed, nor any more than one imparlance: and if any person after notice given that the action depending is grounded and prosecuted upon or by virtue of this Statute shall cause or procure any such action to be stayed or delayed before judgment by colour or means of any order, warrant, power or authority, save only of the court wherein such action as aforesaid shall be brought or depending, or after judgment had upon such action, shall cause or procure the execution of, or upon any such judgment, to be stayed or delayed by colour or means of any order, warrant, power or authority, save only by writ of error or attaint, that then the said persons so offending shall incur and sustain all and every the pains, penalties and forfeitures, limited, ordained and provided in and by the said Statute of Provision and Premunire, made in the 16th of King Richard the Second. And if any Lord Mayor of London shall at any time hereafter commence or prefer any such suit, action or information, and shall happen to die or be removed out of his office before recovery and execution had, that yet not such action, suit or information, sued, commenced or preferred, shall by such displacing or death be abated, discontinued or ended, but that it shall and may be lawful to and for the Lord Mayor of the City of London next succeeding in that office and place, to prosecute, pursue and follow all and every such action, bill, plaint or information for the causes aforesaid, so hanging and depending in such manner and form, and to all intents and purposes, as that Lord Mayor might have done, which first commenced or preferred the same. The fifth part of all and every the forfeitures in this Act mentioned, shall go and be, to, and for the use and behoof of the City of London, and the other four parts and residue to be employed and disposed to, and for such only uses, intents and purposes as by the knights, citizens and burgesses in Parliament assembled, shall be declared, directed and appointed.

Provided that in case the freeholders of any County and inhabitants, or other persons having or claiming power to make election of any knights, citizens, barons or burgesses, shall proceed to making of election of their knights, citizens, barons and burgesses, which election shall afterwards fall out to be adjudged or declared void in law by the House of Commons, by reason of equality of voices or misdemeanour of any person whatsoever, then the said County, City, Cinque Port or Borough shall not incur the penalties in this law, so as an election *de facto* be made.

6. And it is further enacted, that no Parliament henceforth to be assembled shall be dissolved or prorogued within fifty days at least after the time appointed for the meeting thereof, unless it be by assent of His Majesty, his heirs or successors, and of both Houses in Parliament assembled; and that neither the House of Peers nor the House of Commons shall be adjourned within fifty days at least after the meeting thereof, unless it be by the free consent of every the said Houses respectively.

7. And be it further enacted and declared by authority of this present Parliament, that the Peers to be assembled at any Parliament by virtue of this Act, shall and may from time to time, at any time during such their assembly in Parliament, choose and declare such person to be Speaker for the said Peers as they shall think fit. And likewise that the said knights, citizens and burgesses to be assembled at any Parliament by virtue of this Act, shall and may from time to time, at any time during such their assembly in Parliament, choose and declare one of themselves to be Speaker for the said knights, citizens and burgesses of the House of Commons assembled in the said Parliament as they shall think fit; which said Speakers, and every of them, as well for the said Peers as for the said House of Commons respectively, shall, by virtue of this Act, be perfect and complete Speakers for the said Houses respectively, and shall have as full and large power, jurisdiction and privileges, to all intents and purposes, as any Speaker or Speakers of either of the said Houses respectively, heretofore have had or enjoyed.

8. And it is further enacted and declared, that all Parliaments hereafter to be assembled by authority of this Act and every member thereof shall have and enjoy all rights, privileges, jurisdictions and immunities, as any Parliament summoned by writ under the Great Seal of England, or any member thereof might or ought to have; and all and every the members that shall be elected and chosen to serve in any Parliament hereafter to be as-

sembled by authority of this Act as aforesaid, shall assemble and meet in the Commons House of Parliament, and shall enter into the same, and have voices in such Parliament before and without the taking of the several oaths of supremacy and allegiance, or either of them, any law or statute to the contrary thereof in any wise notwithstanding.

9. Provided always, that if the King's Majesty, his heirs or successors, shall at any time during any Parliament hereafter to be assembled by authority of this Act as aforesaid, award or direct any commission or commissions unto any person or persons whatsoever, thereby giving power and authority to him or them to take and receive the oath of supremacy and allegiance, of all or any the members of the Commons House of Parliament, and any the members of that House being duly required thereunto, shall refuse or neglect to take and pronounce the same, that from thenceforth such person so refusing or neglecting shall be deemed no member of that House, nor shall have any voice therein, and shall suffer such pains and penalties as if he had presumed to sit in the same House without election, return or authority.

10. And it is likewise provided and enacted, that this Statute shall be publicly read yearly at every General Sessions of the Peace, to be held next after the Epiphany, and every Assizes then next ensuing by the Clerk of the Peace and Clerk of the Assizes for the time being respectively. And if they or either of them shall neglect or fail to do the same accordingly, then such party so neglecting or failing shall forfeit the sum of one hundred pounds.

11. And it is lastly provided and enacted, that His Majesty's royal assent to this Bill shall not thereby determine this present Session of Parliament, and that all statutes and Acts of Parliament which are to have continuance unto the end of this present Session, shall be of full force after His Majesty's assent, until this present Session be fully ended nd determined; and if this present Session shall determine by dissolution of this present Parliament, then all the Acts and statutes aforesaid shall be continued until the end of the first Session of the next Parliament.

13. The Grand Remonstrance

The Grand Remonstrance was the culmination of the "constitutional revolution" that marked the first year of the Long Parliament. As a series of grievances, many of which had already been addressed and redressed, it represented the program of the parliamentary reform movement. As a

From S. R. Gardiner, *Constitutional Documents of the Puritan Revolution* (Oxford: The Clarendon Press, 1906), pp. 202–16, 221–33.

history of Charles I's reign, it represented a highly emotional account of the fears of the parliamentarian leaders. As propaganda, it represented an appeal for support, especially in London, for further reformation in church and state. The debate over the passage and publication of the Grand Remonstrance was the first watershed of the revolution. Clarendon sought to enter a formal protestation against its passage while Cromwell averred "that if the Remonstrance had been rejected he would have sold all he had the next morning, and never have seen England more." The debate lasted from nine in the morning until well after midnight and the Remonstrance passed by only eleven votes. On the night of 22 November 1641 the royalist party was born.

The Petition of the House of Commons, Which Accompanied the Remonstrance of the State of the Kingdom, When It Was Presented to His Majesty at Hampton Court, December 1, 1641

Most Gracious Sovereign,

Your Majesty's most humble and faithful subjects the Commons in this present Parliament assembled, do with much thankfulness and joy acknowledge the great mercy and favour of God, in giving your Majesty a safe and peaceable return out of Scotland into your kingdom of England, where the pressing dangers and distempers of the State have caused us with much earnestness to desire the comfort of your gracious presence, and likewise the unity and justice of your royal authority, to give more life and power to the dutiful and loyal counsels and endeavours of your Parliament, for the prevention of that eminent ruin and destruction wherein your kingdoms of England and Scotland are threatened. The duty which we owe to your Majesty and our country, cannot but make us very sensible and apprehensive, that the multiplicity, sharpness and malignity of those evils under which we have now many years suffered, are fomented and cherished by a corrupt and ill-affected party, who amongst other their mischievous devices for the alteration of religion and government, have sought by many false scandals and imputations, cunningly insinuated and dispersed amongst the people, to blemish and disgrace our proceedings in this Parliament, and to get themselves a party and faction amongst your subjects, for the better strengthening themselves in their wicked courses, and hindering those provisions and remedies which might, by the wisdom of your Majesty and counsel of your Parliament, be opposed against them.

For preventing whereof, and the better information of your Majesty, your Peers and all other your loyal subjects, we have been necessitated to make a declaration of the state of the kingdom, both before and since the assembly of this Parliament, unto this time, which we do humbly present to your Majesty, without the least intention to lay any blemish upon your royal person, but only to represent how your royal authority and trust have been abused, to the great prejudice and danger of your Majesty, and of all your good subjects. . . .

We, your most humble and obedient subjects, do with all faithfulness and humility beseech your Majesty,—

1. That you will be graciously pleased to concur with the humble desires of your people in a parliamentary way, for the preserving the peace and safety of the kingdom from the malicious designs of the Popish party:—

For depriving the Bishops of their votes in Parliament, and abridging their immoderate power usurped over the Clergy, and other your good subjects, which they have perniciously abused to the hazard of religion, and great prejudice and oppression to the laws of the kingdom, and just liberty of your people:—

For the taking away such oppressions in religion, Church government and discipline, as have been brought in and fomented by them:—

For uniting all such your loyal subjects together as join in the same fundamental truths against the Papists, by removing some oppressions and unnecessary ceremonies by which divers weak consciences have been scrupled, and seem to be divided from the rest, and for the due execution of those good laws which have been made for securing the liberty of your subjects.

2. That your Majesty will likewise be pleased to remove from your council all such as persist to favour and promote any of those pressures and corruptions wherewith your people have been grieved; and that for the future your Majesty will vouchsafe to employ such persons in your great and public affairs, and to take such to be near you in places of trust, as your Parliament may have cause to confide in; that in your princely goodness to your people you will reject and refuse all mediation and solicitation to the contrary, how powerful and near soever.

3. That you will be pleased to forbear to alienate any of the forfeited and escheated lands in Ireland which shall accrue to your Crown by reason of this rebellion, that out of them the Crown may be the better supported, and some satisfaction made to your subjects of this kingdom for the great expenses they are like to undergo [in] this war.

Which humble desires of ours being graciously fulfilled by your Majesty, we will, by the blessing and favour of God, most cheerfully undergo the hazard and expenses of this war, and apply ourselves to such other courses and counsels as may support your real estate with honour and plenty at home, with power and reputation abroad, and by our loyal affections, obedience and service, lay a sure and lasting foundation of the greatness and prosperity of your Majesty, and your royal posterity in future times.

The Grand Remonstrance

The Commons in this present Parliament assembled, having with much earnestness and faithfulness of affection and zeal to the public good of this kingdom, and His Majesty's honour and service, for the space of twelve months wrestled with great dangers and fears, the pressing miseries and calamities, the various distempers and disorders which had not only assaulted, but even overwhelmed and extinguished the liberty, peace and prosperity of this kingdom, the comfort and hopes of all His Majesty's good subjects, and exceedingly weakened and undermined the foundation and strength of his own royal throne, do yet find an abounding malignity and opposition in those parties and factions who have been the cause of those evils, and do still labour to cast aspersions upon that which hath been done, and to raise many difficulties for the hindrance of that which remains yet undone, and to foment jealousies between the King and Parliament, that so they may deprive him and his people of the fruit of his own gracious intentions, and their humble desires of procuring the public peace, safety and happiness of this realm.

For the preventing of those miserable effects which such malicious endeavours may produce, we have thought good to declare the root and the growth of these mischievous designs: the maturity and ripeness to which they have attained before the beginning of the Parliament: the effectual means which have been used for the extirpation of those dangerous evils, and the progress which hath therein been made by His Majesty's goodness and the wisdom of the Parliament: the ways of obstruction and opposition by which that progress hath been interrupted: the courses to be taken for the removing those obstacles, and for the accomplishing of our most dutiful and faithful intentions and endeavours of restoring and establishing the ancient honour, greatness and security of this Crown and nation.

The root of all this mischief we find to be a malignant and pernicious design of subverting the fundamental laws and principles of government, upon which the religion and justice of this kingdom are firmly established. The actors and promoters hereof have been:

1. The Jesuited Papists, who hate the laws, as the obstacles of that change and subversion of religion which they so much long for.

2. The Bishops, and the corrupt part of the Clergy, who cherish formality and superstition as the natural effects and more probable supports of their own ecclesiastical tyranny and usurpation.

3. Such Councillors and Courtiers as for private ends have engaged

themselves to further the interests of some foreign princes or states to the prejudice of His Majesty and the State at home. . . .

4. The first effect and evidence of their recovery and strength was the dissolution of the Parliament at Oxford, after there had been given two subsidies to His Majesty, and before they received relief in any one grievance many other more miserable effects followed.

5. The peace with Spain without consent of Parliament, contrary to the promise of King James to both Houses, whereby the Palatine's cause was deserted and left to chargeable and hopeless treaties, which for the most part were managed by those who might justly be suspected to be no friends to that cause.

6. The charging of the kingdom with billeted soldiers in all parts of it, and the concomitant design of German horse, that the land might either submit with fear or be enforced with rigour to such arbitrary contributions as should be required of them.

7. The dissolving of the Parliament in the second year of His Majesty's reign, after a declaration of their intent to grant five subsidies.

8. The exacting of the like proportion of five subsidies, after the Parliament dissolved, by commission of loan, and divers gentlemen and others imprisoned for not yielding to pay that loan, whereby many of them contracted such sicknesses as cost them their lives.

9. Great sums of money required and raised by privy seals.

10. An unjust and pernicious attempt to extort great payments from the subject by way of excise, and a commission issued under the seal to that purpose.

11. The Petition of Right, which was granted in full Parliament, blasted, with an illegal declaration to make it destructive to itself, to the power of Parliament, to the liberty of the subject, and to that purpose printed with it, and the Petition made of no use but to show the bold and presumptuous injustice of such ministers as durst break the laws and suppress the liberties of the kingdom, after they had been so solemnly and evidently declared.

12. Another Parliament dissolved 4 Car., the privilege of Parliament broken, by imprisoning divers members of the House, detaining them close prisoners for many months together, without the liberty of using books, pen, ink or paper; denying them all the comforts of life, all means of preservation of health, not permitting their wives to come unto them even in the time of their sickness. . . .

18. Tonnage and Poundage hath been received without colour or pretence of law; many other heavy impositions continued against law, and some so unreasonable that the sum of the charge exceeds the value of the goods.

19. The Book of Rates lately enhanced to a high proportion, and such merchants that would not submit to their illegal and unreasonable payments,

were vexed and oppressed above measure; and the ordinary course of justice, the common birthright of the subject of England, wholly obstructed unto them.

20. And although all this was taken upon pretence of guarding the seas, yet a new unheard-of tax of ship-money was devised, and upon the same pretence, by both which there was charged upon the subject near £700,000 some years, and yet the merchants have been left so naked to the violence of the Turkish pirates, that many great ships of value and thousands of His Majesty's subjects have been taken by them, and do still remain in miserable slavery.

21. The enlargements of forests, contrary to *Carta de Foresta,* and the composition thereupon.

22. The exactions of coat and conduct money and divers other military charges.

23. The taking away the arms of trained bands of divers counties. . . .

27. The monopolies of soap, salt, wine, leather, sea-coal, and in a manner of all things of most common and necessary use. . . .

34. Great numbers of His Majesty's subjects for refusing those unlawful charges, have been vexed with long and expensive suits, some fined and censured, others committed to long and hard imprisonments and confinements, to the loss of health in many, of life in some, and others have had their houses broken up, their goods seized, some have been restrained from their lawful callings. . . .

37. The Court of Star Chamber hath abounded in extravagant censures, not only for the maintenance and improvement of monopolies and their unlawful taxes, but for divers other causes where there hath been no offence, or very small; whereby His Majesty's subjects have been oppressed by grievous fines, imprisonments, stigmatisings, mutilations, whippings, pillories, gags, confinements, banishments; after so rigid a manner as hath not only deprived men of the society of their friends, exercise of their professions, comfort of books, use of paper or ink, but even violated that near union which God hath established between men and their wives, by forced and constrained separation, whereby they have been bereaved of the comfort and conversation one of another for many years together, without hope of relief, if God had not by His overruling providence given some interruption to the prevailing power, and counsel of those who were the authors and promoters of such peremptory and heady courses.

38. Judges have been put out of their places for refusing to do against their oaths and consciences; others have been so awed that they durst not do their duties, and the better to hold a rod over them, the clause *Quam diu se bene gesserit* was left out of their patents, and a new clause *Durante bene placito* inserted.

39. Lawyers have been checked for being faithful to their clients; solic-

itors and attorneys have been threatened, and some punished, for following lawful suits. And by this means all the approaches to justice were interrupted and foreclosed. . . .

51. The Bishops and the rest of the Clergy did triumph in the suspensions, excommunications, deprivations, and degradations of divers painful, learned and pious ministers, in the vexation and grievous oppression of great numbers of His Majesty's good subjects.

52. The High Commission grew to such excess of sharpness and severity as was not much less than the Romish Inquisition, and yet in many cases by the Archbishop's power was made much more heavy, being assisted and strengthened by authority of the Council Table. . . .

54. And so afflict and trouble others, that great numbers to avoid their miseries departed out of the kingdom, some into New England and other parts of America, others into Holland, . . .

57. The most public and solemn sermons before His Majesty were either to advance prerogative above law, and decry the property of the subject, or full of such kind of invectives.

58. Whereby they might make those odious who sought to maintain the religion, laws and liberties of the kingdom, and such men were sure to be weeded out of the commission of the peace, and out of all other employments of power in the government of the country.

59. Many noble personages were councillors in name, but the power and authority remained in a few of such as were most addicted to this party, whose resolutions and determinations were brought to the table for countenance and execution, and not for debate and deliberation, and no man could offer to oppose them without disgrace and hazard to himself.

60. Nay, all those that did not wholly concur and actively contribute to the furtherance of their designs, though otherwise persons of never so great honour and abilities, were so far from being employed in any place of trust and power, that they were neglected, discountenanced, and upon all occasions injured and oppressed.

61. This faction was grown to that height and entireness of power, that now they began to think of finishing their work, which consisted of these three parts.

62. I. The government must be set free from all restraint of laws concerning our persons and estates.

63. II. There must be a conjunction between Papists and Protestants in doctrine, discipline and ceremonies; only it must not yet be called Popery.

64. III. The Puritans, under which name they include all those that desire to preserve the laws and liberties of the kingdom, and to maintain religion in the power of it, must be either rooted out of the kingdom with force, or driven out with fear. . . .

106. The multiplied evils and corruption of fifteen years, strengthened by custom and authority, and the concurrent interest of many powerful delinquents, were now to be brought to judgment and reformation. . . .

110. The difficulties seemed to be insuperable, which by the Divine Providence we have overcome. The contrarieties incompatible, which yet in a great measure we have reconciled. . . .

113. The ship-money is abolished, which cost the kingdom about £200,000 a year.

114. The coat and conduct-money, and other military charges are taken away, which in many countries amounted to little less than the ship-money.

115. The monopolies are all suppressed, whereof some few did prejudice the subject, above £1,000,000 yearly. . . .

120. That which is more beneficial than all this is, that the root of these evils is taken away, which was the arbitrary power pretended to be in His Majesty of taxing the subject, or charging their estates without consent in Parliament, which is now declared to be against law by the judgment of both Houses, and likewise by an Act of Parliament.

121. Another step of great advantage is this, the living grievances, the evil counsellors and actors of these mischiefs have been so quelled.

122. By the justice done upon the Earl of Strafford, the flight of the Lord Finch and Secretary Windebanck,

123. The accusation and imprisonment of the Archbishop of Canterbury, of Judge Berkeley; and

124. The impeachment of divers other Bishops and Judges, that it is like not only to be an ease to the present times, but a preservation to the future.

125. The discontinuance of Parliaments is prevented by the Bill for a triennial Parliament, and the abrupt dissolution of this Parliament by another Bill, by which it is provided it shall not be dissolved or adjourned without the consent of both Houses.

126. Which two laws well considered may be thought more advantageous than all the former, because they secure a full operation of the present remedy, and afford a perpetual spring of remedies for the future.

127. The Star Chamber.

128. The High Commission.

129. The Courts of the President and Council in the North were so many forges of misery, oppression and violence, and are all taken away, whereby men are more secured in their persons, liberties and estates, than they could be by any law or example for the regulation of those Courts or terror of the Judges.

130. The immoderate power of the Council Table, and the excessive abuse of that power is so ordered and restrained, that we may well hope that no such things as were frequently done by them, to the prejudice of the

public liberty, will appear in future times but only in stories, to give us and our posterity more occasion to praise God for His Majesty's goodness, and the faithful endeavours of this Parliament.

131. The canons and power of canon-making are blasted by the votes of both Houses.

132. The exorbitant power of Bishops and their courts are much abated, by some provisions in the Bill against the High Commission Court, the authors of the many innovations in doctrine and ceremonies.

133. The ministers that have been scandalous in their lives, have been so terrified in just complaints and accusations, that we may well hope they will be more modest for the time to come; either inwardly convicted by the sight of their own folly, or outwardly restrained by the fear of punishment.

134. The forests are by a good law reduced to their right bounds.

135. The encroachments and oppressions of the Stannary Courts, the extortions of the clerk of the market.

136. And the compulsion of the subject to receive the Order of Knighthood against his will, paying of fines for not receiving it, and the vexatious proceedings thereupon for levying of those fines, are by other beneficial laws reformed and prevented.

137. Many excellent laws and provisions are in preparation for removing the inordinate power, vexation and usurpation of Bishops, for reforming the pride and idleness of many of the clergy, for easing the people of unnecessary ceremonies in religion, for censuring and removing unworthy and unprofitable ministers, and for maintaining godly and diligent preachers through the kingdom. . . .

140. The regulating of courts of justice, and abridging both the delays and charges of law-suits. . . .

143. The oppositions, obstructions and the difficulties wherewith we have been encountered, and which still lie in our way with some strength and much obstinacy, are these; the malignant party whom we have formerly described to be the actors and promotors of all our misery, they have taken heart again.

144. They have been able to prefer some of their own factors and agents to degrees of honour, to places of trust and employment, even during the Parliament.

145. They have endeavoured to work in His Majesty ill impressions and opinions of our proceedings, as if we had altogether done our own work, and not his; and had obtained from him many things very prejudicial to the Crown, both in respect of prerogative and profit.

146. To wipe out this slander we think good only to say thus much: that all that we have done is for His Majesty, his greatness, honour and support, when we yield to give £25,000 a month for the relief of the Northern Counties; this was given to the King, for he was bound to protect his subjects.

147. They were His Majesty's evil counsellors, and their ill instruments that were actors in those grievances which brought in the Scots.

148. And if His Majesty please to force those who were the authors of this war to make satisfaction, as he might justly and easily do, it seems very reasonable that the people might well be excused from taking upon them this burden, being altogether innocent and free from being any cause of it. . . .

154. As to the second branch of this slander, we acknowledge with much thankfulness that His Majesty hath passed more good Bills to the advantage of the subjects than have been in many ages.

155. But withal we cannot forget that these venomous councils did manifest themselves in some endeavours to hinder these good acts.

156. And for both Houses of Parliament we may with truth and modesty say this much: that we have ever been careful not to desire anything that should weaken the Crown either in just profit or useful power.

157. The triennial Parliament for the matter of it, doth not extend to so much as by law we ought to have required (there being two statutes still in force for a Parliament to be once a year), and for the manner of it, it is in the King's power that it shall never take effect, if he by a timely summons shall prevent any other way of assembling.

158. In the Bill for continuance of this present Parliament, there seems to be some restraint of the royal power in dissolving of Parliaments, not to take it out of the Crown, but to suspend the execution of it for this time and occasion only: which was so necessary for the King's own security and the public peace, that without it we could not have undertaken any of these great charges, but must have left both the armies to disorder and confusion, and the whole kingdom to blood and rapine. . . .

162. They have sought to diminish our reputation with the people, and to bring them out of love with Parliaments.

163. The aspersions which they have attempted this way have been such as these:

164. That we have spent much time and done little, especially in those grievances which concern religion.

165. That the Parliament is a burden to the kingdom by the abundance of protections which hinder justice and trade; and by many subsidies granted much more heavy than any formerly endured.

166. To which there is a ready answer; if the time spent in this Parliament be considered in relation backward to the long growth and deep root of those grievances, which we have removed, to the powerful supports of those delinquents, which we have pursued, to the great necessities and other charges of the commonwealth for which we have provided.

167. Or if it be considered in relation forward to many advantages, which not only the present but future ages are like to reap by the good laws

and other proceedings in this Parliament, we doubt not but it will be thought by all indifferent judgments, that our time hath been much better employed than in a far greater proportion of time in many former Parliaments put together; and the charges which have been laid upon the subject, and the other inconveniences which they have borne, will seem very light in respect of the benefit they have and may receive.

168. And for the matter of protections, the Parliament is so sensible of it that therein they intended to give them whatsoever ease may stand with honour and justice, and are in a way of passing a Bill to give them satisfaction.

169. They have sought by many subtle practices to cause jealousies and divisions betwixt us and our brethren of Scotland, by slandering their proceedings and intentions towards us, and by secret endeavours to instigate and incense them and us one against another. . . .

1,76. Only in Ireland, which was farther off, they have had time and opportunity to mould and prepare their work, and had brought it to that perfection that they had possessed themselves of that whole kingdom, totally subverted the government of it, routed out religion, and destroyed all the Protestants whom the conscience of their duty to God, their King and country, would not have permitted to join with them, if by God's wonderful providence their main enterprise upon the city and castle of Dublin had not been detected and prevented upon the very eve before it should have been executed.

177. Notwithstanding they have in other parts of that kingdom broken out into open rebellion, surprising towns and castles, committed murders, rapes and other villainies, and shaken off all bonds of obedience to His Majesty and the laws of the realm.

178. And in general have kindled such a fire, as nothing but God's infinite blessing upon the wisdom and endeavours of this State will be able to quench it.

179. And certainly had not God in His great mercy unto this land discovered and confounded their former designs, we had been the prologue to this tragedy in Ireland, and had by this been made the lamentable spectacle of misery and confusion.

180. And now what hope have we but in God, when as the only means of our subsistence and power of reformation is under Him in the Parliament?

181. But what can we the Commons, without the conjunction of the House of Lords, and what conjunction can we expect there, when the Bishops and recusant lords are so numerous and prevalent that they are able to cross and interrupt our best endeavours for reformation, and by that means give advantage to this malignant party to traduce our proceedings?

182. They infuse into the people that we mean to abolish all Church

government, and leave every man to his own fancy for the service and worship of God, absolving him of that obedience which he owes under God unto His Majesty, whom we know to be entrusted with the ecclesiastical law as well as with the temporal, to regulate all the members of the Church of England, by such rules of order and discipline as are established by Parliament, which is his great council, in all affairs both in Church and State.

183. We confess our intention is, and our endeavours have been, to reduce within bounds that exorbitant power which the prelates have assumed unto themselves, so contrary both to the Word of God and to the laws of the land, to which end we passed the Bill for the removing them from their temporal power and employments, that so the better they might with meekness apply themselves to the discharge of their functions, which Bill themselves opposed, and were the principal instruments of crossing it.

184. And we do here declare that it is far from our purpose or desire to let loose the golden reins of discipline and government in the Church, to leave private persons or particular congregations to take up what form of Divine Service they please, for we hold it requisite that there should be throughout the whole realm a conformity to that order which the laws enjoin according to the Word of God. And we desire to unburden the consciences of men of needless and superstitious ceremonies, suppress innovations, and take away the monuments of idolatry.

185. And the better to effect the intended reformation, we desire there may be a general synod of the most grave, pious, learned and judicious divines of this island; assisted with some from foreign parts, professing the same religion with us, who may consider of all things necessary for the peace and good government of the Church, and represent the results of their consultations unto the Parliament, to be there allowed of and confirmed, and receive the stamp of authority, thereby to find passage and obedience throughout the kingdom. . . .

188. They have strained to blast our proceedings in Parliament, by wresting the interpretations of our orders from their genuine intention.

189. They tell the people that our meddling with the power of episcopacy hath caused sectaries and conventicles, when idolatrous and Popish ceremonies, introduced into the Church by the command of the Bishops, have not only debarred the people from thence, but expelled them from the kingdom.

190. Thus with Elijah, we are called by this malignant party the troublers of the State, and still, while we endeavour to reform their abuses, they make us the authors of those mischiefs we study to prevent.

191. For the perfecting of the work begun, and removing all future impediments, we conceive these courses will be very effectual, seeing the religion of the Papists hath such principles as do certainly tend to the destruc-

tion and extirpation of all Protestants, when they shall have opportunity to effect it.

192. It is necessary in the first place to keep them in such condition as that they may not be able to do us any hurt, and for avoiding of such connivance and favour as hath heretofore been shown unto them.

193. That His Majesty be pleased to grant a standing Commission to some choice men named in Parliament, who may take notice of their increase, their counsels and proceedings, and use all due means by execution of the laws to prevent all mischievous designs against the peace and safety of this kingdom.

194. Thus some good course be taken to discover the counterfeit and false conformity of Papists to the Church, by colour whereof persons very much disaffected to the true religion have been admitted into place of greatest authority and trust in the kingdom.

195. For the better preservation of the laws and liberties of the kingdom, that all illegal grievances and exactions be presented and punished at the sessions and assizes.

196. And that Judges and Justices be very careful to give this in charge to the grand jury, and both the Sheriff and Justices to be sworn to the due execution of the Petition of Right and other laws.

197. That His Majesty be humbly petitioned by both Houses to employ such councillors, ambassadors and other ministers, in managing his business at home and abroad as the Parliament may have cause to confide in, without which we cannot give His Majesty such supplies for support of his own estate, nor such assistance to the Protestant party beyond the sea, as is desired.

198. It may often fall out that the Commons may have just cause to take exceptions at some men for being councillors, and yet not charge those men with crimes, for there be grounds of diffidence which lie not in proof.

199. There are others, which though they may be proved, yet are not legally criminal.

200. To be a known favourer of Papists, or to have been very forward in defending or countenancing some great offenders questioned in Parliament; or to speak contemptuously of either Houses of Parliament or Parliamentary proceedings.

201. Or such as are factors or agents for any foreign prince of another religion; such are justly suspected to get councillors' places, or any other of trust concerning public employment for money; for all these and divers others we may have great reason to be earnest with His Majesty, not to put his great affairs into such hands, though we may be unwilling to proceed against them in any legal way of charge or impeachment.

202. That all Councillors of State may be sworn to observe those laws

which concern the subject in his liberty, that they may likewise take an oath not to receive or give reward or pension from any foreign prince, but such as they shall within some reasonable time discover to the Lords of His Majesty's Council.

203. And although they should wickedly forswear themselves, yet it may herein do good to make them known to be false and perjured to those who employ them, and thereby bring them into as little credit with them as with us.

204. That His Majesty may have cause to be in love with good counsel and good men, by showing him in an humble and dutiful manner how full of advantage it would be to himself, to see his own estate settled in a plentiful condition to support his honour; to see his people united in ways of duty to him, and endeavours of the public good; to see happiness, wealth, peace and safety derived to his own kingdom, and procured to his allies by the influence of his own power and government.

14. The King's Answer to the Grand Remonstrance

The Grand Remonstrance was presented to the king on December 1 but not answered until the 23d. During those four weeks, Charles I was faced with the most extreme alternatives and subject to unrelenting pressures from among his supporters and opponents. His wife, Queen Henrietta Maria, and the leaders of the emerging royalist party demanded that he regain the initiative against Parliament with a bold stroke. Others among his council pleaded that he make this one, last concession and accept the Remonstrance with good grace. In London, mobs were whipped to frenzy with tales of impending calamities. They congregated around Whitehall, where the king resided, and the Palace of Westminster, where the houses of Parliament sat. Their conduct and the potential force that they represented heightened the political tensions. Their presence made it impossible for the bishops to attend the Lords and difficult for others known to support the king. By the time that Charles submitted his response he had determined upon decisive action. On 3 January 1642 he ordered the impeachment of five leaders of the lower house (and the earl of Manchester) and on January 4 he appeared in the Commons himself to arrest them. This bungled attempt on the five members led to the king's withdrawal from London and his subsequent decision to try the mettle of the parliamentary opposition on the field of battle.

From S. R. Gardiner, *Constitutional Documents of the Puritan Revolution* (Oxford: The Clarendon Press, 1906), pp. 233–37.

We having received from you, soon after our return out of Scotland, a long petition consisting of many desires of great moment, together with a declaration of a very unusual nature annexed thereunto, we had taken some time to consider of it, as befitted us in a matter of that consequence, being confident that your own reason and regard to us, as well as our express intimation by our comptroller, to that purpose, would have restrained you from the publishing of it till such time as you should have received our answer to it; but, much against our expectation, finding the contrary, that the said declaration is already abroad in print, by directions from your House as appears by the printed copy, we must let you know that we are very sensible of the disrespect. Notwithstanding, it is our intention that no failing on your part shall make us fail in ours of giving all due satisfaction to the desires of our people in a parliamentary way; and therefore we send you this answer to your petition, reserving ourself in point of the declaration which we think unparliamentary, and shall take a course to do that which we shall think fit in prudence and honour.

To the petition, we say that although there are divers things in the preamble of it which we are so far from admitting that we profess we cannot at all understand them, as of "a wicked and malignant party prevalent in the government"; of "some of that party admitted to our Privy Council and to other employments of trust, and nearest to us and our children"; of "endeavours to sow among the people false scandals and imputations, to blemish and disgrace the proceedings of the Parliament"; all, or any of them, did we know of, we should be as ready to remedy and punish as you to complain of, so that the prayers of your petition are grounded upon such premises as we must in no wise admit; yet, notwithstanding, we are pleased to give this answer to you.

To the first, concerning religion, consisting of several branches, we say that, for preserving the peace and safety of this kingdom from the design of the Popish party, we have, and will still, concur with all the just desires of our people in a parliamentary way: that, for the depriving of the Bishops of their votes in Parliament, we would have you consider that their right is grounded upon the fundamental law of the kingdom and constitution of Parliament. This we would have you consider; but since you desire our concurrence herein in a parliamentary way, we will give no further answer at this time.

As for the abridging of the inordinate power of the clergy, we conceive that the taking away of the High Commission Court hath well moderated that; but if there continue any usurpations or excesses in their jurisdictions, we therein neither have nor will protect them.

Unto that clause which concerneth corruptions (as you style them) in religion, in Church government, and in discipline, and the removing of such unnecessary ceremonies as weak consciences might check at: that for any illegal innovations which may have crept in, we shall willingly concur in the removal of them: that, if our Parliament shall advise us to call a national synod, which may duly examine such ceremonies as give just cause of offence to any, we shall take it into consideration, and apply ourself to give due satisfaction therein; but we are very sorry to hear, in such general terms, corruption in religion objected, since we are persuaded in our consciences that no Church can be found upon the earth that professeth the true religion with more purity of doctrine than the Church of England doth, nor where the government and discipline are jointly more beautified and free from superstition, than as they are here established by law, which, by the grace of God, we will with constancy maintain (while we live) in their purity and glory, not only against all invasions of Popery, but also from the irreverence of those many schismatics and separatists, wherewith of late this kingdom and this city abounds, to the great dishonour and hazard both of Church and State, for the suppression of whom we require your timely aid and active assistance.

To the second prayer of the petition, concerning the removal and choice of councillors, we know not any of our Council to whom the character set forth in the petition can belong: that by those whom we had exposed to trial, we have already given you sufficient testimony that there is no man so near unto us in place or affection, whom we will not leave to the justice of the law, if you shall bring a particular charge and sufficient proofs against him; and of this we do again assure you, but in the meantime we wish you to forbear such general aspersions as may reflect upon all our Council, since you name none in particular.

That for the choice of our councillors and ministers of state, it were to debar us that natural liberty all freemen have; and as it is the undoubted right of the Crown of England to call such persons to our secret counsels, to public employment and our particular service as we shall think fit, so we are, and ever shall be, very careful to make election of such persons in those places of trust as shall have given good testimonies of their abilities and integrity, and against whom there can be no just cause of exception whereon reasonably to ground a diffidence; and to choices of this nature, we assure you that the mediation of the nearest unto us hath always concurred.

To the third prayer of your petition concerning Ireland, we understand your desire of not alienating the forfeited lands thereof, to proceed from much care and love, and likewise that it may be a resolution very fit for us to take; but whether it be seasonable to declare resolutions of that nature before the events of a war be seen, that we much doubt of. Howsoever, we cannot but thank you for this care, and your cheerful engagement for the suppression of that rebellion; upon the speedy effecting whereof, the glory of God in the Protestant profession, the safety of the British there, our honour, and that of the nation, so much depends; all the interests of this kingdom being so involved in that business, we cannot but quicken your affections therein, and shall desire you to frame your counsels, to give such expedition to the work as the nature thereof and the pressures in point of time require; and whereof you are put in mind by the daily insolence and increase of those rebels.

For conclusion, your promise to apply yourselves to such courses as may support our royal estate with honour and plenty at home, and with power and reputation abroad, is that which we have ever promised ourself, both from your loyalties and affections, and also for what we have already done, and shall daily go adding unto, for the comfort and happiness of our people.

From Civil War to Revolution

15. The Nineteen Propositions (1 June 1642)

After the king left London in January 1642 he marched north hoping to attract large crowds of supporters in the vast hinterland of his realm. While he was not disappointed at the enthusiastic assemblies that greeted him on his progress, it was plain that there was as much curiosity as genuine loyalty. During the winter months both king and Parliament jockeyed for position, the king setting out the case for monarchical government against parliamentary usurpation and Parliament setting out the case for the restraint of tyranny and the protection of liberties. This war of words soon gave way to the first tentative steps toward a war of flesh and steel. In June Parliament decided upon a set of conditions, built upon the Ten Propositions of the previous year, under which they would welcome the king back to London. As with all parliamentary peace proposals throughout the Civil War, the Nineteen Propositions were a compromise between the hard line group within Parliament who felt that the king could not be trusted, especially after the attempt on the five members, and must be defeated on the battlefield, and the moderates who believed that any peace treaty was preferable to full-scale fighting. These two groups, of war and of peace, sent contradictory signals to the king and the propositions they produced jointly over the next three years were a

From S. R. Gardiner, *Constitutional Documents of the Puritan Revolution* (Oxford: The Clarendon Press, 1906), pp. 250–55.

curious mixture of sternness and submission; of doubt and defiance; of hope and despair.

Your Majesty's most humble and faithful subjects, the Lords and Commons in Parliament, having nothing in their thoughts and desires more precious and of higher esteem (next to the honour and immediate service of God) than the just and faithful performance of their duty to your Majesty and this kingdom: and being very sensible of the great distractions and distempers, and of the imminent dangers and calamities which those distractions and distempers are like to bring upon your Majesty and your subjects; all which have proceeded from the subtile insinuations, mischievous practices and evil counsels of men disaffected to God's true religion, your Majesty's honour and safety, and the public peace and prosperity of your people, after a serious observation of the causes of those mischiefs, do in all humility and sincerity present to your Majesty their most dutiful petition and advice, that out of your princely wisdom for the establishing your own honour and safety, and gracious tenderness of the welfare and security of your subjects and dominions, you will be pleased to grant and accept these their humble desires and propositions, as the most necessary effectual means, through God's blessing, of removing those jealousies and differences which have unhappily fallen betwixt you and your people, and procuring both your Majesty and them a constant course of honour, peace, and happiness.

The Nineteen Propositions

1. That the Lords and others of your Majesty's Privy Council, and such great officers and Ministers of State, either at home or beyond the seas, may be put from your Privy Council, and from those offices and employments, excepting such as shall be approved of by both Houses of Parliament; and that the persons put into the places and employments of those that are removed may be approved of by both Houses of Parliament; and that the Privy Councillors shall take an oath for the due execution of their places, in such form as shall be agreed upon by both Houses of Parliament.

2. That the great affairs of the kingdom may not be concluded or transacted by the advice of private men, or by any unknown or unsworn councillors, but that such matters as concern the public, and are proper for the High Court of Parliament, which is your Majesty's great and supreme council, may be debated, resolved and transacted only in Parliament, and not elsewhere: and such as shall presume to do anything to the contrary shall be reserved to the censure and judgment of Parliament: and such other matters of state as are proper for your Majesty's Privy Council shall be debated and concluded by such of the nobility and others as shall from time to

time be chosen for that place, by approbation of both Houses of Parliament: and that no public act concerning the affairs of the kingdom, which are proper for your Privy Council, may be esteemed of any validity, as proceeding from the royal authority, unless it be done by the advice and consent of the major part of your Council, attested under their hands: and that your Council may be limited to a certain number, not exceeding five and twenty, nor under fifteen: and if any councillor's place happen to be void in the interval of Parliament, it shall not be supplied without the assent of the major part of the Council, which choice shall be confirmed at the next sitting of Parliament, or else to be void.

3. That the Lord High Steward of England, Lord High Constable, Lord Chancellor, or Lord Keeper of the Great Seal, Lord Treasurer, Lord Privy Seal, Earl Marshall, Lord Admiral, Warden of the Cinque Ports, Chief Governor of Ireland, Chancellor of the Exchequer, Master of the Wards, Secretaries of State, two Chief Justices and Chief Baron, may always be chosen with the approbation of both Houses of Parliament; and in the intervals of Parliament, by assent of the major part of the Council, in such manner as is before expressed in the choice of councillors.

4. That he, or they unto whom the government and education of the King's children shall be committed, shall be approved of by both Houses of Parliament; and in the intervals of Parliament, by the assent of the major part of the Council, in such manner as is before expressed in the choice of councillors; and that all such servants as are now about them, against whom both Houses shall have any just exceptions, shall be removed.

5. That no marriage shall be concluded or treated for any of the King's children, with any foreign prince, or other person whatsoever, abroad or at home, without the consent of Parliament, under the penalty of a premunire, upon such as shall conclude or treat of any marriage as aforesaid; and that the said penalty shall not be pardoned or dispensed with but by the consent of both Houses of Parliament.

6. That the laws in force against Jesuits, priests, and Popish recusants, be strictly put in execution, without any toleration or dispensation to the contrary; and that some more effectual course may be enacted, by authority of Parliament, to disable them from making any disturbance in the State, or eluding the law by trusts or otherwise.

7. That the votes of Popish lords in the House of Peers may be taken away, so long as they continue Papists: and that your Majesty will consent to such a Bill as shall be drawn for the education of the children of Papists by Protestants in the Protestant religion.

8. That your Majesty will be pleased to consent that such a reformation be made of the Church government and liturgy, as both Houses of Parliament shall advise; wherein they intend to have consultations with divines,

as is expressed in their declaration to that purpose; and that your Majesty will contribute your best assistance to them, for the raising of a sufficient maintenance for preaching ministers throughout the kingdom; and that your Majesty will be pleased to give your consent to laws for the taking away of innovations and superstition, and of pluralities, and against scandalous ministers.

9. That your Majesty will be pleased to rest satisfied with that course that the Lords and Commons have appointed for ordering of the militia, until the same shall be further settled by a Bill; and that your Majesty will recall your Declarations and Proclamations against the Ordinance made by the Lords and Commons concerning it.

10. That such members of either House of Parliament as have, during the present Parliament, been put out of any place and office, may either be restored to that place and office, or otherwise have satisfaction for the same, upon the petition of that House whereof he or they are members.

11. That all Privy Councillors and Judges may take an oath, the form whereof to be agreed on and settled by Act of Parliament, for the maintaining of the Petition of Right and of certain statutes made by the Parliament, which shall be mentioned by both Houses of Parliament: and that an enquiry of all the breaches and violations of those laws may be given in charge by the Justices of the King's Bench every Term, and by the Judges of Assize in their circuits, and Justices of the Peace at the sessions, to be presented and punished according to law.

12. That all the Judges, and all the officers placed by approbation of both Houses of Parliament, may hold their places *quam diu bene se gesserint*.

13. That the justice of Parliament may pass upon all delinquents, whether they be within the kingdom or fled out of it; and that all persons cited by either House of Parliament may appear and abide the censure of Parliament.

14. That the general pardon offered by your Majesty may be granted, with such exceptions as shall be advised by both Houses of Parliament.

15. That the forts and castles of this kingdom may be put under the command and custody of such persons as your Majesty shall appoint, with the approbation of your Parliament: and in the intervals of Parliament, with approbation of the major part of the Council, in such manner as is before expressed in the choice of councillors.

16. That the extraordinary guards and military forces now attending your Majesty, may be removed and discharged; and that for the future you will raise no such guards or extraordinary forces, but according to the law, in case of actual rebellion or invasion.

17. That your Majesty will be pleased to enter into a more strict alliance with the States of the United Provinces, and other neighbouring princes

and states of the Protestant religion, for the defence and maintenance thereof, against all designs and attempts of the Pope and his adherents to subvert and suppress it; whereby your Majesty will obtain a great access of strength and reputation, and your subjects be much encouraged and enabled, in a Parliamentary way, for your aid and assistance, in restoring your royal sister and her princely issue to those dignities and dominions which belong unto them, and relieving the other Protestant princes who have suffered in the same cause.

18. That your Majesty will be pleased, by Act of Parliament, to clear the Lord Kimbolton and the five members of the House of Commons, in such manner that future Parliaments may be secured from the consequence of that evil precedent.

19. That your Majesty will be graciously pleased to pass a Bill for restraining peers made hereafter, from sitting or voting in Parliament, unless they be admitted thereunto with the consent of both Houses of Parliament.

And these our humble desires being granted by your Majesty, we shall forthwith apply ourselves to regulate your present revenue in such sort as may be for your best advantage; and likewise to settle such an ordinary and constant increase of it, as shall be sufficient to support your royal dignity in honour and plenty, beyond the proportion of any former grants of the subjects of this kingdom to your Majesty's royal predecessors. We shall likewise put the town of Hull into such hands as your Majesty shall appoint, with the consent and approbation of Parliament, and deliver up a just account of all the magazine, and cheerfully employ the uttermost of our power and endeavours in the real expression and performance of our most dutiful and loyal affections, to the preserving and maintaining the royal honour, greatness and safety of your Majesty and your posterity.

16. The King's Answer to the Nineteen Propositions

Belief by the king and his chief advisors that they were capable of defeating Parliament on the battlefield led to the stinging rejection of the Nineteen Propositions and the publication of the king's response. It is clear, however, that *His Majesties Reply* was not written by Charles I who now relied entirely upon those who urged him to reject all compromise with Parliament. The major part of the reply was a point by point refutation of parliamentary claims of monarchical abuse. It attempted to show that the Nineteen Propositions were a usurpation of all of the legitimate pre-

From *His Majesties Answer to the XIX Propositions of Both Houses of Parliament* (London, 1641).

rogatives of the monarch and would leave the king only a shadow of his regality. The attack upon Parliament contained in the reply was designed for public consumption and it was published in London almost as soon as it was presented to Parliament.

Contained within this document, whether intentionally or not, is the first statement of the idea, which would later become the commonplace upon which the English constitution rested, that the government of the realm was composed of the three estates of King, Lords, and Commons.

. . . We call God to witnesse, that as for Our Subjects sake these Rights are vested in Us, so for their sakes, as well as for Our own, We are resolved not to quit them, nor to subvert (though in a Parliamentary way) the ancient, equall, happy, well-poised and never-enough commended Constitution of the Government of this Kingdom. . . . There being three kindes of Government amongst men, Absolute Monarchy, Aristocracy and Democracy, and all these having their particular conveniences and inconveniencies. The experience and wisdom of your Ancestors hath so moulded this out of a mixture of these, as to give to this Kingdom (as far as humane Prudence can provide) the conveniencies of all three, without the inconveniences of any one, as long as the Balance hangs even between the three Estates, and they run joyntly on in their proper Chanell (begetting Verdure and Fertility in the Meadows on both sides) and the overflowing of either on either side raise no deluge or Inundation. The ill of absolute Monarchy is Tyranny, the ill of Aristocracy is Faction and Division, the ills of Democracy are Tumults, Violence and Licentiousnesse. The good of Monarchy is the uniting a Nation under one Head to resist Invasion from abroad, and Insurrection at home: The good of Aristocracy is the Conjunction of Counsell in the ablest Persons of a State for the publike benefit: The good of Democracy is Liberty, and the Courage and Industry which Liberty begetts.

In this Kingdom the Laws are joyntly made by a King, by a House of Peers, and by a House of Commons chosen by the People, all having free Votes and particular Priviledges: The Government according to these Laws is trusted to the King, Power of Treaties of War and Peace, of making Peers, of chusing Officers and Councellours for State, Judges for Law, Commanders for Forts and Castles, giving Commissions for raising men to make War abroad, or to prevent or provide against Invasions or Insurrections at home, benefit of Confiscations, power of pardoning, and some more of the like kinde are placed in the King. And this kinde of regulated Monarchy having this power to preserve that Authority, without which it would be disabled to preserve the Laws in their Force, and the Subjects in their liberties and proprieties, is intended to draw to him such a Respect and Relation from the great Ones, as may hinder the ills of Division and Faction, and such a Fear and Reverence from the people, as may hinder Tumults, Violence and Licenciousnesse. Again, that the Prince may not make use of this high and perpetuall power to the hurt of those for whose good he hath it, and make use of the name of Publique Necessitie for the gain of his private Favourites and Followers, to the detriment of his People, the House of Commons (an excellent Conserver of Liberty, but never intended for any share in Government, or the chusing of them that should govern) is solely intrusted with the first Propositions concerning the Leavies of Moneys (which is the sinews as well of Peace as War) and the impeaching of those, who for their own ends, though countenanced by any surreptitiously gotten Command of the King, have violated that Law, which he is bound (when he knows it) to protect, and to the protection of which they were bound to advise him, at least not to serve him in the Contrary. And the Lords being trusted with a Judicatorie power, are an excellent Screen and Bank between the Prince and People, to assist each against any Incroachments of the other, and by just Judgements to preserve that Law, which ought to be the Rule of every one of the three. . . .

Since therefore the Power Legally placed in both Houses is more [than] sufficient to prevent and restrain the power of Tyranny, and without the power which is now asked from Us We shall not be able to discharge that Trust which is the end of Monarchy, since this would be a totall Subversion of the Fundamentall Laws, and that excellent Constitution of this Kingdom, which hath made this Nation so many yeers both Famous and Happy to a great degree of Envie; since to the power of punishing (which is already in your hands according to Law) if the power of Preferring be added, We shall have nothing left for Us, but to look on; since the incroaching of one of these Estates upon the power of the other is unhappy in the effects both to them and all the rest; since this power of at most a joynt Government in Us with Our Councellors, (or rather Our Guardians) will return Us to the worst kinde of Minority, and make Us Despicable both at home and abroad, and beget eternall Factions and Dissentions (as destructive to publike Happinesse as War) both in the chosen, and the Houses that chuse them, and the people who chuse the Chusers; since so new a power will undoubtedly intoxicate persons who were not born to it, and beget not onely Divisions among them as equals, but in them contempt of Us as become an equall to them, and Insolence and Injustice towards Our people, as now so much their inferiors, which will be the more grievous unto them, as suffering from those who were so lately of a neerer degree to themselves, and being to have redresse onely from those that placed them, and fearing they may be inclined to preserve what they have made, both out of kindenesse and policie; since all great changes are extreamly inconvenient, and almost infallibly beget yet greater Changes, which beget yet greater Inconveniencies.

Since as great an one in the Church must follow this of the Kingdom; Since the second Estate would in all probability follow the Fate of the first, and by some of the same turbulent spirits Jealousies would be soon raised against them, and the like Propositions for reconciliation of Differences would be then sent to them, as they now have joyned to send to Us, till (all Power being vested in the House of Commons, and their number making them incapable of transacting Affairs of State with the necessary Secrecie and expedition; those being retrusted to some close Committee) at last the Common people (who in the mean time must be flattered, and to whom Licence must be given in all their wilde humours, how contrary soever to established Law, or their own reall Good) discover this *Arcanum Imperii,* That all this was done by them, but not for them, grow weary of Journey-work, and set up for themselves, call Parity and Independence, Liberty; devour that Estate which had devoured the rest; Destroy all Rights and Pro-prieties, all distinctions of Families and Merit; And by this means this splendid and excellently distinguished form of Government end in a dark equall Chaos of Confusion, and the long Line of Our many noble An-cestors in an Jack Cade, or a Wat Tyler.

For all these Reasons to all these demands Our Answer is, *Nolumus Leges Angliae mutari. . . .*

17. J. Sprigge, *Anglia Rediviva* (The Battle of Naseby)

For three years, the fighting in the English Civil War proved inconclusive. The opposing forces were split into armies largely of local character which skirmished with each other but whose victories or defeats could not effect a decisive outcome to the war. The king's forces were raised and financed by locally influential supporters while Parliament directed its war effort from London. Both sides experienced difficulties of finance and supply with neither side able to gain advantage. In the summer of 1644 Parliament tasted the first fruits of its alliance with the Scots, who brought an army into the north of England, but then experienced bitter reversals to its main forces in the south. At the end of the campaign there was widespread belief that Parliament could never win the war without a reorganization of its forces which were under the command of leading peers and members of the House of Commons. The passage of the Self-Denying Ordinance (by the Commons in December and the Lords, under

From J. Sprigge, *Anglia Rediviva* (London, 1647), pp. 27–44.

severe pressure, in April) allowed for the amalgamation of forces and the appointment of new commanders under tighter parliamentary control.

An army of 21,000, the New Model Army, was hastily organized in April and May. This force appeared so weak to the king and his advisers that it was believed a decisive victory could be achieved by defeating it. On 14 June 1645 the largest portion of both royalist and parliamentarian forces met in battle at Naseby, Northamptonshire.

This account of the army and the battle of Naseby comes from Joshua Sprigge's eyewitness report. Sprigge was a chaplain who traveled with the army throughout the campaign of 1645. His hortatory tract was directed at parliamentary supporters in London.

Chapter 5. The Army Commanded to Rise from before *Oxford;* Their Several Marches till the Battel at *Naseby,* with All the Particulars Thereof, Fully Related

Upon the sad news of the losse of *Leicester,* and the danger thereupon of the Kings breaking into the *Associated Counties;* Lieutenant-General *Cromwel* was ordered by the *Committee of both Kingdomes,* to march only with three Troops of horse to secure the Isle of *Ely;* which commands, he, in greater tendernesse of the publique service, then his own honour, in such a time of extremity as that was, disputed not, but fulfilled. And his *Excellency* Sir *Thomas Fairfax* was commanded to rise from before *Oxford,* and to march to defend the *Association;* accordingly Orders were immediately given for the Forces on the other side the river to march to *Islip,* and Major-General *Brown* was desired to put a garison into *Gaunt-house,* being a place that was conceived would much conduce to the straitning of *Oxford;* which accordingly was done, and the bridge lately made, pulled up: and the next day, being *Iune 5.* the Army rose from before *Oxford,* and marched that day to *Marsh-Gibeon,* ten miles. The *General* in his march turned out of the way, to see the siege before *Bostol-house,* where Major-General *Skippon,* according to order, had that morning made some attempt, but the successe was not according to our desires (the Moat being much deeper then we expected.) This night, at the Head quarter, intelligence came that the King was marching from *Leicester* towards *Daventry,* with intention to raise the siege at *Oxford,* as was conceived; which was by order before done to his hand.

Friday, *Iune 6.* the Army marched to *great Brickhill,* twelve miles, where the head-quarter was that night, which was once intended to be at *Stony-Stratford,* but that the intelligence which came that night to us of the Kings horse facing *Northhampton* that day, rendred it not safe so to adventure: whilest the greatest body of our Horse, sent into *Derbyshire,* were not as yet returned.

This night a great fire happened at the Generals [Fairfax's] quarters at *Brickhil,* which was so sudden and violent for the time, that a man and a boy, and three or four horses were burnt in the Barn where the fire began, before the Guard could get to preserve them. It happened most remarkably, in the house of one who expressed no good affection to this Army, and denyed to furnish those conveniences for quarter, (affirming that he had them not,) which afterwards by occasion of the fire, he was enforced to bring out. The next day, *Iune 7.* the Army marched to *Sherrington,* a mile East of *Newport-Pagnel,* to the end the Forces with Colonel *Vermuden* (who upon the Scots retreat to *Westmerland* were recalled, and upon their march back) might more conveniently joyn, but especially to be on that side the River, the better to secure the *Association,* in case the *King,* who the day before had faced *Northhampton,* and seemed to intend that way, should attempt to break into it; wherein it appeared they did not consult their safety and quarter on the back of a garison, as without incurring any great censure they might have done; but rather consulted their honour and the publick service. Expresses were sent to Lieutenant-General *Cromwel* into the Association, to inform him whereabout our Army was, that in case the Association were in danger, he might know how to joyn with us. Lords day, *Iune 8.* the Army resting in their quarters, severall parties of horse were sent out as far as *Tocester,* to gain intelligence of the motions of the *Kings* Army, who brought in some prisoners of Sir *Marmaduke Langdales* Brigade, from whom information was gathered that the Kings Army continued still about *Daventry:* Whereupon the *General* called a Councel of War, to consider of the best way to engage the Enemy. Where taking into consideration of what use Lieutenant-General *Cromwel* would be to them in a time of so great action: The *General* propounded to the Councel of War, and it was by them unanimously consented unto, that a Letter should be writ to the Parliament, to desire that they would please for a time to dispence with L. Gen. *Cromwels* absence from the House; and to give way he might command their Horse, there being like to be very speedily an engagement. Which Letter was sent by Colonel *Hamond,* who went Post the same day to the Parliament, and was instantly returned with an answer according as was desired, to the great content of the *General,* and the whole Army.

This day, Colonel *Vermuden,* who the day before was with his party of Horse returned, and come near to the quarters of the army, himself came to the *General,* desiring (in regard of some speciall occasions which he said he had to draw him beyond seas) that he might have leave to lay down his Commission, which was yielded unto, and accordingly he received his discharge. At this dayes debate, Major-General *Skippon* was desired to draw the form of a battell: and at the same time the Army was divided into severall Brigades of Horse and Foot, in order to their being better disposed for an engagement. The *General*, though not depending upon multitudes, yet serving Providence in the use of all good means; sent one Post after another to Sir *John Gel*, Colonel *Rossiter*, to the Governours of *Coventry, Warwick, Northhampton*, and *Nottingham*, To march with all speed with their Forces to the Army, for that there was likely to be speedily an engagement with the Enemy. In the mean, the Army neglected no time, but on Wednesday, *Iune 11*, though a rainy day, marched from *Stony-Stratford* to *Wootton*, within three miles of *Northampton*, where intelligence still confirmed the *Kings* continuance at *Daventry*, quartering all his Foot and Carriages upon *Burrough-hill;* a place of great advantage (having formerly been an ancient fortification) and making show, as if he had chosen that place to fight upon, in case we durst advance to him. But afterwards it appeared, that his stay there, was only till a part of 1200 horse were returned, which he had sent from his Army to *Oxford*, as a convoy with the plundered cattel & sheep of *Leicestershire, Northamptonshire*, &c. the better to enable *Oxford* to endure a siege, in case it should be attempted again in his absence, himself being intent upon a march for the relief of *Pomfract* and *Scarborough;* which he then apprehended to have smal difficulty in it, understanding the removall of the Scotish army.

The Army being come to *Wotton*, they found there none of the best accommodation for quarter; only, what was wanting that way, was kindly and respectively endeavoured to be supplied by the Major and Magistrates of *Northhampton*, who the same night came to the *General* at the head quarter, upon the errand of a congratulatory visit and present. The next day, the Army marched to *Gilsborough*, (four miles on the west of *Northampton*, and within five miles of *Burrough-hill*, where the Enemy still continued) Marching in very good order; for that they did advance directly upon the place where the enemy had pitcht himself. A commanded party of horse gave the Enemy an alarm, and took some prisoners, by whom they understood the *King* was a hunting, the Souldiers in no order, and their horses all at grasse, having not the least knowledge of our advance, and being in the greatest security that could be; but the alarum was so quickly taken through all their quarters, that our Foot being somewhat behind, and night approaching, it was not thought wisdome to make any further attempt. About twelve that night, the *General* took horse, and rode about both the Horse and Foot guards, till four in the morning (expecting the Enemy would have shewn some gallantry that night, and fallen upon some of his quarters, as he had hindred them in their sport at hunting the day before.) In the very entrance whereof this hard condition befell the General himself; That having forgot the Word, he was stopped at the first Guard; and requiring the Souldier that stood Sentinel, to give it him, he refused to do it, telling him, he was to *demand* the Word from all that past him, but to *give* it to none; and so made the General stand in the wet, till he sent for the Captain of the guard to receive his commission to give the General the word, (In such subjection are the Highest, to those lawes that erst derived their sanction and authority in great part from themselves) and in the end the Souldier was rewarded for his duty and carefulnesse, (as it was interpreted.) As the *General* was riding in the morning about three of the clock, within a mile and half of *Flowre*, where the Enemy kept an horse-guard; He could discern the Enemy riding fast over *Burrough-hill*, to make fires in abundance, as if they were firing their Huts; which gave some cause to believe they were about to march, as indeed it proved afterwards. For,

About five in the morning, *Iune 13.* the General being returned to the head-quarter, the Scoutmaster gen. *Watson* (whose continued diligence in getting timely intelligence of the Enemies motion, then, and alwayes, redounded not a little to the enablement of the Army) brought him certain notice, that the Enemy was drawing off from *Burrough-hill;* had stood in arms all night, and were all amazed that our Army was so neer; it being spread abroad in their army we were gone for security into the *Association;* And four or five more of the Spies came one after another, confirming the same intelligence, adding further, that most of their carriages were drawn from *Burrough-hill* towards *Harborough.* And indeed, the Convoy of horse being returned from *Oxford* the night before, and this unexpected march of the Army close up to them, being in a manner a surprise of them; caused them speedily to resolve upon their forementioned march towards *Pomfract;* either judging, the Army would not follow them, or if they did, they should be able to fight us at more advantage, after they had drawn us further Northward.

About six of the clock in the morning, a Councel of War was called, to consider what attempt to make upon the Enemy. In the middest of the debate, came in Lieutenant-General *Cromwel,* out of the Association, with 600 Horse and Dragoons, who was with the greatest joy received by the *General* and the whole army. Instantly orders were given for Drums to beat, Trumpets to sound to horse, and all our army to draw to a rendezvouz; from whence a good party of Horse were sent towards *Daventry,* under the command of Major *Harrison,* (of whose continued fidelity the Publique hath had sufficient testimony) to bring further intelligence of the Enemies motion: and another strong party of Horse was sent under under the command of Colonel *Ireton,* to fall upon the flank of the Enemy, if he saw cause: and the main body of our Army marched to flank the Enemy in the way to *Harborough,* and came that night to *Gilling;* the Countrey much rejoycing at our comming, having been miserably plundered by the Enemy; and some having had their children taken from them, and sold before their faces to the *Irish* of that Army, whom the parents were enforced to redeem with the price of money. That evening we understood that the Van of the Enemies army was at *Harborough,* the Rear within two miles of *Naseby:* and no sooner was the *General* got to his quarters, but tidings was brought him of the good service done by Colonel *Ireton,* in falling into the Enemies quarters, which they had newly taken up in *Naseby* Town; where he took many prisoners, some of the Princes Life-guard, and *Langdales* Brigade, and gave a sound alarm throughout the Enemies army (the confidence of the Enemy in possessing these quarters, grounded upon their slight esteem of this Army, and want of intelligence, was very remarkable.) Upon this alarm, the *King* (not having notice of it till eleven at night, as he had little imagined the nearnesse of our Army, or that they durst bear up to him) much amazed, left his own quarters at that unseasonable time; and for se-curity went to *Harborough,* where Prince *Rupert* quartered; and so soon as he came thither, sent to call up his Nephew, (resting himself in a chair, in a low-room, in the mean time) who presently arose; a Councel of War was called: the question was put, What was best to be done seeing our Army was so neer, and as they then perceived fully intended to ingage them. It was considered by them, that should they march on to *Leicester,* if the Rear were engaged, the whole Army might be put in hazard; and there was no marching with the Van unlesse they could bring the Rear clear off, which they discerned to be very difficult. Whereupon it was resolved to give bat-tell, taking themselves (as indeed they were) for a more considerable force then we, especially in Horse, on which they chiefly depended; being also as confident, they might relye upon their Infantry for valiant resolute men; & they resolved (as appeared) not to abide in that place till we marched up to them, but in a gallant bravery to seek us out. Herein the Kings Counsel prevailed against the minde of the most of his great Officers, who were of opinion, that it was best to avoid fighting.

Saturday *Iune 14.* The *General* with the Army advanced by three of the clock in the morning, from *Gilling* towards *Naseby,* with an intention to follow close upon the Enemy, and (if possible) retard their march with our Horse, till our foot could draw up to them, in case they should have marched on to *Leicester* (the intelligence being, that they had drawn some of their Carriages in the night through *Harborough*) that way. By five in the morning, the Army was at a Rendezvouz near *Naseby,* where his Excel-lency received intelligence by our Spies, that the Enemy was at *Har-borough;* with this further, that it was still doubtfull, whether he meant to march away, or to stand us. But immediately the doubt was resolved: great Bodies of the Enemies horse were discerned on the top of the hill on this side *Harborough,* which increasing more and more in our view, begat a confidence in the *General,* and the residue of the Officers that he meant not to draw away, as some imagined, but that he was putting his Army in order, either there to receive us, or to come to us, to engage us upon the ground we stood: whilst the *General* was thus observing the countenance of the Enemy, directions were given to put the Army into such a posture, as that if the Enemy came on, we might take the advantage of our ground, and be in readinesse to receive him; or if not, that we might advance towards him. And whilest these things were in consultation and action, the Enemies Army, which before was the greatest part of it out of our view, by reason of the Hill that interposed, we saw plainly advancing in order towards us: and the winde blowing somewhat Westwardly, by the Enemies advance so much on their right hand, it was evident, that he designed to get the winde of us: which occasioned the *General* to draw down into a large fallow field on the Northwest side of *Naseby,* flanked on the left hand with a hedge, which was a convenient place for us to fight the Enemy in. And indeed seeing his resolution to advance upon us, we took the best advantage we could of the ground, possessing the ledge of a Hill, running from East to West; upon which our Army being drawn up, fronted towards the Enemy. But considering it might be of advantage to us to draw up our Army out of sight of the Enemy; who marched upon a plain ground towards us: we retreated about an 100 paces from the ledge of the Hill, that so the Enemy might not perceive in what form our battell was drawn, nor see any confusion therein, and yet we to see the form of their battell; to which we could conform our selves for advantages, and recover the advantage of the Hill when we pleased, which accordingly we did. The Enemy perceiving this retreat, thought (as since they have confessed) we were drawing off to avoid fighting (and just then it was brought to the King, that our Army was flying to *Northhampton*) which did occasion them the more to precipitate; for they made so much haste, that they left many of their Ordnance behinde them.

The *General,* together with the *Major-General,* put the severall Brigades of Foot into order: having committed the Ordering of the Horse to Lieutenant-General *Cromwel,* who did obtain from the *General,* That seeing the Horse were neere 6000. and were to bee fought in two wings; His Excellency would please to make Col. *Ireton* Commissary gen. of horse, and appoint him to command the Left wing, that day; the command of the Right wing being as much as the *Lieutenant-General* could apply himself unto. Which being granted by the *General,* the *Lieutenant-General* assigned him five Regiments of Horse, a Division of 200 Horse of the *Association,* for that Wing; and the Dragoons to line the forementioned hedge, to prevent the enemy from annoying the Left flank of the Army. In the mean time the *Lieutenant-General* having six Regiments of Horse with him for the Right wing, disposed them according as the place gave leave. And the form of the whole Battail you have here inserted.

Upon the Enemies approach, the Parliaments army marcht up to the brow of the hill, having placed a Forlorn of Foot (musquetiers) consisting of about 300. down the steep of the hill towards the enemy, somewhat more then Carbine shot from the Main battail, who were ordered to retreat to the battail, whensoever they should be hard pressed upon by the Enemy. The Enemy this while marched up in good order, a swift march, with a great deal of gallantry and resolution, according to the form here inserted. It is hard to say, whether Wing of our Horse charged first: But the *Lieutenant-General* not thinking it fit to stand and receive the Enemies charge, advanced forward with the Right wing of the Horse, in the same order wherein it was placed. Our Word that day was, *God our strengh;* Their Word was, *Queen Mary.* Colonel *Whaley* being the left hand on the right wing, charged first two Divisions of *Langdales* Horse, who made a very gallant resistance, and firing at a very close charge, they came to the sword: wherein Col. *Whaley's* Divisions routed those two Divisions of *Langdales,* driving them back to Prince *Ruperts* Regiment, being the Reserve of the enemies Foot, whither indeed they fled for shelter, and rallied: the Reserves to Colonel *Whaley* were ordered to second him, which they performed with a great deal of resolution. In the mean time, the rest of the Divisions of the Right wing, being straightned by Furzes on the right hand, advanced with great difficulty, as also by reason of the uneavennesse of the ground, and a Cony-warren over which they were to march, which put them somewhat out of their order, in their advance. Notwithstanding which difficulty, they came up to the engaging the residue of the Enemies horse on the left wing, whom they routed, and put into great confusion, not one body of the enemies horse which they charged, but they routed, and forced to flie beyond all their Foot, except some that were for a time sheltred by the Brigade of Foot before mentioned.

Colonel *Rossiter,* who with his Regiment was just come into the field as the Armies were ready to close; was edg'd in upon the right flank of the right wing of horse, time not permitting a more fitting and equal disposal of him: whose timely comming (according to his Orders) gave him opportunity of such gallant performance in the battel, as deserves an honourable mentioning.

The Horse of the enemies Left wing being thus beaten from their Foot, retreated back about a quarter of a mile beyond the place where the battail was fought. The successe of our Main battail was not answerably; The right hand of the Foot, being the *Generals* Regiment, stood, not being much pressed upon: Almost all the rest of the main Battail being overpressed, gave ground and went off in some disorder, falling behinde the

Reserves; But the Colonels and Officers, doing the duty of very gallant Men, in endeavouring to keep their men from disorder, and finding their attempt fruitless therein, fell into the Reserves with their Colours, choosing rather there to fight and die, then to quit the ground they stood on. The Reserves advancing, commanded by Col. *Rainsborough,* Col. *Hammond,* and Lieut. col. *Pride,* repelled the Enemy, forcing them to a disorderly retreat. Thus much being said of the Right wing and the main battail, it comes next in order, that an account be given of the Left wing of our Horse.

Upon the approach of the Enemies Right wing of Horse, our Left wing drawing down the brow of the hill to meet them, the Enemy comming on fast, suddenly made a stand, as if they had not expected us in so ready a posture: Ours seeing them stand, made a little stand also, partly by reason of some disadvantage of the ground, and untill the rest of the Divisions of Horse might recover their stations. Upon that the Enemy advanced again, whereupon our Left wing sounded a Charge, and fell upon them: The three right hand Divisions of our Left wing made the first onset, and those Divisions of the enemy opposite to them, received the Charge; the two left hand Divisions of the Left wing did not advance equally, but being more backward, the opposite Divisions of the Enemy advanced upon them. Of the three right hand Divisions (before mentioned) which advanced the middlemost charged not home, the other two comming to a close Charge, routed the two opposite Divisions of the Enemy, (And the Commissary Generall seeing one of the enemies Brigades of Foot on his right hand, pressing sore upon our Foot, commanded the Division that was with him, to charge that Body of Foot, and for their better encouragement, he himself with great resolution fell in amongst the Musquetiers, where his horse being shot under him, and himself run through the thigh with a Pike, and into the face with an Halbert, was taken prisoner by the enemy, untill afterwards, when the battell turning, and the enemy in great distraction, he had an happy opportunity to offer his Keeper his liberty, if he would carry him off, which was performed on both parts accordingly.) That Division of the enemies which was between, which the other Division of ours should have charged, was carried away in the disorder of the other two; the one of those right hand Divisions of our Left wing that did rout the front of the enemy, charged the Reserve too, and broke them, the other Reserves of the enemy came on, and broke those Divisions of ours that charged them; the Divisions of the left hand of the right wing were likewise overborn, having much disadvantage, by reason of pits of water, and other pieces of ditches that they expected not, which hindred them in their order to Charge.

The enemy having thus worsted our left wing, pursued their advantage, and Prince *Rupert* himself having prosecuted his successe upon the left wing, almost to *Naseby* town, in his return summoned the Train, offering them quarter, which being well defended with the Fire-locks, and a Rear-guard left for that purpose, who fired with admirable courage on the Princes horse, refusing to hearken to his offer, and the Prince probably perceiving by that time the successe of our Right wing of Horse, he retreated in great haste to the rescue of the Kings Army, which he found in such a general distresse, that instead of attempting any thing in the rescue of them (being close followed in the Rear by some of Commissary Generals, Col. *Riches,* Col. *Fleetwoods,* Major *Huntingtons,* and Col. *Butlers* horse) he made up further, untill he came to the ground where the King was rallying the broken horse of his Left wing, and there joyned with them, and made a stand.

To return again to our right wing, which prosecuting their success, by this time had beaten all the enemies horse quite behinde their foot, which when they had accomplished, the remaining business was with part to keep the enemies horse from coming to the rescue of their foot, which were now all at mercy, except one *Tertia,* which with the other part of the horse we endeavoured to break, but could not, they standing with incredible courage & resolution, although we attempted them in the Flanks, Front and Rear, until such time as the General called up his own Regiment of foot (the Lieut. General being likewise hastening of them) which immediately fell in with them, with But-end of Muskets (the General charging them at the same time with horse) and so broke them. The enemy had now nothing left in the Field, but his horse, (with whom was the King himself) which they had put again into as good order as the shortnesse of their time, and our near pressing upon them would permit.

The Generall (whom God preserved in many hazardous ingagements of his person that day) seeing them in that order, and our whole Army (saving some Bodies of horse which faced the enemy) being busied in the execution upon the foot, and taking, and securing prisoners, endeavoured to put the Army again into as good order as they could receive, to the perfecting of the work that remained: Our foot were somewhat more then a quarter of a mile behinde the horse, and although there wanted no courage nor resolution in the horse themselves alone to have charged the enemy, yet forasmuch as it was not judged fit to put any thing to hazard, the businesse being brought (through the goodnesse of God) to so hopefull an issue, It was ordered our horse should not charge the enemy untill the foot were come up; for by this time our foot that were disordered upon the first Charge, being in shorter time then is well imaginable, rallyed again, were comming up upon a fast march to joyn with our horse, who were again put into two wings, within Carbine shot of the enemy, leaving a wide space for the battail of foot to fall in, whereby there was framed, as it were in a trice, a second good Batalia at the latter end of the day; which the enemy perceiving, and that if they stood, they must expect a second Charge from our Horse, Foot, and Artillery (they having lost all their Foot and Guns before) and our Dragoons having already begun to fire upon their horse, they not willing to abide a second shock upon so great disadvantage as this was like to be, immediatly ran away, both Fronts, and Reserves, without standing one stroke more: Our horse had the Chase of them from that place, within two miles of *Leicester* (being the space of fourteen miles) took many prisoners, and had the execution of them all that way: The number of the slain we had not a certain account of, by reason of the prosecution of our Victory, and speedy advance to the reducing of *Leicester*: the prisoners taken in the field were about five thousand, whereof were six Colonels, eight Lieut. Colonels, eighteen Majors, seventy Captains, eighty Leiutenants, eighty Ensignes, two hundred other inferiour Officers, besides the Kings Footmen, and houshold servants, the rest common Souldiers, four thousand five hundred. The enemy lost very gallant men, and indeed their foot, commanded by the Lord *Astley,* were not wanting in courage; the whole booty of the Field fell to the Souldier, which was very rich and considerable, there being amongst it, besides the riches of the Court, and Officers, the rich plunder of *Leicester.*

Their Train of Artillery was taken, all their Ordnance, (being brasse Guns) whereof two were Demi-Canon, besides two Morter-pieces, (the enemy got away not one Carriage) eight thousand Arms and more, forty Barrels of powder, two hundred horse, with their riders, the Kings Colours, the Duke of *Yorks* Standard, and six of his Colours, four of the *Queens* white Colours, with double Crosses on each of them, and near one hundred other Colours both of horse and foot, the *Kings Cabinet,* the Kings Sumpter, many Coaches, with store of wealth in them: It was not the least mercy in this Victory, that the Cabinet Letters, which discover so much to satisfie all honest men of the intention of the adverse party, fell likewise into our hands, and have been since published by the Authority of the Parliament, to the view of the whole Kingdome.

The Field was about a mile broad where the battail was fought, and from the outmost Flank of the right, to the left Wing, took up the whole ground.

Thus you have a true and exact relation of the work of this happy day.

1. The battail was fought much upon equall advantage, whether you respect the numbers on each side, there being in that not 500. odds, or the ground it was fought upon being on both sides Champaign, and in that respect equal, and the winde at length favouring neither side more then other. But in this the enemy had much the odds of us, that they had on their side not so few as fifteen hundred Officers, that were old souldiers, of great

experience through long experience in forraign parts; when on the other hand, we had not ten Officers that could pretend to any such thing, as the experience of a souldier, save what this war had given them, being for the most part such, whose *Religion, Valour,* and present *Reason* was their best *Conduct;* and herein God went beyond our *Enemies* in their *pride,* and seeming *friends,* in their *contempt* of this Army.

2. Of how great consequence this Victory was to the whole Kingdom: That it may the better appear, let us take a view of it, and suppose we beheld it through the *counter-prospective* of the contrary event, as if the Enemy had had the victory, and we been beaten; and then me thinks I see, not only this Army, the only *guardion* of the Kingdom, lying on a heap, furnishing the enemy with insulting *Trophees,* but also our *party* in the *West* ruined, and the enemy there like a violent *Torrent,* carrying all before him. Me thinks I see the *King* and *Goring* united, making a formidable Army, and marching up to the Walls of *London,* incouraging their souldiers, as formerly, with the promise of the *spoyle* of that *famous* City. And if this successe had been indulged them, and *London* not denyed, (as who should *such* an Army have asked it of) what could have ensued worse or more! When once that City by such a fate had restored an Embleme of undone *Rome,* when *Caesar* came against it, That

> The Senate shooke, the affrighted Fathers leave
> Their Seats, and flying, to the Consuls give
> Directions for the War; where safe to live,
> What place t' avoid they know not, whether ere
> A blest-ripe wit could guide their steps, they bear,
> Th' amazed people forth in Troops, whom nought
> So long had stird.

And who needs any interpretation of this to have been, a being cast in our Cause, and a loosing of our Charges. All this did God mercifully prevent by the successe of that battail, and turned over this condition to the enemy, and thereby laid the happy foundation of all the blessed success we have had since.

He that shall not in this victory look beyond the instrument, will injuriously withhold from God his due: he that doth not behold God in the instruments, will not know how to give him his due; for when he doth actions by instruments, his glory is to be seen in instruments: now had I only to deale with actions, I might possibly by a competent expression give on account of them; but who may undertake to represent the lively frame of an heightened soul, and the working of the affections in such Heroick actions. The General, a man subject to the like infirmities of body, as well as passions of mind with other men, especially to some infirmities (contracted by former wounds) which however at other times they may hinder that puissant and illustrious soul that dwels within, from giving a character of its selfe in his countenance; yet when he hath come upon action, or been near an engagement, it hath been observed, another spirit hath come upon him, another soul hath lookt out at his eyes; I mean he hath been so raised, elevated, and transported, as that he hath been not only unlike himselfe at other times, but indeed more like an Angell, then a man. And this was observed of him at this time: now with what triumphs of faith, with what exultation of spirit, and with what a joynt shout of all the affections God is received into that heart, whose eyes he uses as an Optick to look through, and trouble a proud enemy, it selfe only is privy to? what high transactions, what deep and endearing ingagements passe mutually between God and such a soul? (for certainly the most immediate worship gives not a greater advantage) is better felt experimentally, then described historically; but such a discovery of these things was made in his outward man at this Battel as highly animated his Souldiers.

Lieutenant-General *Cromwel* useth these expressions concerning Him, in his Letter to the House of Commons:

The General served you with all faithfulnesse and honour; and the best commendations I can give of him, is, That I dare say he attributes all to God, and would rather perish, then assume any thing to himself, which is an honest and thriving way; and yet as much for bravery may be given to him in this action, as to a man.

I shall inlarge no further in this particular, but conclude, it was none of the least pledges, none of the lowest speaking Providences betokening good successe to this Army, and promising much happinesse to this Nation; GOD's giving us such a *General,* and so giving out himself to our *General.*

The great share Lieutenant General *Cromwel* had in this action, who commanded the Right wing of Horse, (which did such service, carrying the field before them, as they did at *Marston-moor*) is so known and acknowledged, that envy it self can neither detract, nor deny. One passage relating to his service in this Battel, which I have received from those that well knew it, I shall commend to this Historie: That he being come not above two dayes before out of the Association, and (that day the battel was) attending the General in the field, who was going to draw up for an ingagement; He had the charge and ordering of all the Horse cast upon him by the General unexpectedly, but a little before the Battel; which he had no sooner received, but it was high time to apply himself to the discharge of it: for before the Field-Officers could give a tolerable account of the drawing up of the Army, the Enemy came on amain in passing good order, while our Army was yet in disorder, or the order of it but an Embrio: which the Lieut. General perceiving, was so far from being dismayed at it, that it was the rise and occasion of a most triumphant faith, and joy in him, expecting that GOD would do great things, by small means; and by the things that are not, bring to nought things that are. A happy time, when the Lord of hosts shall make his Tabernacle in the hearts and countenances of our chief Commanders; from thence to laugh his enemies to destruction, and have them in derision to confusion!

Had not Major gen. *Skippon* done gallantly, he had not received such an early wound in his side; and had he not had a Spring of Resolution, he had not stayed in the field, as he did, till the battel was ended; (for being desired by his Excellencie to go off the field, he answered, He would not stirre, so long as a man would stand.) That *I* mention not all those Officers and Souldiers particularly, who behaved themselves so gallantly in this Action, is to avoyd emulation and partiality: *I* shall satisfie my self, to adde concerning them, and the whole businesse, the words of the *General,* and *Lieutenant-General,* in their several Letters to the Speaker of the house of Commons, with which *I* shall conclude. *Honest men served you faithfully in this action; Sir, they are trusty; I beseech you in the name of God, not to discourage them:* (which they have not done, blessed be God, and *I* hope never will.) He proceeds, and wisheth, *This action may beget thankfulnesse and humility in all that are concerned in it;* And concludes thus modestly himself, *He that ventures his life for the liberty of his Country, I wish he trust* GOD for the liberty of his Conscience, and You for the Liberty he fights for, &c. All that *I* desire, sayes the *General,* is, *That the honour of this great, never to be forgotten mercy, may be given to* GOD, *in an extraordinary day of Thanksgiving, and that it may be improved to the good of his Church, which shall be faithfully endeavoured by,* Sir,

> Your most humble Servant,
> *Thomas Fairfax.*

18. Oliver Cromwell to Speaker Lenthall (14 June 1645)

Oliver Cromwell (1599–1658) was a member of the Long Parliament for Huntingdon and a military leader of distinction. During the early years of the Civil War he had served as a colonel of horse in the army of the earl of Manchester and had raised two regiments for Parliament. After the disastrous campaign of 1644 he was ordered to raise additional troops of horse in the eastern counties but his commission lapsed with the passage of the Self-Denying Ordinance in April 1645 which barred all members of Parliament from holding civil or military office. His talent and leader-

From Thomas Carlyle, *Letters and Speeches of Oliver Cromwell, with Elucidations* (New York: Harper Brothers, 1868–71), pp. 168–69.

ship led to a special request from Sir Thomas Fairfax, commander of the New Model Army, that Cromwell be recommissioned for the summer campaign. He arrived at army headquarters just two days before the battle of Naseby and took command, as lieutenant-general of the parliamentary horse.

For the Honorable William Lenthall, Speaker of the Commons House of Parliament: These.

Harborough, 14th June, 1645.

Sir,

Being commanded by you to this service, I think myself bound to acquaint you with the good hand of God towards you and us.

We marched yesterday after the King, who went before us from Daventry to Harborough; and quartered about six miles from him. This day we marched towards him. He drew out to meet us; both armies engaged. We, after three hours fight very doubtful, at last routed his army; killed and took about 5,000,—very many officers, but of what quality we yet know not. We took also about 200 carriages, all he had; and all his guns, being 12 in number, whereof two were demi-cannon, two demi-culverins, and I think the rest sackers. We pursued the enemy from three miles short of Harborough to nine beyond, even to the sight of Leicester, whither the King fled.

Sir, this is none other but the hand of God; and to Him alone belongs the glory, wherein none are to share with Him. The General served you with all faithfulness and honor: and the best commendation I can give him is, That I daresay he attributes all to God, and would rather perish than assume to himself. Which is an honest and a thriving way:—and yet as much for bravery may be given to him, in this action, as to a man. Honest men served you faithfully in this action. Sir, they are trusty: I beseech you, in the name of God, not to discourage them. I wish this action may beget thankfulness and humility in all that are concerned in it. He that ventures his life for the liberty of his country, I wish he trust God for the liberty of his conscience, and you for the liberty he fights for. In this he rests, who is

Your most humble servant,

Oliver Cromwell

19. The Declaration of 30 April 1646

By the beginning of the campaign of 1646 Parliament had all but won the Civil War. It was now in the position, or so it was believed, of dictating

From John Rushworth, *Historical Collections*, 8 vols. (London: 1659–1701), pp. 512–13.

peace terms to the king, and there was much speculation as to what shape the settlement would take. The parliamentary cause was heterogeneous. It was composed of constituencies with contrasting ideas of what was necessary to settle the major issues of the war and to set the nation on a permanent foundation for the future. One of the most vexing issues was that of religion, with Parliament's supporters divided between adherents of a Presbyterian national church along lines similar, but not identical, to that which was established in Scotland and proponents of toleration for individual congregations whose practices and beliefs "differed not in fundamentals." These "tender consciences" had supported parliament financially and as volunteers in its army. Presbyterians had proferred equal support and were better organized to push for their program. The Declaration of 30 April 1646 attempted to speak to adherents of the parliamentary cause and to fearful former royalists who now had to accommodate themselves to a new regime.

A Declaration of the Commons of *England,* assembled in Parliament, of their true Intentions concerning the ancient and fundamental Government of the Kingdom; the Government of the Church; the present Peace; securing the People against all arbitrary Government; and maintaining a right Understanding between the Two Kingdoms of *England* and *Scotland,* according to the Covenant and Treaties.

We the Commons, in Parliament assembled, well remembering, That, in the Beginning of this War, divers Protestations, Declarations, and Suggestions, were spread abroad by the King, and those that did adhere unto him; whereby our sincere Intentions for the Publick Good were misrepresented, and the Minds of many possessed with a Belief, that our Resolutions and Proceedings were grounded upon needless Fears and Jealousies; and that there was no necessary and just Cause of the present War; the Untruth and Deceitfulness whereof, by the good Hand of God, miraculously discovering the Secrets of our Enemies, disposing and blessing our Affairs, Time and Experience have since fully manifested, to the Undeceiving of those, that were seduced thereby; which Mistakes of the People, by this Artifice and Cunning of the Enemy, for some time, much blemished the Justice of this Cause, and not only prolonged the War, but hazarded the Success thereof: And, if the Enemy, by these means, had prevailed, how dangerous the Consequence would have been, is most apparent:

And now observing, that, when it hath pleased God so to bless our Endeavours, and the Actions of our Forces and Armies, as that the Enemy is in Despair to accomplish his Designs by War; and we are brought into good Hopes of attaining and enjoying That, which, with so much Expence of

Blood and Treasure, we have contended for; there are still the same Spirits stirring, and Humours working, as in the Beginning, though under other Disguises, and upon other Grounds; putting false Constructions, as well upon what hath already passed the Houses, as upon the Things under present Debate; and misrepresenting our Intentions in the Use we desire to make of this great Success, which God hath given us, and the happy Opportunity to settle Truth and Peace in the Three Kingdoms; not ceasing, as well in Print, as otherwise, to get a Belief, that we now desire to exceed or swerve from our first Aims and Principles in the undertaking this War, and to recede from the Solemn League and Covenant, and Treaties between the Two Kingdoms; and that we would prolong the uncomfortable Troubles, and bleeding Distractions, in order to alter the fundamental Constitution and Frame of this Kingdom; to leave all Government in the Church loose and unsettled; and ourselves to exercise the same arbitrary Power over the Persons and Estates of the Subjects, which this present Parliament hath thought fit to abolish, by taking away the Star-Chamber, High Commission, and other arbitrary Courts; and the exorbitant power of the Council-Table.

All which being seriously considered by us, although our Actions and Proceedings, from time to time, since the Beginning of this Parliament, and particularly in the manageing this great Cause, are the best Demonstrations of our Sincerity and Faithfulness to the Publick; yet foreseeing, that, if Credit be given to such dangerous Insinuations, and false Surmises, the same will not only continue the present Calamities, and involve us into new and unexpected Embroilments; but likewise inevitably endanger the happy Issue and Success of our Endeavours, which, by God's Blessing, we may otherwise hope for;

We do *Declare*, That our true and real Intentions are, and our Endeavours shall be, to settle Religion in the Purity thereof, according to the Covenant; to maintain the ancient and fundamental Government of this Kingdom; to preserve the Rights and Liberties of the Subject; to lay hold on the first Opportunity of procuring a safe and well-grounded Peace in the Three Kingdoms; and to keep a good Understanding between the Two Kingdoms of *England* and *Scotland*, according to the Grounds expressed in the Solemn League and Covenant, and Treaties; which we desire may be inviolably observed on both Parts.

And, lest these Generals should not give a sufficient Satisfaction, we have thought fit, to the end Men may be no longer abused into a Misbelief of our Intentions, or a Misunderstanding of our Actions, to make this further Inlargement upon the Particulars:

And, first concerning Church-Government; we having so fully declared for a Presbyterial Government, having spent so much Time, taken so much pains, for the Settleing of it, passed most of the Particulars brought to us from the Assembly of Divines (called only to advise of such things as shall be required of them by both or either of the Houses of Parliament) without any material Alteration, saving in the Point of Commissioners; and having published several Ordinances for putting the same in Execution, because we cannot consent to the Granting of an arbitrary and unlimited Power and Jurisdiction to near Ten thousand Judicatories to be erected within this Kingdom, and This demanded in such a Way, as is not consistent with the fundamental Laws and Government of the same, and, by necessary Consequence, excluding the Power of the Parliament of *England* in the Exercise of that Jurisdiction, and whereof we have received no Satisfaction in point of Conscience or Prudence; nor have we yet resolved, how a due Regard may be had, that tender Consciences, which differ not in Fundamentals of Religion, may be so provided for, as may stand with the Word of God, and the Peace of the Kingdom:

It must therefore seem very strange to us, if any sober and modest Man should entertain a Thought, that we should settle no Government in the Church, when our . . . willingness to subject ourselves, and the People of this Land, to this vast Power, hath been a great Cause, that the Government hath not been long since established: And we desire it may be observed, that we have had the more Reason, by no means to part with this Power out of the Hands of the Civil Magistrate, since the Experience of all Ages will manifest, that the Reformation and Purity of Religion, and the Preservation and Protection of the People of God, in this Kingdom, hath, under God, been, by the Parliament, and their Exercise of this Power: And our full Resolutions still are, sincerely, really, and constantly, through the Grace of God, to endeavour the Reformation of Religion in the Kingdoms of *England* and *Ireland,* in Doctrine, Worship, Discipline, and Government, according to the Word of God, and the Example of the best Reformed Churches, and according to our Covenant.

Whence it may appear to all Men, That those Rumours and Aspersions, whereby the Minds of Men are so disturbed, for want of the present Settling of Church-Government, are to be applied to those, who, having a sufficient Power and Direction from the Houses on that behalf, have not as yet put the same in Execution.

And whereas a safe and good Peace is the right End of a just War, there is nothing we have more earnestly desired, nor more constantly laboured after; and, to that Purpose, both Houses of Parliament have framed several Propositions to be sent to the King; such as they hold necessary for the present and future Safety and Good of this Kingdom; some of which are transmitted from both Houses to our Brethren of *Scotland,* where they now remain; whose Consent, that they may speedily be sent to the King, we shall not doubt to obtain, since the Parliament of *England* is, and ought to be, sole and proper Judge of what may be for the Good of this Kingdom, the same Liberty having been always by us admitted to the Kingdom of *Scotland,* in all Things that concern that Kingdom: Wherein we are so far from altering the fundamental Constitution and Government of this Kingdom, by King, Lords, and Commons, that we have only desired, that, with the Consent of the King, such Powers may be settled in the Two Houses, without which we can have no Assurance, but that the like, or greater Mischiefs than these, which God hath hitherto delivered us from, may break out again, and engage us in a Second and more destructive War.

Whereby it plainly appears, our Intentions are not to change the ancient Frame of Government within this Kingdom, but to obtain the End of the primitive Institution of all Government, the Safety and Weal of the People; not judging it wise or safe, after so bitter Experience of the bloody Consequences of a pretended Power of the Militia in the King, to leave any colourable Authority in the same, for the future Attempts of introducing an arbitrary Government over this Nation, and protecting Delinquents, Eenemies of our Religion and Liberties, by Force, from the Justice of the Parliament, the first and chiefest Grounds of the Parliament's taking up Arms in this Cause.

And although the Necessity of War hath given some Disturbance to legal Proceedings; stopped the usual Course of Justice; enforced the Parliament, for the Preservation of this State, to impose and require many great and unusual Payments from the good Subjects of this Kingdom, and to take extraordinary Ways for Procuring of Monies for their many pressing Occasions: It having pleased God to reduce our Affairs into a more hopeful Condition than heretofore, we do *Declare,* That we will not, nor, by any Colour of any Authority derived from us, shall interrupt the ordinary Course of Justice in the several Courts and Judicatories of this Kingdom, nor intermeddle in Cases of private Interest, otherwhere determinable, unless it be Male-administration of Justice; wherein we shall see and provide, that Right be done, and Punishment inflicted, as there shall be Occasion, according to the Laws of the Kingdom, and the Trust reposed in us. And as both Houses have already, for the Ease and Benefit of the People, taken away the Court of Wards and Liveries, with all Tenures *in capite,* and by Knight-Service; so we will take a special Care, that as speedy and as great Ease may be had in future Levies of Money, by Reducing of Garisons, and otherwise, as the pressing Occasions of the Kingdom can possibly admit; and will provide, by bringing Delinquents to due Punishment, who have unnaturally fomented and maintained this present War, against the Parliament and Kingdom, that there may be a fair Possibility of satisfying the Disbursements, clearing the Engagements, and repairing the Losses, of those, who have faithfully and chearfully laid out themselves, and suffered, for the Publick Service; unless, by too great Credulity given to false Suggestions, we be disabled from effecting what we desire.

Lastly, Whereas both Nations have entered into a Solemn League and Covenant, and Treaties have been made and concluded between the Two Kingdoms of *England* and *Scotland:* We have had an especial Regard of the Treaties; and have not (to our best Judgments) failed of the Performance of any thing, which was on our Part to be performed. And, for the Covenant, we have been, and ever shall be, very careful duly to observe the same, that, as nothing hath been done, so nothing shall be done, by us, repugnant to the true Meaning and Intention thereof; and do presume, no Interpretation of it (so far as it concerns the Kingdom of *England*) shall by any be endeavoured to be imposed on us, other than we ourselves do know to be suitable to the first just Ends, for which it was agreed: And we do expect, that the People of *England* should not receive Impressions of any forced Constructions of that Covenant, which, in case of any Doubt arising, is only to be expounded by them, by whose Authority it was established in this Kingdom, who will not depart from those Grounds and Principles, upon which it was framed and founded.

20. The Army's Declaration of 14 June 1647

In 1647 the stalemate between King and Parliament was decisively transformed by the army. After Charles had surrendered his remaining strongholds in June 1646 he refused all parliamentary efforts at recomposition. A peace treaty presented to him at Newcastle was summarily rejected and the king began an effort to play off the contending constituents of the parliamentary cause. After surrendering his forces, he fled north and laid himself on the mercy of the Scots promising them a compromise Presbyterian settlement for their nation if they would help him reconquer England. When this failed and the Scots turned the king over to Parliament, Charles began to send out feelers to the divergent religious groups in England. The parliamentary leaders now believed that the only way to bring an end to the stalemate was to resolve the remaining issues without the king and then force him to accept either rule or imprisonment.

The most important unresolved issues were the suppression of a rebellion in Ireland; the establishment of a standing army in England; and the settlement of religious issues. The first two of these involved the troops of the New Model Army and dissatisfaction over terms, especially the

From John Rushworth, *Historical Collections,* 8 vols. (London: [1659–1701] 1722), 6: 564–70.

failure of Parliament to provide for arrears of pay and to recognize publicly the service that the army had done for the nation, led to a confrontation in the spring of 1647. This dispute, which began over material
grievances and the issue of the army's honor, quickly escalated into a full
scale political confrontation as the soldiers and their officers came to demand a role in deciding the future of the nation. The Declaration of June
14 recounts the history of the dispute between Parliament and army and
sets out the goals of the soldiers as citizens of the nation.

A Declaration, or Representation from His Excellency
Sir Thomas Fairfax, and of the Army under His Command.
Humbly Tendred to the Parliament

That we may no longer be the dissatisfaction of our Friends, the subject of
our Enemies Malice, (to work Jealousies and Misrepresentations upon) and
the suspicion (if not the astonishment) of many in the Kingdom, in our late
or present Transactions and Conduct of Business, we shall in all faithfulness and clearness profess and declare unto you, those Things which have
of late protracted and hindred our disbanding, the present Grievances
which possess our Army, and are yet unremedied, with our Desires as to
the compleat settlement of the Liberties and Peace of the Kingdom, which
is that Blessing of God, than which (of all worldly Things) nothing is more
dear unto us, or more precious in our Thoughts, we having hitherto thought
all our present Enjoyments, whether of Life, or Livelihood, or nearest Relation, a Price but sufficient to the purchase of so rich a Blessing, that we,
and all the free-born People of this Nation may sit down in quiet under our
Vines, under the glorious Administration of Justice and Righteousness,
and in the full possession of those Fundamental Rights and Liberties, without which we can have little hopes (as to humane Considerations) to enjoy
either any Comforts of Life, or so much as Life it self, but at the pleasures
of some Men ruling meerly according to Will and Power.

It cannot be unknown what hath passed betwixt the Parliament and the
Army, as to the Service of *Ireland*. By all which together, with the late
Proceedings against the Army, in relation to their Petition and Grievances,
all Men may judge what hath hindered the Army from a ready engagement
in that Service, and, without further Account or Apology, as to that particular, than what Passages and Proceedings themselves, already made
publick, do afford. We do appeal to your selves, whether those Courses, to
which the Parliament hath (by the Designs and Practices of some) been
drawn, have rationally tended to induce a chearful and unanimous undertaking of the Army to that Service, or rather to break or pull the Army in

pieces with Discontent and Dishonour, and to put such Disobligations and Provocations upon it as might drive it into Distemper; and indeed discourage both this Army and other Soldiers from any further engagement in the Parliament's Service. And we with all Men would, with us, upon the whole Carriage, seriously consider, whether (in the Intentions of those who have by false Informations and Misrepresentations, put the Parliament upon such ways) the timely and effectual relief of *Ireland,* seem really to have been intended, or rather, with the breaking or disbanding of this Army, to draw together, or raise such other Forces, and of such a Temper, as might serve to some desperate and destructive Designs in *England.* For which, besides the probable suspicions from their carriage of the business, we have before-hand, in the transaction thereof, had more than hints of such a Design, by clear Expressions to that purpose, from many of the Officers of the Army, that have been perswaded, and appeared most forward to engage for *Ireland,* on the Terms proposed. And that such a Design hath all along been driven, seems now too evident, by the present disposing of those Forces that have been engaged for *Ireland,* by the endeavours of some to gain a Power from the Parliament, of ordering those Forces for some Service in *England:* And by the private Listings of Men for Service there, without any publick Authority of Parliament. And all this, by the same Persons who have all along appeared most active and violent in the late Proceedings against the Army.

As to the just Discontents and Dissatisfactions of the Army, in relation to their Grievances, and their non-compliance to the late Orders for sudden disbanding by peace-meal, before more full and equal satisfaction were given to the whole, we desire you to look back to the Papers already published, of the Grievances themselves, the Narrative of the Officers, and the late Papers from the General Council of War at *Bury,* and late General Rendezvous near *Newmarket:* And we think your late resuming the Consideration of these things (as to a further satisfaction) doth most justifie the Desires and Proceedings of the Army, in the past Particulars hitherto.

And though had we (upon our first Addresses for our undoubted Rights and Dues) found a free and candid Reception, with a just Consideration and reasonable Satisfaction, or at least a free Answer therein, we should have been easily perswaded to have abated or forborn much of our Dues, and not to have inquired into, or considered (so far as we have) either the possibilities there are for more present satisfaction of Arrears, or the credit of future Securities proposed; yet since upon these former Addresses we have found such hard dealing as in the said Paper is set forth, and those additional (though hitherto but partial) Satisfactions coming so hardly as they have, we find no obliging Reasons in the least to decline or recede from what is our due, but rather still to adhere unto our desires of full and equal satisfaction of all the Things mentioned in the aforesaid Papers not only in behalf of our selves and the Army, but also the whole Soldiery throughout the whole Kingdom, who have concurred, or shall concur with us in the same desires.

And to all our former desires as Soldiers, we cannot but add this (wherein we find our selves so nearly concerned in point of Justice and Reputation) that more care, &c. stricter course may be taken for making good all Articles granted upon Surrenders, according to the true intent and meaning of them. As also for remedy and reparation in case of any Breach; and this without those delays which divers have found as prejudicial to them, or more, than if they had been totally denied the performance of them.

Nor will it now, we hope, seem strange or unseasonable to rational and honest Men, who consider the consequence of our present Case, to their own and the Kingdoms (as well as our) future Concernment in point of Right, Freedom, Peace, and Safety, if from a deep Sense of the high Consequence of our present Case, both to our selves, in future, and all other People, we shall, before disbanding, proceed in our own and the Kingdom's behalf, to propound and plead for some Provision for our and the Kingdom's satisfaction, and future Security, in relation to those things, especially considering, that we were not a meer mercinary Army, hired to serve any Arbitrary Power of a State, but called forth and conjured by the several Declarations of Parliament, to the defence of our own and the People's just Rights and Liberties. And so we took up Arms in Judgment and Conscience to those Ends, and have so continued them, and are resolved, according to your first just desires in your Declarations, and such Principles as we have received from your frequent Informations, and our own common Sense concerning those our fundamental Rights and Liberties, to assert and vindicate the just Power and Rights of this Kingdom in Parliament, for those common Ends premised against all Arbitrary Power, Violence, and Oppression, and against all particular Parties or Interests whatsoever. The said Declarations still directing us to the equitable sense of all Laws and Constitutions, as dispensing with the very Letter of the same, and being supream to it, when the Safety and Preservation of all is concerned, and assuring us, that all Authority is fundamentally seated in the Office, and but ministerially in the Persons; neither do or will these our Proceedings (as we are fully and in Conscience perswaded) amount to any thing not warrantable before God and Men, being thus far much short of the common Proceedings in other Nations, to things of a higher nature than we have yet appeared to. And we cannot but be sensible of the great Complaints that have been made generally to us of the Kingdom, from the People where we march, of Arbitrariness and Injustice, to their great and insupportable Oppressions.

And truly such Kingdoms as have, according both to the Law of Nature and Nations, appear'd to the vindication and defence of their just Rights and Liberties, have proceeded much higher; as our Brethren of *Scotland,* who, in the first beginning of these late Differences, associated in Covenant, from the very same Grounds and Principles (having no visible Form either of Parliament or King to countenance them;) and as they were therein justified and protected by their own and this Kingdom also, so we justly shall expect to be.

We need not mention the States of the *Netherlands,* the *Portugals,* and others, all proceeding from the same Principles of Right and Freedom: And accordingly the Parliament hath declared it is no resistance of Magistracy, to side with the just Principles and the Law of Nature and Nations, being that Law upon which we have assisted you. And that the Soldiery may lawfully hold the Hands of the General, who will turn his Cannon against his Army, on purpose to destroy them; the Seamen the Hands of the Pilot, who wilfully runs the Ship upon a Rock (as our Brethren of *Scotland* argued.) And such were the Proceedings of our Ancestors of famous Memory, to the purchasing of such Rights and Liberties as they have enjoyed, through the Price of their Blood, and we (both by that, and the later Blood of our dear Friends and Fellow-Soldiers, with the hazard of our own) do now lay claim to.

Nor is that supream End (the Glory of God) wanting in these Cases, to set a price upon all such Proceedings of Righteousness and Justice. It being one Witness of God in the World, to carry on a Testimony against the Injustice and Unrighteousness of Men, and against the Miscarriages of Governments, when corrupted or declining from their primitive or original Glory.

These things we mention; but to compare Proceedings, and to shew, that we are so much the more justifiable and warranted in what we do, by how much we come short of that height and measure of Proceedings, which the People in Free Kingdoms and Nations have formerly practised.

Now having thus far cleared our way in this business, we shall proceed to propound such things as we do humbly desire, for the settling and securing of our own and the Kingdom's common Right, Freedom, Peace, and Safety, as followeth.

First, That the Houses may be speedily purged of such Members as for their Delinquency, or for Corruptions, or abuse to the State, or undue Elections, ought not to sit there. Whereof the late Elections in *Cornwal, Wales,* and other parts of the Kingdom, afford too many Examples, to the great prejudice of the People's Freedoms in the said Elections.

Secondly, That those Persons who have in the unjust and high Proceedings against the Army, appeared to have the Will and Confidence, Credit and Power, to abuse the Parliament and the Army, and indanger the Kingdom in carrying on such things against us (while an Army) may be some way speedily disabled from doing the like, or worse to us (when disbanded and disperst, and in the condition of private Men) or to other the free-born People of *England,* in the same Condition with us; and that for that purpose the same Persons may not continue in the same Power (especially as our and the Kingdom's Judges in the highest Trust) but may be made incapable thereof for the future.

And if it be questioned who these are, we thought not fit particularly to name them in this our Representation unto you, but shall very speedily give in their Names, and before long, shall offer what we have to say against them to your Commissioners, wherein we hope so to carry our selves, as that the World shall see we aim at nothing of private Revenge or Animosities, but that Justice may have a free course, and the Kingdom be eased and secured by disabling such Men (at least) from places of Judicature, who desiring to advantage and set up themselves and their Party, in a general Confusion have endeavoured to put the Kingdom into a new flame of War, than which nothing is more abhorring to us.

But because neither the granting of this alone would be sufficient to secure our own, and the Kingdom's Rights, Liberties and Safety, either for the present Age or Posterity, nor would our proposing of this singly, be free from the scandal and appearance of Faction or Design, only to weaken one Party (under the Notion of unjust or oppressive) that we may advance another (which may be imagined more our own) we therefore declare,

That indeed we cannot but wish, That such Men, and such only, might be preferred to the great Power and Trust of the Common-wealth, as are approved at least for moral Righteousness. And of such we cannot but in our Wishes prefer those that appear acted thereunto by a principle of Conscience and Religion in them.

And accordingly we do, and ever shall bless God, for those many such Worthies, who through his Providence have been chosen into this Parliament; and to such Mens endeavours (under God) we cannot but attribute that Vindication in part of the People's Rights and Liberties, and those beginnings of a just Reformation, which the first Proceedings of this Parliament appeared to have driven at and tended to, though of late obstructed, or rather diverted to other Ends and Interests, by the prevailing of other Persons, of other Principles and Conditions.

But yet we are so far from designing or complying to have an absolute or arbitrary Power settled, for continuance, in any Persons whatsoever, as that (if we might be sure to obtain it) we cannot wish to have it so in the Persons of any whom we could most confide in, or who should appear most of our own Opinions or Principles, or whom we might have most personal assurance of, or interest in: But we do and shall much rather wish, that the Authority of this Kingdom in Parliaments (rightly constituted) that is, freely, equally, and successively chosen, according to its original Intention, may ever stand and have its course: And therefore we shall apply our desires chiefly to such things as (by having Parliaments settled in such a right Constitution) may give most hopes of Justice and Righteousness to flow down equally to all in that its ancient Channel, without any Overtures tending either to overthrow that Foundation of Order and Government in this Kingdom, or to engross that Power for Perpetuity into the Hands of any particular Persons or Party whatsoever.

And for that purpose, though (as we have found it doubted by many Men, minding sincerely the publick Good; but not weighing so fully all Consequences of things) it may, and is not unlike to prove, that upon the ending of this Parliament, and the election of a new, the Constitution of succeeding Parliaments, (as to Persons elected) may prove for the worse many ways; yet since neither in the present purging of this Parliament, nor in the election of a new, we cannot promise to our selves, or the Kingdom, an assurance of Justice, or other positive good from the Hands of Men, but those who for present appear most Righteous, or most for common Good, having in them an unlimited Power fixed in them, during Life or Pleasure, in time may become corrupt, or settle into Parties or Factions. Or on the other side, in case of new Elections, those that should so succeed, may prove as bad or worse than the former.

We therefore humbly conceive, that of two Inconveniencies the less being to be chosen, the main thing to be intended in this case (and beyond which humane Providence cannot reach, as to any assurance of positive Good) seems to be this, viz. to provide, That however unjust or corrupt the Persons of Parliament Men, in present or future, may prove, or whatever ill they may do to particular Parties (or to the whole in particular things) during their respective Terms or Periods, yet they shall not have the Temptation or Advantage of an unlimited Power fixed in them, during their own pleasure, whereby to perpetuate Injustice or Oppression upon any, without end or remedy, or to advance or uphold any one particular Party, Faction, or Interest whatsoever, to the oppression or prejudice of the Community, and the enslaving of the Kingdom to all Posterity; but that the People may have an equal hope or possibility, if they have made an ill choice at one time, to mend it in another. And the Members of the House themselves may be in a capacity to taste of Subjection as well as Rule, and may be inclined to consider of other Mens Cases, as what may come to be their own. This we speak of in relation to the House of Commons, as being entrusted on the Peoples behalf for their Interest in that great and supream Power of the Common-wealth, *viz.* the Legislative Power, with the Power of final Judgments, which being in its own Nature so arbitrary, and in a manner so unlimited, unless in point of time, is most unfit and dangerous (as the People's Interest) to be fixt in the Persons of the same Men, during Life, or their own pleasures: Neither by the original Constitution of this State, was it, or ought it to continue so, nor does it (where-ever it is and continues so) render that State any better than a Tyranny, or the People subjected to it any better than Vassals. But in all States where there is any face of common Freedom, and particularly in this State of *England,* (as is most evident both by many positive Laws and ancient constant Custom) the People have a Right to new and successive Elections, unto that great and supream Trust, at certain periods of Time, which is so essential and fundamental to their Freedom, as it cannot or ought not to be denied them, or with-holden from them, and without which the House of Commons is of very little concernment to the Interest of the Commons of *England.* Yet in this we would not be misunderstood in the least, to blame those Worthies of both Houses, whose Zeal to vindicate the Liberties of this Nation, did procure that Act for the continuance of this Parliament, whereby it was secured from being dissolved at the King's pleasure, as former Parliaments had been, as reduced to such a certainty as might enable them the better to assert and vindicate the Liberties of this Nation, immediately before so highly invaded, and then also so much endangered. And this we take to be the principal Ends and Grounds for which in that exigency of Time and Affairs it was procured, and to which we acknowledge it hath happily been made use of; but we cannot think it was by those Worthies intended or ought to be made use of to the perpetuating of that supream Trust and Power in the Persons of any, during their own pleasures, or to the debarring of the People from their Right of Elections, totally now, when these Dangers or Exigencies were past, and the Affairs and Safety of the Common-wealth would admit of such a Change.

Having thus cleared our Grounds and Intentions, as we hope, from all Scruples and Misunderstandings, in what follows we shall proceed further to propose what we humbly desire, for the settling and securing of our own and the Kingdom's Rights and Liberties, (through the Blessing of God) to Posterity; and therefore upon all the Grounds premised, we further humbly desire as followeth.

Thirdly, That some determinate period of Time may be set for the continuance of this and future Parliaments, beyond which none shall continue, and upon which new Writs may of course be issued out, and new Elections successively take place, according to the intent of the Bill for Triennial Parliaments.

And herein we would not be misunderstood to desire a present or sudden Dissolution of this Parliament, but only, as is express'd before, that some certain Period may be set for the determining of it, so as it may not remain, as now, continuable for ever, or during the pleasure of the present Members; and we should desire that the Period be now set for ending this Parliament, may be such as may give sufficient time for provision of what is wanting, and necessary to be passed in point of just Reformation, and for further securing the Rights and Liberties, and settling the Peace of the Kingdom: In order to which we further humbly offer.

Fourthly, That secure Provision may be made for the continuance of future Parliaments, so that they may not be Adjournable or Dissolvable at the King's pleasure, or any other ways, than by their own Consent, during their respective Periods, but at those Periods each Parliament to determine of course as before. This we desire may be now provided for, if it may be, so as to put it out of dispute for future, though we think of Right it ought not to have been otherwise before.

And thus a firm Foundation being laid, in the Authority and Constitution of Parliaments, for the Hopes at least of common and equal Right and Freedom to our selves, and all the free-born People of this Land. We shall hereby, for our part, freely and chearfully commit our Stock or Share of Interest in this Kingdom, into this common Bottom of Parliaments. And though it may, for our Particulars, go ill with us in the Voyage, yet we shall thus hope, if Right be with us, to fare better.

These things we desire may be provided for by Bill or Ordinance of Parliament, to which the Royal Assent may be desired; and when His Majesty in these things, and what else shall be proposed by the Parliament, necessary for securing the Rights and Liberties of the People, and for settling the Militia, and Peace of the Kingdom, shall have given his Concurrence to put them past dispute, we shall then desire, that the Rights of His Majesty, and his Posterity may be considered of, and settled in all things, so far as may consist with the Right and Freedom of the Subject, and with the Security of the same for the future.

Fifthly, We desire, that the Right and Freedom of the People, to represent to the Parliament, by way of humble Petition, their Grievances (in such things as cannot otherwise be remedied than by Parliament) may be cleared and vindicated. That all such Grievances of the People may be freely received, and admitted into Consideration, and put into an equitable and speedy way to be heard, examined, and redressed, if they appear real, and that in such things for which Men have remedy by Law, they may be freely left to the Benefit of the Law, and the regulated course of Justice, without interruption or check from the Parliament, except in case of things done upon the exigency of War, or for the Service and Benefit of the Parliament and Kingdom, in relation to the War, or otherwise, in due pursuance and execution of Ordinances or Orders of Parliament. More particularly, under this Head, we cannot but desire, that all such as are Imprisoned for any pretended Misdemeanor, may be put into a speedy way for a just Hearing and Tryal, and such as shall appear to have been unjustly and unduly Imprisoned, may, with their Liberty, have some reasonable Reparation, according to their Sufferings, and the demerit of their Oppressors.

Sixthly, That the large Powers given to Committees, or Deputy Lieutenants, during the late time of War and Distraction, may be speedily taken into Consideration; that such of those Powers as appear not necessary to be continued, may be taken away, and such of them as are necessary may be put into a regulated way, and left to as little Arbitrariness as the nature and necessity of the things wherein they are conversant will bear.

Seventhly, We could wish that the Kingdom might both be righted and publickly satisfied in point of Accounts for the vast Sums that have been levied and paid; as also in divers other things wherein the Common-wealth may be conceived to have been wronged and abused; but we are loath to press any thing that may tend to lengthen out future Disputes or Contestations, but rather such as may tend to a speedy and general Composure and quieting of Mens Minds, in order to Peace, for which purpose we further propose.

Eighthly, That publick Justice being first satisfied by some few Examples to Posterity, out of the worst of excepted Persons, and other Delinquents, having past their Composition, some course may be taken by a general Act of Oblivion, or otherwise, whereby the Seeds of future War or Fears, either to the present Age or Posterity, may the better be taken away, by easing that Sense of present, and satisfying those Fears of future Ruin or Undoing to Persons or Families, which may drive Men into any desperate ways for Self-Preservation or Remedy; and by taking away the private Remembrances and distinction of Parties, as far as may stand with Safety to the Rights and Liberties we have hitherto fought for.

There are, besides these, many particular things which we would wish to be done, and some to be undone, all in order still to the same Ends of common Right, Freedom, Peace and Safety, but these Proposals aforegoing being the principal things we bottom and insist upon, we shall, as we have said before, for our parts, acquiesce for other Particulars in the Wisdom and Justice of Parliament. And whereas it has been suggested or suspected, That in our late or present Proceedings, our design is to overthrow Presbytery, or hinder the settlement thereof, and to have the Independant Govern-

342 The English Revolution

ment set up, we do clearly disclaim and disavow any such design. We only desire, that according to the Declarations (promising a provision of tender Consciences) there may be some effectual course taken, according to the intent thereof, and that such who upon Conscientious Grounds may differ from the established Forms, may not for that be debarred from the common Rights, Liberties, or Benefits belonging equally to all, as Men and Members to the Common-wealth, while they live soberly and inoffensively towards others, and peaceably and faithfully towards the State.

We have thus freely and clearly declared the depth and bottom of our Hearts and Desires, in order to the Rights, Liberties, and Peace of the Kingdom, wherein we appeal to all Men, whether we seek any thing of advantage to our selves, or any particular Party whatever, to the prejudice of the whole; and whether the Things we wish and seek, do not equally concern and conduce to the Good of others in common with our selves, according to the sincerity of our Desires and Intentions, wherein, as we have already found the concurrent Sense of the People in divers Counties, by their Petitions to the General, expressing their deep resentment of these Things, and pressing us to stand for the Interest of the Kingdom therein, so we shall wish and expect to find their unanimous Concurrence of all others who are equally concerned with us in these Things, and wish well to the Publick.

And so trusting in the Mercy and Goodness of God, to pass by and help any Failings and Infirmities of ours in the Carriage or Proceedings hereupon, we shall humbly cast our selves and the business upon his good pleasure, depending only on his Presence and Blessing for a happy Issue to the Peace and Good of this poor Kingdom; in the accomplishment whereof, we desire and hope, that God will make you blessed Instruments.

Signed, *June* 14, 1647.

By the Appointment of His Excellency Sir Thomas Fairfax, *with the Officers of his Army.*

21. *An Agreement of the People*

As the confrontation between soldiers and statesmen escalated, the army became the last resort for groups of political and religious radicals whose own programs for change had been rejected by Parliament. The army had, throughout the crisis of the summer, kept at arm's length from these groups, the most important of which were called, derisively, the Level-

From A. S. P. Woodehouse, *Puritanism and Liberty*, 2d edition (Chicago: University of Chicago Press, 1951), pp. 88–95. © 1951, The University of Chicago Press.

lers. As army leaders continued to negotiate with both parliamentary leaders and with the king they became more interested in adopting a program that would satisfy grievances which were more widespread than their own mistreatment by Parliament. A call was issued for statements of grievances to be presented to the General Council of the Army, a group composed of both staff officers and of soldiers selected out of the rank and file. But the army leaders were looked upon suspiciously by the radical groups and in September a stinging rebuke, *The Case of the Army Truly Stated,* was published in London accusing its most senior officers of selling out the interests of the nation and sacrificing the just rewards of the soldiers.

An investigation was launched into the charges made by the *Case of the Army* during the course of which Leveller leaders were invited to come to army headquarters and to present their own demands for the settlement of the future of the nation. These were contained in a hastily composed document entitled *An Agreement of the People.*

An Agreement of the People, for a firme and present Peace, upon grounds of Common-Right

Having by our late labours and hazards made it appeare to the world at how high a rate wee value our just freedome, and God having so far owned our cause, as to deliver the Enemies thereof into our hands: We do now hold our selves bound in mutual duty to each other, to take the best care we can for the future, to avoid both the danger of returning into a slavish condition, and the chargable remedy of another war: for as it cannot be imagined that so many of our Country-men would have opposed us in this quarrel, if they had understood their owne good; so may we safely promise to our selves, that when our Common Rights and liberties shall be cleared, their endeavours will be disappointed, that seek to make themselves our Masters: since therefore our former oppressions, and scarce yet ended troubles have beene occasioned, either by want of frequent Nationall meetings in Councell, or by rendring those meetings ineffectuall; We are fully agreed and resolved, to provide that hereafter our Representatives be neither left to an uncertainty for the time, nor made uselesse to the ends for which they are intended: In order whereunto we declare,

I

That the People of England being at this day very unequally distributed by Counties, Cities, & Burroughs, for the election of their Deputies in Parliament, ought to be more indifferently proportioned, according to the number of the Inhabitants: the circumstances whereof, for number, place, and manner, are to be set down before the end of this present Parliament.

II

That to prevent the many inconveniences apparently arising from the long continuance of the same persons in authority, this present Parliament be dissolved upon the last day of September, which shall be in the year of our Lord, 1648.

III

That the People do of course chuse themselves a Parliament once in two years, viz. upon the first Thursday in every 2d. March, after the manner as shall be prescribed before the end of this Parliament, to begin to sit upon the first Thursday in Aprill following at Westminster, or such other place as shall bee appointed from time to time by the preceding Representatives; and to continue till the last day of September, then next ensuing, and no longer.

IV

That the power of this, and all future Representatives of this Nation, is in-feriour only to theirs who chuse them, and doth extend, without the consent or concurrence of any other person or persons; to the enacting, altering, and repealing of Lawes; to the erecting and abolishing of Offices and Courts; to the appointing, removing, and calling to account Magistrates, and Officers of all degrees; to the making War and peace, to the treating with forraigh States: and generally, to whatsoever is not expresly, or implyedly reserved by the represented to themselves. Which are as followeth,

1. That matters of Religion, and the wayes of Gods Worship, are not at all intrusted by us to any humane power, because therein wee cannot remit or exceed a tittle of what our Consciences dictate to be the mind of God, without wilfull sinne: neverthelesse the publike way of instructing the Nation (so it be not compulsive) is referred to their discretion.

2. That the matter of impressing and constraining any of us to serve in the warres, is against our freedome; and therefore we do not allow it in our Representatives; the rather, because money (the sinews of war) being alwayes at their disposall, they can never want numbers of men, apt enough to engage in any just cause.

3. That after the dissolution of this present Parliament, no person be at any time questioned for anything said or done, in reference to the late publike differences, otherwise then in execution of the Judgments of the present Representatives, or House of Commons.

4. That in all Laws made, or to be made, every person may be bound alike, and that no Tenure, Estate, Charter, Degree, Birth, or place, do confer any exemption from the ordinary Course of Legall proceedings, whereunto others are subjected.

5. That as the Laws ought to be equall, so they must be good, and not evidently destructive to the safety and well-being of the people.

These things we declare to be our native Rights, and therefore are agreed and resolved to maintain them with our utmost possibilities, against all opposition whatsoever, being compelled thereunto, not only by the examples of our Ancestors, whose bloud was often spent in vain for the recovery of their Freedomes, suffering themselves, through fraudulent accommodations, to be still deluded of the fruit of their Victories, but also by our own wofull experience, who having long expected, & dearly earned the establishment of these certain rules of Government are yet made to depend for the settlement of our Peace and Freedome, upon him that intended our bondage, and brought a cruell Warre upon us.

For the noble and highly honoured the Free-born People of England, in their respective Counties and Divisions, these.

Deare Country-men, and fellow-Commoners,

For your sakes, our friends, estates and lives, have not been deare to us; for your safety and freedom we have cheerfully indured hard labours and run most desperate hazards, and in comparison to your peace and freedome we neither doe nor ever shall value our dearest bloud and wee professe, our bowells are and have been troubled, and our hearts pained within us, in seeing & considering that you have been so long bereaved of these fruites and ends of all our labours and hazards, wee cannot but sympathize with you in your miseries and oppressions. It's greife and vexation of heart to us; to receive your meate or moneyes, whilest you have no advantage, nor yet the foundations of your peace and freedom surely layed: and therefore upon most serious considerations, that your principall right most essentiall to your well-being is the clearnes, certaintie, sufficiencie and freedom of your power in your representatives in Parliament, and considering that the original of most of your oppressions & miseries hath been either from the obscuritie and doubtfulnes of the power you have committed to your representatives in your elections, or from the want of courage in those whom you have betrusted to claime and exercise their power, which might probably proceed from their uncertaintie of your assistance and maintenance of their power, and minding that for this right of yours and ours wee engaged our lives; for the King raised the warre against you and your Parliament, upon the ground, that hee would not suffer your representatives to provide for your peace safetie and freedom that were then in danger, by disposing

of the Militia and otherwise, according to their trust; and for the maintenance that was deare to us, and God hath borne witnesse to the justice of
our Cause. And further minding that the only effectual meanes to settle a
just and lasting peace, to obtaine remedie for all your greivances, & to prevent future oppressions, is the making clear & secure the power that you
betrust to your representatives in Parliament, that they may know their
trust, in the faithfull execution whereof you wil assist them. Upon all
these grounds, we propound your joyning with us in the agreement herewith sent unto you; that by vertue thereof, we may have Parliaments certainly cal'd and have the time of their sitting & ending certain & their
power or trust cleare and unquestionable, that hereafter they may remove
your burdens, & secure your rights, without oppositions or obstructions, &
that the foundations of your peace may be so free from uncertainty, that
there may be no grounds for future quarrels, or contentions to occasion
warre and bloud-shed; & wee desire you would consider, that as these
things wherein we offer to agree with you, are the fruites & ends of the
Victories which God hath given us: so the settlement of these are the most
absolute meanes to preserve you & your Posterity, from slavery, oppression, distraction, & trouble; by this, those whom your selves shall chuse,
shall have power to restore you to, and secur you in, all your rights; & they
shall be in a capacity to tast of subjection, as well as rule, & so shall be
equally concerned with your selves, in all they do. For they must equally
suffer with you under any common burdens, & partake with you in any
freedoms; & by this they shal be disinabled to defraud or wrong you, when
the lawes shall bind all alike, without priviledge or exemption; & by this
your Consciences shall be free from tyrannie & oppression, & those occasions of endlesse strifes, & bloudy warres, shall be perfectly removed;
without controversie by your joyning with us in this Agreement, all your
particular & common grievances will be redressed forthwith without delay;
the Parliament must then make your reliefe and common good their only
study.

Now because we are earnestly desirous of the peace and good of all our
Country-men, even of those that have opposed us, and would to our utmost
possibility provide for perfect peace and freedome, & prevent all suites,
debates, & contentions that may happen amongst you, in relation to the
late war: we have therefore inserted it into this Agreement, that no person
shall be questionable for any thing done, in relation to the late publike differences, after the dissolution of this present Parliament, further then in
execution of their judgment; that thereby all may be secure from all sufferings for what they have done, & not liable hereafter to be troubled or punished by the judgment of another Parliament, which may be to their ruine,

unlesse this Agreement be joyned in, whereby any acts of indempnity or oblivion shal be made unalterable, and you and your posterities be secure.

But if any shall enquire why we should desire to joyn in an Agreement with the people, to declare these to be our native Rights, & not rather petition to the Parliament for them; the reason is evident: No Act of Parliament is or can be unalterable, and so cannot be sufficient security to save you or us harmlesse, from what another Parliament may determine, if it should be corrupted; and besides Parliaments are to receive the extent of their power, and trust from those that betrust them; and therefore the people are to declare what their power and trust is, which is the intent of this Agreement; and its to be observed, that though there hath formerly been many Acts of Parliament, for the calling of Parliaments every yeare, yet you have been deprived of them, and inslaved through want of them; and therefore both necessity for your security in these freedomes, that are essentiall to your well-being, and wofull experience of the manifold miseries and distractions that have been lengthened out since the war ended, through want of such a settlement, requires this Agreement and when you and we shall be joyned together therein, we shall readily joyn with you, to petition the Parliament, as they are our fellow Commoners equally concerned, to joyn with us.

And if any shall inquire, Why we undertake to offer this Agreement, we must professe, we are sensible that you have been so often deceived with Declarations and Remonstrances, and fed with vain hopes that you have sufficient reason to abandon all confidence in any persons whatsoever, from whom you have no other security of their intending your freedome, then bare Declaration: And therefore, as our consciences witnesse, that in simplicity and integrity of heart, we have proposed lately in the Case of the Army stated, your freedome and deliverance from slavery, oppression, and all burdens: so we desire to give you satisfying assurance thereof by this Agreement whereby the foundations of your freedomes provided in the Case, &c. shall be setled unalterably, & we shall as faithfully proceed to, and all other most vigorous actings for your good that God shall direct and enable us unto; And though the malice of our enemies, and such as they delude, would blast us by scandalls, aspersing us with designes of Anarchy, and community; yet we hope the righteous God will not onely by this our present desire of setling an equall just Government, but also by directing us unto all righteous undertakings, simply for publike good, make our uprightnesse and faithfulnesse to the interest of all our Countreymen, shine forth so clearly, that malice it selfe shall be silenced, and confounded. We question not, but the longing expectation of a firme peace, will incite you to the most speedy joyning in this Agreement: in the prosecution whereof, or of any thing that you shall desire for publike good; you may be confident, you shall never want the assistance of Your most faithfull fellow-Commoners, now in Armes for your service.

Edmond Bear   Robert Everard   LIEUT. GEN. REGIMENT.
George Garret   Thomas Beverly   COM. GEN. REGIMENT.
William Pryor   William Bryan   COL. FLEETWOODS REGIMENT.
Matthew Weale   William Russell   CON. WHALIES REGIMENT.
John Dover   William Hudson   COL. RICHES REGIMENT.

Agents coming from other Regiments unto us, have subscribed the Agreement to be proposed to their respective Regiments, and you.

For Our much honoured, and truly worthy Fellow-Commoners, and Souldiers, the Officers and Souldiers under Command of His Excellencie Sir THOMAS FAIRFAX.

Gentlemen and Fellow Souldiers;
    The deepe sense of many dangers and mischiefes that may befall you in relation to the late War, whensoever this Parliament shall end, unlesse sufficient prevention be now provided, hath constrained Us to study the most absolute & certain means for your security; and upon most serious considerations, we judge that no Act of Indempnity can sufficiently provide for your quiet, ease, and safety; because, as it hath formerly been, a corrupt Party (chosen into the next Parliament by your Enemies meanes) may possibly surprize the house, and make any Act of Indemnity null, seeing they cannot faile of the Kings Assistance and concurrence, in any such actings against you, that conquered him.
    And by the same meanes, your freedome from impressing also, may in a short time be taken from you, though for the present, it should be granted; wee apprehend no other security, by which you shall be saved harmlesse, for what you have done in the late warre, then a mutuall Agreement between the people & you, that no person shall be questioned by any Authority whatsoever, for any thing done in relation to the late publike differences, after the dissolution of the present house of Commons, further then in execution of their judgment; and that your native freedome from constraint to serve in warre, whether domestick or forraign, shall never be subject to the power of Parliaments, or any other; and for this end, we propound the Agreement that we herewith send to you, to be forthwith subscribed.
    And because we are confident, that in judgment and Conscience, ye hazarded your lives for the settlement of such a just and equall Government, that you and your posterities, and all the free borne people of this Nation might enjoy justice & freedome, and that you are really sensible that the distractions, oppressions, and miseries of the Nation, and your

want of your Arreares, do proceed from the Want of the establishment, both of such certain rules of just Government, and foundations of peace, as are the price of bloud, and the expected fruites of all the peoples cost: Therefore in this Agreement wee have inserted the certaine Rules of equall Government, under which the Nation may enjoy all its Rights and Free-domes securely; And as we doubt not but your love to the freedome and lasting peace of the yet distracted Country will cause you to joyn together in this Agreement.

So we question not: but every true English man that loves the peace and freedome of England will concurre with us; and then your Arrears and con-stant pay (while you continue in Armes) will certainly be brought in out of the abundant love of the people to you, and then shall the mouthes of those be stopped, that scandalize you and us, as endeavouring Anarchy, or to rule by the sword; & then will so firm an union be made between the people and you, that neither any homebred or forraigne Enemies will dare to disturbe our happy peace. We shall adde no more but this; that the knowledge of your union in laying this foundation of peace, this Agreement, is much longed for, by

Yours, and the Peoples most faithfull Servants.

22. The Putney Debates

An Agreement of the People was presented at a meeting of the army's Council of Officers and debated over a four-day period. The debate is one of the most remarkable in English history both for the stark contrast in the positions of the antagonists; for the eloquence of the appeals to natu-ral, civil, and divine law; and as expressions of the underlying themes of early modern political theory.

The debates were recorded, in a shorthand cipher, by William Clarke, secretary of the army. Clarke's notes were hastily made, parts of impor-tant speeches are missing as are words and phrases throughout and the cipher was not transcribed by Clarke for over five years. Moreover, the transcriptions which were subsequently bound together are probably not in the proper order.

Among the main speakers, Henry Ireton (1611–51), Cromwell's son-in-law, was commissary-general of cavalry in the army and one of its chief political strategists. He was principally involved in the production of the army's own draft settlement (The Heads of the Proposals) in July.

From A. S. P. Woodehouse, *Puritanism and Liberty,* 2d edition (Chicago: University of Chicago Press, 1951), pp. 99–130. © 1951, The University of Chicago Press.

Ireton came from a modest landed background in Nottinghamshire and he continued to serve Parliament until his death in Ireland in 1651. Thomas Rainsborough, whose immortal speech "the smallest hee in England" has always marked him out as a champion of the common man was, in fact, the son of a wealthy naval officer. He was colonel of a regiment of infantry in the New Model Army and was engaged in a dispute with the senior command over his recent appointment to the fleet which would necessitate his removal from the army. John Wildman (1623–93) was only twenty-four when he came to Putney and he is the most likely candidate for the authorship of both the *Case of the Army* and the *Agreement of the People*. Wildman was to have a remarkable career over the course of the seventeenth century, sitting in Parliament under Charles II and holding the office of postmaster general. He was one of the civilian Levellers who were invited to the council's meeting. Edward Sexby (1616?–58) was one of the original agitators selected by the rank and file in the spring of 1647. Although still noncommissioned in 1647 he would soon rise to the rank of colonel and would serve the Commonwealth as a secret agent on the continent.

From the second day's debate in the General Council of the Army, Putney Church, 29 October 1647. The text is as follows:

The Paper called the Agreement read.

Afterwards the first Article read by itself.

Commissary [General] Ireton: The exception that lies in it is this, it is said, they are to be distributed according to the number of the inhabitants, The People of England, etc. And this doth make me think, that the meaning is that every man that is an inhabitant is to be equally considered, and to have an equal voice in the election of those representers, the persons that are for the general representative, and if that be the meaning then I have something to say against it, but if it be only, that those people, that by the civil constitution of this kingdom, which is original and fundamental, and beyond which I am sure no memory of record does go.

[*Interjection*] Not before the Conquest.

But before the Conquest it was so. If it be intended, that those that by that constitution that was before the Conquest that hath been beyond memory, such persons that have been before that constitution should be the electors I have no more to say against it.

Colonel Rainsborough: Moved, That others might have given their hands to it.

Captain Denne: Denied, That those that were set of their Regiment, that they were their hands.

Ireton: Whether those men whose hands are to it, or those that brought it do know so much of the matter as that they mean that all that had a former right of election, or those that had no right before are to come in?

Commissary [General] Cowling: In the time before the Conquest, and since the Conquest the greatest part of the kingdom was in vassalage.

Mr. Pettus [Maximilian Petty]: We judge, that all inhabitants that have not lost their birthright should have an equal voice in elections.

Rainsborough: I desired that those that had engaged in it, for really I think that the poorest he that is in England hath a life to live as the greatest he; and therefore truly, sir, I think it's clear, that every man that is to live under a government ought first by his own consent to put himself under that government; and I do think that the poorest man in England is not at all bound in a strict sense to that government that he hath not had a voice to put himself under; and I am confident that, when I have heard the reasons against it, that something will be said to answer those reasons, insomuch that I should doubt whether I was an Englishman or no, that should doubt of these things.

Ireton: That's this. Give me leave to tell you, that if you make this the rule, I think you must fly for refuge to an absolute natural right, and you must deny all civil right; and I am sure it will come to that in the consequence. This, I perceive, is pressed as that which is so essential and due, the right of the people of this kingdom, and as they are the people of this kingdom, distinct and divided from other people, as that we must for this right lay aside all other considerations. This is so just; this is so due; this is so right to them; and those that they must thus choose, and that those that they do thus choose, must have such a power of binding all, and loosing all, according to those limitations. This is pressed as so due, and so just, as is argued, that it is an engagement paramount all others, and you must for it lay aside all others; if you have engaged any others, you must break it; so look upon these as thus held out to us; so it was held out by the gentleman that brought it yesterday. For my part, I think it is no right at all. I think that no person hath a right to an interest or share in the disposing of the affairs of the kingdom, and in determining or choosing those that shall determine what laws we shall be ruled by here, no person hath a right to this that hath not a permanent fixed interest in this kingdom, and those persons together are properly the represented of this kingdom, who taken together, and consequently are to make up the representers of this kingdom, are the representers, who taken together do comprehend whatsoever is of real or permanent interest in the kingdom, and I am sure there is otherwise (I cannot tell what), otherwise any man can say why a foreigner coming in amongst us, or as many as will coming in amongst us, or by force or otherwise settling themselves here, or at least by our permission having a being here, why they should not as well lay claim to it as any other.

We talk of birthright. Truly birthright there is thus much claim: men may justly have by birthright, by their very being born in England, that we should not seclude them out of England. That we should not refuse to give them air and place and ground, and the freedom of the highways and other things, to live amongst us, not any man that is born here, though he in birth, or by his birth there come nothing at all that is part of the permanent interest of this kingdom to him. That I think is due to a man by birth. But that by a man's being born here he shall have a share in that power that shall dispose of the lands here, and of all things here, I do not think it a sufficient ground, but I am sure if we look upon that which is the utmost, within man's view, of what was originally the constitution of this kingdom, upon that which is most radical and fundamental, and which if you take away, there is no man hath any land, any goods, you take away any civil interest, and that is this: that those that choose the representers for the making of laws by which this state and kingdom are to be governed, are the persons who taken together, do comprehend the local interest of this kingdom; that is, the persons in whom all land lies, and those in corporations in whom all trading lies. This is the most fundamental constitution of this kingdom, and which if you do not allow, you allow none at all. This constitution hath limited and determined it, that only those shall have voices in elections.

It is true, as was said by a gentleman near me, the meanest man in England ought to have. I say this: that those that have the meanest local interest, that man that hath but forty shillings a year, he hath as great voice in the election of a knight for the shire as he that hath ten thousand a year or more, if he had never so much, and therefore there is that regard had to it. But this still the constitution of this government hath had an eye to, and what other government hath not an eye to this, it doth not relate to the interest of the kingdom if it do not lay the foundation of the power that's given to the representers, in those who have a permanent and a local interest in the kingdom, and who taken altogether do comprehend the whole, and if we shall go to take away this, we shall plainly go to take away all property and interest that any man hath, either in land by inheritance, or in estate by possession, or anything else, if you take away this fundamental part of the civil constitution.

There is all the reason and justice that can be: if I will come to live in a kingdom, being a foreigner to it, or live in a kingdom, having no permanent interest in it, if I will desire as a stranger, or claim as one freeborn here, the air, the free passage of highways, the protection of laws, and all such things, and if I will either desire them, or claim them, I (if I have no permanent interest in that kingdom) must submit to those laws and those rules, who taken together do comprehend the whole interest of the kingdom.

Rainsborough: Truly, sir, I am of the same opinion I was, and am resolved to keep it till I know reason why I should not. I confess my memory is bad, and therefore I am fain to make use of my pen. I remember that in a former speech this gentleman brought before this, he was saying that in some cases he should not value whether a king or no king, whether lords or no lords, whether a property or no property. For my part I differ in that. I do very much care whether a king or no king, lords or no lords, property or no property; and I think, if we do not all take care, we shall all have none of these very shortly. But as to this present business, I do hear nothing at all that can convince me, why any man that is born in England ought not to have his voice in election of burgesses.

It is said that if a man have not a permanent interest, he can have no claim; and we must be no freer than the laws will let us to be, and that there is no chronicle will let us be freer than that we enjoy. Something was said to this yesterday, and I do think that the main cause why Almighty God gave men reason, it was that they should make use of that reason, and that they should improve it for that end and purpose that God gave it them, and truly I think that half a loaf is better than none if a man be an-hungry; yet I think there is nothing that God hath given a man that any else can take from him, and therefore I say, that either it must be the law of God or the law of man that must prohibit the meanest man in the kingdom to have this benefit as well as the greatest.

I do not find anything in the law of God, that a lord shall choose twenty burgesses, and a gentleman but two, or a poor man shall choose none: I find no such thing in the law of nature, nor in the law of nations, but I do find that all Englishmen must be subject to English laws, and I do verily believe that there is no man but will say that the foundation of all law lies in the people, and if in the people, I am to seek for this exemption; and truly I have thought something: in what a miserable distressed condition would many a man that hath fought for the Parliament in this quarrel be? I will be bound to say that many a man whose zeal and affection to God and this kingdom hath carried him forth in this cause, hath so spent his estate that, in the way the state, the army are going this way, he shall not hold up his head, and when his estate is lost, and not worth forty shillings a year, a man shall not have any interest; and there are many other ways by which men have estates (if that be the rule which God in his providence does use) do fall to decay; a man, when he hath an estate, he hath an interest in making laws; when he hath none, he hath no power in it. So that a man cannot lose that which he hath for the maintenance of his family but he must lose that which God and nature hath given him; and therefore I do, and am still of the same opinion, that every man born in England cannot, ought not, neither by the law of God nor the law of nature, to be exempted from the choice of those who are to make laws and for him to live under, and for him (for aught I know) to lose his life under, and therefore I think there can be no great stick in this.

Truly I think that there is not this day reigning in England a greater fruit or effect of tyranny than this very thing would produce, for, sir, what is it, the King he grants a patent under the Broad-Seal of England to such a corporation to send burgesses. He grants to a city to send burgesses. Truly I know nothing free but only the knight of the shire, nor do I know anything in a parliamentary way that is clear from the height and fulness of tyranny, but as for this of corporations, it is as contrary to freedom as may be; when a poor base corporation from the King shall send two burgesses, when five hundred men of estate shall not send one, when those that are to make their laws are called by the King, or cannot act by such a call, truly I think that the people of England have little freedom.

Ireton: I think there was nothing that I said to give you occasion to think that I did contend for this, that such a corporation should have the electing of a man to the parliament. I think I agreed to this matter, that all should be equally distributed, but the question is, whether it should be distributed to all persons, or whether the same persons that are the electors should be the electors still, and it equally distributed amongst them. I do not see anybody else that makes this objection; and if nobody else be sensible of it I shall soon have done. Only I shall a little crave your leave to represent the consequences of it, and clear myself from one misrepresentation of the thing that was misrepresented by the gentleman that sat next me. I think, if the gentleman remember himself, he cannot but remember that what I said was to this effect: that if I saw the hand of God leading so far as to destroy King, and destroy lords, and destroy property, and no such thing at all amongst us, I should acquiesce in it; and so I did not care, if no king, no lords, or no property, how in comparison of the tender care that I have of the honour of God, and of the people of God, whose name is so much concerned in this Army. This I did deliver, and not absolutely.

All the main thing that I speak for, is because I would have an eye to property. I hope we do not come to contend for victory, but let every man consider with himself that he do not go that way to take away all property; for here is the case of the most fundamental part of the constitution of the kingdom, which if you take away, you take away all by that. Here are men of this and this quality are determined to be the electors of men to the parliament, and they are all those who have any permanent interest in the kingdom, and who, taken together, do comprehend the whole interest of the kingdom. I mean by permanent, local, that is not anywhere else. As for instance, he that hath a freehold, and that freehold cannot be removed out of the kingdom. And so there's a corporation, a place which hath the privilege of a market and trading, which if you should allow to all places equally, I do not see how you could preserve any peace in the kingdom, and that is the reason why in the constitution we have but some few market towns. Now those people by the former constitution were looked upon to comprehend the permanent interest of the kingdom, and those are the freemen of corporations; for he that hath his livelihood by his trade, and by his freedom of trading in such a corporation, which he cannot exercise in another, he is tied to that place, his livelihood depends upon it; and secondly, that man hath an interest, hath a permanent interest there, upon which he may live, and live a freeman without dependence. These constitutions this kingdom hath looked at.

Now I wish we may all consider of what right you will challenge, that all the people should have right to elections. Is it by the right of nature? If you will hold forth that as your ground, then I think you must deny all property too, and this is my reason. For thus: by that same right of nature, whatever it be that you pretend, by which you can say, a man hath an equal right with another to the choosing of him that shall govern him, by the same right of nature, he hath the same right in any goods he sees: meat, drink, clothes, to take and use them for his sustenance; he hath a freedom to the land, the ground, to exercise it, till it. He hath the freedom to anything that any one doth account himself to have any propriety in. Why now I say, then if you will, against the most fundamental part of civil constitution (which I have now declared), will plead the law of nature, that a man should, paramount this, and contrary to this, have a power of choosing those men that shall determine what shall be law in this state, though he himself have no permanent interest in the state, whatever interest he hath he may carry about with him, if this be allowed, we are free, we are equal, one man must have as much voice as another. Then show me what step or difference, why by the same right of necessity to sustain nature, it is for my better being, and possibly not for it neither; possibly I may not have so real a regard to the peace of the kingdom as that man who hath a permanent interest in it; but he that hath no permanent interest, that is here to-day and gone tomorrow, I do not see that he hath such a permanent interest. Since you cannot plead to it by anything but the law of nature, but for the end of better being, and that better being is not certain, and more destructive to another; upon these grounds, if you do, paramount all constitutions, hold up this law of nature, I would fain have any man show me their bounds, where you will end, and take away all property?

Rainsborough: I shall now be a little more free and open with you than I was before. I wish we were all true hearted, and that we did all carry ourselves with integrity; if I did mistrust you, I would use such asseverations. I think it doth go on mistrust, and things are thought too matters of reflection that were never intended for my part; as I think you forgot something that was in my speech. You forgot something in my speech, and you do not only yourselves believe, that men are inclining to anarchy, but you would make all men believe that; and, Sir, to say because a man pleads that every man hath a voice, that therefore it destroys the same that there's a property, the law of God says it, else why God made that law, thou shalt not steal. I am a poor man, therefore I must be prest; if I have no interest in the kingdom, I must suffer by all their laws, be they right or wrong. Nay thus, a gentleman lives in a county and hath three or four lordships as some men have, God knows how they got them, and when a parliament is called, he must be a parliament-man; and it may be he sees some poor men they live near, this man he can crush them. I have known an evasion to make sure he hath turned the poor man out of doors, and I would fain know whether the potency of men do not this, and so keep them under the greatest tyranny that was thought of in the world; and therefore I think that to that it is fully answered. God hath set down that thing as to property with this law of his, thou shalt not steal. And for my part I am against any such thought, and I wish you would not make the world believe that we are for anarchy, as for yourselves.

Lieut.-General [Cromwell]: I know nothing but this, that they that are the most yielding have the greatest wisdom; but really Sir, this is not right as it should be. No man says that you have a mind to anarchy, but the consequence of this rule tends to anarchy, must end in anarchy; for where is there any bound or limit set, if you take away this, that men that have no interest but the interest of breathing [should have no voice]. Therefore I am confident on't, we should not be so hot one with another.

Rainsborough: I know that some particular men we debate with [believe—or say—we] are for anarchy.

Ireton: I have, with as much plainness and clearness of reason as I could, showed you how I did conceive the doing of this takes away that which is the most original, the most fundamental civil constitution of this Kingdome, and which is above all that constitution by which I have any property and if you will take away that and set up what ever a man may claim as a thing paramount, that by the law of nature, though it be not a thing of necessity to him for the sustenance of nature, if you do make this your rule, I desire clearly to understand where then remains property.

Now then, that which (I would misrepresent nothing) the great and main answer which had any thing of matter in it that seemed to be the answer upon which that which hath been said against this rests, I profess I must clear myself as to that point; I desire, I would not, I cannot allow my self to lay the least scandal upon any body, and truly for that gentleman that did take so much offence I do not know why he should take it so: we speak to the paper, not to persons, and to the matter of the paper, and I hope that no man is so much engaged to the matter of the paper. I hope our persons, and our hearts, and judgments are not pinned to papers, but that we are ready to hear what good or ill consequence will flow from it. Now then, as I say to that which is to the main answer, that it will not make the breach of property, then that there is a law, thou shalt not steal: the same law says, honour thy father, and mother: and that law doth likewise hold out that it doth extend to all that, in that place where we are in, are our governors, so that by that there is a forbidding of breaking a civil law when we may live quietly under it, and a divine law; and again it is said, indeed before, that there is no law, no divine law that tells us, that such a corporation must have the election of burgesses, of such a shire or the like. Divine law extends not to particular things; and so on the other side, if a man were to demonstrate his property by divine law, it would be very remote, but our property descends from other things, as well as our right of sending burgesses; that divine law doth not determine particulars but generals in relation to man & man, and to property, and all things else, and we should be as far to seek if we should go to prove a property in divine law as to prove that I have an interest in choosing burgesses of the parliament by divine law; and truly under favour I refer it to all whether these be any thing of solution to that objection that I made, if it be understood. I submit it to any man's judgment.

Rainsborough: To the thing itself property, I would fain know how it comes to be the property: as for estates, and those kind of things and other things that belong to men, it will be granted that it is property, but I deny that that is a property, to a lord, to a gentleman, to any man more than another in the kingdom of England, if it be a property, it is a property by a law; neither do I think, that there is very little property in this thing by the law of the land, because I think, that the law of the land in that thing is the most tyrannical law under heaven, and I would fain know what we have fought for; and this is the old law of England and that which enslaves the people of England, that they should be bound by laws in which they have no voice at all. So the great dispute is who is a right father & a right mother. I am bound to know who is my father & mother, and I take it in the same sense you do. I would have a distinction, a character whereby God commands me to honour and for my part I look upon the people of England so, that wherein they have not voices in the choosing of their fathers & mothers, they are not bound to that commandment.

Petty: I desire to add one word, concerning the word property.

It is for something that anarchy is so much talk't of. For my own part I cannot believe in the least, that it can be clearly derived from that paper. 'Tis true, that somewhat may be derived in the paper against the King, the power of the King, and somewhat against the power of the Lords; and the truth is when I shall see God going about to throw down King and Lords and property, then I shall be contented; but I hope that they may live to see the power of the King and the Lords thrown down, that yet may live to see property preserved. And for this of changing the representative of the nation, of changing those that choose the representative, making of them more full, taking more into the number than formerly, I had verily thought we had all agreed in it: that more should have chosen, all that had desired a more equal representation than now we have. For now those only choose who have forty shillings freehold. A man may have a lease for one hundred pounds a year, a man may have a lease for three lives; but for this, that it destroys all right that every Englishman that is an inhabitant of England should choose and have a voice in the representatives, I suppose it is the only means to preserve all property. For I judge every man is naturally free; and I judge the reason why the men when they are in so great numbers that every man could not give his voice, was that they who were chosen might preserve property; and therefore men agreed to come into some form of government that they might preserve property, and I would fain know, if we were to begin a government: you have not forty shillings a year, therefore you shall not have a voice. Whereas before there was a government every man had such a choice, and afterwards, and for this very cause, they did choose representatives, and put themselves into forms of government that they may preserve property, and therefore it is not to destroy it.

Ireton: I think we shall not be so apt to come to a right understanding in this business, if one man, and another man, and another man do speak their several thoughts and conceptions to the same purpose, as if we do consider what the objection is, and where the answer lies to which it is made; and therefore I desire we may do so too. That which this gentleman spake last, the main thing that he seemed to answer was this, that he would make it appear that the going about to establish this government, such a government, is not a destruction of property, nor does not tend to the destruction of property, because the people's falling into a government is for the preservation of property.

What weight there [is] lies in this: since there is a falling into a government, and government is to preserve property, therefore this cannot be against property. The objection does not lie in that, the making of it more equal, but the introducing of men into an equality of interest in this government, who have no property in this kingdom, or who have no local permanent interest in it; for if I had said that I would not wish at all that we should have any enlargement of the bounds of those that are to be the electors, then you might have excepted against it, but that I would not go to enlarge it beyond all bounds, so that upon the same ground you may admit of so many men from foreign states as would outvote you. The objection lies still in this, that I do not mean that I would have it restrained to that proportion, but to restrain it still to men who have a local, a permanent interest in the kingdom, who have such an interest that they may live upon it as freemen, and who have such an interest as is fix't upon a place, and is not the same equally everywhere.

If a man be an inhabitant upon a rack rent for a year, for two years, or twenty years, you cannot think that man hath any fixed permanent interest; that man, if he pay the rent that his land is worth, and he hath no advantage but what he hath by his land, that man is as good a man, may have as much interest in another kingdom, but here I do not speak of an enlarging this at all, but of keeping this to the most fundamental constitution in this kingdom. That is, that no person that hath not a local and permanent interest in the kingdom should have an equal dependence in election; but if you go beyond this law, if you admit any man that hath a breath and being, I did show you how this will destroy property. It may come to destroy property thus: you may have a major part, you may have such men chosen, or at least the major part of them, why those men may not vote against all property. You may admit strangers by this rule, if you admit them once to inhabit, and those that have interest in the land may be voted out of their land; it may destroy property that way, but here is the rule that you go by: for that by which you infer this to be the right of the people, of every inhabitant, and that because this man hath such a right in nature, though it be not of necessity for the preserving of his being; therefore you are to overthrow the most fundamental constitution for this. By the same rule, show me why you will not, by the same right of nature, make use of anything that any man hath, for the necessary sustenance of mee [men?]. Show me what you will stop at, wherein you will fence any man in a property by this rule.

Rainsborough: I desire to know how this comes to be a property in some men, and not in others.

Colonel Rich: I confess that objection that the Commissary-General last insisted upon; for you have five to one in this kingdom that have no permanent interest. Some men [have] ten, some twenty servants, some more, some less; if the master and servant shall be equal electors, then clearly those that have no interest in the kingdom will make it their interest to choose those that have no interest. It may happen, that the majority may by law, not in a confusion, you may destroy property; there may be a law enacted, that there shall be an equality of goods and estate. I think that either of the extremes may be urged to inconveniency; that is, men that have no interest as to estate should have no interest as to election. But there may be a more equal division and distribution than that he that hath nothing should have an equal voice; and certainly there may be some other way thought of, that there may be a representative of the poor as well as the rich, and not to exclude all. I remember there were many workings and revolutions, as we have heard, in the Roman Senate; and there was never a confusion that did appear, and that indeed was come to, till the state came to know this kind of distribution of election: that is how the people's voices were bought and sold, and that by the poor; and thence it came that he that was the richest man, and of some considerable power among the soldiers made himself a perpetual dictator and one they resolved on. And if we strain too far to avoid monarchy in kings that we do not call for emperors to deliver us from more than one tyrant.

Rainsborough: I should not have spoken again. I think it is a fine gilded pill, but there is much danger, and it may seem to some that there is some kind of remedy. I think that we are better as we are, that the poor shall choose many; still the people be in the same case, be over-voted still. And therefore truly, sir, I should desire to go close to the business; and the thing that I am unsatisfied in is how it comes about that there is such a propriety in some freeborn Englishmen, and not others.

Cowling: Whether the younger son have not as much right to the inheritance as the eldest?

Ireton: Will you decide it by the light of nature?

Cowling: Why election was only forty shillings a year, which was more than forty pounds a year now, the reason was: that the Commons of England were overpowered by the Lords, who had abundance of vassals, but that still they might make their laws good against encroaching prerogatives; therefore they did exclude all slaves. Now the case is not so; all slaves have bought their freedoms, they are more free that in the commonwealth are more beneficial. There are men in the country in Staines: there is a tanner in Staines worth three thousand pounds, and another in Reading worth three horseskins.

Ireton: In the beginning of your speech you seem to acknowledge by law, by civil constitution, the propriety of having voices in election was fix't in certain persons. So then your exception of your argument does not prove that by civil constitution they have no such propriety, but your argument does acknowledge by civil propriety. You argue against this law, that this law is not good.

Mr. Wildman: Unless I be very much mistaken we are very much deviated from the first question. And instead of following the first proposition to inquire what is just, I conceive we look to prophecies, and look to what may be the event, and judge of the justness of a thing by the consequence. I desire we may recall whether it be right or no. I conceive all that hath been said against it will be reduced to this, that it is against a fundamental law, and another reason that every person ought to have a permanent interest, because it is not fit that those should choose parliaments that have no lands to be disposed of by parliament.

Ireton: If you will take it by the way, it is not fit that the representees should choose the representees, or the persons who shall make the law in the kingdom, who have not a permanent fix't interest in the kingdom.

Wildman: Sir, I do so take it; and I conceive that that is brought in for the same reason, that foreigners might come as well to have a notice in our elections as well as the native inhabitants.

Ireton: That is upon supposition, that these should be all inhabitants.

Wildman: I shall begin with the last first. The case is different from the native inhabitant and foreigner. If a foreigner shall be admitted to be an inhabitant in the nation, he may so he will submit to that form of government as the natives do; he hath the same right as the natives but in this particular. Our case is to be considered thus: that we have been under slavery, that's acknowledged by all. Our very laws were made by our conquerors; and whereas it's spoken much of chronicles, I conceive there is no credit to be given to any of them; and the reason is because those that were our lords, and made us their vassals, would suffer nothing else to be chronicled. We are now engaged for our freedom; that's the end of parliaments, not to constitute what is already according to the just rules of government. Every person in England hath as clear a right to elect his representative as the greatest person in England. I conceive that's the undeniable maxim of government: that all government is in the free consent of the people. If then upon that account, there is no person that is under a just government, or hath justly his own, unless he by his own free consent be put under that government. This he cannot be unless he be consenting to it, and therefore, according to this maxim, there is never a person in England; if, as that gentleman says be true, there are no laws that in this strictness and rigour of justice, that are not made by those who he doth consent to. And therefore I should humbly move, that if the question be stated, which would soonest bring things to an issue, it might rather be this: Whether any person can justly be bound by law not by his own consent, who doth not give his consent that such persons shall make laws for him.

Ireton: Let the question be so: Whether a man can be bound to any law that he doth not consent to? And I shall tell you, that he may and ought to be, that he doth not give a consent to, nor doth not choose any; and I will make it clear.

If a foreigner come within this kingdom, if that stranger will have liberty who hath no local interest here, he is a man, it's true, hath air that by nature we must not expel our coasts, give him no being amongst us, nor kill him because he comes upon our land, comes up our stream, arrives at our shore. It is a piece of hospitality, of humanity, to receive that man amongst us. But if that man be received to a being amongst us, I think that man may very well be content to submit himself to the law of the land; that is, the law that is made by those people that have a property, a fix't property in the land. I think, if any man will receive protection from this people, though he nor his ancestors, not any betwixt him and Adam, did ever give concurrence to this constitution, I think this man ought to be subject to those laws, and to be bound by those laws, so long as he continues amongst them; that is my opinion.

A man ought to be subject to a law, that did not give his consent, but with this reservation, that if this man do think himself unsatisfied to be subject to this law, he may go into another kingdom; and so the same reason doth extend in my understanding, that a man that hath no permanent interest in the kingdom, if he hath money, his money is as good in another place as here; he hath nothing that doth locally fix him to this kingdom. If that man will live in this kingdom, or trade amongst us, that man ought to subject himself to the law made by the people who have the interest of this kingdom in us. And yet I do acknowledge that which you take to be so general a maxim, that in every kingdom, within every land the original of power, of making laws, of determining what shall be law in the land, does lie in the people that are possess't in the permanent interest in the land. But whoever is extraneous to this, that is, as good a man in another land, that man ought to give such a respect to the property of men that live in the land. They do not determine why should I have any interest of determining what shall be the law of this land.

Major [William] Rainsborough: I think if it can be made to appear that it is a just and reasonable thing, and that it is for the preservation of all the freeborn men, I think it ought to be made good unto them; and the reason is, that the chief end of this government is to preserve persons as well as estates, and if any law shall take hold of my person, it is more dear than my estate.

Colonel Rainsborough: I do very well remember that the gentleman in the window [said] that, if it were so, there were no propriety to be had, because a fifth [five?] part[s] of the poor people are now excluded and would then come in. So I say one on the other side said, if otherwise, then rich men shall be chosen; then, I say, the one part shall make hewers of wood and drawers of water of the other five, and so the greatest part of the nation be enslaved. And truly I think we are where we were still; and I do not hear any argument given but only that it is the present law of the kingdom. I say what shall become still of those many that have laid out themselves for the parliament of England in this present war, that have ruined themselves by fighting, by hazarding all they had. They are Englishmen. They have now nothing to say for themselves.

Rich: I should be very sorry to speak anything here that should give offence, or that may occasion personal reflection that we spoke against just now. I did not urge anything so far as was represented, and I did not at all urge them that there should be a consideration, and that man that is, shall be without consideration, he deserves to be made poor and not to live at all. But all that I urged was this: that I think it worthy of consideration, whether they should have an equality in their interest, but however, I think we have been a great while upon this point, and if we be as long upon all the rest, it were well if there were no greater difference than this.

Mr. Peters [Hugh Peter]: I think that this may be easily agreed on, that is, there may be a way thought of; but I would fain know whether that will answer the work of your meeting. I think you should do well to sit up all night, but I think that three or four might be thought of in this company: you will be forced to put characters upon electors or elected. Therefore I do suppose that if there be any here that can make up a representative to your mind, the thing is gained. But the question is, whether you can state any one question for the present danger of the kingdom, if any one question or no will dispatch the work.

Sir, I desire, that some question may be stated to finish the present work, to cement us wherein lies the distance; and if the thoughts of the commonwealth, the people's freedom, I think that's soon cured; but I desire that all manner of plainness may be used, that we may not go on with the lapwing and carry one another off the nest. There is something else in that must cement us where the awkwardness of our spirits lies.

Rainsborough: For my part, I think we cannot engage one way or other in the Army if we do not think of the people's liberties; if we can agree where the liberty and freedom of the people lies, that will do all.

Ireton: I cannot consent so far before. As I said before, when I see the hand of God destroying King, and Lords, and Commons too, any foundation of human constitution, when I see God hath done it, I shall, I hope, comfortably acquiesce in it; but first, I cannot give my consent to it, because it is not good, and secondly, as I desire that this Army should have regard to engagements wherever they are lawful, so I would have them have regard to this: that they should not bring that scandal upon the name of God, that those that call themselves by that name, those whom God hath owned and appeared with, that we should not represent ourselves to the world as men so far from being of that peaceable spirit which is suitable to the Gospel, as we would have bought peace of the world upon such terms; we would not have peace in the world but upon such terms as should destroy all property. If the principle upon which you move this alteration, or the ground upon which you press that we should make this alteration, do destroy all kind of property or whatsoever a man hath by human constitution. The law of God doth not give me property, nor the law of nature, but property is of human constitution. I have a property and this I shall enjoy.

Constitution founds property. If either the thing itself that you press or the consequence that you press, though I shall acquiesce in having no property, yet I cannot give my heart or hand to it; because it is a thing evil in itself, and scandalous to the world, and I desire this Army may be free from both.

Mr. Sexby: I see that though it [liberty?] were our end, there is a degeneration from it. We have engaged in this kingdom and ventured our lives, and it was all for this: to recover our birthrights and privileges as Englishmen; and by the arguments urged there is none. There are many thousands of us soldiers that have ventured our lives; we have had little propriety in the kingdom as to our estates, yet we have had a birthright; but it seems now, except a man hath a fix't estate in this kingdom, he hath no right in this kingdom. I wonder we were so much deceived. If we had not a right to the kingdom, we were mere mercenary soldiers. There are many in my condition, that have as good a condition; it may be little estate they have at present, and yet they have as much a right as those too who are their lawgivers, as any in this place. I shall tell you in a word my resolution. I am resolved to give my birthright to none, whatsoever may come in the way; and be thought that I will give it to none, if this thing that with so much pressing after. There was one thing spoken to this effect: that if the poor and those in low condition. [. . .] I think this was but a distrust of providence. I do think the poor and meaner of this kingdom, I speak as in that relation in which we are, have been the means of the preservation of this kingdom. I say, in their stations, and really I think that to their utmost possibility; and their lives have not been dear for purchasing the good of the kingdom. Those that act to this end are as free from anarchy or confusion as those that oppose it, and they have the law of God and the law of their conscience. But truly I shall only sum up this in all: I desire that we may not spend so much time upon these things. We must be plain. When men come to understand these things, they will not loose that which they have contended for. That which I shall beseech you is to come to a determination of this question.

Ireton: I am very sorry we are come to this point, that from reasoning one to another we should come to express our resolutions. I profess for my part, what I see is good for the kingdom, and becoming a Christian to contend for, I hope through God I shall have strength and resolution to do my part towards it, and yet I will profess direct contrary in some kind to what that gentleman said. For my part, rather than I will make a disturbance to a good constitution of a kingdom wherein I may live in godliness and honesty, and peace and quietness, I will part with a great deal of my birthright. I will part with my own property rather than I will be the man that shall make a disturbance in the kingdom for my property; and therefore if all the people in this kingdom, or representative of them all together, should meet and should give away my property, I would submit to it, I would give it away. But that gentleman, and I think every Christian spirit, ought to bear that, to carry that in him, that he will not make a public disturbance upon a private prejudice.

Now let us consider where our difference lies. We all agree that you should have a representative to govern, but this representative to be as equal as you can; but the question is, whether this distribution can be made to all persons equally, or whether amongst those equals that have the interest of England in them? That which I have declared my opinion, I think we ought to keep to; that both because it is a civil constitution, it is the most fundamental constitution that we have, and there is so much justice and reason and prudence, as I dare confidently undertake to demonstrate, as that there are many more evils that will follow in case you do alter than there can in the standing of it. But I say but this in the general, that I do wish that they that talk of birthrights, we any of us when we talk of birthrights, would consider what really our birthright is.

If a man me[a]n by birthright, whatsoever he can challenge by the law of nature, suppose there were no constitution at all, supposing no civil law and civil constitution, that that I am to contend for against constitution; you leave no property, nor no foundation for any man to enjoy anything. But if you call that your birthrights which is the most fundamental part of your constitution, then let him perish that goes about to hinder you or any man of the least part of your birthright, or will do it. But if you will lay aside the most fundamental constitution, and I will give you consequence for consequence, of good upon constitution as you for your birthright, which is as good for aught you can discern as anything you can propose, at least it is a constitution; and if you were merely upon pretence of a birthright, of the right of nature, which is only true as for your better being, if you will upon that ground pretend that this constitution, the most fundamental constitution, the thing that hath reason and equity in it, shall not stand in your way, is the same principle to me (say I), but for your better satisfaction you shall take hold of anything that a man calls his own.

Rainsborough: Sir, I see that it is impossible to have liberty but all property must be taken away. If it be laid down for a rule, and if you will say it, it must be so, but I would fain know what the soldiers have fought for all this while; he hath fought to enslave himself, to give power to men of riches, men of estates, to make him a perpetual slave. We do find in all presses that go forth none must be pres't that are freehold men. When these gentlemen fall out among themselves, they shall press the poor shrubs to come and kill them.

Ireton: I must confess I see so much right in the business that I am not easily satisfied with flourishes. If you will lay the stress of the business upon the consideration of reason, or right relating to anything of human constitution, or anything of that nature, but will put it upon consequences, I will show you greater ill consequences; I see enough to say that, to my apprehensions, I can show you greater ill consequences to follow upon that alteration which you would have, by extending to all that have a being in this kingdom, than that by this a great deal. This is a particular ill consequence. This is a general ill consequence, and that is as great as this or any else, though I think you will see that the validity of that argument must lie, that for one ill lies upon that which now is, and I can show you a thousand upon this. Give me leave but this one word. I tell you what the soldier of the kingdom hath fought for.

First, the danger that we stood in was that one man's will must be a law. The people of the kingdom must have this right at least, that they should not be concluded by the representative of those that had the interest of the kingdom. So men fought in this because they were immediately concerned and engaged in it; other men who had no other interest in the kingdom but this, that they should have the benefit of those laws made by the representative, yet that they should have the benefit of this representative. They thought it was better to be concluded by the common consent of those that were fix't men, and settled men, that had the interest of this kingdom, and from that way I shall know a law and have a certainty. And every man that was born in it that hath a freedom is a denizen; he was capable of trading to get money, and to get estates by; and therefore this man, I think, had a great deal of reason to build up such a foundation of interest to himself; that is, that the will of one man should not be a law, but that the law of this kingdom should be by a choice of persons to represent, and that choice to be made by the generality of the kingdom.

Here was a right that induced men to fight, and those men that had not this interest, and though this be not the utmost interest that other men have, yet they had some interest. Now why we should go to plead whatsoever we can challenge by the right of nature against whatsoever any man can challenge by constitution; I do not see where that man will stop, as to point of property, that he shall not use that right he hath by the law of nature against the constitution. I desire any man to show me where there is a difference. I have been answered, now we see liberty cannot stand without property. Liberty may be had and property not be destroyed; first, the liberty of all those that have the permanent interest in the kingdom, that is provided for, and in a general sense liberty cannot be provided for if property be preserved. For, if property be preserved, that I am not to meddle with such a man's estate, his meat, his drink, his apparel, or other goods, then the right of nature destroys liberty. By the right of nature I am to have sustenance rather than perish; yet property destroys it for a man to have by the light of nature, suppose there be no human constitution.

Peter: I will mind you of one thing, that upon the will of one man abusing us, and so forth. So that I profess to you for my part I hope it is not denied by any man, that any wise, discreet man that hath preserved England or the government of it; I do say still under favour there is a way to cure all this debate. I think they will desire no more liberty if there were time to dispute it. I think he will be satisfied and all will be satisfied, and if the safety of the Army be in danger, for my part I am clear it should be amended, the point of election should be mended.

Cromwell: I confess I was most dissatisfied with that I heard Mr. Sexby speak of any man here, because it did savour so much of will. But I desire that all of us may decline that, and if we meet here really to agree to that which is for the safety of the kingdom, let us not spend so much time in such debates as these are, but let us apply ourselves to such things as are conclusive, and that shall be this: everybody here would be willing that the representative might be mended, that is, it might be better than it is. Perhaps it may be offered in that paper too lamely, if the thing be insisted upon too limited; why perhaps there are a very considerable part of copyholders by inheritance that ought to have a voice; and there may be somewhat too reflects upon the generality of the people. I know our debates are endless if we think to bring it to an issue this way, if we may but resolve upon a committee. If I cannot be satisfied to go so far as these gentlemen that bring this paper, I say it again, I profess it, I shall freely and willingly withdraw myself, and I hope to do it in such a manner that the Army shall see that I shall by my withdrawing, satisfying the interest of the Army, the public interest of the kingdom, and those ends these men aim at. And I think if you do bring this to a result it were well.

Rainsborough: If these men must be advanced, and other men set under foot, I am not satisfied; if their rules must be observed, and other men, that are in authority, do not know how this can stand together, I wonder how that should be thought wilfulness in one man that is reason in another; for I confess I have not heard anything that doth satisfy me, and though I have not so much wisdom or notions in my head, but I have so many that I could tell an hundred to the ruin of the people. I am not at all against a committee's meeting; and as you say, and I think every Christian ought to do the same, for my part I shall be ready, if I see the way that I am going, and the thing that I would insist on, will destroy the kingdom, I shall withdraw it as soon as any. And therefore, till I see that, I shall use all the means, and I think it is no fault in any man to sell that which is his birthright.

Sexby: I desire to speak a few words. I am sorry that my zeal to what I apprehend is good should be so ill resented. I am not sorry to see that which I apprehend is truth, but I am sorry the Lord hath darkened some so much as not to see it, and that is in short. Do you think it were a sad and miserable condition, that we have fought all this time for nothing? All here, both great and small, do think that we fought for something. I confess, many of us fought for those ends which, we since saw, was not that which caused us to go through difficulties and straits to venture all in the ship with you; it had been good in you to have advertised us of it, and I believe you would have fewer under your command to have commanded. But if this be the business, that an estate doth make men capable, it is no matter which way they get it, they are capable, to choose those that shall represent them; but I think there are many that have not estates that in honesty have as much right in the freedom their choice as free as any that have great estates. Truly, sir, your putting off this question and coming to some other, I dare say, and I dare appeal to all of them, that they cannot settle upon any other until this be done; it was the ground that we took up arms, and it is the ground which we shall maintain. Concerning my making rents and divisions in this way, as to a particular, if I were but so, I could lie down and be trodden there. Truly I am sent by a regiment; if I should not speak, guilt shall lie upon me, and I think I were a covenant-breaker. And I do not know how we have answered in our arguments, and I conceive we shall not accomplish them to the kingdom when we deny them to ourselves. For my part I shall be loath to make a rent and division, but for my own part unless I see this put to a question, I despair of an issue.

Captain Clarke: The first thing that I shall desire was, and is, this: that there might be a temperature and moderation of spirit within us; that we should speak with moderation, not with such reflection as was boulted one from another, but so speak and so hear as that which may be the droppings of love from one another to another's hearts. Another word I have to say is the grand question of all is, whether or no it be the property of every individual person in the kingdom to have a vote in election; and the ground is the law of nature, which, for my part, I think to be that law which is the ground of all constitutions. Yet really properties are the foundation of constitutions; for if so be there were no property, that the law of nature does give a principle to have a property of what he has, or may have, which is not another man's. This property is the ground of *meum* and *tuum*. Now there may be inconveniences on both hands, but not so great freedom, the greater freedom, as I conceive, that all may have whatsoever. And if it come to pass that there be a difference, and that the one doth oppose the other, then nothing can decide it but the sword, which is the wrath of God.

Captain Audley: I see you have a long dispute that you do intend to dispute here till the tenth of March. You have brought us into a fair pass, and the kingdom into a fair pass, for if your reasons are not satisfied, and we do not fetch all our waters from your wells, you threaten to withdraw yourselves. I could wish, according to our several protestations, we might sit down quietly, and there throw down ourselves where we see reason. I could wish we might all rise, and go to our duties, and see our work in hand. I see both at a stand, and if we dispute here both are lost.

Cromwell: Really, for my own part I must needs say, whilst we say we would not make reflections, we do make reflections; and if I had not come hither with a free heart, to do that that I was persuaded in my conscience is my duty, I should a thousand times rather have kept myself away; for I do think I had brought upon myself the greatest sin that I was guilty of, if I should have come to have stood before God in that former duty which is before you, and if that my saying, which I did say, and shall persevere to say, that I should not, I cannot against my conscience do anything. They that have stood so much for liberty of conscience, if they will not grant that liberty to every man but say it is a deserting I know not what. If that be denied me, I think there is not that equality that I profes't to be amongst us. I said this, and I say no more, that make your businesses as well as you can, we might bring things to an understanding; it was to be brought to a fair composure. And when you have said: if you should put this paper to the question without any qualification, I doubt whether it would pass so freely; if we would have no difference, we ought to put it. And let me speak clearly and freely; I have heard other gentlemen do the like. I have not heard the Commissary-General answered, not in a part to my knowledge, not in a tittle; if therefore, when I see there is an extremity of difference between you, to the end it may be brought nearer to a general satisfaction; and if this be thought a deserting of that interest, if there can be anything more sharply said, I will not give it an ill word. Though we should be satisfied in our consciences in what we do, we are told we purpose to leave the Army, or to leave our commands, as if we took upon us to do it in matter of will. I did hear some gentlemen speak more of will than anything that was spoken for this way, for more was spoken by way of will than of satisfaction; and if there be not a more equality in our minds, I can but grieve for it. I must do no more.

Ireton: I should not speak, bur reflections do necessitate, do call upon us to vindicate ourselves, as if we who have led men into engagements and services, that we had divided because we did not concur with them. I will ask that gentleman whom I love in my heart that spoke, whether when they drew out to serve the Parliament in the beginning, whether when they engaged with the Army at Newmarket, whether then they thought of any more interest or right in the kingdom than this, whether they did think that they should have as great interest in Parliament-Men as freeholders had, or whether from the beginning we did not engage for the liberty of parliaments, and that we should be concluded by the laws that such did make, unless somebody did make you believe before now that you should have an equal interest in the kingdom; unless somebody do make that to be believed, there is no reason to blame men for leading so far as they have done; and if any man was far enough from such an apprehension, that man hath not been deceived. And truly I shall say but this word more for myself in this business, because the whole objection seems to be prest to me and maintained by me.

I will not arrogate that I was the first man that put the Army upon the thought either of successive parliaments or more equal parliaments. Yet there are some here that know who they were put us upon that foundation of liberty, of putting a period to this Parliament, that we might have successive parliaments, and that there might be a more equal distribution of elections. Here are many here that know who were the first movers of that business in the Army. I shall not arrogate that but I can argue this with a clear conscience: that no man hath prosecuted that with more earnestness, and that will stand to that interest more than I do, of having parliaments successive and not perpetual, and the distributions of it; but notwithstanding my opinion stands good, that it ought to be a distribution amongst the fix't and settled people of this nation; it's more prudent and safe, and more upon this ground of right for it. Now it is the fundamental constitution of this kingdom; and that which you take away for matter of wilfulness notwithstanding this universal conclusion, that all inhabitants as it stands, though I must declare that I cannot yet be satisfied. Yet for my part I shall acquiesce; I will not make a distraction in this Army, though I have a property in being one of those that should be an elector; though I have an interest in the birthright, yet I will rather lose that birthright, and that interest, than I will make it my business, if I see but the generality of those whom I have reason to think honest men, and conscientious men, and godly men, to carry them another way. I will not oppose, though I be not satisfied to join with them, and I desire. I am agreed with you, if you insist upon a more equal distribution of elections; I will agree with you, not only to dispute for it, but to fight for it, and contend for it. Thus far I shall agree with you; on the other hand, those who differ their terms, I will not agree with you except you go further; thus far I can go with you; I will go with you as far as I can if you will appoint a committee to consider of some of that, so as you preserve the equitable part of that constitution who are like to be freemen, and men not given up to the wills of others, keeping to the latitude which is the equity of constitutions, I will go with you as far as I can. I will sit down. I will not make any disturbance among you.

Rainsborough: If I do not speak my soul and conscience, I do think that there is not an objection made, but that it hath been answered; but the speeches are so long. I am sorry for some passion and some reflections, and I could wish where it is most taken, the cause had not been given. It is a fundamental constitution of the kingdom; there I would fain know, whether the choice of burgesses in corporations should not be altered. The end wherefore I speak is only this: you think we shall be worse than we are, if we come to a conclusion by a vote. If it be put to the question, we shall all know one another's mind; if it be determined, and the resolutions known we shall take such a course as to put it in execution. This gentleman says, if he cannot go he will sit still. He thinks he hath a full liberty; we think we have not. There is a great deal of difference between us two. If a man hath all he doth desire, but I think I have nothing at all of what I fought for, I do not think the argument holds that I must desist as well as he.

Petty: The rich would very unwillingly be concluded by the poor. And there is as much reason, and indeed no reason, that the rich should conclude the poor as the poor the rich, but there should be an equal share in both. I understood your engagement was, that you would use all your endeavours for the liberties of the people, that they should be secured. If there is a constitution, that the people are not free, that should be annulled. That constitution which is now set up in a constitution of forty shillings a year, but this constitution doth not make people free.

Cromwell: Here's the mistake: whether that's the better constitution in that paper, or that which is. But if you will go upon such a ground as that is, although a better constitution was offered for the removing of the worse, yet some gentlemen are resolved to stick to the worse. There might be a great deal of prejudice upon such an apprehension. I think you are by this time satisfied, that it is a clear mistake; for it is a dispute whether or not this be better, nay whether it be not destructive to the kingdom.

Petty: I desire to speak one word to this business, because I do not know whether my occasions will suffer me to attend it any longer. The great reason that I have heard is the constitution of the kingdom, the utmost constitution of it; and if we destroy this constitution, there is no property. I suppose that if constitutions should tie up all men in this nature, it were very dangerous.

Ireton: First, the thing itself were dangerous, if it were settled to destroy propriety. But I say the principle that leads to this is destructive to property; for by the same reason that you will alter this constitution, merely that there's a greater constitution by nature, by the same reason, by the law of nature, there is a greater liberty to the use of other men's goods, which that property bars you of. And I would fain have any man show me why I should destroy that liberty, which the freeholders and burghers in corporations have in choosing burgesses, that which if you take away, you leave no constitution; and this because there is a greater freedom due to me from some men by the law of nature, more than that I should take another man's goods because the law of nature does allow me.

Rainsborough: I would grant something that the Commissary-General says. But whether this be a just propriety, the propriety says that forty shillings a year enables a man to elect; if it were stated to that, nothing would conduce so much whether some men do agree or no.

Captain Rolfe: I conceive that, as we are met here, there are one or two things mainly to be prosecuted by us; that is especially unity, preservation of unity in the Army, and so likewise to put ourselves into a capacity thereby to do good to the kingdom. And therefore I shall desire that there may be a tender consideration had of that which is so much urged, in that of an equal, as well as of a free, Representative. I shall desire that a medium, or some thoughts of a composure in relation to servants, or to foreigners, or such others as shall be agree upon. I say then, I conceive, excepting those, there may be a very equitable sense resented to us from that offer in our own declarations wherein we do offer the common good of all, unless they have made any shipwreck or loss of it.

Chillenden: In the beginning of this discourse there were overtures made of imminent danger. This way we have taken this afternoon is not the way to prevent it. I should humbly move that we should put a speedy end to this business, and that not only to this main question of the paper, but also according to the Lieutenant-General's motion, that a committee may be chosen seriously to consider the things in that paper, and compare them with divers things in our declarations and engagements, that so as we have all professed, to lay down ourselves before God, if we take this course of debating upon one question a whole afternoon, if the danger be so near as it is supposed, it were the ready way to bring us into it. That things may be put into a speedy dispatch.

Clarke: I presume that the great stick here is this: that if every one shall have his propriety, it does bereave the kingdom of its principal fundamental constitution, that it hath. I presume that all people and all nations whatsoever have a liberty and power to alter and change their constitutions, if they find them to be weak and infirm. Now if the people of England shall find this weakness in their constitution, they may change it if they please. Another thing is this: if the light of nature be only in this, it may destroy the propriety which every man can call his own. The reason is this, because this principle and light of nature doth give all men their own: as for example the clothes upon my back because they are not another man's. If every man hath this propriety of election to choose those whom you fear may beget inconveniencies, I do not conceive that anything may be so nicely and precisely done, but that it may admit of inconveniency. If it be in that wherein it is now, there may those inconveniences rise from them. For my part I know nothing but the want of love in it, and the sword must decide it. I shall desire before the question be stated, it may be moderated as for foreigners.

Sir Hardress Waller: This was that I was saying: I confess I have not spoken yet, and I was willing to be silent, having heard so many speak, that I might learn to. But it is not easy for us to say when this dispute will have an end; but I think it is easy to say when the kingdom will have an end. But if we do not breathe out ourselves, we shall be kicked and spurned of all the world. I would fain know how far the question will decide it; for certainly we must not expect, while we have tabernacles here, to be all of one mind. If it be to be decided by a question, and that all parties are satisfied in that, I think the sooner you hasten to it the better. If otherwise, we shall needlessly discover our dividing opinion, which as long as it may be avoided I desire it may. Therefore I desire to have a period.

Audley: I chanced to speak a word or two. Truly there was more offence taken at it. For my part I spoke against every man living, not only against yourself and the Commissary, but every man that would dispute till we have our throats cut. I profess, if so be there were none but you and the Commissary-General alone to maintain that argument, I would die in any place in England, in asserting that it is the right of every free-born man to elect, according to the rule, *Quod omnibus spectat, ab omnibus tractari debet,* that which concerns all ought to be debated by all. He knew no reason why that law should oblige when he himself had no finger in appointing the law-giver, and therefore I desire I may not lie in any prejudice before your persons.

Captain Bishop: You have met here this day to see if God would show you any way wherein you might jointly preserve the kingdom from its destruction, which you all apprehend to be at the door. God is pleased not to come in to you. There is a gentleman, Mr. Saltmarsh, did desire what he has wrote may be read to the General Council. If God do manifest anything by him, I think it ought to be heard.

Ireton: That you will alter that constitution from a better to a worse, from a just to a thing that is less just in my apprehension; and I will not repeat the reasons of that, but refer to what I have declared before. To me, if there were nothing but this, that there is a constitution, and that constitution which is the very last constitution which if you take away you leave nothing of constitution, and consequently nothing of right or property. I would not go to alter that, though a man could propound that which in some respects might be better, unless it could be demonstrated to me that this were unlawful, or that this were destructive. Truly, therefore, I say for my part, to go on a sudden to make such a limitation as that in general, if you do extend the latitude that any man shall have a voice in election who has not that interest in this kingdom that is permanent and fixed, who hath not that interest upon which he may have his freedom in this kingdom without dependence, you will put it into the hands of men to choose, of men to preserve their liberty who will give it away.

I have a thing put into my heart which I cannot but speak. I profess I am afraid, that if we from such apprehensions as these are, of an imaginable right of nature, opposite to constitution, if we will contend and hazard the breaking of peace upon this enlargement of that business, I am confident our discontent and dissatisfaction, in that if ever they do well they do in this, if there be anything at all that is a foundation of liberty, it is this: that those who shall chose the law makers shall be men freed from dependence upon others. I think if we, from imaginations and conceits, will go about to hazard the peace of the kingdom, to alter the constitution in such a point, I am afraid we shall find the hand of God will follow it; we shall see that that liberty, which we so much talk of and contended for, shall be nothing at all by this our contending for it, by putting it into the hands of those men that will give it away when they have it.

Cromwell: If we should go about to alter these things, I do not think that we are bound to fight for every particular proposition. Servants, while servants, are not included. Then you agree that he that receives alms is to be excluded.

Lieutenant-Colonel Reade: I suppose it's concluded by all, that the choosing of representatives is a privilege; now I see no reason why any man that is a native ought to be excluded that privilege, unless from voluntary servitude.

Petty: I conceive the reason why we would exclude apprentices, or servants, or those that take alms, it is because they depend upon the will of other men and should be afraid to displease. For servants and apprentices, they are included in their masters, and so for those that receive alms from door to door; but if there be any general way taken for those that are not bound, it would do well.

Everard: I being sent from the Agents of five regiments with an answer unto a writing, the committee was very desirous to inquire into the depth of our intentions. Those things that they had there manifested in the paper, I declared it was the Lieutenant-General's desire for an understanding with us, and what I did understand as a particular person, I did declare, and were presuming those things I did declare did tend to unity. And if so, you will let it appear by coming unto us.

We have gone thus far: we have had two or three meetings to declare and hold forth what it is we stand upon, the principles of unity and freedom. We have declared in what we conceive these principles do lie, I shall not name them all because they are known unto you. Now in the progress of these disputes and debates we find that the time spends, and no question but our adversaries are harder at work than we are. I heard that there were meetings (but I had no such testimony as I could take hold of), that there are meetings daily and contrivances against us. Now for our parts I hope you will not say all is yours, but we have nakedly and freely unbosomed ourselves unto you. Though these things have startled many at the first view, yet we find there is good hopes; we have fixed our resolutions, and we are determined, and we want nothing but that only God will direct us to what is just and right. But I understand that all these debates, if we shall agree upon any one thing, This is our freedom; this is our liberty; this liberty and freedom we are debarred of, and we are bereaved of all those comforts. In case we should find half a hundred of these, yet the main business is how we should find them, and how we should come by them. Is there any liberty that we find ourselves deprived of; if we have grievances let us see who are the hindrances, and when we have pitched upon that way.

I conceive I speak humbly in this one thing as a particular person, that I conceive myself, that these delays, these disputes, will prove little encouragement. As it was told me by these gentlemen, that he had great jealousies that we would not come to the trial of our spirits and that perhaps there might happen another design in hand. I said to his Honour again, if they would not come to the light, I would judge they had the works of darkness in hand. Now as they told me again on the other hand, when it was questioned by Colonel Hewson, they told me: These gentlemen, not naming any particular persons, they will hold you in hand, and keep you in debate and dispute till you and we come all to ruin. Now I stood as a moderator between these things. When I heard the Lieutenant-General speak I was marvellously taken up with the plainness of the carriage. I said, I will bring them to you. You shall see if their hearts be so; for my part I see nothing but plainness and uprightness of heart made manifest unto you. I will not judge, nor draw any long discourses upon our disputes this day. We may differ in one thing, that you conceive this debating and disputation will do the work; we must put ourselves into the former privileges which we want.

Waller: I think this gentleman hath dealt very ingenuously and plainly with us. I pray God we may do so too, and for one I will do it. I think our disputings will not do the thing. I think if we do make it our resolution that we do hold it forth to all powers, Parliament or King, or whoever they are, to let them know that these are our rights, and if we have them not we must get them the best way we can.

Cromwell: I think you say very well; and my friend at my back, he tells me that [there] are great fears abroad; and they talk of some things such as are not only specious to take a great many people with, but real and substantial, and such as are comprehensive of that that hath the good of the kingdom in it. And truly if there be never so much desire of carrying on these things, never so much desire of conjunction, yet if there be not liberty of speech to come to a right understanding of things, I think it shall be all one as if there were no desire at all to meet. And I may say it with truth, that I verily believe there is as much reality and heartiness amongst us, to come to a right understanding, and to accord with that, that hath the settlement of the kingdom in it, though when it comes to particulars we may differ in the way. Yet I know nothing but that every honest man will go as far as his conscience will let him; and he that will go farther, I think he will fall back. And I think, when that principle is written in the hearts of us, and when there is not hypocrisy in our dealings, we must all of us resolve upon this, that 'tis God that persuades the heart. If there be a doubt of sincerity, it's the devil that created that effect; and 'tis God that gives uprightness. And I hope with such an heart that we have all met withal; if we have not, God find him out that came without it; for my part I do it.

Ireton: When you have done this according to the number of inhabitants, do you think it is not very variable, I would have us fall to something that is practicable, with as little pains and dissatisfaction as may be. I remember that in the proposals that went out in the name of the Army, it is propounded as a rule to be distributed according to the rates that the counties bear in the kingdom. And remember then you have a rule, and though this be not a rule of exactness for the number will change every day; yet there was something of equality in it, and it was a certain rule, where all are agreed; and therefore we should come to some settling. Now I do not understand wherein the advantage does lie from a sudden danger upon a thing that will continue so long, and will continue so uncertain as this is.

Waller: 'Tis thought there's imminent danger; I hope to God we shall be so ready to agree for the future that we shall all agree for the present to rise as one man if the danger be such, for it is an impossibility to have a remedy in this. The paper says that this Parliament is to continue a year, but will the great burden of the people be ever satisfied with papers? You eat and feed upon them. I shall be glad that there be not any present danger; if not that you will think of some way to ease the burden, that we may take a course, and when we have satisfied the people that we do really intend the good of the kingdom. Otherwise, if the four Evangelists were here, and lay free quarter upon them, they will not believe you.

Colonel Rainsborough: Moved, that the Army might be called to a rendezvous, and things settled.

Ireton: We are called back to engagements. I think the engagements we have made and published, and all the engagements of all sorts, have been better kept by those that did not so much cry out for it than by those that do, and if you will in plain terms better kept than by those that have brought this paper. Give me leave to tell you, in that one point, in the engagement of the Army not to divide, I am sure that he that understands the engagement of the Army not to divide or disband for satisfaction, that we are not to divide for quarters, for the ease of the country, or the satisfaction of service; he that does understand it in that sense, I am not capable of his understanding. But there was another sense in it, and that is, that we should not suffer ourselves to be torn into pieces, such a dividing as is really a disbanding; and for my part I do not know what disbanding is if not that dividing. That I do not see the authors of this paper, the subscribers of that book that is called The Case of the Army, I say that they have gone the way of disbanding. For my part I do not know what disbanding is, if that disbanding of an army is not parting in a place, for if that be so, did not we at that night disband to several quarters? Did we not then send several regiments, and yet the authors of that paper and the subscribers of them, for I cannot think the authors and subscribers all one, we all know, and they may know it, that there is not one part of the Army is divided farther than the outcries of the authors of it. Colonel Scroope's regiment into the West, we know where it was first; Colonel Horton's regiment into Wales for preventing of insurrection there; Colonel Lambert's, Colonel Lilburne's regiment then sent down for strengthening such a place as York? They go to scandalize an engagement or divide. There's no part of the Army is dispersed to quarters farther than that, whereupon that outcry is. But he that will go to understand this to be a dividing that we engaged against, he looks at the name, and not at the time. That dividing which is a disbanding, that dividing which makes no army, and if that dissolving of that order and government which is as essential to an army as life is to a man, which if it be taken away I think that such a company are no more an army than a rotten carcass is a man; and those that have gone to divide the Army.

And what else is there in this paper that we have acted so vigorously for? They do not propose that this Parliament should end till the beginning of September. I say plainly, the way hath been the way of disunion and division, and that of that order and government by which we shall be enabled to act, and I shall appeal to all men: the dividing from that General Council wherein we have all engaged we would be concluded by that, and the endeavouring to draw the soldiers to run this way. When all comes upon the matter, it is but a critical difference and the very substance of that we have declared before. For my part I profess it seriously, that we shall find it in the issue, that the principle of that division, of disbanding is no more than this: whether such or such shall have the managing of the business. And let it be judged whether by this or that way we have taken, or that they have taken be not the same as to the matter. I shall appeal: whether there can be any breach of the Army higher than that breach we have now spoke of, that word dividing the Army; whether we will not divide with such satisfaction, whether that dividing were not more truly and properly in every man's heart, this dividing wherein we do go apart one from another, and consequently those that have gone this way have not broke the Engagement, the other dividing whether that were a dividing a keeping of the Engagement. And those that do judge the one, I do not think that we have been fairly dealt with.

Rainsborough: I do not make any great wonder that this gentleman hath sense above all men in the world. But for these things, he is the man that hath undertaken them all. I say this gentleman hath the advantage of us; he hath drawn up the most part of them; and why he may not keep a sense that we do not know of. It is a huge reflection, a taxing of persons, if this gentleman had declared to us at first that this was the sense of the Army in dividing, and it was meant that men should not divide in opinions. To me that is a mystery, and because I will avoid further reflections, I shall say no more.

Agitator: Whereas you say the Agents did it, the soldiers did put the Agents upon these meetings. It was the dissatisfactions that were in the Army which provoked, which occasioned, those meetings, which you suppose tends so much to dividing; and the reason of such dissatisfactions are because those whom they had to trust to act for them were not true to them.

Ireton: If this be all the effect of your meetings to agree upon this paper, there is but one thing in this that hath not been insisted upon and propounded by the Army heretofore, all along. Here it is put according to the number of inhabitants; here it is put according to the inhabitants, there according to the taxes. This says a period at such a day, the 8th of September; the other says a period within a year at most. That these have the power of making law, and determining what is law, without the consent of another. 'Tis true that Proposals said not that. And for my part, if any man will put that to the question whether we shall concur with it, I am in the same mind if you put it in any other hands than those that are free men. But if you shall put the question and with that limitation that hath been all along acknowledged by the Parliament, till we can acquit ourselves justly from any engagement, old or new, that we stand in, to preserve the person of the King, the persons of Lords, and their rights, so far as they are consistent with the common right—till that be done, I think there is reason that exception should continue, which hath been all along, that is, where the safety of the kingdom is concerned. This they seem to hold out. I would hold to positive constitution where I would not do real mischief. And therefore where I find that the safety of the kingdom is not concerned, I would not for every trifling make that this shall be a law, though neither the Lords, who have a claim to it, nor the King, who hath a claim to it, will consent. But where this is concerned upon the whole matter, let men but consider those that have thus gone away to divide from the Army. Admit that this Agreement of the People be the advantage; it may be we shall agree to that without any limitation. I do agree that the King is bound by his oath at his coronation, is bound at his coronation to agree to the law that the Commons shall choose without Lords or anybody else. But where I see things I would neither be thought to be a wrong-doer or disturber; so long as I can with safety continue a constitution, I will do it. If I can agree any further, that if the King do not confirm with his authority the laws that the people shall choose, we know what will follow.

Petty: I had the happiness sometimes to be at the debate of the Proposals, and my opinion was then as it is now, against the King's vote and the Lords'. But not so as I do desire since it hath pleased God to raise a company of men that do stand up for the power of the House of Commons, which is the representative of the people, and deny the negative voice of King and Lords. For my part I was much unknown to any of them, but only as I heard their principles; and hearing of their principles I cannot but join with them in my judgment, for I think it is reasonable that all laws are made by their consent. Whereas you seem to make the King and Lords so light a thing as that it may be to the destruction of the kingdom to throw them out, and without prejudice; for my part I cannot but think that both the power of King and Lords was ever a branch of tyranny. And if ever a people shall free themselves from tyranny, certainly it is after seven years' war and fighting for their liberty. For my part if the constitution of this kingdom shall be established as formerly, it might rivet tyranny into this kingdom more strongly than before. For when the people shall hear that for seven years together the people were plundered, and after they had overcome the King and kept the King under restraint, and at last the King comes in, then it will rivet the King's interest; and so when any men shall endeavour to free themselves from tyranny, we may do them mischief and no good. I think it's most just and equal, since a number of men have declared against it, they should be encouraged in it, and not discouraged. And I find by the Council that their thoughts are the same against the King and Lords, and if so be that a power may be raised to do that, it would do well.

Wildman: Truly, sir, I being desired by the Agents yesterday to appear at council or committees, either at that time, I suppose I may be bold to make known what I know of their sense, and a little to vindicate them in their way of proceeding, and to show the necessity of this way of proceeding that they have entered upon. Truly, sir, as to breaking of engagements, the Agents do declare their principle, that whensoever any engagement cannot be kept justly, but when they cannot act justly they must break that engagement. Now though its urged they ought to condescend to what the General Council do, I conceive it's true so long as it is for their safety. I conceive just and righteous for them to stand up for some more speedy vigorous actings. I conceive it's no more than what the Army did when the Parliament did not only delay deliverance, but opposed it. And I conceive this way of their appearing hath not appeared to be in the least way anything tending to division, since they proceed to clear the rights of the people; and so long as they proceed upon those righteous principles, I suppose it cannot be laid to their charge that they are dividers. And though it be declared, that the malice of the enemies would have bereaved you of your liberties as Englishmen, therefore as Englishmen they are deeply concerned to regard the due observation of their rights, as I, or any commoner, have right to propound to the kingdom my conceptions what is fit for the good of the kingdom. Whereas it is objected: How will it appear that their proceedings shall tend for the good of the kingdom? The matter is different. Whereas it was said before, it was propounded there must be an end to the Parliament, an equality as to elections, I find it to be their minds when they came there, they found many aversions from matters that they ought to stand to as soldiers and not as Englishmen; and therefore I find it concerning the matter of the thing, I conceive it to be a very vast difference in the whole matter of Proposals. The foundation of slavery was riveted more strongly than before: as where the militia is instated in the King and Lords, and not in the Commons, there is a foundation of a future quarrel constantly laid.

However, the main thing was that the right of the militia was acknowledged by the King. They found in the Proposals propounded, to be before any redress of any one of the people's grievances, any one of their burdens; and so to be brought in as with a negative voice, whereby the people and Army that have fought against him when he had propounded such things. And finding they perceived they were, as they thought, in a sad case; for they thought, he coming in thus with a negative, the Parliament are but as so many ciphers, so many round O's, for if the King would not do it, he might choose, *Sic volo, sic jubeo, Etc.*, and so the corrupt party of the kingdom must be so settled in the King. The godly people are turned over and trampled upon already in the most places of the kingdom. And I find this to be their thoughts. But whereas it is said, How will this paper provide for anything for that purpose? I shall say that this paper doth lay down the foundations of freedom for all manner of people. It doth lay the foundations of soldiers', whereas they found a great uncertainty in the Proposals, that they should go to the King for an Act of Indemnity, and thus the King might command his judges to hang them up for what they did in the wars, because, the present constitution being left as it was, nothing was law but what the King signed, and not any ordinance of Parliament. I speak but the words of the Agents. And considering of this, that they thought it should be by an Agreement with the people, whereby a rule between the Parliament and the people might be set, that so they might be destroyed neither by the King's prerogative nor Parliament's privileges. They are not bound to be subject to the laws as other men; why men cannot recover their estates. They thought there must be a necessity of a rule between the Parliament and the people, so that the Parliament should know what they were entrusted to, and what they were not; and that there might be no doubt for the Parliament's power, to lay foundations of future quarrels. The Parliament shall not meddle with a soldier after indemnity, it is agreed amongst the people. Whereas between a parliament and king, if the King were not under restraint should make an Act of Indemnity, whereas another Parliament cannot alter this. That these foundations might be established, that there might be no dispute between Lords and Commons, but, these things being settled, there should be no more disputes, but that the Parliament should redress the people's grievances. Whereas now all are troubled with King's interests, almost if this were settled, and besides the Parliament should be free from these temptations, which for my own part I do suppose to be a truth. That this very Parliament, by the King's voice in this very Parliament, may destroy, whereas now they shall be free from temptations and the King cannot have an influence upon them as he hath.

Ireton: Gentlemen, I think there is no man is able to give a better account of the sense of the Agents, and so readily; he hath spoke so much as they have in their book, and therefore I say he is very well able to give their sense. And I wish their senses had not been prejudicial to other men's senses, but, as I fear it will prove, really prejudicial to the kingdom, how plausible soever it seems to be carried. That paper of The Case of the Army that doth so abuse the General and General Council of the Army, that such and such things have been done that made them do thus and thus. And first as to the material points of the paper, you know as to the business of the Lords, the way we were then in admitted no other. This gentleman that speaks here, and the other gentleman that spake before, when we were at Reading framing the Proposals, did not think of this way. I am sure they did not think of this way; and according to the best judgments of those that were entrusted by the General Council to draw up the Proposals, it was carried by a question clearly, that we should not. In these Proposals our business was to set forth particulars; we had set forth general declarations, which did come to as much in effect as this: the thing then proposed was, that we should not take away the power of the Lords in this kingdom, and it was concluded in the Proposals. But as to the King we were clear: there is not one thing in the Proposals, nor in what was declared, that doth give the King any negative. And therefore that's part of the scandal amongst others: we do not give the King any negative voice; we do but take the King as a man with whom we have been at a difference; we propound terms of peace. We do not demand that he shall have no negative, but we do not say that he shall have any. There's another thing, that we have, as they say, gone from our engagements in our declarations, in that we go in the Proposals to es-tablish the King's rights before the people's grievances.

In our general declarations we first desire a purging of this Parliament, a period of this Parliament, and provision for the certainty of future parlia-ments; and if the King shall agree in these things and what else the Parlia-ment shall propound, that are necessary for the safety of the kingdom, then we desire his rights may be considered so far as may consist with the rights of the people. We did so in the declarations, and you shall see what we did in the Proposals. In the Proposals, things that are essential to peace, and it distinguishes those from the things that conduce to our better being, and things that lay foundations of an hopeful constitution in the future; when those are passed, then they say that, these things having the King's concur-rence, we desire that his right may be considered.

There were many other grievances and particular matters which we did not think so necessary that they should precede the settling of a peace, which is the greatest grievance of the kingdom. Our way was to take away that. Then we say, these propounding what things we thought in our judg-ments are to be essential and necessary as to peace. And then it says, there yet we desire that the Parliament would lose no time from the consideration of them. These gentlemen would say now we have gone from our declara-tions, that we propose the settling of the King: it stands before those griev-ances. We say, those grievances are not so necessary as that the remedying of them should be before the settling of the peace of the kingdom. What we thought in our consciences to be essential to the peace of the kingdom we did put preceding to the consideration of the King's personal right; and the concurrence of those is a condition without which we cannot have any right at all, and without there can be no peace, and have before named the con-sideration of the King's rights in the settling of a peace, as a thing neces-sary to the constitution of a peace. That, therefore, we should prefer the King's rights before a general good, was as unworthy and as unchristian an injury as ever was done to men that were in society with them, and as merely equivocation.

But it was told you, that the General Council hath seemed to do so and so, to put the soldiers out of the way; and it is suggested that the Engage-ment is broken by our dividing to quarters; and whether that be broken or not, and it is suggested in other things, but it is said that the General Coun-cil hath broken the Engagement in this: that whereas before we were not a mercenary army, now we are. Let any man but speak what hath given the occasion of that. It hath been pressed by some men that we should have subjected to the Parliament, and we should stand to the propositions what-ever they were; but the sense of the General Council was this: that, as they had sent their propositions to the Parliament, that they would see what the

Parliament would do before they would conclude what themselves would do; and that there was respect to that which we have hitherto accounted the fundamental council of the kingdom.

If all the people to a man had subscribed to this, then there would be some security to it, because no man would oppose; but otherwise our concurrence amongst ourselves is no more than our saying ourselves we will be indemnified. But our indemnity must be to something that at least we will uphold, and we see we cannot hold to be a conclusive authority of the kingdom; and for that of going to the King for indemnity, we propose an Act of Oblivion only for the King's party; we propose for ourselves an Act of Indemnity and Justification. Is this the asking of a pardon? Then let us resort to the first petition of the Army, wherein we all were engaged once, which we made the basis of all our proceedings. In that we say, that an ordinance might be passed, to which the royal assent might be desired; but we have declared that, if the royal assent could not be had, we should account the authority of the Parliament valid without it. We have desired, in the General Council, that for security for arrears we might have the royal assent. And let me tell you, though I shall be content to lose my arrears to see the kingdom have its liberty, and if any man can do it, unless it be by putting our liberty into the hands of those that will give it away when they have done; but I say that I do not think that true in this: Whoever talk't either of the endeavours of the soldiers or of any other indemnity by the sword in their hands, is the perpetuating of combustions; so that word cannot take place, and does not suppose the settling of a peace, and by that authority which hath been here, by the legislative power of the kingdom; and he that expects to have the arrears of the soldiers, so I think he does but deceive himself. For my own part I would give up my arrears, and for my part lose my arrears, if we have not settlement; no arrears or want of indemnity, nor anything in the world, shall satisfy me to have a peace upon any terms, wherein that which is really the right of this nation is not as far provided for as can be provided for by men. I could tell you many other particulars wherein there are divers gross injuries done to the General and General Council, and such a wrong as is not fit to be done among Christians, and so wrong and so false that I cannot think that they have gone so far in it.

Wildman: I do not know what reason you have to suppose I should be so well acquainted with The Case of the Army, and the things proposed. I conceive them to be very good and just; but for that which I give as their sense, which you are pleased to say are scandals cast upon the Army. The legislative power had been acknowledged to be in the King with Lords and Commons; and then considering that, and what you said before was a scandal, that you propounded to bring in the King with his negative voice. I do humbly propound to your consideration, when you restrain the King's negative in one particular, which is in restraining unequal distributions, but whereas you do say the legislative power to be now partly in him, and say directly, in these very words, shall be restored to his personal rights.

And therefore I conceive, if I have any reason, the King is proposed to be brought in with his negative voice. And whereas you say it is a scandal for the King to come in with his personal rights, that the King consenting to those things, the King to be restored to all his personal rights.

There's his restoration. Not a bare consideration what his rights are before the people's grievances, but a restoration to his personal rights. These things being done, is the Parliament not to lose their rights; and for that of Indemnity, I do not say it was an asking of the King pardon, it is rendering us up, and therefore it is null in law.

The King and the Monarchy

23. The Army Agreement (15 January 1649)

The decisive break between army and Parliament came after the second civil war in 1648. This was a pathetic affair in England with brief uprisings in Kent and Essex easily suppressed by Fairfax and his troops. It was a rather more serious matter in Scotland where Cromwell and a large contingent of the New Model Army found themselves fighting some of the crack Scottish regiments. The bloodshed of the second civil war made a compromise settlement with the king impossible for the army. But the fear of continued uprisings and unrest led parliamentary moderates to desire a compromise settlement ever more desperately. When Parliament again offered Charles I peace terms (watered down from those offered the previous year) and continued to negotiate with him, the army presented its own demands. These were an amalgam of old army issues, constitutional and parliamentary reforms, and a new hard line toward the king all wrapped up in the Leveller device of an agreement of the people. When Parliament put off debating and accepting the Army Agreement, the soldiers intervened with force. On 5 December 1648 troops of the New Model Army under the command of Colonel Thomas Pride surrounded the houses of Parliament and refused entry to a majority of the MPs who came to debate the peace treaty. "Pride's Purge" left a core of MPs willing to follow the army's lead and a larger group willing to conform to whatever decisions were taken as long as Parliament itself was not dis-

From *The Parliamentary or Constitutional History of England,* 23 vols. (London, 1751–62), 18:516–20, 522, 525–27, 531–37.

solved. This "rump" of the Long Parliament voted, in accordance with the army's demands, for the trial of "Charles Stuart, that man of blood."

To the Honourable the Commons of England, in Parliament assembled, The Humble Petition of His Excellency Thomas Lord Fairfax, and the General Council of Officers of the Army under his Command

Whitehall, Jan. 15, 1648

In our late Remonstrance, of the 16th of *November* last, we propounded, next after the Matters of public Justice, some Foundations for a general Settlement of Peace in the Nation, which we therein desired might be formed and established in the Nature of a general Contract or Agreement of the People; and since then, the Matters so propounded being wholly rejected, or no Consideration of them admitted in Parliament, tho' visibly of highest Moment to the Public, and all ordinary Remedies being denied, we were necessitated to an extrodinary Way of Remedy; whereby, to avoid the Mischiefs then at hand, and set you in a Condition, without such Obstructions or Diversions by corrupt Members, to proceed to Matters of public Justice and general Settlement.

Now, as nothing did, in our own Hearts, more justify our late Undertakings towards many Members in this Parliament, than the Necessity thereof in order to a found Settlement in the Kingdom, and the Integrity of our Intentions to make use of it only to that End; so we hold ourselves obliged to give the People all Assurance possible, That our opposing the corrupt Closure endeavoured with the King, was not in Design to hinder Peace or Settlement, thereby to render our Employments, as Soldiers, necessary to be continued; and that neither that extraordinary Course we have taken, nor any other Proceedings of ours, have been intended for the setting up of any particular Party or Interest, by or with which to uphold ourselves in Power and Dominion over the Nation; but that it was, and is, the Desire of our Hearts, in all we have done, with the hindering of that imminent Evil and destructive Conjunction with the King, to make Way for the Settlement of a Peace and Government of the Kingdom upon Grounds of common Freedom and Safety; and therefore, because our former Overtures for that Purpose (being only in general Terms, and not reduced to a Certainty of Particulars fit for Practice) might possibly be understood but as plausible Pretences, not intended really to be put into Effect; we have thought it our Duty, to draw out these Generals into an intire Frame of Particulars, ascertained with such Circumstances as may make it effectively practicable; and, for that End, while your Time hath been taken up in other Matters of high and present Importance, we have spent much of ours in preparing and perfecting such a Draught of Agreement, and in all Things so circumstantiated, as to render it ripe for your speedier Consideration, and the Kingdom's Acceptance and Practice, if approved; and so we do herewith humbly present it to you.

Now, to prevent Misunderstanding of our Intentions therein, we have but this to say, That we are far from such a Spirit, as positively to impose our private Apprehensions upon the Judgments of any in the Kingdom, that have not forfeited their Freedom, and much less upon yourselves: Neither are we apt in anywise to insist upon circumstantial Things, or ought that is not evidently fundamental to that Public Interest for which you and we have declared and engaged; but, in this Tender of it, we humbly desire,

1. That, whether it shall be fully approved by you and received by the People, as it now stands or not, it may yet remain upon Record, before you, a perpetual Witness of our real Intentions and utmost Endeavours for a sound and equal Settlement; and as a Testimony whereby all Men may be assured what we are willing and ready to acquiesce in; and their Jealousies satisfied or Mouths stopt, who are apt to think or say, We have no Bottom.

2. That, with all the Expedition which the immediate and pressing great Affairs will admit, it may receive your most mature Consideration and Resolutions upon it; not that we desire either the whole, or what you shall like in it, should be by your Authority imposed as a Law upon the Kingdom, for so it would lose the intended Nature of *An Agreement of the People;* but that, so far as it concurs with your own Judgments, it may receive your Seal of Approbation only.

3. That, according to the Method propounded therein, it may be tendered to the People in all Parts, to be subscribed by those that are willing, as Petitions and other Things of a voluntary Nature are; and that, in the mean while the Ascertaining of those Circumstances, which are referred to Commissioners in the several Counties, may be proceeded upon in a Way preparatory to the Practice of it: And if, upon the Account of Subscriptions (to be returned by those Commissioners in *April* next) there appears a general or common Reception of it amongst the People, or by the Well-affected of them, and such as are not obnoxious for Delinquency, it may then take Place and Effect, according to the Tenor and Substance of it.

By the Appointment of his Excellency, and the General Council of Officers of the Army,

Jo. Rushworth, *Secr.*

An Agreement of the People of England, and the Places therewith Incorporated, for a Secure and Present Peace, upon Grounds of Common Right, Freedom, and Safety

Having, by our late Labours and Hazards, made it appear to the World at how high a Rate we value our just Freedom; and God having so far owned our Cause as to deliver the Enemies thereof into our Hands, we do now hold ourselves bound, in mutual Duty to each other, to take the best Care we can, for the future, to avoid both the Danger of returning into a slavish Condition, and the chargeable Remedy of another War: For as it cannot be imagined that so many of our Countrymen would have opposed us in this Quarrel, if they had understood their own Good, so may we hopefully promise to ourselves, that when our common Rights and Liberties shall be cleared, their Endeavours will be disappointed that seek to make themselves our Masters; since therefore our former Oppressions and not-yet-ended Troubles, have been occasioned either by want of frequent National Meetings in Council, or by the undue or unequal Constitution thereof, or by rendering those Meetings ineffectual, we are fully agreed and resolved, God willing, to provide, That hereafter our Representatives be neither left to an Uncertainty for Time, nor be unequally constituted, nor made useless to the Ends for which they are intended. In order whereunto we declare and agree,

First, That, to prevent the many Inconveniences apparently arising from the long Continuance of the same Persons in Supreme Authority, this present Parliament end and dissolve upon, or before, the last Day of *April,* in the Year of our Lord 1649.

Secondly, That the People of *England* (being at this Day very unequally distributed by Counties, Cities, and Boroughs, for the Election of their Representatives) be indifferently proportioned; and, to this End, that the Representative of the whole Nation shall consist of 400 Persons, or not above; and in each County, and the Places thereto subjoined, there shall be chosen, to make up the said Representative at all Times, the several Numbers here mentioned. . . .

Provided, That the first or second Representative may, if they see Cause, assign the Remainder of the 400 Representers, not hereby assigned, or so many of them as they shall see Cause for, unto such Counties as shall appear in this present Distribution to have less than their due Proportion.

Provided also, That where any City or Borough, to which one Representer or more is assigned, shall be found, in a due Proportion, not competent alone to elect a Representer, or the Number or Representers assigned thereto, it is left to future Representatives to assign such a Number of Parishes or Villages near adjoining to such City or Borough, to be joined therewith in the Elections, as may make the same proportionable.

Thirdly, That the People do, of course, choose themselves a Representative once in two Years, and shall meet for that Purpose upon the first *Thursday* in every second *May,* by Eleven of the Clock in the Morning; and the Representatives so chosen to meet upon the second *Thursday* in the *June* following, at the usual Place in *Westminster,* or such other Place as, by the foregoing Representative, or the Council of State in the Interval, shall be, from Time to Time, appointed and published to the People, at the least twenty Days before the Time of Election: And to continue their Sessions there, or elsewhere, untill the second *Thursday* in *December* following, unless they shall adjourn, or dissolve themselves sooner; but not to continue longer. The Election of the first Representative to be on the first *Thursday* in *May,* 1649; and that, and all future Elections, to be according to the Rules prescribed for the same Purpose in this Agreement, *viz.*

1. That the Electors in every Division shall be Natives or Denizens of *England;* not Persons receiving Alms, but such as are assessed ordinarily towards the Relief of the Poor; not Servants to, and receiving Wages from, any particular Person. And in all Elections, except for the Universities, they shall be Men of one and twenty Years of Age, or upwards, and Housekeepers, dwelling within the Division for which the Election is: Provided, That (untill the End of seven Years next ensuing the Time herein limited for the End of this present Parliament) no Person shall be admitted to, or have any Hand or Voice in, such Elections, who hath adhered unto or assisted the King against the Parliament in any of the late Wars or Insurrections; or who shall make, or join in, or abet, any forcible Opposition against this *Agreement.*

2. That such Persons, and such only, may be elected to be of the Representative, who, by the Rule aforesaid, are to have Voice in Elections in one Place or other.

Provided, That of those none shall be eligible for the first or second Representative, who have not voluntarily assisted the Parliament against the King, either in Person before the 14th of *June,* 1645, or else in Money, Plate, Horse, or Arms, lent upon the Propositions, before the End of *May,* 1643; or who have joined in, or abetted, the treasonable Engagement in *London,* in the Year 1647; or who declared or engaged themselves for a Cessation of Arms with the *Scots* that invaded this Nation the last Summer; or for Compliance with the Actors in any Insurrections of the same Summer; or with the Prince of *Wales,* or his Accomplices, in the revolted Fleet.

Provided also, That such Persons as, by the Rules in the preceding Article, are not capable of electing untill the End of seven Years, shall not be capable to be elected untill the End of fourteen Years next ensuing. And we desire and recommend it to all Men, that, in all Times, the Persons to be chosen for this great Trust may be Men of Courage, fearing God and hating Covetousness; and that our Representatives would make the best Provisions for that End.

3. That whoever, by the Rules in the two preceding Articles, are incapable of electing, or to be elected, shall presume to vote in, or be present at, such Election for the first or second Representative; or, being elected, shall presume to sit or vote in either of the said Representatives, shall incur the Pain of Confiscation of the Moiety of his Estate, to the Use of the Public, in case he have any visible Estate to the Value of 50 £ and if he has not such an Estate, than shall incur the Pain of Imprisonment for three Months: And if any Person shall forcibly oppose, molest, or hinder the People, capable of electing as aforesaid, in their quiet and free Election of Representers, for the first Representative, then each Person so offending shall incur the Penalty of Confiscation of his whole Estate, both Real and Personal; and, if he has not an Estate to the Value of 50 £ shall suffer Imprisonment during one whole Year without Bail or Mainprize.

Provided, That the Offender in each such Case be convicted within three Months next after the committing of his Offence: And the first Representative is to make further Provision for the avoiding of these Evils in future Elections.

4. That to the end all Officers of State may be certainly accountable, and no Factions made to maintain corrupt Interests, no Member of a Council of State, nor any Officer of any Salary-Forces in Army or Garrison, nor any Treasurer or Receiver of public Money, shall, while such, be elected to be of a Representative: And in case any such Election shall be, the same to be void. And in case any Lawyer shall be chosen into any Representative, or Council of State, then he shall be incapable of Practice as a Lawyer during that Trust. . . .

This Course is to hold for the first Representative, which is to provide for the ascertaining of these Circumstances in order to future Representatives.

Fourthly That 150 Members at least be always present in each Sitting of the Representative, at the passing of any Law, or doing of any Act whereby the People are to be bound; saving, That the Number of 60 may make a House for Debates or Resolutions that are preparatory thereunto.

Fifthly, That each Representative shall, within twenty Days after their first Meeting, appoint a Council of State for the managing of public Affairs, untill the tenth Day after the Meeting of the next Representative, unless that next Representative thinks fit to put an End to that Trust sooner.

And the same Council to act and proceed therein, according to such Instructions and Limitations as the Representative shall give, and not otherwise.

Sixthly, That, in each Interval betwixt biennial Representatives, the Council of State, in case of imminent Danger or extreme Necessity, may summon a Representative to be forthwith chosen, and to meet; so as the Session thereof continue not above eighty Days; and so as it dissolve, at least, fifty Days before the appointed Time for the next biennial Representative; and upon the fiftieth Day so preceeding it shall dissolve of course, if not otherwise dissolved sooner.

Seventhly, That no Member of any Representative be made either Receiver, Treasurer, or other Officer, during that Employment, saving to be a Member of the Council of State.

Eighthly, That the Representatives have, and shall be understood to have, the supreme Trust in order to the Preservation and Government of the whole; and that their Power extend, without the Consent or Concurrence of any other Person or Persons, to the erecting and abolishing of Courts of Justice and public Offices, and to the enacting, altering, repealing, and declaring of Laws, and the highest and final Judgment, concerning all Natural or Civil Things; but not concerning Things Spiritual or Evangelical.

Provided that, even in Things Natural and Civil, these six Particulars next following are, and shall be, understood to be excepted and reserved from our Representatives, *viz.*

1. We do not impower them to impress or constrain any Person to serve in foreign War, either by Sea or Land, nor for any military Service within the Kingdom; save that they may take Order for the forming, training, and exercising of the People in a military Way, to be in Readiness for resisting of foreign Invasions, suppressing of sudden Insurrections, or for assisting in Execution of the Laws; and may take Order for the employing and conducting of them for those Ends; provided, That, even in such Cases, none be compellable to go out of the County he lives in, if he procure another to serve in his room.

2. That, after the Time herein limited for the Commencement of the First Representative, none of the People may be at any Time questioned for any Thing said or done in relation to the late Wars or public Differences, otherwise than in Execution or Pursuance of the Determinations of the present House of Commons, against such as have adhered to the King, or his Interest, against the People; and saving, that Accomptants for public Monies received, shall remain accountable for the same.

3. That no Securities given, or to be given, by the Public Faith of the Nation, nor any Engagements of the Public Faith for Satisfaction of Debts and Damages, shall be made void or invalid by the next, or any future Rep-

resentatives; except to such Creditors as have, or shall have, justly forfeited the same: And saving, That the next Representative may confirm or make null, in part or in whole, all Gifts of Lands, Monies, Offices, or otherwise, made by the present Parliament to any Member or Attendant of either House.

4. That, in any Laws hereafter to be made, no Person, by virtue of any Tenure, Grant, Charter, Patent, Degree, or Birth, shall be priviledged from Subjection thereto, or from being bound thereby, as well as others.

5. That the Representative may not give Judgment upon any Man's Person or Estate, where no Law hath before provided; save only in calling to Account, and punishing public Officers for abusing or failing in their Trust.

6. That no Representative may in any wise render up, or give, or take away, any of the Foundations of Common Right, Liberty, and Safety contained in this Agreement; nor level Men's Estates, destroy Property, or make all Things common; and that, in all Matters of such fundamental Concernment, there shall be a Liberty to particular Members of the said Representatives to enter their Dissents from the major Vote.

Ninthly, Concerning Religion, we agree as followeth:

1. It is intended that the Christian Religion be held forth and recommended, as the public Profession in this Nation, which we desire may, by the Grace of God, be reformed to the greatest Purity in Doctrine, Worship, and Discipline, according to the Word of God; the instructing of the People thereunto in a public Way, so it be not compulsive; as also the maintaining of able Teachers for that End, and for the Confutation or Discovery of Heresy, Error, and whatsoever is contrary to sound Doctrine, is allowed to be provided for by our Representatives; the Maintenance of which Teachers may be out of a public Treasury, and, we desire, not by Tithes. Provided, That Popery or Prelacy be not held forth as the public Way or Profession in this Nation.

2. That, to the public Profession so held forth, none be compelled by Penalties or otherwise; but only may be endeavoured to be won by sound Doctrine, and the Example of a good Conversation.

3. That such as profess Faith in God by Jesus Christ, however differing in Judgment from the Doctrine, Worship, or Discipline publickly held forth, as aforesaid, shall not be restrained from, but shall be protected in, the Profession of their Faith and Exercise of Religion, according to their Consciences, in any Place except such as shall be set apart for the public Worship; where we provide not for them, unless they have Leave; so as they abuse not this Liberty to the civil Injury of others, or to actual Disturbance of the public Peace on their Parts. Nevertheless, it is not intended to be hereby provided, That this Liberty shall necessarily extend to Popery or Prelacy.

4. That all Laws, Ordinances, Statutes, and Clauses in any Law, Statute, or Ordinance to the contrary of the Liberty herein provided for, in the two Particulars next preceding concerning Religion, be, and are hereby, repealed and made void.

Tenthly, It is agreed, That whosoever shall, by Force of Arms, resist the Orders of the next or any future Representative (except in case where such Representative shall evidently render up or give, or take away the Foundations of Common Right, Liberty, and Safety contained in this *Agreement*) he shall forthwith, after his or their such Resistance, lose the Benefit and Protection of the Laws, and shall be punishable with Death, as an Enemy and Traitor to the Nation.

Of the Things expressed in this *Agreement:* The certain Ending of this Parliament, as in the first Article; the equal or proportionable Distribution of the Number of the Representers to be elected, as in the second; the Certainty of the People's Meeting to elect for Representatives biennal, and their Freedom in Elections; with the Certainty of Meeting, Sitting, and Ending of Representatives so elected, which are provided for in the third Article; as also the Qualifications of Persons to elect or be elected, as in the first and second Particulars under the third Article; also the Certainty of a Number for passing a Law or preparatory Debates, provided for in the fourth Article; the Matter of the fifth Article, concerning the Council of State; and of the sixth, concerning the Calling, Sitting, and Ending of Representatives extraordinary; also the Power of Representatives to be, as in the eighth Article, and limited, as in the six Reserves next following the same: Likewise the second and third Particulars under the ninth Article concerning Religion, and the whole Matter of the tenth Article:

All these we do account and declare to be fundamental to our Common Right, Liberty, and Safety; and therefore do both agree thereunto, and resolve to maintain the same, as God shall enable us. The rest of the Matters in this *Agreement,* we account to be useful and good for the Public; and the particular Circumstances of Numbers, Times, and Places expressed in the several Articles, we account not fundamental; but we find them necessary to be here determined, for the making the *Agreement* certain and practicable; and do hold these most convenient that are here set down; and therefore do positively agree thereunto.

By the Appointment of his Excellency the Lord-General and his General Council of Officers.

John Rushworth, *Secr.*

24. The Trial of Charles I

The decision of the purged Parliament to accept the army's demand that the king be brought to answer for the tyrannies that had been committed and the blood that had been shed led to the appointment of a high court of justice. It was always the army's intention that the king be brought to trial rather than that he be deposed or executed surreptitiously. This was one of the main arguments in favor of purging rather than dissolving the Long Parliament. Without Parliament there would have been no legitimately constituted body to nominate a court of justice. Both the army leaders and those who remained in the House of Commons (with a handful of lords who continued to occupy the upper house) wanted a public charge, a public defense, and a public verdict. Galleries were built in the palace to accommodate spectators and a number of reports of the proceedings of the trial, fairly recorded as far as can be judged, were licensed by the parliamentary authorities. The king was brought to the bar in the name of the nation and the nation was to have its opportunity to judge him.

The appointment of the court, however, proved difficult. Four eminent parliamentarian-lawyers refused the office of president of the court which was finally accepted by John Bradshaw (1602–59). One hundred and thirty-two commissioners were appointed to hear the evidence and judge the king. The group was composed of MPs, army officers, and civilians. Barely half attended any individual session and even fewer could be induced, after the verdict was rendered, to sign the death warrant. Those who did have passed into history as the regicides.

The Charge Against the King

That the said Charles Stuart, being admitted King of England, and therein trusted with a limited power to govern by and according to the laws of the land, and not otherwise; and by his trust, oath, and office, being obliged to use the power committed to him for the good and benefit of the people, and for the preservation of their rights and liberties; yet, nevertheless, out of a wicked design to erect and uphold in himself an unlimited and tyrannical power to rule according to his will, and to overthrow the rights and liberties of the people, yea, to take away and make void the foundations thereof, and of all redress and remedy of misgovernment, which by the fundamen-

From *State Trials*, edited by H. L. Stephens (London: 1899), pp. 371–80.

tal constitutions of this kingdom were reserved on the people's behalf in the right and power of frequent and successive Parliaments, or national meetings in Council; he, the said Charles Stuart, for accomplishment of such his designs, and for the protecting of himself and his adherents in his and their wicked practices, to the same ends hath traitorously and maliciously levied war against the present Parliament, and the people therein represented, particularly upon or about the 30th day of June, in the year of our Lord 1642, at Beverley, in the County of York; and upon or about the 24th day of August in the same year, at the County of the Town of Nottingham, where and when he set up his standard of war; and also on or about the 23rd day of October in the same year, at Edgehill or Keynton-field, in the County of Warwick; and upon or about the 30th day of November in the same year, at Brentford, in the County of Middlesex; and upon or about the 30th day of August, in the year of our Lord 1643, at the Caversham Bridge, near Reading, in the County of Berks; and upon or about the 30th day of October in the year last mentioned, at or upon the City of Gloucester; and upon or about the 30th day of November in the year last mentioned, at Newbury, in the County of Berks; and upon or about the 31st day of July, in the year of our Lord 1644, at Cropredy Bridge, in the County of Oxon; and upon or about the 30th day of September in the last year mentioned, at Bodmin and other places near adjacent, in the County of Cornwall; and upon or about the 30th day of November in the year last mentioned, at Newbury aforesaid; and upon or about the 8th day of June, in the year of our Lord 1645, at the Town of Leicester; and also upon the 14th day of the same month in the same year, at Naseby-field, in the County of Northampton. At which several times and places, or most of them, and at many other places in this land, at several other times within the years aforementioned, and in the year of our Lord 1646, he, the said Charles Stuart, hath caused and procured many thousands of the free people of this nation to be slain; and by divisions, parties, and insurrections within this land, by invasions from foreign parts, endeavoured and procured by him, and by many other evil ways and means, he, the said Charles Stuart, hath not only maintained and carried on the said war both by land and sea, during the years beforementioned, but also hath renewed, or caused to be renewed, the said war against the Parliament and good people of this nation in this present year 1648, in the Counties of Kent, Essex, Surrey, Sussex, Middlesex, and many other Counties and places in England and Wales, and also by sea. And particularly he, the said Charles Stuart, hath for that purpose given commission to his son the Prince, and others, whereby, besides multitudes of other persons, many such as were by the Parliament entrusted and employed for the safety of the nation (being by him or his agents corrupted to the betraying of their trust, and revolting from the Parliament), have had entertainment and commission for the continuing and renewing of war and hostility against the said Parliament and people as aforesaid. By which cruel and unnatural wars, by him, the said Charles Stuart, levied, continued, and renewed as aforesaid, much innocent blood of the free people of this nation hath been spilt, many families have been undone, the public treasure wasted and exhausted, trade obstructed and miserably decayed, vast expense and damage to the nation incurred, and many parts of this land spoiled, some of them even to desolation. And for further prosecution of his said evil designs, he, the said Charles Stuart, doth still continue his commissions to the said Prince, and other rebels and revolters, both English and foreigners, and to the Earl of Ormond, and the Irish rebels and revolters associated with him; from whom further invasions upon this land are threatened, upon the procurement, and on the behalf of the said Charles Stuart.

All which wicked designs, wars, and evil practices of him, the said Charles Stuart, have been, and are carried on for the advancement and upholding of a personal interest of will, power, and pretended prerogative to himself and his family, against the public interest, common right, liberty, justice, and peace of the people of this nation, by and from whom he was entrusted as aforesaid.

By all which it appeareth that the said Charles Stuart hath been, and is the occasioner, author, and continuer of the said unnatural, cruel and bloody wars; and therein guilty of all the treasons, murders, rapines, burnings, spoils, desolations, damages and mischiefs to this nation, acted and committed in the said wars, or occasioned thereby.

The King's Reasons for Declining the Jurisdiction of the High Court of Justice

Having already made my protestations, not only against the illegality of this pretended Court, but also, that no earthly power can justly call me (who am your King) in question as a delinquent, I would not any more open my mouth upon this occasion, more than to refer myself to what I have spoken, were I in this case alone concerned: but the duty I owe to God in the preservation of the true liberty of my people will not suffer me at this time to be silent: for, how can any free-born subject of England call life or anything he possesseth his own, if power without right daily make new, and abrogate the old fundamental laws of the land which I now take to be the present case? Wherefore when I came hither, I expected that you would have endeavoured to have satisfied me concerning these grounds which hinder me to answer to your pretended impeachment. But since I see that nothing I can say will move you to it (though negatives are not so naturally proved as affirmatives) yet I will show you the reason why I am confident you cannot judge me, nor indeed the meanest man in England: for I will not (like you) without showing a reason, seek to impose a belief upon my subjects.

There is no proceeding just against any man, but what is warranted, either by God's laws or the municipal laws of the country where he lives. Now I am most confident this day's proceeding cannot be warranted by God's laws; for, on the contrary, the authority of obedience unto Kings is clearly warranted, and strictly commanded in both the Old and New Testament, which, if denied, I am ready instantly to prove.

And for the question now in hand, there it is said, that "where the word of a King is, there is power; and who may say unto him, what dost thou?" Eccles. viii. 4. Then for the law of this land, I am no less confident, that no learned lawyer will affirm that an impeachment can lie against the King, they all going in his name: and one of their maxims is, that the King can do no wrong. Besides, the law upon which you ground your proceedings, must either be old or new: if old, show it; if new, tell what authority, warranted by the fundamental laws of the land, hath made it, and when. But how the House of Commons can erect a Court of Judicature, which was never one itself (as is well known to all lawyers) I leave to God and the world to judge. And it were full as strange, that they should pretend to make laws without King or Lords' House, to any that have heard speak of the laws of England.

And admitting, but not granting, that the people of England's commission could grant your pretended power, I see nothing you can show for that; for certainly you never asked the question of the tenth man in the kingdom, and in this way you manifestly wrong even the poorest ploughman, if you demand not his free consent; nor can you pretend any colour for this your pretended commission, without the consent at least of the major part of every man in England of whatsoever quality or condition, which I am sure you never went about to seek, so far are you from having it. Thus you see that I speak not for my own right alone, as I am your King, but also for the true liberty of all my subjects, which consists not in the power of government, but in living under such laws, such a government, as may give themselves the best assurance of their lives, and property of their goods; nor in this must or do I forget the privileges of both Houses of Parliament, which this day's proceedings do not only violate, but likewise occasion the greatest breach of their public faith that (I believe) ever was heard of, with which I am far from charging the two Houses; for all the pretended crimes laid against me bear date long before this Treaty at Newport, in which I having concluded as much as in me lay, and hopefully expecting the Houses' agreement thereunto, I was suddenly suprised and hurried from thence as a prisoner; upon which account I am against my will brought hither, where since I am come, I cannot but to my power defend the ancient laws and liberties of this kingdom, together with my own just right. Then for anything I can see, the higher House is totally excluded; and for the House of Commons, it is too well known that the major part of them are detained or deterred from sitting; so as if I had no other, this were sufficient for me to protest against the lawfulness of your pretended Court. Besides all this, the peace of the kingdom is not the least in my thoughts; and what hope of settlement is there, so long as power reigns without rule or law, changing the whole frame of that government under which this kingdom hath flourished for many hundred years? (nor will I say what will fall out in case this lawless, unjust proceeding against me do go on) and believe it, the Commons of England will not thank you for this change; for they will remember how happy they have been of late years under the reigns of Queen Elizabeth, the King my father, and myself, until the beginning of these unhappy troubles, and will have cause to doubt, that they shall never be so happy under any new: and by this time it will be too sensibly evident, that the arms I took up were only to defend the fundamental laws of this kingdom against those who have supposed my power hath totally changed the ancient government.

Thus, having showed you briefly the reasons why I cannot submit to your pretended authority, without violating the trust which I have from God for the welfare and liberty of my people, I expect from you either clear reasons to convince my judgment, showing me that I am in an error (and then truly I will answer) or that you will withdraw your proceedings.

This I intended to speak in Westminster Hall, on Monday, January 22, but against reason was hindered to show my reasons.

The Trial of Charles I

On Saturday, being the 20th day of January 1649, the Lord President of the High Court of Justice, with near fourscore of the members of the said Court, having sixteen gentlemen with partizans, and a sword, and a mace, with their and other officers of the said Court, marching before them, came to the place ordered to be prepared for their sitting at the west-end of the great Hall at Westminster; where the Lord President, in a crimson velvet chair, fixed in the midst of the Court, placed himself, having a desk with a crimson-velvet cushion before him; the rest of the members placing themselves on each side of him upon several seats, or benches, prepared and hung with scarlet for that purpose; and the partizans dividing themselves on each side of the court before them.

The Court being thus sat, and Silence made, the great gate of the said

Hall was set open, to the end that all persons without exception, desirous to see or hear, might come into it. Upon which the Hall was presently filled, and silence again ordered.

This done, colonel Thomlinson, who had the charge of the Prisoner, was commanded to bring him to the Court; who within a quarter of an hour's space brought him, attended with about twenty officers with partizans, marching before him, there being other gentlemen, to whose care and custody he was likewise committed, marching in his rear.

Being thus brought up within the face of the Court, the Serjeant at Arms, with his mace, receives and conducts him strait to the bar, having a crimson-velvet chair set before him. After a stern looking upon the Court, and the people in the galleries on each side of him, he places himself, not at all moving his hat, or otherwise shewing the least respect to the court; but presently rises up again, and turns about, looking downwards upon the guards placed on the left side, and on the multitude of spectators on the right side of the said great Hall. After silence made among the people, the Act of Parliament for the trying of Charles Stuart, king of England, was read over by the Clerk of the Court, who sat on one side of a table covered with a rich Turkey-carpet, and placed at the feet of the said Lord President; upon which table was also laid the sword and mace.

After reading the said Act, the several names of the Commissioners were called over, every one who was present, being eighty, as aforesaid, rising up, and answering to his call.

Having again placed himself in his Chair, with his face towards the Court, silence being again ordered, the Lord President stood up, and said,

Lord President: Charles Stuart, king of England, the Commons of England assembled in Parliament being deeply sensible of the calamities that have been brought upon this nation, which is fixed upon you as the principal author of it, have resolved to make inquisition for blood; and according to that debt and duty they owe to justice, to God, the kingdom, and themselves, and according to the fundamental power that rests in themselves, they have resolved to bring you to Trial and Judgment; and for that purpose have constituted this High Court of Justice, before which they are brought.

This said, Mr. Cook, Solicitor for the Commonwealth standing within a bar on the right hand of the Prisoner, offered to speak; but the king having a staff in his hand, held it up, and laid it on the said Mr. Cook's shoulder two or three times, bidding him hold. Nevertheless, the Lord President ordering him to go on, he said,

Mr. Cook: My lord, I am commanded to charge Charles Stuart King of England, in the name of the Commons of England, with Treason and High Misdemeanors; I desire the said Charge may be read.

The said Charge being delivered to the Clerk of the Court, the Lord President ordered it should be read; but the king bid him hold. Nevertheless, being commanded by the Lord President to read it, the Clerk begun, and the Prisoner sat down again in his chair, looking sometimes on the High Court, sometimes up to the Galleries; and having risen again, and turned about to behold the guards and spectators, sat down, looking very sternly, and with a countenance not at all moved, till these words, viz.:— "Charles Stuart to be a Tyrant and Traitor," etc. were read; at which he laughed, as he sat, in the face of the Court.

The Charge being read, the Lord President replied;

Lord President: Sir, You have now heard your Charge, containing such matter as appears in it; you find, that in the close of it, it is prayed to the Court, in the behalf of the commons of England, that you answer to your Charge. The Court expects your Answer.

King: I would know by what power I am called hither; I was not long ago in the Isle of Wight; how I came there, is a longer story than I think it fit at this present time for me to speak of; but there I entered into a Treaty with both houses of Parliament, with as much public faith as it is possible to be had of any people in the world. I treated there with a number of honorable lords and gentlemen, and treated honestly and uprightly; I cannot say but they did very nobly with me, we were upon the conclusion of the Treaty. Now I would know by what authority, I mean lawful; there are many unlawful authorities in the world, thieves and robbers by the highways; but I would know by what authority I was brought from thence, and carried from place to place, and I know not what; and when I know what lawful authority, I shall answer. Remember I am your king, your lawful king, and what sins you bring upon your heads, and the judgment of God upon this land; think well upon it, I say, think well upon it, before you go further from one sin to a greater; therefore let me know by what lawful authority I am seated here, and I shall not be unwilling to answer. In the mean time, I shall not betray my trust; I have a trust committed to me by God, by old and lawful descent; I will not betray it, to answer to a new unlawful authority; therefore resolve me that and you shall hear more of me.

Lord President: If you had been pleased to have observed what was hinted to you by the Court, at your first coming hither, you would have known by what authority; which authority requires you, in the name of the people of England, of which you are elected king, to answer them.

King: No. Sir, I deny that.

Lord President: If you acknowledge not the authority of the Court, they must proceed.

King: I do tell them so; England was never an elective kingdom, but an hereditary kingdom, for near these thousand years; therefore let me know by what authority I am called hither. I do stand more for the Liberty of my people, than any here that come to be my pretended Judges; and therefore let me know by what lawful authority I am seated here, and I will answer it; otherwise I will not answer it.

Lord President: Sir, how really you have managed your trust, is known: your way of answer is to interrogate the Court, which beseems not you in this condition. You have been told of it twice or thrice.

King: Here is a gentleman, lieutenant-colonel Cobbet; ask him, if he did not bring me from the Isle of Wight by force. I do not come here as submitting to the Court: I will stand as much for the privilege of the house of commons, rightly understood, as any man here whatsoever. I see no house of lords here that may constitute a parliament; and the king too should have been. Is this the bringing of the king to his parliament? Is this the bringing an end to the Treaty in the public faith of the world? Let me see a legal authority warranted by the Word of God, the Scriptures, or warranted by the Constitutions of the kingdom, and I will answer.

Lord President: Sir; You have propounded a question, and have been answered. Seeing you will not answer, the Court will consider how to proceed; in the mean time, those that brought you hither, are to take charge of you back again. The Court desires to know, whether this be all the Answer you will give or no.

King: Sir, I desire that you would give me, and all the world, satisfaction in this: let me tell you, it is not a slight thing you are about, I am sworn to keep the peace, by that duty I owe to God and my country, and I will do it to the last breath of my body; and therefore ye shall do well to satisfy first God, and then the country, by what authority you do it; if you do it by an usurped authority, you cannot answer. There is a God in Heaven, that will call you, and all that give you power, to account. Satisfy me in that, and I will answer; otherwise I betray my Trust, and the Liberties of the people: and therefore think of that, and then I shall be willing. For I do avow, that it is as great a sin to withstand lawful authority, as it is to submit to a tyrannical, or any other ways unlawful authority; and therefore satisfy me that, and you shall receive my answer.

Lord President: The Court expects you should give them a final Answer; their purpose is to adjourn to Monday next; if you do not satisfy yourself, though we do tell you our authority, we are satisfied with our authority, and it is upon God's authority and the kingdom's; and that peace you speak of will be kept in the doing of justice, and that is our present work.

King: For answer, let me tell you, you have shewn no lawful authority to satisfy any reasonable man.

Lord President: That is, in your apprehension; we are satisfied that are your Judges.

King: It is not my apprehension, nor yours neither, that ought to decide it.

Lord President: The Court hath heard you, and you are to be disposed of as they have commanded.

The Court adjourns to the Painted Chamber, on Monday at ten of the clock in the forenoon, and thence hither. . . .

At the High Court of Justice sitting in Westminster Hall, Monday, January 22, 1649.

O Yes! made; Silence commanded; the Court called, and answered to their names. Silence commanded upon pain of imprisonment, and the Captain of the Guard to apprehend all such as make disturbance. Upon the king's coming in, a shout was made. Command given by the Court to the Captain of the Guard, to fetch and take into his custody those who make any disturbance.

Mr. Solicitor: May it please your lordship, my Lord President; I did at the last court in the behalf of the Commons of England, exhibit and give in to this court a Charge of High Treason, and other High Crimes, against the prisoner at the bar whereof I do accuse him in the name of the People of England; and the Charge was read unto him, and his Answer required. My lord, He was not then pleased to give an Answer, but instead of answering, did there dispute the Authority of this high Court. My humble motion to this high Court in behalf of the kingdom of England is, That the prisoner may be directed to make a positive Answer, either by way of confession, or negation; which if he shall refuse to do, that the matter of the Charge may be taken *pro confesso,* and the Court may proceed according to justice.

Lord President: Sir, You may remember at the last Court you were told the occasion of your being brought hither, and you heard a Charge read against you, containing a Charge of High Treason and other high crimes against this realm of England: you heard likewise, that it was prayed in the behalf of the People, that you should give an Answer to that Charge, that thereupon such proceedings might be had, as should be agreeable to justice. You were then pleased to make some scruples concerning the authority of this Court, and knew not by what authority you were brought hither; you did divers times propound your questions, and were as often answered. That it was by authority of the Commons of England assembled in parliament, that did think fit to call you to account for those high and capital Misdemeanours wherewith you were then charged. Since that the Court hath taken into consideration what you then said; they are fully satisfied with their own authority, and they hold it fit you should stand satisfied with it too; and they do require it, that you do give a positive and particular Answer to this Charge that is exhibited against you; they do expect you should either confess or deny it; if you deny, it is offered in the behalf of the kingdom to be made good against you; their authority they do avow to the whole world, that the whole kingdom are to rest satisfied in, and you are to rest satisfied with it. And therefore you are to lose no more time, but to give a positive Answer thereunto.

King: When I was here last, it is very true, I made that question; truly if it were only my own particular case, I would have satisfied myself with the protestation I made the last time I was here against the Legality of this Court, and that a king cannot be tried by any superior jurisdiction on earth; but it is not my case alone, it is the Freedom and the Liberty of the people of England; and do you pretend what you will, I stand more for their Liberties. For if power without law may make laws, may alter the fundamental laws of the kingdom, I do not know what subject he is in England, that can be sure of his life, or any thing that he calls his own: therefore when that I came here, I did expect particular reasons to know by what law, what authority you did proceed against me here. And therefore I am a little to seek what to say to you in this particular, because the affirmative is to be proved, the negative often is very hard to do: but since I cannot persuade you to do it, I shall tell you my reasons as short as I can—My Reasons why in conscience and the duty I owe to God first, and my people next, for the preservation of their lives, liberties, and estates I conceive I cannot answer this, till I be satisfied of the legality of it. All proceedings against any man whatsoever—

Lord President: Sir, I must interrupt you, which I would not do, but that what you do is not agreeable to the proceedings of any court of justice: You are about to enter into argument, and dispute concerning the Authority of this Court, before whom you appear as a Prisoner, and are charged as an high Delinquent: if you take upon you to dispute the Authority of the Court, we may not do it, nor will any court give way unto it: you are to submit unto it, you are to give a punctual and direct Answer, whether you will answer your charge or no, and what your Answer is.

King: Sir, By your favour, I do not know the forms of law: I do know law and reason, though I am no lawyer professed; but I know as much law as any gentleman in England; and therefore (under favour) I do plead for the Liberties of the People of England more than you do: and therefore if I should impose a belief upon any man, without reasons given for it, it were unreasonable: but I must tell you, that that reason that I have, as thus informed, I cannot yield unto it.

Lord President: Sir, I must interrupt you, you may not be permitted; you speak of law and reason; it is fit there should be law and reason, and there is both against you. Sir, the Vote of the Commons of England assembled in parliament, it is the reason of the kingdom, and they are these that have given to that law, according to which you should have ruled and reigned. Sir, you are not to dispute our Authority, you are told it again by the Court.

Sir, it will be taken notice of, that you stand in contempt of the Court, and your contempt will be recorded accordingly.

King: I do not know how a king can be a Delinquent; but by any law that ever I heard of, all men (Delinquents, or what you will), let me tell you, they may put in Demurrers against any proceeding as legal: and I do demand that, and demand to be heard with my Reasons: if you deny that, you deny reason.

Lord President: Sir, you have offered something to the Court: I shall speak something unto you, the Sense of the Court. Sir, neither you nor any man are permitted to dispute that point, you are concluded, you may not demur to the jurisdiction of the Court: if you do, I must let you know, that they over-rule your Demurrer; they sit here by the authority of the Commons of England, and all your predecessors and you are responsible to them.

King: I deny that; shew me one precedent.

Lord President: Sir, you ought not to interrupt while the Court is speaking to you. This point is not to be debated by you, neither will the Court permit you to do it; if you offer it by way of Demurrer to the Jurisdiction of the Court, they have considered of their Jurisdiction, they do affirm their own Jurisdiction.

King: I say, Sir, by your favour, that the Commons of England was never a Court of Judicature: I would know how they came to be so.

Lord President: Sir, you are not to be permitted to go on in that Speech and these discourses.

Then the clerk of the Court read as followeth:—

"Charles Stuart, king of England, You have been accused on behalf of the People of England of High Treasons, and other high Crimes; the Court have determined that you ought to answer the same."

King: I will answer the same so soon as I know by what Authority you do this.

Lord President: If this be all that you will say, then Gentlemen, you that brought the Prisoner hither, take charge of him back again.

King: I do require that I may give in my Reasons why I do not answer, and give me time for that.

Lord President: Sir, it is not for Prisoners to require.

King: Prisoners! Sir, I am not an ordinary prisoner.

Lord President: The Court hath considered of their jurisdiction, and they have already affirmed their jurisdiction; if you will not answer, we shall give order to record your default.

King: You never heard my Reasons yet.

Lord President: Sir, your Reasons are not to be heard against the highest jurisdiction.

King: Shew me that Jurisdiction where reason is not to be heard.

Lord President: Sir, we shew it you here. The Commons of England; and the next time you are brought, you will know more of the pleasure of the Court; and, it may be, their final determination.

King: Shew me where ever the House of Commons was a Court of Judicature of that kind.

Lord President: Serjeant, take away the Prisoner.

King: Well, Sir, remember that the king is not suffered to give in his Reasons for the Liberty and Freedom of all his Subjects.

Lord President: Sir, you are not to have Liberty to use this language; How great a friend you have been to the Laws and Liberties of the people, let all England and the world judge.

King: Sir, under favour, it was the Liberty, Freedom, and Laws of the subject, that ever I took—defended myself with arms; I never took up arms against the people, but for the laws.

Lord President: The command of the Court must be obeyed; no Answer will be given to the Charge.

King: Well, Sir! . . .

At the High Court of Justice sitting in Westminster Hall, Tuesday, January 23, 1649.

O Yes made, Silence commanded, the Court called, 73 persons present. The King comes in with his guard, looks with an austere countenance upon the Court, and sits down. The second O Yes made, and Silence commanded.

Mr. Cook, Solicitor-General: May it please your lordship, my lord President; this is now the third time, that by the great grace and favour of this High Court, the Prisoner hath been brought to the bar before any issue joined in the cause. My lord, I did at the first court exhibit a Charge against him, containing the highest Treasons that ever was wrought upon the theatre of England; That a king of England trusted to keep the law, that had taken an oath so to do, that had tribute paid him for that end, should be guilty of a wicked Design to subvert and destroy our Laws, and introduce an Arbitrary and Tyrannical Government, in defiance of the Parliament and their Authority, set up his standard for War against his Parliament and People: And I did humbly pray, in the behalf of the people of England, that he might speedily be required to make an Answer to the Charge. But my lord, instead of making any Answer, he did then dispute the Authority of this High Court. Your lordship was pleased to give him a further day to consider, and to put in his Answer; which day being Yesterday, I did humbly move, that he might be required to give a direct and positive Answer, either by denying or confession of it; But, my lord, he was then pleased for to demur to the Jurisdiction of the Court; which the court did then over-rule, and commanded him to give a direct and positive Answer. My lord, besides this great delay of justice, I shall now humbly move your lordship for speedy Judgment against him. My lord, I might press your lordship upon the whole, that according to the known rules of the law of the land, That if a Prisoner shall stand as contumacious in contempt, as I shall not put in an issuable plea, Guilty or not Guilty of the Charge given against him, whereby he may come to a fair trial; that, as by an implicit confession, it may be taken *pro confesso,* as it hath been done to those who have deserved more favour than the Prisoner at the bar has done. But, besides, my lord, I shall humbly press your lordship upon the whole fact. The house of commons, the supreme Authority and Jurisdiction of the kingdom, they have declared, That it is notorious that the matter of the Charge is true, as it is in truth, my lord, as clear as crystal, and as the sun that shines at noonday: which if your lordship and the Court be not satisfied in, I have notwithstanding, on the people of England's behalf, several Witnesses to produce. And therefore I do humbly pray, and yet I must confess it is not so much I, as the innocent blood that hath been shed, the cry whereof is very great for justice and judgment; and therefore I do humbly pray, that speedy Judgment be pronounced against the Prisoner at the bar.

Lord President: Sir, you have heard what is moved by the Counsel on the behalf of the kingdom against you. Sir, you may well remember, and if you do not, the Court cannot forget, what dilatory dealings the Court hath found at your hands. You were pleased to propound some Questions, you have had our Resolutions upon them. You were told, over and over again, That the Court did affirm their own jurisdiction; that it was not for you, nor any other man, to dispute the jurisdiction of the supreme and highest Authority of England, from which there is no appeal, and touching which there must be no dispute; yet you did persist in such carriage, as you gave no manner of obedience, nor did you acknowledge any authority in them, nor the High Court that constituted this Court of Justice. Sir, I must let you know from the Court, that they are very sensible of these delays of yours, and that they ought not, being thus authorised by the supreme Court of England, to be thus trifled withal; and that they might in justice, if they pleased, and according to the rules of justice, take advantage of these delays and proceed to pronounce judgment against you; yet nevertheless they are pleased to give direction, and on their behalfs I do require you, that you make a positive Answer unto this Charge that is against you, Sir, in plain terms, for Justice knows no respect of persons; you are to give your positive and final Answer in plain English, whether you be Guilty or Not Guilty of these Treasons laid to your charge.

The King, after a little pause, said,

King: When I was here yesterday, I did desire to speak for the Liberties of the people of England; I was interrupted; I desire to know yet whether I may speak freely or not.

Lord President: Sir, you have had the Resolution of the Court upon the like question the last day, and you were told that having such a Charge of so high a nature against you, and your work was, that you ought to acknowledge the jurisdiction of the Court, and to answer to your Charge. Sir, if you answer to your Charge, which the Court gives you leave now to do, though they might have taken the advantage of your contempt; yet if you be able to answer to your Charge, when you have once answered, you shall be heard at large, make the best defence you can. But, Sir, I must let you know from the Court, as their commands, that you are not to be permitted to issue out into any other discourses, till such time as you have given a positive Answer concerning the matter that is charged upon you.

King: For the Charge, I value it not a rush; it is the Liberty of the People of England that I stand for. For me to acknowledge a new Court that I never heard of before, I that am your King, that should be an example to all the people of England for to uphold justice, to maintain the old laws: indeed I do not know how to do it. You spoke very well the first day that I came here (on Saturday) of the obligations that I had laid upon me by God, to the maintenance of the Liberties of my people; the same obligation you spake of, I do acknowledge to God that I owe to him, and to my people, to defend as much as in me lies the ancient laws of the kingdom: therefore, until that I may know that this is not against the fundamental Laws of the kingdom, by your favour I can put in no particular Charge. If you will give me time, I will shew you my Reasons why I cannot do it, and this—

Here, being interrupted, he said,

By your favor, you ought not to interrupt me: How I came here, I know not; there's no law for it to make your king your prisoner. I was in a Treaty upon the public faith of the kingdom, that was the known . . . two Houses of Parliament that was the representative of the kingdom; and when that I had almost made an end of the Treaty, then I was hurried away, and brought hither: and therefore—

Here the Lord President said, Sir, you must know the pleasure of the Court.

King: By your favour, sir.

Lord President: Nay, sir, by your favour, you may not be permitted to fall into those discourses; you appear as a Delinquent, you have not acknowledged the authority of the Court, the Court craves it not of you; but once more they command you to give your positive Answer.—Clerk, do your duty.

King: Duty, Sir!

The Clerk reads.

"Charles Stuart, king of England, you are accused in behalf of the commons of England of divers Crimes and Treasons, which Charge hath been read unto you: the Court now requires you to give your positive and final Answer, by way of confession or denial of the Charge."

King: Sir, I say again to you, so that I might give satisfaction to the people of England of the clearness of my proceeding, not by way of Answer, not in this way, but to satisfy them that I have done nothing against that trust that has been committed to me, I would do it; but to acknowledge a new Court, against their Privileges, to alter the fundamental laws of the kingdom—sir, you must excuse me.

Lord President: Sir, this is the third time that you have publicly disowned this Court, and put an affront upon it. How far you have preserved the privileges of the people, your actions have spoke it; but truly, Sir, men's intentions ought to be known by their actions; you have written your meaning in bloody characters throughout the whole kingdom. But, Sir, you understand the pleasure of the Court.—Clerk, Record the Default.—And, Gentlemen, you that took charge of the Prisoner, take him back again.

King: I will only say this one word more to you: If it were only my own particular, I would not say any more, nor interrupt you.

Lord President: Sir, you have heard the pleasure of the Court, and you are (notwithstanding you will not understand it) to find that you are before a court of justice. . . .

Cryer: God bless the kingdom of England!

The Proceedings of the High Court of Justice sitting in Westminster Hall, on Saturday the 27th of January 1649.

O Yes made: Silence commanded; the court called; Serjeant Bradshaw Lord President (in a scarlet robe), with sixty-eight other members of the court.

As the King comes in, a Cry made in the Hall for Execution! Justice! Execution!

King: I shall desire a word to be heard a little, and I hope I shall give no occasion of interruption.

Lord President: You may answer in your time, hear the Court first.

King: If it please you, Sir, I desire to be heard, and I shall not give any occasion of interruption, and it is only in a word: a sudden Judgment.

Lord President: Sir, you shall be heard in due time, but you are to hear the Court first.

King: Sir, I desire—it will be in order to what I believe the Court will say; and therefore, Sir, an hasty Judgment is not so soon recalled.

Lord President: Sir, you shall be heard before the Judgment be given, and in the mean time you may forbear.

King: Well, Sir, shall I be heard before the Judgment be given?

Lord President: Gentlemen, it is well known to all, or most of you here present, that the Prisoner at the Bar hath been several times convened and brought before the Court to make answer to a Charge of Treason, and other high Crimes exhibited against him in the name of the people of England

[Here a malignant lady (Lady Fairfax) interrupted the Court, saying "Not half the People"; but she was soon silenced. See the Trial of Daniel Axtell, Oct. 15, 1660]; to which Charge being required to answer he hath been so far from obeying the commands of the Court by submitting to their justice, as he began to take upon him to offer reasoning and debate unto the Authority of the Court, and of the highest court that constituted them to try and judge him: but being over-ruled in that, and required to make his Answer, he was still pleased to continue contumacious, and to refuse to submit or answer. Hereupon the Court, that they may not be wanting to themselves, to the trust reposed in them, nor that any man's wilfulness prevent justice, they have thought fit to take the matter into their consideration, they have considered of the Charge, they have considered of the Contumacy, and of that Confession, which in law doth arise upon that contumacy; they have likewise considered of the notoriety of the fact charged upon this Prisoner, and upon the whole matter they are resolved, and have agreed upon a Sentence to be now pronounced against this Prisoner; but in respect he doth desire to be heard, before the Sentence be read and pronounced, the Court hath resolved that they will hear him. Yet, Sir, thus much I must tell you beforehand, which you have been minded of at other courts, that if that you have to say be to offer any debate concerning jurisdiction, you are not to be heard in it; you have offered it formerly, and you have indeed struck at the root, that is, the power and supreme authority of the Commons of England, which this Court will not admit a debate of; and which indeed is an irrational thing in them to do, being a court that acts upon authority derived from them, that they should presume to judge upon their superior, from whom there is no appeal. But, sir, if you have anything to say in defence of yourself concerning the matter charged, the Court hath given me in command to let you know they will hear you.

King: Since that I see that you will not hear anything of debate concerning that which I confess I thought most material for the Peace of the Kingdom, and for the Liberty of the Subject, I shall waive it; I shall speak nothing to it, but only I must tell you, that this many a day all things have been taken away from me, but that, that I call more dear to me than my life, which is my conscience and my honour: and if I had respect to my life more than the Peace of the Kingdom, the Liberty of the Subject, certainly I should have made a particular Defence for myself; for by that at leastwise I might have delayed an ugly Sentence, which I believe will pass upon me. Therefore certainly, Sir, as a man that hath some understanding, some knowledge of the world, if that my true zeal to my country had not overborne the care that I have of my own preservation, I should have gone another way to work than that I have done. Now, Sir, I conceive, that an hasty Sentence once passed, may sooner be repented than recalled; and truly, the self-same desire that I have for the Peace of the Kingdom, and the Liberty of the subject more than my own particular, does make me now at last desire, that having something for to say that concerns both, I desire before Sentence be given, that I may be heard in the Painted Chamber before the Lords and Commons. This delay cannot be prejudicial to you, whatsoever I say; if that I say no reason, those that hear me must be judges: I cannot be judge of that, which I have: if it be reason, and really for the welfare of the kingdom, and the liberty of the subject, I am sure on't, very well it is worth the hearing; therefore I do conjure you, as you love that which you pretend, I hope it is real, the Liberty of the Subject, the Peace of the kingdom, that you will grant me the hearing, before any Sentence be past. I only desire this, that you will take this into your consideration, it may be you have not heard of it before-hand; if you will, I'll retire, and you may think of it; but if I cannot get this liberty I do here protest, that so fair shews of Liberty and Peace are pure shews, and not otherwise, since you will not hear your king.

Lord President: Sir, you have now spoken.

King: Yes, Sir.

Lord President: And this that you have said is a further declining of the Jurisdiction of this Court, which was the thing wherein you were limited before.

King: Pray excuse me, Sir, for my interruption, because you mistake me; it is not a declining of it, you do judge me before you hear me speak; I say it will not, I do not decline it, though I cannot acknowledge the Jurisdiction of the Court; yet, Sir, in this give me leave to say, I would do it, though I do not by this acknowledge it, I do protest it is not the declining of it, since I say, if that I do say any thing, but that which is for the Peace of the Kingdom, and the Liberty of the Subject, then the shame is mine. Now I desire that you will take this into your consideration; if you will, I'll withdraw.

Lord President: Sir, this is not altogether new that you have moved unto us, not altogether new to us, though it is the first time in person you have offered it to the Court. Sir, you say you do not decline the Jurisdiction of the Court.

King: Not in this that I have said.

Lord President: I understand you well, Sir; but nevertheless, that which you have offered seems to be contrary to that saying of yours; for the Court are ready to give a Sentence; It is not as you say, That they will not hear your king; for they have been ready to hear you, they have patiently waited your pleasure for three Courts together, to hear what you would say to the People's Charge against you, to which you have not vouchsafed to give any Answer at all. Sir, this tends to a further delay; truly, Sir, such delays as these, neither may the kingdom nor justice well bear, you have had three several days to have offered in this kind what you would have pleased. This Court is founded upon that Authority of the Commons of England in whom rests the supreme jurisdiction; that which you now tender is to have another jurisdiction, and a co-ordinate jurisdiction. I know very well you express yourself, Sir, that notwithstanding that you would offer to the Lords and Commons in the Painted Chamber, yet nevertheless you would proceed on here, I did hear you say so. But, Sir, that you would offer there, whatever it is, it must needs be in delay of the Justice here; so as if this Court be re-solved, and prepared for the Sentence, this that you offer they are not bound in justice to grant; But, Sir, according to what you seem to desire, and because you shall know the further pleasure of the Court upon that which you have moved, the Court will withdraw for a time.

King: Shall I withdraw?

Lord President: Sir, you shall know the pleasure of the Court presently.

[The Court withdrew for half an hour into the Court of Wards.]

Serjeant-at-Arms: The Court gives command, that the Prisoner be with-drawn; and they give order for his return again.

[The Court withdrew for half an hour and returned.]

Lord President: Serjeant-at-Arms, send for your Prisoner.

Sir, you were pleased to make a motion here to the Court to offer a de-sire of yours, touching the propounding of somewhat to the Lords in the Painted Chamber, for the peace of the kingdom; Sir, you did, in effect, re-ceive an Answer before the Court adjourned; truly, Sir, their withdrawing, and adjournment was *pro forma tantum:*[1] for it did not seem to them that there was any difficulty in the thing; they have considered of what you have moved, and have considered of their own Authority, which is founded, as hath been often said, upon the supreme Authority of the Commons of En-gland assembled in parliament: the Court acts according to their Commis-sion. Sir, the return I have to you from the Court, is this: That they have been too much delayed by you already, and this that you now offer hath occasioned some little further delay; and they are Judges appointed by the highest Judges; and Judges are no more to delay, than they are to deny Jus-tice: they are good words in the great old Charter of England; *Nulli nega-bimus, nulli vendemus, nulli differemus Justitiam.*[2] There must be no de-lay; but the truth is, Sir, and so every man here observes it, that you have much delayed them in your Contempt and Default, for which they might long since have proceeded to Judgment against you; and notwithstanding

1. pro forma only
2. We shall not deny, sell, or defer justice to anyone.

what you have offered, they are resolved to proceed to Punishment, and to Judgment, and that is their unanimous Resolution.

King: Sir, I know it is in vain for me to dispute, I am no sceptic for to deny the Power that you have; I know that you have Power enough: Sir, I confess, I think it would have been for the kingdom's peace, if you would have taken the pains for to have shewn the lawfulness of your Power; for this Delay that I have desired, I confess it is a delay, but it is a delay very important for the Peace of the Kingdom; for it is not my person that I look on alone, it is the kingdom's welfare, and the kingdom's peace; it is an old Sentence, That we should think long, before we resolve of great matters. Therefore, Sir, I do say again, that I do put at your doors all the inconveniency of an hasty Sentence. I confess I have been here now, I think, this week; this day eight days was the day I came here first, but a little Delay of a day or two further may give Peace; whereas an hasty Judgment may bring on that trouble and perpetual inconveniency to the kingdom, that the child that is unborn may repent it; and therefore again, out of the duty I owe to God, and to my country, I do desire that I may be heard by the Lords and Commons in the Painted Chamber, or any other chamber that you will appoint me.

Lord President: Sir, you have been already answered to what you even now moved, being the same you moved before, since the Resolution and the Judgment of the Court in it; and the Court now requires to know whether you have any more to say for yourself than you have said, before they proceed to Sentence?

King: I say this, Sir, That if you will hear me, if you will give but this Delay, I doubt not but I shall give some satisfaction to you all here, and to my People after that; and therefore I do require you, as you will answer it at the dreadful Day of Judgment, that you will consider it once again.

Lord President: Sir, I have received direction from the Court.

King: Well, Sir.

Lord President: If this must be re-enforced, or any thing of this nature, your Answer must be the same; and they will proceed to Sentence, if you have nothing more to say.

King: Sir, I have nothing more to say, but I shall desire, that this may be entered what I have said.

Lord President: The Court then, Sir, hath something else to say to you; which, although I know it will be very unacceptable, yet notwithstanding they are willing, and are resolved to discharge their duty. Sir, You speak very well of a precious thing, which you call Peace; and it had been much to be wished that God had put it into your heart, that you had as effectually and really endeavoured and studied the Peace of the kingdom, as now in words you seem to pretend; but, as you were told the other day, actions must expound intentions; yet actions have been clean contrary. And truly, Sir, it doth appear plainly enough to them, that you have gone upon very erroneous principles: The kingdom hath felt it to their smart; and it will be no case to you to think of it; for, Sir, you have held yourself, and let fall such language, as if you had been no way subject to the Law, or that the law had not been your superior. Sir, the Court is very sensible of it, and I hope so are all the understanding people of England, that the law is your superior; that you ought to have ruled according to the law; you ought to have so. Sir, I know very well your pretence hath been that you have done so; but, Sir, the difference hath been who shall be the expositors of this law: Sir, whether you and your party, out of courts of justice, shall take upon them to expound law, or the courts of justice, who are the expounders? Nay, the Sovereign and the High Court of Justice, the Parliament of England, that are not only the highest expounders, but the sole makers of the law? Sir, for you to set yourself with your single judgment, and those that adhere unto you, to set yourself against the highest Court of Justice, that is not law. Sir, as the Law is your Superior, so truly, Sir, there is something that is superior to the Law, and that is indeed the Parent or Author of the Law, and that is the people of England: for, Sir, as they are those that at the first (as other countries have done) did chuse to themselves this form of government even for Justice sake, that justice might be administered, that peace might be preserved; so, Sir, they gave laws to their governors, according to which they should govern; and if those laws should have proved inconvenient or prejudicial to the public, they had a power in them, and reserved to themselves, to alter as they shall see cause. Sir, it is very true what some of your side have said, *"Rex non habet parem in regno,"* [3] say they: This Court will say the same, while King, that you have not your peer in some sense, for you are *major singulis;* [4] but they will aver again that you are *minor universis.* [5] And the same Author tells you that, *"non debet esse major eo in regno suo in exhibitione juris, minimus autem esse debet in judicio suscipiendo"* [6] [Bract., *De Leg.,* lib. I. c. viii.]

This we know to be law, *Rex habet superiorem, Deum et legem, etiam et curiam;* [7] so says the same author. And truly, Sir, he makes bold to go a little further, *Debent ei ponere froenum:* [8] they ought to bridle him. And, Sir, we know very well the stories of old: those wars that were called the

---

3. The king has no equal in the kingdom.   4. greater than each

5. smaller than all

6. No one in his kingdom must be greater in displaying justice, but he must be the least in undertaking judgment.

7. The king has a superior: God and the law, and even the court.

8. They must put reins on him.

Barons' War, when the nobility of the land did stand out for the Liberty and Property of the Subject, and would not suffer the kings, that did invade, to play the tyrants freer, but called them to account for it; we know that truth, that they did *froenum ponere*.[9] But, sir, if they do forbear to do their duty now, and are not so mindful of their own honour and the kingdom's good as the Barons of England of old were, certainly the Commons of England will not be unmindful of what is for their preservation, and for their safety; *Justitiae fruendi causa reges constituti sunt.*[10] This we learn: The end of having kings, or any other governors, it is for the enjoying of justice; that is the end. Now, Sir, if so be the king will go contrary to that end, or any other governor will go contrary to the end of his government; Sir, he must understand that he is but an officer in trust, and he ought to discharge that trust; and they are to take order for the animadversion and punishment of such an offending governor.

This is not law of yesterday, Sir (since the time of the division betwixt you and your people), but it is law of old. And we know very well the Authors and the Authorities that do tell us what the law was in that point upon the Election of Kings upon the Oath that they took unto their people: And if they did not observe it, there were those things called Parliaments; the Parliaments were they that were to adjudge (the very Words of the Author) the plaints and wrongs done of the king and the queen, or their children; such wrongs especially, when the people could have no where else any Remedy. Sir, that hath been the people of England's case: they could not have their Remedy elsewhere but in parliament.

Sir, Parliaments were ordained for that purpose, to redress the Grievances of the people; that was their main end. And truly, Sir, if so be that the kings of England had been rightly mindful of themselves, they were never more in majesty and state than in the Parliament: But how forgetful some have been, Stories have told us, we have a miserable, a lamentable, a sad experience of it. Sir, by the old laws of England, I speak these things the rather to you, because you were pleased to let fall the other day, You thought you had as much knowledge in the Law as most gentlemen in England: it is very well, Sir. And truly, Sir, it is very fit for the gentlemen of England to understand that Law under which they must live, and by which they must be governed. And then, Sir, the Scripture says, "They that know their master's will and do it not" what follows? The Law is your master, the acts of parliament.

The Parliaments were to be kept antiently, we find in our old Author, twice in the year, that the Subject upon any occasion might have a ready

9. put reins on
10. Kings were set up for the enjoyment of justice.

Remedy and Redress for his Grievance. Afterwards, by several acts of parliament in the days of your predecessor Edward the third, they should have been once a year. Sir, what the Intermission of parliaments hath been in your time, it is very well known, and the sad consequences of it; and what in the interim instead of these Parliaments hath been by you by an high and arbitrary hand introduced upon the People, that likewise hath been too well known and felt. But when God by his Providence had so far brought it about, that you could no longer decline the calling of a Parliament, Sir, yet it will appear what your ends were against the antient and your native kingdom of Scotland: the Parliament of England not serving your ends against them, you were pleased to dissolve it. Another great necessity occasioned the calling of this parliament; and what your Designs, and Plots, and Endeavours all along have been, for the crushing and confounding of this Parliament, hath been very notorious to the whole kingdom. And truly, Sir, in that you did strike at all; that had been a sure way to have brought about That that this Charge lays upon you, your intention to subvert the Fundamental Laws of the Land; for the great bulwark of the Liberties of the People is the Parliament of England; and to subvert and root up that, which your aim hath been to do, certainly at one blow you had confounded the Liberties and the Property of England.

Truly, Sir, it makes me to call to mind; I cannot forbear to express it; for, Sir, we must deal plainly with you, according to the merits of your cause; so is our Commission; it makes me to call to mind (these proceedings of yours) That that we read of a great Roman Emperor, by the way let us call him a great Roman tyrant, Caligula, that wished that the people of Rome had had but one neck, that at one blow he might cut it off. And your proceedings have been somewhat like to this; for the body of the people of England hath been (and where else) represented but in the Parliament; and could you but have confounded that, you had at one blow cut off the neck of England. But God hath reserved better things for us, and hath pleased for to confound your designs, and to break your forces, and to bring your person into custody, that you might be responsible to justice.

Sir, we know very well that it is a question much on your side press'd, By what Precedent we shall proceed? Truly, Sir, for Precedents, I shall not upon these occasions institute any long discourse; but it is no new thing to cite precedents almost of all nations, where the people (where the power hath been in their hands) have made bold to call their Kings to account; and where the change of government hath been upon occasion of the Tyranny and Misgovernment of those that have been placed over them, I will not spend time to mention either France, or Spain, or the Empire, or other countries; volumes may be written of it. But truly, Sir, that of the kingdom of Arragon, I shall think some of us have thought upon it, where they have the justice of Arragon, that is, a man, *tanquam in medio positus*,[11] betwixt the King of Spain and the people of the country; that if wrong be done by the King, he that is king of Arragon, the justice, hath power to reform the wrong; and he is acknowledged to be the king's superior, and is the grand preserver of their privileges, and hath prosecuted kings upon their miscarriages.

Sir, what the Tribunes of Rome were heretofore, and what the Ephori were to the Lacedemonian State, we know that is the Parliament of England to the English state; and though Rome seemed to lose its liberty when once the Emperors were; yet you shall find some famous acts of justice even done by the Senate of Rome; that great Tyrant of his time, Nero, condemned and judged by the Senate. But truly, Sir, to you I should not need to mention these foreign examples and stories: If you look but over Tweed, we find enough in your native kingdom of Scotland. If we look to your first King Fergus, that your Stories make mention of, he was an elective king; he died, and left two sons, both in their minority; the kingdom made choice of their uncle, his brother, to govern in the minority. Afterwards the elder brother, giving small hope to the people that he would rule or govern well, seeking to supplant that good uncle of his that governed them justly, they set the elder aside, and took to the younger. Sir, if I should come to what your Stories make mention of, you know very well you are the hundred and ninth king of Scotland; for not to mention so many kings as that kingdom, according to their power and privileges, have made bold to deal withal, some to banish, and some to imprison, and some to put to death, it would be too long: and as one of your own authors says, it would be too long to recite the manifold examples that your own stories make mention of. *Reges,* etc. (say they) we do create: we created kings at first: *Leges,* etc., we imposed laws upon them. And as they are chosen by the suffrages of the People at the first, so upon just occasion, by the same suffrages they may be taken down again. And we will be bold to say, that no kingdom hath yielded more plentiful experience than that your native kingdom of Scotland hath done concerning the Deposition and the Punishment of their offending and transgressing kings.

It is not far to go for an example: near you—Your grandmother set aside, and your Father, an infant, crowned. And the State did it here in England; here hath not been a want of some examples. They have made bold (the Parliament and the People of England) to call their Kings to account; there are frequent examples of it in the Saxons' time, the time before the Conquest. Since the Conquest there want not some Precedents neither; King Edward the Second, King Richard the Second, were dealt with

11. placed as it were in the middle

so by the Parliament, as they were deposed and deprived. And truly, Sir, whoever shall look into their Stories, they shall not find the Articles that are charged upon them to come near to that height and capitalness of Crimes that are laid to your Charge; nothing near.

Sir, you were pleased to say, the other day, wherein they dissent; and I did not contradict it. But take all together, Sir; If you were as the Charge speaks, and no otherwise, admitted king of England; but for that you were pleased then to alledge, how that for almost a thousand years these things have been, Stories will tell you, if you go no higher than the time of the Conquest; if you do come down since the Conquest, you are the twenty-fourth king from William called the Conqueror, you shall find one half of them to come merely from the state, and not merely upon the point of descent. It were easy to be instanced to you; but time must not be lost that way. And truly, Sir, what a grave and learned Judge said in his time, and well known to you, and is since printed for posterity, That although there was such a thing as a descent many times, yet the kings of England ever held the greatest assurance of their Titles when it was declared by Parliament. And, Sir, your Oath, the manner of your Coronation, doth shew plainly, that the kings of England, although it is true, by the law the next person in blood is designed: yet if there were just cause to refuse him, the people of England might do it. For there is a Contract and a bargain made between the King and his people, and your Oath is taken; and certainly, Sir, the bond is reciprocal; for as you are the Liege Lord, so they Liege Subjects. And we know very well, that hath been so much spoken of, *Ligeantia est duplex.*[12] This we know, now, the one tie, the one bond, is the Bond of Protection that is due from the sovereign; the other is the Bond of Subjection that is due from the Subject. Sir, if this bond be once broken, farewell sovereignty! *Subjectio trahit,*[13] etc.

These things may not be denied, Sir; I speak it rather, and I pray God it may work upon your heart, that you may be sensible of your Miscarriages. For whether you have been, as by your office you ought to be, a Protector of England, or the Destroyer of England, let all England judge, or all the world, that hath look'd upon it. Sir, though you have it by inheritance in the way that is spoken of, yet it must not be denied that your office was an office of trust, and indeed an office of the highest trust lodged in any single person; For as you were the Grand Administrator of Justice, and others were, as your delegates, to see it done throughout your realms; if your greatest office were to do Justice, and preserve your People from wrong, and instead of doing that, you will be the great Wrong-doer yourself; if

12. Allegiance is twofold.   13. Subjection draws

instead of being a Conservator of the Peace, you will be the grand Disturber of the Peace; surely this is contrary to your office, contrary to your trust. Now, Sir, if it be an office of inheritance, as you speak of, your Title by Descent, let all men know that great offices are seizable and forfeitable, as if you had it but for a year, and for your life. Therefore, Sir, it will concern you to take into your serious consideration your great Miscarriages in this kind. Truly, Sir, I shall not particularize the many Miscarriages of your reign whatsoever, they are famously known: It had been happy for the kingdom, and happy for you too, if it had not been so much known, and so much felt, as the Story of your Miscarriages must needs be, and hath been already.

Sir, That which we are now upon, by the command of the highest Court, hath been and is to try and judge you for these great offences of yours. Sir, the Charge hath called you Tyrant, a Traitor, a Murderer, and a Public Enemy to the Commonwealth of England. Sir, it had been well if that any of all these terms might rightly and justly have been spared, if any one of them at all.

King: Ha!

Lord President: Truly, Sir, We have been told *"Rex est dum bene regit, Tyrannus qui populum opprimit"*: [14] And if so be that be the definition of a Tyrant, then see how you come short of it in your actions, whether the highest Tyrant, by that way of arbitrary government, and that you have sought for to introduce, and that you have sought to put, you were putting upon the people? Whether that was not as high an Act of Tyranny as any of your predecessors were guilty of, nay, many degrees beyond it?

Sir, the term Traitor cannot be spared. We shall easily agree it must denote and suppose a Breach of Trust; and it must suppose it to be done to a superior. And therefore, Sir, as the people of England might have incurred that respecting you, if they had been truly guilty of it, as to the definition of law; so on the other side, when you did break your trust to the kingdom, you did break your trust to your superior; For the kingdom is that for which you were trusted. And therefore, sir, for this breach of Trust when you are called to account, you are called to account by your superiors. *"Minimus ad majorem in judicium vocat."* [15] And, Sir, the People of England cannot be so far wanting to themselves, God having dealt so miraculously and gloriously for them: but that having power in their hands, and their great enemy, they must proceed to do justice to themselves and to you: For, Sir, the Court could heartily desire, that you would lay your hand upon your

14. He is a king while he rules well, and a tyrant if he oppresses the people.
15. The smallest is called to the greater for judgment.

heart, and consider what you have done amiss, that you would endeavour to make your peace with God. Truly, Sir, these are your High-Crimes, Tyranny and Treason.

There is a third thing too, if those had not been, and that is Murder, which is laid to your charge. All the bloody Murders, which have been committed since this time that the division was betwixt you and your people, must be laid to your charge, which have been acted or committed in these late wars. Sir, it is an heinous and crying sin: And truly, Sir, if any man will ask us what Punishment is due to a Murderer, let God's Law, let man's law speak. Sir, I will presume that you are so well read in Scripture, as to know what God himself hath said concerning the shedding of man's blood: Gen. ix., Numb. xxxv. will tell you what the punishment is: And which this Court, in behalf of the whole kingdom, are sensible of, of that innocent blood that has been shed, whereby indeed the land stands still defiled with that blood; and, as the text hath it, it can no way be cleansed but with the shedding of the Blood of him that shed this blood. Sir, we know no dispensation from this blood in that Commandment "Thou shalt do no Murder": We do not know but that it extends to kings as well as to the meanest peasants, the meanest of the people: the command is universal. Sir, God's law forbids it: Man's law forbids it: Nor do we know that there is any manner of exception, not even in man's laws, for the punishment of murder in you. It is true, that in the case of kings every private hand was not to put forth itself to this work for their reformation and punishment; But, Sir, the people represented having power in their hands, had there been but one wilful act of murder by you committed, had power to have convened you, and to have punished you for it.

But then, Sir, the weight that lies upon you in all those respects that have been spoken, by reason of your Tyranny, Treason, Breach of Trust, and the Murders that have been committed; surely, Sir, it must drive you into a sad consideration concerning your eternal condition. As I said at first, I know it cannot be pleasing to you to hear any such things as these are mentioned unto you from this Court, for so we do call ourselves, and justify ourselves to be a Court, and a high Court of Justice, authorized by the highest and solemnest court of the kingdom, as we have often said; And although you do not yet endeavour what you may to discourt us, yet we do take knowledge of ourselves to be such a Court as can administer Justice to you: and we are bound, Sir, in duty to do it. Sir, all I shall say before the reading of your Sentence, it is but this: The Court does heartily desire that you will seriously think of those evils that you stand guilty of. Sir, you said well to us the other day, you wished us to have God before our eyes. Truly Sir, I hope all of us have so: That God, who we know is a King of Kings, and Lord of Lords; that God with whom there is no respect of Persons; that

God, who is the Avenger of innocent Blood; We have that God before us; that God, who does bestow a curse upon them that with-hold their hands from shedding of blood, which is in the case of guilty malefactors, and that do deserve death: That God we have before our eyes. And were it not that the conscience of our duty hath called us unto this place, and this imployment, Sir, you should have had no appearance of a Court here. But, Sir, we must prefer the discharge of our duty unto God, and unto the kingdom, before any other respect whatsoever. And although at this time many of us, if not all of us, are severely threatened by some of your party, what they intend to do, Sir, we do here declare, That we shall not decline or forbear the doing of our duty in the administration of Justice, even to you, according to the merit of your Offence although God should permit those men to effect all that bloody design in hand against us. Sir, we will say, and we will declare it, as those Children in the Fiery Furnace, that would not worship the golden image, that Nebuchadnezzar had set up, "That their God was able to deliver them from that danger that they were near unto"; But yet if he would not do it, yet notwithstanding that they would not fall down and worship the Image. We shall thus apply it; That though we should not be delivered from those bloody hands and hearts that conspire the overthrow of the kingdom in general, of us in particular, for acting in this great Work of Justice, though we should perish in the Work, yet by God's grace, and by God's strength, we will go on with it. And this is all our resolutions, Sir, I say for yourself, we do heartily wish and desire that God would be pleased to give you a sense of your sins, that you would see wherein you have done amiss, that you may cry unto him, that God would deliver you from Blood-guiltiness. A good king was once guilty of that particular thing, and was clear otherwise, saving in the matter of Uriah. Truly, Sir, the Story tells us that he was a repentant king: and it signifies enough, that he had died for it, but that God was pleased to accept of him, and to give him his pardon, "Thou shalt not die, but the child shall die: Thou hast given cause to the enemies of God to blaspheme."

King: I would desire only one word before you give Sentence; and that is, that you would hear me concerning those great Imputations that you have laid to my charge.

Lord President: Sir, You must give me now leave to go on; for I am not far from your Sentence, and your time is now past.

King: But I shall desire you will hear me a few words to you: For truly, whatever Sentence you will put upon me in respect of those heavy imputations, that I see by your Speech you have put upon me; Sir, It is very true, that—

Lord President: Sir, I must put you in mind: Truly, Sir, I would not willingly, at this time especially, interrupt you in anything you have to say, that is proper for us to admit of; but, Sir, you have not owned us as a Court, and you look upon us as a sort of people met together; and we know what language we receive from your party.

King: I know nothing of that.

Lord President: You disavow us as a Court; and therefore for you to address yourself to us, not acknowledging us as a Court to judge of what you say, it is not to be permitted. And the truth is, all along, from the first time you were pleased to disavow and disown us, the Court needed not to have heard you one word; For unless they be acknowledged a Court, and engaged, it is not proper for you to speak. Sir, we have given you too much liberty already, and admitted of too much delay, and we may not admit of any farther. Were it proper for us to do it, we should hear you freely; and we should not have declined to hear you at large, what you could have said or proved on your behalf, whether for totally excusing, or for in part excusing those great and heinous Charges, that in whole or in part are laid upon you. But, Sir, I shall trouble you no longer; your sins are of so large a dimension, that if you do but seriously think of them, they will drive you to a sad consideration of it, and they may improve in you a sad and serious repentance; And that the Court doth heartily wish that you may be so penitent for what you have done amiss, that God may have mercy, at leastwise, upon your better part: Truly, Sir, for the other, it is our parts and duties to do that, which the law prescribes. We are not here *jus dare* but *jus dicere.* We cannot be unmindful of what the Scripture tells us; "For to acquit the Guilty is of equal Abomination, as to condemn the Innocent." We may not acquit the Guilty. What sentence the law affirms to a Traitor, Tyrant, a Murderer, and a public Enemy to the Country, that Sentence you are now to hear read unto you; and that is the Sentence of the Court.

[The Lord President commanded the sentence to be read. The Clerk read the Sentence, which was drawn up in Parchment.]

"Whereas the Commons of England in Parliament had appointed them an High Court of Justice, for the Trying of Charles Stuart, King of England, before whom he had been three times convened; and at the first time a Charge of High-Treason, and other Crimes and Misdemeanors, was read in the behalf of the Kingdom of England," etc. [Here the Clerk read the Charge.] "Which Charge being read unto him, as aforesaid, he the said Charles Stuart was required to give his Answer: But he refused so to do; and so expressed the several Passages of his Trial in refusing to answer. For all which Treasons and Crimes this Court doth adjudge, That the said Charles Stuart, as a Tyrant, Traitor, Murderer, and a Public Enemy, shall be put to Death, by the severing his Head from His Body."

After the Sentence read, the Lord President said, This Sentence now read and published, is the Act, Sentence, Judgment, and Resolution of the whole Court.

Here the Court stood up, as assenting to what the President said.

King: Will you hear me a word, Sir?

Lord President: Sir, you are not to be heard after the Sentence.

King: No, Sir?

Lord President: No, Sir; by your favour, Sir. Guard, withdraw your Prisoner.

King: I may speak after the Sentence—By your Favour, Sir, I may Speak after the Sentence ever.

By your Favour (Hold!) the Sentence, Sir,—

I say, Sir, I do—

I am not suffered for to speak: Expect what Justice other People will have.

O yes: All manner of Persons that have any thing else to do, are to depart at this time, and to give their attendance in the Painted Chamber; to which place this Court doth forthwith adjourn itself.

The Sentence of the High Court of Justice upon the King

Whereas the Commons of England assembled in Parliament, have by their late Act intituled an Act of the Commons of England assembled in Parliament, for erecting an High Court of Justice for the trying and judging of Charles Stuart, King of England, authorised and constituted us an High Court of Justice for the trying and judging of the said Charles Stuart for the crimes and treasons in the said Act mentioned; by virtue whereof the said Charles Stuart hath been three several times convented before this High Court, where the first day, being Saturday, the 20th of January instant, in pursuance of the said Act, a charge of high treason and other high crimes was, in the behalf of the people of England, exhibited against him, and read openly unto him, wherein he was charged, that he, the said Charles Stuart, being admitted King of England, and therein trusted with a limited power to govern by, and according to the law of the land, and not otherwise; and by his trust, oath, and office, being obliged to use the power committed to him for the good and benefit of the people, and for the preservation of their rights and liberties; yet, nevertheless, out of a wicked design to erect and uphold in himself an unlimited and tyrannical power to rule according to his will, and to overthrow the rights and liberties of the people, and to take away and make void the foundations thereof, and of all redress and remedy of misgovernment, which by the fundamental constitutions of this kingdom were reserved on the people's behalf in the right and power of frequent and successive Parliaments, or national meetings in Council; he, the said Charles Stuart, for accomplishment of such his designs, and for the protecting of himself and his adherents in his and their wicked practices, to the same end hath traitorously and maliciously levied war against the present Parliament, and people therein represented, as with the circumstances of time and place is in the said charge more particularly set forth; and that he hath thereby caused and procured many thousands of the free people of this nation to be slain; and by divisions, parties, and insurrections within this land, by invasions from foreign parts, endeavoured and procured by him, and by many other evil ways and means, he, the said Charles Stuart, hath not only maintained and carried on the said war both by sea and land, but also hath renewed, or caused to be renewed, the said war against the Parliament and good people of this nation in this present year 1648, in several counties and places in this kingdom in the charge specified; and that he hath for that purpose given his commission to his son the Prince, and others, whereby, besides multitudes of other persons, many such as were by the Parliament entrusted and employed for the safety of this nation, being by him or his agents corrupted to the betraying of their trust, and revolting from the Parliament, have had entertainment and commission for the continuing and renewing of the war and hostility against the said Parliament and people: and that by the said cruel and unnatural war so levied, continued and renewed, much innocent blood of the free people of this nation hath been spilt, many families undone, the public treasure wasted, trade obstructed and miserably decayed, vast expense and damage to the nation incurred, and many parts of the land spoiled, some of them even to desolation; and that he still continues his commission to his said son, and other rebels and revolters, both English and foreigners, and to the Earl of Ormond, and to the Irish rebels and revolters associated with him, from whom further invasions of this land are threatened by his procurement and on his behalf; and that all the said wicked designs, wars, and evil practices of him, the said Charles Stuart, were still carried on for the advancement and upholding of the personal interest of will, power, and pretended prerogative to himself and his family, against the public interest, common right, liberty, justice, and peace of the people of this nation; and that he thereby hath been and is the occasioner, author, and continuer of the said unnatural, cruel, and bloody wars, and therein guilty of all the treasons, murders, rapines, burnings, spoils, desolations, damage, and mischief to this nation, acted and committed in the said wars, or occasioned thereby; whereupon the proceedings and judgment of this Court were prayed against him, as a tyrant, traitor, and murderer, and public enemy to the Commonwealth, as by the said charge more fully appeareth. To which charge, being read unto him as aforesaid, he, the said Charles Stuart, was required to give his answer; but he refused so to do, and upon Monday, the 22nd day of January instant, being again brought before this Court, and there required to answer directly to the said charge, he still refused so to do; whereupon his default and contumacy was entered; and the next day, being the third time brought before the Court, judgment was then prayed against him on the behalf of the people of England for his contumacy, and for the matters contained against him in the said charge, as taking the same for confessed, in regard of his refusing to answer thereto: yet notwithstanding this Court (not willing to take advantage of his contempt) did once more require him to answer to the said charge; but he again refused so to do; upon which his several defaults, this Court might justly have proceeded to judgment against him, both for his contumacy and the matters of the charge, taking the same for confessed as aforesaid.

Yet nevertheless this Court, for its own clearer information and further satisfaction, have thought fit to examine witnesses upon oath, and take notice of other evidences, touching the matters contained in the said charge, which accordingly they have done.

Now, therefore, upon serious and mature deliberation of the premises, and consideration had of the notoriety of the matters of fact charged upon him as aforesaid, this Court is in judgment and conscience satisfied that he, the said Charles Stuart, is guilty of levying war against the said Parliament and people, and maintaining and continuing the same; for which in the said charge he stands accused, and by the general course of his government, counsels, and practices, before and since this Parliament began (which have been and are notorious and public, and the effects whereof remain abundantly upon record) this Court is fully satisfied in their judgments and consciences, that he has been and is guilty of the wicked design and endeavours in the said charge set forth; and that the said war hath been levied, maintained, and continued by him as aforesaid, in prosecution, and for accomplishment of the said designs; and that he hath been and is the occasioner, author, and continuer of the said unnatural, cruel, and bloody wars, and therein guilty of high treason, and of the murders, rapines, burnings, spoils, desolations, damage, and mischief to this nation acted and committed in the said war, and occasioned thereby. For all which treasons and crimes this Court doth adjudge that he, the said Charles Stuart, as a tyrant, traitor, murderer, and public enemy to the good people of this nation, shall be put to death by the severing of his head from his body.

The Death Warrant of Charles I

At the High Court of Justice for the trying and judging of Charles Stuart, King of England, Jan. 29, Anno Domini 1648.

Whereas Charles Stuart, King of England, is, and standeth convicted, attainted, and condemned of high treason, and other high crimes; and sentence upon Saturday last was pronounced against him by this Court, to be put to death by the severing of his head from his body; of which sentence, execution yet remaineth to be done; these are therefore to will and require you to see the said sentence executed in the open street before Whitehall, upon the morrow, being the thirtieth day of this instant month of January, between the hours of ten in the morning and five in the afternoon of the same day, with full effect. And for so doing this shall be your sufficient warrant. And these are to require all officers, soldiers, and others, the good people of this nation of England, to be assisting unto you in this service.

To Col. Francis Hacker, Col. Huncks, and Lieut.-Col. Phayre, and to every of them.

> Given under our hands and seals.
> JOHN BRADSHAW.
> THOMAS GREY.
> OLIVER CROMWELL.
> &c. &c.

25. *King Charles, His Speech on the Scaffold*

Refusing to recognize the authority of the court that tried him, Charles I awaited its illegal judgment before requesting the right to address his accusers. This was denied to him. His reflective comments were therefore left for the scaffold and are reported in this contemporary tract published within hours of the execution. Although the anonymous author of the pamphlet inserted obviously pro-Parliament marginal notes, he appears to have reported faithfully the king's final words.

Charles I was executed on the afternoon of 30 January 1649. The scaffold was erected outside of the windows of the second floor of the royal banqueting house providing both a good view of the event for the people who were allowed to fill the courtyard below and also offering security from the crowd. The diarist John Evelyn remembered the stroke of the axe and the dismal groan that went up within the crowd when the executioner held the head aloft and pronounced the ritual words, "behold the head of a traitor."

King Charles, His Speech Made upon the Scaffold at Whitehall-Gate Immediately before his execution (30 January 1648)

About ten in the morning the King was brought from St. James's, walking on foot through the park, with a regiment of foot, part before and part be-

From *Trial of Charles I*, edited by J. G. Muddiman (Edinburgh: Wm. Hodge and Co., 1928), pp. 260–65.

hind him, with colours flying, drums beating, his private guard of partizans with some of his gentlemen before and some behind bareheaded, Dr. Juxon next behind him and Col. Thomlinson (who had the charge of him) talking with the King bareheaded, from the Park up the stairs into the gallery and so into the cabinet chamber where he used to lie.

[Marginal note. "It is observed the King desired to have the use of the cabinet and the little room next it where there was a trap door."]

Where he continued at his devotion, refusing to dine, (having before taken the Sacrament) only about an hour before he came forth, he drank a glass of claret wine and eat a piece of bread about twelve at noon.

From thence he was accompanied by Dr. Juxon, Col. Thomlinson and other officers formerly appointed to attend him and the private guard of partizans, with musketeers on each side, through the Banqueting house adjoining to which the scaffold was erected between Whitehall Gate and the Gate leading into the gallery from St. James's.

[Marginal note. "It was near (if not in) the very place where the first blood in the beginning of the late troubles was shed, when the Kings Cavaliers fell upon the citizens, killed one, and wounded about 50 others."]

The scaffold was hung round with black and the floor covered with black and the Ax and block laid in the middle of the scaffold. There were divers companies of foot, and troops of horse placed on the one side of the scaffold towards Kings Street and on the other side towards Charing Cross, and the multitudes of people that came to be spectators, very great.

The King being come upon the scaffold, look'd very earnestly upon the block and ask'd Col. Hacker if there were no higher. And then spake thus, directing his speech chiefly to Col. Thomlinson.

King: I shall be very little heard of anybody here, I shall therefore speak a word unto you here. Indeed I could hold my peace very well, if I did not think that holding my peace would make some men think I did submit to the guilt as well as to the punishment. But I think it is my duty to God first and to my country for to clear myself both as an honest man and a good King, and a good christian. I shall begin first with my innocency. In troth I think it not very needful for me to insist long upon this, for all the world knows that I never did begin a war with the two Houses of Parliament. And I call God to witness, to whom I must shortly make an account, that I never did intend for to encroach upon their privileges. They began upon me, it is the Militia they began upon, they confest that the Militia was mine, but they thought it fit for to have it from me. And, to be short, if any body will look to the dates of Commissions, of their commissions and mine, and likewise to the Declarations, will see clearly that they began these unhappy troubles, not I. So that as the guilt of these enormous crimes that are laid against me I hope in God that God will clear me of it, I will not, I am in charity. God forbid that I should lay it upon the two Houses of Parliament; there is no necessity of either, I hope that they are free of this guilt. For I do believe that ill instruments between them and me has been the chief cause of all this bloodshed. So that, by way of speaking, as I find myself clear of this, I hope (and pray God) that they may too. Yet, for all this, God forbid that I should be so ill a christian as not to say God's judgments are just upon me. Many times he does pay justice by an unjust sentence, that is ordinary. I will only say this that an unjust sentence [Marginal note. "Strafford."] that I suffered for to take effect, is punished now by an unjust sentence upon me. That is, so far as I have said, to show you that I am an innocent man.

Now for to show you that I am a good christian. I hope there is [Marginal note. "Pointing to D. Juxon."] a good man that will bear me witness that I have forgiven all the world, and even those in particular that have been the chief causes of my death. Who they are, God knows, I do not desire to know, God forgive them. But this is not all, my charity must go further. I wish that they may repent, for indeed they have committed a great sin in that particular. I pray God with St. Stephen, that this be not laid to their charge. Nay, not only so, but that they may take the right way to the peace of the kingdom, for my charity commands me not only to forgive particular men, but my charity commands me to endeavour to the last gasp the Peace of the Kingdom. So, Sirs, I do wish with all my soul, and I do hope there is some here [Marginal note. "Turning to some gentlemen that wrote."] that will carry it further, that they may endeavour the peace of the Kingdom.

Now, Sirs, I must show you both how you are out of the way and will put you in a way. First, you are out of the way, for certainly all the way you have ever had yet, as I could find by anything, is by way of conquest. Certainly this is an ill way, for conquest, Sir, in my opinion is never just, except there be a good just cause, either for matter of wrong or just title. And then if you go beyond it, the first quarrel that you have to it, that makes it unjust at the end that was just at the first. But if it be only matter of conquest, there is a great robbery; as a Pirate said to Alexander that he was the great robber, he was but a petty robber: and so, Sir, I do think the way that you are in is much out of the way. Now, Sir, for to put you in the way. Believe it you will never do right, nor God will never prosper you, until you give God his due, the King his due (that is, my successors) and the people their due, I am as much for them as any of you. You must give God his due by regulating rightly His Church (according to the Scripture) which is now out of order. For to get you in a way particularly now I cannot, but onely this. A national synod freely called, freely debating among themselves, must settle this, when that every opinion is freely and clearly heard.

For the King, indeed I will not, then turning to a gentleman that touched the Ax, said, hurt not the ax, that may hurt me [Marginal note. "Meaning if he did blunt the edge"]. For the King, the laws of the land will clearly instruct you for that. Therefore because it concerns my own particular, I onely give you a touch of it.

For the people. And truly I desire their liberty and freedom as much as anybody whomsoever. But I must tell you that their liberty and freedom consists in having of government; those laws by which their life and their goods may be most their own. It is not for having share in government, Sir, that is nothing pertaining to them. A subject and a soveraign are clean different things, and therefore until they do that, I mean, that you do put the people in that liberty as I say, certainly they will never enjoy themselves.

Sirs. It was for this that now I am come here. If I would have given way to an arbitrary way, for to have all laws changed according to the power of the sword I needed not to have come here. And, therefore, I tell you, and I pray God it be not laid to your charge, that I am the martyr of the people.

In troth, Sirs, I shall not hold you much longer, for I will only say thus to you. That in truth I could have desired some little time longer, because I would have put then that I have said in a little more order, and a little better digested than I have done. And, therefore, I hope that you will excuse me.

I have delivered my conscience. I pray God that you do take those courses that are best for the good of the Kingdom and your own salvations.

Dr. Juxon: Will your Majesty, though it may be very well known, your Majesties affections towards religion, yet it may be expected that you should say somewhat for the world's satisfaction?

King: I thank you very heartily, my lord, for that I had almost forgotten it. In troth, Sirs, my conscience in religion I think is very well knowne to all the world: and, therefore, I declare before you all that I die a christian, according to the profession of the Church of England, as I found it left me by my father. And this honest man [Marginal note. "Pointing to Dr. Juxon"] I think will witness it.

Then turning to the officers, said, "Sirs, excuse me for this same, I have a good cause and I have a gracious God. I will say no more."

Then turning to Colonel Hacker, he said "Take care that they do not put me to pain. And Sir, this, and it please you—" But then a gentleman coming near the Ax, the King said "Take heed of the Ax. Pray take heed of the Ax."

Then the King, speaking to the Executioner said "I shall say but very short prayers, and when I thrust out my hands—"

Then the King called to Dr. Juxon for his night-cap, and having put it on said to the executioner "Does my hair trouble you?" Who desired him to put it all under his cap. Which the King did accordingly, by the help of the executioner and the bishop.

Then the King turning to Dr. Juxon said, "I have a good cause, and a gracious God on my side."

Doctor Juxon: There is but one stage more. This stage is turbulent and troublesome; it is a short one. But you may consider, it will soon carry you a very great way. It will carry you from Earth to Heaven. And there you shall find a great deal of cordial joy and comfort.

King: I go from a corruptible to an incorruptible crown; where no disturbance can be, no disturbance in the world.

Doctor Juxon: You are exchanged from a temporal to an eternal crown, a good exchange.

The King then said to the Executioner, "Is my hair well?" Then the King took off his cloak and his George, giving his George to Dr. Juxon, saying "Remember—." [Marginal note. "It is thought for to give it to the Prince."]

Then the King put off his dublet and being in his wastcoat, put his cloak on again. Then looking upon the block, said to the Executioner "You must set it fast."

Executioner: It is fast, Sir.

King: It might have been a little higher.

Executioner: It can be no higher, Sir.

King: When I put out my hands this way [Marginal note. "Stretching them out"] then—

After having said two or three words, as he stood, to himself with hands and eyes lift up. Immediately stooping down laid his neck on the block. And then the executioner again putting his hair under his cap, the King said "Stay for the sign" [Marginal note. "Thinking he had been going to strike."]

Executioner: Yes I will and it please your Majesty.

And after a very little pause, the King stretching forth his hands, the executioner at one blow severed his head from his body. That [*sic*] when the Kings head was cut off, the executioner held it up and shewed it to the spectators.

And his body was put in a coffin covered with black velvet for that purpose.

The King's body now lies in his lodging chamber in Whitehall. *Sic transit gloria Mundi.*

26. John Gauden, *Eikon Basilike*

Eikon Basilike or the King's Image was published, without license, within hours of the King's execution. It was one of the most influential pamphlets of the revolutionary period, achieving forty-six English editions within a year. Contemporary belief was that Charles I had authored the

From John Gauden, *Eikon Basilike* (London, 1649).

piece during his captivity, but after the Restoration a clergyman named John Gauden asserted that he had written the pamphlet on direction from the king, and that it was based upon notes and writings given to him by Charles I. This story, and the evidence that he produced to support it, resulted in his elevation to the bishopric of Winchester in 1660. Why Charles I should have chosen this obscure East Anglian clergyman for so important a task remains a mystery. Gauden was born in 1605, attended Bury School, St. John's College, Cambridge, and received his divinity training at Oxford. His writings before the publication of *Eikon Basilike* were on narrow theological topics. There continues to be a vigorous historical debate over just how much editing or composing Gauden did on the *Eikon*, though recent opinion gives him more credit than the king for the final product.

Upon His Majesty's Calling This Last Parliament

This last Parliament I called, not more by others' advice and necessity of my affairs than by my own choice and inclination, who have always thought the right way of Parliaments most safe for my crown and best pleasing to my people. And although I was not forgetful of those sparks which some men's distempers formerly studied to kindle in Parliaments (which, by forbearing to convene for some years, I hoped to have extinguished), yet resolving with myself to give all just satisfaction to modest and sober desires, and to redress all public grievances in church and state, I hoped, by my freedom and their moderation, to prevent all misunderstandings and miscarriages in this; in which, as I feared affairs would meet with some passion and prejudice in other men, so I resolved they should find least of them in myself, not doubting but by the weight of reason I should counterpoise the overbalancings of any factions.

I was indeed sorry to hear with what partiality and popular heat elections were carried in many places; yet, hoping that the gravity and discretion of other gentlemen would allay and fix the Commons to a due temperament, guiding some men's well-meaning zeal by such rules of moderation as are best both to preserve and restore the health of all states and kingdoms, no man was better pleased with the convening of this Parliament than myself; who, knowing best the largeness of my own heart toward my people's good and just contentment, pleased myself most in that good and firm understanding which would hence grow between me and my people.

All jealousies being laid aside, my own and my children's interests gave me many obligations to seek and preserve the love and welfare of my subjects, the only temporal blessing that is left to the ambition of just monarchs, as their greatest honor and safety, next God's protection. I cared not to lessen myself in some things of my wonted prerogative, since I knew I could be no loser if I might gain but a recompense in my subjects' affections.

I intended not only to oblige my friends, but mine enemies also, exceeding even the desires of those that were factiously discontented, if they did but pretend to any modest and sober sense.

The odium and offenses which some men's rigor or remissness in church and state had contracted upon my government I resolved to have expiated by such laws and regulations for the future as might not only rectify what was amiss in practice but supply what was defective in the constitution, no man having a greater zeal to see religion settled and preserved in truth, unity, and order than myself, whom it most concerns both in piety and policy; as knowing that no flames of civil dissensions are more dangerous than those which make religious pretensions the grounds of factions.

I resolved to reform what I should, by free and full advice in Parliament, be convinced to be amiss, and to grant whatever my reason and conscience told me was fit to be desired. I wish I had kept myself within those bounds and not suffered my own judgment to have been overborne in some things, more by others' importunities than their arguments. My confidence had less betrayed myself and my kingdoms to those advantages which some men sought for who wanted nothing but power and occasion to do mischief.

But, our sins being ripe, there was no preventing of God's justice from reaping that glory in our calamities which we robbed Him of in our prosperity. . . .

Upon His Majesty's Going to the House of Commons

My going to the House of Commons to demand justice upon the five members was an act which my enemies loaded with all the obloquies and exasperations they could.

It filled indifferent men with great jealousies and fears; yea, and many of my friends resented it as a motion rising rather from passion than reason, and not guided with such discretion as the touchiness of those times required.

But these men knew not the just motives and pregnant grounds with which I thought myself so furnished that there needed nothing to such evidence as I could have produced against those I charged, save only a free and legal trial, which was all I desired.

Nor had I any temptation of displeasure or revenge against those men's persons further than I had discovered those, as I thought, unlawful correspondencies they had used and engagements they had made to embroil my kingdoms; of all which I missed but little to have produced writings under some men's own hands who were the chief contrivers of the following innovations.

Providence would not have it so; yet I wanted not such probabilities as were sufficient to raise jealousies in any king's heart who is not wholly stupid and neglective of the public peace; which to preserve by calling in question half a dozen men in a fair and legal way (which God knows was all my design) could have amounted to no worse effect, had it succeeded, than either to do me and my kingdom right, in case they had been found guilty, or else to have cleared their innocency and removed my suspicions; which, as they were not raised out of any malice, so neither were they in reason to be smothered.

What flames of discontent this spark (though I sought by all speedy and possible means to quench it) soon kindled, all the world is witness. The aspersion which some men cast upon that action, as if I had designed by force to assault the House of Commons and invade their privilege, is so false that, as God best knows, I had no such intent; so none that attended could justly gather from anything I then said or did the least intimation of any such thoughts.

That I went attended with some gentlemen, as it was no unwonted thing for the majesty and safety of a king so to be attended, especially in discontented times, so were my followers at that time short of my ordinary guard and no way proportionable to hazard a tumultuary conflict. Nor were they more scared at my coming that I was unassured of not having some affronts cast upon me, if I had none with me to preserve a reverence to me. For many people had, at that time, learned to think those hard thoughts which they have since abundantly vented against me, both by words and deeds.

The sum of that business was this: those men and their adherents were then looked upon by the affrighted vulgar as greater protectors of their laws and liberties than myself, and so worthier of their protection. I leave them to God and their own consciences, who, if guilty of evil machinations, no present impunity or popular vindications of them will be subterfuge sufficient to rescue them from those exact tribunals.

To which, in the obstructions of justice among men, we must religiously appeal, as being an argument to us Christians of that after unavoidable judgment which shall rejudge what among men is but corruptly decided or not at all.

I endeavored to have prevented, if God had seen fit, those future commotions, which I foresaw would in all likelihood follow some men's activity, if not restrained, and so now hath done, to the undoing of many thousands; the more is the pity.

But to overawe the freedom of the Houses or to weaken their just authority by any violent impressions upon them was not at all my design. I thought I had so much justice and reason on my side as should not have needed so rough assistance; and I was resolved rather to bear the repulse with patience than to use such hazardous extremities. . . .

Upon His Majesty's Passing the Bill for the Triennial Parliaments: and, After Settling This, During the Pleasure of the Two Houses

That the world might be fully confirmed in my purposes at first to contribute what in justice, reason, honor, and conscience I could to the happy success of this Parliament, which had in me no other design but the general good of my kingdoms, I willingly passed the Bill for Triennial Parliaments; which, as gentle and seasonable physic, might, if well applied, prevent any distempers from getting any head or prevailing, especially if the remedy proved not a disease beyond all remedy.

I conceived this Parliament would find work with convenient recesses for the first three years, but I did not imagine that some men would thereby have occasioned more work than they found to do by undoing so much as they found well done to their hands. Such is some men's activity that they will needs make work rather than want it and choose to be doing amiss rather than do nothing.

When that first act seemed too scanty to satisfy some men's fears and compass public affairs, I was persuaded to grant that bill of sitting during the pleasure of the Houses, which amounted in some men's sense to as much as the perpetuating this Parliament. By this act of highest confidence I hoped forever to shut out and lock the door upon all present jealousies and future mistakes; I confess I did not thereby intend to shut myself out of doors as some men have now requited me.

True, it was an act unparalleled by any of my predecessors, yet cannot in reason admit of any worse interpretation than this, of an extreme confidence I had that my subjects would not make ill use of an act by which I declared so much to trust them as to deny myself in so high a point of my prerogative.

For good subjects will never think it just or fit that my condition should be worse by my bettering theirs; nor, indeed, would it have been so in the events if some men had known as well with moderation to use, as with earnestness to desire, advantages of doing good or evil.

A continual Parliament, I thought, would but keep the commonweal in tune by preserving laws in their due execution and vigor; wherein my interest lies more than any man's, since by those laws my rights as a king would be preserved no less than my subjects, which is all I desired. More than the law gives me, I would not have; and less, the meanest subject should not.

Some, as I have heard, gave it out that I soon repented me of that settling act, and many would needs persuade me I had cause so to do; but I could not easily nor suddenly suspect such ingratitude in men of honors that, the more I granted them, the less I should have and enjoy with them. I still counted myself undiminished by my largest concessions if by them I might gain and confirm the love of my people.

Of which I do not yet despair but that God will still bless me with increase of it when men shall have more leisure and less prejudice, that so with unpassionate representations they may reflect upon those, as I think, not more princely than friendly contributions which I granted toward the perpetuating of their happiness; who are now only miserable in this, that some men's ambition will not give them leave to enjoy what I intended for their good.

Nor do I doubt but that in God's due time the loyal and cleared affections of my people will strive to return such retributions of honor and love to me or my posterity as may fully compensate both the acts of my confidence and my sufferings for them; which, God knows, have been neither few, nor small, nor short, occasioned chiefly by a persuasion I had that I could not grant too much or distrust too little to men that, being professedly my subjects, pretended singular piety and religious strictness.

The injury of all injuries is that which some men will needs load me withal, as if I were a willful and resolved occasioner of my own and my subjects' miseries; while (as they confidently, but God knows, falsely divulge) I, repining at the establishment of this Parliament, endeavored by force and open hostility to undo what by my royal assent I had done. Sure it had argued a very short sight of things and extreme fatuity of mind in me so far to bind my own hands at their request if I had shortly meant to have used a sword against them. God knows, though I had then a sense of injuries, yet not such as to think them worth vindicating by a war. I was not then compelled, as since, to injure myself by their not using favors with the same candor wherewith they were conferred. The tumults, indeed, threatened to abuse all acts of grace and turn them into wantonness; but I thought at length their own fears, whose black arts first raised up those turbulent spirits, would force them to conjure them down again.

Nor, if I had justly resented any indignities put upon me or others, was I then in any capacity to have taken just revenge in an hostile and warlike way upon those whom I knew so well fortified in the love of the meaner sort of the people that I could not have given my enemies greater and more desired advantages against me than by so unprincely inconstancy to have assaulted them with arms, thereby to scatter them whom but lately I had solemnly settled by an act of Parliament.

God knows I longed for nothing more than that myself and my subjects might quietly enjoy the fruits of my many condescendings.

It had been a course full of sin as well as of hazard and dishonor for me to go about the cutting up of that by the sword which I had so lately planted, so much, as I thought, to my subjects' content, and mine own too, in all probability, if some men had not feared where no fear was, whose security consisted in scaring others.

I thank God I know so well the sincerity and uprightness of my own heart in passing that great bill which exceeded the very thoughts of former times; that although I may seem less a politician to men, yet I need no secret distinctions or evasions before God. Nor had I any reservations in my own soul when I passed it, nor repentings after, till I saw that my letting some men go up to the pinnacle of the temple was a temptation to them to cast me down headlong.

Concluding that, without a miracle, monarchy itself, together with me, could not but be dashed in pieces by such a precipitous fall as they intended; whom God in mercy forgive, and make them see at length that as many kingdoms as the devil showed our Saviour, and the glory of them (if they could be at once enjoyed by them), are not worth the gaining by ways of sinful ingratitude and dishonor, which hazards a soul worth more worlds than this hath kingdoms.

But God hath hitherto preserved me and made me to see that it is no strange thing for men left to their own passions either to do much evil themselves or abuse the overmuch goodness of others, whereof an ungrateful surfeit is the most desperate and incurable disease.

I cannot say properly that I repent of that act, since I have no reflections upon it as a sin of my will, though an error of too charitable a judgment; only I am sorry other men's eyes should be evil because mine were good. . . .

Upon the Nineteen Propositions First Sent to the King, and More Afterwards

Although there be many things they demand, yet if these be all, I am glad to see at what price they set my own safety and my people's peace, which I cannot think I buy at too dear a rate, save only the parting with my conscience and honor. If nothing else will satisfy, I must choose rather to be as miserable and inglorious as my enemies can make or wish me.

Some things here propounded to me have been offered by me; others are easily granted. The rest, I think, ought not to be obtruded upon me with the point of the sword nor urged with the injuries of a war when I have already declared that I cannot yield to them without violating my conscience. 'Tis strange there can be no method of peace but by making war upon my soul.

Here are many things required of me, but I see nothing offered to me by the way of grateful exchange of honor or any requital for those favors I have or can yet grant them.

This honor they do me, to put me on the giving part, which is more princely and divine. They cannot ask more than I can give, may I but reserve to myself the incommunicable jewel of my conscience and not be forced to part with that whose loss nothing can repair or requite.

Some things which they are pleased to propound seem unreasonable to me; and while I have any mastery of my reason, how can they think I can consent to them, who know they are such as are inconsistent with being either a king or a good Christian? My yielding so much as I have already makes some men confident I will deny nothing.

The love I have of my people's peace hath, indeed, great influence upon me; but the love of truth and inward peace hath more.

Should I grant some things they require, I should not so much weaken my outward state of a king as wound that inward quiet of my conscience, which ought to be, is, and ever shall be, by God's grace, dearer to me than my kingdoms.

Some things which a king might approve, yet in honor and policy are at some time to be denied to some men lest he should seem not to dare to deny anything and give too much encouragement to unreasonable demands or importunities.

But to bind myself to a general and implicit consent to whatever they shall desire or propound, for such is one of their propositions, were such a latitude of blind obedience as never was expected from any freeman nor fit to be required of any man, much less of a king by his own subjects, any of whom he may possibly exceed as much in wisdom as he doth in place and power.

This were as if Samson should have consented not only to bind his own hands and cut off his hair but to put out his own eyes, that the Philistines might with the more safety mock and abuse him; which they chose rather to do than quite to destroy him when he was become so tame an object and fit occasion for their sport and scorn.

Certainly, to exclude all power of denial seems an arrogancy least of all becoming those who pretend to make their addresses in an humble and loyal way of petitioning; who by that sufficiently confess their own inferiority, which obligeth them to rest, if not satisfied, yet quieted with such an answer as the will and reason of their superior thinks fit to give; who is acknowledged to have a freedom and power of reason to consent or dissent; else it were very foolish and absurd to ask what, another having not liberty to deny, neither hath power to grant.

But if this be my right, belonging to me in reason as a man and in honor as a sovereign king (as undoubtedly it doth), how can it be other than extreme injury to confine my reason to a necessity of granting all they have a mind to ask, whose minds may be as differing from mine both in reason and honor as their aims may be and their qualities are? Which last, God and the laws have sufficiently distinguished, making me their sovereign and them my subjects, whose propositions may soon prove violent oppositions if once they gain to be necessary impositions upon the regal authority, since no man seeks to limit and confine his king in reason who hath not a secret aim to share with him or usurp upon him in power and dominion.

But they would have me trust to their moderation and abandon mine own discretion; that so I might verify what representations some have made of me to the world that I am fitter to be their pupil than their prince. Truly I am not so confident of my own sufficiency as not willingly to admit the counsel of others. But yet I am not so diffident of myself as brutishly to submit to any men's dictates and at once to betray the sovereignty of reason in my soul and the majesty of my own crown to any of my subjects.

Least of all have I any ground of credulity to induce me fully to submit to all the desires of those men who will not admit, or do refuse and neglect to vindicate, the freedom of their own and others' sitting and voting in Parliament.

Besides, all men that know them know this, how young statesmen the most part of these propounders are; so that till experience of one seven years hath showed me how well they can govern themselves and so much power as is wrested from me, I should be very foolish indeed, and unfaithful in my trust, to put the reins of both reason and government wholly out of my own into their hands, whose driving is already too much like Jehu's and whose forwardness to ascend the throne of supremacy portends more of Phaëthon than of Phoebus. God divert the omen, if it be His will.

They may remember that at best they sit in Parliament as my subjects, not my superiors; called to be my counselors, not dictators. Their summons extends to recommend their advice, not to command my duty.

When I first heard of propositions to be sent me, I expected either some good laws, which had been antiquated by the course of time or overlaid by the corruption of manners, had been desired to a restoration of their vigor and due execution; or some evil customs preterlegal and abuses personal had been to be removed; or some injuries done by myself and others to the commonweal were to be repaired; or some equable overtures were to be tendered to me, wherein the advantages of my crown, being considered by them, might fairly induce me to condescend to what tended to my subjects' good without any great diminution of myself, whom nature, law, reason, and religion bind me, in the first place, to preserve, without which 'tis impossible to preserve my people according to my place.

Or, at least, I looked for such moderate desires of due reformation of what was indeed amiss in church and state as might still preserve the foundation and essentials of government in both, not shake and quite overthrow either of them without any regard to the laws in force, the wisdom and piety of former Parliaments, the ancient and universal practice of Christian churches, the rights and privileges of particular men; nor yet anything offered in lieu or in the room of what must be destroyed, which might at once reach the good end of the other's institution and also supply its pretended defects, reform its abuses, and satisfy sober and wise men, not with soft and specious words, pretending zeal and special piety, but with pregnant and solid reasons, both divine and human, which might justify the abruptness and necessity of such vast alterations.

But in all their propositions I can observe little of these kinds, or to these ends; nothing of any laws disjointed which are to be restored, of any right invaded, of any justice to be unobstructed, of any compensations to be made, of any impartial reformation to be granted; to all or any of which reason, religion, true policy, or any other human motives might induce me.

But as to the main matters propounded by them at any time, in which is either great novelty or difficulty, I perceive that what were formerly looked upon as factions in the state and schisms in the church, and so punishable by the laws, have now the confidence, by vulgar clamors and assistance chiefly, to demand not only tolerations of themselves in their vanity, novelty, and confusion but also abolition of the laws against them and a total extirpation of that government whose rights they have a mind to invade.

This as to the main. Other propositions are for the most part but as waste paper in which those are wrapped up to present them somewhat more handsomely.

Nor do I so much wonder at the variety and horrible novelty of some propositions, there being nothing so monstrous which some fancies are not prone to long for.

This casts me into not an admiration but an ecstasy how such things should have the fortune to be propounded in the name of the two Houses of the Parliament of England, amongst whom I am very confident there was not a fourth part of the members of either House, whose judgments—free, single, and apart—did approve or desire such destructive changes in the government of the church.

I am persuaded there remains in far the major part of both Houses, if free and full, so much learning, reason, religion, and just moderation as to know how to sever between the use and the abuse of things, the institution and the corruption, the government and the misgovernment, the primitive patterns and the aberrations or blottings of aftercopies.

Sure they could not all, upon so little or no reason as yet produced to the contrary, so soon renounce all regard to the laws in force, to antiquity, to the piety of their reforming progenitors, to the prosperity of former times in this church and state, under the present government of the church.

Yet, by a strange fatality, these men suffer either by their absence, or silence, or negligence, or supine credulity (believing that all is good which is gilded with shows of zeal and reformation), their private dissenting in judgment to be drawn into the common sewer or stream of the present vogue and humor; which hath its chief rise and abetment from those popular clamors and tumults, which served to give life and strength to the infinite activity of those men who studied with all diligence and policy to improve to their innovating designs the present distractions.

Such armies of propositions having so little, in my judgment, of reason, justice, and religion on their side as they had tumult and faction for their rise, must not go alone but ever be backed and seconded with armies of soldiers. Though the second should prevail against my person, yet the first shall never overcome me, further than I see cause; for I look not at their number and power so much as I weigh their reason and justice.

Had the two Houses first sued out their livery and once effectually redeemed themselves from the wardship of the tumults, which can be no other than the hounds that attend the cry and hollo of those men who hunt after factious and private designs to the ruin of church and state.

Did my judgment tell me that the propositions sent to me were the results of the major part of their votes who exercise their freedom as well as they have a right to sit in Parliament, I should then suspect my own judgment for not speedily and fully concurring with every one of them.

For I have charity enough to think there are wise men among them, and humility to think that, as in some things I may want, so 'tis fit I should use their advice, which is the end for which I called them to a Parliament. But yet I cannot allow their wisdom such a completeness and inerrability as to exclude myself, since none of them hath that part to act, that trust to discharge, nor that estate and honor to preserve as myself; without whose reason concurrent with theirs (as the sun's influence is necessary in all nature's productions), they cannot beget or bring forth any one complete and authoritative act of public wisdom, which makes the laws.

But the unreasonableness of some propositions is not more evident to me than this is, that they are not the joint and free desires of those in their major number who are of right to sit and vote in Parliament.

For many of them savor very strong of that old leaven of innovations, masked under the name of reformation, which in my two last famous predecessors' days heaved at and sometime threatened both prince and Parliaments, but, I am sure, was never wont so far to infect the whole mass of the nobility and gentry of this kingdom, however it dispersed among the vulgar. Nor was it likely so suddenly to taint the major part of both Houses as that they should unanimously desire and affect so enormous and dangerous innovations in church and state, contrary to their former education, practice, and judgment.

Not that I am ignorant how the choice of many members was carried by much faction in the countries, some thirsting after nothing more than a passionate revenge of whatever displeasure they had conceived against me, my court, or the clergy.

But all reason bids me impute these sudden and vast desires of change to those few who armed themselves with the many-headed and many-handed tumults.

No less doth reason, honor, and safety, both of church and state, command me to chew such morsels before I let them down. If the straitness of my conscience will not give me leave to swallow down such camels as others do of sacrilege and injustice both to God and man, they have no more cause to quarrel with me than for this, that my throat is not so wide as theirs. Yet by God's help I am resolved that nothing of passion, or peevishness, or list to contradict, or vanity to show my negative power, shall have any bias upon my judgment to make me gratify my will by denying anything which my reason and conscience commands me not.

Nor, on the other side, will I consent to more than reason, justice, honor, and religion persuade me to be for God's glory, the church's good, my people's welfare, and my own peace.

I will study to satisfy my Parliament and my people, but I will never, for fear or flattery, gratify any faction, how potent soever; for this were to nourish the disease and oppress the body.

Although many men's loyalty and prudence are terrified from giving me that free and faithful counsel which they are able and willing to impart and I may want, yet none can hinder me from craving of the counsel of that mighty Counselor, Who can both suggest what is best and incline my heart steadfastly to follow it. . . .

Meditations upon Death, After the Votes of Nonaddresses and His Majesty's Closer Imprisonment in Carisbrooke Castle

As I have leisure enough, so I have cause more than enough to meditate upon and prepare for my death; for I know there are but few steps between the prisons and graves of princes.

It is God's indulgence which gives me the space but man's cruelty that gives me the sad occasions for these thoughts.

For besides the common burden of mortality, which lies upon me as a man, I now bear the heavy load of other men's ambitions, fears, jealousies, and cruel passions, whose envy or enmity against me makes their own lives seem deadly to them while I enjoy any part of mine.

I thank God my prosperity made me not wholly a stranger to the contemplations of mortality.

Those are never unseasonable, since this is always uncertain, death being an eclipse which oft happeneth as well in clear as cloudy days.

But my now long and sharp adversity hath so reconciled in me those natural antipathies between life and death which are in all men that I thank God the common terrors of it are dispelled and the special horror of it, as to my particular, much allayed. For although my death at present may justly be represented to me with all those terrible aggravations which the policy of cruel and implacable enemies can put upon it (affairs being drawn to the very dregs of malice), yet, I bless God, I can look upon all those stings as unpoisonous, though sharp, since my Redeemer hath either pulled them out or given me the antidote of His death against them; which, as to the immaturity, unjustice, shame, scorn, and cruelty of it, exceeded whatever I can fear.

Indeed, I never did find so much the life of religion, the feast of a good conscience, and the brazen wall of a judicious integrity and constancy as since I came to these closer conflicts with the thoughts of death.

I am not so old as to be weary of life, nor, I hope, so bad as to be either afraid to die or ashamed to live. True, I am so afflicted as might make me sometime even desire to die, if I did not consider that it is the greatest glory of a Christian's life to die daily, in conquering, by a lively faith and patient hopes of a better life, those partial and quotidian deaths which kill us, as it were, by piecemeals and make us overlive our own fates; while we are deprived of health, honor, liberty, power, credit, safety, or estate, and those other comforts of dearest relations which are as the life of our lives.

Though as a king I think myself to live in nothing temporal so much as in the love and good will of my people, for which, as I have suffered many deaths, so I hope I am not in that point as yet wholly dead; notwithstanding my enemies have used all the poison of falsity and violence of hostility to destroy first the love and loyalty which is in my subjects and then all that content of life in me which from these I chiefly enjoyed.

Indeed, they have left me but little of life, and only the husk and shell, as it were, which their further malice and cruelty can take from me, having bereaved me of all those worldly comforts for which life itself seems desirable to men.

But, O my soul, think not that life too long or tedious wherein God gives thee any opportunities, if not to do, yet to suffer with such Christian patience and magnanimity in a good cause as are the greatest honor of our lives and the best improvement of our deaths.

I know that in point of true Christian valor it argues pusillanimity to desire to die out of weariness of life, and a want of that heroic greatness of spirit which becomes a Christian in the patient and generous sustaining those afflictions which as shadows necessarily attend us while we are in this body, and which are lessened or enlarged as the sun of our prosperity moves higher or lower, whose total absence is best recompensed with the dew of heaven.

The assaults of affliction may be terrible like Samson's lion, but they yield much sweetness to those that dare to encounter and overcome them; who know how to overlive the witherings of their gourds without discontent or peevishness while they may yet converse with God.

That I must die as a man is certain. That I may die a king by the hands of my own subjects, a violent, sudden, and barbarous death, in the strength of my years, in the midst of my kingdoms, my friends and loving subjects being helpless spectators, my enemies insolent revilers and triumphers over me, living, dying, and dead, is so probable in human reason that God hath taught me not to hope otherwise as to man's cruelty. However, I despair not of God's infinite mercy.

I know my life is the object of the devil's and wicked men's malice, but yet under God's sole custody and disposal; Whom I do not think to flatter for longer life by seeming prepared to die, but I humbly desire to depend upon Him and to submit to His will both in life and death in what order soever He is pleased to lay them out to me. I confess it is not easy for me to contend with those many horrors of death wherewith God suffers me to be tempted; which are equally horrid either in the suddenness of a barbarous assassination or in those greater formalities whereby my enemies (being more solemnly cruel) will, it may be, seek to add (as those did who crucified Christ) the mockery of justice to the cruelty of malice. That I may be destroyed, as with greater pomp and artifice so with less pity, it will be but a necessary policy to make my death appear as an act of justice done by subjects upon their sovereign; who know that no law of God or man invests them with any power of judicature without me, much less against me; and who, being sworn and bound by all that is sacred before God and man to endeavor my preservation, must pretend justice to cover their perjury.

It is indeed a sad fate for any man to have his enemies to be accusers, parties, and judges, but most desperate when this is acted by the insolence of subjects against their sovereign, wherein those who have had the chiefest hand and are most guilty of contriving the public troubles must, by shedding my blood, seem to wash their own hands of that innocent blood whereof they are now most evidently guilty before God and man and, I believe, in their own consciences too; while they carried on unreasonable demands, first by tumults, after by armies. Nothing makes mean spirits more cowardly cruel in managing their usurped power against their lawful superiors than this, the guilt of their unjust usurpation; notwithstanding those specious and popular pretensions of justice against delinquents, applied only to disguise at first the monstrousness of their designs who despaired indeed of possessing the power and profits of the vineyard till the heir whose right it is be cast out and slain.

With them my greatest fault must be that I would not either destroy myself with the church and state by my word, or not suffer them to do it unresisted by the sword; whose covetous ambition no concessions of mine could ever yet either satisfy or abate.

Nor is it likely they will ever think that kingdom of brambles which some men seek to erect (at once weak, sharp, and fruitless either to God or man) is like to thrive till watered with the royal blood of those whose right the kingdom is.

Well, God's will be done. I doubt not but my innocency will find Him both my protector and my advocate, Who is my only judge; Whom I own as King of Kings not only for the eminency of His power and majesty above them, but also for that singular care and protection which He hath over them; Who knows them to be exposed to as many dangers (being the greatest patron of law, justice, order, and religion on earth) as there be either men or devils which love confusion.

Nor will He suffer those men long to prosper in their Babel who build it with the bones and cement it with the blood of their kings.

I am confident they will find avengers of my death among themselves. The injuries I have sustained from them shall be first punished by them who agreed in nothing so much as in opposing me.

Their impatience to hear the loud cry of my blood shall make them think no way better to expiate it than by shedding theirs who, with them, most thirsted after mine.

The sad confusions following my destruction are already presaged and confirmed to me by those I have lived to see since my troubles; in which God alone (Who only could) hath many ways pleaded my cause, not suffering them to go unpunished whose confederacy in sin was their only security; who have cause to fear that God will both further divide and by mutual vengeance afterward destroy them.

My greatest conquest of death is from the power and love of Christ, Who hath swallowed up death in the victory of His Resurrection and the glory of His Ascension.

My next comfort is that He gives me not only the honor to imitate His example in suffering for righteousness' sake (though obscured by the foulest charges of tyranny and injustice), but also that charity which is the noblest revenge upon, and victory over, my destroyers. By which, I thank God, I can both forgive them and pray for them, that God would not impute my blood to them further than to convince them what need they have of Christ's blood to wash their souls from the guilt of shedding mine.

At present, the will of my enemies seems to be their only rule, their power the measure, and their success the exactor of what they please to call justice; while they flatter themselves with the fancy of their own safety by my danger and the security of their lives' designs by my death; forgetting that, as the greatest temptations to sin are wrapped up in seeming prosperities, so the severest vengeances of God are then most accomplished when men are suffered to complete their wicked purposes.

I bless God I pray not so much that this bitter cup of a violent death may pass from me as that of His wrath may pass from all those whose hands by deserting me are sprinkled or by acting and consenting to my death are imbrued with my blood.

The will of God hath confined and concluded mine. I shall have the pleasure of dying without any pleasure of desired vengeance.

This, I think, becomes a Christian toward his enemies and a king toward his subjects.

They cannot deprive me of more than I am content to lose when God sees fit by their hands to take it from me; Whose mercy, I believe, will more than infinitely recompense whatever by man's injustice He is pleased to deprive me of.

The glory attending my death will far surpass all I could enjoy or conceive in life.

I shall not want the heavy and envied crowns of this world when my God hath mercifully crowned and consummated His graces with glory and exchanged the shadows of my earthly kingdoms among men for the substance of that heavenly kingdom with Himself.

For the censures of the world, I know the sharp and necessary tyranny of my destroyers will sufficiently confute the calumnies of tyranny against me. I am persuaded I am happy in the judicious love of the ablest and best of my subjects, who do not only pity and pray for me, but would be content even to die with me or for me.

These know how to excuse my failings as a man and yet to retain and pay their duty to me as their king; there being no religious necessity binding any subjects, by pretending to punish, infinitely to exceed the faults and errors of their princes, especially there where more than sufficient satisfaction hath been made to the public, the enjoyment of which private ambitions have hitherto frustrated.

Others, I believe, of softer tempers and less advantaged by my ruin, do already feel sharp convictions and some remorse in their consciences; where they cannot but see the proportions of their evil dealings against me in the measure of God's retaliations upon them, who cannot hope long to enjoy their own thumbs and toes, having under pretense of paring others' nails been so cruel as to cut off their chiefest strength.

The punishment of the more insolent and obstinate may be like that of

Korah and his complices (at once mutinying against both prince and priest) in such a method of divine justice as is not ordinary; the earth of the lowest and meanest people opening upon them and swallowing them up in a just disdain of their ill-gotten and worse-used authority, upon whose support and strength they chiefly depended for their building and establishing their designs against me, the church, and state.

My chiefest comfort in death consists in my peace, which, I trust, is made with God, before Whose exact tribunal I shall not fear to appear as to the cause so long disputed by the sword between me and my causeless enemies; where I doubt not but His righteous judgment will confute their fallacy, who from worldly success (rather like sophisters than sound Christians) draw those popular conclusions for God's approbation of their actions; Whose wise providence, we know, oft permits many events which His revealed Word (the only clear, safe, and fixed rule of good actions and good consciences) in no sort approves.

I am confident the justice of my cause and clearness of my conscience before God and toward my people will carry me as much above them in God's decision as their successes have lifted them above me in the vulgar opinion; who consider not that many times those undertakings of men are lifted up to heaven in the prosperity and applause of the world whose rise is from hell as to the injuriousness and oppression of the design. The prosperous winds which oft fill the sails of pirates doth not justify their piracy and rapine.

I look upon it with infinite more content and quiet of soul to have been worsted in my enforced contestation for and vindication of the laws of the land, the freedom and honor of parliaments, the rights of my crown, the just liberty of my subjects, and the true Christian religion in its doctrine, government, and due encouragements than if I had with the greatest advantages of success overborne them all, as some men have now evidently done, whatever designs they at first pretended.

The prayers and patience of my friends and loving subjects will contribute much to the sweetening of this bitter cup, which I doubt not but I shall more cheerfully take and drink as from God's hand (if it must be so) than they can give it to me whose hands are unjustly and barbarously lifted up against me.

And as to the last event, I may seem to owe more to my enemies than my friends; while those will put a period to the sins and sorrows attending this miserable life, wherewith these desire I might still contend.

I shall be more than conqueror through Christ enabling me, for Whom I have hitherto suffered, as He is the author of truth, order, and peace; for all which I have been forced to contend against error, faction, and confusion.

If I must suffer a violent death with my Saviour, it is but mortality crowned with martyrdom, where the debt of death which I owe for sin to nature shall be raised as a gift of faith and patience offered to God.

Which I humbly beseech Him mercifully to accept. And although death be the wages of my own sin as from God, and the effect of others' sins as men both against God and me, yet, as I hope my own sins are so remitted that they shall be no ingredients to embitter the cup of my death, so I desire God to pardon their sins who are most guilty of my destruction.

The trophies of my charity will be more glorious and durable over them than their ill-managed victories over me.

Though their sin be prosperous, yet they had need to be penitent, that they may be pardoned; both which I pray God they may obtain, that my temporal death unjustly inflicted by them may not be revenged by God's just inflicting eternal death upon them. For I look upon the temporal destruction of the greatest king as far less deprecable than the eternal damnation of the meanest subject.

Nor do I wish other than the safe bringing of the ship to shore when they have cast me overboard, though it be very strange that mariners can find no other means to appease the storm themselves have raised but by drowning their pilot.

I thank God my enemies' cruelty cannot prevent my preparation; whose malice in this I shall defeat, that they shall not have the satisfaction to have destroyed my soul with my body; of whose salvation, while some of them have themselves seemed and taught others to despair, they have only discovered this, that they do not much desire it.

Whose uncharitable and cruel restraints, denying me even the assistance of any of my chaplains, hath rather enlarged than any way obstructed my access to the throne of heaven.

27. John Milton, *Eikonoklastes*

John Milton (1608–74), one of England's greatest poets, is best known as author of *Paradise Lost*. During the revolution, however, his literary talents were turned toward issues of social and religious reform such as the abolition of censorship and the sanctioning of divorce. He also became a skilled polemicist in the sectarian debates over religious toleration. By 1649 he was established as the ablest of all of the writers who supported the revolution. After the startling success of *Eikon Basilike* Milton was commissioned by the Council of State to prepare a reply that would overcome the widespread sympathy that had grown for Charles I after his

From *The Prose Works of John Milton*, edited by J. A. St. John (London: G. Bell and Sons, Ltd., 1910).

execution. "I was ordered to answer it and opposed the Iconoclast to his Icon," Milton later recalled. *Eikonoklastes* or Image-Breaking, published in 1649, was a chapter-by-chapter refutation of *Eikon Basilike*.

Milton's Preface

To descant on the misfortunes of a person fallen from so high a dignity, who hath also paid his final debt both to nature and his faults, is neither of itself a thing commendable, nor the intention of this discourse. Neither was it fond ambition, nor the vanity to get a name, present or with posterity, by writing against a king, I never was so thirsty after fame, nor so destitute of other hopes and means, better and more certain to attain it; for kings have gained glorious titles from their favourers by writing against private men, as Henry VIII did against Luther; but no man ever gained much honour by writing against a king, as not usually meeting with that force of argument in such courtly antagonists, which to convince might add to his reputation. Kings most commonly, though strong in legions, are but weak at argument; as they who ever have accustomed from their cradle to use their will only as their right hand, their reason always as their left. Whence unexpectedly constrained to that kind of combat, they prove but weak and puny adversaries: nevertheless, for their sakes, who through custom, simplicity, or want of better teaching, have not more seriously considered kings, than in the gaudy name of majesty, and admire them and their doings, as if they breathed not the same breath with other mortal men, I shall make no scruple to take up (for it seems to be the challenge both of him and all his party) to take up this gauntlet, though a king's, in the behalf of liberty and the commonwealth.

And further, since it appears manifestly the cunning drift of a factious and defeated party, to make the same advantage of his book which they did before of his regal name and authority, and intend it not so much the defence of his former actions, as the promoting of their own future designs; (making thereby the book their own rather than the king's, as the benefit now must be their own more than his;) now the third time to corrupt and disorder the minds of weaker men, by new suggestions and narrations, either falsely or fallaciously representing the state of things to the dishonour of this present government, and the retarding of a general peace, so needful to this afflicted nation, and so nigh obtained; I suppose it no injury to the dead, but a good deed rather to the living, if by better information given them, or, which is enough, by only remembering them the truth of what they themselves know to be here misaffirmed, they may be kept from entering the third time unadvisedly into war and blood shed. For as to any moment of solidity in the book itself (save only that a king is said to be the author, a name than which there needs no more among the blockish vulgar, to make it wise, and excellent, and admired, nay to set it next the Bible, though otherwise containing little else but the common grounds of tyranny and popery, dressed up the better to deceive, in a new protestant guise, trimly garnished over), or as to any need of answering, in respect of staid and well-principled men, I take it on me as a work assigned rather, than by me chosen or affected: which was the cause both of beginning it so late, and finishing it so leisurely in the midst of other employments and diversions.

And though well it might have seemed in vain to write at all, considering the envy and almost infinite prejudice likely to be stirred up among the common sort, against whatever can be written or gainsaid to the king's book, so advantageous to a book it is only to be a king's; and though it be an irksome labour, to write with industry and judicious pains, that which, neither weighed nor well read, shall be judged without industry or the pains of well-judging, by faction and the easy literature of custom and opinion; it shall be ventured yet, and the truth not smothered, but sent abroad, in the native confidence of her single self, to earn, how she can, her entertainment in the world, and to find out her own readers: few perhaps, but those few, of such value and substantial worth, as truth and wisdom, not respecting numbers and big names, have been ever wont in all ages to be contented with.

And if the late king had thought sufficient those answers and defences made for him in his lifetime, they who on the other side accused his evil government, judging that on their behalf enough also hath been replied, the heat of this controversy was in all likelihood drawing to an end; and the further mention of his deeds, not so much unfortunate as faulty, had in tenderness to his late sufferings been willingly forborne; and perhaps for the present age might have slept with him unrepeated, while his adversaries, calmed and assuaged with the success of their cause, had been the less unfavourable to his memory. But since he himself, making new appeal to truth and the world, hath left behind him this book, as the best advocate and interpreter of his own actions, and that his friends, by publishing, dispersing, commending, and almost adoring it, seem to place therein the chief strength and nerves of their cause; it would argue doubtless in the other party great deficience and distrust of themselves, not to meet the force of his reason in any field whatsoever, the force and equipage of whose arms they have so often met victoriously. And he who at the bar stood excepting against the form and manner of his judicature, and complained that he was not heard; neither he nor his friends shall have that cause now to find fault, being met and debated with in this open and monumental court of his erecting; and not only heard uttering his whole mind at large, but answered:

which to do effectually, if it be necessary, that to his book nothing the more respect be had for being his, they of his own party can have no just reason to exclaim.

For it were too unreasonable that he, because dead, should have the liberty in his book to speak all evil of the parliament; and they, because living, should be expected to have less freedom, or any for them, to speak home the plain truth of a full and pertinent reply. As he, to acquit himself, hath not spared his adversaries to load them with all sorts of blame and accusation, so to him, as in his book alive, there will be used no more courtship than he uses; but what is properly his own guilt, not imputed any more to his evil counsellors, (a ceremony used longer by the parliament than he himself desired), shall be laid here without circumlocutions at his own door. That they who from the first beginning, or but now of late, by what unhappiness I know not, are so much affatuated, not with his person only, but with his palpable faults, and dote upon his deformities, may have none to blame but their own folly, if they live and die in such a stricken blindness, as next to that of Sodom hath not happened to any sort of men more gross, or more misleading. Yet neither let his enemies expect to find recorded here all that hath been whispered in the court, or alleged openly, of the king's bad actions; it being the proper scope of this work in hand, not to rip up and relate the misdoings of his whole life, but to answer only and refute the missayings of his book.

First, then, that some men (whether this were by him intended, or by his friends) have by policy accomplished after death that revenge upon their enemies, which in life they were not able, hath been oft related. And among other examples we find, that the last will of Caesar being read to the people, and what bounteous legacies he had bequeathed them, wrought more in that vulgar audience to the avenging of his death, than all the art he could ever use to win their favour in his lifetime. And how much their intent, who published these over-late apologies and meditations of the dead king, drives to the same end of stirring up the people to bring him that honour, that affection, and by consequence that revenge to his dead corpse, which he himself living could never gain to his person, it appears both by the conceited portraiture before his book, drawn out of the full measure of a masking scene, and set there to catch fools and silly gazers; and by those Latin words after the end, *Vota dabunt quae bella negarunt;* intimating that what he could not compass by war he should achieve by his meditations: for in words which admit of various sense, the liberty is ours, to choose that interpretation, which may best mind us of what our restless enemies endeavour, and what we are timely to prevent.

And here may be well observed the loose and negligent curiosity of those, who took upon them to adorn the setting out of this book; for though the picture set in front would martyr him and saint him to befool the people, yet the Latin motto in the end, which they understand not, leaves him, as it were, a politic contriver to bring about that interest, by fair and plausible words, which the force of arms denied him. But quaint emblems and devices, begged from the old pageantry of some twelfthnight's entertainment at Whitehall, will do but ill to make a saint or martyr: and if the people resolve to take him sainted at the canonizing, I shall suspect their calendar more than the Gregorian. In one thing I must commend his openness, who gave the title to this book, Εἰκὼν Βασιλικὴ, that is to say, The King's Image; and by the shrine he dresses out for him, certainly would have the people come and worship him. For which reason this answer also is entitled, *Eikonoklastes*, the famous surname of many Greek emperors, who, in their zeal to the command of God, after long tradition of idolatry in the church, took courage and broke all superstitious images to pieces. . . .

Chapter 1: Upon the King's Calling This Last Parliament

That which the king lays down here as his first foundation, and as it were the head-stone of his whole structure, that "he called this parliament, not more by others' advice, and the necessity of his affairs, than by his own choice and inclination," is to all knowing men so apparently not true, that a more unlucky and inauspicious sentence, and more betokening the downfall of his whole fabric, hardly could have come into his mind. For who knows not, that the inclination of a prince is best known either by those next about him, and most in favour with him, or by the current of his own actions? Those nearest to this king, and most his favourites, were courtiers and prelates; men whose chief study was to find out which way the king inclined, and to imitate him exactly: how these men stood affected to parliaments cannot be forgotten. No man but may remember, it was their continual exercise to dispute and preach against them; and in their common discourse nothing was more frequent, than that "they hoped the king should now have no need of parliaments any more." And this was but the copy which his parasites had industriously taken from his own words and actions, who never called a parliament but to supply his necessities; and having supplied those, as suddenly and ignominiously dissolved it, without redressing any one grievance of the people, sometimes choosing rather to miss of his subsidies, or to raise them by illegal courses, than that the people should not still miss of their hopes to be relieved by parliaments.

The first he broke off at his coming to the crown, for no other cause than to protect the Duke of Buckingham against them who had accused him, besides other heinous crimes, of no less than poisoning the deceased king, his father; concerning which declaration of "No more addresses" hath sufficiently informed us. And still the latter breaking was with more affront and indignity put upon the house and her worthiest members, than the former. Insomuch that in the fifth year of his reign, in a proclamation, he seems offended at the very rumour of a parliament divulged among the people; as if he had taken it for a kind of slander, that men should think him that way exorable, much less inclined: and forbids it as a presumption, to prescribe him any time for parliaments; that is to say, either by persuasion or petition or so much as the reporting of such a rumour: for other manner of prescribing was at that time not suspected. By which fierce edict, the people, forbidden to complain, as well as forced to suffer, began from thenceforth to despair of parliaments. Whereupon such illegal actions, and especially to get vast sums of money, were put in practice by the king and his new officers, as monopolies, compulsive knighthoods, coat, conduct, and ship-money, the seizing not of one Naboth's vineyard, but of whole inheritances, under the pretence of forest or crown-lands; corruption and bribery compounded for, with impunities granted for the future, as gave evident proof, that the king never meant, nor could it stand with the reason of his affairs, ever to recal parliaments; having brought by these irregular courses the people's interest and his own to so direct an opposition, that he might foresee plainly, if nothing but a parliament could save the people, it must necessarily be his undoing.

Till eight or nine years after, proceeding with a high hand in these enormities, and having the second time levied an injurious war against his native country, Scotland; and finding all those other shifts of raising money, which bore out his first expedition, now to fail him, not "of his own choice and inclination," as any child may see, but urged by strong necessities, and the very pangs of state, which his own violent proceedings had brought him to, he calls a parliament; first in Ireland, which only was to give him four subsidies, and so to expire; then in England, where his first demand was but twelve subsidies, to maintain a Scots war, condemned and abominated by the whole kingdom: promising their grievances should be considered afterwards. Which when the parliament, who judged that war itself one of their main grievances, made no haste to grant, not enduring the delay of his impatient will, or else fearing the conditions of their grant, he breaks off the whole session, and dismisses them and their grievances with scorn and frustration.

Much less therefore did he call this last parliament by his own choice and inclination; but having first tried in vain all undue ways to procure money, his army of their own accord being beaten in the north, the lords petitioning, and the general voice of the people almost hissing him and his ill-acted regality off the stage, compelled at length both by his wants and by his fears, upon mere extremity he summoned this last parliament. And how is it possible, that he should willingly incline to parliaments, who never was perceived to call them but for the greedy hope of a whole national bribe, his subsidies; and never loved, never fulfilled, never promoted the true end of parliaments, the redress of grievances; but still put them off, and prolonged them, whether gratified or not gratified; and was indeed the author of all those grievances? To say, therefore, that he called this parliament of his own choice and inclination, argues how little truth we can expect from the sequel of this book, which ventures in the very first period to affront more than one nation with an untruth so remarkable; and presumes a more implicit faith in the people of England, than the pope ever commanded from the Romish laity; or else a natural sottishness fit to be abused and ridden: while in the judgment of wise men, by laying the foundation of his defence on the avouchment of that which is so manifestly untrue, he hath given a worse soil to his own cause, than when his whole forces were at any time overthrown. They, therefore, who think such great service done to the king's affairs in publishing this book, will find themselves in the end mistaken; if sense and right mind, or but any mediocrity of knowledge and remembrance, hath not quite forsaken men.

But to prove his inclination to parliaments, he affirms here, "to have always thought the right way of them most safe for his crown, and best pleasing to his people." What he thought, we know not, but that he ever took the contrary way we saw; and from his own actions we felt long ago what he thought of parliaments or of pleasing his people: a surer evidence than what we hear now too late in words.

He alleges, that "the cause of forbearing to convene parliaments was the sparks which some men's distempers there studied to kindle." They were indeed not tempered to his temper; for it neither was the law, nor the rule, by which all other tempers were to be tried; but they were esteemed and chosen for the fittest men, in their several counties, to allay and quench those distempers, which his own inordinate doings had inflamed. And if that were his refusing to convene, till those men had been qualified to his temper, that is to say, his will, we may easily conjecture what hope there was of parliaments, had not fear and his insatiate poverty, in the midst of his excessive wealth, constrained him.

"He hoped by his freedom and their moderation to prevent misunderstandings." And wherefore not by their freedom and his moderation? But freedom he thought too high a word for them, and moderation too mean a word for himself; this was not the way to prevent misunderstandings. He still "feared passion and prejudice in other men;" not in himself: "and doubted not by the weight of his" own "reason,["] to counterpoise any faction; it being so easy for him, and so frequent, to call his obstinacy reason, and other men's reason, faction. We in the meanwhile must believe that wisdom and all reason came to him by title with his crown; passion, prejudice, and faction came to others by being subjects.

"He was sorry to hear, with what popular heat elections were carried in many places." Sorry rather, that court-letters and intimations prevailed no more to divert or to deter the people from their free election of those men whom they thought best affected to religion and their country's liberty, both at that time in danger to be lost. And such men they were, as by the kingdom were sent to advise him, not sent to be cavilled at, because elected, or to be entertained by him with an undervalue and misprision of their temper, judgment, or affection. In vain was a parliament thought fittest by the known laws of our nation, to advise and regulate unruly kings, if they, instead of hearkening to advice, should be permitted to turn it off, and refuse it by vilifying and traducing their advisers, or by accusing of a popular heat those that lawfully elected them.

"His own and his children's interest obliged him to seek, and to preserve the love and welfare of his subjects." Who doubts it? But the same interest, common to all kings, was never yet available to make them all seek that which was indeed best for themselves and their posterity. All men by their own and their children's interest are obliged to honesty and justice: but how little that consideration works in private men, how much less in kings, their deeds declare best.

"He intended to oblige both friends and enemies, and to exceed their desires, did they but pretend to any modest and sober sense;" mistaking the whole business of a parliament; which met not to receive from him obligations, but justice; nor he to expect from them their modesty, but their grave advice, uttered with freedom in the public cause. His talk of modesty in their desires of the common welfare, argues him not much to have understood what he had to grant, who misconceived so much the nature of what they had to desire. And for "sober sense," the expression was too mean, and recoils with as much dishonour upon himself, to be a king where sober sense could possibly be so wanting in a parliament.

"The odium and offences, which some men's rigour, or remissness in church and state, had contracted upon his government, he resolved to have expiated with better laws and regulations." And yet the worst of misdemeanours committed by the worst of all his favourites in the height of their dominion, whether acts of rigour or remissness, he hath from time to time continued, owned, and taken upon himself by public declarations, as often as the clergy, or any other of his instruments, felt themselves overburdened with the people's hatred. And who knows not the superstitious rigour of his Sunday's chapel, and the licentious remissness of his Sunday's theatre; accompanied with that reverend statute for dominical jigs and maypoles, published in his own name, and derived from the example of his father, James? Which testifies all that rigour in superstition, all that remissness in religion, to have issued out originally from his own house, and from his own authority.

Much rather then may those general miscarriages in state, his proper sphere, be imputed to no other person chiefly than to himself. And which of all those oppressive acts or impositions did he ever disclaim or disavow, till the fatal awe of this parliament hung ominously over him? Yet here he smoothly seeks to wipe off all the envy of his evil government upon his substitutes and under officers; and promises, though much too late, what wonders he purposed to have done in the reforming of religion: a work wherein all his undertakings heretofore declared him to have had little or no judgment: neither could his breeding, or his course of life, acquaint him with a thing so spiritual. Which may well assure us what kind of reformation we could expect from him; either some politic form of an imposed religion, or else perpetual vexation and persecution to all those that complied not with such a form.

The like amendment he promises in state; not a step further "than his reason and conscience told him was fit to be desired;" wishing "he had kept within those bounds, and not suffered his own judgment to have been overborne in some things," of which things one was the Earl of Strafford's execution. And what signifies all this, but that still his resolution was the same, to set up an arbitrary government of his own, and that all Britain was to be tied and chained to the conscience, judgment, and reason of one man; as if those gifts had been only his peculiar and prerogative, entailed upon him with his fortune to be a king? Whenas doubtless no man so obstinate, or so much a tyrant, but professes to be guided by that which he calls his reason and his judgment, though never so corrupted; and pretends also his conscience. In the meanwhile, for any parliament or the whole nation to have either reason, judgment, or conscience, by this rule was altogether in vain, if it thwarted the king's will; which was easy for him to call by any other plausible name. He himself hath many times acknowledged to have no right over us but by law; and by the same law to govern us: but law in a free nation hath been ever public reason, the enacted reason of a parliament; which he denying to enact, denies to govern us by that which ought to be our law; interposing his own private reason, which to us is no law. And thus we find these fair and specious promises, made upon the experience of many hard sufferings, and his most mortified retirements, being

454 The English Revolution

thoroughly sifted, to contain nothing in them much different from his former practices, so cross, and so reverse to all his parliaments, and both the nations of this island. What fruits they could in likelihood have produced in his restorement, is obvious to any prudent foresight.

And this is the substance of his first section, till we come to the devout of it, modelled into the form of a private psalter. Which they who so much admire, either for the matter or the manner, may as well admire the archbishop's late breviary, and many other as good manuals and handmaids of devotion, the lip-work of every prelatical liturgist, clapped together and quilted out of Scripture phrase, with as much ease and as little need of Christian diligence or judgment, as belongs to the compiling of any ordinary and saleable piece of English divinity, that the shops value. But he who from such a kind of psalmistry, or any other verbal devotion, without the pledge and earnest of suitable deeds, can be persuaded of a zeal and true righteousness in the person, hath much yet to learn; and knows not that the deepest policy of a tyrant hath been ever to counterfeit religious. And Aristotle, in his Politics, hath mentioned that special craft among twelve other tyrannical sophisms. Neither want we examples: Andronicus Comnenus, the Byzantine emperor, though a most cruel tyrant, is reported by Nicetas to have been a constant reader of Saint Paul's Epistles; and by continual study had so incorporated the phrase and style of that transcendent apostle into all his familiar letters, that the imitation seemed to vie with the original. Yet this availed not to deceive the people of that empire, who, notwithstanding his saint's vizard, tore him to pieces for his tyranny. . . .

They who are yet incredulous of what I tell them for a truth, that this philippic prayer is no part of the king's goods, may satisfy their own eyes at leisure in the third book of Sir Philip's Arcadia, p. 248, comparing Pamela's prayer with the first prayer of his majesty, delivered to Dr. Juxon immediately before his death, and entitled a Prayer in Time of Captivity, printed in all the best editions of his book. And since there be a crew of lurking railers, who in their libels, and their fits of railing up and down, as I hear from others, take it so currishly, that I should dare to tell abroad the secrets of their Ægyptian Apis; to gratify their gall in some measure yet more, which to them will be a kind of alms, (for it is the weekly vomit of their gall, which to most of them is the sole means of their feeding,) that they may not starve for me, I shall gorge them once more with this digression somewhat larger than before: nothing troubled or offended at the working upward of their sale-venom thereupon, though it happen to asperse me; being, it seems, their best livelihood, and the only use or good digestion that their sick and perishing minds can make of truth charitably told them.

However, to the benefit of others much more worth the gaining, I shall proceed in my assertion; that if only but to taste wittingly of meat or drink offered to an idol be in the doctrine of St. Paul judged a pollution, much more must be his sin who takes a prayer so dedicated into his mouth, and offers it to God. Yet hardly it can be thought upon (though how sad a thing!) without some kind of laughter at the manner and solemn transaction of so gross a cozenage, that he, who had trampled over us so stately and so tragically, should leave the world at last so ridiculously in his exit, as to bequeath among his deifying friends that stood about him such a precious piece of mockery to be published by them, as must needs cover both his and their heads with shame, if they have any left. Certainly, they that will may now see at length how much they were deceived in him, and were ever like to be hereafter, who cared not, so near the minute of his death, to deceive his best and dearest friends with the trumpery of such a prayer, not more secretly than shamefully purloined; yet given them as the royal issue of his own proper zeal. And sure it was the hand of God to let them fall, and be taken in such a foolish trap, as hath exposed them to all derision; if for nothing else, to throw contempt and disgrace in the sight of all men upon this his idolized book, and the whole rosary of his prayers; thereby testifying how little he accepted them from those who thought no better of the living God than of a buzzard idol, fit to be so served and worshipped in reversion, with the polluted orts and refuse of Arcadias and romances, without being able to discern the affront rather than the worship of such an ethnic prayer.

But leaving what might justly be offensive to God, it was a trespass also more than usual against human right, which commands, that every author should have the property of his own work reserved to him after death, as well as living. Many princes have been rigorous in laying taxes on their subjects by the head; but of any king heretofore that made a levy upon their wit, and seized it as his own legitimate, I have not whom besides to instance. True it is, I looked rather to have found him gleaning out of books written purposely to help devotion. And if in likelihood he have borrowed much more out of prayer-books than out of pastorals, then are these painted feathers, that set him off so gay among the people, to be thought few or none of them his own. But if from his divines he have borrowed nothing, nothing out of all the magazine, and the rheum of their mellifluous prayers and meditations, let them who now mourn for him as for Thammuz, them who howl in their pulpits, and by their howling declare themselves right wolves, remember and consider in the midst of their hideous faces, when they do only not cut their flesh for him like those rueful priests whom Elijah mocked; that he who was once their Ahab, now their Josiah, though feigning outwardly to reverence churchmen, yet here hath so extremely set at nought both them and their praying faculty, that being at a loss himself what to pray in captivity, he consulted neither with the liturgy, nor with the directory, but, neglecting the huge fardell of all their honeycomb devotions, went directly where he doubted not to find better praying to his mind with Pamela, in the Countess's Arcadia.

What greater argument of disgrace and ignominy could have been thrown with cunning upon the whole clergy, than that the king, among all his priestery, and all those numberless volumes of their theological distillations, not meeting with one man or book of that coat that could befriend him with a prayer in captivity, was forced to rob Sir Philip and his captive shepherdess of their heathen orisons, to supply in any fashion his miserable indigence, not of bread, but of a single prayer to God? I say therefore not of bread, for that want may befall a good man, and yet not make him totally miserable: but he who wants a prayer to beseech God in his necessity, it is inexpressible how poor he is; far poorer within himself than all his enemies can make him. And the unfitness, the indecency of that pitiful supply which he sought, expresses yet further the deepness of his poverty.

Thus much be said in general to his prayers, and in special to that Arcadian prayer used in his captivity; enough to undeceive us what esteem we are to set upon the rest. For he certainly, whose mind could serve him to seek a Christian prayer out of a pagan legend, and assume it for his own, might gather up the rest God knows from whence; one perhaps out of the French Astraea, another out of the Spanish Diana; Amadis and Palmerin could hardly scape him. Such a person we may be sure had it not in him to make a prayer of his own, or at least would excuse himself the pains and cost of his invention, so long as such sweet rhapsodies of heathenism and knight-errantry could yield him prayers. How dishonourable then, and how unworthy of a Christian king, were these ignoble shifts to seem holy, and to get a saintship among the ignorant and wretched people; to draw them by this deception, worse than all his former injuries, to go a whoring after him! And how unhappy, how forsook of grace, and unbeloved of God that people who resolve to know no more of piety or of goodness, than to account him their chief saint and martyr, whose bankrupt devotion came not honestly by his very prayers; but having sharked them from the mouth of a heathen worshipper, (detestable to teach him prayers!) sold them to those that stood and honoured him next to the Messiah, as his own heavenly compositions in adversity; for hopes no less vain and presumptuous (and death at that time so imminent upon him) than by these goodly reliques to be held a saint and martyr in opinion with the cheated people!

And thus far in the whole chapter we have seen and considered, and it cannot but be clear to all men, how, and for what ends, what concernments and necessities, the late king was no way induced, but every way constrained to call this last parliament; yet here in his first prayer he trembles not to avouch, as in the ears of God, "That he did it with an upright intention to his glory, and his people's good": of which dreadful attestation, how sincerely meant, God, to whom it was avowed, can only judge; and he hath judged already, and hath written his impartial sentence in characters legible to all Christendom; and besides hath taught us, that there be some, whom he hath given over to delusion, whose very mind and conscience is defiled; of whom St. Paul to Titus makes mention. . . .

Chapter 3: Upon His Going to the House of Commons

Concerning his inexcusable and hostile march from the court to the house of commons, there needs not much be said; for he confesses it to be an act, which most men, whom he calls "his enemies," cried shame upon, "indifferent men grew jealous of and fearful, and many of his friends resented, as a motion arising rather from passion than reason." He himself, in one of his answers to both houses, made profession to be convinced, that it was a plain breach of their privilege; yet here, like a rotten building newly trimmed over, he represents it speciously and fraudulently, to impose upon the simple reader; and seeks by smooth and supple words, not here only, but through his whole book, to make some beneficial use or other even of his worst miscarriages.

"These men," saith he, meaning his friends, "knew not the just motives and pregnant grounds with which I thought myself furnished;" to wit, against the five members, whom he came to drag out of the house. His best friends indeed knew not, nor could ever know, his motives to such a riotous act; and had he himself known any just grounds, he was not ignorant how much it might have tended to his justifying, had he named them in this place, and not concealed them. But suppose them real, suppose them known, what was this to that violation and dishonour put upon the whole house, whose very door, forcibly kept open, and all the passages near it, he beset with swords and pistols cocked and menaced in the hands of about three hundred swaggerers and ruffians, who but expected, nay, audibly called for, the word of onset to begin a slaughter.

"He had discovered, as he thought, unlawful correspondences, which they had used, and engagements to embroil his kingdoms;" and remembers not his own unlawful correspondences and conspiracies with the Irish army of papists, with the French to land at Portsmouth, and his tampering both with the English and Scots army to come up against the parliament: the least of which attempts, by whomsoever, was no less than manifest treason against the commonwealth.

If to demand justice on the five members were his plea, for that which they with more reason might have demanded justice upon him, (I use his own argument,) there needed not so rough assistance. If he had "resolved to bear that repulse with patience," which his queen by her words to him at his return little thought he would have done, wherefore did he provide against it, with such an armed and unusual force? but his heart served him not to undergo the hazard that such a desperate scuffle would have brought him to. But wherefore did he go at all, it behoving him to know there were two statutes that declared he ought first to have acquainted the parliament, who were the accusers, which he refused to do, though still professing to govern by law, and still justifying his attempts against law? And when he saw it was not permitted him to attaint them but by a fair trial, as was offered him from time to time, for want of just matter which yet never came to light, he let the business fall of his own accord; and all those pregnancies and just motives came to just nothing.

"He had no temptation of displeasure or revenge against those men": none but what he thirsted to execute upon them, for the constant opposition which they made against his tyrannous proceedings, and the love and reputation which they therefore had among the people; but most immediately, for that they were supposed the chief, by whose activity those twelve protesting bishops were but a week before committed to the Tower.

"He missed but little to have produced writings under some men's own hands." But yet he missed, though their chambers, trunks, and studies were sealed up and searched; yet not found guilty. "Providence would not have it so." Good Providence! that curbs the raging of proud monarchs, as well as of mad multitudes. "Yet he wanted not such probabilities" (for his pregnant is come now to probable) "as were sufficient to raise jealousies in any king's heart." And thus his pregnant motives are at last proved nothing but a tympany, or a Queen Mary's cushion; for in any king's heart, as kings go now, what shadowy conceit or groundless toy will not create a jealousy?

"That he had designed to insult the house of commons," taking God to witness, he utterly denies; yet in his answer to the city, maintains that "any course of violence had been very justifiable." And we may then guess how far it was from his design: however, it discovered in him an excessive eagerness to be avenged on them that crossed him; and that to have his will, he stood not to do things never so much below him. What a becoming sight it was, to see the king of England one while in the house of commons, and by and by in the Guildhall among the liveries and manufacturers, prosecuting so greedily the track of five or six fled subjects; himself not the solicitor only, but the pursuivant and the apparitor of his own partial cause! And although in his answers to the parliament, he hath confessed, first that his manner of prosecution was illegal, next "that as he once conceived he had ground enough to accuse them, so at length that he found as good cause to desert any prosecution of them;" yet here he seems to reverse all, and against promise takes up his old deserted accusation, that he might have something to excuse himself, instead of giving due reparation, which he always refused to give them whom he had so dishonoured.

"That I went," saith he of his going to the house of commons, "attended with some gentlemen;" gentlemen indeed! the ragged infantry of stews and brothels; the spawn and shipwreck of taverns and dicing-houses: and then he pleads, "it was no unwonted thing for the majesty and safety of a king to be so attended, especially in discontented times." An illustrious majesty no doubt, so attended! a becoming safety for the king of England, placed in the fidelity of such guards and champions! happy times, when braves and hacksters, the only contented members of his government, were thought the fittest and the faithfullest to defend his person against the discontents of a parliament and all good men! Were those the chosen ones to "preserve reverence to him," while he entered "unassured," and full of suspicions, into his great and faithful council! Let God then and the world judge, whether the cause were not in his own guilty and unwarrantable doings: the house of commons, upon several examinations of this business, declared it sufficiently proved, that the coming of those soldiers, papists and others, with the king, was to take away some of their members; and in case of opposition or denial, to have fallen upon the house in a hostile manner.

This the king here denies; adding a fearful imprecation against his own life, "if he purposed any violence or oppression against the innocent, then," saith he, "let the enemy prosecute my soul, and tread my life to the ground, and lay mine honour in the dust." What need then more disputing? He appealed to God's tribunal, and behold! God hath judged and done to him in the sight of all men according to the verdict of his own mouth: to be a warning to all kings hereafter how they use presumptuously the words and protestations of David, without the spirit and conscience of David. And the king's admirers may here see their madness, to mistake this book for a monument of his worth and wisdom, whenas indeed it is his dooms-day book; not like that of William the Norman, his predecessor, but the record and memorial of his condemnation; and discovers whatever hath befallen him to have been hastened on from divine justice by the rash and inconsiderate appeal of his own lips. But what evasions, what pretences, though never so unjust and empty, will he refuse in matters more unknown, and more involved in the mists and intricacies of state, who, rather than not justify himself in a thing so generally odious, can flatter his integrity with such frivolous excuses against the manifest dissent of all men, whether enemies, neuters, or friends? But God and his judgments have not been mocked; and good men may well perceive what a distance there was ever like to be between him and his parliament, and perhaps between him and all amendment, who for one good deed, though but consented to, asks God forgiveness; and from his worst deeds done, takes occasion to insist upon his righteousness! . . .

Chapter 5: Upon the Bill for Triennial Parliaments, and for Settling This, &c

The bill for a triennial parliament was but the third part of one good step toward that which in times past was our annual right. The other bill for settling this parliament was new indeed, but at that time very necessary; and, in the king's own words, no more than what the world "was fully confirmed he might in justice, reason, honour, and conscience grant them;" for to that end he affirms to have done it.

But whereas he attributes the passing of them to his own act of grace and willingness, (as his manner is to make virtues of his necessities,) and giving to himself all the praise, heaps ingratitude upon the parliament, a little memory will set the clean contrary before us; that for those beneficial acts we owe what we owe to the parliament, but to his granting them neither praise nor thanks. The first bill granted much less than two former statutes yet in force by Edward the Third; that a parliament should be called every year, or oftener, if need were; nay, from a far ancienter law-book, called the "Mirror," it is affirmed in a late treatise called "Rights of the Kingdom;" that parliaments by our old laws ought twice a year to be at London. From twice in one year to once in three years, it may be soon cast up how great a loss we fell into of our ancient liberty by that act, which in the ignorant and slavish minds we then were, was thought a great purchase.

Wisest men perhaps were contented (for the present, at least) by this act to have recovered parliaments, which were then upon the brink of danger to be for ever lost. And this is that which the king preaches here for a special token of his princely favour, to have abridged and overreached the people five parts in six what their due was, both by ancient statute and originally. And thus the taking from us all but a triennial remnant of that English freedom which our fathers left us double, in a fair annuity enrolled, is set out, and sold to us here for the gracious and over-liberal giving of a new enfranchisement. How little, may we think, did he ever give us, who in the bill of his pretended givings writes down imprimis that benefit or privilege once in three years given us, which by so giving he more than twice every year illegally took from us: such givers as give single to take away sixfold, be to our enemies! for certainly this commonwealth, if the statutes of our ancestors be worth aught, would have found it hard and hazardous to thrive under the damage of such a guileful liberality.

The other act was so necessary, that nothing in the power of man more seemed to be the stay and support of all things from that steep ruin to which he had nigh brought them, than that act obtained. He had by his ill-stewardship, and, to say no worse, the needless raising of two armies, intended for a civil war, beggared both himself and the public; and besides had left us upon the score of his needy enemies for what it cost them in their own defence against him. To disengage him and the kingdom great sums were to be borrowed, which would never have been lent, nor could ever be repaid, had the king chanced to dissolve this parliament as heretofore. The errors also of his government had brought the kingdom to such extremes, as were incapable of all recovery without the absolute continuance of a parliament. I had been else in vain to go about the settling of so great distempers, if he, who first caused the malady, might, when he pleased, reject the remedy. Notwithstanding all which, that he granted both these acts unwillingly, and as a mere passive instrument, was then visible even to most of those men who now will see nothing.

At passing of the former act he himself concealed not his unwillingness; and testifying a general dislike of their actions, which they then proceeded in with great approbation of the whole kingdom, he told them with a masterly brow, that "by this act he had obliged them above what they had deserved," and gave a piece of justice to the commonwealth six times short of his predecessors, as if he had been giving some boon or begged office to a sort of his desertless grooms.

That he passed the latter act against his will, no man in reason can hold it questionable. For if the February before he made so dainty, and were so loath to bestow a parliament once in three years upon the nation, because this had so opposed his courses, was it likely that the May following he should bestow willingly on this parliament an indissoluble sitting, when they had offended him much more by cutting short and impeaching of high-treason his chief favourites? It was his fear then, not his favour, which drew from him that act, lest the parliament, incensed by his conspiracies against them, about the same time discovered, should with the people have resented too heinously those his doings, if to the suspicion of their danger from him he had also added the denial of this only means to secure themselves.

From these acts therefore in which he glories, and wherewith so oft he upbraids the parliament, he cannot justly expect to reap aught but dishonour and dispraise; as being both unwillingly granted, and one granting much less than was before allowed by statute, the other being a testimony of his violent and lawless custom, not only to break privileges, but whole parliaments; from which enormity they were constrained to bind him first of all his predecessors; never any before him having given like causes of distrust and jealousy to his people. As for this parliament, how far he was from being advised by them as he ought, let his own words express.

He taxes them with "undoing what they found well done" and yet knows they undid nothing in the church, but lord bishops, liturgies, ceremonies, high-commission, judged worthy by all true protestants to be thrown out of the church. They undid nothing in the state but irregular and grinding courts, the main grievances to be removed; and if these were the things which in his opinion they found well done, we may again from hence be informed with what unwillingness he removed them; and that those gracious acts, whereof so frequently he makes mention, may be Englished more properly acts of fear and dissimulation against his mind and conscience.

The bill preventing dissolution of this parliament he calls "an unparel-leled act, out of the extreme confidence that his subjects would not make ill use of it." But was it not a greater confidence of the people, to put into one man's hand so great a power, till he abused it, as to summon and dissolve parliaments? He would be thanked for trusting them, and ought to thank them rather for trusting him: the trust issuing first from them, not from him.

And that it was a mere trust, and not his prerogative, to call and dissolve parliaments at his pleasure; and that parliaments were not to be dissolved, till all petitions were heard, all grievances redressed, is not only the asser-tion of this parliament, but of our ancient law-books, which aver it to be an unwritten law of common right, so engraven in the hearts of our ancestors, and by them so constantly enjoyed and claimed, as that it needed not en-rolling. And if the Scots in their declaration could charge the king with breach of their laws for breaking up that parliament without their consent, while matters of greatest moment were depending; it were unreasonable to imagine, that the wisdom of England should be so wanting to itself through all ages, as not to provide by some known law, written or unwritten, against the not calling, or the arbitrary dissolving, of parliaments; or that they who ordained their summoning twice a year, or as oft as need re-quired, did not tacitly enact also, that as necessity of affairs called them, so the same necessity should keep them undissolved, till that were fully satisfied.

Were it not for that, parliaments, and all the fruit and benefit we receive by having them, would turn soon to mere abusion. It appears then, that if this bill of not dissolving were an unparalleled act, it was a known and common right, which our ancestors under other kings enjoyed as firmly as if it had been graven in marble; and that the infringement of this king first brought it into a written act: who now boasts that as a great favour done us, which his own less fidelity than was in former kings constrained us only of an old undoubted right to make a new written act. But what needed written acts, whenas anciently it was esteemed part of his crown oath, not to dis-solve parliaments till all grievances were considered? whereupon the old "Modi of Parliament" calls it flat perjury, if he dissolve them before: as I find cited in a book mentioned at the beginning of this chapter, to which and other law tractates I refer the more lawyerly mooting of this point, which is neither my element, nor my proper work here; since the book which I have to answer, pretends reason, not authorities and quotations: and I hold reason to be the best arbitrator, and the law of law itself.

It is true, that "good subjects think it not just, that the king's condition should be worse by bettering theirs." But then the king must not be at such a distance from the people in judging what is better and what worse; which might have been agreed, had he known (for his own words condemn him) "as well with moderation to use, as with earnestness to desire his own advantages." "A continual parliament, he thought, would keep the commonwealth in tune." Judge, commonwealth! what proofs he gave, that this boasted profession was ever in his thought. "Some," saith he, "gave out, that I repented me of that settling act." His own actions gave it out beyond all supposition; for doubtless it repented him to have established that by law, which he went about so soon after to abrogate by the sword.

He calls those acts, which he confesses "tended to their good, not more princely than friendly contributions." As if to do his duty were of courtesy, and the discharge of his trust a parcel of his liberality; so nigh lost in his esteem was the birthright of our liberties, that to give them back again upon demand, stood at the mercy of his contribution. "He doubts not but the affections of his people will compensate his sufferings for those acts of confidence": and imputes his sufferings to a contrary cause. Not his confidence, but his distrust, was that which brought him to those sufferings, from the time that he forsook his parliament; and trusted them never the sooner for what he tells "of their piety and religious strictness," but rather hated them as puritans, whom he always sought to extirpate.

He would have it believed, that "to bind his hands by these acts, argued a very short foresight of things, and extreme fatuity of mind in him," if he had meant a war. If we should conclude so, that were not the only argument: neither did it argue that he meant peace; knowing that what he granted for the present out of fear, he might as soon repeal by force, watching his time; and deprive them the fruit of those acts, if his own designs, wherein he put his trust, took effect.

Yet he complains, "that the tumults threatened to abuse all acts of grace, and turn them into wantonness." I would they had turned his wantonness into the grace of not abusing scripture. Was this becoming such a saint as they would make him, to adulterate those sacred words from the grace of God to the acts of his own grace? Herod was eaten up of worms for suffering others to compare his voice to the voice of God; but the borrower of this phrase gives much more cause of jealousy, that he likened his own acts of grace to the acts of God's grace.

From profaneness he scarce comes off with perfect sense. "I was not then in a capacity to make war," therefore, "I intended not." "I was not in a capacity," therefore "I could not have given my enemies greater advantage, than by so unprincely inconstancy to have scattered them by arms, whom but lately I had settled by parliament." What place could there be for his inconstancy in that thing whereto he was in no capacity? Otherwise his inconstancy was not so unwonted, or so nice, but that it would have easily found pretences to scatter those in revenge, whom he settled in fear.

"It had been a course full of sin, as well as of hazard and dishonour." True; but if those considerations withheld him not from other actions of like nature, how can we believe they were of strength sufficient to withhold him from this? And that they withheld him not, the event soon taught us. "His letting some men go up to the pinnacle of the temple, was a temptation to them to cast him down headlong." In this simile we have himself compared to Christ, the parliament to the devil, and his giving them that act of settling, to his letting them go up to the "pinnacle of the temple." A tottering and giddy act rather than a settling. This was goodly use made of scripture in his solitudes: but it was no pinnacle of the temple, it was a pinnacle of Nebuchadnezzar's palace, from whence he and monarchy fell headlong together.

He would have others see that "all the kingdoms of the world are not worth gaining by ways of sin which hazard the soul;" and hath himself left nothing unhazarded to keep three. He concludes with sentences, that, rightly scanned, make not so much for him as against him, and confesses, that "the act of settling was no sin of his will;" and we easily believe him, for it hath been clearly proved a sin of his unwillingness. With his orisons I meddle not, for he appeals to a high audit. This yet may be noted, that at his prayers he had before him the sad presage of his ill success, "as of a dark and dangerous storm, which never admitted his return to the port from whence he set out." Yet his prayer-book no sooner shut, but other hopes flattered him; and their flattering was his destruction. . . .

Chapter 11: Upon the Nineteen Propositions, &c

Of the nineteen propositions he names none in particular, neither shall the answer: but he insists upon the old plea of "his conscience, honour, and reason;" using the plausibility of large and indefinite words, to defend himself at such a distance as may hinder the eye of common judgment from all distinct view and examination of his reasoning. "He would buy the peace of his people at any rate, save only the parting with his conscience and honour." Yet shews not how it can happen that the peace of a people, if otherwise to be bought at any rate, should be inconsistent or at variance with the conscience and honour of a king. Till then, we may receive it for a better sentence, that nothing should be more agreeable to the conscience and honour of a king, than to preserve his subjects in peace; especially from civil war.

And which of the propositions were "obtruded on him with the point of the sword," till he first ["]with the point of the sword," thrust from him both the propositions and the propounders? He never reckons those violent and merciless obtrusions, which for almost twenty years he had been forcing upon tender consciences, by all sorts of persecution, till through the multitude of them that were to suffer, it could no more be called a persecution, but a plain war. From which when first the Scots, then the English, were constrained to defend themselves, this their just defence is that which he calls here, "their making war upon his soul."

He grudges that "so many things are required of him, and nothing offered him in requital of those favours which he had granted." What could satiate the desires of this man, who being king of England, and master of almost two millions yearly, what by hook or crook, was still in want; and those acts of justice which he was to do in duty, counts done as favours; and such favours as were not done without the avaricious hope of other rewards besides supreme honour, and the constant revenue of his place?

"This honour," he saith, "they did him, to put him on the giving part." And spake truer than he intended, it being merely for honour's sake that they did so; not that it belonged to him of right: for what can he give to a parliament, who receives all he hath from the people, and for the people's good? Yet now he brings his own conditional rights to contest and be preferred before the people's good; and yet, unless it be in order to their good, he hath no rights at all; reigning by the laws of the land, not by his own; which laws are in the hands of parliament to change or abrogate as they see best for the commonwealth, even to the taking away of kingship itself, when it grows too masterful and burdensome.

For every commonwealth is in general defined, a society sufficient of itself, in all things conducible to well-being and commodious life. Any of which requisite things, if it cannot have without the gift and favour of a single person, or without leave of his private reason or his conscience, it cannot be thought sufficient of itself, and by consequence no commonwealth, nor free; but a multitude of vassals in the possession and domain of one absolute lord, and wholly obnoxious to his will. If the king have power to give or deny anything to his parliament, he must do it either as a person several from them, or as one greater: neither of which will be allowed him: not to be considered severally from them; for as the king of England can do no wrong, so neither can he do right but in his courts and by his courts; and what is legally done in them, shall be deemed the king's assent, though he as a several person shall judge or endeavour the contrary; so that indeed without his courts, or against them, he is no king. If therefore he obtrude upon us any public mischief, or withhold from us any general good, which is wrong in the highest degree, he must do it as a tyrant, not as a king of England, by the known maxims of our law. Neither can he, as one greater, give aught to the parliament which is not in their own power, but he must be greater also than the kingdom which they represent: so that to honour him with the giving part was a mere civility, and may be well termed the courtesy of England, not the king's due.

But the "incommunicable jewel of his conscience" he will not give, "but reserve to himself." It seems that his conscience was none of the crown jewels; for those we know were in Holland, not incommunicable, to buy arms against his subjects. Being therefore but a private jewel, he could not have done a greater pleasure to the kingdom, than by reserving it to himself. But he, contrary to what is here professed, would have his conscience not an incommunicable, but a universal conscience, the whole kingdom's conscience. Thus what he seems to fear lest we should ravish from him, is our chief complaint that he obtruded upon us; we never forced him to part with his conscience, but it was he that would have forced us to part with ours.

Some things he taxes them to have offered him, "which, while he had the mastery of his reason, he would never consent to." Very likely; but had his reason mastered him as it ought, and not been mastered long ago by his sense and humour, (as the breeding of most kings hath been ever sensual and most humoured,) perhaps he would have made no difficulty. Meanwhile at what a fine pass is the kingdom, that must depend in greatest exigencies upon the phantasy of a king's reason, be he wise or fool, who arrogantly shall answer all the wisdom of the land, that what they offer seems to him unreasonable!

He prefers his "love of truth" before his love of the people. His love of truth would have led him to the search of truth, and have taught him not to lean so much upon his own understanding. He met at first with doctrines of unaccountable prerogative; in them he rested, because they pleased him; they therefore pleased him because they gave him all; and this he calls his love of truth, and prefers it before the love of his people's peace.

Some things they proposed, "which would have wounded the inward peace of his conscience." The more our evil hap that three kingdoms should be thus pestered with one conscience; who chiefly scrupled to grant us that, which the parliament advised him to, as the chief means of our public welfare and reformation. These scruples to many perhaps will seem pretended; to others, upon as good grounds, may seem real; and that it was the just judgment of God, that he who was so cruel and so remorseless to other men's consciences, should have a conscience within him as cruel to himself; constraining him, as he constrained others, and ensnaring him in such ways and counsels as were certain to be his destruction.

"Other things though he could approve, yet in honour and policy he thought fit to deny, lest he should seem to dare deny nothing." By this means he will be sure, what with reason, honour, policy, or punctilios, to be found never unfurnished of a denial; whether it were his envy not to be overbounteous, or that the submissness of our asking stirred up in him a certain pleasure of denying. Good princes have thought it their chief happiness to be always granting; if good things, for the things' sake; if things indifferent, for the people's sake; while this man sits calculating variety of excuses how he may grant least; as if his whole strength and royalty were placed in a mere negative.

Of one proposition especially he laments him much, that they would bind "to a general and implicit consent for whatever they desired." Which though I find not among the nineteen, yet undoubtedly the oath of his coronation binds him to no less; neither is he at all by his office to interpose against a parliament in the making or not making of any law; but to take that for just and good legally, which is there decreed, and to see it executed accordingly. Nor was he set over us to vie wisdom with his parliament, but to be guided by them; any of whom possibly may as far excel him in the gift of wisdom, as he them in place and dignity. But much nearer is it to impossibility, that any king alone should be wiser than all his council; sure enough it was not he, though no king ever before him so much contended to have it thought so. And if the parliament so thought not, but desired him to follow their advice and deliberation in things of public concernment, he accounts it the same proposition as if Samson had been moved "to the putting out his eyes, that the Philistines might abuse him." And thus out of an unwise or pretended fear, lest others should make a scorn of him for yielding to his parliament, he regards not to give cause of worse suspicion, that he made a scorn of his regal oath.

But "to exclude him from all power of denial seems an arrogance;" in the parliament he means: what in him then to deny against the parliament? None at all, by what he argues: for "by petitioning, they confess their inferiority, and that obliges them to rest, if not satisfied, yet quieted with such an answer as the will and reason of their superior thinks fit to give." First, petitioning, in better English, is no more than requesting or requiring; and men require not favours only, but their due; and that not only from superiors, but from equals, and inferiors also. The noblest Romans, when they stood for that which was a kind of regal honour, the consulship, were wont in a submissive manner to go about, and beg that highest dignity of the meanest plebeians, naming them man by man; which in their tongue was called *petitio consulatus*. And the parliament of England petitioned the king, not because all of them were inferior to him, but because he was inferior to any one of them, which they did of civil custom, and for fashion's sake, more than of duty; for by plain law cited before, the parliament is his superior.

But what law in any trial or dispute enjoins a freeman to rest quieted, though not satisfied with the will and reason of his superior? It were a mad law that would subject reason to superiority of place. And if our highest consultations and purposed laws must be terminated by the king's will, then is the will of one man our law, and no subtlety of dispute can redeem the parliament and nation from being slaves: neither can any tyrant require more than that his will or reason, though not satisfying, should yet be rested in, and determine all things. We may conclude, therefore, that when the parliament petitioned the king, it was but merely form, let it be as "foolish and absurd" as he pleases. It cannot certainly be so absurd as what he requires, that the parliament should confine their own and all the kingdom's reason to the will of one man, because it was his hap to succeed his father. For neither God nor the laws have subjected us to his will, nor set his reason to be our sovereign above law, (which must needs be, if he can strangle it in the birth,) but set his person over us in the sovereign execution of such laws as the parliament establish. The parliament, therefore, without any usurpation, hath had it always in their power to limit and confine the exorbitancy of kings, whether they call it their will, their reason, or their conscience.

But this above all was never expected, nor is to be endured, that a king, who is bound by law and oath to follow the advice of his parliament, should be permitted to except against them as "young statesmen," and proudly to suspend his following their advice, "until his seven years' experience had shewn him how well they could govern themselves." Doubtless the law never supposed so great an arrogance could be in one man; that he whose seventeen years' unexperience had almost ruined all, should sit another seven years schoolmaster to tutor those who were sent by the whole realm to be his counsellors and teachers. But with what modesty can he pretend to be a statesman himself, who with his father's king-craft and his own did never that of his own accord which was not directly opposite to his professed interest both at home and abroad; discontenting and alienating his subjects at home, weakening and deserting his confederates abroad, and with them the common cause of religion; so that the whole course of his reign, by an example of his own furnishing, hath resembled Phaeton more than Phoebus, and forced the parliament to drive like Jehu; which omen taken from his own mouth, God hath not diverted?

And he on the other side might have remembered, that the parliament sit in that body, not as his subjects, but as his superiors, called, not by him, but by the law; not only twice every year, but as oft as great affairs require, to be his counsellors and dictators, though he stomach it; nor to be dissolved at his pleasure, but when all grievances be first removed, all petitions heard and answered. This is not only reason, but the known law of the land.

"When he heard that propositions would be sent him," he sat conjecturing what they would propound; and because they propounded what he expected not, he takes that to be a warrant for his denying them. But what did he expect? He expected that the parliament would reinforce "some old laws." But if those laws were not a sufficient remedy to all grievances, nay, were found to be grievances themselves, when did we lose that other part of our freedom to establish new? "He thought some injuries done by himself and others to the commonwealth were to be repaired." But how could that be, while he, the chief offender, took upon him to be sole judge both of the injury and the reparation?

"He stayed till the advantages of his crown considered, might induce him to condescend to the people's good." Whenas the crown itself with all those advantages were therefore given him, that the people's good should be first considered; not bargained for, and bought by inches with the bribe of more offertures and advantages to his crown. He looked "for moderate desires of due reformation;" as if any such desires could be immoderate. He looked for such a reformation, "both in church and state, as might preserve" the roots of every grievance and abuse in both still growing, (which he calls "the foundation and essentials,") and would have only the excrescences of evil pruned away for the present, as was plotted before, that they might grow fast enough between triennial parliaments, to hinder them, by work enough besides, from ever striking at the root.

He alleges, "They should have had regard to the laws in force, to the wisdom and piety of former parliaments, to the ancient and universal practice of Christian churches." As if they who come with full authority to redress public grievances, which ofttimes are laws themselves, were to have their hands bound by laws in force, or the supposition of more piety and wisdom in their ancestors, or the practice of churches heretofore; whose fathers, notwithstanding all these pretences, made as vast alterations to free themselves from ancient popery. For all antiquity that adds or varies from the scripture, is no more warranted to our safe imitation, than what was done the age before at Trent. Nor was there need to have despaired of what could be established in lieu of what was to be annulled, having before his eyes the government of so many churches beyond the seas; whose pregnant and solid reasons wrought so with the parliament, as to desire a uniformity rather with all other Protestants, than to be a schism divided from them under a conclave of thirty bishops, and a crew of irreligious priests that gaped for the same preferment.

And whereas he blames those propositions for not containing what they ought, what did they mention, but to vindicate and restore the rights of parliament invaded by cabin councils, the courts of justice obstructed, and the government of the church innovated and corrupted? All these things he might easily have observed in them, which he affirms he could not find; but found "those demanding" in parliament, who were "looked upon before as factious in the state, and schismatical in the church; and demanding not only toleration for themselves in their vanity, novelty, and confusion, but also an extirpation of that government, whose rights they had a mind to invade." Was this man ever likely to be advised, who with such a prejudice and disesteem sets himself against his chosen and appointed counsellors? likely ever to admit of reformation, who censures all the government of other Protestant churches, as bad as any papist could have censured them? And what king had ever his whole kingdom in such contempt, so to wrong and dishonour the free elections of his people, as to judge them, whom the nation thought worthiest to sit with him in parliament, few else but such as were "punishable by the laws?" yet knowing that time was, when to be a protestant, to be a Christian, was by law as punishable as to be a traitor; and that our Saviour himself, coming to reform his church, was accused of an intent to invade Caesar's right, as good a right as the prelate bishops ever had: the one being got by force, the other by spiritual usurpation; and both by force upheld.

He admires and falls into an ecstasy, that the parliament should send him such a "horrid proposition," as the removal of episcopacy. But expect from him in an ecstasy no other reasons of his admiration than the dream and tautology of what he hath so often repeated, law, antiquity, ancestors, prosperity, and the like, which will be therefore not worth a second answer, but may pass with his own comparison into the common sewer of other popish arguments.

"Had the two houses sued out their livery from the wardships of tumults," he could sooner have believed them. It concerned them first to sue out their livery from the unjust wardship of his encroaching prerogative. And had he also redeemed his overdated minority from a pupilage under bishops, he would much less have mistrusted his parliament; and never would have set so base a character upon them, as to count them no better than the vassals of certain nameless men, whom he charges to be such as "hunt after faction with their hounds, the tumults." And yet the bishops could have told him that Nimrod, the first that hunted after faction, is reputed by ancient tradition the first that founded monarchy; whence it appears, that to hunt after faction is more properly the king's game; and those hounds, which he calls the vulgar, have been often hallooed to from court, of whom the mongrel sort have been enticed; the rest have not lost their scent, but understood aright that the parliament had that part to act, which he had failed in; that trust to discharge, which he had broken; that estate and honour to preserve, which was far beyond his, the estate and honour of the commonwealth, which he had embezzled.

Yet so far doth self-opinion or false principles delude and transport him, as to think "the concurrence of his reason" to the votes of parliament, not only political, but natural, "and as necessary to the begetting," or bringing forth of any one "complete act of public wisdom as the sun's influence is necessary to all nature's productions." So that the parliament, it seems, is but a female, and without his procreative reason, the laws which they can produce are but wind-eggs; wisdom, it seems, to a king is natural, to a parliament not natural, but by conjunction with the king; yet he professes to hold his kingly right by law; and if no law could be made but by the great council of a nation, which we now term a parliament, then certainly it was a parliament that first created kings; and not only made laws before a king was in being, but those laws especially whereby he holds his crown.

He ought then to have so thought of a parliament, if he count it not male, as of his mother, which to civil being created both him and the royalty he wore. And if it hath been anciently interpreted the presaging sign of a future tyrant, but to dream of copulation with his mother, what can it be less than actual tyranny to affirm waking, that the parliament, which is his mother, can neither conceive or bring forth "any authoritative act" without his masculine coition? Nay, that his reason is as celestial and lifegiving to the parliament, as the sun's influence is to the earth: what other notions but these, or such like, could swell up Caligula to think himself a god?

But to be rid of these mortifying propositions, he leaves no tyrannical evasion unessayed; first, "that they are not the joint and free desires of both houses, or the major part;" next, "that the choice of many members was carried on by faction." The former of these is already discovered to be an old device put first in practice by Charles V, since the Reformation: who, when the protestants of Germany for their own defence joined themselves in league, in his declarations and remonstrances laid the fault only upon some few (for it was dangerous to take notice of too many enemies), and accused them, that under colour of religion they had a purpose to invade his and the church's right; by which policy he deceived many of the German cities, and kept them divided from that league, until they saw themselves brought into a snare. That other cavil against the people's choice puts us in mind rather what the court was wont to do, and how to tamper with elections: neither was there at that time any faction more potent or more likely to do such a business, than they themselves who complain most.

But "he must chew such morsels as propositions, ere he let them down." So let him; but if the kingdom shall taste nothing but after his chewing, what does he make of the kingdom but a great baby? "The straitness of his conscience will not give him leave to swallow down such camels of sacrilege and injustice as others do." This is the pharisee up and down: "I am not as other men are." But what camels of injustice he could devour all his three realms were witness, which was the cause that they almost perished for want of parliaments. And he that will be unjust to man, will be sacrilegious to God; and to bereave a Christian conscience of liberty, for no other reason than the narrowness of his own conscience, is the most unjust measure to man, and the worst sacrilege to God.

That other, which he calls sacrilege, of taking from the clergy that superfluous wealth, which antiquity as old as Constantine, from the credit of a divine vision, counted "poison in the church," hath ever been most opposed by men, whose righteousness in other matters hath been least observed. He concludes, as his manner is, with high commendation of his own "unbiassed rectitude," and believes nothing to be in them that dissent from him but faction, innovation, and particular designs. Of these repetitions I find no end, no, not in his prayer; which being founded upon deceitful principles, and a fond hope that God will bless him in those errors, which he calls "honest," finds a fit answer of St. James: "Ye ask and receive not, because ye ask amiss." As for the truth and sincerity, which he prays may be always found in those his declarations to the people, the contrariety of his own actions will bear eternal witness, how little careful or solicitous he was what he promised or what he uttered there. . . .

Chapter 28: Entitled, Meditations upon Death

It might be well thought by him who reads no further than the title of this last essay, that it required no answer. For all other human things are disputed, and will be variously thought of to the world's end. But this business of death is a plain case, and admits no controversy: in that centre all opinions meet. Nevertheless, since out of those few mortifying hours that should have been entirest to themselves, and most at peace from all passion and disquiet, he can afford spare time to inveigh bitterly against that justice which was done upon him; it will be needful to say something in defence of those proceedings, though briefly, in regard so much on this subject hath been written lately.

It happened once, as we find in Esdras and Josephus, authors not less believed than any under sacred, to be a great and solemn debate in the court of Darius, what thing was to be counted strongest of all other. He that could resolve this, in reward of his excellent wisdom, should be clad in purple, drink in gold, sleep on a bed of gold, and sit next Darius. None but they, doubtless, who were reputed wise had the question propounded to them; who after some respite given them by the king to consider, in full assembly of all his lords and gravest counsellors, returned severally what they thought. The first held that wine was strongest; another, that the king was strongest; but Zorobabel, prince of the captive Jews, and heir to the crown of Judah, being one of them, proved women to be stronger than the king, for that he himself had seen a concubine take his crown from off his head to set it upon her own; and others beside him have likewise seen the like feat done, and not in jest. Yet he proved on, and it was so yielded by the king himself, and all his sages, that neither wine, nor women, nor the king, but truth of all other things was the strongest.

For me, though neither asked, nor in a nation that gives such rewards to wisdom, I shall pronounce my sentence somewhat different from Zorobabel; and shall defend that either truth and justice are all one, (for truth is but justice in our knowledge, and justice is but truth in our practice); and he indeed so explains himself, in saying that with truth is no accepting of persons, which is the property of justice, or else if there be any odds, that justice, though not stronger than truth, yet by her office, is to put forth and exhibit more strength in the affairs of mankind. For truth is properly no more than contemplation; and her utmost efficiency is but teaching: but justice in her very essence is all strength and activity; and hath a sword put into her hand, to use against all violence and oppression on the earth. She it is most truly, who accepts no person, and exempts none from the severity of her stroke. She never suffers injury to prevail, but when falsehood first prevails over truth; and that also is a kind of justice done on them who are so deluded. Though wicked kings and tyrants counterfeit her sword, as some did that buckler fabled to fall from heaven into the capitol, yet she communicates her power to none but such as, like herself, are just, or at least will do justice. For it were extreme partiality and injustice, the flat denial and overthrow of herself, to put her own authentic sword into the hand of an unjust and wicked man, or so far to accept and exalt one mortal person above his equals, that he alone shall have the punishing of all other men transgressing, and not receive like punishment from men, when he himself shall be found the highest transgressor.

We may conclude, therefore, that justice, above all other things, is and ought to be the strongest; she is the strength, the kingdom, the power, and majesty of all ages. Truth herself would subscribe to this, though Darius and all the monarchs of the world should deny. And if by sentence thus written it were my happiness to set free the minds of Englishmen from longing to return poorly under that captivity of kings from which the strength and supreme sword of justice hath delivered them, I shall have done a work not much inferior to that of Zorobabel; who, by well-praising and extolling the force of truth, in that contemplative strength conquered Darius, and freed his country and the people of God from the captivity of Babylon. Which I shall yet not despair to do, if they in this land, whose minds are yet captive, be but as ingenuous to acknowledge the strength and supremacy of justice, as that heathen king was to confess the strength of truth: or let them but, as he did, grant that, and they will soon perceive that truth resigns all her outward strength to justice; justice therefore must needs be strongest, both in her own, and in the strength of truth. But if a king may do among men whatsoever is his will and pleasure, and notwithstanding be unaccountable to men, then, contrary to his magnified wisdom of Zorobabel, neither truth nor justice, but the king, is strongest of all other things, which that Persian monarch himself, in the midst of all his pride and glory, durst not assume.

Let us see, therefore, what this king hath to affirm, why the sentence of justice, and the weight of that sword, which she delivers into the hands of men, should be more partial to him offending, than to all others of human race. First, he pleads, that "no law of God or man gives to subjects any power of judicature without or against him." Which assertion shall be proved in every part to be most untrue. The first express law of God given to mankind was that to Noah, as a law, in general, to all the sons of men. And by that most ancient and universal law, "Whosoever sheddeth man's blood, by man shall his blood be shed," we find here no exception. If a king therefore do this, to a king, and that by men also, the same shall be done. This in the law of Moses, which came next, several times is repeated, and in one place remarkably, Numb. xxxv. "Ye shall take no satisfaction for the life of a murderer, but he shall surely be put to death: the land cannot be cleansed of the blood that is shed therein, but by the blood of him that shed it." This is so spoken as that which concerned all Israel, not one man alone, to see performed; and if no satisfaction were to be taken, then certainly no exception. Nay, the king, when they should set up any, was to observe the whole law, and not only to see it done, but to "do it; that his heart might not be lifted up above his brethren;" to dream of vain and useless prerogatives or exemptions, whereby the law itself must needs be founded in unrighteousness.

And were that true, which is most false, that all kings are the Lord's anointed, it were yet absurd to think that the anointment of God should be, as it were, a charm against law, and give them privilege, who punish others, to sin themselves unpunishably. The high-priest was the Lord's anointed as well as any king, and with the same consecrated oil; yet Solomon had put to death Abiathar, had it not been for other respects than that anointment. If God himself say to kings, "Touch not mine anointed," meaning his chosen people, as is evident in that Psalm, yet no man will argue thence, that he protects them from civil laws if they offend; then certainly, though David, as a private man, and in his own cause, feared to lift his hand against the Lord's anointed, much less can this forbid the law, or disarm justice from having legal power against any king. No other supreme magistrate, in what kind of government soever, lays claim to any such enormous privilege; wherefore then should any king, who is but one kind of magistrate, and set over the people for no other end than they?

Next in order of time to the laws of Moses are those of Christ, who declares professedly his judicature to be spiritual, abstract from civil managements, and therefore leaves all nations to their own particular laws, and way of government. Yet because the church hath a kind of jurisdiction within her own bounds, and that also, though in process of time much corrupted and plainly turned into a corporal judicature, yet much approved by this king; it will be firm enough and valid against him, if subjects, by the laws of church also, be "invested with a power of judicature" both without and against their king, though pretending, and by them acknowledged, "next and immediately under Christ supreme head and governor." Theodosius, one of the best Christian emperors, having made a slaughter of the Thessalonians for sedition, but too cruelly, was excommunicated to his face by St. Ambrose, who was his subject; and excommunion is the utmost of ecclesiastical judicature, a spiritual putting to death.

But this, ye will say, was only an example. Read then the story; and it will appear, both that Ambrose avouched it for the law of God, and Theodosius confessed it of his own accord to be so; "and that the law of God was not to be made void in him, for any reverence to his imperial power." From hence, not to be tedious, I shall pass into our own land of Britain; and show that subjects here have exercised the utmost of spiritual judicature, and more than spiritual, against their kings, his predecessors. Vortiger, for committing incest with his daughter, was by St. German, at that time his subject, cursed and condemned in a British council, about the year 448; and thereupon soon after was deposed. Mauricus, a king in Wales, for breach of oath and murder of Cynetus, was excommunicated and cursed, with all his offspring, by Oudoceus, bishop of Llandaff, in full synod, about the year 560, and not restored till he had repented. Morcant, another king in Wales, having slain Frioc his uncle, was fain to come in person, and receive judgment from the same bishop and his clergy; who

476 The English Revolution

upon his penitence acquitted him, for no other cause than lest the kingdom should be destitute of a successor in the royal line.

These examples are of the primitive, British, and episcopal church; long ere they had any commerce or communion with the church of Rome. What power afterwards of deposing kings, and so consequently of putting them to death, was assumed and practised by the canon law, I omit, as a thing generally known. Certainly, if whole councils of the Romish church have in the midst of their dimness discerned so much of truth, as to decree at Constance, and at Basil, and many of them to avouch at Trent also, that a council is above the pope, and may judge him, though by them not denied to be the vicar of Christ; we in our clearer light may be ashamed not to discern further, that a parliament is by all equity and right above a king, and may judge him, whose reasons and pretensions to hold of God only, as his immediate vicegerent, we know how far-fetched they are, and insufficient.

As for the laws of man, it would ask a volume to repeat all that might be cited in this point against him from all antiquity. In Greece, Orestes, the son of Agamemnon, and by succession king of Argos, was in that country judged and condemned to death for killing his mother: whence escaping, he was judged again, though a stranger, before the great council of Areopagus in Athens. And this memorable act of judicature was the first that brought the justice of that grave senate into fame and high estimation over all Greece for many ages after. And in the same city tyrants were to undergo legal sentence by the laws of Solon.

The kings of Sparta, though descended lineally from Hercules, esteemed a god among them, were often judged, and sometimes put to death, by the most just and renowned laws of Lycurgus; who, though a king, [thought] it most unequal to bind his subjects by any law, to which he bound not himself. In Rome, the laws made by Valerius Publicola, soon after the expelling of Tarquin and his race, expelled without a written law, the law being afterward written; and what the senate decreed against Nero, that he should be judged and punished according to the laws of their ancestors, and what in like manner was decreed against other emperors, is vulgarly known; as it was known to those heathen, and found just by nature ere any law mentioned it. And that the Christian civil law warrants like power of judicature to subjects against tyrants, is written clearly by the best and [most famous] civilians. For if it was decreed by Theodosius, and stands yet firm in the code of Justinian, that the law is above the emperor, then certainly the emperor being under law, the law may judge him; and if judge him, may punish him, proving tyrannous: how else is the law above him, or to what purpose? These are necessary deductions; and thereafter hath been done in all ages and kingdoms, oftener than to be here recited.

But what need we any further search after the law of other lands, for that which is so fully and so plainly set down lawful in our own? Where ancient books tell us, Bracton, Fleta, and others, that the king is under law, and inferior to his court of parliament; that although his place "to do justice" be highest, yet that he stands as liable "to receive justice" as the meanest of his kingdom. Nay, Alfred, the most worthy king, and by some accounted first absolute monarch of the Saxons here, so ordained; as is cited out of an ancient law-book called "the Mirror;" in "Rights of the Kingdom," p. 31, where it is complained of, "as the sovereign abuse of all," that the king should be deemed above the law, whereas he ought to be subject to it by his oath. Of which oath anciently it was the last clause, that the king "should be as liable, and obedient to suffer right, as others of his people." And indeed it were but fond and senseless, that the king should be accountable to every petty suit in lesser courts as we all know he was, and not be subject to the judicature of parliament in the main matters of our common safety or destruction; that he should be answerable in the ordinary course of law for any wrong done to a private person, and not answerable in court of parliament for destroying the whole kingdom.

By all this, and much more that might be added, as in an argument over-copious rather than barren, we see it manifest that all laws, both of God and man, are made without exemption of any person whomsoever; and that if kings presume to overtop the law by which they reign for the public good, they are by law to be reduced into order; and that can no way be more justly, than by those who exalt them to that high place. For who should better understand their own laws, and when they are transgressed, than they who are governed by them, and whose consent first made them? And who can have more right to take knowledge of things done within a free nation than they within themselves?

Those objected oaths of allegiance and supremacy we swore, not to his person, but as it was invested with his authority; and his authority was by the people first given him conditionally, in law, and under law, and under oath also for the kingdom's good, and not otherwise; the oaths then were interchanged, and mutual; stood and fell together; he swore fidelity to his trust; (not as a deluding ceremony, but as a real condition of their admitting him for king; and the Conqueror himself swore it oftener than at his crowning); they swore homage and fealty to his person in that trust. There was no reason why the kingdom should be further bound by oaths to him, than he by his coronation oath to us, which he hath every way broken: and having broken, the ancient crown oath of Alfred above mentioned conceals not his penalty.

As for the covenant, if that be meant, certainly no discreet person can imagine it should bind us to him in any stricter sense than those oaths formerly. The acts of hostility, which we received from him, were no such dear obligements, that we should owe him more fealty and defence for being our enemy, than we could before when we took him only for a king. They were accused by him and his party, to pretend liberty and reformation, but to have no other end than to make themselves great, and to destroy the king's person and authority. For which reason they added that third article, testifying to the world, that as they were resolved to endeavour first a reformation in the church, to extirpate prelacy, to preserve the rights of parliament, and the liberties of the kingdom, so they intended, so far as it might consist with the preservation and defence of these, to preserve the king's person and authority; but not otherwise. As far as this comes to, they covenant and swear in the sixth article to preserve and defend the persons and authority of one another, and all those that enter into that league; so that this covenant gives no unlimitable exemption to the king's person, but gives to all as much defence and preservation as to him, and to him as much as to their own persons, and no more; that is to say, in order and subordination to those main ends, for which we live and are a nation of men joined in society either Christian, or, at least, human.

But if the covenant were made absolute, to preserve and defend any one whomsoever, without respect had, either to the true religion, or those other superior things to be defended and preserved however, it cannot then be doubted, but that the covenant was rather a most foolish, hasty, and unlawful vow, than a deliberate and well-weighed covenant; swearing us into labyrinths and repugnances, no way to be solved or reconciled, and therefore no way to be kept; as first offending against the law of God, to vow the absolute preservation, defence, and maintaining of one man, though in his sins and offences never so great and heinous against God or his neighbour; and to except a person from justice, whereas his law excepts none. Secondly, it offends against the law of this nation, wherein, as hath been proved, kings in receiving justice, and undergoing due trial, are not differenced from the meanest subject.

Lastly, it contradicts and offends against the covenant itself, which vows in the fourth article to bring to open trial and condign punishment all those that shall be found guilty of such crimes and delinquencies, whereof the king, by his own letters, and other undeniable testimonies not brought to light till afterward, was found and convicted to be chief actor in what they thought him, at the time of taking that covenant, to be overruled only by evil counsellors; and those, or whomsoever they should discover to be principal, they vowed to try, either by their own "supreme judicatories," (for so even then they called them), "or by others having power from them to that effect." So that to have brought the king to condign punishment hath not broke the covenant, but it would have broke the covenant to have saved him from those judicatories, which both nations declared in that covenant to be supreme against any person whatsoever.

And besides all this, to swear in covenant the bringing of his evil counsellors and accomplices to condign punishment, and not only to leave unpunished and untouched the grand offender, but to receive him back again from the accomplishment of so many violences and mischiefs, dipped from head to foot, and stained over with the blood of thousands that were his faithful subjects, forced to their own defence against a civil war by him first raised upon them; and to receive him thus, in this gory pickle, to all his dignities and honours, covering the ignominious and horrid purple robe of innocent blood, that sat so close about him, with the glorious purple of royalty and supreme rule, the reward of highest excellence and virtue here on earth, were not only to swear and covenant the performance of an unjust vow, the strangest and most impious to the face of God, but were the most unwise and unprudential act as to civil government.

For so long as a king shall find by experience that, do the worst he can, his subjects, overawed by the religion of their own covenant, will only prosecute his evil instruments, nor dare to touch his person; and that whatever hath been on his part offended or transgressed, he shall come off at last with the same reverence to his person, and the same honour as for well doing, he will not fail to find them work; seeking far and near, and inviting to his court all the concourse of evil counsellors, or agents, that may be found: who, tempted with preferments and his promise to uphold them, will hazard easily their own heads, and the chance of ten to one but they shall prevail at last over men so quelled and fitted to be slaves by the false conceit of a religious covenant. And they in that superstition neither wholly yielding, nor to the utmost resisting, at the upshot of all their foolish war and expense, will find to have done no more but fetched a compass only of their miseries, ending at the same point of slavery, and in the same distractions wherein they first began.

But when kings themselves are made as liable to punishment as their evil counsellors, it will be both as dangerous from the king himself as from his parliament, to those that evil counsel him: and they, who else would be his readiest agents in evil, will then not fear to dissuade or to disobey him, not only in respect of themselves and their own lives, which for his sake they would not seem to value, but in respect of that danger which the king himself may incur, whom they would seem to love and serve with greatest fidelity. On all these grounds therefore of the covenant itself, whether religious or political, it appears likeliest, that both the English parliament and the Scotch commissioners, thus interpreting the covenant, (as indeed at that time they were the best and most authentical interpreters joined together), answered the king unanimously, in their letter dated January the 13th, 1645, that till security and satisfaction first given to both kingdoms for the blood spilled, for the Irish rebels brought over, and for the war in Ireland by him fomented, they could in nowise yield their consent to his return.

Here was satisfaction, full two years and upward after the covenant taken, demanded of the king by both nations in parliament for crimes at least capital, wherewith they charged him. And what satisfaction could be given for so much blood, but justice upon him that spilled it? till which done, they neither took themselves bound to grant him the exercise of his regal office by any meaning of the covenant which they then declared, (though other meanings have been since contrived), nor so much regarded the safety of his person, as to admit of his return among them from the midst of those whom they declared to be his greatest enemies; nay, from himself as from an actual enemy, not as from a king, they demanded security. But if the covenant, all this notwithstanding, swore otherwise to preserve him than in the preservation of true religion and our liberties, against which he fought, if not in arms, yet in resolution, to his dying day, and now after death still fights again in this his book, the covenant was better broken, than he saved. And God hath testified by all propitious and the most evident signs, whereby in these latter times he is wont to testify what pleases him, that such a solemn and for many ages unexampled act of due punishment was no mockery of justice, but a most grateful and well-pleasing sacrifice. Neither was it to cover their perjury, as he accuses, but to uncover his perjury to the oath of his coronation.

The rest of his discourse quite forgets the title; and turns his meditations upon death into obloquy and bitter vehemence against his "judges and accusers;" imitating therein, not our Saviour, but his grandmother, Mary queen of Scots, as also in the most of his other scruples, exceptions, and evasions; and from whom he seems to have learnt, as it were by heart, or else by kind, that which is thought by his admirers to be the most virtuous, most manly, most Christian, and most martyr-like, both of his words and speeches here, and of his answers and behaviour at his trial.

"It is a sad fate," he saith, "to have his enemies both accusers, parties, and judges." Sad indeed, but no sufficient plea to acquit him from being so judged. For what malefactor might not sometimes plead the like? If his own crimes have made all men his enemies, who else can judge him? They of the powder-plot against his father might as well have pleaded the same. Nay, at the resurrection it may as well be pleaded, that the saints, who then shall judge the world, are "both enemies, judges, parties, and accusers."

So much he thinks to abound in his own defence, that he undertakes an unmeasurable task, to bespeak "the singular care and protection of God over all kings," as being the greatest patrons of law, justice, order and religion on earth. But what patrons they be, God in the Scripture oft enough hath expressed; and the earth itself hath too long groaned under the burden of their injustice, disorder, and irreligion. Therefore "to bind their kings in chains, and their nobles with links of iron," is an honour belonging to his saints; not to build Babel, (which was Nimrod's work, the first king, and the beginning of his kingdom was Babel), but to destroy it, especially that spiritual Babel: and first to overcome those European kings, which receive their power, not from God, but from the beast; and are counted no better than his ten horns. "These shall hate the great whore," and yet "shall give their kingdoms to the beast that carries her; they shall commit fornication with her," and yet "shall burn her with fire," and yet "shall lament the fall of Babylon," where they fornicated with her. Rev. xvii. xviii.

Thus shall they be to and fro, doubtful and ambiguous in all their doings, until at last, "joining their armies with the beast," whose power first raised them, they shall perish with him by the "King of kings," against whom they have rebelled; and "the fowls shall eat their flesh." This is their doom written, Rev. xix., and the utmost that we find concerning them in these latter days; which we have much more cause to believe, than his unwarranted revelation here, prophesying what shall follow after his death, with the spirit of enmity, not of St. John.

He would fain bring us out of conceit with the good success, which God vouchsafed us. We measure not our cause by our success, but our success by our cause. Yet certainly in a good cause success is a good confirmation; for God hath promised it to good men almost in every leaf of scripture. If it argue not for us, we are sure it argues not against us; but as much or more for us, than ill success argues for them; for to the wicked God hath denounced ill success in all they take in hand.

He hopes much of those "softer tempers," as he calls them, and "less advantaged by his ruin, that their consciences do already" gripe them. It is true, there be a sort of moody, hotbrained, and always unedified consciences; apt to engage their leaders into great and dangerous affairs past retirement, and then upon a sudden qualm and swimming of their conscience, to betray them basely in the midst of what was chiefly undertaken for their sakes. Let such men never meet with any faithful parliament to hazard for them; never with any noble spirit to conduct and lead them out: but let them live and die in servile condition and their scrupulous queasiness, if no instruction will confirm them! Others there be, in whose consciences the loss of gain, and those advantages they hoped for, hath sprung a sudden leak. These are they that cry out, "The covenant broken!" and, to keep it better, slide back into neutrality, or join actually with incendiaries and malignants. But God hath eminently begun to punish those, first in Scotland, then in Ulster, who have provoked him with the most hateful kind of mockery, to break his covenant under pretence of strictest keeping it; and hath subjected them to those malignants, with whom they scrupled not to be associates. In God therefore we shall not fear what their false fraternity can do against us.

He seeks again with cunning words to turn our success into our sin: but might call to mind, that the scripture speaks of those also, who "when God slew them, then sought him;" yet did but "flatter him with their mouth, and lied to him with their tongues: for their heart was not right with him." And there was one, who in the time of his affliction trespassed more against God. This was that king Ahaz.

He glories much in the forgiveness of his enemies; so did his grandmother at her death. Wise men would sooner have believed him, had he not so often told us so. But he hopes to erect "the trophies of his charity over us." And trophies of charity no doubt will be as glorious as trumpets before the alms of hypocrites; and more especially the trophies of such an aspiring charity, as offers in his prayer to share victory with God's compassion, which is over all his works. Such prayers as these may haply catch the people, as was intended: but how they please God is to be much doubted, though prayed in secret, much less written to be divulged. Which perhaps may gain him after death, a short, contemptible, and soon fading reward; not what he aims at, to stir the constancy and solid firmness of any wise man, or to unsettle the conscience of any knowing Christian, (if he could ever aim at a thing so hopeless, and above the genius of his cleric elocution), but to catch the worthless approbation of an inconstant, irrational, and image-doting rabble; that like a credulous and hapless herd, begotten to servility, and enchanted with these popular institutes of tyranny, subscribed with a new device of the king's picture at his prayers, hold out both their ears with such delight and ravishment to be stigmatized and bored through, in witness of their own voluntary and beloved baseness. The rest, whom perhaps ignorance without malice, or some error, less than fatal, hath for the time misled, on this side sorcery or obduration, may find the grace and good guidance, to bethink themselves and recover.

From Commonwealth to Restoration

28. The Establishment of the Commonwealth

The Commonwealth of England was officially established by three pieces
of legislation which, because they did not receive the royal assent, are
properly called ordinances rather than acts. They were the ordinance
abolishing the office of the king (17 March 1649); the ordinance abolishing the House of Lords (19 March 1649); and the ordinance declaring
England to be a commonwealth (19 May 1649). In these brief pieces of
legislation a new theory of government was enunciated.

The Act Abolishing the Office of King

Whereas Charles Stuart, late King of England, Ireland, and the territories
and dominions thereunto belonging, hath by authority derived from Parliament been and is hereby declared to be justly condemned, adjudged to die,
and put to death, for many treasons, murders, and other heinous offences
committed by him, by which judgment he stood, and is hereby declared to
be attainted of high treason, whereby his issue and posterity, and all others
pretending title under him, are become incapable of the said Crowns, or of
being King or Queen of the said kingdom or dominions, or either or any of
them; be it therefore enacted and ordained, and it is enacted, ordained, and
declared by this present Parliament, and by authority thereof, that all the
people of England and Ireland, and the dominions and territories thereunto
belonging, of what degree or condition soever, are discharged of all fealty,
homage, and allegiance which is or shall be pretended to be due unto any
of the issue and posterity of the said late King, or any claiming under him;
and that Charles Stuart, eldest son, and James called Duke of York, second
son, and all other the issue and posterity of him the said late King, and
all and every person and persons pretending title from, by, or under him,
are and be disabled to hold or enjoy the said Crown of England and Ireland,
and other the dominions thereunto belonging, or any of them; or to have the
name, title, style, or dignity of King or Queen of England and Ireland,
Prince of Wales, or any of them; or to have and enjoy the power and domin-

From S. R. Gardiner, *Constitutional Documents of the Puritan Revolution* (Oxford: The
Clarendon Press, 1906), pp. 384–88.

ion of the said kingdom and dominions, or any of them, or the honors, manors, lands, tenements, possessions, and hereditaments belonging or appertaining to the said Crown of England and Ireland, and other the dominions aforesaid, or to any of them; or to the Principality of Wales, Duchy of Lancaster or Cornwall, or any or either of them, any law, statute, ordinance, usage, or custom to the contrary hereof in any wise notwithstanding.

And whereas it is and hath been found by experience, that the office of a King in this nation and Ireland, and to have the power thereof in any single person, is unnecessary, burdensome, and dangerous to the liberty, safety, and public interest of the people, and that for the most part, use hath been made of the regal power and prerogative to oppress and impoverish and enslave the subject; and that usually and naturally any one person in such power makes it his interest to incroach upon the just freedom and liberty of the people, and to promote the setting up of their own will and power above the laws, that so they might enslave these kingdoms to their own lust; be it therefore enacted and ordained by this present Parliament, and by authority of the same, that the office of a King in this nation shall not henceforth reside in or be exercised by any one single person; and that no one person whatsoever shall or may have, or hold the office, style, dignity, power, or authority of King of the said kingdoms and dominions, or any of them, or of the Prince of Wales, any law, statute, usage, or custom to the contrary thereof in any wise notwithstanding.

And it is hereby enacted, that if any person or persons shall endeavour to attempt by force of arms or otherwise, or be aiding, assisting, comforting, or abetting unto any person or persons that shall by any ways or means whatsoever endeavour or attempt the reviving or setting up again of any pretended right of the said Charles, eldest son to the said late King, James called Duke of York, or of any other the issue and posterity of the said late King, or of any person or persons claiming under him or them, to the said regal office, style, dignity, or authority, or to be Prince of Wales; or the promoting of any one person whatsoever to the name, style, dignity, power, prerogative, or authority of King of England and Ireland, and dominions aforesaid, or any of them; that then every such offence shall be deemed and adjudged high treason, and the offenders therein, their counsellors, procurers, aiders and abettors, being convicted of the said offence, or any of them, shall be deemed and adjudged traitors against the Parliament and people of England, and shall suffer, lose, and forfeit, and have such like and the same pains, forfeitures, judgments, and execution as is used in case of high treason.

And whereas by the abolition of the kingly office provided for in this Act, a most happy way is made for this nation (if God see it good) to return to its just and ancient right, of being governed by its own representatives or national meetings in council, from time to time chosen and entrusted for that purpose by the people, it is therefore resolved and declared by the Commons assembled in Parliament, that they will put a period to the sitting of this present Parliament, and dissolve the same so soon as may possibly stand with the safety of the people that hath betrusted them, and with what is absolutely necessary for the preserving and upholding the Government now settled in the way of a Commonwealth; and that they will carefully provide for the certain choosing, meeting, and sitting of the next and future representatives, with such other circumstances of freedom in choice and equality in distribution of members to be elected thereunto, as shall most conduce to the lasting freedom and good of this Commonwealth.

And it is hereby further enacted and declared, notwithstanding any thing contained in this Act, no person or persons of what condition and quality soever, within the Commonwealth of England and Ireland, dominion of Wales, the islands of Guernsey and Jersey, and town of Berwick-upon-Tweed, shall be discharged from the obedience and subjection which he and they owe to the Government of this nation, as it is now declared, but all and every of them shall in all things render and perform the same, as of right is due unto the supreme authority hereby declared to reside in this and the successive representatives of the people of this nation, and in them only.

An Act Abolishing the House of Lords

The Commons of England assembled in Parliament, finding by too long experience that the House of Lords is useless and dangerous to the people of England to be continued, have thought fit to ordain and enact, and be it ordained and enacted by this present Parliament, and by the authority of the same, that from henceforth the House of Lords in Parliament shall be and is hereby wholly abolished and taken away; and that the Lords shall not from henceforth meet or sit in the said House called the Lords' House, or in any other house or place whatsoever, as a House of Lords; nor shall sit, vote, advise, adjudge, or determine of any matter or thing whatsoever, as a House of Lords in Parliament: nevertheless it is hereby declared, that neither such Lords as have demeaned themselves with honour, courage, and fidelity to the Commonwealth, nor their posterities who shall continue so, shall be excluded from the public councils of the nation, but shall be admitted thereunto, and have their free vote in Parliament, if they shall be thereunto elected, as other persons of interest elected and qualified thereunto ought to have.

And be it further ordained and enacted by the authority aforesaid, that no Peer of this land, not being elected, qualified and sitting in Parliament as aforesaid, shall claim, have, or make use of any privilege of Parliament,

486   The English Revolution

aforesaid, shall claim, have, or make use of any privilege of Parliament, either in relation to his person, quality, or estate, any law, usage, or custom to the contrary notwithstanding.

An Act Declaring England to Be a Commonwealth

Be it declared and enacted by this present Parliament, and by the authority of the same, that the people of England, and of all the dominions and territories thereunto belonging, are and shall be, and are hereby constituted, made, established, and confirmed, to be a Commonwealth and Free State, and shall from henceforth be governed as a Commonwealth and Free State by the supreme authority of this nation, the representatives of the people in Parliament, and by such as they shall appoint and constitute as officers and ministers under them for the good of the people, and that without any King or House of Lords.

29. The Adultery Act (1650)

The abolition of bishops and the reform of the church left many matters that were once the jurisdiction of the ecclesiastical courts under the power of civil law. The Rump Parliament struggled to produce social legislation that would reflect more accurately the vision of godly justice espoused by the Commonwealth. It failed in most of its major efforts, especially in the area of law reform, but did succeed in passing bills to license civil marriage and to regulate social conduct. One of the more interesting pieces of social legislation was the Adultery Act of 1650. The issues of incest and adultery were serious ecclesiastical issues, for even among the more extreme religious groups it was believed that such acts were evidence of damnation and were grounds for expulsion from the congregation. Not surprisingly, the Rump Parliament adopted a stern attitude to the problem. The effectiveness of the Adultery Act is difficult to gauge but there is no evidence to suggest that anyone suffered the full rigors of its prescribed penalties.

From *Acts and Ordinances of the Interregnum, 1642–1660*, edited by C. H. Firth and R. S. Rait (London: HMSO, 1911), pp. 387–89.

An Act for Suppressing the Detestable Sins of Incest, Adultery and Fornication (10 May, 1650)

For the suppressing of the abominable and crying sins of Incest, Adultery and Fornication, wherewith this Land is much defiled, and Almighty God highly displeased; Be it Enacted by the Authority of this present Parliament, That if any person or persons whatsoever, shall from and after the Four and twentieth day of June, in the year of our Lord One thousand six hundred and fifty, Marry, or have the carnal knowledge of the Body of his or her Grandfather or Grandmother, Father or Mother, Brother or Sister, Son or Daughter, or Grandchilde, Fathers Brother or Sister, Mothers Brother or Sister, Fathers Wife, Mothers Husband, Sons Wife, Daughters Husband, Wives Mother or Daughter, Husbands Father or Son; all and every such Offences are hereby adjudged and declared Incest: And every such Offence shall be, and is hereby adjudged Felony; and every person offending therein, and confessing the same, or being thereof convicted by verdict upon Indictment or Presentment, before any Judge or Justices at the Assize or Sessions of the Peace, shall suffer death as in case of Felony, without benefit of Clergy: And all and every such Marriage and Marriages are hereby declared and adjudged to be void in Law, to all intents and purposes; and the Children begotten between such persons, notwithstanding any contract or solemnization of Marriage, to be illegitimate, and altogether disabled to claim or inherit any Lands or Inheritance whatsoever, by way of descent from, or to receive or challenge any Childes Portion in any Goods or Chattels of their said Parents, or any other Ancestor of such Parents.

And be it further Enacted by the authority aforesaid, That in case any married woman shall from and after the Four and twentieth day of June aforesaid, be carnally known by any man (other then her Husband) (except in Case of Ravishment) and of such offence or offences shall be convicted as aforesaid by confession or otherwise, every such Offence and Offences shall be and is hereby adjudged Felony: and every person, as well the man as the woman, offending therein, and confessing the same, or being thereof convicted by verdict upon Indictment or Presentment as aforesaid, shall suffer death as in case of Felony, without benefit of Clergy.

Provided, That this shall not extend to any man who at the time of such offence committed, is not knowing that such woman with whom such Offence is committed, is then married.

Provided also, That the said penalty in the case of Adultery aforesaid, shall not extend to any woman whose Husband shall be continually remaining beyond the Seas by the space of three years, or shall by common fame be reputed to be dead; nor to any woman whose husband shall absent himself from his said wife by the space of three years together, in any parts or places whatsoever, so as the said wife shall not know her said husband to be living within that time.

And be it further Enacted by the authority aforesaid, That if any man shall from and after the Four and twentieth day of June aforesaid, have the carnal knowledge of the body of any Virgin, unmaried Woman or Widow, every such man so offending, and confessing the same, or being thereof convicted by verdict upon Indictment or Presentment, as also every such woman so offending, and confessing the same, or being thereof convict as aforesaid, shall for every such offence be committed to the common Gaol, without Bail or Mainprize, there to continue for the space of three Moneths; and until he and she respectively shall give security, to be taken by one or more Justice or Justices of the Peace before whom such Confession or Conviction shall be had, to be of the good behavior for the space of one whole year then next ensuing.

And be if further Enacted by the authority aforesaid, That all and every person and persons who shall from and after the Four and twentieth day of June aforesaid, be convicted as aforesaid, by confession or otherwise, for being a common Bawd, be it man or woman, or wittingly keeping a common Brothel or Bawdy-house, shall for his or her first offence be openly whipped and set in the Pillory, and there marked with a hot Iron in the forehead with the Letter B and afterwards committed to Prison or the House of Correction, there to work for his or her living for the space of three years, without Bail or Mainprize, and until he or she shall put in sufficient Sureties for his or her good behavior during his or her life: And if any person by confession or otherwise shall be convicted of committing, after such Conviction, any of the said last recited offences, every such second offence shall be, and is hereby adjudged Felony; and the person and persons so offending shall suffer death, as in case of Felony, without benefit of Clergy.

And be it further Enacted by the authority aforesaid, That the Justices of Assize in their respective Circuits, and the Justices of Peace in every County, at their usual and General Sessions, are hereby authorized and required to give in charge to the Grand Jury to enquire of all and every the Crimes aforesaid: And the said Justices of Assize, Justices of the Peace in their General Sessions, and all and every Major and Justices of Peace of any City, Borough or Town Corporate, that have power to hear and determine Felonies at their usual Sessions, shall have full power and authority to enquire by verdict of twelve or more good and lawful men, within the said respective Counties and places aforesaid, of all and every the crimes and offences aforesaid, and upon Indictment or Presentment, to hear and determine the same, as in other cases of Felony or Trespass, Any Law, Usage or Custom to the contrary notwithstanding.

Provided, That no Attainder for any offence made Felony by this Act, shall make or work any corruption of Blood, loss of Dower, forfeiture of Goods, disinherison of Heir or Heirs.

Provided also, That no person or persons shall incur any of the penalties in this Act mentioned, unless the said person or persons be thereof indicted within twelve Moneths after the offence committed.

Provided also, That it shall be lawful for any person or persons who shall be indicted for any the offences aforesaid, to produce at their respective Tryals any witness or witnesses, for the clearing of themselves from the said offences whereof they shall be so indicted: And the Justices before whom such Tryal shall be so had, shall have power, and are hereby Authorized to Examine the said Witnesses upon Oath.

Provided, That no parties confession shall be taken as Evidence within this Act against any other, but onely against such party so confessing; nor the husband shall be taken as a Witness against his wife, nor the wife against her husband, for any offence punishable by this Act.

30. The Instrument of Government

The Instrument of Government was the first written constitution in English history. Its provisions can be compared with the Agreement of the People of 1647 and the Army Agreement of 1649 to gauge the development of both theoretical and practical solutions to the problems of government without the king. The Instrument followed the forcible dissolution of the Rump Parliament by Cromwell in 1653 and the dismal failure of a scheme to have a nominated parliament of godly men on the model of the Israelites (Barebones Parliament). It was largely the work of John Lambert who had been a Colonel in the New Model Army and who, along with Henry Ireton had been the army's chief tactician throughout the revolution. Lambert had urged the establishment of a written constitution before the dissolution of the Rump Parliament, but did not gain the support of other elements of the army. With the failure of Barebones Parliament, Lambert's proposal of grounding civil government in institutions rather than on individuals appealed to Cromwell who became, under its provisions, Lord Protector of England.

From *Acts and Ordinances of the Interregnum, 1642–1660,* edited by C. H. Firth and R. S. Rait (London: HMSO, 1911), pp. 405–17.

The government of the Commonwealth of England, Scotland, and Ireland, and the dominions thereunto belonging.

1. That the supreme legislative authority of the Commonwealth of England, Scotland, and Ireland, and the dominions thereunto belonging, shall be and reside in one person, and the people assembled in Parliament: the style of which person shall be the Lord Protector of the Commonwealth of England, Scotland, and Ireland.

2. That the exercise of the chief magistracy and the administration of the government over the said countries and dominions, and the people thereof, shall be in the Lord Protector, assisted with a council, the number whereof shall not exceed twenty-one, nor be less than thirteen.

3. That all writs, processes, commissions, patents, grants, and other things, which now run in the name and style of the keepers of the liberty of England by authority of Parliament, shall run in the name and style of the Lord Protector, from whom, for the future, shall be derived all magistracy and honours in these three nations; and have the power of pardons (except in case of murders and treason) and benefit of all forfeitures for the public use; and shall govern the said countries and dominions in all things by the advice of the council, and according to these presents and the laws.

4. That the Lord Protector, the Parliament sitting, shall dispose and order the militia and forces, both by sea and land, for the peace and good of the three nations, by consent of Parliament; and that the Lord Protector, with the advice and consent of the major part of the council, shall dispose and order the militia for the ends aforesaid in the intervals of Parliament.

5. That the Lord Protector, by the advice aforesaid, shall direct in all things concerning the keeping and holding of a good correspondency with foreign kings, princes, and states; and also, with the consent of the major part of the council, have the power of war and peace.

6. That the laws shall not be altered, suspended, abrogated, or repealed, nor any new law made, nor any tax, charge, or imposition laid upon the people, but by common consent in Parliament, save only as is expressed in the thirtieth article.

7. That there shall be a Parliament summoned to meet at Westminster upon the third day of September, 1654, and that successively a Parliament shall be summoned once in every third year, to be accounted from the dissolution of the present Parliament.

8. That neither the Parliament to be next summoned, nor any successive Parliaments, shall, during the time of five months, to be accounted from the day of their first meeting, be adjourned, prorogued, or dissolved, without their own consent.

9. That as well the next as all other successive Parliaments shall be summoned and elected in manner hereafter expressed; that is to say, the persons

to be chosen within England, Wales, the Isles of Jersey, Guernsey, and the town of Berwick-upon-Tweed, to sit and serve in Parliament, shall be, and not exceed, the number of four hundred. The persons to be chosen within Scotland, to sit and serve in Parliament, shall be, and not exceed, the number of thirty; and the persons to be chosen to sit in Parliament for Ireland shall be, and not exceed, the number of thirty.

10. That the persons to be elected to sit in Parliament from time to time, for the several counties of England, Wales, the Isles of Jersey and Guernsey, and the town of Berwick-upon-Tweed, and all places within the same respectively, shall be according to the proportions and numbers hereafter expressed: [list follows].

The distribution of the persons to be chosen for Scotland and Ireland, and the several counties, cities, and places therein, shall be according to such proportions and number as shall be agreed upon and declared by the Lord Protector and the major part of the council, before the sending forth writs of summons for the next Parliament.

11. That the summons to Parliament shall be by writ under the Great Seal of England, directed to the sheriffs of the several and respective counties, with such alteration as may suit with the present government, to be made by the Lord Protector and his council, which the Chancellor, Keeper, or Commissioners of the Great Seal shall seal, issue, and send abroad by warrant from the Lord Protector. If the Lord Protector shall not give warrant for issuing of writs of summons for the next Parliament, before the first of June, 1654, or for the Triennial Parliaments, before the first day of August in every third year, to be accounted as aforesaid; that then the Chancellor, Keeper, or Commissioners of the Great Seal for the time being, shall, without any warrant or direction, within seven days after the said first day of June, 1654, seal, issue, and send abroad writs of summons (changing therein what is to be changed as aforesaid) to the several and respective Sheriffs of England, Scotland, and Ireland, for summoning the Parliament to meet at Westminster, the third day of September next; and shall likewise, within seven days after the said first day of August, in every third year, to be accounted from the dissolution of the precedent Parliament, seal, issue, and send forth abroad several writs of summons (changing therein what is to be changed) as aforesaid, for summoning the Parliament to meet at Westminster the sixth of November in that third year. That the said several and respective Sheriffs shall, within ten days after the receipt of such writ as aforesaid, cause the same to be proclaimed and published in every market-town within his county upon the market-days thereof, between twelve and three of the clock; and shall then also publish and declare the certain day of the week and month, for choosing members to serve in Parliament for the body of the said county, according to the tenor

of the said writ, which shall be upon Wednesday five weeks after the date of the writ; and shall likewise declare the place where the election shall be made: for which purpose he shall appoint the most convenient place for the whole county to meet in; and shall send precepts for elections to be made in all and every city, town, borough, or place within his county, where elections are to be made by virtue of these presents, to the Mayor, Sheriff, or other head officer of such city, town, borough, or place, within three days after the receipt of such writ and writs; which the said Mayors, Sheriffs, and officers respectively are to make publication of, and of the certain day for such elections to be made in the said city, town, or place aforesaid, and to cause elections to be made accordingly.

12. That at the day and place of elections, the Sheriff of each county, and the said Mayors, Sheriffs, Bailiffs, and other head officers within their cities, towns, boroughs, and places respectively, shall take view of the said elections, and shall make return into the chancery within twenty days after the said elections, of the persons elected by the greater number of electors, under their hands and seals, between him on the one part, and the electors on the other part; wherein shall be contained, that the persons elected shall not have power to alter the government as it is hereby settled in one single person and a Parliament.

13. That the Sheriff, who shall wittingly and willingly make any false return, or neglect his duty, shall incur the penalty of 2000 marks of lawful English money; the one moiety to the Lord Protector, and the other moiety to such person as will sue for the same.

14. That all and every person and persons, who have aided, advised, assisted, or abetted in any war against the Parliament, since the first day of January, 1641 (unless they have been since in the service of the Parliament, and given signal testimony of their good affection thereunto) shall be disabled and incapable to be elected, or to give any vote in the election of any members to serve in the next Parliament, or in the three succeeding Triennial Parliaments.

15. That all such, who have advised, assisted, or abetted the rebellion of Ireland, shall be disabled and incapable for ever to be elected, or give any vote in the election of any member to serve in Parliament; as also all such who do or shall profess the Roman Catholic religion.

16. That all votes and elections given or made contrary, or not according to these qualifications, shall be null and void; and if any person, who is hereby made incapable, shall give his vote for election of members to serve in Parliament, such person shall lose and forfeit one full year's value of his real estate, and one full third part of his personal estate; one moiety thereof to the Lord Protector, and the other moiety to him or them who shall sue for the same.

17. That the persons who shall be elected to serve in Parliament, shall be such (and no other than such) as are persons of known integrity, fearing God, and of good conversation, and being of the age of twenty-one years.

18. That all and every person and persons seised or possessed to his own use, of any estate, real or personal, to the value of £200, and not within the aforesaid exceptions, shall be capable to elect members to serve in Parliament for counties.

19. That the Chancellor, Keeper, or Commissioners of the Great Seal, shall be sworn before they enter into their offices, truly and faithfully to issue forth, and send abroad, writs of summons to Parliament, at the times and in the manner before expressed: and in case of neglect or failure to issue and send abroad writs accordingly, he or they shall for every such offence be guilty of high treason, and suffer the pains and penalties thereof.

20. That in case writs be not issued out, as is before expressed, but that there be a neglect therein, fifteen days after the time wherein the same ought to be issued out by the Chancellor, Keeper, or Commissioners of the Great Seal; that then the Parliament shall, as often as such failure shall happen, assemble and be held at Westminster, in the usual place, at the times prefixed, in manner and by the means hereafter expressed; that is to say, that the sheriffs of the several and respective counties, sheriffdoms, cities, boroughs, and places aforesaid within England, Wales, Scotland, and Ireland, the Chancellor, Masters, and Scholars of the Universities of Oxford and Cambridge, and the Mayor and Bailiffs of the borough of Berwick-upon-Tweed, and other places aforesaid respectively, shall at the several courts and places to be appointed as aforesaid, within thirty days after the said fifteen days, cause such members to be chosen for their said several and respective counties, sheriffdoms, universities, cities, boroughs, and places aforesaid, by such persons, and in such manner, as if several and respective writs of summons to Parliament under the Great Seal had issued and been awarded according to the tenor aforesaid: that if the sheriff, or other persons authorised, shall neglect his or their duty herein, that all and every such sheriff and person authorised as aforesaid, so neglecting his or their duty, shall, for every such offence, be guilty of high treason, and shall suffer the pains and penalties thereof.

21. That the clerk, called the clerk of the Commonwealth in Chancery for the time being, and all others, who shall afterwards execute that office, to whom the returns shall be made, shall for the next Parliament, and the two succeeding triennial Parliaments, the next day after such return, certify the names of the several persons so returned, and of the places for which he and they were chosen respectively, unto the Council; who shall peruse the said returns, and examine whether the persons so elected and

returned be such as is agreeable to the qualifications, and not disabled to be elected: and that every person and persons being so duly elected, and being approved of by the major part of the Council to be persons not disabled, but qualified as aforesaid, shall be esteemed a member of Parliament, and be admitted to sit in Parliament, and not otherwise.

22. That the persons so chosen and assembled in manner aforesaid, or any sixty of them, shall be, and be deemed the Parliament of England, Scotland, and Ireland; and the supreme legislative power to be and reside in the Lord Protector and such Parliament, in manner herein expressed.

23. That the Lord Protector, with the advice of the major part of the Council, shall at any other time than is before expressed, when the necessities of the State shall require it, summon Parliaments in manner before expressed, which shall not be adjourned, prorogued, or dissolved without their own consent, during the first three months of their sitting. And in case of future war with any foreign State, a Parliament shall be forthwith summoned for their advice concerning the same.

24. That all Bills agreed unto by the Parliament, shall be presented to the Lord Protector for his consent; and in case he shall not give his consent thereto within twenty days after they shall be presented to him, or give satisfaction to the Parliament within the time limited, that then, upon declaration of the Parliament that the Lord Protector hath not consented nor given satisfaction, such Bills shall pass into and become laws, although he shall not give his consent thereunto; provided such Bills contain nothing in them contrary to the matters contained in these presents.

25. That Henry Lawrence, Esq., &c., or any seven of them, shall be a Council for the purposes expressed in this writing; and upon the death or other removal of any of them, the Parliament shall nominate six persons of ability, integrity, and fearing God, for every one that is dead or removed; out of which the major part of the Council shall elect two, and present them to the Lord Protector, of which he shall elect one; and in case the Parliament shall not nominate within twenty days after notice given unto them thereof, the major part of the Council shall nominate three as aforesaid to the Lord Protector, who out of them shall supply the vacancy; and until this choice be made, the remaining part of the Council shall execute as fully in all things, as if their number were full. And in case of corruption, or other miscarriage in any of the Council in their trust, the Parliament shall appoint seven of their number, and the Council six, who, together with the Lord Chancellor, Lord Keeper, or Commissioners of the Great Seal for the time being, shall have power to hear and determine such corruption and miscarriage, and to award and inflict punishment, as the nature of the offence shall deserve, which punishment shall not be pardoned or remitted

by the Lord Protector; and, in the interval of Parliaments, the major part of the Council, with the consent of the Lord Protector, may, for corruption or other miscarriage as aforesaid, suspend any of their number from the exercise of their trust, if they shall find it just, until the matter shall be heard and examined as aforesaid.

26. That the Lord Protector and the major part of the Council aforesaid may, at any time before the meeting of the next Parliament, add to the Council such persons as they shall think fit, provided the number of the Council be not made thereby to exceed twenty-one, and the quorum to be proportioned accordingly by the Lord Protector and the major part of the Council.

27. That a constant yearly revenue shall be raised, settled, and established for maintaining of 10,000 horse and dragoons, and 20,000 foot, in England, Scotland and Ireland, for the defence and security thereof, and also for a convenient number of ships for guarding of the seas; besides £200,000 per annum for defraying the other necessary charges of administration of justice, and other expenses of the Government, which revenue shall be raised by the customs, and such other ways and means as shall be agreed upon by the Lord Protector and the Council, and shall not be taken away or diminished, nor the way agreed upon for raising the same altered, but by the consent of the Lord Protector and the Parliament.

28. That the said yearly revenue shall be paid into the public treasury, and shall be issued out for the uses aforesaid.

29. That in case there shall not be cause hereafter to keep up so great a defence both at land or sea, but that there be an abatement made thereof, the money which will be saved thereby shall remain in bank for the public service, and not be employed to any other use but by consent of Parliament, or, in the intervals of Parliament, by the Lord Protector and major part of the Council.

30. That the raising of money for defraying the charge of the present extraordinary forces, both at sea and land, in respect of the present wars, shall be by consent of Parliament, and not otherwise: save only that the Lord Protector, with the consent of the major part of the Council, for preventing the disorders and dangers which might otherwise fall out both by sea and land, shall have power, until the meeting of the first Parliament, to raise money for the purposes aforesaid; and also to make laws and ordinances for the peace and welfare of these nations where it shall be necessary, which shall be binding and in force, until order shall be taken in Parliament concerning the same.

31. That the lands, tenements, rents, royalties, jurisdictions and hereditaments which remain yet unsold or undisposed of, by Act or Ordinance of

Parliament, belonging to the Commonwealth (except the forests and chases, and the honours and manors belonging to the same; the lands of the rebels in Ireland, lying in the four counties of Dublin, Cork, Kildare, and Carlow; the lands forfeited by the people of Scotland in the late wars, and also the lands of Papists and delinquents in England who have not yet compounded), shall be vested in the Lord Protector, to hold, to him and his successors, Lords Protectors of these nations, and shall not be alienated but by consent in Parliament. And all debts, fines, issues, amercements, penalties and profits, certain and casual, due to the Keepers of the liberties of England by authority of Parliament, shall be due to the Lord Protector, and be payable into his public receipt, and shall be recovered and prosecuted in his name.

32. That the office of Lord Protector over these nations shall be elective and not hereditary; and upon the death of the Lord Protector, another fit person shall be forthwith elected to succeed him in the Government; which election shall be by the Council, who, immediately upon the death of the Lord Protector, shall assemble in the Chamber where they usually sit in Council; and, having given notice to all their members of the cause of their assembling, shall, being thirteen at least present, proceed to the election; and, before they depart the said Chamber, shall elect a fit person to succeed in the Government, and forthwith cause proclamation thereof to be made in all the three nations as shall be requisite; and the person that they, or the major part of them, shall elect as aforesaid, shall be, and shall be taken to be, Lord Protector over these nations of England, Scotland and Ireland, and the dominions thereto belonging. Provided that none of the children of the late King, nor any of his line or family, be elected to be Lord Protector or other Chief Magistrate over these nations, or any the dominions thereto belonging. And until the aforesaid election be past, the Council shall take care of the Government, and administer in all things as fully as the Lord Protector, or the Lord Protector and Council are enabled to do.

33. That Oliver Cromwell, Captain-General of the forces of England, Scotland and Ireland, shall be, and is hereby declared to be, Lord Protector of the Commonwealth of England, Scotland and Ireland, and the dominions thereto belonging, for his life.

34. That the Chancellor, Keeper or Commissioners of the Great Seal, the Treasurer, Admiral, Chief Governors of Ireland and Scotland, and the Chief Justices of both the Benches, shall be chosen by the approbation of Parliament; and, in the intervals of Parliament, by the approbation of the major part of the Council, to be afterwards approved by the Parliament.

35. That the Christian religion, as contained in the Scriptures, be held forth and recommended as the public profession of these nations; and that, as soon as may be, a provision, less subject to scruple and contention, and more certain than the present, be made for the encouragement and mainte-

nance of able and painful teachers, for the instructing the people, and for discovery and confutation of error, hereby, and whatever is contrary to sound doctrine; and until such provision be made, the present maintenance shall not be taken away or impeached.

36. That to the public profession held forth none shall be compelled by penalties or otherwise; but that endeavours be used to win them by sound doctrine and the example of a good conversation.

37. That such as profess faith in God by Jesus Christ (though differing in judgment from the doctrine, worship or discipline publicly held forth) shall not be restrained from, but shall be protected in, the profession of the faith and exercise of their religion; so as they abuse not this liberty to the civil injury of others and to the actual disturbance of the public peace on their parts: provided this liberty be not extended to Popery or Prelacy, nor to such as, under the profession of Christ, hold forth and practise licentiousness.

38. That all laws, statutes and ordinances, and clauses in any law, statute or ordinance to the contrary of the aforesaid liberty, shall be esteemed as null and void.

39. That the Acts and Ordinances of Parliament made for the sale or other disposition of the lands, rents and hereditaments of the late King, Queen, and Prince, of Archbishops and Bishops, &c., Deans and Chapters, the lands of delinquents and forest-lands, or any of them, or of any other lands, tenements, rents and hereditaments belonging to the Commonwealth, shall nowise be impeached or made invalid, but shall remain good and firm; and that the securities given by Act and Ordinance of Parliament for any sum or sums of money, by any of the said lands, the excise, or any other public revenue; and also the securities given by the public faith of the nation, and the engagement of the public faith for satisfaction of debts and damages, shall remain firm and good, and not be made void and invalid upon any pretence whatsoever.

40. That the Articles given to or made with the enemy, and afterwards confirmed by Parliament, shall be performed and made good to the persons concerned therein; and that such appeals as were depending in the last Parliament for relief concerning bills of sale of delinquents' estates, may be heard and determined the next Parliament, any thing in this writing or otherwise to the contrary notwithstanding.

41. That every successive Lord Protector over these nations shall take and subscribe a solemn oath, in the presence of the Council, and such others as they shall call to them, that he will seek the peace, quiet and welfare of these nations, cause law and justice to be equally administered; and that he will not violate or infringe the matters and things contained in this writing, and in all other things will, to his power and to the best of his

understanding, govern these nations according to the laws, statutes and customs thereof.

42. That each person of the Council shall, before they enter upon their trust, take and subscribe an oath, that they will be true and faithful in their trust, according to the best of their knowledge; and that in the election of every successive Lord Protector they shall proceed therein impartially, and do nothing therein for any promise, fear, favour or reward.

31. Sir Henry Vane, *A Healing Question Propounded* (1656)

The establishment of the Protectorate further fragmented the revolutionary movement. Many of those who were instrumental in forming the Commonwealth had become republicans by the 1650s. They resented Cromwell's forcible dissolution of the Rump Parliament in 1653 and helped bring about the collapse of the Barebones Parliament and the failure of the Parliament of 1654. Principally, republicans believed that the only legitimate center of authority in the nation was Parliament. They attacked Cromwell and the army in the same terms as they had Charles I and his ministers. In consequence, Cromwell struck back excluding them from positions of trust in his government.

Sir Henry Vane, Jr. (1613–62) was among the most remarkable men of his age. He came from a wealthy Essex family, and his father was a successful courtier under Charles I. The younger Vane, after a traditional education, underwent a religious conversion, and emigrated to the new world. There he was elected governor of the colony of Massachusetts at the age of twenty-three. He returned to England and was selected a Member of the Long Parliament for Hull. An early leader of the more radical reformers, he was instrumental in the execution of the earl of Strafford, and in negotiating the treaty signed with the Scots (The Solemn League and Covenant) in 1643; but as the army's power grew, Vane's influence waned. He did not take an active role in the central events of the revolution, but continued a champion of religious freedom, first against the Presbyterians and then against the Cromwellian protectorate. He was imprisoned by Cromwell, and at the Restoration was excluded from the general pardon. Tried and convicted, he was executed for his part in the revolution.

From *Somer Tracts*, edited by Sir Walter Scott, 13 vols. (London, 1748–52), 6:304–15.

A Healing Question propounded and resolved upon Occasion of the late publique and seasonable Call to Humiliation, in order to Love and Union amongst the honest Party, and with a Desire to apply Balsome to the Wound before it become incurable

The question propounded is, What possibility doth yet remain (all things considered) of reconciling and uniting the dissenting judgments of honest men within the three nations, who still pretend to agree in the spirit, justice, and reason of the same good cause, and what is the means to effect this?

Answ. If it be taken for granted (as on the magistrates part, from the ground inviting the people of England and Wales to a solemn day of fasting and humiliation, may not be despaired of) that all the dissenting parties agree still in the spirit and reason of the same righteous cause, the resolution seems very clear in the affirmative; arguing not only for a possibility, but a great probability hereof, nay a necessity daily approaching neerer and neerer to compel it, if any or all of the dissenting parties intend or desire to be safe from the danger of the common enemy, who is not out of work, though at present much out of sight and observation.

The grounds of this are briefly these: First, the cause hath still the same goodness in it as ever; and is or ought to be as much in the hearts of all good people that have adhered to it; it is not less to be valued now, then when neither blood nor treasure were thought too dear to carry it out and hold it up from sinking; and hath the same omnipotent God, whose great name is concerned in it, as well as his peoples outward safety and welfare; who knows also how to give a revival to it when secondary instruments and visible means fail, or prove deceitful.

Secondly, The persons concerned and engaged in this cause are still the same as before, with the advantage of being more tried, more enured to danger and hardship, and more endeared to one another, by their various and great experiences, as well of their own hearts as their fellow brethrens: These are the same still in heart, and desire after the same thing, which is, that, being freed out of the hands of their enemies, they may serve the Lord without fear in holiness and righteousness all the daies of their life.

As they have had this great good finally in their aims (if declarations to men and appeals to God signifie any thing) so as a requisite to attain this, they did with great cheerfulness and unanimity, draw out themselves to the utmost in the maintenance of a war, when all other means first essayed proved ineffectual. In the management of this war it pleased God, the righteous Judge, (who was appealed to in the controversie) so to bless the council and forces of the persons concerned and engaged in this cause, as in the end to make them absolute and compleat conquerors over their common enemy; and by this means they had added unto the natural right which was in them before (and so declared by their representatives in parliament assembled) the right of conquest for the strengthning of their just claim to be governed by national councils, and successive representatives of their own election and setting up. This they once thought they had been in possession of when it was ratified, as it were, in the blood of the last king: But of late a great interruption having happened unto them in their former expectations, and instead thereof, something rising up that seems rather accommodated to the private and selfish interest of a particular part (in comparison) then truly adequate to the common good and concern of the whole body engaged in this cause: Hence it is that this compacted body is now falling asunder into many dissenting parts (a thing not unforeseen, nor unhoped for, by the common enemy all along as their last relief) and if these breaches be not timely healed, and the offences (before they take too deep root) removed, they will certainly work more to the advantage of the common enemy, than any of their own unwearied endeavours and dangerous contrivances in forraign parts put all together.

A serious discussion and sober enlarging upon these grounds will quickly give an insight into the state of the question, and naturally tend to a plain and familiar resolution thereof.

That which is first to be opened is the nature and goodness of the cause; which had it not carried in it its own evidence, would scarce have found so many of the people of God adherers to it within the three nations, contributing either their counsels, their purses, their bodily pains, or their affections and prayers, as a combined strength, without which the military force alone would have been little available to subdue the common enemy, and restore to this whole body their just natural rights in civil things, and true freedom in matters of conscience.

The two last mentioned particulars, rightly stated, will evidence sufficiently the nature and goodness of this cause.

For the first of these, that is to say, the naturall right, which the whole party of honest men adhering to this cause, are by the success of their armes restored unto, fortified in, and may claim as their undeniable priviledge, that righteously cannot be taken from them, nor they debarred from bringing into exercise: it lies in this.

They are to have and enjoy the freedom (by way of dutiful compliance and condiscention from all the parts and members of this society) to set up meet persons in the place of supreme judicature and authority amongst them; whereby they may have the use and benefit of the choisest light and wisdom of the nation, that they are capable to call forth, for the rule and government under which they will live, and through the orderly exercise of such measure of wisdom and counsel as the Lord in this way shall please to give unto them, to shape and form all subordinate actings and administrations of rule and government, so as shall best answere the publique welfare and safety of the whole.

This in substance is the right and freedom contained in the nature and goodnesse of the cause wherein the honest party have been engaged: For in this all the particulars of our civil right and freedom are comprehended, conserved in, and derived from their proper root; in which whilst they grow, they will ever thrive, flourish, and increase: Whereas on the contrary, if there be never so many fair branches of liberty planted on the root of a private and selfish interest, they will not long prosper, but must within a little time wither and degenerate into the nature of that whereinto they are planted. And hence indeed sprung the evill of that government which rose in and with the Norman conquest.

The root and bottom upon which it stood was not publique interest, but the private lust and will of the conquerour, who by force of armes did at first detain the right and freedom which was, and is, due to the whole body of the people; for whose safety and good, government it self is ordained by God, not for the particular benefit of the rulers, as a distinct and private interest of their own; which yet for the most part is not onely preferred before the common good, but upheld in opposition thereunto. And as at first the conquerour did by violence and force deny this freedom to the people, which was their natural right and priviledge, so he and his successours all along lay as bars and impediments to the true national interest and publique good, in the very national councils and assemblies themselves; which were constituted in such a manner as most served for the upholding of the private interest of their families. And this being challenged by them as their prerogative, was found by the people assembled in parliament most unrighteous, burdensome, and destructive to their liberty. And when they once perceived that by this engine all their just rights were like to be destroyed, especially being backed, as it was, with the power of the militia, which the late king for that purpose had assumed into his hands, and would not upon the peoples application to him in parliament part with into the hands of that great council, who were best to be in trusted with the nations safety: This was the ground of the quarrel, upon a civil account, between the king and his party, and the whole body of adherents to the cause of the peoples true liberty; whereof this short touch hath been given, and shall suffice for the opening of the first branch of this clause.

The second branch which remains briefly to be handled, is that which also upon the grounds of naturall right is to be laid claime unto, but distinguishes it self from the former, as it respects a more heavenly and excellent object, wherein the freedom is to be exercised and enjoined; that is to say, matters of religion, or that concern the service and worship of God.

Unto this freedom, the nations of the world have right and title, by the purchase of Christ's blood, who, by vertue of his death and resurrection, is become the sole Lord and Ruler in and over the conscience; for to this end Christ died, rose, and revived, that he might be Lord both of the dead and the living, and that every one might give an account of himself in all matters of Gods worship, unto God and Christ alone, as their own master; unto whom they stand or fall in judgment, and are not in these things to be oppressed, or brought before the judgment-seats of men. For why shouldest thou set at naught thy brother in matters of his faith and conscience, and herein intrude into the proper office of Christ, since we are all to stand at the judgment-seat of Christ, whether governors or governed, and by his decision only are capable of being declared with certainty, to be in the right or in the wrong?

By vertue then of this supream law, sealed and confirmed in the blood of Christ unto all men, (whose souls he challenges a propriety in, to bring under his inward rule in the service and worship of God) it is that all magistrates are to feare and forbear intermedling with, giving rule, or imposing in those matters; they are to content themselves with what is plain in their commission, as ordained of God to be his minister unto men for good, whilest they approve themselves the doers of that which is good in the sight of men, and whereof earthly and worldly judicatures are capable to make a clear and perfect judgment: in which case, the magistrate is to be for praise and protection to them. In like manner he is to be a minister of terrour and revenge to those that doe evil in matters of outward practice, converse, and dealings in the things of this life between man and man, for the cause whereof the judicatures of men are appointed and set up. But to exceed these limits, as it is not safe nor warrantable for the magistrate, (in that he who is higher then the highest, regards and will shew himselfe displeased at it,) so neither is it good for the people, who hereby are nourished up in a biting, devouring, wrathful spirit, one against another, and are found transgressors of that royal law which forbids us to doe that unto another which we would not have them do unto us, were we in their condition.

This freedome then is of high concern to be had and enjoyed, as well for the magistrates sake as for the peoples common good; and it consists, as hath been said, in the magistrates forbearing to put forth the power of rule and coercion in things that God hath exempted out of his commission. So that all care requisite for the peoples obtaining this may be exercised with great ease, if it be taken in its proper season, and that this restraint be laid upon the supream power before it be erected, as a fundamental constitution among others, upon which the free consent of the people is given to have the persons brought into the exercise of supreme authority over them, and on their behalf; and if besides, as a further confirmation hereunto, it be acknowledged the voluntary act of the ruling power, when once brought into a capacity of acting legislatively, that herein they are bound up and judge it their duty so to be, (both in reference to God the institor of magistracy, and in reference to the whole body by whom they are entrusted) this great blessing will hereby be so well provided for, that we shall have no cause to fear, as it may be ordered.

By this means a great part of the outward exercise of antichristian tyranny and bondage will be plucked up by the very roots, which, till some such course be held in it, will be alwayes apt to renew and sprout out afresh under some new forme or refined appearances, as by late years experience we have been taught. For, since the fall of the bishops and persecuting presbyteries, the same spirit is apt to arise in the next sort of clergy that can get the ear of the magistrate, and pretend to the keeping and ruling the conscience of the governours: although this spirit and practice hath been all along decried by the faithful adherents to this cause, as a most sore oppression and insufferable yoke of bondage, most unrighteously kept up over the consciences of the people, and therefore judged by them most needful to be taken out of the way. And in this matter the present governours have been willing very eminently to give their testimony in their publique declarations; however, in practice there is much of grievance yet found among us, though more in probability, from the officiousnesse of subordinate ministers, then any clear purpose or designe of the chief in power.

Having thus shewed what the true freedom is, in both branches of it that shines forth in the righteous cause, wherein the good people of these nations have so deeply engaged, it will not be improper in the next place to consider two particulars more that give still further light into the matter in question; as, first, The qualifications of the persons that have adhered to this cause. Secondly, The capacity wherein they have been found from time to time carrying it on.

As to their qualification, they have in the general distinguished themselves and been made known by a forwardness to assist and own the publique welfare and good of the nation, for the attaining and preserving the just rights and liberties thereof, asserted and witnessed unto in the true stating of this cause, according to the two branches thereof already spoken to. They have shewed themselves upon all occasions desirers and lovers of true freedom, either in civils or in spirituals, or in both. To express their value thereof and faithfulness to the same, they have largely contributed, in one kind or other, what was proper to each in his place to doe; which actions of theirs proceeding from hearts sincerely affected to the cause, created in them a right to be of an incorporation and society by themselves, under the name of *The Good Party;* having been, from the beginning unto this day, publiquely and commonly so acknowledged by way of distinction from all neuters, close and open enemies, and deceitful friends or apostates. These, in order to the maintaining of this cause, have stood by the army, in defence and support thereof, against all opposition whatever, as those that, by the growing light of these times, have been taught and led forth in their experiences to look above and beyond the letter, forme, and outward circumstances of government, into the inward reason and spirit thereof, herein only to fix and terminate, to the leaving behind all empty shadows that would obtrude themselves in the place of true freedom.

Secondly, As to the capacity wherein these persons thus qualified have acted, it hath been very variable and subject to great changes; sometimes in one form, and sometimes in another, and very seldome, if ever at all, so exactly and in all points consonant to the rule of former laws and constitutions of government, as to be clearly and fully justified by them any longer then the law of successe and conquest did uphold them who had the inward warrant of justice and righteousnesse to encourage them in such their actings.

The utmost and last reserve, therefore, which they have had, in case all other failed, hath been their military capacity, not only strictly taken for the standing army, but in the largest sense, wherein the whole party may (with the army, and under that military constitution and conduct, which by the providence of God they shall then be found in,) associate themselves in the best order they can for the common defence and safety of the whole. As not ignorant, that, when once embodied in this their military posture, in such manner as by common consent shall be found requisite for the safety of the body, they are most irresistible, absolute, and comprehensive in their power; having that wherein the substance of all government is contained, and under the protection whereof, and safety that may be maintained thereby, they can contrive and determine in what manner this irresistible, absolute, and boundless power, unto which they are now arrived in this their military capacity, shall have just and due limits set unto it, and be drawn out in a meet and orderly way of exercise, for the commonwealth and safety of the whole body, under the rule and oversight of a supreame judicature; unto the wisdome of whose laws and orders, the sword is to become most entirely subject and subservient, and this without the least cause of jealousie or unsafety, either to the standing army or any member thereof, or unto the good people adhering to this cause, or any one of them; since the interest of both, by this mutual action of either, will be so combined together in one, (even in that wherein before they were distinct) that all just cause of difference, fear, animosity, emulation, jealousie, or the like, will be wholly abolished and removed.

For when once the whole body of the good people find that the military interest and capacity is their own, and that into which necessity at the last may bring the whole party (whereof of right a place is to be reserved for them) and that herein they are so far from being in subjection or slavery, that in this posture they are most properly soveraign and possesse their right of natural soveraignty, they will presently see a necessity of continuing ever one with their army, raised and maintained by them, for the promoting this cause against the common enemy; who in his next attempt will put for all with greater desperatenesse and rage then ever.

Again, when once the standing army and their governours shall also find that, by setting and keeping up themselves in a divided interest from the rest of the body of honest men, they withhold from themselves those contributions in all voluntary and cheerful assistances by the affections and prayers, by the persons and purses of the good party, in the weakening themselves thereby; as to any vigorous support from them in the times of most imminent danger, (whereof the late king had an experience, that will not suddenly be out of memory, when he undertook the war in the beginning of these troubles against the Scots, and was, in a manner, therein deserted by all the good party in England,) they will then find (if they stay not till it be too late) they, by espousing the interests of the people, in submitting themselves with their fellow adherents to the cause, under the rule and authority of their own supream judicature, they lose not their power or sovereignty, but, becoming one civil or politique incorporation with the whole party of honest men, they doe therein keep the sovereignty, as originally seated in themselves, and part with it only but as by deputation and representation of themselves; when it is brought into an orderly way of exercise, by being put into the hands of persons chosen and entrusted by themselves to that purpose.

By this mutual and happy transition which may be made between the party of honest men in the three nations virtually in arms, and those actually so now in power at the head of the army, how suddenly would the union of the whole body be consolidated, and made so firm as it will not need to fear all the designs and attempts of the common enemy; especially, if herein they unite themselves in the first place to the Lord, as willing to follow his providence, and observe his will in the way and manner of bringing this to passe. In which case we shall not need to fear what all the gates of hell are able to do in opposition thereunto.

It is not then the standing and being of the present army and military forces in the three nations that is lyable to exception of offence from any dissenting judgments at this time amongst the honest well-affected party: in and with them, under God, stand the welfare and outward safety of the whole body, and to be enemies to them, or wish them hurt, were to doe it to themselves, and, by trying such conclusions, to play the game of the common enemy, to the utter ruine and destruction, not onely of the true freedom aimed at and contended for in the late wars, but of the very persons themselves that have been in any sort active or eminent promoters thereof.

The army, considered as it is in the hands of an honest and wise general and sober faithful officers, embodied with the rest of the party of honest men, and espousing still the same cause, and acting in their primitive simplicity, humility, and trust in reference to the welfare and safety of the whole body, is the only justifyable and most advantagious posture and capacity that the good party at present can find themselves in, in order to the obtaining that true freedom they have fought for, and possessing of it in the establishment thereof upon the true basis and foundation, as hath been shewed of right government.

That therein the offence lies, and which causes such great thoughts of heart amongst the honest party (if it may be freely expressed, as sure it may, when the magistrate himself professes he doth but desire and wait for conviction therein,) is in short this:

That when the right and priviledge is returned, nay is restored by conquest unto the whole body, (that forfeited not their interest therein) of freely disposing themselves in such a constitution of righteous government as may best answer the end held forth in this cause; that nevertheless, either through delay they should be withheld as they are, or through design they should come at last to be utterly denied the exercise of this their right, upon pretence that they are not in capacity as yet to use it; which indeed hath some truth in it, if those that are now in power and have the command of the arms do not prepare all things requisite thereunto, as they may, and, like faithful guardians to the commonwealth, admitted to be in its nonage, they ought.

But if the bringing of true freedom into exercise amongst men, yea, so refined a party of men, be impossible, why hath this been concealed all this while? and why was it not thought on before so much blood was spilt and treasure spent? Surely such a thing as this was judged real and practicable, not imaginary and notional.

Besides, Why may it not suffice to have been thus long delayed and withheld from the whole body, at least as to its being brought by them into exercise now at last? Surely the longer it is withheld the stronger jealousies do increase, that it is intended to be assumed and ingrossed by a party onely, to the leaving the rest of the body, (who in all reason and justice ought to be equally participants with the other in the right and benefit of the conquest, for as much as the war was managed at the expence and for the safety of the whole) in a condition almost as much exposed, and subject to be imposed upon as if they been enemies and conquered, not in any sense conquerors.

If ever such an unrighteous, unkinde, and deceitful dealing with brethren should happen, although it might continue above the reach of question from humane judicature, yet can we think it possible it should escape and go unpunished by the immediate hand of the righteous Judge of the whole world, when he ariseth out of his place to do right to the oppressed?

Nay, if in stead of favouring and promoting the peoples common good and welfare, self-interest and private gain should evidently appear to be the things we have aimed at all along; if those very tyrannical principles and antichristian reliques which God by us hath punished in our predecessors, should again revive, spring up afresh, and shew themselves lodged also and retained in our bosomes, rendring us of the number of those that have forgot they were purged from their old sins, and declaring us to be such as to please a covetous mind, do withhold from destruction that which God hath designed to the curse of his vengeance. If all those great advantages of serving the Lords will and design in procuring and advancing his peoples true welfare and outward safety, which (as the fruit of his blessing upon our armies) have so miraculously fallen into our hands, shall at last be wrested and mis-improved to the enriching and greatning of our selves: If these things should ever be found amongst us, (which the Lord in mercy forbid) shall we need to look any further for the accursed thing? Will not our consciences shew us, from the light of the word and spirit of God, how neer a conformity these actions would hold therewith? which sin, (Josh. 7) became a curse to the camp, and withheld the Lord from going any more amongst them, or going out with their forces. And did the action of Achan import any more than these two things? First, he saved and kept from destruction the goodly Babylonish garment, which was devoted by God thereunto. Secondly, he brought not in the fruit and gain of the conquest into the Lords treasure, but covetously went about to convert it to his own proper use. To do this is to take of the accursed thing, which (Josh. 7) all Israel was said to do in the sin of Achan, and to have stolen and dissembled likewise, and to put it amongst their own stuffe. This caused the anger of the Lord to kindle against Israel, and made them unable to stand before their enemies, but their hearts melted as water. And thus far the Lord is concerned, if such an evil as this shall lie hid in the midst of us. But to return to what we were upon before.

The matter which is in question among the dissenting parts of the whole body of honest men, is not so trivial and of such small consequences as some would make it. 'Tis in effect the main and whole of the cause, without which all the freedome which the people have or can have, is in comparison but shadow and in name onely, and therefore can never give that peace and satisfaction to the body, which is requisite unto a durable and solid settlement. This is that which makes all sound and safe at the root, and gives the right ballance necessary to be held up between soveraignty and subjection, in the exercise of all righteous government; applying the use of the sword to the promoting and upholding the publick safety and welfare of the whole body, in preference, and, if need be, in opposition, unto any of the parts; whilst yet, by its equal and impartiall administration in reference unto each, it doth withall maintaine the whole body in a most delightful harmony, welfare, and correspondency. The sword never can, nor is it to be expected ever will do this, while the soveraignty is admitted and placed any where else than in the whole body of the people that have adhered to the cause, and by them be derived unto their successive representatives, as the most equal and impartial judicature for the effecting hereof.

Where there is then a righteous and good constitution of government, there is first an orderly union of many understandings together, as the publick and common supream judicature or visible soveraignty set in a way of free and orderly exercise, for the directing and applying the use of the ruling power or the sword, to promote the interest and common welfare of the whole, without any disturbance or annoyance from within or without. And then, secondly, there is a like union and readinesse of will in all the individuals in their private capacities, to execute and obey (by all the power requisite and that they are able to put forth) those soveraign laws and orders issued out by their own deputies and trustees.

A supream judicature, thus made the representative of the whole, is that which we say will most naturally care, and most equally provide for the common good and safety. Though by this it is not denied but that the supream power, when by free consent 'tis placed in a single person, or in some few persons, may be capable also to administer righteous government; at least the body that gives this liberty, when they need not, are to thank themselves if it prove otherwise: but when this free and naturall access unto government is interrupted and declined, so as a liberty is taken by any particular member, or number of them, that are to be reputed but a part in comparison of the whole, to assume and engrosse the office of soveraign rule and power, and to impose themselves as the competent publick judge of the safety and good of the whole, without their free and due consent; and to lay claim unto this as those that find themselves possessed of the sword, (and that so advantagiously, as it cannot be recovered again out of their hands, without more apparent danger and damage to the whole body than such attempts are worth,) this is that anarchy that is the first rise and step to tyranny, and laies grounds of manifest confusion and disorder, exposing the ruling power to the next hand that on the next opportunity can lay hold on the sword; and so, by a kind of necessity, introduces the highest imposition and bondage upon the whole body, in compelling all the parts, though never so much against the true publick interest, to serve and obey as their soveraign rule and supream authority, the arbitrary will and judgment of those that bring themselves into rule by the power of the sword, in the right onely of a part that sets up it self in preference before, or at least in competition with the welfare of the whole.

And if this, which is so essential to the well being and right constitution of government, were once obtained, the disputes about the form would not prove so difficult, nor find such opposition as to keeping the bone of contention and dis-union, with much danger to the whole: for if, as the foundation of all, the soveraignty be acknowledged to reside originally in the whole body of adherents to this cause, (whose naturall and inherent right thereunto is of a far ancienter date than what is obtained by successe of their arms, and so cannot be abrogated even by conquest it self if that were the case) and then if, in consequence hereof, a supream judicature be set up and orderly constituted, as naturally arising and resulting from the free choice and consent of the whole body taken out from among themselves, as flesh of their flesh, and bone of their bone, of the same publick spirit and nature with themselves, and the main be by this means secured, what could be propounded afterwards, as to the form of administration that would much stick?

Would a standing council of state setled for life in reference to the safety of the commonwealth, and for the maintaining intercourse and commerce with foreign states, under the inspection and oversight of the supream judicature, but of the same fundamental constitution with themselves, would this be disliked? Admitting their orders were binding in the intervals of supream national assemblies, so far only as consonant to the setled laws of the commonwealth; the vacancy of any of which, by death or otherwise, might be supplied by the vote of the major part of themselves. Nay, would there be any just exception to be taken, if (besides both these) it should be agreed (as another part of the fundamental constitution of the government) to place that branch of soveraignty which chiefly respects the execution of laws in a distinct office from that of the legislative power, (and yet subordinate to them and to the laws) capable to be intrusted into the hands of one single person, if need require, or in a greater number, as the legislative power should think fit; and for the greater strength and honour unto this office, that the execution of all laws and orders (that are binding) may go forth in his or their name; and all disobedience thereunto, or contempt thereof, be taken as done to the peoples soveraignty, whereof he or they bear the image or representation, subordinate to the legislative power, and at their will to be kept up and continued in the hands of a single person or more, as the experience of the future good or evil of it shall require.

Would such an office as this, thus stated, carry in it any inconsistency with a free state? Nay, if it be well considered, would it not rather be found of excellent use to the well-being of magistracy founded upon this righteous bottom, that such a lieutenancy of the peoples soveraignty in these three nations, may alwayes reside in some one or more persons, in whose administration that which is reward and punishment may shine forth?

And if now it shall be objected, that (notwithstanding all these cautions) should once this soveraignty be acknowledged to be in the diffused body of the people, (though the adherents to this cause, not onely as their natural, but as their acquired right by conquest) they would suddenly put the use and exercise of the legislative power into such hands, as would, through their ill quallifiednesse to the work, spoil all by male-administration thereof, and hereby loose the cause instead of upholding and maintaining it.

The answer unto this is, first, that God by his providence hath eased our minds much in this solicitude, by the course he hath already taken to fit and prepare a choice and selected number of the people unto this work, that are tryed and refined by their inward and outward experiences in this great quarrel, and the many changes they have passed through; in respect whereof, well qualified persons are to be found, if due care be taken in the choice of them. And if herein the people of the Lord shall be waiting upon him for his guidance and presence with them, we may have grounds and hope that God (whose name hath all along been called upon in the maintaining of this cause) will pour out so abundantly of his spirit upon his people attending on him in righteous wayes, and will also so move their hearts to choose persons bearing his image in the magistracy, that a more glorious product may spring up out of this, than at first we can expect to the setting up of the Lord himself, as chief judge and lawgiver amongst us. And unto this the wisdome and honesty of the persons now in power may have an opportunity eminently to come into discovery; for in this case, and upon the grounds already layd, the very persons now in power are they unto whose lot it would fall to set about this preparatory work, and by their orders and directions to dispose the whole body and bring them into the meetest capacity to effect the same. The most natural way for which would seem to be by a generall councill, or convention of faithfull, honest, and discerning men, chosen for that purpose by the free consent of the whole body of adherents to this cause in the several parts of the nations, and observing the time and place of meeting appointed to them (with other circumstances concerning their election) by order from the present ruling power, but considered as generall of the army.

Which convention is not properly to exercise the legislative power, but only to debate freely, and agree upon the particulars; that, by way of fundamentall constitutions, shall be laid and inviolably observed as the conditions upon which the whole body so represented doth consent to cast it self into a civil and politick incorporation, and under the visible form and administration of government therein declared, and to be by each individuall member of the body subscribed in testimony of his or their particular consent given thereunto. Which conditions so agreed (and amongst them an act of oblivion for one) will be without danger of being broken or departed from; considering of what it is they are the conditions and the nature of the convention wherein they are made, which is of the people represented in their highest state of soveraignty, as they have the sword in their hands unsubjected unto the rules of civill government, but what themselves orderly assembled for that purpose do think fit to make. And the sword upon these conditions subjecting it self to the supreme judicature, thus to be set up: how suddenly might harmony, righteousnesse, love, peace, and safety unto the whole body follow hereupon, as the happy fruit of such a settlement, if the Lord have any delight to be amongst us.

And this once put in a way, and declared for by the general and army, as that which they are clearly convinced in the sight of God is their duty to bring about, and which they engage accordingly to see done, how firmly and freely would this oblige the hearts and persons, the counsels and purses, the affections and prayers, with all that is in the power of this whole party to do, in way of assistance and strengthning the hands of those now in power, whatever straits and difficulties they may meet with in the maintenance of the publick safety and peace?

This then being the state of our present affairs and differences, let it be acknowledged on all hands, and let all be convinced that are concerned, that there is not only possibility but probability, yea a compelling necessity of a firm union in this great body, the setting of which in joynt and tune again by a spirit of meekness and fear of the Lord, is the work of the present day, and will prove the onely remedy under God to uphold and carry on this blessed cause and work of the Lord in the three nations, that is already come thus far onwards in its progresse to its desired and expected end, of bringing in Christ the desire of all nations as the chief ruler amongst us.

Now unto this re-uniting work let there be a readiness in all the dissenting parts from the highest to the lowest, by chearfully coming forth to one another in a spirit of self-denial and love, instead of warre and wrath, and to cast down themselves before the Lord, who is the father of all their spirits, in self-abasement and humiliation for the mutual offence they have [been] in for sometime past, one unto another, and great provocation unto God and reproach unto his glorious name, who expected to have been served by them with reverence and godly fear, for our God is a consuming fire.

And as an inducement unto this, let us assure ourselves the means of effecting it will not prove so difficult as other things that have been brought about in the late war, if the minds and spirits of all concerned were once well and duely prepared hereunto by a kindly work of self-denial and self-abasement, set home by the spirit of the Lord upon their consciences, which, if he please, he may do we know not how soon. Nay we shall behold with a discerning eye the inside of that work which God hath been doing amongst us the three years last past, it would seem chiefly to have been his aim to bring his people into such a frame as this is. For in this tract of time, there hath been (as we may say) a great silence in heaven, as if God were pleased to stand still and be a looker on to see what his people would be in their later end, and what work they would make of it if left to their owne wisdome and politick contrivances. And as God hath had the silent part, so men, and that good men too, have had the active and busy part, and have like themselves made a great sound and noise, like the shout of a king in a mighty hoast; which whilest it hath been a sound onely and no more, hath not done much hurt as yet; but the fear and jealousie thereby caused, hath put the whole body out of frame, and made them apt to fall into great confusions and disorder.

And if there be thus arisen a general dissent and disagreement of parts (which is not, nor ought to be accounted the less considerable, because it lies hid and kept in under a patient silence) why should there not be as general a confession and acknowledgment of what each may find themselves overtaken in, and cannot but judge themselves faulty for? This kind of vent being much better than to have it break out in flames of a forward and untimely wrathful spirit, which never works the righteousness of God. Especially since what hath been done amongst us may probably have been more the effect of temptation than the product of any malicious design; and this sort of temptation is very common and incident to men in power (how good soever they may be) to be overtaken, and thereupon do sudden unadvised actions, which the Lord pardons and over rules for the best: evidently making appear that it is the work of the weak and fleshly part, which his own people carry about with them too much unsubdued. And therefore the Lord thinks fit by this means to shew them the need of being beholding to their spiritual part, to restore them again, and bring them into their right temper and healthful constitution.

And thus whilst each dissenting part is aggravating upon itself faultiness and blame, and none excusing, but all confessing they deserve, in one sort or other, reproof if not before men, yet in Gods sight: Who knows how soon it may please God to come into this broken, contrite, and self-denying frame of spirit in the good people within the three nations, and own them thus truly humbled and abased, for his temple and the place of his habitation and rest, wherein he shall abide for ever? of whom it may be said God is in the midst of her, she shall not be moved; God shall help her and that right early, or with his morning appearance. At which time he will sit silent no longer, but heaven will speak again, and become active and powerful in the spirits and hearts of honest men, and in the works of his providences, when either they go out to fight by sea or by land, or remain in counsel and debates at home for the publick weal, and again hear the prayers of his people, and visibly own them as a flock of holy men, as Jerusalem in her solemn feasts. "I will yet for this be enquired of by the house of Israel, saith the Lord, to do it for them:" And then they shall know that I the Lord their God am with them, and that they are my people, and that ye my flock, the flock of my pasture, are men that have shewed your selves weak sinful men, and I am your God that have declared myself an all-wise and powerful God, saith the Lord God.

Postscript

Reader,

Upon the perusal of this discourse thou wilt quickly perceive that these two things are principally aimed at in it by the author. First, to answer in some measure that which is called for by those in power, when they publickly profess they desire nothing more than conviction, and to find out the hidden provocations which either have or yet may bring forth the Lord against these nations, in the way which at present they are in.

Secondly, To remove out of the minds and spirits of the honest party, that still agree in the reason and justice of the good old cause, all things of a private nature and selfish concern (the tendency whereof serves but to foment and strengthen wrath and divisions amongst them) and in place thereof to set before them that common and publick interest, which (if with sincerity imbraced) may be the means of not only procuring a firm union amongst them, but also of conserving them herein.

In order to this, the author hath not been willing so much to declare his own opinion, or deliver any positive conclusions, as to discusse the business by way of question and answer, and thereby make as near a conjecture as he can, of that, wherein the several dissenting parts may with better satisfaction meet together, and agree upon a safe and righteous bottome, than to remain at the distance they do, to the apparent advantage of the common enemy, the approaching ruine of themselves, and needless hazard (if not loss) of the cause they have been so deeply engaged in. Especially considering, that when once they shall be found beginning to come forth to one another in such a condescending self-denying spirit, cleansed from the stain of hypocrisie and deceit, they may be well assured that light will spring up amongst them more and more unto a perfect day; and then those things which at present we have next in view, will prove as shadows ready to flee away before the morning brightness of Christs heavenly appearance and second coming; through which they will be heightened and improved to their full maturity, to the bringing in that kingdom of his that shall never be moved.

And because an essay hath been already made in a private way to obtain the first thing, that is to say, conviction, which chiefly is in the hand of the Lord to give; the same obligation lies upon the author, with respect to the second, for the exposing of it as now it is unto publick view, and therein leaving it also with the Lord, for his blessing thereunto.

32. Cromwell's Speech to the Parliament of 1656 (17 September 1656)

The Parliament of 1656 was the second called by Cromwell under the provisions of the Instrument of Government. It met on the 17th of September amidst foreign and domestic crises: A naval war with Spain; the interminable occupation of Ireland (now under the direction of his son, Henry); and the aftermath of several serious royalist uprisings, all occupied Cromwell's thoughts. In an effort to ensure a productive and cooperative session, the Council of State had refused to validate the elections of known republicans and other critics of the regime, and to ensure domestic tranquillity the nation had been placed under direct military rule for the first time since the civil wars. Major-generals were appointed to act as regional governors to prevent further proto-royalist activities. Both the legality of the Instrument of Government and the rule of the Major-generals became central issues of this Parliament.

Gentlemen,

When I came hither, I did think that a duty was incumbent upon me a little to pity myself; because (this being a very extraordinary occasion), I thought I had very many things to say unto you, and was somewhat burdened and straitened thereby. But truly now, seeing *you* in such a condition as you are, I think I must turn off my pity in this, as I hope I shall in everything else;—and consider [you] as certainly not being able long to bear that condition and heat that you are now in.—So far as possible, on this large subject, let us be brief; not studying the Art of Rhetoricians. Rhetoricians, whom I do not pretend to much concern with; neither with them, nor with what they use to deal in: Words!

From Thomas Carlyle, *Letters and Speeches of Oliver Cromwell, with Elucidations* (New York: Harper Brothers, 1868–71), pp. 509–11, 513–15, 519–21, 525–26, 529–30, 532–37, 540–42, 546–51. Footnotes and Carlyle's comments deleted.

Truly *our* business is to speak Things! The dispensations of God that are upon us do require it; and that subject upon which we shall make our discourse is somewhat of very great interest and concernment, both for the glory of God, and with reference to His Interest in the world. I mean His peculiar, His most peculiar Interest, His Church, the Communion of the faithful Followers of Christ;—and that will not teach any of us to exclude His general Interest, which is the concernment of the Living People, not as Christians but as human creatures, within these three Nations, and with all the dependencies thereupon. I have told you I should speak to *things;* things that concern these Interests: The Glory of God, and His Peculiar Interest in the world,—which latter is more extensive, I say more extensive, than the People of all these three Nations with their appurtenances, or the countries and places belonging unto them.

The first thing, therefore, that I shall speak to is *That* that is the first lesson of Nature, which is Being and Preservation. . . . As to that of Being, I do think I do not ill style it the *first* consideration that Nature teacheth the Sons of Adam:—and then I think we shall enter into a field large enough when we come to consider that of Well-being. But if Being itself be not first well laid, I think the other will hardly follow.

Now in order to this, to the Being and Subsistence of these Nations with all their Dependencies: The conservation of that, namely of our National Being, is first to be viewed with respect to those who seek to undo it, and so make it *not to be;* and then very naturally we shall come to the consideration of what will make it *be,* of what will *keep* its being and its subsistence.

Now that which plainly seeks the destruction of the Being of these Nations is, out of doubt: The endeavour and design of all the common Enemies of them. I think, truly, it will not be hard to find out who those Enemies are; nor what hath made them so! I think, They are all the wicked men of the world, whether abroad or at home, that are the Enemies to the very Being of these Nations;—and that upon a common account, from that very enmity that's in them to all such things; whatsoever should serve the glory of God and the interest of His People,—which they see to be more eminently, yea more eminently patronised and professed in this Nation (we will not speak it with vanity) than in all the Nations in the world: *this* is the common ground of the common enmity entertained against the prosperity of these Nations, against the very Being of them.—But we shall not, I think, take up much time, in contemplating who these Enemies are, and what they are, in the general notion: we will labour to *specificate* our Enemies; to know what persons and bodies of persons they practically are that seek the very destruction and Being of these Three Nations.

And truly I would not have laid this foundation but to this end: that I might very particularly communicate with you about that same matter. For which end above others, I think, you are called thither at this time:—That I might particularly communicate with you of the many dangers that these Nations stand in, in respect of Enemies both abroad and at home; and also to advise with you about the remedies and means to obviate these dangers. Dangers which, say I,—and I shall leave it to you whether you will join with me or no,—strike at the very Being and vital interest of these Nations. And therefore, coming to particulars, I will shortly represent to you the estate of your affairs in that respect: in respect namely of the Enemies you are engaged with; and how you come to be engaged with those Enemies, and how they come to be, *as* heartily, I believe, engaged against you. . . .

Why, truly, your great Enemy is the Spaniard. He is. He is a natural enemy. He is naturally so; he is naturally so throughout, by reason of that enmity that is in him against whatsoever is of God. Whatsoever is of God which is in *you,* or which may be in you, contrary to that that *his* blindness and darkness, led on by superstition, and the implicitness of his faith in submitting to the See of Rome, actuate him unto!—With this King and State, I say, you are at this present in hostility. . . .

No sooner did this Nation reform that which is called (unworthily) the Reformed Religion after the death of Queen Mary, by the Queen Elizabeth of famous memory,—we need not be ashamed to call her so!—but the Spaniard's design became, by all unworthy, unnatural means, to destroy that Person, and to seek the ruin and destruction of these Kingdoms. . . .

So that a State that you can neither have peace with nor reason from,—is that State with whom you have enmity at this time, and against whom you are engaged. And give me leave to say this unto you, because it is truth, and most men know it, That the Long Parliament did endeavour, but could not obtain satisfaction from the Spaniard all the time they sat: for their Messenger was murdered: and when they asked satisfaction for the blood of your poor people unjustly shed in the West Indies . . . and for the wrongs done elsewhere; when they asked liberty of conscience for your people that traded thither,—satisfaction in none of these things would be given, but was denied. . . .

Now if this be so, why truly then there is some little foundation laid to justify the War that has been entered upon with the Spaniard! And not only so: but the plain truth of it is, Make any peace with any State that is Popish and subjected to the determination of Rome and of the Pope himself,—you are bound, and they are loose. . . .

And now farther,—as there is a complication of these Interests abroad, so there is a complication of them here. Can we think that Papists and Cavaliers shake not hands in England? It is unworthy, unchristian, un-English-like, say you. Yes; but it doth serve to let you see, and for that end I tell it you that you may see, your danger, and the source thereof. Nay it is not only thus, that we stand in this condition of hostility, towards Spain; and towards all that Interest that would make void and frustrate everything that has been doing for you; namely, towards the Popish Interest, Papists and Cavaliers;—but it is also . . . That is to say, your danger is *so great,* if you will be sensible of it, from Persons that pretend *other* things! . . . Yet all men know, and must know, that discontented parties are among us somewhere! They must expect backing and support somewhere. They must end at the Interest of the Cavalier at the long-run. That must be their support! . . .

Certain it is there was, not long since, an endeavour to make an insurrection in England [Penruddock's rising, in 1655]. . . . It was so for some time before it broke out. It was so before the last Parliament sat, the last. Nay, it was so from the time not only of the undertaking of this Government; but the spirit and principle of it did work in the Long-Parliament time. From that time till to this hath there been nothing but enterprising and designing against you. And its no strange nor new thing to tell you: Because its true and certain that the Papists, the Priests and Jesuits, have a great influence upon the Cavalier Party; they and the Cavalier party upon the discontented spirits of the Nation,—who are not all so apt to see where the dangers lie, nor to what the management of affairs tend. Those Papists and Cavaliers do foment all things that tend to disservice; to propagate discontentments upon the minds of men. And if we would instance in particulars those that have manifested this, we could tell you that Priests and Jesuits have insinuated themselves into the society of men; pretending the same things that *they* have pretended; . . .

If this be our condition,—with respect had to this, truly let us go a little farther. For I would lay open the danger, wherein, I think in my conscience, we stand; and if God give not you hearts to see and discern that which is obvious, we shall sink, and the house will fall about our ears,— upon even what are called such sordid attempts as these are! Truly there are a great many people in this Nation, that would not reckon up every pitiful thing that may be, perhaps like a mouse nibbling at the heel; but only considerable dangers! I will tell you plainly what to me seems dangerous;—for it is not a time for compliments nor rhetorical speeches.—I have none, truly;—but to tell you how we *find* things.

There is a generation of men in this Nation that cry up nothing but righteousness and justice and liberty . . . ; and these are diversified in to several sects, and sorts of men; and though they may be contemptible in respect they are many, and so not like to make a solid vow to do you mischief,—yet they are apt to agree *in aliquo tertio.* They are known (yea, well enough) to shake hands with,—I should be loath to say with Cavaliers—but with all the scum and dirt of this Nation, to put you to trouble. . . .

We think it our duty to tell you of these things; and we can make them good. Here is your danger; that is it! And here is a poor Nation that hath wallowed in its blood;—though, thanks be to God, we have had Peace these four or five years: yet here is the condition we stand in. And I think I should be false to you, if I did not give you this true representation of it.

I am to tell you, by the way, a word to justify a Thing . . . that, I hear, is much spoken of. When we knew all these Designs before mentioned; when we found that the Cavaliers would not be quiet—No quiet; there is "no peace to the wicked," saith the Scriptures, the Fifty-seventh of *Isaiah:* "They are like the troubled sea, that cannot rest; whose waters cast up mire and dirt." They cannot rest,—they have no Peace with God and Jesus Christ in the remission of sins! They do not know what belongs to it . . . therefore they know not how to be at rest; therefore they can no more cease from their actions than they can cease to be,—nor so easily neither!— Truly when this Insurrection was, and we saw it in all the roots and grounds of it, we did find out a little poor Invention, which I hear has been much regretted. . . . I say, there was a little thing invented; which was, the erecting of your Major-Generals . . . To have a little inspection upon the People thus divided, thus discontented, thus dissatisfied, split in to divers interests,—by the workings of the Popish Party! . . .

How the Major-Generals have behaved themselves in that work? I hope they are men, as to their persons, of known integrity and fidelity; and men that have freely adventured their blood and lives for that good Cause,—if it still be thought such, and it was well stated, this morning, against all the new humours and fancies of men!—And truly England doth yet receive one day more of Lengthening-out its tranquillity, by that same service of theirs,—

Well; your danger is as you have seen. And truly I am sorry it is so great. But I wish it might cause no despondency;—as truly, I think, it will not: because we are Englishmen; that is one good account. And if God give a Nation the property of valour and courage, it is honour and a mercy from Him, . . . and much more than English! Because you all, I hope, are Christian Men, Christian men that know Jesus Christ . . . and know that Cause that hath been mentioned to you this day.

Having declared to you my sense and my knowledge,—pardon me if I say so, my knowledge, of the condition of these poor Nations, for it hath an influence upon them all, it concerns them all very palpably; I should be to blame if I should not a little offer to you the Remedies. . . . I would comprehend them under two considerations. They are both somewhat general. The one is, Considering all things that may be done, and ought to be done, in order to Security; that's one. And truly the other is a common head, a general, nay a universal consideration,—the other is, Doing all things that ought to be done in order to Reformation. . . .

First, however, for that of Security outwardly considered. We shall speak a little distinctly to that. You see where your War is. It is with the Spaniard. You have Peace with all other Nations, or the most of them; Swede, Dane, Dutch. At present, I say, it is well; it is at present so. And so likewise with the Portugal, with France,—the Mediterranean Sea. Both those States, both Christian and Profane; the Mahometans;—you have Peace with them all. Only with Spain, I say, you have a difference, you have a War. I pray consider it. Do I come to tell you that I would *tie* you to this War? No. According as you shall find your spirits and reasons grounded in what hath been said, so let you and me join in the prosecution of that War,—according as we are satisfied, and as the cause will appear to our consciences in the sight of the Lord. But if you *can* come to prosecute it, prosecute it vigorously, or do not do it at all! . . .

As to those lesser Distempers of people that pretend Religion, yet, from the whole consideration of Religion, which would fall under as one of the heads of Reformation, I had rather put it under this head; and I shall the less speak to it, because you have been so well spoken-to this day already elsewhere. I will tell you the truth: Our practice since the last Parliament hath been, To let all this Nation see that whatever pretensions to Religion would continue quiet, peaceable, they should enjoy conscience and liberty to themselves;—and *not* make Religion a pretence for arms and blood, truly we have suffered them, and that cheerfully, so to enjoy their own liberties. Whatsoever is contrary, and not peaceable, let the pretence be never so specious,—if it tend to combination, to interests and factions, we shall not care, by the grace of God, *whom* we meet withal, though never so specious, though never so quiet! And truly I am against all liberty of conscience repugnant to *this*. I am. If men will profess,—be they those under Baptism, be they those of the Independent judgment simply, and of the Presbyterian judgment,—in the name of God, encourage them, countenance them; so long as they do plainly continue to be thankful to God, and to make use of the liberty given them to enjoy their own consciences! . . .

That men that believe in Jesus Christ—that's the Form that gives the being to true religion, Faith in Christ and walking in a profession answerable to that Faith;—men that believe the remission of sins through the blood of Christ, and free justification by the blood of Christ, and live upon the grace of God: that those men that are certain they are so, . . . they are members of Jesus Christ, and are to Him as the apple of His eye. Whoever hath this Faith, let his Form be what it will; he walking peaceably, without the prejudicing of others under another Form:—it is a debt due to God and Christ; and He will require it, if he that Christian may not enjoy this liberty . . . and those abuses that are in this Nation through disorder, is a thing which should be much in your hearts. It is that, that I am confident is a description and character of that Interest you have been engaged against [and pressing to as any other,] the Cavalier Interest: against the badge and character of countenancing Profaneness, Disorder and Wickedness in all places, . . . In my conscience, it was a shame to be a Christian, within these fifteen, sixteen or seventeen years, in this Nation, either in Caesar's house, or elsewhere! It was a shame, it was a reproach to a man; and the badge of Puritan was put upon it. . . . If it lives in us, therefore; I say, if it be in the general heart of the nation, it is a thing I am confident our liberty and prosperity depends upon,—Reformation. To make it a shame to see men to be bold in sin and profaneness,—and God will bless you. You will be a blessing to the Nation; and by this, will be more repairers of breaches than by anything in the world. Truly these things do respect the souls of men, and the spirits,— which *are* the men. The mind is the man. If that be kept pure, a man signifies somewhat; if not, I would very fain see what difference there is betwixt him and a beast. . . .

There are some things which respect the Estates of men; and there is one general Grievance in the Nation. It is the Law. Not that the Laws are a grievance; but there are Laws that are a grievance; and the great grievance lies in the execution and administration. I think I may say it, I have as eminent Judges in this land as have been had, or that the Nation has had, for these many years. . . . Truly I could be particular as to the executive part of it, to administration of the Law; but that would trouble you. But the truth of it is, There are wicked and abominable Laws, that it will be in your power to alter. To hang a man for six pence, thirteen pence, I know not what; to hang for a trifle, and pardon murder,—is in the ministration of the Law, through the ill-framing of it. I have known in my experience abominable murders acquitted. And to come and see men lose their lives for petty matters: this is a thing that God will reckon for. . . . And I wish it may not lie upon this Nation a day longer than you have an opportunity to give a remedy; and I hope I shall cheerfully join with you in it. This hath been a great grief to many honest hearts and conscientious people; and I hope it is all in your hearts to rectify it.

I have little more to say to you, being very weary; and I know you are so too. Truly I did begin with that that I thought was the means to carry on this War (if you will carry it on), That we may join together in that vigorously. . . .

Therefore I pray, aye and beseech you, in the name of Christ, Show yourselves to be men; quit yourselves like men! It doth not infer any reproach if you do show yourselves men: *Christian* men,—which *will* only make you quit yourselves. I do not think that, to this work you have in hand, a neutral spirit will do it. That is a Laodicean spirit; and we know what God said of that Church: it was lukewarm, and therefore He would spew it out of His mouth! It is not a neutral spirit that is incumbent upon you. And if not a neutral spirit, it is much less a stupefied spirit, inclining you, in the least disposition, the *wrong* way! Men are, in their private consciences, every day making shipwreck and it's no wonder if these can shake hands with men of reprobate Interests:—such, give me leave to think, are the Popish Interests. For the Apostle brands them so, Having seared consciences. Though I do not judge every man:—but the ringleaders are such. The Scriptures foretold they should be such. It is not such a spirit will carry the work on! It is men in a Christian state that have *works* with *faith;* that know how to lay hold on Christ for remission of sins, till a man be brought to glory in hope. Such an hope kindled in men's spirits will actuate them to such ends as you are tending to: and so many as are partakers of this, and do own your standings, wherein the Providence of God hath set and called you to this work, so many will carry it on. . . .

Give me leave to tell you,—those that are called to this work, it will not depend for them upon formalities, nor notions, nor speeches! I do not look the work should be done by these. No; but by men of honest hearts, engaged to God; strengthened by Providence; enlightened in His words, to know His Word,—to which He hath set His Seal, sealed with the blood of His Son, in the blood of His Servants: *that* is such a spirit as will carry on this work. . . .

Therefore I beseech you, I beseech you, do not dispute of unnecessary and unprofitable things that may divert you from carrying on of so glorious a work as this is. I think *every* objection that ariseth is not to be answered; nor have I time for it. I say, Look up to God; have peace among yourselves. Know assuredly that if I have interest, I am by the voice of the People the Supreme Magistrate; and, it may be, do know somewhat that may satisfy my conscience, if I stood in doubt! But it is an union, really it is an union, this between you and me: and both of us united in faith and love to Jesus Christ, and to His peculiar Interest in the world,—*that* must ground this work. And in *that,* if I have any peculiar Interest that's personal to myself, that is not subservient to the Public end,—it were no extravagant thing for me to *curse* myself: because I know God will curse me, if I have! . . . And I have learned too much of God, not to dally with Him, and to be bold with Him, in these things. And I never was and I hope I never shall be bold with Him;—though I can be bold with men, if Christ be pleased to assist!—

I say if there be love between us, so that the Nations may say, These are knit together in one bond, to promote the glory of God against the Common Enemy; to suppress everything that is Evil, and encourage whatsoever is of Godliness,—yea, the Nation will bless you! And really, really, that and nothing else will work-off these Disaffections from the minds of men; which are as great,—if not greater—than all the other oppositions you can meet with. I do know what I say. When I speak of these things, I speak my heart before God;—and, as I said before, I dare not be bold before Him. I have a little faith: I have a little lived by faith, and therein I may be bold. If I spoke other than the affections and secrets of my heart, I know He would not bear it at my hands! Therefore in the fear and name of God: Go on, with love and integrity, against whatever arises contrary to these ends which you have known and been told of; and the blessing of God go with you,—the blessing of God *will* go with you!

I have but this one thing to say more. I know it is troublesome:—But I did read a Psalm yesterday; which truly may not unbecome both me to tell you of, and you to observe. It is the Eighty-fifth Psalm, that's very instructive and very significant: and though I do but a little touch upon it, I desire your perusal at your pleasure.

It begins: "Lord, Thou hast been very favourable unto Thy Land; Thou hast brought back the captivity of Jacob. Thou hast forgiven the iniquity of Thy People; Thou hast covered all their sins. Thou hast taken away all (the fierceness of) Thy wrath: Thou hast turned Thyself from the fierceness of Thine anger. Turn us, O God of our salvation, and cause Thine anger toward us to cease. Wilt Thou be angry with us forever; wilt Thou draw out Thine anger to all generations? Wilt thou not revive us again, that Thy People may rejoice in Thee?" Then he calls upon God as "the God of his salvation," and then saith he: "I will hear what God the Lord will speak: for He will speak 'peace' unto His People, and to His Saints; but let them not turn again to folly. Surely His salvation is nigh them that fear Him;" Oh—"that glory may dwell in our land! Mercy and Truth are met together; Righteousness and Peace have kissed each other. Truth shall spring out of the Earth, and Righteousness shall look down from Heaven. Yea the Lord shall give that which is good, and our Land shall yield its increase. Righteousness shall go before Him, and shall set us in the way of His steps." . . .

Truly I wish that this Psalm, as it is written in the Book, might be better written in our hearts, that we might say as David, "*Thou* hast done this," and "Thou hast done that;" "Thou hast pardoned our sins; Thou hast taken away our iniquities!" Whither can we go to a better God? For "He hath done it." It is to Him any Nation may come in their extremity, for the taking away of His wrath. How did He do it? By pardoning their sins, and taking away their iniquities! If we can but cry unto Him, He will turn and take away *our* sins.—Then let us listen to Him, and then let us consult, and meet in Parliament; and ask Him counsel, and hear what He saith, for He will speak peace unto His People. If you be the People of God [and be for the people of God,] He will speak *peace;*—and we will not again return to folly. . . .

33. The Declaration of Breda

The death of Oliver Cromwell in 1658 marked the effective end of the revolution. His son Richard was briefly installed as Lord Protector, but he had none of his father's charisma and none of his experience. Most vitally, he could not exercise control over the army, which remained the center of political power. Nevertheless, the Restoration of Charles II was by no means a foregone conclusion. Presbyterians, republicans, and old rumpers all believed that the collapse of the protectorate was but another stage in the constitutional experimentation that had characterized the revolution. Charles II's return to England was thus the result of shrewd political maneuvers and hard political bargaining. Both are revealed in the declaration made before he set sail to return to his kingdom.

Charles R.

Charles, by the grace of God, King of England, Scotland, France and Ireland, Defender of the Faith, &c. To all our loving subjects, of what degree or quality soever, greeting.

If the general distraction and confusion which is spread over the whole kingdom doth not awaken all men to a desire and longing that those wounds which have so many years together been kept bleeding, may be bound up, all we can say will be to no purpose; however, after this long silence, we have thought it our duty to declare how much we desire to contribute thereunto; and that as we can never give over the hope, in good time, to obtain the possession of that right which God and nature hath made our due, so we do make it our daily suit to the Divine Providence, that He will, in compassion to us and our subjects, after so long misery and sufferings, remit and put us into a quiet and peaceable possession of that our right, with as little blood and damage to our people as is possible; nor do we desire more to enjoy what is ours, than that all our subjects may enjoy what by law is theirs, by a full and entire administration of justice throughout the land, and by extending our mercy where it is wanted and deserved.

And to the end that the fear of punishment may not engage any, con-

From S. R. Gardiner, *Constitutional Documents of the Puritan Revolution* (Oxford: The Clarendon Press, 1906), pp. 465–67.

scious to themselves of what is past, to a perseverance in guilt for the future, by opposing the quiet and happiness of their country, in the restoration of King, Peers and people to their just, ancient and fundamental rights, we do, by these presents, declare, that we do grant a free and general pardon, which we are ready, upon demand, to pass under our Great Seal of England, to all our subjects, of what degree or quality soever, who, within forty days after the publishing hereof, shall lay hold upon this our grace and favour, and shall, by any public act, declare their doing so, and that they return to the loyalty and obedience of good subjects; excepting only such persons as shall hereafter be excepted by Parliament, those only to be excepted. Let all our subjects, how faulty soever, rely upon the word of a King, solemnly given by this present declaration, that no crime whatsoever, committed against us or our royal father before the publication of this, shall ever rise in judgment, or be brought in question, against any of them, to the least endamagement of them, either in their lives, liberties or estates, or (as far forth as lies in our power) so much as to the prejudice of their reputations, by any reproach or term of distinction from the rest of our best subjects; we desiring and ordaining that henceforth all notes of discord, separation and difference of parties be utterly abolished among all our subjects, whom we invite and conjure to a perfect union among themselves, under our protection, for the re-settlement of our just rights and theirs in a free Parliament, by which, upon the word of a King, we will be advised.

And because the passion and uncharitableness of the times have produced several opinions in religion, by which men are engaged in parties and animosities against each other (which, when they shall hereafter unite in a freedom of conversation, will be composed or better understood), we do declare a liberty to tender consciences, and that no man shall be disquieted or called in question for differences of opinion in matter of religion, which do not disturb the peace of the kingdom; and that we shall be ready to consent to such an Act of Parliament, as, upon mature deliberation, shall be offered to us, for the full granting that indulgence.

And because, in the continued distractions of so many years, and so many and great revolutions, many grants and purchases of estates have been made to and by many officers, soldiers and others, who are now possessed of the same, and who may be liable to actions at law upon several titles, we are likewise willing that all such differences, and all things relating to such grants, sales and purchases, shall be determined in Parliament, which can best provide for the just satisfaction of all men who are concerned.

And we do further declare, that we will be ready to consent to any Act or Acts of Parliament to the purposes aforesaid, and for the full satisfaction of all arrears due to the officers and soldiers of the army under the command of General Monk; and that they shall be received into our service upon as good pay and conditions as they now enjoy.

Given under our Sign Manual and Privy Signet, at our Court at Breda, this 4/14 day of April, 1660, in the twelfth year of our reign.

3
The Scientific Revolution

The New Cosmos and the Old

34. Galileo Galilei

Born in Pisa in 1564 of a distinguished Florentine family, Galileo Galilei began his scientific career in 1589 as an underpaid mathematics professor at the University of Pisa, where he had obtained much of his scientific training before embarking on an elaborate program of self-instruction. Soon after his appointment, the same talent for involving himself in controversies that is noted in the present documents got him into trouble with colleagues inconvenienced by his insistence on exposing the absurdity of current Aristotelian physical theories in practical demonstrations or in imaginary practical problems. Fortunately, his contract at Pisa ran out just when the Venetian Senate, in an effort to increase its own prestige as a patron of science and to augment its available resources in technical fields, had begun an effort to attract the most promising scholars to the University of Padua by offering them large salaries. At Padua from 1592 to 1610, in increasingly fortunate circumstances, Galileo introduced what new ideas he could regarding geometry, fortifications, ballistics, and mechanics into a standard mathematics curriculum based on Euclid, and, in the intervals between classes and private lessons, made many of the discoveries—including the laws of falling bodies—that later brought him lasting fame. The immediate cause of his sudden celebrity in 1610, however, was his masterful exploitation of the newly invented telescope. After

From Galileo Galilei, *Il Saggiatore* (Milan: Feltrinelli, 1965), pp. 2–3, 5–17, 261–67. Translated for this volume by Brendan Dooley. Footnotes are translator's notes. Letters from Mario Guiducci and Benedetto Castelli to Galileo are from *Edizione Nazionale delle opere di Galileo Galilei* (Florence: Barbera, 1929–39), 13:265–66, 400–402. Translated for this volume by Eric Cochrane.

perfecting his own version, he went into business to produce it in quantity for presentation to powerful prospective patrons. And by using it to undertake the first telescopic astronomical observations on record, he discovered the four largest moons of Jupiter and named them after Cosimo de'Medici in a public relations coup that helped earn him a place as "official mathematician"—later "philosopher"—to the Tuscan grand duke.

Galileo devoted the next years to an energetic publishing campaign, of which *The Assayer* (*Il Saggiatore,* 1623) is a perfect example, for converting the public—both scientists and laymen—to the heliocentric universe and to the quantitative approach to physics. True, he suffered some setbacks, such as when a few disgruntled Roman theologians managed to steer the scientific debate toward the theological questions they thought they understood and convinced the Holy Office and Pope Paul V to cooperate in condemning Copernicus' *De Revolutionibus* "until it is corrected." But with friends like Roberto Bellarmino and Sforza Pallavicino, two of the most influential Jesuits in Italy, the members of philanthropist Federico Cesi's newly-formed Roman Accademia dei Lincei (i.e., "The Lynxes")— one of the first official scientific academies in Europe—and many of the best philosophers and scientists of the time, the prospects for success looked bright; and Galileo accordingly continued to teach and demonstrate the validity of heliocentrism without fear of official censure. Prospects looked even brighter in 1623 with the arrival on the papal throne of Maffeo Barberini (Urban VIII), who apparently desired nothing more than to surpass all previous popes as a patron of the arts and sciences, and who proved the sincerity of his intentions by awarding Galileo two ecclesiastical pensions. Galileo thereupon widened his campaign in order to convert the Church and the theologians along with everyone else in a masterful work of popular science written according to the best traditions of humanist prose, the *Dialogue Concerning the Two Chief World Systems* (1632), which he sent to all the cardinals, bishops and university professors whom he believed might find it provocative.

Contrary to Galileo's expectations, Urban VIII was far less interested in philosophy than he was in reinforcing the papal bargaining position in the Thirty Years' War, turning Rome into the artistic and architectural wonder of the age, and carving out a prinicipality for his family in Italy. So he left the problem of the conflict between Galileo and his theological adversaries to the obscure papal bureaucrats who handled most of the uninteresting administrative details of his monarchical rule—the same bureaucrats whom Mario Guiducci, one of Galileo's students and staunch supporters, here calls "frati" (with derogatory connotations) and with whom another, Benedetto Castelli, tried to reason. And when these bureaucrats managed to pull enough passages from Galileo's works out of context and build a case that they believed would cut Galileo down to size and at the same time build up their own prestige, the pope offered no resistance. Galileo's only possible refuge lay with Grand Duke Ferdinand II of Tuscany, who had succeeded his father in 1621. And when the Grand Duke, whose territory was in the throes of the worst depression and plague since the fourteenth century, forgot philosophy temporarily in favor of more urgent projects, Galileo's cause was lost. After a retraction of his heliocentrism in Rome in 1633, Galileo went back to Florence to teach it and all the other new ideas he supported—not to the public, as before, but to a small circle of friends and admirers including Paolo Sarpi and Thomas Hobbes, and not from the podium of official lectures but from the comfortable estate in Arcetri where the condemnation decreed that he should spend his retirement.

The Assayer (written in the form of a letter to Virginio Cesarini, the pope's chamberlain) demonstrates Galileo's method in action, illustrates the issues in his quarrel with Aristotelian qualitative physics and shows his support for a few ideas that apparently have little to do with modern science.

___

The Assayer of Signor Galileo Galilei

I have never been able to understand, Your Excellency, how it came about that whenever I have had to make my studies public to please or to serve others, they have always encountered the animosity of those who sought to diminish, defraud and vilify the small return I believed was due me—if not from the work itself, at least from the intention. My *Starry Messenger* [*Sidereus Nuncius,* 1610], in which I revealed so many new and marvellous discoveries for which all lovers of the true philosophy should have been grateful, had only just been printed when immediately from all sides conspirators emerged who sought for themselves the praises due to my discoveries; there were even some who cared nothing about bringing into doubt, just to contradict my statements, the things they saw plainly and repeatedly. The Most Serene Grand Duke Cosimo II, my lord of glorious memory, commanded me to write my opinion about the floating and sinking of things in water; and, to satisfy this command, having written down on paper everything that came to mind besides the doctrine of Archimedes—everything, perhaps, that can truthfully be said about the subject— suddenly the print shops filled with invectives against my *Discourse on Floating Bodies* [*Discorso intorno alle cose che stanno in su l'acqua. . . ,* 1612]; and heedless of the geometrical demonstrations that supported my arguments, they contradicted my statements, not noticing (such was the force of their passion) that to contradict geometry is openly to deny the truth. And by how many and in how many ways was the *Letter on Sunspots* [*Istoria e dimostrazioni intorno alle macchie solari. . . ,* 1613] combatted? And the material there, which ought to provide manifold opportunities for exposing intellects to wonderful speculations, was either not believed or not esteemed, and entirely vilified and derided by many; others, who did not want to believe my ideas [*concetti*], produced ridiculous and impossible opinions against me; and some, compelled and convinced by my reasons, tried to take away from me that glory that was surely mine and, pretending not to have seen my writings, tried after me to make themselves the first inventors of such stupendous marvels. I will not mention a few of my private discourses, demonstrations and statements, many of which were never published by me in print, that have been evilly impugned or denigrated as nothing; some of these have even encountered persons who cleverly tried to usurp honor by pretending to have invented them by their own genius [*ingegni*].

I could name not a few such usurpers; but I wish to pass over them in silence now, since the first robbery is usually punished less than the next ones. But I shall no longer remain silent about the second robbery committed with excessive audacity by the same man who committed another one many years ago in appropriating my invention of the "geometrical compass," which I had much earlier shown and communicated to many and finally made public in print.[1] And this time let me be pardoned if I react perhaps too bitterly and declaim, against my nature, my custom and my intention, about something I have remained silent about for many years. I speak of Simon Mayr of Guntzenhausen,[2] who translated my description of my said compass into the Latin language while I was in Padua, and attributing it to himself, gave it to a disciple to print under his own name and immediately, perhaps to escape punishment, went back to his own country, leaving his scholar, as they say, in the lurch; against whom I had to proceed, in the absence of Simon Mayr, in the manner explained in the *Defense against the Calumnies and Impostures of Baldessar Capra* [*Difesa . . . contro le calunnie. . . ,* 1607] that I wrote and published at the time. This same man, four years after the publication of the *Starry Messenger,* desiring to have himself decorated by the work of others, was not ashamed to make himself out to be the author of the things I discovered and published there; and printing under the title of *World of Jupiter* and so

1. Galileo invented this device, a kind of sector marked off for determining any area bounded by straight lines and curves, around 1597, set up a shop to build it in quantity, took in students interested in learning how to use it, and published a description of it nine years later in perfect Tuscan Italian, *Le operazioni del compasso geometrico e militare* (1606).

2. Also called Simon Mayer (1570–1624).

forth,[3] he has temerariously affirmed that he observed the Medicean stars[4] that circle around Jupiter before I did. But because the truth rarely permits itself to be suppressed by lies, he himself gives me now in the same work, because of carelessness or lack of intelligence, the opportunity to expose him with irrefutable testimonies and manifestly to demonstrate his error, proving that not only did he not observe the said stars before I did, but he did not even see them two years later; indeed, it can probably be said that he never observed them at all. And even though I could draw from many passages in his book very evident proofs of what I say, I reserve this for another occasion, so as not to go into it too deeply and thereby detract from my present intention; I shall therefore discuss only one.

Simon Mayr, in the second part of his *World of Jupiter,* on considering the sixth phenomenon,[5] writes of his diligent observation that the four planets of Jupiter are never on a straight line parallel to the ecliptic except when they are at their maximum digressions from Jupiter; but that when they are not in these maximum digressions, they always decline with notable difference from such a line; they decline, according to him, from that [line] always toward the north when they are in the lower parts of their circles and, on the contrary, incline to the south in the upper parts; and to save these appearances he establishes that their circles are inclined from the plane of the ecliptic toward the south in their upper parts and toward the north in their lower parts.[6] But this doctrine of his is full of falsehoods, which openly demonstrate and testify to his fraud.

First of all, it is not true that the four circles of the Medicean stars incline from the plane of the ecliptic; indeed, they are always parallel to it. Secondly, it is not true that the same stars are never exactly on a straight line except when they are at the maximum digression from Jupiter; indeed, it occasionally happens that at whatever distance they happen to be, maximum, medium or minimum, and when they are in contrary movements[7] very close to Jupiter, finding themselves on an exactly straight line and en-

3. I.e., *Mundus Jovialis Anno 1609 Detectus Ope Perspicilli Belgici* . . . (Nuremburg: 1614).

4. I.e., the four large satellites that Galileo named and described in *The Starry Messenger.*

5. I.e., the sixth configuration of the four large satellites, during which none is eclipsed by the planet.

6. Keep in mind the following definitions: *Ecliptic*—the line traced by the sun in its apparent annual movement across the sky through the constellations. (Nowadays, the celestial line of reference is the celestial equator, a projection of the Earth's equator on the celestial sphere inclined about 23 degrees from the ecliptic.) *Decline* and derivatives—to depart or diverge from a celestial line or plane. *Digressions*—apparent distances between heavenly bodies. *North*—except where noted, toward the Pole Star (Polaris).

7. I.e., as they appear on successive days of observation. They revolve, of course, in the same direction.

countering each other, they join together exactly so that two appear one. Finally, it is false to say that while they are away from the plane of the ecliptic, they always incline toward the south in the upper halves of their circles and toward the north in the lower halves; indeed, they only occasionally decline from the straight line in this manner, and at other times they decline to the contrary—that is, toward the north when they are in the upper half-circles, and toward the south when they are in the lower half-circles. But Simon Mayr, since he neither understood nor observed this affair, has inadvertently made his mistake manifest. The real explanation is as follows:

The four circles of the Medicean stars are always parallel to the plane of the ecliptic; and because we are located in the same plane,[8] it happens that whenever Jupiter has no latitude and is therefore on the ecliptic,[9] the movements of these stars will seem to be on the same straight line, and their conjunctions in any place will always be corporal—that is, without any declination.[10] But when Jupiter itself is outside the plane of the ecliptic, to which the four circles of the Medicean stars are always parallel, and its latitude is north of this plane, the parts of the planets' circles that seem to be further above us[11] as we observe them from the plane of the ecliptic—where we ourselves are always located—will seem to incline toward the south with respect to the lower parts and the lower parts will seem more northern. On the other hand, when the latitude of Jupiter is southern, the superior parts of the same circles will seem more northern than the lower parts; so that the declinations of the Medicean stars will seem to be contrary when Jupiter has northern latitude to their declinations when Jupiter is southern. Therefore, the Medicean stars in the first case will seem to decline toward the south when they are at the upper halves of their circles and toward the north when they are in the lower halves; and these declinations will be greater or lesser according to the greater or lesser latitude of Jupiter. Now, when Simon Mayr writes about having observed that the said four stars always decline toward the south when they are at the upper half of their circles, it must be that his observations were made at a time when Jupiter had northern latitude. But when I made my first observations, Jupiter was southern; and it remained that way for a long time without be-

8. Imagine a plane slicing through the ecliptic and through the Earth where you are sitting.

9. I.e., when Jupiter has latitude zero in relation to the ecliptic, which happens when it is on the ecliptic. Celestial latitude is measured nowadays in relation to the celestial equator.

10. *Conjunctions* between two or more celestial bodies occur in this context when they appear to be in the same astrological sign. When there is no declination between such bodies, that is, when they have the same latitude with respect to the ecliptic and therefore seem to touch, their conjunctions are said to be *corporal*.

11. I.e., further out in the general direction of the plane of the ecliptic.

coming northern, and thereby allowing the latitudes of the four stars to show that which Simon writes about, until more than two years afterward. Therefore, if he ever saw and observed them, it could only have been two years after me.

See him thus caught in a lie already by his own testimony that he made such observations before me. But I should like to add more. There is probable reason to believe that he never made the observations at all, since he affirms never to have observed or seen the planets exquisitely arranged one after another in a straight line except when they were at their maximum distances from Jupiter; for the truth is that for four months—that is, from mid-February to mid-June 1611, during which the latitude of Jupiter was little or nothing—the arrangement of these four stars in all of their positions was always in a straight line. Notice, moreover, the sagacity by which he tries to prove he preceded me. I wrote in my *Starry Messenger* that I made my first observation on 7 January 1610, and followed this with others on the following nights. Simon Mayr comes along and, appropriating my observations, prints in the title of his book and also in the work itself that he made his observations at the end of the year 1609 to demonstrate his alleged priority to his readers. Nevertheless, the oldest observation he produces as having been made by himself is the second one made by me; but he claims to have made it in the year 1609, neglecting to caution his readers that he is separated from our Church and did not accept the Gregorian emendation, so that the only precedence of his pretended observations consists in this: that the 7th of January of 1610 of our Catholics is the same as the 28th of December of 1609 of those heretics.[12] He also falsely claims to have discovered the Medicean stars' periodic motions, which I myself discovered after long vigils and great efforts and made public both in my *Letters on Sunspots* and in the tract *On Floating Bodies* that Simon obviously used as the basis for his own account.

But I find that I have allowed myself to be drawn into an excessively long digression—longer, perhaps, than the present opportunity required. However, returning to where I left off, I should note that since such clear proofs prevented me from ignoring disaffection toward and obstinate opposition to my works, I had decided to avoid the displeasure I felt from being the target of such frequent sarcasms by keeping entirely silent, thus removing from others the temptation to exercise such a blameworthy faculty. It is true that I should never have lacked occasion to produce other works, perhaps no less unexpected in the philosophical schools and of no

12. In order to bring the calendar into parity with astronomical events, Pope Gregory XIII in 1582 established that the 4th of October would be followed immediately by the 15th of the same month.

less consequence in natural philosophy than those published to date, but because of these occasions I am content to enjoy the opinion and favorable judgment of only a few gentlemen, my real and sincere friends, with whom, by communicating and discussing my thoughts, I have experienced the pleasure of contributing whatever the intellect occasionally provides, while avoiding at the same time a renewal of the injuries that caused me so much pain. Indeed, these gentlemen, my friends, demonstrating general approval for my ideas, attempted with various reasonings to steer me away from such a proposition. And they first tried to persuade me that I should scorn such impertinent attempts to contradict me, since these attempts all turned in the end against their own authors and thus reinforced and amplified my reasoning, giving a clearer argument that my compositions were not mediocre. They added to this the common opinion that vulgarity and mediocrity, since they are little if ever esteemed, fall by the wayside and that human intellects only go where they discover marvellous and exalted things, which instead in immoderate minds excite envy, and, in turn, slander. And even though these and similar reasonings, which I adopted on the authority of these gentlemen, nearly turned me away from my resolve to write no longer, nevertheless my desire to live in quiet away from so many contests subsequently took over; and thus established in my resolve, I thought I could shut up all the tongues that have until now shown such a desire to contradict me. But this design turned out to be vain, and I have not been able in any way to reduce this obstinate influence of mine by which there is always someone who desires to write against and quarrel with me.

Keeping quiet did not help me at all, since these detractors, in their willingness to torment me, had recourse to the stratagem of making me the author of the writings of others; and when I violently objected, they then did something that no one ever does without giving clear evidence of being an emotional and unreasonable soul. And why should not Signor Mario Guiducci have been able to speak in his Academy,[13] according to the position he enjoyed there [as Consul], and subsequently publish his *Discourse on Comets* [*Discorso delle comete*, 1619], without having Lottario Sarsi, a person entirely unknown, turn against me and, with total disregard for its real author, make me the author of that *Discourse* in which I had no other part except the esteem and honor the author gave to me by agreeing with my view,[14] heard by Signor Guiducci in the above-mentioned frequent

13. The famous Accademia Fiorentina had been established in 1540 by Cosimo I de' Medici for promoting Tuscan literature.

14. Guiducci's agreement with Galileo was hardly surprising, since the *Discourse* in question was really Galileo's own work with a few minor additions by Guiducci.

meetings he had with those gentlemen, my friends? And even if the entire *Discourse on Comets* was my work (and no one who knows the work of Signor Mario could ever entertain such a notion), what kind of behavior was this of Sarsi, who pulled off the mask and impudently exposed me when I showed such a desire to remain unknown? Finding myself constrained by this unexpected and unusual behavior, I break my established resolution not to publicize my writings again; and by doing my best to make sure that the inconvenience of this fact should not go unrecognized, I hope to make someone wish he did not wake up the sleeping mastiff by picking a quarrel with him who was silent.

Although I know this name Lottario Sarsi, never heard before in the world, is a disguise for someone who wishes to remain unknown, I will not try to penetrate the disguise as Sarsi did, since I believe this action neither deserves my imitation nor promises to support my arguments.[15] In fact, dealing with him as an unknown person might make my own arguments clearer and give me more freedom to explain my ideas. Those who wear disguises are either low-class persons who desire to have the esteem due only to lords or gentlemen in order to use the honor that nobility brings for their own ends; or else they are gentlemen who, surrendering the respectable dignity appropriate to their station, allow themselves, according to the custom of many cities of Italy, to talk freely about everything with everyone, taking equal pleasure from allowing any person, whoever he may be, to talk and dispute with them without any fear. And I believe that the wearer of this disguise of Lottario Sarsi is among the latter (since if he were among the former, he could derive little pleasure from passing this work off as being greater than it is). Moreover, since he was induced to say something against me in disguise that bare-faced he perhaps would have kept to himself, he ought not to complain when, taking advantage of the liberties allowed against those who wear disguises, I deal with him freely; nor should the expressions I use while I exploit this liberty be taken amiss by him or by others.

I wish Your Excellency to see my reply first since, as a person well-versed in the subject and impartial because of your noble qualities, you ought to be sympathetic to my cause. I shall not neglect to reprimand the audacity of those who, defective in their ignorance but not in their possession of impassioned sentiment (since I have little to fear from the others), viciously misrepresented my arguments among the undiscerning vulgar. When I first read Sarsi's work, I intended to put my reply in the form of a simple letter to Your Excellency; nevertheless, when I began writing, the

15. His antagonist was Orazio Grassi (1582–1654), professor of mathematics at the Jesuit Collegio Romano.

things worthy of comment somehow multiplied in my hands and eventually exceeded by far the limits of a letter. However, I kept my resolution to speak and write to Your Excellency regardless of the eventual form of this response, which I have decided to entitle *The Assayer,* using Sarsi's own metaphor.[16] But it seemed to me that in weighing the propositions of Signor Guiducci, he used a gross and inaccurate steelyard; therefore, I wish to use the tiny scales of the goldsmiths—so exact that they sense less than a six-tieth of a grain. Using the latter with the greatest diligence, I will take account of every proposition produced by the former and test each, annotating and numbering it so that if Sarsi ever sees this and wishes to respond, he can easily avoid neglecting anything.

But coming finally to particulars, it would be well perhaps to say something, so that nothing should remain unpondered, about the title of the work, which Signor Lottario Sarsi calls *Libra Astronomica e Philosophica.* He adds in an epigram that he was moved to use this title because the birth and appearance of the same comet in the sign of Libra mysteriously indicated to him that he should librate in a good scale-pan[17] and ponder the things contained in Signor Mario Guiducci's treatise on comets. Here I note that Signor Sarsi confidently begins to change things as soon as he possibly can to accommodate them to his intention, according to the style he maintains in the entire work. After he got this idea into his head about punning on the correspondence between his *Libra* and the celestial Libra, the appearance of the comet in Libra seemed to add wit to his metaphor, so he liberally[18] says it was born there, not caring to contradict the truth and indeed himself, since this goes against the affirmation of his own master,[19] who draws the following conclusion in his *Disputation* at facsicle 7: "Indeed, whatever seems to be the first light of the comet, it always comes from Scorpio"; and twelve lines later, "this is so, because it was born in Scorpio—that is, in the principal house of Mars"; and a bit further, "I have inquired about its house and affirm, for my part, that it was Scorpio, as everyone agrees." Therefore, with much more propriety and truth, judging by what he says inside the book, he ought to have entitled it, *The Astro-*

16. Grassi called his work *Libra Astronomica ac Philosophica* [1619], playing on the similarity between the common Latin title-word "Liber" or book and "Libra," which refers both to the astronomical sign in which he incorrectly assumed that a comet of the previous year had first appeared and to the scales used for weighing objects. Galileo plays with this pun throughout the following passages, insisting particularly upon the metaphor "weigh" and its various meanings—think, ponder, etc.

17. In the original, *lance,* from Latin *lanx* that forms half of a *bi-lances* or scales. The Italian word for "librate" was not archaic, but this translation approximates the pun.

18. The pun with Libra works better in the Italian.

19. Grassi, of whom Sarsi pretended to be a disciple.

nomical and Philosophical Scorpio, which constellation the sovereign poet Dante calls the

> . . . image of the cold animal
> Who stings and worries people with his tail
> > *(Purgatorio,* IX: 5–6)

It now remains for me, according to the promise I made above to Your Excellency, to say what I think about the proposition, "motion is the cause of heat," showing the instances in which I believe it to be true. But first I must make a few remarks concerning that which we call *heat,* about which I believe the universally held concept is very far from the truth—namely, that it is a true accident, affection, and quality that actually resides in the matter by which we feel ourselves heated.

Whenever I perceive a corporeal material or substance, I feel myself much drawn by necessity to conceive of it at the same time as being bounded by and in the form of some figure, as being large or small in relation to others, as existing in a particular time, as moving or staying still, as touching or not touching another body, as being one, few, or many; and I cannot by any imagination separate it from these considerations. But as to whether it is white or red, bitter or sweet, noisy or silent, or of a pleasing or unpleasing odor, I do not feel that my mind is compelled to understand that it is necessarily accompanied by these conditions; indeed, without guidance from our senses, perhaps neither language nor imagination would ever invent them. I therefore think these tastes, odors, colors, etc., that seem to us to reside in the subject[20] are nothing other than pure names, residing in the sensitive body alone, so that all these qualities are taken away and annihilated when the animal is removed; nevertheless, since we have given them particular names that differ from those of the other first and real accidents, we would like to believe that the latter are truly and really different from the former.

With a few examples I believe I can better explain my idea. I move my hand first over a marble statue, then over a living man. As far as the hand's action is concerned, with respect to the hand it is the same over both subjects—that is, of those first accidents, motion and touching, and we do not call it by any other name; but the living body that receives such operations feels diverse affections according as it is touched in diverse parts. And when it is touched, for example, under the heels of the feet, over the knees, or under the arms, it feels another affection besides the common touching, to which we have given the particular name, "tickling." This affection is wholly ours and is not in the hand; and it seems that whoever should say

20. Why does he use "subject" rather than the more obvious "object"?

that the hand, besides motion and touching, should have in itself another faculty different from these—such as tickling, where tickling is considered to be an accident that resides within the hand—would be making a serious error. A bit of paper or a feather, rubbed lightly over any part of our body, completes, with respect to itself, everywhere the same operation—that is, moving and touching. But in us, when it touches between our eyes, our nose, and below our nostrils, it causes an almost intolerable titillation; and in other parts of the body it can hardly be felt. Now that titillation comes entirely from us and not from the feather; and when the living and sensitive body is removed, it is no longer anything but a pure name. Many qualities that are attributed to natural bodies, such as tastes, odors, colors, etc., exist, I believe, in a similar way and no more.

A solid and, so to speak, very material body, moved and applied to any part of my person produces in me that sensation that we call *touch,* which, even though it occupies the entire body, nevertheless seems principally to reside in the palms of the hands, and especially in the fleshy tips of the fingers, by which we feel very small differences of roughness, smoothness, softness and hardness that we do not distinguish as well with other parts of the body. Some of these sensations are more pleasing and others are less, according as the figures of the touched bodies are smooth, rough, sharp or dull, hard or yielding. This sense, since it is more material than the others and comes from the solidity of the matter, seems to have something to do with the element earth.[21] Since some bodies are continuously dissolving into tiny particles [*particelle minimi*], of which those that are heavier than air descend and those that are lighter ascend, perhaps two other senses come into being when these particles touch two parts of our body that are more sensitive than the skin, impervious as it is to the incursions of such subtle, tenuous, and yielding matter. The descending particles, received over the superior parts of the tongue and penetrating in a mixture of its substance and humidity, bring tastes—pleasant or unpleasant according to the diversity of the touching of the various shapes of these tiny particles and according as they are few or many and fast or slow. The ascending particles, entering at the nose, strike some tiny protuberances that are the instrument of smell, and there in a similar fashion their contact and passage are received with pleasure or displeasure according to their shape and according as their movements are slow or fast and as their quantity is small or large. One sees the tongue and the canals of the nose very appropriately situated: the former extended below to receive the incursions that descend

21. Galileo's association of each of the five elements—earth, air, fire, water and the so-called "fifth essence"—with one of the five senses was a commonplace of the chemistry and psychology of the time, but you can guess how these associations were described before Galileo.

and the latter situated to receive those that rise. Perhaps fluids that descend from the air accommodate themselves by a kind of analogy to the stimulation of taste and the fires that ascend accommodate themselves to odors. The remaining element of air is for sounds, which come to us indiscriminately from above, from below, and from the sides, since we are located in the air, whose movement in its own region is itself uniformly disposed on all sides. The situation of the ear is accommodated, as far as possible, to all positions; and we feel that sounds are made (and they do not require any sonorous or sound-resistant qualities) when a frequent tremor of the air, rippled into very minute waves, moves some cartilage of a certain drum in our ear. Furthermore, there are many external means to cause this rippling of the air, all of which may be reduced perhaps to the tremor of some body that ripples the air by beating against it, so that the waves extend throughout with great velocity, from the frequency of which arises the highness of the sound and from the rarity of which arises the lowness of the sound. But I do not believe that something else in the external bodies is required besides greatness, shape, quantity and slow or fast movements, in order for them to excite in us tastes, odors, and sounds; and I think that if the ears, the tongues and the noses were taken away, there would remain the shapes, the quantities, and the movements but not the odors nor the tastes nor the sounds, which I do not believe are anything other than names when considered apart from the living animal, just as tickling and titillation are nothing but names when the underarms and the skin around the nose are removed. And just as the four elements are related to the four senses under consideration, so I believe that sight, a sense far superior to the others, is related to light, but in that proportion of excellence which obtains between the finite and the infinite, between the temporary and the instantaneous, between that which has quantity and that which is indivisible, between light and darkness: I do not pretend to understand more than a small amount regarding this sensation and the things pertaining to it; but to explain—or, more exactly, to sketch out on paper—that very small amount would take much time, so I therefore leave it in silence.

To return to my original purpose in this section, having noted that many affections reputed to be qualities residing in external subjects really have no existence except in ourselves, and outside of us are nothing but names, I should like to add that I am very much inclined to believe that heat is of this kind, and that the matter which produces and makes us feel heat, called by the general name of *fire,* consists of a multitude of tiny particles, shaped in such a way and moved with such a velocity as to penetrate our body through their extreme fineness when they encounter it; and that their touching, which we feel during their passage through our substance, is the affection that we call *heat,* agreeable or annoying according to the quantity and greater or lesser velocity of these tiny particles that prick and penetrate us. Thus, penetration is agreeable when it aids our necessary and imperceptible perspiration, and annoying when it causes our substance to be altered excessively in opening up during it and closing afterwards. Thus, the action of fire is nothing other than to penetrate, by its movement, all bodies with its extreme fineness, dissolving them sooner or later according to the quantity and velocity of the *ignicoli*[22] and the density or rarity of the matter of these bodies; and there are many of these bodies that, when they disintegrate, turn for the most part into other *ignicoli,* and keep dissolving in this fashion as long as soluble matter remains. But I do not believe that there are other qualities in fire besides shape, multitude, motion, penetration and touch, or that heat is one of these; and I believe that this heat depends so much upon us that heat is nothing other than a simple word when the living and sensitive body is removed. And since the *ignicoli* produce this affection in us by their passage and touching through our substance, it is manifest that when they are immobile, their operation should be nil; and indeed, a quantity of fire contained in the porosity and anfractuousness of a stone after it has been heated does not heat us, though we hold the stone in our hand, because the fire remains at rest. But when the stone is put in water, where the weight of the fire is less of a hindrance to its movement, and where the water passages are more open than those of the air, the *ignicoli* escape and encounter our hand, penetrate it, and we feel heat.

Since the presence of *ignicoli* is insufficient alone to excite heat but some movement is also required, I therefore believe motion was very justly said to be the cause of heat. This motion causes arrows and other wooden things burn and lead and other metals liquefy, since the tiny particles of fire, moved quickly either by themselves or, when their own force is not enough, chased by an impetuous wind from a bellows, penetrate all bodies; and of those bodies, some dissolve into other tiny flying *ignicoli* and some into very fine dust, and others liquefy and produce fluids. But if this proposition is taken according to the common view, which supposes that a stone or piece of metal or wood when moved becomes heated, I believe it is pompous idiocy. Now rubbing and scrubbing two hard bodies together, either by dissolving a part into tiny flying and very fine particles or by opening a passage to the *ignicoli* inside, excites the *ignicoli* eventually to motion; and when these encounter our bodies and penetrate and flow through them, the sensitive soul, feeling their touch with their passage, experiences that agreeable or annoying affection that we call *heat, burning,* or *scalding.* Perhaps when the dissolution and attrition continues and is contained within the smallest quantity of *ignicoli,* their motion is temporary and their

---

22. Literally, "little fires"—Galileo's word for the tiny particles of heat.

operation is calorific only; and when they arrive at the last and highest dissolution into really indivisible atoms, they create light, which moves or, better, expands and diffuses instantaneously and is powerful enough—due to that which I should call its subtlety, rarity, and immateriality or perhaps due to another condition yet unnamed and different from all these—to fill immense spaces.

I do not wish, Your Excellency, to set out inadvertently into an infinite ocean, where I should not be able to return to port; nor do I wish, as I attempt to clear up one difficulty, to cause another hundred to arise, which I fear might happen even with this small distance that I have gone from the shore. Therefore, I shall save the rest for a more opportune occasion.

Mario Guiducci to Galileo in Florence (Rome, 18 April 1625)

Most Excellent Sir:

It has been several weeks since I have written you or received letters from you, although I have always had news of you and of your well-being and of your continuing to work on your *Dialogues*.

I have been several times with the Prince of Sant'Angelo [Federico Cesi], talking about you and of the works you have written and are writing. On the advice of His Excellency, I have put off giving Ingoli the letter written to him, and I will continue to put it off until you, notwithstanding the arguments of the Prince, order me to do the contrary. My considerations are these. First: several months ago at the Congregation of the Holy Office it was proposed by a pious person to have prohibited or corrected the *Saggiatore,* saying that in it is praised the doctrine of Copernicus concerning the movement of the earth. About this affair a cardinal undertook the responsibility to inform himself about the case and report back. By good luck, it happened that he commissioned the task to P. [Giovanni di] Guevara, general of a kind of Theatines that I believe are called Minimi. The said father then went to France with the Cardinal Legate [Francesco Barberini]. He read the work diligently; and since it pleased him very much, he praised and commended it to the cardinal. What's more, he put on paper several points in defense of it according to which that doctrine of the motion, if it indeed was asserted there, seemed to him ought not to be condemned. And thus the question quieted down for the time being. Now, not having the support that we might expect from that cardinal, it does not seem worth risking some sort of reproach. For in the letter to Ingoli, Copernicus's opinion is defended ex professo; and even though it is said clearly that a superior light has revealed it to be false, nonetheless, the insincere will not believe it in this way and will cause trouble again. Since we do not have the protection of Cardinal Barbarino, who is out of town, since in this matter

we have against us another important person who once was a strong supporter, and since this war-like confusion has considerably annoyed the
pope—to the point, indeed, where no one would be able to talk to him
about it, the matter would certainly remain at the discretion and the mind
of the *frati*. For all these reasons it seems best, as I said, to quiet down the
question and let it sleep a while, rather than keep it awake with persecu-
tions and have to defend it against those who can give harsh blows. After
all, time will assist the cause.

As I wrote you, Sarsi's work has still not been printed, and I believe that
he, in these times of trouble at Genoa, is worried about his homeland.

I hope to be there before mid-May. When I leave, I will put the letter to
Ingoli in the hands of Mr. Filippo Magalotti so that he can present it when
you wish.

Prince Cesi told me that the Accademia dei Lincei has done me the singular favor of admitting me among its members. I know that this has been
your principal motive; hence I recognize that the favor has come from you,
and in time I will thank you. In the meanwhile, let this be a beginning, or
rather an expression of thanks for the news given me. And finally, I kiss
your hands and pray that the Lord God will give you all happiness.

(P.S.) Yesterday I was for some time with the Illustrious Cardinal (Alessandro) Orsini, who asked me how good Cosimo Lotti was at building
fountains, for he has been proposed to him as a singular man in this profession. I answered that I knew he was a painter but that I knew nothing else.
He then asked me if I knew some excellent person in this service, and I
said that I knew no one but that I had heard you say that in Rome there was
someone who was very ingenious and inventive, but that I did not know if
he were still alive. If you have anyone to propose in this matter, let me
know, and send me some information about Cosimo Lotti, who I have heard
has worked at [Villa di] Castello. The cardinal is still very affectionate toward you, but he is on the side of the Illustrious Mr. Apelle [Cristoforo
Scheiner].

Benedetto Castelli to Galileo in Florence (Rome, 2 October 1632)

My most illustrious Patron and Lord:

I returned to Rome last Wednesday and found your letter, about which I
had heard while still out of town; and he who informed you that the letter
had arrived told me that he had assured you what the truth is, that I did not
fail to do everything in order to avoid a deliberation against your noble,
useful, and great work, declaring openly that not proceeding in the manner
proper to this high and holy tribunal, everything would have turned against

the reputation and the reverence that is owed it, and that what I said was not intended to prevent its prohibiting and condemning the book, but only that it proceed in such a way that after the fact they could say what it was they had prohibited; and in this manner I spoke forcibly, and with all reverence, to the Reverend Father Maestro and his companions, in whom I found in appearance a very good disposition. I added that if a decision was taken against one who had written very modestly, reverendly, and reservedly, that would cause others to write recklessly and resolutely, pointing out to these Fathers that, although it was their job to prohibit or not to prohibit the pages written by the hand of men, still their authority did not extend to the point of prohibiting God and nature from revealing at one time or another their recondite secrets in a thousand different ways. And now, having returned to Rome, I spoke for some time with the Reverend Father Commissioner [Vincenzo Maculano], offering to save him trouble by explaining to him the book of the Dialogues in that part and principally in those places where the point about the motion of the earth is treated. Indeed, since this Father is a very sharp person, and a very good friend of mine, I took care to speak to him in these words: "Father Commissioner, I find written in Saint Augustine expressly that this question, whether the earth moves or not, has been carefully examined by holy writers, but not determined or taught, since it has nothing whatever to do with the salvation of souls. Indeed, after the passage of many centuries since [the time of] Saint Augustine, there came into the world the high genius of N. Copernicus, who with Herculean labors and hard work wrote the volume of the Revolution of the Heavenly Orbs, and, encouraged by the great Cardinal Nicholas Schomberg and other Catholic, pious, and well educated bishops, he published his book, dedicating it to the most learned pontiff, who was Paul III; and on the basis of these suppositions, with the aid of his tables, the Holy Mother Church completed the reform of the calendar, in such a way that the work of N. Copernicus has been, it could be said, approved by the authority of the Holy Church." Moved by these things, I confessed to not having any scruples about holding what I have been persuaded by most efficacious reasons and by many proofs of experience and observation: that the earth moves according to those movements assigned to it by Copernicus; and in all this I have many times conversed with pious and very intelligent theologians who have shown me no scruples whatever. Hence, given these things, I saw no reason at all why your *Dialogues* should be prohibited. The said Father answered that, although he was of the same opinion, this question should not end with the authority of the sacred Scriptures, and he said indeed that he intended to write a memo on the subject and that he would show it to me. I want nothing more in this matter, only that your book be read and understood, for I am certain that this is the way to avoid precipitating into an unreasonable sentence. . . .

35. Agostino Scilla, *Vain Speculations Undeceived by the Senses*

After studying in Rome under Andrea Sacchi, one of the leaders of the "classical" or "Carraccian" school of baroque painting, Agostino Scilla (pronounced "Shilla", 1629–1700) became a successful painter (as he himself points out), particularly of portraits, in his native city of Messina, Sicily. Like many of his Renaissance predecessors, Scilla was also a widely-read man of letters and an active member of the local learned society, the Accademia della Fucina, in which he took the ironic academic name "Lo Scolorito"—"One who has been deprived of color." Although he does not mention Galileo by name, it is obvious that he was as much impressed by the methodological innovations of Galileo and his later disciples as were the members of the contemporary Accademia degli Investiganti in neighboring Naples, who had recently invoked it in an all-out war against the remnants of Aristotelian metaphysics. He was forced to flee after the failure of the four-year rebellion of Messina against the viceregal government in Palermo, and hence against the king of Spain, who was also king of Sicily and of Naples. After a brief residence at the court of Turin, he settled in Rome, where he continued his career as an artist by collaborating with Cirro Ferri, then the leading painter of the prestigious art academy of San Luca (Saint Luke). He also continued to pursue his scientific interests by assembling a large collection of coins and natural curiosities, probably in imitation of the several late Renaissance collectors he mentions in the text.

Vain Speculations is Scilla's only published work, and it was published only once during his lifetime. But it was cited with approval by several of the leading philosophers of the age, most notably Leibniz, and a synopsis of it, published in English the following year, was presented to the Royal Society in London in 1696. After the appearance of a somewhat truncated Latin translation of the book in Rome in 1752, Scilla was largely forgotten: his name appears in none of the standard histories of Italian literature.

The Author to the Reader:

Courteous reader, I know that I should exchange a few words with you, now that my letter is in print, but I will not imitate the style of some authors who are quick to take the occasion to blame their own errors on the

From Agostino Scilla, *La vana speculazione disingannata del senso* (Naples: Andrea Colicchia, 1670). Translated for this volume by Lydia G. Cochrane. Footnotes are translator's notes.

printer. I have never understood why it should be customary for even the coarsest persons to insult an honest man instead of thanking him when his work is finished, and to pass him off as slovenly, half-asleep, and ignorant, when making mistakes comes so easily to everyone that it is hard to imagine anything less laborious or less exclusive to writers. Let me put an end to the question by saying that if you are a man of learning and familiar with proper writing, you will certainly take pity on both the printer and myself and rectify our errors—his and mine alike. If you are not, everything will seem just fine to you, in which case I see no reason to offer excuses. In any event, I beg you to consider that this letter is by no means a treatise on rhetoric or on good manners, but on natural things; and I would prefer to obey the natural inclinations of my speech than crack my skull wondering whether a word should be written in one way or another. Therefore I have put things down as I understood them, and if I have explained an idea so that it can be easily grasped by anyone, that is enough for me. As a matter of fact, I am not blind enough to imitate some writers who are persuaded that they have written in the finest Florentine only because they have put words together following the rules of the Crusca,[1] because I know that you have to get the sentence right as well, which is extremely difficult for anyone not born in Tuscany. It is difficult, I tell you, to be born outside that land and write with the precision and the polish that are the ornament of the *Essays on Natural Experiments* of the respected members of the Academy of the Cimento, dedicated to his most serene highness, the Grand Duke,[2] or with the coherence of Signor Francesco Redi's most accurate *History of the Insects*.[3] My only remaining task, then, is to state what my

1. I.e., the Accademia della Crusca, of Florence, founded in 1582: it compiled the first full dictionary of a modern European language, namely, the literary Tuscan Italian in which Petrarch and Boccaccio had written their poems and stories and that had been codified by Pietro Bembo in the early sixteenth century. The first edition of the *Vocabolario* was published in Venice in 1612.

2. The Accademia del Cimento, the first academy in Europe dedicated specifically to promoting experimental science, was founded by the first generation of Galileo's disciples in Florence in 1657 under the protection of Cardinal Leopoldo dei Medici, brother of Grand Duke Ferdinando II (who was in his spare time an experimental scientist). Many of the experiments conducted by the academy were published by its secretary, Lorenzo Magalotti, as the *Saggi,* or *Essays concerning the Experiments of the Academy* (1667).

3. Redi was the leader of the first generation of Galileian scientists in Florence after the dissolution of the Accademia del Cimento, and the leader of the anti-Aristotelian "deconstructionists"—those experimental scientists who set out to destroy conventional scientific categories without proposing others in their place. His *On Vipers* (1664) banished the notion that snake venom was fatal when injected into the human body in any manner; his still more famous *On the Generation of Insects* destroyed the theory of spontaneous generation—i.e., that insects and some rodents could be generated from the bits of "soul" still present in the decaying flesh of other animals.

intentions may have been when I made much of some philosopher and called him "great" or some such thing—most particularly Epicurus, inasmuch as I do not take him to be a miserable glutton, as the common herd scornfully perceives him, one of the most self-possessed of the ancient philosophers, as the moral Seneca, the erudite Gassendi, and a hundred other grave Men of Letters have asserted. Be that as it may, I declare that the praise and the judgments expressed here are to be understood within the limits of these authors' capacities and of what is permitted to discourse on the liberal sciences. I am a Catholic, and I submit everything with true and prompt resignation to the censorship of my Superiors; and I intend, with God's grace, to live and die under the dictates of the Holy Roman Church. Keep well!

To the most illustrious and excellent Lord and most observant Patron, Signor Doctor N. N., Most illustrious and excellent sir;

. . . This is the sort of man I am—unadorned by belles lettres—and my only good quality is my desire not to live by hazard. For that reason I have stuck it in my brain that doubting about things is the best and the only means to knowing them less remotely or with more probability. I confess, moreover, that I am not so enamored of speculative philosophy as to think that I cannot enjoy this world without its mediation: I have a great love for philosophy; I yearn for it, more as something all men need to help them avoid being taken in by others than for any other reason. For me, the philosopher judged the best is the one who has expressed his concepts the most gracefully, and the philosophers who have founded the most lasting schools are the ones who have constructed the least imperfect systems out of their fantasies.

Nor would I hesitate to state that every one of the master philosophers was quite aware of the incertitude of the notions he propagated, and I would consider it an intellectual blunder to accept their opinions as if they reported true causes, when in reality they are nothing but passing fancies and fine ways of explaining what we can in no way understand. If some statement—or, better, some system—seems probable to us, this is due to our judgment, and not to things in fact being so.

The fact of the matter is that it was the great Democritus[4] who put an odd thought in my head when he speaks of losing his temper at a serving girl because she had pointed out something to him, teaching him what he had wanted to arrive at through lofty speculations. This confirms my mind's doubting habits, for I believe that the philosophers' profession has been to investigate avidly and to search for pastures for their fine minds—

4. Greek philosopher of the fifth century B.C. according to whom all substances were composed of small particles, or atoms: hence, the founder of the atomistic explanation of matter.

that is, to subject everything, rightly or wrongly, to their intellect—rather than teaching us the truth fully (if they could have done so). I am not ashamed of my perplexity, and the more I reflect on the hypotheses concerning the great machine of the universe, the less I say. One of these hypotheses was presented most forcefully by Ptolemy,[5] who, with clear and worthy proofs separated its parts, stable and revolving. Another, with no less clarity of demonstration, collapsed the whole of it, unhinged the earth, and stopped celestial motion itself, belying what every living man sees with his eyes. Nor would human ingenuity lack other ways to philosophize, negating both these systems and preaching many others, should innovation and not the obligation to track down the truth be the purpose of its speculations. . . .

It would have been a waste of effort if I had cultivated letters, because if I followed the Peripatetics[6] I would have to fool myself into thinking that I knew everything, which would not be true. If I followed the great Democritus I would have something more reasonable to say, thanks to his fine work on atoms. Still, how confidently he confesses, "The cause we do not know, for truth is an abyss." If I followed the impeccable Plato, any matter discussed would lead to an eternal and indeterminate dispute, but why waste so many words? If I lent an ear to Zeno, I would not know whether I could walk or move, and with the others it would be even worse. To end the list, with Euripides I would have to sing, with a beautiful Spanish guitar flourish, "Who knows whether this life is death, or death is what we call life?" One thing is certain: if I were prohibited observation and the study of the anatomy of the things that we see and handle, and if I had to encourage the melancholy humors of those who put their own eyes out so they can dedicate themselves exclusively to the abstractions of speculative philosophy, I would have to confess the desperation and confusion of my soul and would become a passionate supporter of my fellow professor, Pyrrus, stubbornly insisting, with Empedocles, "All things are hidden. We can perceive nothing with our senses; discern nothing; discover the nature of nothing." This will not happen, though, because in the consideration of natural bodies (in which some vestige of truth can be detected) there is no need to turn to the murky abstractions of the Metaphysicians. However, if the difficulty of the material that I have a mind to trace should cloud my faculty of sense, I will realize that I must doubt: my "that's how it seems to me" will never lead me into the mistaken and stolid presumption of others,

5. Greek mathematician of the second century A.D., author of, among other works, a *Geography,* which remained authoritative through the fifteenth century, and of the earth-centered system of planetary and stellar motion rejected in favor of a heliocentric system first by Copernicus and then by Galileo.

6. I.e., Aristotelians.

who, guided by insubstantial sophistic quibblings, pronounce "that's how it is."

I will say, to finish, halfway blushing for my simplicity, that I would like things that are subjected to sense to be established uniquely by what sense determines. I would also like it if philosophy could include a modicum of history, and things that have no need of long, drawn-out speculations not carry us on flights of fancy to distant and spacious pastures of the possible, as is the habit of some of the noblest minds of today, who consistently disdain mere history.

This is what I would like, and in particular in the case before me—that is, in the consideration of the glossopetrae of Malta, about which I will frankly say that my mind, totally unpreoccupied by opinion and not impelled by the authority of any master, but borne along by chance, believed them bits of different petrified animals. I will tell the tale here, and will explain how this happened. I cannot promise you that I will use art in the telling, nor will I take pains over the organization of the parts of my discourse, as happens in a proper treatise. Rather, I will explain pell-mell and as best I can what occurs to me, counting on your courtesy to kindly excuse my errors. My justification is that I have not rashly made up my mind on any opinion mentioned, nor arrived at it without first thinking diligently. If then I was mistaken, error is a fault common to all men.

While walking in southern Calabria a few miles above the city of Reggio, on the road that leads to a place called Musorrima [now Mosorrofa], I spied a considerable mound of snail shells, striated clam shells, and similar shells, not at that point petrified. This seemed to me an important fact, and I decided to take a good look at the surrounding terrain, where I could find no sign of such shells. I could not get enough of looking at them and of digging them out, since it seemed to me extraordinary that they could have been so well conserved and for such a long time so far from the sea and so high above sea level, more than six miles' walk up the steep slopes of those mountains. Out of curiosity I asked about them of the peasants who live in those parts, and they answered promptly that the shells had been carried there by the sea at the time of the Flood. I pitied those simple people and marveled at such extreme credulity, noting that in their homespun fashion and in total tranquillity they attributed the effect of those things of unknown origin to a cause that outstripped all human memory. Still, in the end I realized that "greater wisdom has the common herd, because it has only as much as it needs," as some philosopher has said, which means that one must pay great respect to simple and natural statements, since truth is above all things easy to understand. And if at times it does not appear so, it is probably our own obstinacy that makes understanding difficult.

Then, preoccupied and marveling much at what I had seen, I returned to

Messina, where, continuing in my leisure hours to read about ancient coins, a favorite pastime, I came across a passage in Strabo[7] that aroused my curiosity. Philosophizing on the true reason for unusual and sudden marine inundations, he cites several passages from other works, one of which says that far from the sea "in many places a great number of mussel shells, oyster shells, and scallop shells are found; and there are salt marshes around the temple of Ammon and the road, three thousand stadia long, which leads to it. . . . Near it, too, fragments of seafaring ships can be seen which, they say, issued forth from the gaping earth. They say that upon small columns sleep dolphins bearing this inscription: 'Of ambassadors from Cyrene.'" After saying this he [Eratosthenes] commends the opinion of the natural philosopher, Strato, and that of the Lydian, Xanthus. . . . "And [Xanthus says] that he himself had seen in many places quite far from the sea small mussel shells, pecten shells, and the shapes of testacea fixed in rocks; and [he had seen] salt marshes in Armenia and Matiene and lower Phrygia; and for these reasons was convinced that those places were at one time sea." I found the account acceptable, but not the conclusion, thinking it full of a number of sizable ambiguities, since these shells could be the remains of animals from fresh water or brackish lakes, dried by some accident, or they could have been transported by the sea during sudden inundations (news of which has failed to reach us) and left there. Similarly, a fragment of a ship might be found in the ground far from the sea, but it might have been carried in a triumphal parade, or made inland for use in boat jousts, as was practiced in Rome, where many a cutwater of a ship's prow has been found. This is no reason to conclude that such a terrain was once Neptune's domain. And so forth, with a hundred similar objections.

But let us go back a bit. This passage in Strabo reminded me that in our own Sicily there are many places—for example, in the hills near Messina—where most of the stone dug out of the rock quarries is little more than a conglomeration of ocean-tossed shells and gravels alien to the place, combined with an infinite number of other marine bodies.

I believed the whole lot to be true marine animal shells, nor did I admit any doubt in my discourse—all the more so since Cardano,[8] who could

7. Greek geographer of the first century A.D., author of a historical-topical description, in seventeen books, of the world known to Romans of his day.

8. Girolamo Cardano (c. 1501–76), physician and professor of medicine at the University of Pavia, author of numerous works on mathematics, physics, metaphysics, medicine, and magic, as well as of an apologetical autobiography (1575). The reference here is to the most widely read of his works in his own day, *De Subtilitate,* a "mastrodontic encyclopedia of the natural sciences" according to his most recent biographer, Marino Gliozzi (*DBI*), published in Nuremberg in 1550 and in Frankfurt-am-Main in 1556.

hardly be called inept, speaks of such shells and, citing a passage in Pausanius, gives his opinion that this could easily happen: "For when the shells of conchylia are among stones for a long time, and are beneath the earth, in many places they turn to stone, with their shape intact but their substance altered." I would have liked it if he had not only touched on the question but discussed why in some places these shells become petrified and in others no, for experience persuades me, since I have concrete evidence continually before my eyes, that in many places they can conglomerate and even become like stone. Both along the arm of the Port of Messina that faces east and in the Gregale, one can easily observe quarries that produce mill wheels out of a rock that is most certainly a mixture of various sorts of multicolored small stones resembling sea-washed gravel. It can happen that the hole left when the wheels are quarried fills up again with loose gravel, and in a short time appears as a mass that incorporates whatever shells may have fallen into it. I would obviously be mad if I chose to believe that these shells were born there, and I can see without a shade of doubt that this is true for all like shells along the entire coast when it comes their turn to be regurgitated by the sea and suffer the same imprisonment.

I understood from this, as I was saying, not only how easy it is to observe snail shells in stone, but also how this rock comes to be composed and amassed (although the exact composition varies according to chance and location). I completely rejected the other opinion as requiring a great deal of faith and as lacking proof, since it is backed up by no demonstration or evidence except the weakest sort of conjecture. I am speaking of the opinion, reported in your most learned letter, of those who insist that all stone—or at least metallic ore—grows. I believe this is true, though not because the ore struggles its way out of the propagating viscera of rocky minerals, but by means of an agglomeration caused by some salt, some exudation, some exhalation, some heat due to fermentation—unknown to me—that exists in that place and that binds the sediment into stone, converting it into its own disposition and nature.

To be sure, it would not be much to believe that nature makes mineral deposits grow by themselves because some ingenious mind has expressed this concept so well that it seems to explain the hindrances other writers see. The same cannot be said, however, of some who follow Aristotle's writings superstitiously and do not blush to assign vegetable qualities to bits of metal sown like grains of wheat simply because he says as much in chapters forty and forty-one of his work *On Admirable Things*. "But I fear," the learned Maiolo writes,[9] and I do not doubt him, but have the

9. Simone Maiolo, or Majolo (1520–c. 1598), cited in his *Dies Caniculares, seu Colloquia Tria & Viginti* ("Colloquia in which Many Admirable Things of Nature Are Described,

utmost respect for him, "that this is too much to believe; for in that book [Aristotle's chapter 41] too, this less probable thing is contained. . . . In Cyprus, he says, near the place called Tyrrias, copper is produced. Cutting this into small bits, they plant it and it grows with the rains and comes forth and is finally collected. This is his account. If it is so, I attribute it to a miracle of God." Still, Maiolo resolves this problem well: "But in our region of Italy, things of this sort are held to be tall tales; for everywhere it is considered ridiculous that metals, when sown, grow with the rains." According to what I have read on the subject, which has been but little, I understand that mineral deposits often run out because, as Georgio Agricola writes in his treatise on the *Art of Metals*,[10] they have their heads and their tails. In all mines, however, it is true that the miners make every effort to reach the principal veins of the deposit, since these are richer in metals, which are, so to speak, ramified in the earth, twisting through and insinuating themselves into the viscera of the rock. This shows us that the deposit is a particular disposition of such a place in which the intrinsic virtue, almost like a root, follows its nature and converts and distends the veins of metal. If this were not so, miners on the island of Elba would not have to wait twenty years in order to extract minerals from the mines that are now exhausted, either because the best has been taken out, or perhaps because the excessive depth of the mine shafts makes them difficult to work. For all these reasons I am disinclined to accept the opinion of those who insist that mines replenish themselves with fresh, burgeoning metal within an assigned time period. No matter what they say, one has either to concede that the ground grows together with the minerals, or that the latter vegetate, producing a pure vein of a size equal to the given space, which is not true. If it were true, some of these mines could be abandoned for twice the usual time—for forty years, that is—and if the mineral indeed coagulated like saltpeter seepages and no other substance were needed, pure metal should come from them, and in double the quantity produced in twenty years. This would most certainly be marvelously convenient, since what people strive for with such wearisome effort could be had for the taking lying layered up about the countryside or piled high in prodigal and precious pyramids. We all know that material of varying purity is taken out of the same deposit because the veins are of differing perfection, or perhaps because they are to

Both in the Air and in Europe, Asia, and Africa"), first published in Rome, 1583, republished in 1597, 1600, 1607, and 1614; it is here cited in colloquy 19, chap. 41. Maiolo also wrote a world history for the purpose of defending the use of sacred images (1585).

10. Agricola's (1490–1555) *De Re Metalica* (1556) was based on his experiences as a physician in a mining town in Bohemia and contained a section on diseases common to mine workers.

a greater or lesser degree mixed with the earth along the veins. Anyone can deduce from this that the hollow places rumored to have been refilled never did produce any intrinsic growth, but were filled up with material that collected there. Because, if material gushed up out of the heart of the rock, it ought to take the form of the space left empty and fill it completely, and not be mixed with pebbles and earth—relatively unproductive materials because not yet converted and transfused by the effluvium active in such a place. Thus I have to say that I most reasonably agreed with those who assert that this is all done by combination of the various parts, and that it is more likely to happen in places in which the terrain is propitious, as it is on the island of Elba, where the soil is like the lodestone, and consequently, since it is impregnated with the sort of ferment that makes iron, is more apt to ripen. . . .

I remembered that Strabo and the philosophers he cites devoted considerable thought to how the sea could at some time have deposited those confirmations of its awesome wanderings so far inland, and also to whether the shells and similar bodies were the remains of marine animals or were stones so configured in the absolute, produced by nature in inland areas and in the mountains. They speak almost as if this was so clear to sense perception that there was nothing to quarrel about. Recalling this, I resolved to believe and to defend what my eyes had taught me. For that reason, I thought an unsubstantial notion the idea of those who "ascribe these things either to the soul of the world or, in general, to nature, which, since it is everywhere the same and contains everywhere the ideas of all the things it brings forth, forms stones from suitable moisture, and in the midst of the land, that externally resemble mussel shells, just as it is wont to produce fish in the middle of a remote sea." [11] Since this opinion is denied by immense amounts of evidence, it seemed to me better not to follow it. Moreover, it seemed to me impossible that it not have been excoriated by many authors. I proved not to have been mistaken, for when I thought to seek out the sentiments of some serious writers, leafing through a number of books, that was exactly what I found. Francesco Calzolari, [12] who writes judiciously on the question, has ideas similar to my own, and my first

11. Pierre Gassendi (1592–1655), scientist, metaphysician, and priest of the Oratoire in France. In a series of courses in philosophy he presented at Aix-en-Provence in 1617–23, subsequently published as *Exercitationes Paradoxica adversus Aristotelos,* he rejected Aristotelian physics. He adopted Galileo's Copernican astronomy and was a frequent correspondent of Galileo from 1625 on. In his *Observations* on the ancient biographer of the philosophers, Diogenes Laertius, he proposed an atomistic theory of matter. His theses on all these questions are summed up in his greatest work, the *Syntagma Philosophia* of 1658, referred to here are the chapters *De Lapidibus ac Metallis* ("On Stones and Metals").

12. The reference is to the catalogue of the natural history museum assembled by Francesco Calzolari of Verona (1552–1609) and by his son Francesco Jr.; it was published as *Mus-*

552 The Scientific Revolution

thought was that I had on my side a writer of solid authority—in fact a truly authoritative voice, because he was backed up by Fracastoro, famous among men of letters, whom he declares "said that he thought that these [things]"—that is, the petrified bodies under discussion, "had once been real, living things, tossed there by the sea and born in the sea." The erudite Simone Maiolo was of like opinion: "Indeed, I should not think it so marvelous that mussel shells and the bones of living things are found within stones or rocks, since those bones dug up from the bowels of the earth, hardened by the long passage of time, and solidified in the earth itself, have been preserved there from the universal flood, or even from some other catastrophe. Things of this sort are found, as Georg Braun relates in his work on that region, in the district of Zichem on the Meuse." [13] The same idea is confirmed by the virtuous and candid Ludovico Moscardo. He provides a number of drawings of petrified animals, along with observations on "various species of fish, such as bream, eels, and others, which are hardened inside a sort of many-layered stone, which, when these layers are split, always leave the fish half on one side and the other half attached to the other. When the fish remains split in half in this manner, [you can see] all its bones from its head to its tail." [14] If I transcribed all the passages from authors who agree with my view, there would be no end to it. If you want to go to the trouble, read for yourself Pietro Maffeo, Paolo Orosio, Andrea Cesalpino, Athanasius Kircher, Pierre Potier, Fabio Colonna, Ferrante Imperato, Alessandro d'Alessandro, [15] and many others, while I take

---

aeum Francisci Calceolari in Verona, 1622. The sixteenth-century philosopher-poet-physician Girolamo Fracastoro is quoted in the *Musaeum*, sec. 3.

13. Colloquy 18 in the book cited above at n. 9.

14. Ludovico (or Lodovico) Moscardo was a patrician and leading member of the musical Accademia dei Filarmonici of Verona. His most important book was a history of his native city from its origins to 1668, published at Verona in the latter year. He was also an ardent collector of miscellaneous rarities. Scilla here quotes from the catalogue he himself prepared and published in 1656 as *Note, overo Memoria del museo di Lodovico Moscardo.* The author published a second, and much enlarged, edition in 1672, which, of course, Scilla could not have seen; like the first, it was divided into three sections: (1) "ancient things," (2) rocks and minerals, and (3) "corals, sea-shells, animals, and fruits."

15. Giovan Pietro (and not just Pietro) Maffei (b. 1535), a Jesuit and professor at the Collegio Romano; he wrote biographies of King Manuel of Portugal and Ignatius of Loyola and a commentary on the pontificate of Gregory XIII as well as, after an eleven-year research expedition to Portugal, his most famous work (six editions after the first of 1588), *Historiae Indicae* ("A History of the Indies"). Paolus Orosius, a disciple of Augustine, wrote (or rather cribbed from available compendia) a history of the world from the Creation to 417 A.D., which was used as a standard reference work throughout the Middle Ages. Andrea Cesalpino (1524/25–1603) was prefect of the botanical garden of the University of Pisa and after 1592 physician to Pope Clement VIII and professor of medicine at the Sapienza in Rome. Under the guise of a defense of Aristotelian metaphysics (*Quaestiones Peripateticae,* 1569), he

the liberty of citing Melchiore Guilandino on the opinions of Plutarch and Olympiadorus: "Plutarch too writes, in Isis and Osiris, and Olympiadorus agrees [in his commentary] on the first book of the Meteora, that Egypt had been sea, since it is found to this day to have many shells in its pits and mountains." [16] To tell it plainly, I thought my ideas on this point agreed with both the truth and the scholars contradictory to the vain opinion of those "who think that they alone have devoured Minerva [i.e. wisdom] whole." [17] Even if the writings of others had not backed me up, the authority of the most learned and most erudite Gassendi would have sufficed. Although he denies that the sea could have reached so far inland, after summarizing and examining various opinions, he concludes: "Since, indeed, it frequently happens, either because of an earthquake or by some other cause, that those pooled waters flow out through cracks, or that the waters which were flowing into them are diverted elsewhere, it can therefore come about that fish and shellfish remain on land, and that moisture gathers there as the

---

produced the first explanation of the circulation of the blood; in two successive works on botany he proposed a completely new system for the classification of plants. Athanasius Kircher was born in Saxony in 1601 and was professor of mathematics, physics, and oriental languages in Rome from 1634 until his death in 1690. He wrote numerous works on even more numerous scientific and pseudoscientific subjects: Egyptian hieroglyphics, magnets, optics, astronomy (in which he supported the Tycho Brahe system espoused by the Society of Jesus, of which he was a member), and volcanoes. Pierre Potier (Petrus Poterius) was a chemist and physicist of the early seventeenth century; his *Opera Omnia* were published at Frankfurt-am-Main in 1698 and at Venice in 1741. Scilla probably has in mind his "Hundred Singular Observations of Various Kinds of Diseases" of 1616 and his *Pharmacopaea*, published at Bologna in 1635, as well as his 1643 work on fevers (*Libri due de febribus*). Fabio Colonna (1567–1640) belonged to the Neapolitan branch of the powerful Roman family of the same name and belonged to the Neapolitan branch of the Accademia dei Lincei of Rome to which Galileo belonged. He wrote a number of works on fossils as well as medicine that make him one of the most direct ancestors of Scilla. Ferrante Imperato was a Neapolitan druggist of the late sixteenth century whose huge encyclopedia of natural history was published in Naples in 1599 and again in 1672. His importance in the metaphysical speculations of Galileo's contemporaries is underscored in Nicola Badaloni's study of one of them, Colantonio Stelliola, in *Studi storici*, XXVI (1985), 160. The *Genialium Dierum Libri VI* (1552) of Alessandro d'Alessandro, or Alessandri (1461–1523) was correctly described by its eighteenth century editor as "an enormous universal warehouse of goods of all kinds arranged with no discernible order."

16. Plutarch is best known in the context of this course for his biographies of famous Greeks and Romans. He also wrote some sixty other works, generally collected under the title *Moralia;* the one referred to here is "On Isis and Osiris" (the Egyptian gods). Olympiodorus was an Aristotelian philosopher of Alexandria in the second half of the second century A.D. who wrote a commentary, still extant, on Aristotle's *Meteorologica.*

17. Teodoro Folengo, alias Merlin Cocai (1491–1544), author of numerous poems in what he, and everyone thereafter, called "macaronic" Latin, i.e., various dialects of Italian pressed into Latin grammatical and syntactical forms. Scilla here quotes from his *Opus Maccaronicum,* book 5.

ground hardens, and that when the moisture is sucked up, stones retaining their former shape can be made from them. Moreover, it is known that stones of this sort can be found by digging, or can become uncovered when torrents come down the sides of mountains, or can be revealed by an earthquake, or, finally, can emerge in some other way." [18]

In reading the authors mentioned above, however, I observed that a more reasonable problem was posed: were the shellfish, echinodermata, fish, and other similar bodies that we find on land thrown up from the sea, or should we think that they were generated where we find them, in some river, lake, or underground pool? Although this is an extremely curious problem, it does not pertain to my principal concern. Nor will I insist on one opinion on the matter, though you should know by now that this letter will present as more likely the point of view that all these objects were thrown up by the sea. For the moment it is enough for me that we all agree that the objects of our investigation were once real animals and are not tricks of nature, simply generated out of stony substance.

I must add that before I received your most courteous letter I had taken the trouble to read a few authors, ancient and modern, who happen to hold the opinion that I hold indefensible (and impossible), for I wanted to know what their arguments were in order to judge their worth more clearly. When I did so I forced myself to suspend my own passions and preconceptions. I reached the point where I doubted both my own eyes and the opinions of many illustrious men of letters, and I realized from their example that we are often fooled, not only by authoritative writers, but by experience and by our own senses, when our mind is prejudiced and occupied by some preconceived principle of our own choosing. This is usually the greatest or the only impediment to reaching and embracing the truth. Aware of all this, I went in search, as I have said, of the source of this school of thought among the ancient philosophers. I soon found that even in those ancient times the world was thought to be animal. It was with a curious sort of pleasure, however, that I noted the philosophers' confusion, because when they come to decide who is the resident master (or, to use their terms, the soul) of the great machine of the world that distributes so many and such astonishing effects throughout the universe, the only thing that they really prove is the ignorance of men.

At least I learned from their disagreement the need to doubt their vagaries, and I resolved to cultivate my ignorance as before, and to leave my mind be. I did so all the more tranquilly when I saw that the learned Guilandino, in a letter about to be published, [19] champions the opinion that

18. Gassendi quoted from the same *De Lapidibus* cited above at n. 11.
19. Melchiorre Guilandino, an Italianized Prussian who traveled widely in the Near East and was professor and custodian of the botanical garden at the University of Padua until his

was not to my taste, and he either supports his arguments poorly or gives us to understand the contrary of what he states his points to be. I can say in my favor and for everyone's benefit that he is unproductive as an authority, and that if the others who defend the same position have no better way to prove it, reading them is a waste of time. Guilandino's principal point is that animals can be born and be generated in the viscera of the earth (you could almost say in places unreachable by the breath of respiration), and all he offers us as proof of what he adduces is a tale or two. . . .

This is what Guilandino has swallowed, and it may well be true. All I ask is to speak of thoroughgoing animals, not of the generation of stones configured to look like sea animals. This is the point on which I continued my diligent search, for I wanted to satisfy my mind. In fact, I thought I had found what I wanted in Oswald Croll,[20] one of the renowned writers who believe, preach, and teach that this fortunate generating virtue is similar for all things and in all places. But good Lord! I discovered that he saw in plants a design that no one else, for all that we have eyes, will ever be able to see. I am a painter, and I swear on my honor as a poor man that you would put together a ghastly figure if the parts of a body were shaped like some grass or other, which Croll describes as comparable to human parts. But if this might perhaps inspire fear, his brief ninth entry, "De Genitalium signat," would raise a good laugh. He says: "Grapes bear the signature of the genitalia of both sexes"—a fine conclusion!—"which is why the ancients say, not without cause, that without Bacchus Venus is cold." The complete adage ought to have warned him to speak with better sense, since "Without Ceres and Bacchus Venus is cold" corresponds with the words of the philosopher Krates,[21] "Hunger allays love."

For me, the other famous names tread the same path. I will pay them little heed and will leave to others the liberty to believe as they will, conceding to them that the marine ball, the Hermodactylus, the phallus, and the "boratmets" resemble the chestnut more than a grape stalk, the hand more than the knee, the god of the orchards, Priapus, more than the human

---

death in 1589. The letter here mentioned was published in an anthology, *Scelta di lettere memorabili,* edited by the local and religious historian of the early seventeenth century, Michele Giustiniani, cited by Scilla in the second edition of Naples, 1683.

20. Crollius (c. 1560–1609) was a German physician who frequently traveled in Italy; he was appointed physician to Emperor Rudolf II on the eve of his death. His anti-Paracelsan *Basilica Chymica* published in 1612 described his own chemical experiments and gave recipes for the use of chemicals in medical cures.

21. Krates, not to be confused with the actor and playwright of the same name, was a disciple and the successor of Ptolemy at the Academy in Athens. His philosophical writings have been lost and are now known only through what is said about them by Diogenes Laertius.

breast, and, to finish, a lamb more than a snake, but certainly not that they are these very same things in their form. It would take much to persuade me that they could be produced from a same seed or from one coherent formative virtue.

I clearly understood that whoever follows such a way of philosophizing is doing his utmost to move away from knowledge of the truth. These are frivolities, as you know as well as I. . . .

I wrote, in total confusion as is my wont, to the virtuous Father Paolo Boccone, asking him to help me to procure some *linguette* and various other shells from the quarries of Malta. He sent me a lightning bolt that I little expected—your letter—which arrived trailing splendor, much activity, and a fearsome noise. It hit me like a thunderbolt, and in it you dismembered and consumed my thoughts in a flash. Still, since it is the habit of celestial fire to leave intact the shell of the things it strikes, there is an external effigy of what I was before that is still recognizable in me today.

Do not attribute all this to my defect of an almost overwhelmingly suspicious mind: you have blamed me for this and you may be right. We see the legal works of such persons as Alciati, Cujas,[22] and other learned doctors refused acceptance in the canonical courts with the explanation that we should be suspicious of the art of men of such ingenious minds and such subtle understanding because their knowledge can so easily pervert pure truth. And what mischief (say I) should I suspect from your letter? Would it be possible to find one more ornate, more cleverly assembled, or more vehement? I do not think so. Nevertheless, I resolve to strip it of its many, highly subtle, and most handsome amplifications and consider only the numerous learned arguments and vigorous proofs that it contains. If my feeble capacities lead me into some difficulty, rest assured that I will recant freely, after which, if it suits you, you may offer me your aid, along with medicine more appropriate to the melancholy humor from which I suffer.

First I shall make a reasonable demand or two so that I can then express my thoughts without interruption, come what may. To begin with, I request that you not be angry with someone who thinks that the island of Malta was formed after the creation of the world and who believes that the glossopetrae found there are shattered animal parts, seeming to agree with certain persons who would like to diminish the reputation of that soil and cast doubt upon both the great age of that island and the special property it is

---

22. Andrea Alciati of Milan (1492–1550) and Jacques Cujas (1522–90) were the founders of the neocultist or historical school of Roman jurisprudence in the early sixteenth century. They insisted that the single articles of the Justinian code be explained according to the rules of philology—i.e., according to the language and the institutions of the times in which they were first promulgated—and that they not be arbitrarily applied to the very different institutions and practices of other ages.

believed to have. I protest that I have no such thought. Quite to the contrary: I believe Malta to have been made after many other islands, following Father Kircher and others, and I recognize it as one of the most perfect, indeed the very most perfect island in the universe. If we carefully observe the method of a painter or a sculptor, we realize that first he makes sketches of everything, the last of which will be the most graceful and made with the surest hand. When we consider the operations of the Great Artificer and Creator, who used graceful light to color this world perfectly and who sculpted it marvelously with his omnipotent right hand, we are forced to admire this island as one of the strokes most clearly reserved to the power of God in His intent to beautify the noblest part of the great body of this earth with a striking and vivid light. Is this perhaps adulation? But is not the island of Malta one of the most famous, even the most glorious in all the world? Is it not the honor of Christendom, the impregnable shield of faith, the temple of the Catholic Mars?[23] This is how the Omnipotent conceived it; this is how all view it; this is how it sits in state in the Mediterranean. But if someone believes it to be a heap of teeth and various other things, will it do Malta any harm? Not in the least, because the supreme providence of the Maker left room for the operation of chance—in no way discordant with His will—which includes the accidents that petrified those bones. Perhaps He intended to show us that Time the destroyer would not dent Malta the invincible, marvelously jagged, beautiful monster that it is, and which will last for a thousand centuries, inspiring delight in its friends and fear in the rabid invidious Ottoman dog. This is what I tell myself in my heart. I ask to be believed, but I also ask to be allowed to reason at liberty.

Second, I would like to see acceptance of the accidents that are not only possible, but also are attested by many historians, both sacred and gentile. By this I refer to the many particular and sudden inundations (I know that we all believe in the universal one). The case is not closed, however, as to whether they happened by the ocean overflowing, through emanations from under the sea, or for some other reason favored by these authors. Indeed, to deny such inundations would be unreasonable and purely capricious. If this is conceded, as I ask, I would like the right to affirm as clearly as human discourse permits that the force of those floods transported different and infinitely mixed, and originally scattered things.

Third, I would like our eyes to have more power of decision about the

23. After the surrender of Rhodes to the Turks in 1521, the crusading order that had previously ruled that island moved to Malta and was thereafter known as the order of the Knights of Malta. With the help of reinforcements from Spain and several Italian states, they successfully resisted a fierce Turkish onslaught in 1567 and therefore prevented the Turks from penetrating permanently the western Mediterranean: hence Scilla's epithet.

things that strike them than speculative philosophy, since they are an instrument less apt to commit errors. Further, I would like philosophy to remain silent a bit when discussion turns to demonstration, not speculation. Let me explain what I mean. In your most learned letter you state, "If after all this someone still wanted to contend that these figured stones of ours cannot bear forms similar to animals, snails, bones, teeth, and so forth, except by having once been what they now represent, you must first explain to me, according to your principle, the varied and admirable figures that can be seen as if painted or in relief on some animals and plants. What do you make of the black half-moon so clearly drawn on the panther's right shoulder? Or of the musical notes on the species of marine shells that for that reason are commonly called *musicali?*" I still ask leave to discuss my opinion concerning the glossopetrae of Malta—that they are fragments of various sorts of animals—not as a reward for having figured out from what turbid heaven the black half-moon so sharply imprinted on the right shoulder of the panther might have fallen, nor what choir master could have penned the notes on the shell of the musical conch, but rather because it seems right to me to speak of a thing that we see without being obliged to speculate or guess about other things that do not fit the case and that surpass human judgment. When I happen to see a fur exactly like the coat of a living animal, I will say without hesitation that it was once part of a beast of that species. But if I am supposed to know why the panther's shoulder bears a half-moon and not his head, I will answer that I absolutely do not know, and that probably no one else does either.

Fourth, I ask that we speak only of things that I have seen or that we can both see. In mine shafts I have observed and delighted in many lovely aspects of gems and stones painted by nature, but on hearing the report—or, more accurately, the exaggerations—given of them, I am left with good reason not to trust anyone's words. . . .

It seems to me that a conjecture such as yours remains valid until its underlying presupposition—which I have never conceded—can be disproven and removed. If we consider attentively the objects under discussion, we will realize (as far as the glossopetrae are concerned) that the teeth of the Lamia [i.e., the shark], the Canicola [dogfish], and the like are pointed, quite thick, and highly polished, and are thus well designed to avoid contact with other bodies that could harm or crack them. Secondly, I do not suppose or think that the sea rolled them over lazily into the rivers, but rather that the violent shock of an ocean swollen by divine anger threw them up, and as great dams formed to block the waters, immense numbers of them were stopped, collected as chance dictated, and were left far inland, along with animals (or their skeletons) and other detritus that had lain in the way of the floods. In that case, it would be reasonable to expect a greater proportion of broken pieces than worn ones. Indeed, only a small number of whole, well-conserved glossopetrae are found, compared to the many broken and dismembered ones that are quarried.

We also need to ask what part of the tooth best resists time, the destroyer of all things. Anyone of solid judgment will agree this to be the highly-polished hard outside crust, and not the inside, which is of a rarer and more humor-laden substance, subject to decay and obliteration. Thus even if I conceded to those who disagree with me that the glossopetrae—the teeth, that is—were rubbed on all sides, it would not help much that they cannot be found in the rock filed down and worn by this conjectured rubbing. We cannot deny that time could easily have destroyed what was left of the animals' bodies once they remained stripped of the covering that alone could conserve them, sparing only the teeth, which were either preserved separated from the body, or were transported with the animals or their skeletons. In the mud, and pressed down as the muck compacted, these bodies relaxed their hold and scattered their fractured teeth to join the masses of bones, vertebrae, teeth, mollusk shells, and turbinidae, gravels, stones, and infinite amounts of other objects, lying in total disorder, smashed, whole, and broken pieces inextricably mixed.

Another consideration is why the miners gather these so-called glossopetrae. It is not, as we can easily surmise, to philosophize over them, but rather to turn a profit on them. They do not gather the disfigured or worn ones, but the clean, whole ones, since the first are scorned and worth little, while the latter have a commercial value and are sought after for some supposed virtue. But there is little reason to linger over the matter, since I am not obliged to show that all the glossopetrae were worn by a motion imagined by those contrary to my ideas (a motion never conceded by some, nor by myself, in spite of my habit of satisfying everyone and of accepting others' views). I can show to anyone who wants to see them glossopetrae that are corroded, filed down, worn away (for the most part at the root, which was never protected by a crust), broken into pieces, or whole: all of them, however, are not only similar but identical to shark teeth, dogfish teeth and the like. I can submit to examination a great many testacea excavated from boulders or found in the mountains, which I find it hard to believe fit the same case as teeth, as is claimed, since they are light bodies that float and would respond to the slightest movement of the current. Consequently, they ought to show only damage due to weight and humidity, and in fact we can see that almost all are flattened, stripped of their spines, and without ligaments (these being membranous, they would easily have dissolved in the wet silt). If all this leads to a conclusion in my favor, we can well pass on to the next problem. . . .

While I am at it, I would love to see certain people abandon their prattle (after hasty observation) about small mollusks and turbinidea found with soft shells, or about bigger ones so tender on one side that they can be dented with a fingernail while the other side is of a hard, rock-like substance, almost as if they had hardened gradually and had reached perfection after they had grown to a good size. This vain discourse gives rise to the presumption that, unless they are all simply produced where they are found, one should be able to find some small animals petrified in their shells. Although it should be enough to cite the words of Francesco Calzolaro, who, in agreement with the famous Fracastoro, answers shrewd questions of the sort by saying, "The reason is, that flesh that in itself was soft and designed to contract, soon solidified into stone after being covered round by much earth." [24] . . .

Let me add that the world is ancient: the authors speak of many separate inundations. I do not believe that when God created the universe, He established the island of Malta in the form in which we see it today (as Father Kircher would have it), [25] but that at first it lay low on the water, and after was brought, by several moves, to the state we so appreciate today. I also think it easy to imagine marine detritus, combined proportionally with thousands of millions of silt particles, giving a hundred islands like Malta at each of the floods reported by highly serious authors (and who also merit our confidence in historical matters), or at the one that is certain—the universal deluge. But this is no answer to the problem of why glossopetrae are seen only in Malta and not on the neighboring shores.

This is a question that I remember having asked myself as I observed that mound of striated shells in Musorrima about which I have spoken, for I found it astonishing not to find a single one in the surrounding terrain, which resembles an island. I did the same at the sight of marine animal shells that we call *piedi di porco* [pigs' feet], *piedi di capra* [goats' hoofs], *conchigliette* [little shells], *turbini* [turban shells], *bastoncini* [sticks], *echini* [sea urchins], and of infinite numbers of other things (as you shall see) far from the sea, three miles' hike into the mountains—to be exact, on the road to the Madonna di Buonviaggio. But as far as I could see, this collection contained a mixture of several sorts of objects, even though the majority were of one species. This led me to think that not chance alone, but the configuration of the shells might have had some share in what mystifies us. That is, chance could have determined the site by the formation

---

24. Above, n. 12. Girolamo Fracastoro (1484–1553) was a logician, poet, astronomer, and physicist who taught for many years at the University of Padua. The reference here is to his book on *Contagion and Contagious Diseases* of 1546.

25. Kircher (above, n. 15) in his *Ars Magnesia*, "On the Nature of the Strength and Prodigious Strength of the Magnet" (1631), and *Magnes, sive De Arte Magnetica* (1641).

of obstructions to stop up the immense inundations, and when the animals struck those barriers, the shape of their shell or some other cause could have grouped them together.

Let me explain what I mean. If we take a large tidal pool that contains a number of things capable of impeding the water's flow and we deposit into it quantities of eggs, eggshells, dry grasses, small stones, shells, and various other things of different shapes, I would think that if we then introduce irregular and violent movement in that water, whirlpools will form as the water strikes those barriers and, when the motion subsides, the greater part of the various things floating in it will most probably be deposited, according to their shape and size. Furthermore, not only will they collect in those whirlpools, but they will be abandoned in other places as chance dictates the gradual formation of the jams. I would say the same is also true of much larger-scale phenomena. Please think about this a bit for my sake, and tell me where you see difficulties in it. For the moment all I can say is that this is a queer thought of mine, born unexpectedly, and not yet come to maturity with proper proofs. On the other hand, if glossopetrae are not seen on the neighboring coasts, I think the reason may perhaps lie in the difference in terrain, which in Malta is propitious to their conservation, but elsewhere, where the soil is composed of loose sand, is unpropitious, so after a time they tend to be consumed. Or perhaps it is because the teeth are heavy bodies that must have come to rest on the bottom before the others. This would explain why it is difficult to find them in the superimposed [e.g. stratified] mountains in our parts. Here one can see quantities of the sort that float easily, similar to those also found on Malta, but very few teeth. I have found only five, with all my diligence, and of those five three are just shells without their internal substance, filled instead with fine, light marl.

On your island, to the contrary, since it is flatter and not very high, it is easy, almost effortless, to penetrate to the base on which the heavier bodies were the first to be deposited. This seems very likely to me, and perhaps I will prepare a brief summary of my views on the subject for you, for they are not to be scorned, and I am almost certain to encounter fish teeth as large as yours at the base of one of these hills.For now, the true cause is the same for the striated shells imprisoned in rock in Musorrima, for the clam shells, sea urchin shells, *colonnette* [little columns], *piedi di capra,* and the many other things in the hills of Messina—things left there and not elsewhere nor in the surrounding areas—and for certain things found in Malta and not in Sicily. This is difficult to deny, and I will draw a good argument from it. If the glossopetrae of Malta are subject to the same fate as the objects in Musorrima and Messina, and if some obstinately insist that the latter were born underground and inside the rock (as you shall see), then either the same argument applies to the other places, or we must go about speculating that in certain places nature generates on the highest mountains, not stones similar to marine objects, but real marine animals and their shells. . . .

I will change my discourse to suit you, then, protesting that I thought Salas's handsome and subtle labors more fantastic than true. As for me, I believe and will continue to believe in the universal inundation, just as Moses told it, and also that the waters covered the entire earth: "The waters continued to recede," and "on the first day of the . . . month the tops of the mountains appeared"—the mountain from which the dove could fly; the mountains of the earth, which remained mountains after the Flood as before—and "there in her mouth was a green olive leaf" [Gen. 8:5, 11].

This is not a fantastic hypothesis; it is the truth. Therefore I would serve my purpose badly indeed if I decided to abandon this opinion to follow the imaginings of the author in question. Do not waste your breath, then, in trying to urge him on me, for I have no use for this argument to support my views. I am so against extravagant flights of fancy that it disappointed me to see you subscribing to the fantastic and unsubstantial opinions of those who state and insist that marine animal shells can be generated in the midst of the rocks, either by other shells or by means of waters from the sea impregnated by who knows what sort of ostracodermi. What Agricola reports (but which I myself have not seen) seems to me likely or perfectly possible—that is, that one can see toads and serpents in rocks, or even dogs, according to William of Newburgh.[26] "It may well be said that as time went on they were petrified in place," you write, "but it does not satisfy my thinking." Why not? "Because even now similar animals would be found live in the midst of rocks." Not so. All we need is to imagine them alive in their lairs in the ground and that somehow they remained shut in there, dead and petrified, and this would satisfy all requirements. Their only task is to testify to their misfortune, which was to have been surprised by some accident that managed to gather together and agglutinate that mud and silt, along with them, and to compact the whole into a rock mass. In another passage you seem not to deny that things petrify. You say, "But I do not mean by that to deny that there are really animals, wood, bones, shellfish, and similar petrified things in some parts of the world where there was a lapidescent fluid that slowly filtered into their pores, and that, when the original substance had corroded or putrified, replaced it with its own earthy substance. Thus converted wholly into stone, they kept only their former shape." You add a condition, however: "I believe this to be ex-

26. William Petit, or Gulielmus Neubrigensis (d. c. 1201), author of a chronicle first published in Antwerp in 1567 with the title *Rerum Anglicarum Libri Quinque*.

tremely rare, and not adaptable to the innumerable quantities of figured stones that are excavated from this island."

I know, however, that this would not seem so very rare to you should you care to glance at the enormous number of stories gathered and cited approvingly by the above-mentioned Johann Daniel Major and Philipp Jacob Sachs,[27] for both of these authors' works contain a copious index on the strange effects of petrification. For me it is enough that nature can and habitually does operate in this manner. I would also be at a loss to say how we could prescribe or limit its activity. I think, what is more, that nature toils just as much to petrify a shellfish as a mountain when it dictates its formula for doing so to the accidents of chance, its ministers. I have no idea what discretion these ministers have when they feel inclined to turn to stone what they embrace, nor whether they can leave one part petrified and the rest not, just as I know no way to satisfy your desire to see examples of what once were true mollusk shells half petrified and half unaltered. I will say, however, that in many places poorly disposed for turning things into stone, everything remains unpetrified, and where such a disposition is found, everything is petrified, since it is subjected to one activity for the same period of time. Perhaps I can console you, though, not only with a few petrified shellfish, but with some petrified in part and even with the animal inside (extremely rare)—all in the grip of strongest rock. This way I hope you will grant my view some small indulgence, and will have good reason to doubt the others' opinions. . . .

To conclude, all these considerations, together with the evidence given above, oblige me to believe that the shellfish, sea urchins and other echinodermata, teeth (which are called glossopetrae), vertebrae, corals, sponges, crabs, spatangina, and turbinidae, along with many other objects that some have judged to be generated out of pure stone and tricks of nature, used to be not only animals and bodies of that species, but bodies and animals quite appropriate to the sea, which arrived by some accident within the earth with the matter they contained, and which we now see raised up in hills and mountains, either of sand and gravel or of marl, tuff, or hard stone. This material also arrived from elsewhere, as I have already shown, but because it has been there from time immemorial, it is taken to be native to the place—indeed, to have been exposed with the bedrock to the first rays of the sun—by those who do not care to or are unable to look with their own eyes at the true history that the Omnipotent clearly registered in His works everywhere and offers to our view.

27. Johann Daniel Major, *Dissertatio Epistolica de Cancris et Serpentibus Petrefactis,* published with Phil. Iac Sachs *De Miranda Lapidum Natura* (Jena, 1664). Major also edited one of Fabio Colonna's (above, n. 15) works (1675) dedicated in particular to fossils.

Do not be scandalized if I have treated such high and difficult matters with deliberate scorn for speculation and with stubborn dependence on the observation of things alone, for to tell the truth, I have little inclination for high flights of philosophy. I also thought there no need for sublime intellect in discourses that aim at discovering the pure and simple truth underlying the teachings of sense perception. If it has led me astray, to whom should I turn?

What must be held to be of greater surety than sense? Should I perhaps turn someone else's speculations? No, because they will turn out to be true or false when approved or rejected by the senses.

Unless they are true, all reason too becomes false.[28]

Thus my reasoning is confirmed and as long as I know at least some things with certainty, my ignorance of many others is no threat to it. I will be satisfied with knowing (because both they themselves and the circumstances of the place in which they are now found clearly tell us so) that the bodies that have been the object of our disquisition and that can be found in Musorrima and in the valley of the Sperone (in fact, in all Calabria), in the hills of Messina and throughout Sicily, in Malta, and even elsewhere were formerly true shells or parts of real animals that once lived in the sea or are forms produced by them. If anyone wants to ignore this fact and go about investigating whether nature can generate, underground, stony figures similar (better, identical) to animals that live in the sea, or can generate in the seas things that usually grow on dry land, and then, in spite of much contrary evidence, if he wants to conclude from such a vain opinion that everything is native to its site and generated out of stone, let him do so. Let him believe it, let him investigate. But let him not force me to agree before he can make me understand clearly, with good arguments and proofs equal to the others (and proof in fact denies it) how such things were generated in rock on dry land and how nature continues to make them. This is certainly a difficult task, because, according to Plutarch, nature, speaking through Isis, says: "I am everything that has been, is, and will be; and my cloak no mortal has yet removed." Better still, he speaks for us all.

28. Lucretius, *De Rerum Natura* ("On the Nature of Things"), 4:482–83 and 485; Cyral Bailey translation (Oxford: Clarendon Press, 1947).

36. Blaise Pascal, *Pensées* XV, Transition from Knowledge of Man to Knowledge of God

Blaise Pascal, one of the most enigmatic intellectual figures of seventeenth-century Europe, was born at Clermont-Ferrand in 1623. His father occupied a modest position in the local *noblesse de robe*—the section of the French nobility engaged in bureaucratic and judicial service. Benefiting from an unorthodox education, Pascal showed signs of scientific genius from an early age. His most important work was in mathematics: at age seventeen he produced an essay on conic sections which provoked the jealousy of Descartes; later, he helped lay the foundations for probability theory, and came close to discovering the calculus. In physics, Pascal involved himself in the controversy over the existence of the vacuum: an experiment he had carried out on the mountain of Puy-de-Dome earned him a reputation across Europe. In a more practical vein, he designed and built an adding machine that has some claim to being the first digital calculator. By the end of his relatively brief life, in 1662, Pascal had established himself as one of the pioneers of the Scientific Revolution.

At the same time, Pascal, along with other members of his family, gradually became involved with Jansenism, a Catholic reform movement which was to be of fundamental importance for French religion and politics. A reaction against the Counter-Reformation Church, Jansenism reiterated themes associated with Protestant reformers: original sin, predestination, the necessity of grace for salvation. Though persecuted, the Jansenists never abandoned Catholicism, and the movement later became associated with the defense of the independence of the French Church and with opposition to the French monarchy. The initial result of Pascal's Jansenism was the *Lettres provinciales,* a mordant attack on the Jesuits, the chief enemies of the movement. Prized for its grace and wit, this work quickly attained the status of a classic of French prose writing.

Pascal next embarked on a more ambitious project: a full-scale *Apology for the Christian Faith*. With astonishing clairvoyance, Pascal recognized the challenges that the intellectual revolution of Early Modern Europe had posed for traditional Christian belief. His response, in an attempt to meet these challenges, was to rehabilitate the perennial themes of Augustinian Christianity, themselves the products of an age of crisis. One of Pascal's main targets was humanist skepticism, represented by the genial figure of Montaigne. It was against this opponent that he mounted

From Blaise Pascal, *Pensées,* translated by W. F. Trotter (London: J. M. Dent & Sons, Ltd., Everyman's Library, 1908), pp. 10–11, 16–21, 28, 30, 61, 97, 198.

the notorious "wager" argument: if there is no God, the skeptic loses
nothing by believing in him; if God exists, the skeptic loses eternal life
by not believing in him. The *Apology*, however, was never finished by
Pascal. What remains is the collection of notes for it, which comes down
to us under the misleading title of *Pensées*. The selection below, with its
anguished perception of the "disproportion" of man and nature, shows
one of Pascal's most characteristic themes: the insurmountable limitations—intellectual and physical—of man without God. This kind of reversion to theology was, of course, the norm rather than the exception for
the major scientific figures of the seventeenth century—Newton himself
is a good example. But no other thinker of the period showed so great an
awareness of the stakes involved in the emergence of the new scientific
culture of Europe.

37

Since we cannot be universal and know all that is to be known of everything, we ought to know a little about everything. For it is far better to
know something about everything than to know all about one thing. This
universality is the best. If we can have both, still better; but if we must
choose, we ought to choose the former. And the world feels this and does
so; for the world is often a good judge.

72

Man's disproportion.—This is where our innate knowledge leads us. If it
be not true, there is no truth in man; and if it be true, he finds therein great
cause for humiliation, being compelled to abase himself in one way or another. And since he cannot exist without this knowledge, I wish that, before entering on deeper researches into nature, he would consider her both
seriously and at leisure, that he would reflect upon himself also, and knowing what proportion there is. . . . Let man then contemplate the whole of
nature in her full and grand majesty, and turn his vision from the low objects which surround him. Let him gaze on that brilliant light, set like an
eternal lamp to illumine the universe; let the earth appear to him a point in
comparison with the vast circle described by the sun; and let him wonder at
the fact that this vast circle is itself but a very fine point in comparison with
that described by the stars in their revolution round the firmament. But if
our view be arrested there, let our imagination pass beyond; it will sooner
exhaust the power of conception than nature that of supplying material for
conception. The whole visible world is only an imperceptible atom in the

ample bosom of nature. No idea approaches it. We may enlarge our conceptions beyond all imaginable space; we only produce atoms in comparison with the reality of things. It is an infinite sphere, the centre of which is everywhere, the circumference nowhere. In short it is the greatest sensible mark of the almighty power of God, that imagination loses itself in that thought.

Returning to himself, let man consider what he is in comparison with all existence; let him regard himself as lost in this remote corner of nature; and from the little cell in which he finds himself lodged, I mean the universe, let him estimate at their true value the earth, kingdoms, cities, and himself. What is a man in the Infinite?

But to show him another prodigy equally astonishing, let him examine the most delicate things he knows. Let a mite be given him, with its minute body and parts incomparably more minute, limbs with their joints, veins in the limbs, blood in the veins, humours in the blood, drops in the humours, vapours in the drops. Dividing these last things again, let him exhaust his powers of conception, and let the last object at which he can arrive be now that of our discourse. Perhaps he will think that here is the smallest point in nature. I will let him see therein a new abyss. I will paint for him not only the visible universe, but all that he can conceive of nature's immensity in the womb of this abridged atom. Let him see therein an infinity of universes, each of which has its firmament, its planets, its earth, in the same proportion as in the visible world; in each earth animals, and in the last mites, in which he will find again all that the first had, finding still in these others the same thing without end and without cessation. Let him lose himself in wonders as amazing in their littleness as the others in their vastness. For who will not be astounded at the fact that our body, which a little while ago was imperceptible in the universe, itself imperceptible in the bosom of the whole, is now a colossus, a world, or rather a whole, in respect of the nothingness which we cannot reach? He who regards himself in this light will be afraid of himself, and observing himself sustained in the body given him by nature between those two abysses of the Infinite and Nothing, will tremble at the sight of these marvels; and I think that, as his curiosity changes into admiration, he will be more disposed to contemplate them in silence than to examine them with presumption.

For in fact what is man in nature? A Nothing in comparison with the Infinite, an All in comparison with the Nothing, a mean between nothing and everything. Since he is infinitely removed from comprehending the extremes, the end of things and their beginning are hopelessly hidden from him in an impenetrable secret; he is equally incapable of seeing the Nothing from which he was made, and the Infinite in which he is swallowed up.

What will he do then, but perceive the appearance of the middle of things, in an eternal despair of knowing either their beginning or their end. All things proceed from the Nothing, and are borne towards the Infinite. Who will follow these marvellous processes? The Author of these wonders understands them. None other can do so.

Through failure to contemplate these Infinites, men have rashly rushed into the examination of nature, as though they bore some proportion to her. It is strange that they have wished to understand the beginnings of things, and thence to arrive at the knowledge of the whole, with a presumption as infinite as their object. For surely this design cannot be formed without presumption or without a capacity infinite like nature.

If we are well informed, we understand that, as nature has graven her image and that of her Author on all things, they almost all partake of her double infinity. Thus we see that all the sciences are infinite in the extent of their researches. For who doubts that geometry, for instance, has an infinite infinity of problems to solve? They are also infinite in the multitude and fineness of their premises; for it is clear that those which are put forward as ultimate are not self-supporting, but are based on others which, again having others for their support, do not permit of finality. But we represent some as ultimate for reason, in the same way as in regard to material objects we call that an indivisible point beyond which our senses can no longer perceive anything, although by its nature it is infinitely divisible.

Of these two Infinites of science, that of greatness is the most palpable, and hence a few persons have pretended to know all things. "I will speak of the whole," said Democritus.

But the infinitely little is the least obvious. Philosophers have much oftener claimed to have reached it, and it is here they have all stumbled. This has given rise to such common titles as *First Principles, Principles of Philosophy,* and the like, as ostentatious in fact, though not in appearance, as that one which blinds us, *De omni scibili.*

We naturally believe ourselves far more capable of reaching the centre of things than of embracing their circumference. The visible extent of the world visibly exceeds us; but as we exceed little things, we think ourselves more capable of knowing them, And yet we need no less capacity for attaining the Nothing than the All. Infinite capacity is required for both, and it seems to me that whoever shall have understood the ultimate principles of being might also attain to the knowledge of the Infinite. The one depends on the other, and one leads to the other. These extremes meet and reunite by force of distance, and find each other in God, and in God alone.

Let us then take our compass; we are something, and we are not everything. The nature of our existence hides from us the knowledge of first beginnings which are born of the Nothing; and the littleness of our being conceals from us the sight of the Infinite.

Our intellect holds the same position in the world of thought as our body occupies in the expanse of nature.

Limited as we are in every way, this state which holds the mean between two extremes is present in all our impotence. Our senses perceive no extreme. Too much sound deafens us; too much light dazzles us; too great distance or proximity hinders our view. Too great length and too great brevity of discourse tend to obscurity; too much truth is paralysing (I know some who cannot understand that to take four from nothing leaves nothing). First principles are too self-evident for us; too much pleasure disagrees with us. Too many concords are annoying in music; too many benefits irritate us; we wish to have the wherewithal to over-pay our debts. *Beneficia eo usque laeta sunt dum videntur exsolvi posse; ubi multum antevenere, pro gratia odium redditur.* We feel neither extreme heat nor extreme cold. Excessive qualities are prejudicial to us and not perceptible by the senses; we do not feel but suffer them. Extreme youth and extreme age hinder the mind, as also too much and too little education. In short, extremes are for us as though they were not, and we are not within their notice. They escape us, or we them.

This is our true state; this is what makes us incapable of certain knowledge and of absolute ignorance. We sail within a vast sphere, ever drifting in uncertainty, driven from end to end. When we think to attach ourselves to any point and to fasten to it, it wavers and leaves us; and if we follow it, it eludes our grasp, slips past us, and vanishes for ever. Nothing stays for us. This is our natural condition, and yet most contrary to our inclination; we burn with desire to find solid ground and an ultimate sure foundation whereon to build a tower reaching to the Infinite. But our whole groundwork cracks, and the earth opens to abysses.

Let us therefore not look for certainty and stability. Our reason is always deceived by fickle shadows; nothing can fix the finite between the two Infinites, which both enclose and fly from it.

If this be well understood, I think that we shall remain at rest, each in the state wherein nature has placed him. As this sphere which has fallen to us as our lot is always distant from either extreme, what matters it that man should have a little more knowledge of the universe? If he has it, he but gets a little higher. Is he not always infinitely removed from the end, and is not the duration of our life equally removed from eternity, even if it lasts ten years longer?

In comparison with these Infinites all finites are equal, and I see no reason for fixing our imagination on one more than on another. The only comparison which we make of ourselves to the finite is painful to us.

If man made himself the first object of study, he would see how incapable he is of going further. How can a part know the whole? But he may perhaps aspire to know at least the parts to which he bears some proportion. But the parts of the world are all so related and linked to one another, that I believe it impossible to know one without the other and without the whole.

Man, for instance, is related to all he knows. He needs a place wherein to abide, time through which to live, motion in order to live, elements to compose him, warmth and food to nourish him, air to breathe. He sees light; he feels bodies; in short, he is in a dependent alliance with everything. To know man, then, it is necessary to know how it happens that he needs air to live, and, to know the air, we must know how it is thus related to the life of man, etc. Flame cannot exist without air; therefore to understand the one, we must understand the other.

Since everything then is cause and effect, dependent and supporting, mediate and immediate, and all is held together by a natural though imperceptible chain, which binds together things most distant and most different, I hold it equally impossible to know the parts without knowing the whole, and to know the whole without knowing the parts in detail.

The eternity of things in itself or in God must also astonish our brief duration. The fixed and constant immobility of nature, in comparison with the continual change which goes on within us, must have the same effect.

And what completes our incapability of knowing things, is the fact that they are simple, and that we are composed of two opposite natures, different in kind, soul and body. For it is impossible that our rational part should be other than spiritual; and if any one maintain that we are simply corporeal, this would far more exclude us from the knowledge of things, there being nothing so inconceivable as to say that matter knows itself. It is impossible to imagine how it should know itself.

So if we are simply material, we can know nothing at all; and if we are composed of mind and matter, we cannot know perfectly things which are simple, whether spiritual or corporeal. Hence it comes that almost all philosophers have confused ideas of things, and speak of material things in spiritual terms, and of spiritual things in material terms. For they say boldly that bodies have a tendency to fall, that they seek after their centre, that they fly from destruction, that they fear the void, that they have inclinations, sympathies, antipathies, all of which attributes pertain only to mind. And in speaking of minds, they consider them as in a place, and attribute to them movement from one place to another; and these are qualities which belong only to bodies.

Instead of receiving the ideas of these things in their purity, we colour them with our own qualities, and stamp with our composite being all the simple things which we contemplate.

Who would not think, seeing us compose all things of mind and body, but that this mixture would be quite intelligible to us? Yet it is the very thing we least understand. Man is to himself the most wonderful object in nature; for he cannot conceive what the body is, still less what the mind is, and least of all how a body should be united to a mind. This is the consummation of his difficulties, and yet it is his very being. *Modus quo corporibus adhaerent spiritus comprehendi ab hominibus non potest, et hoc tamen homo est.* . . .

86

My fancy makes me hate a croaker, and one who pants when eating. Fancy has great weight. Shall we profit by it? Shall we yield to this weight because it is natural? No, but by resisting it. . . .

98

Bias leading to error.—It is a deplorable thing to see all men deliberating on means alone, and not on the end. Each thinks how he will acquit himself in his condition; but as for the choice of condition, or of country, chance gives them to us.

It is a pitiable thing to see so many Turks, heretics, and infidels follow the way of their fathers for the sole reason that each has been imbued with the prejudice that it is the best. And that fixes for each man his conditions of locksmith, soldier, etc.

Hence savages care nothing for Providence.

206

The eternal silence of these infinite spaces frightens me.

208

Why is my knowledge limited? Why my stature? Why my life to one hundred years rather than to a thousand? What reason has nature had for giving me such, and for choosing this number rather than another in the infinity of those from which there is no more reason to choose one than another, trying nothing else?

347

Man is but a reed, the most feeble thing in nature; but he is a thinking reed. The entire universe need not arm itself to crush him. A vapour, a drop of water suffices to kill him. But, if the universe were to crush him, man would still be more noble than that which killed him, because he knows that he dies and the advantage which the universe has over him; the universe knows nothing of this.

All our dignity consists, then, in thought. By it we must elevate ourselves, and not by space and time which we cannot fill. Let us endeavour, then, to think well; this is the principle of morality.

516

Comfort yourselves. It is not from yourselves that you should expect grace; but, on the contrary, it is in expecting nothing from yourselves, that you must hope for it.

693

And what crowns all this is prediction, so that it should not be said that it is chance which has done it.

Whosoever, having only a week to live, will not find out that it is expedient to believe that all this is not a stroke of chance. . . .

Now, if the passions had no hold on us, a week and a hundred years would amount to the same thing.

37. Roger Cotes, Preface to Newton's *Principia*

Because Newtonian physics is so inextricably associated with the origins of modern science, it may be difficult for the modern reader to understand that, to many of Newton's contemporaries—some on the cutting edge of scientific and philosophical developments—the physics of universal gravitation appeared as a reversion to a more primitive way of thinking. The "mechanical philosophy," popularized by René Descartes and later upheld by such great men as Leibniz and Huygens, rested on the assumption that all physical interaction must be mediated by the direct impact of particles; the ultimate aim of physical science was therefore to find an underlying corpuscular mechanism to explain all observable physical phenomena. To assert, as Newton did, that large bodies could exert forces on each other across immense distances seemed, from this

From Cotes's Preface to the 2d (1713) edition of Sir Isaac Newton's *Mathematical Principles of Natural Philosophy,* translated by Andrew Motte, rev. Florian Cajori, pp. xx–xxxiii. © 1934, 1962, The Regents of the University of California Press, used by permission of the University of California Press.

thoroughly mechanical and modern point of view, like a return to Aristotelian "occult qualities."

In order to defend Newton's theory from this criticism, to refute the Cartesian ideas, and to explain the virtues of the Newtonian scientific method, Roger Cotes (1682–1716) wrote his preface to the second edition of Newton's *Principia* (1713). Cotes was uniquely suited to this task, for he was one of only a few English mathematicians at that time who were capable of appreciating and building upon Newton's highly mathematical point of view. Born in Leicestershire, England in 1682, he showed great mathematical promise as a child; he earned his B.A. from Trinity College, Cambridge in 1702 and his M.A. in 1706, when he also was named the first Plumian Professor of Astronomy and Natural Philosophy. He published little in his lifetime, but a posthumous collection of many of his works, the *Harmonia mensurarum* (1722), contained original contributions to integration and differentiation theory as well as to the theory of logarithmic functions. In addition, as Newton's collaborator on the second edition of the *Principia,* he contributed greatly to improving the mathematical precision of the work, particularly as regards the lunar theory and the theory of comets. Of his death, at only thirty-three years of age, Newton remarked, "Had Cotes lived, we might have learned something."

We hereby present to the benevolent reader the long-awaited new edition of *Newton's* Philosophy, now greatly amended and increased. The principal contents of this celebrated work may be gathered from the adjoining Table. What has been added or modified is indicated in the author's Preface. There remains for us to add something relating to the method of this philosophy.

Those who have treated of natural philosophy may be reduced to about three classes. Of these some have attributed to the several species of things, specific and occult qualities, according to which the phenomena of particular bodies are supposed to proceed in some unknown manner. The sum of the doctrine of the Schools derived from *Aristotle* and the *Peripatetics* is founded on this principle. They affirm that the several effects of bodies arise from the particular natures of those bodies. But whence it is that bodies derive those natures they don't tell us; and therefore they tell us nothing. And being entirely employed in giving names to things, and not in searching into things themselves, they have invented, we may say, a philosophical way of speaking, but they have not made known to us true philosophy.

Others have endeavored to apply their labors to greater advantage by rejecting that useless medley of words. They assume that all matter is homogeneous, and that the variety of forms which is seen in bodies arises from some very plain and simple relations of the component particles. And by going on from simple things to those which are more compounded they certainly proceed right, if they attribute to those primary relations no other relations than those which Nature has given. But when they take a liberty of imagining at pleasure unknown figures and magnitudes, and uncertain situations and motions of the parts, and moreover of supposing occult fluids, freely pervading the pores of bodies, endued with an all-performing subtilty, and agitated with occult motions, they run out into dreams and chimeras, and neglect the true constitution of things, which certainly is not to be derived from fallacious conjectures, when we can scarce reach it by the most certain observations. Those who assume hypotheses as first principles of their speculations, although they afterwards proceed with the greatest accuracy from those principles, may indeed form an ingenious romance, but a romance it will still be.

There is left then the third class, which possess experimental philosophy. These indeed derive the causes of all things from the most simple principles possible; but then they assume nothing as a principle, that is not proved by phenomena. They frame no hypotheses, nor receive them into philosophy otherwise than as questions whose truth may be disputed. They proceed therefore in a twofold method, synthetical and analytical. From some select phenomena they deduce by analysis the forces of Nature and the more simple laws of forces; and from thence by synthesis show the constitution of the rest. This is that incomparably best way of philosophizing, which our renowned author most justly embraced in preference to the rest, and thought alone worthy to be cultivated and adorned by his excellent labors. Of this he has given us a most illustrious example, by the explication of the System of the World, most happily deduced from the Theory of Gravity. That the attribute of gravity was found in all bodies, others suspected, or imagined before him, but he was the only and the first philosopher that could demonstrate it from appearances, and make it a solid foundation to the most noble speculations.

I know indeed that some persons, and those of great name, too much prepossessed with certain prejudices, are unwilling to assent to this new principle, and are ready to prefer uncertain notions to certain. It is not my intention to detract from the reputation of these eminent men; I shall only lay before the reader such considerations as will enable him to pass an equitable judgment in this dispute.

Therefore, that we may begin our reasoning from what is most simple and nearest to us, let us consider a little what is the nature of gravity in earthly bodies, that we may proceed the more safely when we come to consider it in the heavenly bodies that lie at the remotest distance from us. It is now agreed by all philosophers that all circumterrestrial bodies gravitate towards the earth. That no bodies having no weight are to be found, is now confirmed by manifold experience. That which is relative levity is not true levity, but apparent only, and arises from the preponderating gravity of the contiguous bodies.

Moreover, as all bodies gravitate towards the earth, so does the earth gravitate again towards all bodies. That the action of gravity is mutual and equal on both sides, is thus proved. Let the mass of the earth be divided into any two parts whatever, either equal or unequal; now if the weights of the parts towards each other were not mutually equal, the lesser weight would give way to the greater, and the two parts would move on together indefinitely in a right line towards that point to which the greater weight tends, which is altogether contrary to experience. Therefore we must say that the weights with which the parts tend to each other are equal; that is, that the action of gravity is mutual and equal in contrary directions.

The weights of bodies at equal distances from the centre of the earth are as the quantities of matter in the bodies. This is inferred from the equal acceleration of all bodies that fall from a state of rest by their weights; for the forces by which unequal bodies are equally accelerated must be proportional to the quantities of the matter to be moved. Now, that all falling bodies are equally accelerated, appears from this, that when the resistance of the air is taken away, as it is under an exhausted receiver of Mr. *Boyle,* they describe equal spaces in equal times; but this is yet more accurately proved by the experiments with pendulums.

The attractive forces of bodies at equal distances are as the quantities of matter in the bodies. For since bodies gravitate towards the earth, and the earth again towards bodies with equal moments, the weight of the earth towards each body, or the force with which the body attracts the earth, will be equal to the weight of the same body towards the earth. But this weight was shown to be as the quantity of matter in the body; and therefore the force with which each body attracts the earth, or the absolute force of the body, will be as the same quantity of matter.

Therefore the attractive force of the entire bodies arises from and is composed of the attractive forces of the parts, because, as was just shown, if the bulk of the matter be augmented or diminished, its power is proportionately augmented or diminished. We must therefore conclude that the action of the earth is composed of the united actions of its parts, and therefore that all terrestrial bodies must attract one another mutually, with absolute forces that are as the matter attracting. This is the nature of gravity upon earth; let us now see what it is in the heavens.

That every body continues in its state either of rest or of moving uniformly in a right line, unless so far as it is compelled to change that state

by external force, is a law of Nature universally received by all philosophers. But it follows from this that bodies which move in curved lines, and
are therefore continually bent from the right lines that are tangents to their
orbits, are retained in their curvilinear paths by some force continually acting. Since, then, the planets move in curvilinear orbits, there must be some
force operating, by the incessant actions of which they are continually
made to deflect from the tangents.

Now it is evident from mathematical reasoning, and rigorously demonstrated, that all bodies that move in any curved line described in a plane,
and which, by a radius drawn to any point, whether at rest or moved in any
manner, describe areas about that point proportional to the times, are urged
by forces directed towards that point. This must therefore be granted.
Since, then, all astronomers agree that the primary planets describe about
the sun, and the secondary about the primary, areas proportional to the
times, it follows that the forces by which they are continually turned aside
from the rectilinear tangents, and made to revolve in curvilinear orbits, are
directed towards the bodies that are placed in the centres of the orbits. This
force may therefore not improperly be called centripetal in respect of the
revolving body, and in respect of the central body attractive, from whatever
cause it may be imagined to arise.

Moreover, it must be granted, as being mathematically demonstrated,
that, if several bodies revolve with an equable motion in concentric circles,
and the squares of the periodic times are as the cubes of the distances from
the common centre, the centripetal forces will be inversely as the squares
of the distances. Or, if bodies revolve in orbits that are very nearly circular
and the apsides of the orbits are at rest, the centripetal forces of the revolving bodies will be inversely as the squares of the distances. That both these
facts hold for all the planets, all astronomers agree. Therefore the centripetal forces of all the planets are inversely as the squares of the distances
from the centres of their orbits. If any should object, that the apsides of the
planets, and especially of the moon, are not perfectly at rest, but are carried progressively with a slow kind of motion, one may give this answer,
that, though we should grant that this very slow motion arises from a slight
deviation of the centripetal force from the law of the square of the distance,
yet we are able to compute mathematically the quantity of that aberration,
and find it perfectly insensible. For even the ratio of the lunar centripetal
force itself, which is the most irregular of them all, will vary inversely as a
power a little greater than the square of the distance, but will be well-nigh
sixty times nearer to the square than to the cube of the distance. But we
may give a truer answer, by saying that this progression of the apsides
arises not from a deviation from the law of inverse squares of the distance,
but from a quite different cause, as is most admirably shown in this work.

It is certain then that the centripetal forces with which the primary planets tend to the sun, and the secondary planets to their primary, are accurately as the inverse squares of the distances.

From what has been hitherto said, it is plain that the planets are retained in their orbits by some force continually acting upon them; it is plain that this force is always directed towards the centres of their orbits; it is plain that its intensity is increased in its approach and is decreased in its recession from the centre, and that it is increased in the same ratio in which the square of the distance is diminished, and decreased in the same ratio in which the square of the distance is augmented. Let us now see whether, by making a comparison between the centripetal forces of the planets and the force of gravity, we may not by chance find them to be of the same kind. Now, they will be of the same kind if we find on both sides the same laws and the same attributes. Let us then first consider the centripetal force of the moon, which is nearest to us.

The rectilinear spaces which bodies let fall from rest describe in a given time at the very beginning of the motion, when the bodies are urged by any forces whatsoever, are proportional to the forces. This appears from mathematical reasoning. Therefore the centripetal force of the moon revolving in its orbit is to the force of gravity at the surface of the earth, as the space which in a very small interval of time the moon, deprived of all its circular force and descending by its centripetal force towards the earth, would describe, is to the space which a heavy body would describe, when falling by the force of its gravity near to the earth, in the same small interval of time. The first of these spaces is equal to the versed sine of the arc described by the moon in the same time, because that versed sine measures the translation of the moon from the tangent, produced by the centripetal force, and therefore may be computed, if the periodic time of the moon and its distance from the centre of the earth are given. The last space is found by experiments with pendulums, as Mr. *Huygens* has shown. Therefore by making a calculation we shall find that the first space is to the latter, or the centripetal force of the moon revolving in its orbit will be to the force of gravity at the surface of the earth, as the square of the semidiameter of the earth, to the square of the semidiameter of the orbit. But by what was shown before, the very same ratio holds between the centripetal force of the moon revolving in its orbit, and the centripetal force of the moon near the surface of the earth. Therefore the centripetal force near the surface of the earth is equal to the force of gravity. Therefore these are not two different forces, but one and the same; for if they were different, these forces united would cause bodies to descend to the earth with twice the velocity they would fall with by the force of gravity alone. Therefore it is plain that the centripetal force, by which the moon is continually either impelled or attracted out of the tangent and retained in its orbit, is the very force of terrestrial gravity reaching up to the moon. And it is very reasonable to believe that this force should extend itself to vast distances, since upon the tops of the highest mountains we find no sensible diminution of it. Therefore the moon gravitates towards the earth; but on the other hand, the earth by a mutual action equally gravitates towards the moon, which is also abundantly confirmed in this philosophy, where the tides in the sea and the precession of the equinoxes are treated of, which arise from the action both of the moon and of the sun upon the earth. Hence lastly, we discover by what law the force of gravity decreases at great distances from the earth. For since gravity is noways different from the moon's centripetal force, and this is inversely proportional to the square of the distance, it follows that it is in that very ratio that the force of gravity decreases.

Let us now go on to the other planets. Because the revolutions of the primary planets about the sun and of the secondary about Jupiter and Saturn are phenomena of the same kind with the revolution of the moon about the earth, and because it has been moreover demonstrated that the centripetal forces of the primary planets are directed towards the centre of the sun and those of the secondary towards the centres of Jupiter and Saturn, in the same manner as the centripetal force of the moon is directed towards the centre of the earth, and since, besides, all these forces are inversely as the squares of the distances from the centres, in the same manner as the centripetal force of the moon is as the square of the distance from the earth, we must of course conclude that the nature of all is the same. Therefore as the moon gravitates towards the earth and the earth again towards the moon, so also all the secondary planets will gravitate towards their primary, and the primary planets again towards their secondary, and so all the primary towards the sun, and the sun again towards the primary.

Therefore the sun gravitates towards all the planets, and all the planets towards the sun. For the secondary planets, while they accompany the primary, revolve the meanwhile with the primary about the sun. Therefore, by the same argument, the planets of both kinds gravitate towards the sun and the sun towards them. That the secondary planets gravitate towards the sun is moreover abundantly clear from the inequalities of the moon, a most accurate theory of which, laid open with a most admirable sagacity, we find explained in the third Book of this work.

That the attractive force of the sun is propagated on all sides to prodigious distances and is diffused to every part of the wide space that surrounds it, is most evidently shown by the motion of the comets, which, coming from places immensely distant from the sun, approach very near to it, and sometimes so near that in their perihelia they almost touch its body.

The theory of these bodies was altogether unknown to astronomers till in our own times our excellent author most happily discovered it and demonstrated the truth of it by most certain observations. So that it is now apparent that the comets move in conic sections having their foci in the sun's centre, and by radii drawn to the sun describe areas proportional to the times. But from these phenomena it is manifest and mathematically demonstrated, that those forces by which the comets are retained in their orbits are directed towards the sun and are inversely proportional to the squares of the distances from its centre. Therefore the comets gravitate towards the sun, and therefore the attractive force of the sun not only acts on the bodies of the planets, placed at given distances and very nearly in the same plane, but reaches also the comets in the most different parts of the heavens, and at the most different distances. This therefore is the nature of gravitating bodies, to exert their force at all distances to all other gravitating bodies. But from thence it follows that all the planets and comets attract one another mutually, and gravitate towards one another, which is also confirmed by the perturbation of Jupiter and Saturn, observed by astronomers, and arising from the mutual actions of these two planets upon each other, as also from that very slow motion of the apsides, above taken notice of, which arises from a like cause.

We have now proceeded so far, that it must be acknowledged that the sun, and the earth, and all the heavenly bodies attending the sun, attract one another mutually. Therefore all the least particles of matter in every one must have their several attractive forces proportional to their quantities of matter, as was shown above of the terrestrial bodies. At different distances these forces will be also inversely as the squares of their distances; for it is mathematically demonstrated, that globes attracting according to this law are composed of particles attracting according to the same law.

The foregoing conclusions are grounded on this axiom which is received by all philosophers, namely, that effects of the same kind, whose known properties are the same, take their rise from the same causes and have the same unknown properties also. For if gravity be the cause of the descent of a stone in *Europe,* who doubts that it is also the cause of the same descent in *America?* If there is a mutual gravitation between a stone and the earth in *Europe,* who will deny the same to be mutual in *America?* If in *Europe* the attractive force of a stone and the earth is composed of the attractive forces of the parts, who will deny the like composition in *America?* If in *Europe* the attraction of the earth be propagated to all kinds of bodies and to all distances, why may we not say that it is propagated in like manner in *America?* All philosophy is founded on this rule; for if that be taken away, we can affirm nothing as a general truth. The constitution of particular things is known by observations and experiments; and when that is done, no general conclusion of the nature of things can thence be drawn, except by this rule.

Since, then, all bodies, whether upon earth or in the heavens, are heavy, so far as we can make any experiments or observations concerning them, we must certainly allow that gravity is found in all bodies universally. And in like manner as we ought not to suppose that any bodies can be otherwise than extended, movable, or impenetrable, so we ought not to conceive that any bodies can be otherwise than heavy. The extension, mobility, and impenetrability of bodies become known to us only by experiments; and in the very same manner their gravity becomes known to us. All bodies upon which we can make any observations, are extended, movable, and impenetrable; and thence we conclude all bodies, and those concerning which we have no observations, are extended and movable and impenetrable. So all bodies on which we can make observations, we find to be heavy; and thence we conclude all bodies, and those we have no observations of, to be heavy also. If anyone should say that the bodies of the fixed stars are not heavy because their gravity is not yet observed, they may say for the same reason that they are neither extended nor movable nor impenetrable, because these properties of the fixed stars are not yet observed. In short, either gravity must have a place among the primary qualities of all bodies, or extension, mobility, and impenetrability must not. And if the nature of things is not rightly explained by the gravity of bodies, it will not be rightly explained by their extension, mobility, and impenetrability.

Some I know disapprove this conclusion, and mutter something about occult qualities. They continually are cavilling with us, that gravity is an occult property, and occult causes are to be quite banished from philosophy. But to this the answer is easy: that those are indeed occult causes whose existence is occult, and imagined but not proved; but not those whose real existence is clearly demonstrated by observations. Therefore gravity can by no means be called an occult cause of the celestial motions, because it is plain from the phenomena that such a power does really exist. Those rather have recourse to occult causes, who set imaginary vortices of a matter entirely fictitious and imperceptible by our senses, to direct those motions.

But shall gravity be therefore called an occult cause, and thrown out of philosophy, because the cause of gravity is occult and not yet discovered? Those who affirm this, should be careful not to fall into an absurdity that may overturn the foundations of all philosophy. For causes usually proceed in a continued chain from those that are more compounded to those that are more simple; when we are arrived at the most simple cause we can go no farther. Therefore no mechanical account or explanation of the most simple cause is to be expected or given; for if it could be given, the cause were not the most simple. These most simple causes will you then call occult, and reject them? Then you must reject those that immediately depend upon them, and those which depend upon these last, till philosophy is quite cleared and disencumbered of all causes.

Some there are who say that gravity is preternatural, and call it a perpetual miracle. Therefore they would have it rejected, because preternatural causes have no place in physics. It is hardly worth while to spend time in answering this ridiculous objection which overturns all philosophy. For either they will deny gravity to be in bodies, which cannot be said, or else, they will therefore call it preternatural because it is not produced by the other properties of bodies, and therefore not by mechanical causes. But certainly there are primary properties of bodies; and these, because they are primary, have no dependence on the others. Let them consider whether all these are not in like manner preternatural, and in like manner to be rejected; and then what kind of philosophy we are like to have.

Some there are who dislike this celestial physics because it contradicts the opinions of *Descartes,* and seems hardly to be reconciled with them. Let these enjoy their own opinion, but let them act fairly, and not deny the same liberty to us which they demand for themselves. Since the *Newtonian* Philosophy appears true to us, let us have the liberty to embrace and retain it, and to follow causes proved by phenomena, rather than causes only imagined and not yet proved. The business of true philosophy is to derive the natures of things from causes truly existent, and to inquire after those laws on which the Great Creator actually chose to found this most beautiful Frame of the World, not those by which he might have done the same, had he so pleased. It is reasonable enough to suppose that from several causes, somewhat differing from one another, the same effect may arise; but the true cause will be that from which it truly and actually does arise; the others have no place in true philosophy. The same motion of the hour-hand in a clock may be occasioned either by a weight hung, or a spring shut up within. But if a certain clock should be really moved with a weight, we should laugh at a man that would suppose it moved by a spring, and from that principle, suddenly taken up without further examination, should go about to explain the motion of the index; for certainly the way he ought to have taken would have been actually to look into the inward parts of the machine, that he might find the true principle of the proposed motion. The like judgment ought to be made of those philosophers who will have the heavens to be filled with a most subtile matter which is continually carried round in vortices. For if they could explain the phenomena ever so accurately by their hypotheses, we could not yet say that they have discovered true philosophy and the true causes of the celestial motions, unless they could either demonstrate that those causes do actually exist, or at least that no others do exist. Therefore if it be made clear that the attraction of all bodies is a property actually existing *in rerum natura,* and if it be also shown how the motions of the celestial bodies may be solved by that property, it would be very impertinent for anyone to object that these motions ought to be accounted for by vortices; even though we should allow such an explication of those motions to be possible. But we allow no such thing; for the phenomena can by no means be accounted for by vortices, as our author has abundantly proved from the clearest reasons. So that men must be strangely fond of chimeras, who can spend their time so idly as in patching up a ridiculous figment and setting it off with new comments of their own.

If the bodies of the planets and comets are carried round the sun in vortices, the bodies so carried, and the parts of the vortices next surrounding them, must be carried with the same velocity and the same direction, and have the same density, and the same inertia, answering to the bulk of the matter. But it is certain, the planets and comets, when in the very same parts of the heavens, are carried with various velocities and various directions. Therefore it necessarily follows that those parts of the celestial fluid, which are at the same distances from the sun, must revolve at the same time with different velocities in different directions; for one kind of velocity and direction is required for the motion of the planets, and another for that of the comets. But since this cannot be accounted for, we must either say that all celestial bodies are not carried about by vortices, or else that their motions are derived, not from one and the same vortex, but from several distinct ones, which fill and pervade the spaces round about the sun.

But if several vortices are contained in the same space, and are supposed to penetrate one another, and to revolve with different motions, then because these motions must agree with those of the bodies carried about by them, which are perfectly regular, and performed in conic sections which are sometimes very eccentric, and sometimes nearly circles, one may very reasonably ask how it comes to pass that these vortices remain entire, and have suffered no manner of perturbation in so many ages from the actions of the conflicting matter. Certainly if these fictitious motions are more compounded and harder to be accounted for than the true motions of the planets and comets, it seems to no purpose to admit them into philosophy, since every cause ought to be more simple than its effect. Allowing men to indulge their own fancies, suppose any man should affirm that the planets and comets are surrounded with atmospheres like our earth, which hypothesis seems more reasonable than that of vortices; let him then affirm that these atmospheres by their own nature move about the sun and describe conic sections, which motion is much more easily conceived than that of the vortices penetrating one another; lastly, that the planets and comets are carried about the sun by these atmospheres of theirs: and then applaud his own sagacity in discovering the causes of the celestial motions. He that rejects this fable must also reject the other; for two drops of water are not more like than this hypothesis of atmospheres, and that of vortices.

Galileo has shown that when a stone projected moves in a parabola, its deflection into that curve from its rectilinear path is occasioned by the gravity of the stone towards the earth, that is, by an occult quality. But now somebody, more cunning than he, may come to explain the cause after this manner. He will suppose a certain subtile matter, not discernible by our sight, our touch, or any other of our senses, which fills the spaces which are near and contiguous to the surface of the earth, and that this matter is carried with different directions, and various, and often contrary, motions, describing parabolic curves. Then see how easily he may account for the deflection of the stone above spoken of. The stone, says he, floats in this subtile fluid, and following its motion, can't choose but describe the same figure. But the fluid moves in parabolic curves, and therefore the stone must move in a parabola, of course. Would not the acuteness of this philosopher be thought very extraordinary, who could deduce the appearances of Nature from mechanical causes, matter and motion, so clearly that the meanest man may understand it? Or indeed should not we smile to see this new *Galileo* taking so much mathematical pains to introduce occult qualities into philosophy, from whence they have been so happily excluded? But I am ashamed to dwell so long upon trifles.

The sum of the matter is this: the number of the comets is certainly very great; their motions are perfectly regular and observe the same laws with those of the planets. The orbits in which they move are conic sections, and those very eccentric. They move every way towards all parts of the heavens, and pass through the planetary regions with all possible freedom, and their motion is often contrary to the order of the signs. These phenomena are most evidently confirmed by astronomical observations, and cannot be accounted for by vortices. Nay, indeed, they are utterly irreconcilable with the vortices of the planets. There can be no room for the motions of the comets, unless the celestial spaces be entirely cleared of that fictitious matter.

For if the planets are carried about the sun in vortices, the parts of the vortices which immediately surround every planet must be of the same density with the planet, as was shown above. Therefore all the matter contiguous to the perimeter of the earth's orbit must be of the same density as the earth. But this great orb and the orb of Saturn must have either an equal or a greater density. For to make the constitution of the vortex permanent, the parts of less density must lie near the centre, and those of greater density must go farther from it. For since the periodic times of the planets vary as the 3/2th powers of their distances from the sun, the periods of the parts of the vortices must also preserve the same ratio. Thence it will follow that the centrifugal forces of the parts of the vortex must be inversely as the squares of their distances. Those parts therefore which are more remote from the centre endeavor to recede from it with less force; whence, if their density be deficient, they must yield to the greater force with which the parts that lie nearer the centre endeavor to ascend. Therefore the denser parts will ascend, and those of less density will descend, and there will be a mutual change of places, till all the fluid matter in the whole vortex be so adjusted and disposed, that being reduced to an equilibrium its parts become quiescent. If two fluids of different density be contained in the same vessel, it will certainly come to pass that the fluid of greater density will sink the lower; and by a like reasoning it follows that the denser parts of the vortex by their greater centrifugal force will ascend to the higher places. Therefore all that far greater part of the vortex which lies without the earth's orb, will have a density, and by consequence an inertia, answering to the bulk of the matter, which cannot be less than the density and inertia of the earth. But from hence will arise a mighty resistance to the passage of the comets, such as must be very sensible, not to say enough to put a stop to and absorb their motions entirely. But it appears from the perfectly regular motion of the comets, that they suffer no resistance that is in the least sensible, and therefore that they do not meet with matter of any kind that has any resisting force or, by consequence, any density or inertia. For the resistance of mediums arises either from the inertia of the matter of the fluid, or from its want of lubricity. That which arises from the want of lubricity is very small, and is scarcely observable in the fluids commonly known, unless they be very tenacious like oil and honey. The resistance we find in air, water, quicksilver, and the like fluids that are not tenacious, is almost all of the first kind, and cannot be diminished by a greater degree of subtility, if the density and inertia, to which this resistance is proportional, remains, as is most evidently demonstrated by our author in his noble theory of resistances in the second Book.

Bodies in going on through a fluid communicate their motion to the ambient fluid by little and little, and by that communication lose their own motion, and by losing it are retarded. Therefore the retardation is proportional to the motion communicated, and the communicated motion, when the velocity of the moving body is given, is as the density of the fluid; and therefore the retardation or resistance will be as the same density of the fluid; nor can it be taken away, unless the fluid, coming about to the hinder parts of the body, restore the motion lost. Now this cannot be done unless the impression of the fluid on the hinder parts of the body be equal to the impression of the fore parts of the body on the fluid; that is, unless the relative velocity with which the fluid pushes the body behind is equal to the velocity with which the body pushes the fluid; that is, unless the absolute velocity of the recurring fluid be twice as great as the absolute velocity with which the fluid is driven forwards by the body, which is impossible. Therefore the resistance of fluids arising from their inertia can by no means be taken away. So that we must conclude that the celestial fluid has no inertia, because it has no resisting force; that it has no force to communicate motion with, because it has no inertia; that it has no force to produce any change in one or more bodies, because it has no force wherewith to communicate motion; that it has no manner of efficacy, because it has no faculty wherewith to produce any change of any kind. Therefore certainly this hypothesis may be justly called ridiculous and unworthy a philosopher, since it is altogether without foundation and does not in the least serve to explain the nature of things. Those who would have the heavens filled with a fluid matter, but suppose it void of any inertia, do indeed in words deny a vacuum, but allow it in fact. For since a fluid matter of that kind can noways be distinguished from empty space, the dispute is now about the names and not the natures of things. If any are so fond of matter that they will by no means admit of a space void of body, let us consider where they must come at last.

For either they will say that this constitution of a world everywhere full was made so by the will of God to this end, that the operations of Nature might be assisted everywhere by a subtile ether pervading and filling all things; which cannot be said, however, since we have shown from the phenomena of the comets, that this ether is of no efficacy at all; or they will say, that it became so by the same will of God for some unknown end, which ought not be said, because for the same reason a different constitution may be as well supposed; or lastly, they will not say that it was caused by the will of God, but by some necessity of its nature. Therefore they will at last sink into the mire of that infamous herd who dream that all things are governed by fate and not by providence, and that matter exists by the necessity of its nature always and everywhere, being infinite and eternal. But supposing these things, it must be also everywhere uniform; for variety of forms is entirely inconsistent with necessity. It must be also unmoved; for if it be necessarily moved in any determinate direction, with any determinate velocity, it will by a like necessity be moved in a different direction with a different velocity; but it can never move in different directions with different velocities; therefore it must be unmoved. Without all doubt this world, so diversified with that variety of forms and motions we find in it, could arise from nothing but the perfectly free will of God directing and presiding over all.

From this fountain it is that those laws, which we call the laws of Nature, have flowed, in which there appear many traces indeed of the most wise contrivance, but not the least shadow of necessity. These therefore we must not seek from uncertain conjectures, but learn them from observations and experiments. He who is presumptuous enough to think that he can find the true principles of physics and the laws of natural things by the force alone of his own mind, and the internal light of his reason, must either suppose that the world exists by necessity, and by the same necessity follows the laws proposed; or if the order of Nature was established by the will of God, that himself, a miserable reptile, can tell what was fittest to be done. All sound and true philosophy is founded on the appearances of things; and if these phenomena inevitably draw us, against our wills, to such principles as most clearly manifest to us the most excellent counsel and supreme dominion of the All-wise and Almighty Being, they are not therefore to be laid aside because some men may perhaps dislike them. These men may call them miracles or occult qualities, but names maliciously given ought not to be a disadvantage to the things themselves, unless these men will say at last that all philosophy ought to be founded in atheism. Philosophy must not be corrupted in compliance with these men, for the order of things will not be changed.

Fair and equal judges will therefore give sentence in favor of this most excellent method of philosophy, which is founded on experiments and observations. And it can hardly be said or imagined, what light, what splendor, hath accrued to that method from this admirable work of our illustrious author, whose happy and sublime genius, resolving the most difficult problems, and reaching to discoveries of which the mind of man was thought incapable before, is deservedly admired by all those who are somewhat more than superficially versed in these matters. The gates are now set open, and by the passage he has revealed we may freely enter into the knowledge of the hidden secrets and wonders of natural things. He has so clearly laid open and set before our eyes the most beautiful frame of the System of the World, that if King *Alphonso* were now alive, he would not complain for want of the graces either of simplicity or of harmony in it. Therefore we may now more nearly behold the beauties of Nature, and entertain ourselves with the delightful contemplation; and, which is the best and most valuable fruit of philosophy, be thence incited the more profoundly to reverence and adore the great Maker and Lord of all. He must be blind who from the most wise and excellent contrivances of things cannot see the infinite Wisdom and Goodness of their Almighty Creator, and he must be mad and senseless who refuses to acknowledge them.

Newton's distinguished work will be the safest protection against the attacks of atheists, and nowhere more surely than from this quiver can one draw forth missiles against the band of godless men. This was felt long ago and first surprisingly demonstrated in learned English and Latin discourses by *Richard Bentley,* who, excelling in learning and distinguished as a patron of the highest arts, is a great ornament of his century and of our academy, the most worthy and upright Master of our *Trinity College.* To him in many ways I must express my indebtedness. And you too, benevolent reader, will not withhold the esteem due him. For many years an intimate friend of the celebrated author (since he aimed not only that the author should be esteemed by those who come after, but also that these uncommon writings should enjoy distinction among the literati of the world), he cared both for the reputation of his friend and for the advancement of the sciences. Since copies of the previous edition were very scarce and held at high prices, he persuaded by frequent entreaties and almost by chidings, the splendid man, distinguished alike for modesty and for erudition, to grant him permission for the appearance of this new edition, perfected throughout and enriched by new parts, at his expense and under his supervision. He assigned to me, as he had a right, the not unwelcome task of looking after the corrections as best I could.

ROGER COTES
Fellow of Trinity College,
Plumian Professor of Astronomy
and Experimental Philosophy.

Cambridge, May 12, 1713.

38. Isaac Newton, *Principia Mathematica*

Isaac Newton's work represents not only the culmination of what is known as the Scientific Revolution, but also a scientific and philosophical revolution in itself. His *Principia Mathematica Philosophiae Naturalis* certainly synthesized the best results of Newton's predecessors in physics, but, more important, it reinterpreted them and integrated them into an original and still fruitful approach to scientific investigation and explanation.
Born in Lincolnshire, England, in 1642, he took his B.A. at Trinity College, Cambridge in 1665 and his M.A. in 1668, and in 1669 he replaced Isaac Barrow as Lucasian Professor of Mathematics; by this time he had already formulated the differential and integral calculus, some insightful speculations on the force of gravity, and a controversial "new theory of light and colors," which revealed that white light actually consists of

From Isaac Newton, *Mathematical Principles of Natural Philosophy,* translated by Andrew Motte (London: B. Motte, 1729).

differently-colored rays. In 1687 he published his *Principia*, which contained two achievements of incalculable worth: it gave a complete and mathematically precise form to the laws of mechanics, and it showed that the weight of terrestrial bodies, the shape of the earth, the phenomena of tides, the motion of the moon, and Kepler's laws of planetary motion could all be explained and precisely predicted on the basis of a single, universal force of gravitation.

The second achievement only hints at the dimensions of Newton's contributions to physics; in addition to showing the explanatory power of the force of gravity, Newton also succeeded in clarifying, as no one had before him, the very concept of physical force and its role in physical interaction. For by establishing physics on a coherent conceptual foundation—both recognizing and supplying the need for a clear understanding of concepts like force and mass, inertia and acceleration—Newton commands respect not only as a mathematical genius, but as a deep and penetrating philosopher.

Newton's philosophy is embodied in his scientific investigations rather than explicitly set forth in a philosophical treatise. In the following selections from the *Principia*, however, some of his most important philosophical principles and preoccupations become apparent, principles concerning, for example, the role of God in the universe as well as the foundations of knowledge and of scientific method. Especially for those of his contemporaries who came to admire him, but who could not follow the mathematical subtleties of his physics, general themes such as these seemed to capture the essence of that "Newtonian spirit" which became such an important feature of the science and culture of the Enlightenment.

Since the Ancients (as we are told by *Pappus*) esteemed the science of mechanics of greatest importance in the investigation of natural things, and the moderns, rejecting substantial forms and occult qualities, have endeavored to subject the phenomena of nature to the laws of mathematics, I have in this treatise cultivated mathematics as far as it relates to philosophy. . . . Geometry is founded in mechanical practice, and is nothing but that part of universal mechanics which accurately proposes and demonstrates the art of measuring. But since the manual arts are chiefly employed in the moving of bodies, it happens that geometry is commonly referred to their magnitude, and mechanics to their motion. In this sense rational mechanics will be the science of motions resulting from any forces whatsoever, and of the forces required to produce any motions, accurately proposed and demonstrated. This part of mechanics, as far as it extended to the five powers which relate to manual arts, was cultivated by the ancients who considered gravity (it not being a manual power) no otherwise than in moving weights by those powers. But I consider philosophy rather than arts and write not concerning manual but natural powers, and consider chiefly those things which relate to gravity, levity, elastic force, the resistance of fluids, and the like forces, whether attractive or impulsive; and therefore I offer this work as the mathematical principles of philosophy, for the whole burden of philosophy seems to consist in this—from the phenomena of motions to investigate the forces of nature, and then from these forces to demonstrate the other phenomena; and to this end the general propositions in the first and second Books are directed. In the third Book I give an example of this in the explication of the System of the World; for by the propositions mathematically demonstrated in the former Books, in the third I derive from the celestial phenomena the forces of gravity with which bodies tend to the sun and the several planets. Then from these forces, by other propositions which are also mathematical, I deduce the motions of the planets, the comets, the moon, and the sea. I wish we could derive the rest of the phenomena of Nature by the same kind of reasoning from mechanical principles, for I am induced by many reasons to suspect that they may all depend upon certain forces by which the particles of bodies, by some causes hitherto unknown, are either mutually impelled towards one another, and cohere in regular figures, or are repelled and recede from one another. These forces being unknown, philosophers have hitherto attempted the search of Nature in vain; but I hope the principles here laid down will afford some light either to this or some truer method of philosophy. . . .

Rules of Reasoning in Philosophy

Rule 1. *We are to admit no more causes of natural things than such as are both true and sufficient to explain their appearances.*

To this purpose the philosophers say that Nature does nothing in vain, and more is in vain when less will serve; for Nature is pleased with simplicity, and affect not the pomp of superfluous causes.

Rule 2. *Therefore to the same natural effects we must, as far as possible, assign the same causes.*

As to respiration in a man and in a beast; the descent of stone in *Europe* and in *America;* the light of our culinary fire and of the sun; the reflection of light in the earth, and in the planets.

Rule 3. *The qualities of bodies, which admit neither intensification nor remission of degrees, and which are found to belong to all bodies within the reach of our experiments, are to be esteemed the universal qualities of all bodies whatsoever.*

For since the qualities of bodies are only known to us by experiments, we are to hold for universal all such as universally agree with experiments; and such as are not liable to diminution can never be quite taken away. We are certainly not to relinquish the evidence of experiments for the sake of dreams and vain fictions of our own devising; nor are we to recede from the analogy of Nature, which is wont to be simple, and always consonant to itself. We no other way know the extension of bodies than by our senses, nor do these reach it in all bodies; but because we perceive extension in all that are sensible, therefore we ascribe it universally to all others also. That abundance of bodies are hard, we learn by experience; and because the hardness of the whole arise from the hardness of the parts, we therefore justly infer the hardness of the undivided particles not only of the bodies we feel but of all others. That all bodies are impenetrable, we gather not from reason, but from sensation. The bodies which we handle we find impenetrable, and thence conclude impenetrability to be a universal property of all bodies whatsoever. That all bodies are movable, and endowed with certain powers (which we call the inertia) of persevering in their motion, or in their rest, we only infer from the like properties observed in the bodies which we have seen. The extension, hardness, impenetrability, mobility, and inertia of the whole, result from the extension, hardness, impenetrability, mobility, and inertia of the parts; and hence we conclude the least particles of all bodies to be also all extended, and hard and impenetrable, and movable, and endowed with their proper inertia. And this is the foundation of all philosophy. Moreover, that the divided but contiguous particles of bodies may be separated from one another, is matter of observation; and, in the particles that remain undivided, our minds are able to distinguish yet lesser parts, as is mathematically demonstrated. But whether the parts so distinguished, and not yet divided, may, by the powers of Nature, be actually divided and separated from one another, we cannot certainly determine. Yet, had we the proof of but one experiment that any undivided particle, in breaking a hard and solid body, suffered a division, we might by virtue of this rule conclude that the undivided as well as the divided particles may be divided and actually separated to infinity.

Lastly, if it universally appears, by experiments and astronomical observations that all bodies about the earth gravitate towards the earth, and that in proportion to the quantity of matter which they severally contain; that the moon likewise, according to the quantity of its matter, gravitates towards the earth; and all the planets one towards another; and the comets in like manner towards the sun; we must, in consequence of this rule, universally allow that all bodies whatsoever are endowed with a principle of mutual gravitation. For the argument from the appearances concludes with more force for the universal gravitation of all bodies than for their impene-

trability; of which, among those in the celestial regions, we have no experiments, nor any manner of observation. Not that I affirm gravity to be
essential to bodies; by their *vis insita* I mean nothing but their inertia. This
is immutable. Their gravity is diminished as they recede from the earth.

Rule 4. *In experimental philosophy we are to look upon propositions
inferred by general induction from phenomena as accurately or very nearly
true, notwithstanding any contrary hypotheses that may be imagined, till
such time as other phenomena occur, by which they may either be made
more accurate, or liable to exceptions.*

This rule we must follow, that the argument of induction may not be
evaded by hypotheses. . . .

(General Scholium.) The six primary planets are revolved about the sun
in circles concentric with the sun, and with motions directed towards the
same parts, and almost in the same plane. Ten moons are revolved about
the earth, Jupiter, and Saturn, in circles concentric with them, with the
same direction of motion, and nearly in the planes of the orbits of these
planets; but it is not to be conceived that mere mechanical causes could
give birth to so many regular motions, since the comets range over all parts
of the heavens in very eccentric orbits; for by that kind of motion they pass
easily through the orbs of the planets, and with great rapidity; and in their
aphelions, where they move the slowest, and are detained the longest, they
recede to the greatest distances from each other, and hence suffer the least
disturbance from their mutual attractions. This most beautiful system of
the sun, planets, and comets, could only proceed from the counsel and dominion of an intelligent and powerful Being. And if the fixed stars are the
centres of other like systems, these, being formed by the like wise counsel,
must be all subject to the dominion of One; especially since the light of the
fixed stars is of the same nature with the light of the sun, and from every
system light passes into all the other systems: and lest the systems of the
fixed stars should, by their gravity, fall on each other, he hath placed those
systems at immense distances from one another. . . .

Hitherto we have explained the phenomena of the heavens and of our sea
by the power of gravity, but have not yet assigned the cause of this power.
This is certain, that it must proceed from a cause that penetrates to the very
centres of the sun and planets, without suffering the least diminution of its
force; that operates not according to the quantity of the surfaces of the particles upon which it acts (as mechanical causes used to do), but according
to the quantity of solid matter which they contain, and propagates its virtue
on all sides to immense distances, decreasing always as the inverse square
of the distances. Gravitation towards the sun is made up out of the gravita-
tions toward the several particles of which the body of the sun is composed;
and in receding from the sun decreases accurately as the inverse square of

the distances as far as the orbit of Saturn, as evidently appears from the quiescence of the aphelion of the planets; nay, and even to the remotest aphelion of the comets if those aphelions are also quiescent. But hitherto I have not been able to discover the cause of those properties of gravity from phenomena, and I frame no hypotheses; for whatever is not deduced from the phenomena is to be called an hypothesis; and hypotheses, whether metaphysical or physical, whether of occult qualities or mechanical, have no place in experimental philosophy. In this philosophy particular propositions are inferred from the phenomena, and afterwards rendered general by induction. Thus it was that the impenetrability, the mobility, and the impulsive forces of bodies, and the laws of motion and gravitation, were discovered. And to us it is enough that gravity does really exist, and acts according to the laws which we have explained, and abundantly serves to account for all the motions of the celestial bodies, and of our sea.

And now we might add something concerning a certain most subtle spirit which pervades and lies hid in all gross bodies; by the force and action of which spirit the particles of bodies attract one another at near distances, and cohere, if contiguous; and electric bodies operate to greater distances, as well repelling as attracting the neighboring corpuscles; and light is emitted, reflected, refracted, inflected, and heats bodies; and all sensation is excited, and the members of animal bodies move at the command of the will, namely, by the vibrations of this spirit, mutually propagated along the solid filaments of the nerves, from the outward organs of sense to the brain, and from the brain into the muscles. But these are things that cannot be explained in a few words, nor are we furnished with that sufficiency of experiments which is required to an accurate determination and demonstration of the laws by which this electric and elastic spirit operates.

From Colbert, *Lettres, instructions et mémoires,* edited by Pierre Clement (Paris: Imprimerie impériale, 1868), pp. 513–14, 563–64. Notes are from the original edition. Translated for this volume by Lydia G. Cochrane.

The Institutions of Science

39. Letters and Memoranda to Colbert

Printed below are documents which reveal some of the initiatives and strategies of French absolutism in the area of cultural affairs. French absolutism reached the summit of its power and authority in the second half of the seventeenth century, under the rule of Louis XIV. Although the confident young king was determined to govern without a prime minister, he nevertheless drew on the talents of a brilliant group of administrators. By far the most celebrated of these was Jean-Baptiste Colbert (1619–83), who was born into a merchant family at Reims. Through indefatigable work and unimpeachable loyalty to the monarch, Colbert gradually assumed the posts of minister of finances, secretary of state for the navy, and superintendant of construction. His supreme achievement was the restoration of French finances in the decade betweeen 1661 and 1671: net revenues for the state were doubled in these years. Colbert also sponsored a program of state intervention into the economy, inspired by the economic doctrines we know as "mercantilism," whose ultimate goal was to augment the wealth of France at the expense of other nations. The fruits of these labors were the beginnings of French colonial expansion overseas, and four decades of ruinous war against the Dutch Republic and England.

The organizational ambitions of French absolutism extended well beyond the frontiers of politics and the economy. The whole range of French cultural production—in both the arts and sciences—was to be mobilized for a single overarching purpose, the enhancement of the power and glory of the monarchy. The main organ of governmental supervision in these areas came to be the "academy," modeled on the great academies of Antiquity and on the learned societies of the Italian Renaissance, and funded by the state. The Académie Française, which attempted to place the French language itself under its direction, was a pioneering example: founded under Richelieu, it came under firm royal control after 1671. But it was Colbert who presided over the great multiplication of cultural academies. He sponsored the creation of an Academy of Inscriptions and Belles Lettres in 1663; the Academy of Sciences in 1666; the Royal Academy of Architecture in 1671; as well as the Academy of France in Rome, which dictated the aesthetic standards of French classicism in painting and sculpture.

The first document presented here is an anonymous memorandum to Colbert which suggests not only the overriding concern with subordinating the arts and sciences to the needs of the state, but also a preoccupation with a thorny problem, that of determining exactly *who* deserved to be considered a "scientist." Our second document is a letter from Daguesseau, the intendant in the southern city of Montepellier, which reveals Colbert's involvement in a more pedestrian, but no less vital pursuit: the retrieval of documents to be used to protect the "rights" of the French king. The system of intendants (appointed officials who acted as representatives of the crown in the provinces) had been created under Richelieu, and was one of the chief instruments in the extension of centralized authority across the breadth of France. The French monarchy, for all its pretensions to absolutism, still had to contend with a chaotic mass of traditional law and local custom, and thus the establishment and reinforcement of its power often depended on the control of the kind of documents and charters mentioned by Daguesseau. The letter may also reflect, to some extent, Colbert's famous mania for paperwork: "to direct the affairs of France with all the thoroughness of a good private accountant."

Note to Colbert on the Establishment of the Academy of Arts and Sciences[1]

There is talk of creating an academy for the sciences and the arts. This enterprise is worthy of the king's magnificence and M. Colbert's attentions; and although prudence has dictated that the generous project of a universal reform start with things that regard the continued existence and the tranquillity of the state, reason would like to bring it to completion with things capable of maintaining abundance and virtue in the state. All who cultivate the sciences and the arts ought to make an effort to encourage such a handsome project. My own contribution will necessarily be minor, but I feel obliged to say what I know in this connection, and if I cannot show all the capacities of the great philosophers, I shall at least demonstrate that I share their open sincerity.

I believe, first, that no project for a royal academy should be drawn up from ideas alone, and that a surer method is to consider the example of all the academies that have been created thus far; for even though this is to be incomparably above all the best that we have seen of the sort, nevertheless, it is a fact that the proportion that exists between lesser and greater things of the same nature makes it necessary to consider the practice of the other academies if we want to judge clearly what should be done in this one. We can always add to it what is needed to raise it above all others and give it such advantages as to show by what hand it is supported. Thus I believe

1. This memorandum, which is not without interest, is not signed.

that we should invite other persons from the various academies to present a model of their academy.

In the second place, I think it imperative to hold consultations concerning the choice of the scholars who are to make up this illustrious company, and to remember that those who enjoy the greatest reputation at court are not always the best choices. Anyone with even a scant acquaintance with scholars knows why this is so, but people who are deeply occupied with public affairs have no way of knowing this secret. Nonetheless, it is important, on an occasion such as this, to bring it out into the open and to point out to M. Colbert that there are in this world scholars of two sorts: some give themselves over to the sciences because they find pleasure in them. They are content if the knowledge they acquire is the sole fruit of their labors; they do not attempt to have them published. And if these scholars are well known, it is only among the persons with whom they converse, without ambition and for mutual instruction. These men are scholars in good faith and persons one cannot do without in a project as great as that of the royal academy. There are other scholars who only cultivate the sciences as they would a field that feeds them; and as they see that the greatest recompense is given exclusively to those who make the most clamor in the world, they take great pains, not to make new discoveries, for thus far these have had little recompense, but to cultivate whatever can make them most visible. Above all, they pretend to be well known at court: they form cliques [*cabales*] for that purpose, in which there is an unspoken agreement to have nothing but praise for certain people and to speak ill, or at least coldly, of all who do not belong to those ambitious circles. Such men are scholars of the beau monde and they are the most famous. It is to them that all turn for a proper judgment of works or authors. It is well and good that they do so; still, one should not expect them always to name the finest person, since they often are more interested in helping the least capable to advance.

I offer no particulars for fear that someone might imagine that I have specific persons in mind, when all I want to do is to warn of an evil that has always existed and that is to be avoided in this instance. Thus let me say merely that it is very important to be sure that this not occur in an enterprise that, if it fails, will cause scandal throughout the world and compromise the honor of France. Petty interests and the petty vanity of scholars must not prevent all who belong in this assembly from being called to it. Furthermore, it seems that the best that we can do to ascertain who the best scholars are is to rely on the judgment of persons of a quality sufficiently eminent to be above all such foibles, but also of a sufficiently profound knowledge to be able to distinguish clearly between the different talents of those who are appropriate for carrying out an experiment and those who can draw all its useful consequences, between those who possess sufficient clarity of mind to gather together such consequences and, finally, all those who have the variety of talents that could make the royal academy as brilliant as it is useful. Instead of which, if we turn to professional scholars, it will doubtless be true that out of interest or prejudice such men will exclude those whose ability they fear or who are not of their own opinion, to the extent that the most illustrious enterprise that ever was will fail to fulfill its principal reason for coming into existence, which is to use experiment alone to banish prejudice from the sciences; to find some sort of certainty in them; to rid them of all chimeras; to prepare a smooth path to the truth for all who will cultivate the sciences in the future, insofar as God has given men to know the truth for their benefit. What glory there would be for the King, and what honor for M. Colbert, if this could be so! But what misfortune will it bring if, deluding the generosity of the prince and the efforts of the minister, most of the best candidates for this Company are excluded! If instead of reforming the sciences—the abuses of which are perhaps even greater, even if this is not commonly thought to be so, than those of the law and of finance—and instead of discovering new things, we remain in our ancient errors. But the destruction of ignorance is a victory no less glorious than the defeat of pettifoggery [la chicane] and irrational taxation [la Maltôte], and since the King has already suffocated these two monsters, he seems destined to defeat the third. Thus I hope that close watch will be kept, and that in admitting to this illustrious academy only talents worthy of it, we will soon see the sciences and the arts at the peak of their perfection.[2]

Daguesseau, Intendant of Montpellier, to Colbert on Local Libraries and Archives

(*Montpellier, 14 April 1679.*) I sent off yesterday by the messenger, to your address, a case containing various papers taken, thanks to the efforts of M. Boudon, *trésorier* [archivist] of France, from the archives of a number of chapters and abbeys in this province.[3] He has just discovered a great quantity of others at Narbonne; which have not been seen by M. Doat[4] and which are curious from a historical point of view. In order to facilitate the task of continuing this work, however, he needs a commission, a draft for

2. *See* in the *Lettres de Chapelain,* p. 587, the report addressed to Colbert on the foundation of an academy of inscriptions and belles-lettres.

3. The eleventh of the following month Colbert answered Daguesseau: "I have received the box of diverse pieces that were extracted under M. Boudon's direction from several chapters and abbeys of Languedoc, for which I thank you. You will do me an express pleasure by urging him to continue with this work." (*Mélanges Clairambault,* vol. 426 fol. 486).

4. Doat was president of the chambre des comptes of Navarre; Colbert had sent him to the provinces of the South to supervise the copying of old papers of historical interest.

which I am sending you based on the one[5] that you had sent for M. Doat. I hope that by next summer we can make good progress with this material and make some fine discoveries. I will contribute to this end in all that falls under my charge, making sure, in the voyages that I undertake, to go to the places in which this sort of documentation is found, taking M. Boudon with me to have copies made of the most important papers, and to have the originals when possible.

In the meanwhile, as the said Boudon has already incurred a certain number of expenses, both for travel and for the copyists he has employed and whom he will still need to employ in quantity in the future, it may please you to free such funds as you deem appropriate for this expense, which will be spent with all possible care and for which Boudon will send you an accounting. . . .

40. Academy of Sciences (Académie royale des sciences), Statutes

By and large, the events and discoveries we know as the Scientific Revolution took place outside the institutional framework of the university. The vanguard intellectual life of the seventeenth century was instead

5. The text of this commission runs as follows: "We commission you, order you, and delegate you to take yourself to all the treasuries containing our charters and to all the archives of cities, towns, archbishoprics, bishoprics, abbeys, priories, commanderies, and other communities, ecclesiastical and lay . . . and in the archives of the archbishops, bishops, abbots, priors, and commanders who may have [papers] separated from those of their chapter, to have described and delivered to you all the documents that you judge necessary for the conservation of the rights of our crown and the service of history, in order to make copies which you will have your clerk gather together in your presence and for which you will sign the inventories. . . . We desire, to this effect, that the keepers of the treasuries of our charters and of the archives of our provinces of Guyenne and Languedoc and of the country of Foix and all others who may have charge of such documents and have them under their power be obliged to describe them to you and to deliver up to you the ones of which you have chosen to have copies made . . . in order, when this is done, to have the copies thus taken by you sent to the keeper of our royal library."

The commissioners carried out their mandate with care; the documents they sent fill nearly forty volumes.

"This is an abundant harvest," Le Prince said, "which was even further enlarged later, and today forms one of the largest collections of modern manuscripts in His Majesty's library. [It is] all the more priceless for noble families and for communities because, should the originals be lost, these copies, made and gathered through *lettres patentes,* would bear full authenticity" (*Essai historique sur la bibliothèque du roi,* p. 54).

From *L'Institut de France: Lois, statuts, et règlements concernant les anciennes académies et l'institut,* edited by Leon Aucoc (Paris: Imprimerie nationale, 1889), pp. lxxiv–xcii. Translated for this volume by Lydia G. Cochrane.

focused on the kinds of academies discussed above, and the abundant creation of these all across Europe coincided with the emergence of "science" as an autonomous activity and discipline, distinct from natural philosophy or metaphysics. The most famous such organizations were the Royal Academy in England and the Academy of Sciences in France. The former grew out of the informal meetings of a group of London scholars; though it took on the title of "Royal" in 1662, it never received more than trifling support from the English government, and remained a primarily private, relatively undisciplined group. The French Academy of Sciences, by contrast, was a creature of the French state from the start. The document which follows, from 1699, is the earliest extant charter for the academy, but the original organization founded by Colbert in 1666 was in all likelihood very similar. The fascinating contrast between the disciplined, elitist character of the French Academy and the anarchic amateurism of its English counterpart, has given rise to an endless debate among historians over their relative efficiency as promoters of science. Amply funded by the king, the French Academy was able to undertake experiments (such as the most accurate measurement of the earth's size of the time) well beyond the reach of any other scientific body of the age. Nevertheless, the lead in the development of modern science had, by 1700, passed from France to England, where the Royal Academy could boast of its support for the most illustrious scientist of the epoch, Isaac Newton.

Decree on the order of the King for the Royal Academy of Sciences, Versailles, 26 January 1699

Wishing to continue to show marks of his affection to the Royal Academy of Sciences, His Majesty the King has resolved the present decree, which he wishes and expects to be observed with due exactitude.

1. The Royal Academy of Sciences will remain always under the protection of the King and will receive its orders through whichever of the Secretaries of State to whom it will please His Majesty to give charge of it.

2. The said Academy will always be composed of four sorts of members: honorary, pensioned, associate, and student. The first class will be composed of ten persons and the three others of twenty persons each, and no one will be admitted into any of these four classes except by the choice or the assent of His Majesty.

3. The honorary members are all to be native-born and commendable for their accomplishments in mathematics or in physics. One of their number will act as president, and none of them can become pensioned members.

4. The pensioned members are all to be established in Paris: three geometers, three astronomers, three mechanists, three anatomists, three chemists, three botanists, a secretary, and a treasurer. Should it happen that one of their number be called to a post or a commission that requires his residence outside Paris, he will be removed from his post as if it had been vacated by death.

5. The associate members are to be in equal number, twelve among them being native-born. Two will specialize in geometry, two in astronomy, two in mechanics, two in anatomy, two in chemistry, two in botany; the other eight may be foreigners and can apply themselves to those among these various sciences for which they have the most inclination and talent.

6. All the students are to be established in Paris, each specializing in the type of science professed by the pensioned academician to whom he is attached. If a student passes on to employment that requires residence outside Paris, his place will be filled as if it had been vacated by death.

7. To fill the seat of an honorary member, the assembly will elect, by majority vote, a worthy candidate whom it will propose to His Majesty for his assent.

8. To fill the seat of a pensioned member, the Academy will elect three candidates, at least two of whom are to be associates or students, and they will be proposed to His Majesty so that it may please him to choose one.

9. To fill the places of the associates, the Academy will elect two candidates, at least one of whom can be taken from among the students, and they will be proposed to His Majesty so that it may please him to choose one.

10. To fill the places of the students, each one of the pensioned members may choose one person, whose name he will present to the Company. After discussion, if he is acceptable, by majority vote, his name will be proposed to His Majesty.

11. No one may be proposed to His Majesty to fill any of the said places as members of the Academy if he is not of good habits and recognized probity.

12. Similarly, no one can be proposed if he is of the regular clergy or attached to a religious order, unless it is to fill a position as honorary member.

13. No one can be proposed to His Majesty for a position as pensioned or associate member unless he is known for some considerable printed work, some course given with brilliance, some machine of his invention, or some specific discovery.

14. No one can be proposed for a position as pensioned or associate member who is not at least twenty-five years of age.

15. No one can be proposed for a position as student who is not at least twenty years of age.

16. The ordinary meetings of the Academy will be held in the King's Library on Wednesday and Saturday of every week. If these days coincide with a feast day, the meetings will be held the preceding day.

17. The sessions of the said meetings will last at least two hours—that is, from three to five o'clock.

18. The vacations of the Academy will begin 8 September and end 11 November; it will also be on vacation during the two weeks of Easter, the week of Pentecost, and from Christmas through Epiphany.

19. Members will attend the meetings of the Academy assiduously, and no pensioned member can be absent more than two months on personal business, vacations excluded, without the express permission of His Majesty.

20. Experience having taught that there are too many drawbacks to projects on which the entire Academy might work in common, each member will instead choose some particular object for his studies, and by the account he gives of it in the meetings he will attempt to enrich all the members of the Academy with his enlightenment and to profit from their remarks.

21. At the beginning of every year, each pensioned member will be obligated to state to the company in writing his principal object of study; the other members will be invited to give a similar declaration of their projects.

22. Although every member of the Academy is obligated to concentrate principally on the particular science he has chosen, all will nevertheless be encouraged to extend their research to everything that may be useful or curious in the various sections of mathematics, in the different ways of pursuing the arts, and in all that might regard a topic in natural history or in some manner pertain to physics.

23. At each meeting at least two members, in turn, will be obligated to offer some observations concerning their studies. The associates will always be at liberty to propose their observations in like fashion, and all those present—honorary members, pensioners, or associates—will have an opportunity, in turn according to their science, to offer remarks on the topic proposed, but the students will speak only when invited to do so by the president.

24. Members will leave with the secretary, in writing, all the observations that they put before the meeting so that they can be referred to when necessary.

25. All experiments reported on by a member are to be verified by him during the meeting, if possible, or at least in private, in the presence of several other members.

26. The Academy will take great care to assure, should several members

be of different opinions, that they use no scornful or biting terms against one another, either in their discourses or in their writings, and that even when members combat the sentiments of any scholar whatsoever, the Academy will exhort them to speak of them in civil terms.

27. The Academy will take pains to keep up correspondence with the various scholars of Paris and the provinces of the kingdom or even of foreign lands in order to be informed promptly of things of interest that may be occurring there in mathematics and physics, and in elections to fill academic positions it will give marked preference to the scholars who have been promptest in this sort of correspondence.

28. The Academy will charge one of its members to read important works in physics or mathematics that may appear in France and elsewhere, and the member charged with this reading will make his report to the company without criticizing the work, but simply noting if there are views in it from which it might profit.

29. The Academy will repeat noteworthy experiments that have been carried out elsewhere and will note in its proceedings the conformity or differences between its own results and those in question.

30. The Academy will examine the works that the members propose to have printed. It will give its approval only after the entire text has been read in the meetings, or at least after examination has been made and a report given by persons whom the company charges with such an examination. No member of the Academy may put the title of academician in the works he publishes if the work has not been approved in this manner by the Academy.

31. The Academy will examine, should the king so command, all the machines for which patents are solicited from His Majesty. It will certify whether such machines are new and useful, and the inventors of the ones that are approved will be under obligation to leave a model with the Academy.

32. The honorary, pensioned, and associate members will have the right to speak when science alone is under discussion.

33. Only the honorary and pensioned members will have the right to speak regarding elections or business concerning the Academy, and such deliberations will be governed by vote.

34. Persons who are not of the Academy cannot attend nor be admitted to the ordinary meetings, except when they are brought by the secretary in order to propose some discovery or some new machine.

35. All persons will be admitted to the public meetings, which will be held twice each year, one on the day following Saint Martin's Day [11 November] and the other the day after Easter.

36. The president will be placed at the high end of the table with the

honorary members, the pensioned members will occupy the two sides of the table, the associates the lower end, and the students will be behind the academician supervising their studies.

37. The president will take particular care that proper order be faithfully observed at every meeting and in all that concerns the Academy. He will be held strictly accountable in this to His Majesty or to the secretary of state to whom the king has given charge of the Academy.

38. At all the meetings, the president will hold debate on the various questions, will take note of the opinions of those who have voice in the company, in order of their seat, and will announce the resolutions that have been passed by majority vote.

39. The president will be named by His Majesty January 1 of each year, but although a new nomination is thus necessary every year, the president's tenure can be continued as long as it pleases His Majesty. Since it could happen, through indisposition or the press of personal affairs, that the president miss several sessions, His Majesty will at the same time name another member to preside in the absence of the said president.

40. The secretary will take pains to gather the substance of all that is proposed, argued, examined, and resolved in the company, to write it in his records under each meeting date, and to include the treatises that have been read. He will sign the minutes of proceedings, which will be distributed to the members of the company and to others interested in having them. At the end of December of every year, he will give the public a summary of his records or a narrative account of the more remarkable things that have occurred in the Academy during the year.

41. The record books and papers, official and unofficial, concerning the Academy will remain always in the hands of the secretary, to whom they will be given immediately by means of a new inventory that the president will draw up, and in December of every year the president will review this inventory and note everything to be added to it for the entire year.

42. The secretary will be perpetual. When, through sickness or any other imperative reason he cannot attend the meetings, he will commission, as he sees fit, a member of the Academy to keep the records in his stead.

43. The treasurer will keep all the books, furnishings, instruments, machines, and other curiosities that belong to the Academy. When he takes on this task, the president will give these into his charge, accompanied by an inventory, and in the month of December of every year the said president will review the said inventory in order to add acquisitions made during the entire year.

44. When scholars ask to see any of the things committed to the treasurer's safekeeping, he will see to it that they are shown to them but will not

permit them to be transported out of the rooms in which they are kept without a written order of the Academy.

45. The treasurer's charge will be perpetual, and when for some legitimate reason he cannot satisfy all the duties of his function, he will name some member of the Academy to do so.

46. To facilitate the printing of the various works that the members of the Academy may compose, His Majesty permits the Academy to choose a bookseller to whom the King will, in consequence, send the privileges necessary to print and distribute the members' works approved by the Academy.

47. In order to encourage the members of the Academy to pursue their labors, His Majesty will continue to see that they are paid their ordinary pensions and even extraordinary gratifications, according to the merit of their works.

48. In order to aid the members in their studies and to help them perfect their knowledge, the king will continue to furnish the funds necessary for the various experiments and research projects that the members may carry out.

49. In order to reward assiduous attendance, at each meeting of the Academy His Majesty will distribute forty tokens, to be divided among the pensioned members present.

50. His Majesty wishes the present decree to be read at the next meeting and to be entered into the record so as to be observed scrupulously, in its form and in its tenor; and if it should happen that some member of the Academy fails to conform to some part of it, His Majesty will order that he be punished according to the severity of the case.

Given at Versailles the twenty-sixth day of January one thousand six hundred ninety-nine.

(*signed*)   Louis
(*lower*)   Phelypeaux

Index